Innovative and Agile Contracting for Digital Transformation and Industry 4.0

Mohammad Ali Shalan
Aqarat Real Estate Development Company, Saudi Arabia

Mohammed Ayedh Algarni
Information and Documents Center, Institute of Public Administration, Saudi Arabia

IGI Global
PUBLISHER of TIMELY KNOWLEDGE

A volume in the Advances in Business Information Systems and Analytics (ABISA) Book Series

Published in the United States of America by
IGI Global
Business Science Reference (an imprint of IGI Global)
701 E. Chocolate Avenue
Hershey PA, USA 17033
Tel: 717-533-8845
Fax: 717-533-8661
E-mail: cust@igi-global.com
Web site: http://www.igi-global.com

Library of Congress Cataloging-in-Publication Data

Names: Shalan, Mohammad Ali, 1972- editor. | Algarni, Mohammed Ayedh, 1975- editor.
Title: Innovative and agile contracting for digital transformation and industry 4.0 / Mohammad Ali Shalan and Mohammed Ayedh Algarni, editors.
Description: Hershey, PA : Business Science Reference, [2021] | Includes bibliographical references and index. | Summary: "This book introduces innovative contracting to fit the era of digital transformation and industry 4.0 by addressing the motivations to promote such a new style of contracting and listing the shortcomings of traditional contracting"-- Provided by publisher.
Identifiers: LCCN 2020024125 (print) | LCCN 2020024126 (ebook) | ISBN 9781799845010 (hardcover) | ISBN 9781799865261 (paperback) | ISBN 9781799845027 (ebook)
Subjects: LCSH: Contracting out--Management. | Contracting out--Technological innovations. | Business planning.
Classification: LCC HD2365 .I55 2021 (print) | LCC HD2365 (ebook) | DDC 658.4/058--dc23
LC record available at https://lccn.loc.gov/2020024125
LC ebook record available at https://lccn.loc.gov/2020024126

This book is published in the IGI Global book series Advances in Business Information Systems and Analytics (ABISA) (ISSN: 2327-3275; eISSN: 2327-3283)

British Cataloguing in Publication Data
A Cataloguing in Publication record for this book is available from the British Library.

All work contributed to this book is new, previously-unpublished material. The views expressed in this book are those of the authors, but not necessarily of the publisher.

For electronic access to this publication, please contact: eresources@igi-global.com.

Advances in Business Information Systems and Analytics (ABISA) Book Series

Madjid Tavana
La Salle University, USA

ISSN:2327-3275
EISSN:2327-3283

Mission

The successful development and management of information systems and business analytics is crucial to the success of an organization. New technological developments and methods for data analysis have allowed organizations to not only improve their processes and allow for greater productivity, but have also provided businesses with a venue through which to cut costs, plan for the future, and maintain competitive advantage in the information age.

The **Advances in Business Information Systems and Analytics (ABISA) Book Series** aims to present diverse and timely research in the development, deployment, and management of business information systems and business analytics for continued organizational development and improved business value.

Coverage

- Data Analytics
- Business Models
- Geo-BIS
- Business Information Security
- Strategic Information Systems
- Legal information systems
- Algorithms
- Data Governance
- Business Intelligence
- Statistics

IGI Global is currently accepting manuscripts for publication within this series. To submit a proposal for a volume in this series, please contact our Acquisition Editors at Acquisitions@igi-global.com or visit: http://www.igi-global.com/publish/.

The Advances in Business Information Systems and Analytics (ABISA) Book Series (ISSN 2327-3275) is published by IGI Global, 701 E. Chocolate Avenue, Hershey, PA 17033-1240, USA, www.igi-global.com. This series is composed of titles available for purchase individually; each title is edited to be contextually exclusive from any other title within the series. For pricing and ordering information please visit http://www.igi-global.com/book-series/advances-business-information-systems-analytics/37155. Postmaster: Send all address changes to above address.

Titles in this Series

For a list of additional titles in this series, please visit: www.igi-global.com/book-series

Opportunities and Strategic Use of Agribusiness Information Systems
Ferdinand Ndifor Che (W3-Research, USA & APPC Research, Australia) Kenneth David Strang (W3-Research, USA & APPC Research, Australia) and Narasimha Rao Vajjhala (University of New York Tirana, Albania)
Business Science Reference • © 2021 • 333pp • H/C (ISBN: 9781799848493) • US $195.00

Integration Challenges for Analytics, Business Intelligence, and Data Mining
Ana Azevedo (CEOS, ISCAP, Polytechnic of Porto, Portugal) and Manuel Filipe Santos (Algoritmi Centre, University of Minho, Guimarães, Portugal)
Engineering Science Reference • © 2021 • 250pp • H/C (ISBN: 9781799857815) • US $225.00

Managing Business in the Civil Construction Sector Through Information Communication Technologies
Bithal Das Mundhra (Simplex Infrastructures Ltd, India) and Rajesh Bose (Simplex Infrastructures Ltd, India)
Business Science Reference • © 2021 • 254pp • H/C (ISBN: 9781799852919) • US $195.00

Achieving Organizational Agility, Intelligence, and Resilience Through Information Systems
Hakikur Rahman (Institute of Computer Management and Science, Bangladesh)
Business Science Reference • © 2021 • 300pp • H/C (ISBN: 9781799847991) • US $195.00

Handbook of Research on User Experience in Web 2.0 Technologies and Its Impact on Universities and Businesses
Jean-Éric Pelet (ESCE International Business School, INSEEC U Research Center, Paris, France)
Business Science Reference • © 2021 • 426pp • H/C (ISBN: 9781799837565) • US $295.00

Empowering Businesses With Collaborative Enterprise Architecture Frameworks
Tiko Iyamu (Cape Peninsula University of Technology, South Africa)
Business Science Reference • © 2021 • 309pp • H/C (ISBN: 9781522582298) • US $195.00

Natural Language Processing for Global and Local Business
Fatih Pinarbasi (Istanbul Medipol University, Turkey) and M. Nurdan Taskiran (Istanbul Medipol University, Turkey)
Business Science Reference • © 2021 • 452pp • H/C (ISBN: 9781799842408) • US $225.00

Applications of Big Data and Business Analytics in Management
Sneha Kumari (Vaikunth Mehta National Institute of Cooperative Management, India) K. K. Tripathy (Vaikunth Mehta National Institute of Cooperative Management, India) and Vidya Kumbhar (Symbiosis International University (Deemed), India)
Business Science Reference • © 2020 • 300pp • H/C (ISBN: 9781799832614) • US $225.00

IGI Global
PUBLISHER of TIMELY KNOWLEDGE

701 East Chocolate Avenue, Hershey, PA 17033, USA
Tel: 717-533-8845 x100 • Fax: 717-533-8661
E-Mail: cust@igi-global.com • www.igi-global.com

Table of Contents

Detailed Table of Contents

As we delve into value deconstruction, the number of contractors will increase a great deal, and every specialty will have its own parameters. The contract by its own will not be able to accommodate all clauses and conditions that may be due for changes. Now imagine, what would happen if important information like trade secrets of any corporation or business were to be leaked to competitors? And wouldn't it be so much better to legally oblige to privacy and urge those who consent to keep the information in question completely under wraps? For this reason, it is important to have an ecosystem of agreements such as NDAs, SLAs, and others to complete the chain and allow for efficient governance and risk management considerations. NDAs and confidentiality provisions have groundbreaking propensity. The design of such agreements is fundamental and various parameters must be considered. This chapter directs attention to these subjects and concerns by discussing the various types of complementary agreements and how they can be attached to the original contract to add value and reduce risk.

Contract management depends on document-driven processes that, in a paper-based environment, can be laborious and inefficient. The time it takes to approve a contract can be as significant as the content preparation of the contract. Slow, manual contract processing reflects negatively on an organization's ability to provide excellent service. The contract lifecycle is defined differently from an organization to organization or even form department to another. The number of contracts and the associated documents are ramping up in this era of digital transformation. An automated, digital contract lifecycle management (CLM) can reduce the administrative burden on employees and allows legal, financial, sales, and other professionals to make better use of their expertise. This chapter shows how automation can change the organizations' behaviors to view contracts as opportunities for operational improvement and competitive advantage. It shows also how CLM can be integrated with business intelligence (BI) and data analytics systems to provide contract insights and dashboards.

Risk management is a very crucial aspect in contracting; it has been an issue since the early days. This is becoming more and more challenging as new dimensions have entered the arena. With a lot of stakeholders working together to produce value, this includes contracts, providers, customers, and end users. The risk management paradigm has shifted and transformed multiple times in the recent years. This chapter is trying to touch on the risks associated with traditional contracts, then move ahead to suggest a design model for risks in innovative contracts. In between, the chapter is touching on points related to outsourcing and governance.

The selection and employment processes are considered among the complicated jobs that the human resources department performs. It is related to making specific decisions that are often difficult to withdraw or undo, such decision determine the fate of the organization in terms of human competencies that is selected to conduct the business functions. The employee selection and contracting are changing heavily in the digital transformation era, HR department needs to transform and find new ways to hire and retire based on technology tools. More professionals are looking at limited time jobs rather than permanent jobs as shown in the gig economy. The main objective of this chapter is to highlight hiring, training, and contracting of professionals in this era along with development stages, types, and strategies. In addition, it shows how such activities contributes to increase the effectiveness of employment process as well the organization effectiveness. In the last part will be presented the conclusions, recommendations, and future research suggestions.

The complexity of business and competitive environment enforces organizations to adopt innovative ways for doing business. This drives a new trend of agile organizations that are adaptable to market and technology changes. As a result, 75% of organizations recognized agility as one of the key drivers for their IT strategies. As organizations start adopting digital transformation initiatives, they recognize the necessity to adapt agility in their IT departments as well. However, moving to an agile organization and an agile IT department is more complex than adapting an agile software. This chapter aims to provide an in-depth explanation of agile IT department specifying its features, roles, and differentiation elements from the traditional IT department. Emerging technologies that are crucial in the movement towards an agile IT department are also discussed with possible change management process to facilitate the transition of the agile IT department into profit center that is contracted to add value for the whole organization while working in a feasible partnership mode with the business.

Artificial intelligence (AI) will continue to disrupt everything in the future; in the authors' view, AI needs a couple of years for perfect implementation. We need to minimize future AI negative impacts by passing suitable risk avoidance mechanisms for reaching global human satisfaction. Artificial intelligence has a critical role in converting the unstructured documents into structured enterprise data. Through implementing AI in contractual management, enterprises can get assistance in assessing risks and opportunities of businesses. The mission will be to develop and implement an AI strategy for the organization by selecting the best AI techniques and methodology for advancing legal documents' manipulation to assist managers in implementing and generating contracts and contracting analysis.

Digital transformation is the core value of the 4th industrial revolution or Industry 4.0. Although the efforts are focused on utilization and usage of technologies like artificial intelligence, internet of things,

The construction sector is large; it engages a variety of professions thus it is a main provider of employment and has a diverse market. The construction sector has a reputation for being conservative, problematic, and inefficient. This should change as we are moving toward industry 4.0 and smart cities that is injecting new tools and business dynamics. This chapter is trying to find methodologies to make an equilibrium between value produced by the contract, the flexibility of contract terms and contracting conditions thus contractors can be controlled in a reasonable matter. We are in here applying concepts and techniques from statics science and structural engineering to calculate PORD or PRCD (the Percentage Profit On Realistic Cashflow Duration) as a new financial modeling parameter that can help financial planners and decision makers to take more realistic decision. This parameter can be used jointly with other financial parameters such as ROI, IRR and NPV.

Chapter 16
Basic Concepts of Electric Power System Planning: Contracting for Reliability and Cost Effectiveness 306
Abdullah Alshaalan, King Saud University, Saudi Arabia

Power systems' planning, particularly in developing countries, faces enormous challenges and problems such as defining the future load growth in the face of uncertainties. Renewable energies are coming to the arena and affecting the planning of power and energy systems. The relation between power generation, transmission, and distribution entities, as well as the need for consolidating the dispersed electric utilities in the isolated regions is a prerequisite for future planning. Plenty of technologies, systems, and contractors are coming off the road while an optimal reliability levels need to be achieved. This chapter attempts to display the most tedious and prominent problems and challenges that face innovating the electric power systems which must be based on two major factors, namely reliability and cost. This chapter will help in drafting a new contracting style that mitigate obstacles that face power systems planners and concerned agencies while planning and operating electric power facilities.

Chapter 17
The Transformation of Supplier-Client Relationship: Real Stories About Tire Business Solutions .. 326
Ghassan Wahbe, BridgeStone, UAE

Industry 4.0 has affected everything around us. Today we have entered an era where we must move our focus away from traditional business relations and shift instead to solutions that support the virtual enterprise in which independent businesses align to share skills and resources to sharpen their responses to external business opportunities. Manufacturers, suppliers, and clients need to work jointly to create value and share risk instead of settings tight conditions, KPIs that are hard to implement, and start blaming each other. Business solutions are representing a new wave that is built on technology to overcome the inward-looking nature of old systems and promises a great wave of efficiency and reduced costs by streamlining the management processes of external relationships that is based on trust and governed by innovative contracts. This chapter is describing a real virtual enterprise from the business showing how digital transformation is changing the supplier-client contracting relationship.

Chapter 18
The Inspiring Contracts: How to Create Value Through Contracting 345
Momen Nashar, Oracle, Lebanon

Foreword

Digital Transformation is becoming the heart of every innovation or future planning. It can be defined as a journey to adopt and deploy digital technologies and business models to improve business performance. Major driving factors include agility, sustainability, disruption avoidance and enhanced user experience. Contracts have organized the business relations since long time, but the contracting process was more of a manual, lengthy process handled by administration and legal counsel.

The new business dynamics that have been imposed by industry 4.0 such as the increased business velocity, the layered partnerships and the ascending dependance on temporary workers are forcing the recognition of effective contract management as a need-to-have necessity across every enterprise. New contracting types are invented, and contracts started to operate as an integral management tool for business operation and professional practice integrity.

A deeper knowledge of the contract outcomes is required today for contracts in place, and for the identification and predictions of future results. Modern contract management stands at the heart of modern business, acting as the real glue behind many inter-dependent and inter-locking entities and business processes. The contracts are positioned now as critical business assets.

An increased collaboration across industries, organizations and temporary workers are required to handle clashing or moving expectations regarding timing, training, governance, and quality. As a result, the contracting processes need to be more flexible and agile to align and adapt continuously. A strong ecosystem will be beneficial to all stakeholders to foster continuous value creation.

Technology will never replace the human touch, but rather transform, enrich, and automate the contract management process. Digital transformation created a huge potential for better systematized contract management styles, behaviors, and workflows, that can utilize analytical tools and artificial intelligence systems. Such systems are expected to accommodate data extraction and enhanced insights for individual agreements and contractual networks.

This book provides a valuable window on contract management and new contracting styles. It covers the necessary components from building the contracting roadmap toward creating innovative contracts that can accommodate challenges and variables in modern business styles, emerging technologies, and the contracting arena. Additionally, this book provides practical business cases from the field to show the value of innovative contracting and how contracts can inspire the business and create a Win-Win situation.

One unique point in an edited book is the diversity of authors, who are coming from different countries, universities, and business organizations. Every author is tackling one topic from different perspective and mindset as a researcher or as a working professional. This diversity enriched the view and here come the editors' role to successfully align the book theme and avoid duplications.

The bottom line is that as business complexities increase and timeframes shrink, more potential will exist to build smart, collaborative, and efficient contract management powered by technology and innovation. New contract types and contracting methodologies have been invented and will continue. The deeper the understanding of contract elements and business behaviors are, the more significant the achieved results will be and the satisfaction levels among stakeholders who will have enhanced ability to act timely and precisely.

Adding new layers of business intelligence and data analytics will enhance the ability to approach and manage the contracting objectives that are specific, measurable, attainable, relevant, and time-based both at enterprise-wide scale, or lower levels. An automated processing and reporting function with more actionable insights will help organizations in managing upwards of hundreds to thousands of contracts each year, which may contain multi-stream, global scale workflows.

While innovative contracts are becoming a reality, the world is ultimately moving toward fully smart contracts that have some use cases today but are expected to take place in plenty of industries. Agile contracting and innovative contracts are becoming a solid figure that will have more maturity and adoption levels.

Saad S. Alkahtani
Institute of Public Administration, Saudi Arabia

Saad S. Alkahtani, *Associate Professor of Applied Statistics at the Institute of Public Administration (IPA), Saudi Arabia, earned his PhD in Applied Statistics in 2010 from the University of Northern Colorado, USA. He has published, presented and reviewed plenty of scientific research studies and working papers, as well as authored and translated a number of books. The most important of which is an authored book entitled "Applied Statistics" published in 2015 in Arabic language, and two translated books from English to Arabic language about Structural Equation Modeling using AMOS and Scale Development. Alkahtani worked as a part-time statistician consultant for a number of government agencies. He chaired and was a member of many scientific and advisory committees inside and outside the IPA. He holds a number of professional certificates and many practical practices in the field of data analytics, survey design and performance measurement.*

Preface

Digital Transformation and Industry 4.0 is a trend of automation and data exchange that affects everything in our lives. It is blurring the lines between physical, biological, and digital. In the new environment technology and humans are so closely integrated and boundaries are changing every day.

Modern schools are much more than a pencil and a book. Today's teachers express their vision by multiple dimensions of audio, video, reporting, and technology effects to create a rich experience. To conduct a class today you will require an ecosystem that comprise a complex and highly adaptable network of collaborators who come with a highly personalized experience.

This ecosystem behaviors are occurring in every industry today. An automaker run various partnerships to access the technology and intellectual properties needed for connected cars and related digital services. Smart cities utilize plenty emerging technologies from various partners to have a connected, resilient, and safe city.

It is obvious now that delivering unique value will require radical connectivity, an open mind, and a wide range of players. The collaboration itself and the interplay of different elements create a unique value. Contracts are increasingly needed to manage such complex scenarios and are progressively recognized as an imperative asset to the enterprise. Business architectures and orchestrators should be careful in choosing partners who are skilled enough and have the tools or technologies for the desired functionality.

This situation inspires companies to recognize the contracts' impact and value that is directly interrelated to improving overall business performance. More inspirations are added due to the increased number of contracts resulted from business value deconstruction and the flexible human capital. Moreover, the complexity of contracts is ramping up with every specialty have its own parameters and activities that are transforming rapidly in an agile, speedy manner.

Traditionally, contracts used to exist as paper-based documents with manual or email-based routing for reviews. Once terms were defined, shared, and agreed upon with relevant stakeholders, they were signed in ink, and either stored away in a file cabinet or scanned into an electronic document repository. Contract control was primarily focused around risk prevention in contract terms. Access to contract documents was likely limited to counsel and separated from scrutiny to actual business performance, obligations, or measurements.

Today the actual performance needs to be verified continuously against the business terms contained within the contract and the business relationships can scarcely function without parties being able to accommodate themselves to inevitable changes during the lifetime of the contract. The friction between the legal mindsets of tight control and the business flexibility perspective has endured for decades but it is discussed more in this futuristic era where technology is innovating exponentially putting everything on change.

The editors have identified the contracting gap that is uncovered causing plenty of hassle while moving to the new business environments. The editors have discussed the new business dynamics with many professionals and academic circles. Plenty of people were looking forward for different contracts and contracting styles that can improve efficiencies, cope with the organization needs, and at the same time facilitate faster, more-secure, soft, and real time transactions. This inspired the editors to look actively for well-respected authors who can contribute a piece of their research or practical experience in this unique field and the book journey was ignited.

CHALLENGES OF TRADITIONAL CONTRACTS

On 17 January 2018, UK infrastructure giant Carillion announced it was going into liquidation. According to (Colhoun, 2018), its collapse was caused in part by cost overruns on some of its large contracts. The failure is often due to inadequate contract management systems that are frequently not integrated with materials management solutions and the design software tools. This was a strong case to embed and enforce proven contractual discipline to better manage interface with the contractors and avoid contract leakage.

Traditionally, contracts formalize arm's length transactions that is implying a strictly professional relationship between parties. Usually standard contracts are straightforward agreements based on each party agreeing to fulfill its contractually obligated duty in exchange for the other party's fulfillment of a duty. However, these contracts have accumulated challenges that can be categorized as legal, administrative, functional, financial, quality.

Some companies are losing serious money in their sale-side and procurement contracts. (Marttinen, 2019) defined contract value leakage as the difference between the value expected from a contract and the value realized in its implementation during its lifetime. Good contract development and management could improve profitability by the equivalent of a massive 9% of annual revenue. In a study mentioned at (Cummins, IACCM, 2012), almost 77% of International Association for Contract & Commercial Management member' companies indicated that project delays or cost overruns represent a regular source of loss; a further 53% highlighted claim and dispute settlements, with 26% experiencing losses and delays from contract cancellation and a similar percentage facing revenue leakage from liquidated damages.

MOTIVATIONS FOR A NEW CONTRACTING STYLE

The contracting process used to be lengthy, manual, and handled as a legal or administrative function. Today more contracts are coming into action and organizations are looking for contracts' agility and stability while responding to the new market trends and keeping up with legal obligations. The mission that seems impossible from first glance.

The human capital preparations for new contracting styles should be different. Futuristic issues in business ecosystem challenge legal practitioners on creating a fit between technology based operational activities and adaptive functional strategies. There is a solid need for skillful legal practitioners who can extract actionable information and utilize advanced technology tools to build the required contracting paradigm.

Throughout the contract lifecycle, teams of people must collaborate on various tasks both pre-execution and post-execution. This includes collaboration among several different departments across an enterprise and even multiple external vendors or resources. Even more, the main contractors may hire second-degree contractors for certain activities. The challenge is to make the collaboration smooth and transparent, so that costly mistakes can be avoided through the implemented system of control, collaboration, and governance.

According to (Ellis, Molloy, Cohen, & Crozier, 2019), waterfall projects proceed in a 'straight line' with clear sequencing, milestones, and pre-defined delivery outcomes. Contracting for them is therefore relatively simple. But agile projects which are more common today works through a continual process of review, in a series of small increments or sprints, and with flexible desired outcomes that may change as the project progresses. Innovative contracting is invited to handle such situations.

Moreover, businesses have become more dependent on external suppliers whose performance determine by the quality of operations across an 'interdependent network' or virtual enterprise. Complex environments require a disciplined approach to manage with proper digital integration. This will enhance the contract management and associated costing while enhancing the contract visibility (Ball, 2017).

Many ecosystems are set up to bring in expertise from other industries. Organizations in an ecosystem need to share expertise, data, technology, and intellectual property with partners who may be subject to less stringent regulations, rules and contractual commitments (Lang, Szczepanski, & Wurzer, 2019). Innovative contracting will help in setting up flexible ecosystems that can be formed, changed, or dissolved easily. This setup will be able to respond quickly to changing preferences, emerging technologies, and regulatory changes.

However, flexibility means that an organization need to have a clear strategy map that can identify the potential participants, and clearly defines all roles, responsibilities, contributions, and interactions upfront the journey. In addition, an effective governance model needs to be well established. Such a platform has so many contributors, thus, the orchestrator must set up a standard and often an automated model of governance, interaction, and financial exchange.

Innovative contracts are introduced to comprise a set of approaches which includes the smart contracts that can automate rule-based functions, frictionless contracts that can facilitate many different activities and opportunity contracts that enhance the collaboration between stakeholders and combine several factors to produce an effective contract (Shalan & Anaim, 2017).

Contracts move along their lifecycles with a clear delineation of beginning, in-state, and end-state purposes. This will enable extraction of data across contract portfolios, offering not just efficiencies, but also far greater insight into the effectiveness of alternative contract types or terms, as well as management of contractual networks, not just individual agreements. Organizations will then be able to accomplish complex tasks in different environments and ecosystems with relative ease (Barnaud & Antona, 2019).

The book authors have identified shifts in technology and business dynamics that invite the new approach of contracts which include the following pillars:

- The changed ownership of systems and solution with the introduction of giant powerhouses
- The massive data flow in the organizations
- The increased dependency on contractors and temporary skilled workers
- The break of silos mentality towards fully integrated behaviors among business units
- The inevitable agility, transformation, and change management practices

- Viable variations in business areas that enforces cultural shifts, technology innovations and collaborative business.

Considering such movements, innovative contracts play a vital role in building trust among partners which is critical for fluidity and flexibility. This trusted contracting will foster the setup of agile arrangements in which the ecosystem can respond quickly to changes in the business landscape and form partnerships as required. This emphasizes the need to study the complex interdependences underlying the ecosystem dynamics. (Barnaud & Antona, 2019).

Overall, this will portray the future trends for virtual enterprises and ecosystem buildups in a way to improve quality, reduce project cost, diminish complexity in vendor relationships, and enhance collaboration (Shalan M., 2010). Governance should handle the fear of disclosing confidential information, expanding services without compensation, or losing operational autonomy. Innovative contracting is very crucial to manage the evolution of these emerging relationships cooperatively while sharing the benefits correspondingly among the stakeholders.

An innovative contract needs to balance the creation of a collaborative culture that allows for continuous delivery and embraces change, with the provision of sufficient commercial protection for all parties. It needs to incentivize all stakeholders to work together and take a shared responsibility for success.

THE BOOK STRUCTURE

This book has three main sections the first part represents the innovative contracts' roadmap and ecosystem from concept to regulation while illustrating few motivations. It also elaborates on associated risks, human resources movements, information technology transformation and contracting lifecycle management to enrich the journey. The second part shows emerging technology contracting and the third part describes practical case studies from the field.

Dr. Hana Yamani and Dr. Waleed Elsigini started the journey, they set up the stage by defining industry 4.0 and summarizing the dimensions of digital transformation which includes technologies, data, processes, and human factors among other vital components for vision planning and implementation. Emerging technologies, execution strategies, challenges and future behaviors are also discussed.

Mr. Mohamed Bassyouni dives into the anatomy of traditional contracts, specifying their rights, relationships, and major types such as Fixed Price (FBC), Cost Plus (CPC), and Time and Materials (T&M) Contracts. History and hurdles were also discussed before moving to describe new contracting styles such as the vested outsourcing that introduce rules to enhance partnership and value-based contracts (VBC) that is used in healthcare. This will help to select and negotiate a contract.

Dr. Hasan Tayyeb debate building an ecosystem around the contract to handle specialty topics that have its own parameters. The contract by its own may not accommodate all clauses and conditions that are due for change and control. This ecosystem of agreements includes non-disclosure (NDAs), service level (SLAs) and annexes to complete the chain, add value, reduce risk, and handle forward changes.

Dr. Mohammed Algarni illustrate how to change contract into data and utilize business intelligence (BI) and data analytics to generate insights. This will stop the old style of manual, slow processing that reflects negatively on an organization's ability to provide excellent service. The automated, digital Contract Lifecycle Management (CLM) was explored to reduce the administrative burden on employees and allows legal, financial, and other professionals to make better use of their expertise.

Mr. Omar Shalan discussed the risk management for the traditional and innovative contracts in addition to outsourcing and governance. Risks have transformed multiple times in recent years and become more challenging as new dimensions and stakeholders have entered the arena. This is obvious in construction and digital transformation contracts where the cost of poor contracts can be more obvious.

Dr. Akif Al-Khasawneh review the employee contracts and the hiring process which may result in decisions that are difficult to withdraw or undo. This includes the human resources department transformation from hire to retire considering the trend of professionals' preferencing limited duration jobs. This will require enhanced contracting, monitoring and selection activities to hire more effectively and quickly.

Dr. Fawaz Alharbi touch the other side of the resources required to support the innovative contracting. He defined how the technology department can be more agile, business oriented, customer centric and data driven. This will facilitate communication, align with the organization strategy, and enable more flexible contracts that can be correlated with real time performance tools

Dr. Fatmah Baothman verified the role of artificial intelligence (AI) in converting the unstructured contracts into structured enterprise data. She explained how this will benefit the enterprises in assessing risks and opportunities within the business's contracts. This will encourage and advance legal practices and assist managers in generating and implementing new contracts and advanced contracting analysis.

In the last chapter of part one, Mr. Belal Hafnawi elaborated on regulating the innovative contracts and emerging technologies. He explained how solid regulatory frameworks can remove uncertainties in development, investment, and implementation of technologies. As the transformation is so fast, some regulators are keen to test the consequences immediately utilizing a sandbox thinking to evaluating the impact at a small scale. Others are more conservative to act even if this generate unnecessary boarders.

The second part of the book discussed how technology is standing at the heart of new business value generation. It showed how to transform, implement, and contract for the human resources solutions (HRMs), blockchain based systems, internet of things (IoT) and the business solutions including the enterprise resource planning (ERP) to cope with the digital transformation era.

Dr Malek Elayan suggestted some modifications in the electronic human resources management solution (eHRMS) to allow accommodating the gig workers contracting. The eHRMSs have been important to support strategic decisions, create value and maintain business continuity. The suggested methodologies are important to retain progression and development considering the new dynamics and behaviors.

Dr. Sara Alotaibi set out definitions and criteria related to smart contracts advantages and limitations. She illustrates how blockchain can be used to build smart contracts that is self-executable piece of code based on a trigger. Smart contracts replace the idea of 'credit intermediation' in dealing such as notary or bank with another thought based on a peer-to-peer system to increase contractual security and speed.

Mr. Saeed Baselm studied the contracting for the internet of things (IoT) and the implementation methodologies. This has a particular importance since it is a vertical integration where business expands by contracting with another company that operates before or after them in the supply chain. Vertical diffusion is becoming more common in Industry 4.0 era compared to the traditional horizontal integration.

Mr. Mohamed Raouf explored an interesting topic that have been thought by all types of organizations. The decision to innovate or build an Enterprise Resource Planning (ERP) software is a big decision that can make or break the business. He started with the difficult part of defining a workable scope before considering the full journey of transformation up to contracting, implementation and enhancement.

The third part bring plenty of real stories and case studies to show how innovative contracting can make a great difference. The first two cases are coming from real estate industry showing the effect of new technologies on enhancing the touch points associated with the architecture design and the contracting equilibrium between value and cashflow. The other two cases described the inter-contracting between power generation, transmission, and distribution entities while the last one illustrated the move to virtual enterprise. The last chapter displayed inspiring contracting stories collected from around the world.

A well know architect in Saudi Arabia, Mr. Solaiman Elkhereiji started the third part by explaining the effects of industry 4.0 technologies on architecture and design offices contracting. It is interesting to see how advanced means are facilitating new mindsets in design architects and construction industry. Customer expectations are already elevated and new touch points with stakeholders are to be managed.

Mr. Mohamad Raafat focused on construction sector reputation as being conservative, problematic, and inefficient while he is calling for innovation. New tools, techniques and business dynamics are identified to make equilibrium between value produced by the contract, the flexibility of contract terms and contracting conditions. The realistic cashflow duration method (RCD) is suggested to enhance cashflow sensation for projects and tenders.

Dr. Abdullah M. Al-Shaalan simplifies a very complex topic related to the power systems' planning, and renewable energies. The relation between power generation, transmission, and distribution entities have been tedious focusing on two major factors reliability and cost. This chapter is drafting a new contracting style that mitigate obstacles that face power systems planners and concerned agencies.

One more case study is coming from the tire industry, where Mr. Ghassan Wahbe described the move from traditional business relations in tire industry to business solutions that foster the virtual enterprise setup. This case illustrated enhancing the businesses alignment, sharing skills, moving resources, and refining the responses to business opportunities. Manufacturers, suppliers, and clients work jointly to create value and share risk instead of settings tight contracting conditions.

The last chapter in the book was chosen to stick in mind. Dr. Momen Nachar raised the bar by telling inspiring stories to show powerful contracts that reshaped the business and encompass additional stakeholders. Loose-loose scenarios turned into successful win-win relationships through contracting. Ukraine saved huge amounts through open contracting, Dell-FedEx relationship was sustained form the edge and Henry Ford challenge the employee contracting philosophy.

MOVING TOWARD THE NEW ERA

As we have entered the era of blurred lines, we expect the borders between business units and partners to be detached or reshaped. The concept of virtual enterprise is being more enforced with horizontal and vertical diffusions. Business performance relies predominantly on the strength and efficiency of external relationships, effective contracting and innovation capabilities. According to (Cummins, Contracting-Excellence-Journal, 2019) streamlining these commercial operations help organizations to reduce operational costs by at least 20% and generate improved revenues and savings from their relationships.

A virtual enterprise is formed by independent resources that is aligned to share properties, hire gig workers, and sharpen the responses to opportunities and deconstructed values. According to (Vitasek, 2018) the most successful deals move away toward the "two-in-a-box" concept where organizations work together and collaborate as they govern/manage aspects of the business. This includes having peer-to-peer relationships at multiple levels as a part of a tiered management structure.

According to the IACCM, the International Association for Contract and Commercial Management, key aspects of the contracting process will be undertaken through technology (Howard, 2016). Contracts themselves will increasingly be core business assets and sources of valuable business information. The future of contracting will be multi-dimensional with technology at heart. However, there's a blockage of incumbent contracts and commercial staff who need to be repositioned and equipped with new skills.

Innovative contracting will be able to govern the dynamic business relationships and achieve the advanced obligations while monitoring shared data streams and controlling the value generation. According to (Cummins, Contracting-Excellence-Journal, 2019) (Vitasek, 2018), emerging technologies and digital transformation will be a driver for multiple contracting insights and trends that are maturing which includes:

- **Considering Contracts as Data Sets**: The traditional view of contracts as 'documents' is fast giving away toward considering them as a critical source of 'data', at transactional and portfolio levels.
- **Abandoning Risk Transfer Mindset:** The contracts are becoming instruments for mutual economic value. This is leading to formality in relationships and behaviors, with growing focus on outputs and outcomes, rather than inputs and risk transfers.
- **Moving Toward Pathways:** Contracts tend traditionally to set boundaries to impose responsibilities and establish protections. The new era is increasingly open, transparent data flows; thus, contracts need to establish pathways through enhanced collaboration structures.
- **Leveraging Pooled Resources:** Parties can capitalize on each other's strengths to align strategic outputs. Collaboration enables maximal leverage of the resources of each partner. Mutual benefits will be attained.
- **Hunting for the Future:** New contracting relationships are focused on long or short partnerships that foster strategic collaboration to mutually facilitate the achievement of a futuristic goal. The goal may not be central to the ultimate success or direction of both organizations.
- **Inheriting Innovation:** The innovative contracting need to encourage the desire to innovate and work toward the delivery or provision of a new products or services in alignment with corporate goals, strategies, and priorities.

Well defined quality parameters and solid governance structures need to cope up with the moving business dynamics and contracting challenges. The innovative contracting is expected to provide sufficient structure to protect all parties and achieve the desired mission outcomes, while offering flexibility for adaptation of requirements within the agreed-on scope.

CONCLUSION

Digital transformation has shaped everything around us, and contracting is not an exception. The key is to have a well governed structure that shape the approach to drive satisfaction and productivity. This book is navigating the prescribed situation in contracts, contracting and related human, business, and technology factors. Plenty of touch points will be described and investigated.

Related emerging technologies will provide several important enablers to contract design and structure, some examples are the visualization trends, blockchain, robotic process automation (RPA) and business Intelligence (BI). Ultimately, we will be moving to create platforms that generate visibility across the contracting environment while accelerating the push towards smart self-service contracts.

Innovative contracts will keep aligning with businesses dynamics to become nimbler and more responsive to market signals through accelerated development and pivoting. Without innovative contracting, an agile project or a flexible research may become an exercise in stop-start frustration.

The human touch will remain, and the contracting officer will continue to fall squarely in the middle of defining the appropriate balance between the two sides of contracting tenet "Customer collaboration over contract negotiation." (Wrubel & Gross, 2015).

In due course, we are moving toward full automation to have innovated smart self-executable contracts that are built on deconstructed value, mutual trust, real risk sharing and tiered management and is powered by emerging technologies, featured process automation and business intelligence.

REFERENCES

Ball, B. (2017, July 1). *Contract Management: How the Best-in-Class Maximize Their Potential.* Retrieved August 01, 2020, from https://naviant.com/wp-content/uploads/2020/04: https://naviant.com/wp-content/uploads/2020/04/Aberdeen-ContractManagement-Whitepaper-2015.pdf

Barnaud, C., & Antona, M. (2019, May 23). Deconstructing ecosystem services: Uncertainties and and controversies around a socially constructed concept. *Geoforum*, 113–123. https://www.sciencedirect.com/science/article/abs/pii/S0016718514001547

Colhoun, C. (2018, January 22). *Poor-contract-management-fails-uk-infrastructure-giant-carillion.* Retrieved July 30, 2020, from https://sw.aveva.com/blog/poor-contract-management-fails-uk-infrastructure-giant-carillion

Cummins, T. (2012, October 23). *IACCM.* Retrieved July 27, 2020, from https://blog.iaccm.com/commitment-matters-tim-cummins-blog/2012/10/23/poor-contract-management-costs-companies-9-bottom-lin

Cummins, T. (2019, December 16). *Contracting-Excellence-Journal.* Retrieved from https://journal.iaccm.com/contracting-excellence-journal/the-next-big-thing-relationship-resource-planning-rrp-1

Ellis, W., Molloy, M., Cohen, J., & Crozier, P. (2019, July 1). *Ontracting-for-agile.pdf.* Retrieved August 2, 2020, from https://assets.kpmg/content/dam/kpmg/uk/pdf/2019/08/contracting-for-agile.pdf

Howard. (2016, June 22). *The-contract-management-best-practice-gap/.* https://thedmcollaborators.com/2016/06/22/the-contract-management-best-practice-gap/

Lang, N., Szczepanski, K. v., & Wurzer, C. (2019, January 16). *Emerging-art-ecosystem-management.* Retrieved August 1, 2020, from https://www.bcg.com/publications/2019/emerging-art-ecosystem-management

Marttinen, T. (2019, August 21). *Are you familiar with the concept of Contract Value Leakage?* Retrieved from https://www.linkedin.com/pulse/you-familiar-concept-contract-value-leakage-teemu-marttinen/

Shalan, M. (2010). Managing IT Risks in Virtual Enterprise Networks: A Proposed Governance Framework. In Managing Risk in Virtual Enterprise Networks: Implementing Supply Chain Principles (pp. 115-136). IGI Global. doi:10.4018/978-1-61520-607-0.ch006

Shalan, M., & Anaim, N. (2017). The SMAC Opportunity Contracts: Generating Value From Responsive Agile Risk-Oriented Techniques. In Mobile Platforms, Design, and Apps for Social Commerce (pp. 115-134). IGI Global.

Vitasek, K. (2018, June 4). *Adopt a "two-in-a-box" partner for efficient outsourcing governance*. Retrieved from https://futureofsourcing.com/adopt-a-two-in-a-box-partner-for-efficient-outsourcing-governance

Wrubel, E., & Gross, J. (2015). *Contracting for Agile Software Development in the Department of Defense: An Introduction.* Carnegie Mellon's University, Software Engineering Institute. Retrieved from https://resources.sei.cmu.edu/library/asset-view.cfm?assetid=442499

Section 1

The Roadmap Toward Innovative Contracting

Chapter 1
Digital Transformation and Industry 4.0

Hanaa Abdulraheem Yamani
Umm Al-Qura University, Saudi Arabia

Waleed Tageldin Elsigini
https://orcid.org/0000-0003-0247-7817
Umm Al-Qura University, Saudi Arabia

ABSTRACT

The current era is witnessing many changes on various levels. The information and communication revolutions are considered one of the important changes which has cast a shadow over how different institutions in society work via the phenomenon of digitization. As some of the most important institutions of society, industrial companies have been responding to this phenomenon of digital transformation to improve products and customer service while achieving a significant profitable return. This response by these institutions to the digital transformation has resulted in the emergence of the so-called fourth industrial revolution. In this context, this chapter reviews the definition of digital transformation as well as its dimensions, benefits, and obstacles. It also comments on the future of digital transformation and its relationship with industry. Ultimately it presents the fourth industrial revolution in terms of its definition, history, criteria, benefits, and the challenges it faces moving into the future.

INTRODUCTION

There is no doubt that the process of technological development known as digitization occurred in the last quarter of the previous century and has affected the concept of industrial production. This development has led to a group of information and communication technologies which allow for the combination of the physical and digital worlds. It has affected all society sectors by employing new digital technologies such as big data, social networks, internet of things, artificial intelligence, blockchain and many more. These changes have led to a new industrial revolution (Industry 4.0) also called "The Fourth Industrial

DOI: 10.4018/978-1-7998-4501-0.ch001

Revolution". This revolution plays a noteworthy role in making the most of digitalization opportunities in all the phases of service systems and production (Ustundsag and Cevikcan, 2018).

The word "Industry 4.0" appeared in Germany and it does not represent a set of technologies but rather a political program developed by the German government, trade unions, and businesses. It mentions, "We are behind the train of the ICT revolution. We want to be those who produce smart robots that allow the production of a smart industry and thus create a kind of aristocratic work in the world, which is high wage and is able to design these things"(Dosi, 2017).

Returning to Industry 4.0 and the age of digital revolution, the World Economic Forum listed twelve different technologies which enhanced business models and brought forth new production techniques. It would be of special interest to know that these changes have significantly affected and changed the global production system. These technologies are artificial intelligence (AI) and robotics, internet of things (IoT), additive manufacturing (3D printing), virtual and augmented reality (VR, AR), blockchain and distributed ledger technology, energy capture, advanced materials and nano-materials, new computing technology, storage and transmission, geo-engineering, bio-technologies, neurotechnology and space technologies (World Economic Forum, 2018).

Foro de Empresas Innovadoras (2018), added some other technologies, such as machine learning technology and big data to the previous list. Other studies summarize the technologies in three branches: internet of things (connectivity), additive manufacturing (3D printing), and advanced robotics (flexible automation) (Eurofound 2017, 2018).

In light of the foregoing, this chapter reviews the digital transformation with regards to its definition, dimensions, obstacles, and future. Ultimately it concludes with The Fourth Industrial Revolution or Industry 4.0 benefits, boundaries, criteria, challenges and future expectations.

Furthermore, this chapter reviews suggestions of how to implement digital transformation in institutions through several steps including: analyzing the new business processes, identifying the main technologies, developing an innovative system, building an efficient team, and defining a roadmap and evaluation. It also addresses the future trends of digital transformation through the increase in digital transformation strategies, investment in IT and the new skill requirements. The barriers of successful implementation are also addressed along with how to overcome such obstacles.

BACKGROUND

The digital transformation is one of the areas that attracted the attention of many researchers in various fields due to the growing role that information and communication technology plays in various sectors of society.

Several studies and literature have reviewed the concept of digital transformation:(Mazzone, 2014), (Schallmo, Williams, and Boardman, 2017), (Ismail, Khater and Zaki, 2017), (Schwertner, 2017), (Bloomberg, 2018) did so with regards to its dimensions; (Seres, Pavlicevic and Tumbas, 2018), (Verina and Titko, 2019), (Turchi, 2018) its application; and (Matt, Hess and Benliam,2015), (Ismail, Khater and Zaki, 2017), (Schallmo, Williams,and Boardman, 2017), also analyze these items. The research indicates that the different definitions of digital transformation center around the use of technology to improve institutional business, and that the dimensions of digital transformation are varied between strategy, implementation, technology (Turchi, 2018), activities, processes, data, business models, clients, leaders, and employees (Verina and Titko, 2019). But the different classifications converge into four main dimensions: technologies - data - processes - individuals.

As for the strategies for implementing the digital transformation, most neglect the aspect of analysis in the light of strategic planning, where the factors of strengths, weaknesses, opportunities, and threats must be identified.

Some researches focused on highlighting the relationship between the digital transformation and the industrial sector, which is represented in the concept of The Fourth Industrial Revolution, where the revolution is characterized by the use of specific enabling technologies such as big data, IOT, cloud, robots, 3D Printing, augmented reality, and simulation to improve the production process and gain customer satisfaction (Gadi, 2016), (Mcginnis,2018), (Petrillo, De Felice, Cioffi and Zomparelli, 2018), (Rossi,2018).

DIGITAL TRANSFORMATION OR THE INDUSTRY 4.0

Both terms are used interchangeably a lot of times, however they have different origins but describing a similar way forward to utilize emerging technologies to create a new business future. Digital transformation is discussed more with normal business structures while Industry 4.0 is used more in the context of manufacturing industry.

Digital Transformation Definition

There are many definitions of digital transformation where (Ismail, Khater, & Zaki, 2017) define digital transformation as a process whereby companies converge through different new digital technologies, improved by communication everywhere, with the goal of achieving superior performance and sustainable competitive advantage. This would be achieved by transforming the multiple dimensions of business (including customer experience, digital enabled products and services, and business models), process (including operations and decision-making), and at the same time influencing people (including talent and culture skills) and networks (including the entire value system).

Schwertner (2017) defines the digital transformation as the application of technology to develop software, process, system, and new business models in order to obtain greater competitive advantage, more profitable revenue, and increased efficiency; while Deloitte (2018) defines it as using technology to fundamentally improve an organization's performance in a digitally transformed business as digital technologies improve interactive talent and new business models. Furthermore, OECD (2018) referred to it as the conversion of data and analog processes to a machine-readable format. Digitization is the use of digital technologies and data as well as their interconnection which ultimately leads to new changes in existing activities.

Digital transformation can be defined as a combination of advanced technologies with the integration of physical and digital systems, the dominance of the innovative business model and new processes, and the creation of smart products and services (European Commission, 2019). At its simplest level, digital transformation means transforming the core business of an organization where it uses technology and data to better meet customer needs (Clark,2019).

Thus, we can define the concept of digital transformation as a system of technologies, data, processes, and individuals that aims to improve the performance of organizations and make all of their members and customers more satisfied.

Digital Transformation Dimensions

According to most authors, the digital transformation of business has six dimensions (Seres, Pavlicevic and Tumbas, 2018):

- An acceptable organizational strategy and approach to applying innovation.
- Collaborative processes adaptable to the modern business model.
- Full automation of business processes.
- Analysis and research in customer decision making.
- Information technology that supports all organizational processes.
- Usable and relevant data with the use of data analysis as the basis for the decision making

Verina and Titko (2019) and McKeown (2019) illustrated the elements of digital transformation that should be addressed at any institute as shown in figure (1).

Figure 1. Elements of digital transformation.
(Verina and Titko,2019)

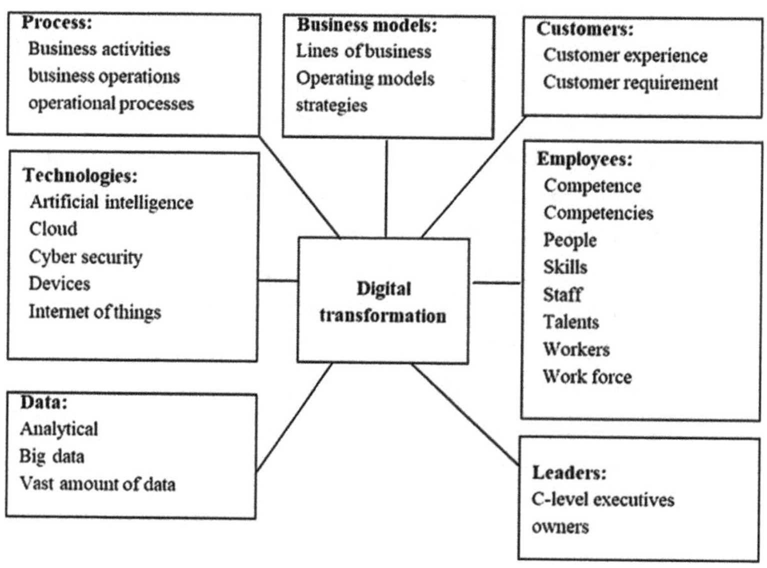

In light of the above we can summarize the dimensions of digital transformation at any institution as follows:

- **Technologies**: While it is generally accepted that digital transformation should not only focus technology, it is significant to understand that technology is a crucial element in the journey of digital transformation. Technology here refers to a system of devices, data, storage media, programs and networks that operate within technical environments and information centers and allow the use of all assets with continuous operational efficiency.
- **Data**: It is highly accepted that the sufficient use of data and analytics for decision making is a vital component to succeed in digital transformation. Institutions work to regularly and effectively manage and analyze data to provide qualitative, reliable, and complete data; as well as to provide and develop appropriate tools for statistical analysis, data search, and future prediction. This is conducted while constantly monitoring data to ensure its continued flow in order to benefit from it in line with the goals of the institution and its expectations.
- **Processes**: Institutions must establish an effective technical construction that allows performance development to ensure the optimal application of digital transformation considering the available capabilities and resources. This includes the establishment of a technical construction that includes policies and procedures covering all of the institution's activities and operations interconnected with the necessary technologies, developed applications, and processing data.
- **Individuals**: Individuals are vital components of the digital transformation system wherein qualified cadres must be provided to use data and analyze them to make effective decisions. Vision planning and implementation requires human competencies with scientific and practical experiences as well as a belief in change and development while taking into account the experiences and requirements of the institution's customers.

Figure 2. The digital transformation pyramid.
(Turchi, 2018)

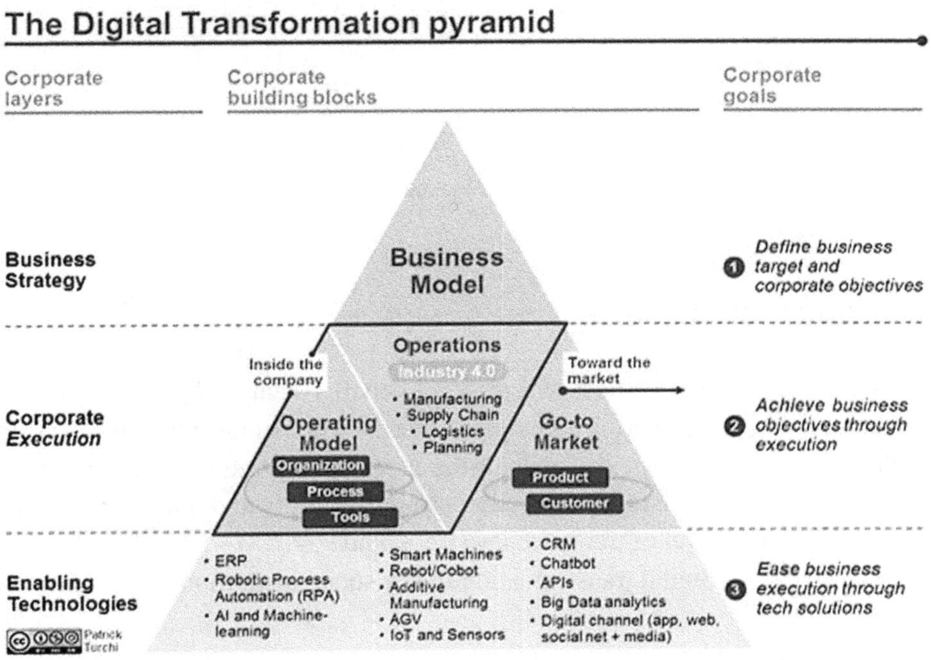

Turchi (2018) emphasizes that there are three important levels which should be addressed by the digital transformation framework: strategy, execution, and technology; as shown in figure(2).

The digital transformation blocks from which they are adapted are shown in figure(3) (Turchi, 2018).

As shown by the digital transformation pyramid, an effective digital transformation framework has to approach these three levels. The three elements have different sub-elements in each layer. These are combined and described as follows:

- **Strategy**: This layer includes the business model (business strategy) and defines it in a digital environment as a strategy that evaluates the impacts and opportunities of the digital business model, such as marketplace and platform business, owner model evaluation, value-added services after employing digital technology, and data-based products and services.
- **Execution**: This element should effectively work inside the organization and outside it, and it includes three different blocks: (the corporate operating model, the operating model of operations, and the go-to-market approach.
- **Technology**: A mentioned before, technology is not considered the core of digital transformation, rather its essential enabler, as it drives the changes and improvements required by each layer in the digital transformation pyramid.

Figure 3. The Digital Transformation Pyramid
Adapted from (Turchi, 2018)

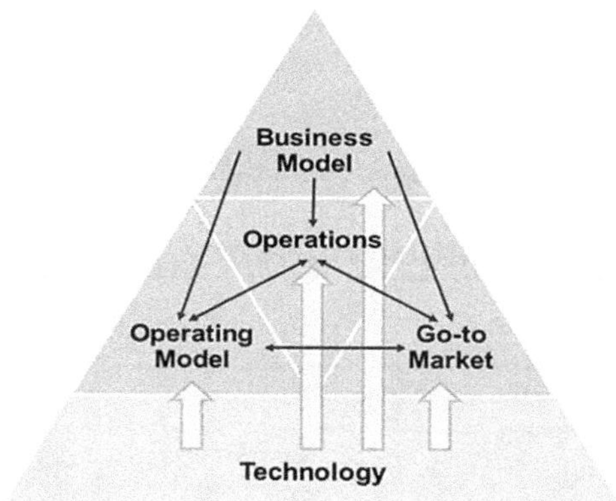

Digital Transformation Benefits

Digital transformation comes with a host of high-level benefits such as digitizing business processes, managing greater resources, empowering employees, greater customer insights, a better customer experience, creating digital products and services, opening the door to globalization, facilitating and encouraging cooperation across the divisions of institutions, increasing flexibility and innovation, enhancing digital culture, and providing a new level of transparency (Bookbinder, 2018).

In general, the benefits of digital transformation in any social institution can be identified as:

- Increased confidence and comfort in dealing.

- Less dependence on geographical location.
- Increased availability of information.
- Instant communication, even over large distances or between countries.
- Enhanced processing speed and improved decision making (Roseell, 2019).

Digital Transformation Implementation

By reviewing many articles and studies (Matt, Hess and Benliam, 2015), (Ismail, Khater and Zaki, 2017), (Sales, 2017), (McKeown,2019), this chapter can identify the framework for successful digital transformation as follows:

- **Analyzing the new business process:** Analyze the current status of the institution and its internal data (Strengths, Weaknesses, Opportunities, and Threats) to find the processes that have a scope for optimization.
- **Identifying the main technologies:** While there are many modern technologies that are growing rapidly, this does not mean that all of them need to be implemented at work. The focus should be on employing technologies that appropriately fit business and development goals and implementing them effectively.
- **Developing an innovative system:** When starting digital transformation, it is unlikely that you will find the appropriate efficacy on the first attempt. Consequently, there is a need for a mechanism to implement new innovations that requires the institute to move from the traditional administrative hierarchy to engaging more with staff at the lower end of the chain.

It also means redefining culture to create a dynamic environment in which the opinions and changes of all the members of the institute are embraced rather than suppressed.

- **Building an efficient team:** There is a need for skillful and dynamic people who are ready to shape ideas in an actionable plan. Without skilled IT experts, it will be difficult to apply innovative technologies.
- **Defining a roadmap:** It is a time to define the roadmap for implementation. Implementation should be done in stages; it is preferred to test the implementation progress on a small scale before the generalization stage of your plan.
- **Evaluation**: To measure the effectiveness of the implementation plan, there is a need to prepare some KPIs. These metrics will demonstrate the plan's effectiveness and will also guide future decision-making.

Once all steps of the digital transformation have been completed, it is important to update the strategy of implementing the digital transformation considering the conditions of the institute.

Digital Transformation Obstacles

Bayern (2018) referred to the most significant barriers when working towards a better digital transformation, according to her survey study as follows:

- Budget restrictions (51%)
- Old or very complex IT infrastructure (45%)
- Lack of complete visibility about the digital or end user experience (40%)
- Lack of suitable staff (39%)
- Leaders' lack of prioritization of digital initiatives (37%)

Miroslava (2018) illustrates the obstacles for the implementation of digital transformation, including a lack of competencies and capabilities within the organization, an inability to lead programs for digital transformation and change within the organization, and the lack of budgets allocated to these programs. Also, to be considered are concerns about information security risks due to the use of technology, especially if the assets are of high value.

These obstacles can be overcome by communicating the value of digital transformation to stakeholders within the institute while fostering a culture of continuous learning among individuals. Up-skilling the staff will help to make the most of available talent. Understanding and analyzing the data will create a clear digital vision for decision makers and help them to define the processes and tasks required to advance towards a successful digital transformation. These leaders will be enabled to work in collaboration with all key stakeholders within the institution to decide on software and infrastructure budgets and implement changes.

The Future of Digital Transformation

According to Newman (2016), Thierry (2017), IDG (2018), and Obeng (2019), the future trends of the digital transformation in society's institutions are determined as follows:

- **Increased implementation of digital transformation strategies:** The State of Digital Business Transformation's survey conducted by IDG in 2018 demonstrated that 89% of organizations implemented digital business strategies are in the process of this implementation. It is of interest to know that there are different technologies which have been adopted in different proportions; including mobile technology, public cloud, private cloud, analytics/big data, and APIs with an estimated rate of 59%, 45%, 53%, 58%, and 40% respectively.
- **Increased investment in IT and new skill requirements:** Gartner, Forrester, and IDC conducted a joint survey in order to investigate the surrender situation and the future indicators of IT. They emphasized that digital transformation initiatives are continuously increasing. This has led to the devotion of up to 50% of these organizations' budgets to the IT sector to date. Subsequently, organizations which have digitalized themselves will concentrate on attracting specialists in digital skills to assist the organization throughout their digital transformation journey. These skills include, but are not limited to, analytical skills, design, thinking, and mobile app development.
- **Big data analytics:** Data analytics is a cornerstone of the initiative for various digital institutions because it has the potential ability by 2020 to increase yearly savings by more than $60 billion. Big data provides organizations with data that increases employee productivity, process development, process effectiveness, and profits. Indeed, according to the IDG (2018), survey, an estimated 70% of IT managers believe that big data plays a significant role in revenue growth.
- **Significance of the internet of things (IoT):** In 2018, there were around 22 billion different IoT devices globally which have made significant contributions towards the creation of around

200,000 different apps and services. Recently, organizations have their digital transformation strategies greatly affected by the great proliferation of IoT devices. IDG (2018), stated that around 61% of organizations pointed out that their digital transformation strategies have been greatly affected by IoT. IoT has been devoted to assisting different digital processes, such as monitoring equipment (53%); collecting products and gathering customers data (41%); and managing compliance, security, monitoring performance and risk of IT assets (57%). The study indicated that IoT technology has been adapted by around 73% of the manufacturing industry in their general digitalization process, with 69% of the sample pointing out that IoT has been employed in their organization to monitor equipment and machinery.

- **Artificial intelligence (AI):** This concept is nothing new for those who are familiar with using devices which are capable of performing tasks which would normally require a human, such as Apple's Siri, Microsoft's Cortana, Amazon's Alexa, and Google Assistant. Recently, artificial intelligence has been acquiring prominence in marketing, customer service, and analytics. Institutions use artificial intelligence to perform tasks such as communicating efficiently with their customers. Undoubtedly, such digital services provided by AI have the ability to provide such services in a cheap, fast, and smart way. Artificial intelligence is the way ahead with different companies like Salesforce Einstein, IBM Watson, and SAP Leonardo that integrate it into their websites, systems, and operations.

The Fourth Industrial Revolution Definition:

The industrial system has gone through several stages, beginning with the first industrial revolution, which crystallized at the end of the eighteenth century and continues until the present time. The triggers behind these changes are the increasing individualization of demands, the short periods of product development, and resource efficiency (Ustundsag and Cevikcan, 2018). Digital transformation has been playing an important role in the development of the industrial system since we have come to live under the so-called Fourth Industrial Revolution.

Recently, Industry 4.0 has significantly attracted attention because of its enormous technological developments, such as smartphones, apps, Web 2.0, 3D printers, and laptops. There are so many technologies which have created significant potential in all sectors of society (Ustundsag and Cevikcan, 2018).

Industry 4.0 is a term which refers to a "further development stage in the organization and management of the entire value chain process involved in the manufacturing industry" (ATCC Finance, 2015). Gadi (2016) referred to industry 4.0 as "Organizing production processes based on technology, especially the Internet, and on the use of devices such as sensors and chips, which communicate independently with each other with complementarity between them both in the production process itself and in the final products, which led to the emergence of new types of goods and services.

The Fourth Industrial Revolution is a method for describing the melting of the boundaries between the physical, digital, and biological worlds. It is a blend of advances in artificial intelligence (AI), robotics, internet of things (IoT), 3D printing, genetic engineering, quantum computing, and other technologies. It is the collective strength behind many products and services that have become indispensable to modern life (Mcginnis, 2018).

Industry 4.0 is the combining of robots, interconnected devices, and fast data networks within the factory environment in order to make the plant more productive and to carry out the routine tasks that robots are best able to perform (Rossi, 2018).

And we can define the concept of industry 4.0 as "a system that integrates human capabilities and innovative technology such as artificial intelligence (AI), robotics, the internet of things (IoT), 3D printing, genetic engineering, and quantum computing to improve the processes of production and services while also satisfying customer needs.

The History of Industry 4.0 and Its Criteria

Luenendonk (2017) illustrated the history behind the 4th industry as described below:

- **The First Industrial Revolution:** The Industrial Revolution in Britain came at the end of the eighteenth century (1760-1840) to introduce machines into production; this included the transition from manual production to the use of steam and water engines as an energy source.
- **The Second Industrial Revolution:** The second industrial revolution dates back to between 1870 and 1914, and perhaps the distinguishing feature of this period is the introduction of mass production due to the electrification of factories and the introduction of the rail system. This revolution continued until the beginning of the First World War.
- **The Third Industrial Revolution:** Perhaps this revolution is the most familiar to us today as it is defined by industries relying on the digital technologies that are well-known in today's society. Moreover, this era of industrial revolution is dated between the year 1950 and 1970. Some also call it the information age, a direct result of the phenomenal development of computers and information and communication technologies.
- **The Fourth Industrial Revolution:** The fourth industrial revolution (also called Industry 4.0) integrates IT systems with physical systems to in order to obtain a cyber-physical system that adopts the real world into a virtual reality (Petrillo, De Felice, Cioffi, and Zomparelli, 2018).

These Cyber-Physical Systems (CPS) are controlled by computer-based algorithms and integrate between networking, computation, and physical process to be able to monitor physical processes efficiently. These systems use embedded storage systems, smart machines, and production branches to enable and exchange executing actions and information and also control each other separately (Luenendonk, 2017; Francisco, 2015). The development of such systems consists of three phases (Francisco,2015):

- **Identification**: Unique identification is essential in the manufacturing process. This is the primary language through which a machine can efficiently communicate. Radio Frequency Identification (RFID) is a significant example of this as it adapts an electromagnetic field to identify a specific tag attached to an object. This is a unique example of how Industry 4.0 worked initially.
- **The integration of sensors and actuators**: The combination of sensors and actuators simply means that the movement of a specific device can be highly controlled and that it can observe changes in the environment. On the other hand, the process of integrating actuators and sensors is still limited and they do not have the ability to communicate with each other.
- **The development of sensors and actuators:** Machines are able to store and analyze data due to this movement. CPS, for example, are equipped with different actuators and sensors allowing them to network and communicate in order to exchange information.

And as mentioned by Petrillo, De Felice, Cioffi and Zomparelli (2018). Industry 4.0 is identified by the utilization of multiple specific enabling technologies. These technologies could be depicted as follows:

- **Big data:** Big data is definitely one of the most important technologies adopted in Industry 4.0. It consists of collecting, processing, and analyzing a large amount of data while providing a number of new opportunities for companies.
- **Cloud:** Cloud computing allows the management of huge amounts of data in open systems and ensures real-time communication within the production process system by allowing access to information from anywhere in the world at any time, thus increasing flexibility.
- **The internet of things:** The internet of things is a type of network which connects anything with the internet through information sensing tools to facilitate communication and the exchange of information in order to achieve smart recognition, monitoring, and management.
- **Cybersecurity**: Cybersecurity plays a major role in the new industrial revolution. This is because data is sent digitally in a smart factory, so the security and confidentiality of the information exchange must be maintained.
- **Robots:** Robots are directly managed by the smart factory and connected to the rest of the systems. In general, automatic robots are used for difficult or very demanding tasks.
- **Additive manufacturing:** The evolution of technological systems and the increasingly personalized demands of customers have led to the evolution of techniques and 3D printing. Through this technique, it is possible to build prototypes and also finished products in three sizes for wide variety of purposes. With prototypes, it is possible to test the material while the finished products are used.
- **Augmented reality**: It is possible to educate operators by teaching them the right operations to perform for maintenance or machine setup. The augmented reality system aims to replace old paper manuals that are difficult to understand.
- **Horizontal and vertical integration**: Technology enables the integration between computer and command processes across networks.
- **Simulation**: Simulation systems and software are also very important. Through these tools, it is possible to simulate the manufacturing processes by analyzing system input and output in real time and obtain a detailed report about the process.

Additionally, Industry 4.0 covers three fundamental aspects (Petrillo, De Felice, Cioffi, and Zomparelli, 2018):

- **Digitization and increased integration of vertical and horizontal value chains:** This comprises the development of custom products, the customer's digital orders, automatic data transfer, and the integration of customer service systems.
- **Digitization of product and service offerings:** Complete descriptions of the product and its related services are shared across smart networks.
- **Introduction of innovative digital business models:** The high level of interaction between systems and technological opportunities creates the integration and real-time availability and control of systems across the enterprise.

The Benefits and Challenges of Industry 4.0

The advantages of Industry 4.0 are a decrease production costs by 10-30%, logistic costs by 10-30%, and quality management costs by 10-20%. Also, it facilitates shorter time–to-market for new products, improves customer representativeness, and enables a customer mass production without significantly (Rojko,2017).

Manda and Dhaou (2019) define the advantages of Industry 4.0 as follows:

- **Optimization**: Optimizing production is a major advantage of Industry 4.0. A smart factory containing unlimited smart devices that are able to self-optimize production will lead to almost zero down-time in production. This is extremely important for industries that use high end, expensive manufacturing equipment.
- **Customization**: Creating a flexible market that is customer-oriented will quickly and easily meet the needs of the population. It will also cancel the gap between the manufacturer and the customer. Communication will take place between both directly.
- **Pushing Research**: The evolution of Industry 4.0 technologies will push research in many fields such as IT security and will have an effect on different sectors, especially education. This is due to the fact that smart industry will require a new set of skills. Education and training will take a new shape that provides such an industry with the required skilled labor.

On the other hand, (Manda and Dhaou 2019) also illustrate the challenges that face Industry 4.0 which includes:

- **Security**: IT security risk represents the most challenging aspect of implementing Industry 4.0 techniques. Cyber theft should also be put into consideration.
- **Capital**: Such transformation will require a great investment in new technology. The decision to implement these major changes will have to be made on the CEO level. Even then, the risks must be calculated and taken seriously. In addition, this transformation will require a huge amount of capital, which may alienate smaller businesses and cost them their future market share.
- **Employment**: It is necessary to say that workers will need to acquire new skill sets. This may help employment rates go up, but it will also alienate a big sector of workers. Different forms of education must be offered, but this still won't solve the problem for the elder portion of workers.
- **Privacy**: In such an interconnected smart industry, producers need to collect and analyze data about their customers, and this might be taken as a threat to their privacy. Bridging the gap between the consumer and the producer will be a huge challenge for both parties.

Moreover, the researchers can summarize the challenges of implementing Industry 4.0 as the lack of training for all members of the institute including workers, operators, and managers; the funding required to plan and implement it at the national or regional level; and the security of computer data, where a standard will be required to ensure communication between intelligent systems while avoiding any external intrusion.

The Future of Industry 4.0

Industry 4.0 will start to move towards Industry 5.0 when it begins to allow customers to customize what they want. The fifth industrial revolution, or industry 5.0, will be focused on the cooperation and the integration between human begins and machines, as human intelligence. By putting humans back into the manufacturing process with collaborative robots, workers will be upskilled to provide value-added tasks in production, leading to mass customization and personalization for customers (Rossi, 2018).

(Petrillo, De Felice, Cioffi and Zomparelli, 2018) are illustrating the extent of industry development and its evolution toward industry 5.0 where machines will work side by side with humans as a coworkers.

FUTURE RESEARCH DIRECTIONS

Digital Transformation and Industry 4.0 are reshaping the future. Everyday new emerging technologies are invented, and new business cases are utilized. However, best benefits and worst drawbacks of such technologies are debatable. Even the boundaries and terminologies are being reshaped. One big hurdle in using these new innovations is how to manage the stakeholders who are working on such initiatives to create the required values. This chapter attempts to penetrate the discussion in a manner that will eventually lead to an increased number of research studies in the field of digital transformation and industry 4.0.

This chapter illustrates that the field of digital transformation is a continuous movement and is still itself under development. The field is still open for further modernization through new employment strategies in the field of technology.

One research dimension that need to be addressed is the contracting methodologies associated with the digital transformation and industry 4.0. This is a hot topic that will add huge benefits ad add great value to every stakeholder. This is particularly important as boundaries of every emerging technology and digital journey are being reshaped. Big research opportunities can be found in those subjects and especially when being applied to certain scenarios and industries.

CONCLUSION

By reviewing the studies and literature that deal with digital transformation and the fourth industrial revolution, in this chapter, the concept of digital transformation was reached as a system comprising technologies, data, processes, and individuals that aims to improve the performance of organizations, work and make all the members and customers more satisfied. Furthermore, the dimensions of the digital transformation were found to be represented in technologies, data, processes and individuals; while its benefits were reviewed in terms of increasing confidence and comfort in dealing, less dependence on geographical location, an increase the availability of information, instant communication, and the speed of processing and decision making.

The relationship between the digital transformation and The Fourth Industrial Revolution was also reached. This was illustrated in terms of the definition of The Fourth Industrial Revolution as a system that integrates human capabilities and innovative technology such as artificial intelligence (AI), robotics, the Internet of Things (IoT), 3D printing, genetic engineering, and quantum computing in order to improve the processes of production, services, and to satisfy customer needs. And also, we understand this relationship from its history, as the first evolution at the end of the eighteenth introduced machines into production. Lastly, this revolution is defined by its criteria, which includes digitization and increased integration of vertical and horizontal value chains, the digitization of product and service offerings, and the introduction of innovative digital business models.

Also included is a review of its benefits which include optimization, customization, pushing research, as well as its challenges; such as a lack of training for all members of the institute, the funds required to start planning and implementation, and the security of computer data.

And finally, we looked into a future where Industry 4.0 starts to move towards Industry 5.0 and begins to allow customers to customize what they want while focusing on the integration between human and machine as human intelligence.

REFERENCES

Alamada-Lobo, F. (2015). The Industry 4.0 revolution and the future of manufacturing execution systems (MES). *Journal of Innovation Management.*, *3*(4), 16–21. doi:10.24840/2183-0606_003.004_0003

Antonella, P., De Felice, F., Cioffi, R., & Zomparelli, F. (2018). *Fourth Industrial Revolution: Current Practices, Challenges, and Opportunities, Digital Transformation in Smart Manufacturing*. Retrieved on February 16,2020 from https://www.intechopen.com/books/digital-transformation-in-smart-manufacturing/fourth-industrial-revolution-current-practices-challenges-and-opportunities

Bayern, M. (2018). *The 5 biggest challenges to digital transformation and how to overcome them*. Retrieved on January 16,2020 from https://www.techrepublic.com/article/the-5-biggest-challenges-to-digital-transformation-and-how-to-overcome-them

Bloomberg, J. (2018). *Digitization and Digital Transformation: Confuse Them at Your Peril*. Retrieved on December 25,2019 from https://www.forbes.com/sites/jasonbloomberg/2018/04/29/digitization-digitalization-and-digital-transformation-confusethem-at-your-peril/#2dd1ce842f2c

Bookbinder, S. (2018). *The Benefits of Digital Transformation (& What They Mean for Sales Professionals)*. Retrieved on March5,2020 from https://www.impactbnd.com/blog/benefits-of-digital-transformation-sales-professionals

Clark, E. (2018).*D igital Transformation:W hat is it?* Retrieved on December 22.2019 from https://er.educause.edu/articles/2018/5/digital-transformation-what-is-it

Deloitte. (2018). *Digital enablement turning your transformation into a successful journey*. Retrieved on December 23,2019 from https://www2.deloitte.com/content/dam/Deloitte/ie/Documents/Technology/IE_C_HC_campaign.pdf

Dosi, G. (2017). The blade runner scenario. In La Nueva Revolución de la Producción: La Transformación Digital. Revista de Ciencias y Humanidades (pp. 71–74). Fundación Ramón Areces.

Eurofound. (2017). *Digitisation of processes. Literature review*. Luxembourg: Publications Office of the European Union.

Eurofound. (2018a). *Game changing technologies: Exploring the impact on production processes and work*. Luxembourg: Publications Office of the European Union.

European Commission. (2019). *Digital transformation*. Retrieved on December 20,2019 from https://ec.europa.eu/growth/industry/policy/digitaltransformation_en

Finance, A. T. C. C. (2015). Industry 4.0 Challenges and Solutions for the Digital Transformation and Use do Exponential Technologies [Audit Tax Consulting Corporate Finance Report]. Zurich, Switzerland: Author.

Foro de Empresas Innovadoras. (2018). Re-industrialización en España: Industria 4.0 y ecosistemas de innovación. Madrid: Author.

Gadi, M. (2016). Left industrial policy and industry 4.0. At progressive industrial policy for the EU? Out-manoeuvring liberalism. Rosa Luxemburgo Stiftung. Brussels Office.

IDG. (2018). *State of Digital Business Transformation 2018*. Retrieved on December 15,2019 from https://cdn2.hubspot.net/hubfs/1624046/Digital%20Business%20Executive%20Summary_FINAL.pdf

Ismail, M. H., Khater, M., & Zaki, M. (2017). *Digital business transformation and strategy: What do we know so far?* Retrieved on January 11,2020 from https://pdfs.semanticscholar.org/35b2/bd95aeb8e-6ca0ea0652d0d7fc697eda3362a.pdf

Javier-Braña, F. (2019). A fourth industrial revolution? Digital transformation, labor and work organization: A view from Spain. *Economia e Politica Industriale*, *46*(3), 415–430. doi:10.100740812-019-00122-0

Luenendonk, M. (2017). *Industry 4.0: Definition, Design Principles, Challenges, and the Future of Employment*. Retrieved on February 28,2020 from https://www.cleverism.com/industry-4-0/

Manda, M., & Dhaou, S. (2019). Responding to challenges and opportunities in the 4th industrial revolution in developing countries. *I EGOV2019*.

Matt, C., Hess, H., & Benliam, A. (2015). Digital Transformation Strategies. *Business & Information Systems Engineering*, *57*(5), 339–343. doi:10.100712599-015-0401-5

Mazzone, D. M. (2014). *Digital or Death: Digital Transformation – The Only Choice for Business to Survive Smash and Conquar* (1st ed.). Smashbox Consulting Inc.

Mcginnis, D. (2018). *What Is the Fourth Industrial Revolution?* Retrieved on February 20,2020 from https://www.salesforce.com/blog/2018/12/what-is-the-fourth-industrial-revolution-4IR.html

McKeown, N. (2019).*A step- by- step guide to digital Transformation*. Retrieved on December 20,2019 from https://www.ionology.com/wp-content/uploads/2017/03/StepbyStepGuideToDigitalTransformation.pdf

Miroslava, B. (2018).*Challenges Related to the Digital Transformation of Business Companies*. Paper presented to 6th International Conference: Innovation Management, Entrepreneurship and sustainability(IMES).

Newman, D. (2016). *Exploring The Future Of Digital Transformation And Disruption*. Retrieved on January 3,2020 from https://www.forbes.com/sites/danielnewman/2016/03/01/exploring-the-future-of-digital-transformation-and-disruption/#2eeddc375bdc

Obeng, E. (2019). *Looking beyond Digital Transformation to the Future of Work.* Retrieved on January 18, 2020 from https://www.eddieobeng.com/wp-content/uploads/2017/02/Future_of_work_in_a-post-Digital_World.pdf

OECD. (2019). *Measuring the Digital Transformation: A Roadmap for the future.* Paris: OECD Publishing. Retrieved on January 3,2020 from www.oecd.org/going-digital/measurment-roadmap.pdf

Rojko, A. (2014). Industry 4.0 Concepts: Background and Overview. *Journal of Innovation Management, 11*(5).

Rosell, C. D. (2019). *Why Digital Transformation is a Vital Priority for Educational Institutions Today.* Retrieved on January 15,2020 from https://www.cae.net/why-digital-transformation-is-a-vital-priority-for-educational-institutions-today

Rossi, B. (2018). *What will Industry 5.0 mean for manufacturing?* Retrieved on February 25,2020 from https://www.raconteur.net/technology/manufacturing-gets-personal-industry-5-0

Sales. (2017). *6 Steps Framework to Implement Digital Transformation in Business.* Retrieved on December 26,2019 from https://www.newgenapps.com/blog/what-is-digital-transformation-steps-to-implement-digital-transformation

Schallmo, D., Williams, C., & Boardman, L. (2017). Digital Transformation of Business Model-Best Practice, Enablers and Roadmap. International Journal of Innovation Management, 21(8).

Schwertner, K. (2017). Digital transformation of business. *Trakia Journal of Sciences, 15*(1, Suppl.1), 388–393. doi:10.15547/tjs.2017.s.01.065

Seres, L., Pavlicevic, V., & Tumbas, P. (2018).Digital Transformation of Higher Education Competing on Analytics. *Proceeding of INTED conference.* 10.21125/inted.2018.2348

Thierrt, I. (2017). *Companies of the Future: The Issues of Digital Transformation.* Retrieved on December 25, 2019 from https://www.researchgate.net/profile/Isckia_Thierry/publication/313105824_White_paper_Companies_of_the_future_The_Issues_of_Digital_Transformation/links/5890566ea6fdcc2351c08eeb/White-paper-Companies-of-the-future-The-Issues-of-Digital-Transformation.pdf?origin=publication_detail

Turchi, P. (2018). *The Digital Transformation Pyramid: A business-driven Approach for Corporate Initiatives.* Retrieved on February 1, 2018 from https://www.thedigitaltransformationpeople.com/channels/the-case-for-digital-transformation/digital-transformation-pyramid-business-driven-approach-corporate-initiatives/

Ustundsag, A. & Cevikcan, E. (2018). *Industry 4.0: Managing The Digital Transformation.* . doi:10.1007/978-3-319-57870-5

Verina, N., & Titko, D. (2019). Digital Transformation: Conceptual Framework. *International scientific conference "Contemporary Issues in Business, Management,and Economics engineering' 2019.*

World Economic Forum. (2018). *Readiness for the future of production report 2018.* Geneva, Switzerland: Author.

ADDITIONAL READING

Abram, T. (2009). The hidden values of it risk management. Information Systems Audit and Control Association (ISACA). *Journal, 2009*(2), 40–45. PMID:19480123

Ben Halpert, B. (2011). *Auditing Cloud Computing: A Security and Privacy Guide*. John Wiley & Sons. doi:10.1002/9781118269091

Dallas, G. (Ed.). (2004). Governance and risk. New York: McGraw-Hill Companies Inc.

Shalan, M., & Anaim, N. (2017). The SMAC Opportunity Contracts: Generating Value From Responsive Agile Risk-Oriented Techniques. Mobile Platforms, Design, and Apps for Social Commerce (pp. 115-134). Hershy: IGI Global.

Shalan, M. A., & Anaim, N. A. (2017). The SMAC Opportunity Contracts: Generating Value From Responsive Agile Risk-Oriented Techniques. In *Mobile Platforms, Design, and Apps for Social Commerce* (pp. 115–134). IGI Global. doi:10.4018/978-1-5225-2469-4.ch008

York, A., Dunham, L., & Ahn, M. (2012, January). Vertical Versus Horizontal Integration in the Biopharma Industry. *Advances in Mergers and Acquisitions*, *10*, 121–143. doi:10.1108/S1479-361X(2012)0000010010

Zheng, Z., Xie, S., Dai, H.-N., Chen, W., Chen, X., Weng, J., & Imran, M. (2019). An Overview on Smart Contracts: Challenges, Advances and Platforms. *Future Generation Computer Systems*, 1–19. doi:10.1016/j.future.2019.12.019

KEY TERMS AND DEFINITIONS

Boundaries: As digital transformation is reshaping the boundaries of utilizing various emerging technologies are being shaped, and this will define the value that can be created out of a digital journey.

Customer Experience: One of the main pillars in digital transformation and Industry 4.0 which is focusing on customer as adopting "customer-centric" approaches to stretch the value provided to the customers.

Digital Transformation: A process whereby companies converge through different new digital technologies, improved by communication everywhere, with the goal of achieving superior performance and sustainable competitive advantage.

Emerging Technologies: A set of technologies that are being generated and tested as a result of the successive innovations. It forms an important part in the digital transformation journey.

Industry 4.0: An equivalent term to digital transformation but are used mainly in the industry and described as a further development stage in the organization and management of the entire value chain process involved in the manufacturing industry.

Strategy: An important layer in the digital transformation journey that includes the business model and defines the impacts and opportunities of the business to create value-added services after employing digital technology, and data-based products and services.

Chapter 2
Contracts and Contracting Styles:
Existing and Future Types

Mohamed Bassyouni
Aqarat Real Estate Development Company, Saudi Arabia

ABSTRACT

From service management to vendor agreements, contracts take many forms. They establish partnership and accountability between parties and often require considerable negotiation before being finalized. Traditionally, a wide variety of contract types was created to fit the needs of contractors, supplies, and clients. These types vary according to the degree of risk sharing, timing, and responsibilities assumed by the contractor for the costs of performance; and the amount and nature of the profit incentive offered to the contractor for achieving or exceeding specified standards or goals. As we delve into the digital transformation era, various business aspects have been revisited. Innovation, transformation, and change management become major players in all business relations, and they need to be considered in the contracting arena as well. This chapter is discussing various types of traditional contracts specifying the differences of each type and how and when to utilize it. It also describes the pros and cons of each one.

INTRODUCTION

Contracts are core business assets and a source of valuable business information. It is essential for the customer and supplier to select a commercial model that both appropriately shares risk and drives the quality achievements and benefit sharing. However, without a solid contracting, a business relation or project may become an exercise of frustration. Typically, the supplier and client teams work separately to select the contracting approach to drive satisfaction and productivity.

Traditionally, there have been three major types of contracts fixed price contracts (FBC), cost plus contracts (CPC) and time and materials (T&M). Which was selected based on project maturity and contractor capabilities. Contract obligations was easy to set and follow.

DOI: 10.4018/978-1-7998-4501-0.ch002

As we delve into digital transformation era, the verdict is clear that the future of contracting will be multi-dimensional with technology at its heart. New contracting styles are leading the way considering the increased business agility, change management styles and levels of innovation. There will be a need to handle a blockage of incumbent contracts and commercial staff who are not well positioned and lack skills.

Virtual enterprises are being the norm especially when related to Digital Transformation. Ecosystems are being used more frequently to support wider types of projects and operation. It may not be easy to find the right partner, but if or when it does happen, it can help companies forge a long-term plan. Value based contracting, opportunity contracts and agile contracting has been introduced by various researchers as to manage the new norm.

The selection of contract types is important to the contractors to provide needed flexibility in acquiring the large variety and volume of supplies and services. Contract types may vary according to the degree and timing of the responsibility assumed by the contractor for the costs of performance; and the amount and nature of the profit incentive offered to the contractor for achieving or exceeding specified standards or goals in addition to the nature of the project, its time frames and deliverables.

This chapter is summarizing the traditional contracts and describing the new contracting styles. It also indicates the defining parameters. It shows also how the new contracts can provide sufficient structure to protect all parties and achieve the desired mission outcomes, while offering flexibility for adaptation of requirements within the agreed-on scope of the system.

BACKGROUND

Contracting is a traditional story to manage the relation between suppliers and clients. There is usually a bonus as well as a penalty depending on which side of the project budget the contractor ends up. This relation is progressing up to real-time contracts and forward contracts as discussed by (Morstyn, Teytelboym, & Mcculloch, 2019) to resolve the coordination between the owners of large-scale and small-scale energy resources at different levels of the power system. (Lumineau, 2017) stated that two main governance mechanisms are at play in interorganizational relationships. However, this background will focus on new contracting methodologies and describe few real scenarios of existing contracts.

The contractor is insulated from major changes in the contract, but their incentive to find efficiencies in the performance of the work is greatly increased. (Lumineau & Quelin, 2012) discuss contracts as a first stream focuses on the role of the formal contract as a safeguard against opportunism and conflict. A second stream focuses on relational governance, and trust, as a mechanism regulating interorganizational exchange (Heide, 1994).

In recent years, the increasing number of transport services offered in cities and the advancements in Technology and ICT have introduced an innovative Mobility as a Service (MaaS) concept. (Jittrapirom, et al., 2017). Flexibility in contracting is increasingly required as discussed by (Du, Gelenbe, Jiang, Zhang, & Ren, 2017) who suggested offloading contracts as a mechanism to incentivized traffic and encourage each small-cell base stations to select the contract that achieves its own maximum utility. (Hietanen, 2014) discussed the different transport modes to offer a tailored mobility package, like a monthly mobile phone contract and includes other complementary services.

As more e-tailers or platforms are allowing manufacturers direct access to customers, two common contracts are offered by platforms to manufacturers: the revenue sharing contract where a platform appropriates a portion of the manufacturer's revenue, and the fixed fee contract where a platform charges a fixed rent for each sale (Zhang, Cao, & He, 2019). Deep learning methods are used today to extract contract elements such as termination date, legalization reference, contracting parties, payment schedule (Chalkidis & Androutsopoulos, 2017).

Servicing was discussed by (Toffel, 2008) as a novel business practice that sells product functionality rather than products. (Chalkidis, Androutsopoulos, & Michos, Extracting contract elements, 2018) describe and experimentally compare several contract element extraction methods that use manually written rules and linear classifiers to help automating contracts.

(Yu, 2020) dive into the aircraft and aviation valuation and leasing. Discussing the dynamics between the related ecosystem of the owner, financier, and user. The owner can be the airline or lessor. The operator is the ultimate user of the aircraft and one of the main stakeholders in the aircraft leasing industry. To operate as an airline, it needs to buy or obtain the use of one or multiple aircraft and other large fixed assets in addition to many smaller items. The operator has a variety of options that are assessed to complete this objective.

This last example enforces the need for new contracting styles in conjunction with other examples in this background. These complex scenarios and the increasing number of contracts that cross borders bring more focus to contract negotiations as discussed by (Chatterjee, 2000) (Kuppa, 2018)

THE CONTRACT RIGHTS

Despite the scholarly interest in contracts and trust governing interorganizational relationships, an understanding of how contracts influence trust remains limited by the way in which the interaction between the two constructs is conceptualized (Lumineau, 2015). Contract rights may be expressly written such as the exclusive right to use copyrighted material. Contract rights may also be inferred, such as the right to fair and equal disclosure of material.

Both parties of an agreement have contract rights. For instance, one party may have the right to buy a product, while the other party has the right to supply it. Naturally, contracts address different rights, depending on the parties' needs.

Explicit Contract Rights

A concept related to contract rights is "contract duties," which refers to a party's obligations under the agreement terms. Contract rights typically involve business matters, such as providing products and services. However, these rights may also involve other subject matters. Contract obligations and contract duties may be used interchangeably in the professional world. However, there may be some distinctions between the two concepts in certain types of contracts.

Contract obligations are those duties that each party is legally responsible for in a contract agreement. In a contract, each party exchanges something of value, whether it be a product, services, money, etc. On both sides of the agreement, each party has various obligations in connected with this exchange. (Kronman, 1985)

An example of contract obligations is with the sale of a product such as a car. One party has the obligation to transfer ownership of the car, while the other has the obligation to pay for it. The contract will specify the terms that regulate the obligations, such as the method and amount of payment, and the time/place of delivery.

If either party fails to perform their contractual obligations according to the contract terms, it will usually result in a breach of contract. This may result in a damages award to reimburse the non-breaching party for their economic losses.

Implicit Contract Rights

Along with expressly stated contract rights are "implied contract rights," which exist based on current contract laws and policies. While they can be written into the agreement, they're usually simply implied by governmental laws. They include the following:

- **Good Faith and Fair Dealing:** All parties in valid agreements are expected to act in good faith and with fair dealing. This means they don't act misleadingly. They're expected to disclose all relevant information under the agreement (O'Byrne, 2007).
- **Right to Be Free from Pressure:** Contracts that are formed under power — when one party is forced to sign — are invalid. All parties should be free and informed enough to enter into an agreement (Gluck, 1979).
- **Right to Be Free From Fraud:** Parties have the right to be free from fraudulent information or misrepresentation (Sefton-Green, 2005).

What If Contract Rights Are Violated?

All parties to a contract have certain rights. Some are expressly stated, and others are implied. An organization might have legal claim if they feel someone has violated the contract rights (wong, 2006). In the case of a breach of contract, the non-breaching party can still enforce the contract and sue for damages. The non-breaching party might be entitled to the following remedies:

- Specific performance
- Damages
- Contract cancellation
- Restitution for benefits conferred to the breaching party

CONTRACT STRUCTURES AND PURPOSES

Usually the contract includes a combinations of contract clauses that correlate to high operational performance. Which affect the design, methodology and approach of the contract. according to (Kapsali, Roehrich, & Akhtar, 2018), the classical, relational, and/or associational contract structures should be used in different context to enhance the contract performance as follows

Classical Structure

Used for safeguard and formal control substantive agreements thus it is court enforceable (Fried, 2015). It allocates decision rights over task selection and control rights over task execution on predicted circumstances. It is usually assigned to one central agent and is highly prescriptive and transactional. Its suitable to short, discrete, nonrepeatable contracts.

Relational Structure

Establish a relation of recognition and respect, substantive agreements that are informal and self-enforceable (Darrington & Howell, 2011). It uses informal control through extracontractual means to repair some of the failures of classical contracting. It is suitable for long-term relations, moderately uncertain, repeated transactions.

Associational Structure

A new class of "associational" and "constitutional" contract, resource based rather than action based, is singled out as particularly fit to the governance of innovation (Grandori & Furlotti, 2009). This structure ensure action in contingencies using a procedural agreement formal thus it is court enforceable. Its clauses emulate discretion of action, resource lock-in and allocate decision-making among multiple parties. It is procedural and suitable for long-term relations, highly uncertain results and enable transactions change over time

According to (Kapsali, Roehrich, & Akhtar, 2018), the analysis produced two theoretical implications: first, that better performing contracts are created when combining relational and associational contract clauses; and second, that in projects, relational and classical contract clauses are not complementary with regards to realizing high operational performance.

Contract Classifications

A contract is a legally binding agreement between two or more parties in which an exchange of value is made. The contract's purpose is to set out the terms of the agreement and provide a record of that agreement which may be enforceable in a court of law (Reuer & Ariño, 2007). Contracts may come in many forms, each with its own use and purpose.

Unilateral vs. Bilateral

In a unilateral contract only one party promises something (McCullough, 2020). For instance, if a car dealer tells a customer, "I will give you that car if you give me $15,000," he has made an offer for a unilateral contract—the contract will only be created if the customer accepts the offer by paying the $15,000. If the dealer says, "I will promise to give you the car if you promise to pay me $15,000," a bilateral contract has been proposed because both parties must make a promise. The concept of unilateral contracts is important because it has been used by courts to hold a party liable for a promise even when consideration was not given by the other party. For instance, an employer may be liable for providing pension benefits that it promised to an employee, even if the worker gave no promise and did nothing in return.

Expressed vs. Implied

Contracts may also be classified as "expressed" or "implied." Expressed contracts are those in which both parties have explicitly stated the terms of their bargain, either orally or in writing, at the time that the contract was created (Legal Dictionary, 2017). In contrast, implied contracts result from surrounding facts and circumstances that suggest an agreement. For instance, when a person takes a car to a repair shop, he expects the shop to exercise reasonable care and good faith in fixing the car and charging for repairs. Likewise, the shop expects the customer to pay for its services. Although no formal agreement is created, an implied contract exists.

Quasi-Contracts

In addition to express and implied contracts are "quasi-contracts," which arise from unique circumstances. Quasi-contracts are obligations imposed by law to avoid injustice (Bidkar, 2020). When no enforceable contract exists, the court may imply one to avoid unjust enrichment on a benefiting party. This could happen if a party conferred a benefit onto another party, with the benefiting party knowing that the first party expects compensation for this service. Courts usually let the party recover reasonable value for services even if there's no valid agreement in place.

For instance, suppose that a man hires a contractor to paint his house. By accident, the contractor paints the wrong house. The owner of the house knows that he is painting it by mistake but, happy to have a free paint job, says nothing. The painter would likely be able to collect something from the homeowner because he knowingly was "unjustly enriched" at his expense. Had the contractor painted his house while he was on vacation, he would be under no obligation to the contractor.

Validity and Voidability

Contracts may also be categorized as valid, unenforceable, voidable, and void (Schaefer, 2001). Valid contracts are simply those that meet all legal requirements. Unenforceable contracts are those that meet the basic requirements but fail to fulfill some other law. For instance, if a country has special requirements for contracts related to lending money, failure to comply could make the contract unenforceable. Voidable contracts occur when one or both parties have a legal right to cancel their obligation(s). A contract entered under duress, for example, would be voidable at the request of the injured party. Void contracts are those that fail to meet basic criteria and are therefore not contracts at all. An illegal contract, for example, is void.

Promissory Estoppel

A separate type of contract, and one that overtly exemplifies the trend away from strict interpretation and toward fairness, is created by promissory estoppel. Promissory estoppel is the legal principle that a promise is enforceable by law, even if made without formal consideration when a promisor has made a promise to a promisee who then relies on that promise to his subsequent detriment (Baird, 2019).

Under the theory of promissory estoppel, a party can rely on a promise made by another party despite the nonexistence of a formal, or even implied, contract. Promissory estoppel can be evoked if allowing a promisor to claim freedom from liability because of a lack of consideration (or some other contractual element) would result in injustice (Leacock, 2011). Suppose that a business owner promised an employee that he would eventually give him the business if he worked there until he (the owner) retired. Then, after 20 years of faithful service by the employee, the owner decides to give the business to his son-in-law. The owner could be "estopped" from claiming in court that a true contract did not exist, because the worker relied on the owner's promise.

CONVENTIONAL (TRADITIONAL) CONTRACTING

Conventional contracting is characterized by the aim of own profit maximization (at the expense of the other contract party, if necessary) using reactive provisions. According to (Petersen & Østergaard, 2017), the primary objectives of those provisions are to:

- Transfer risks, liability, and undertakings to the other party.
- Regulate how disputes are settled.
- Stipulate conditions for the dissolution of the collaboration.
- Instruct how assets are to be divided between the parties if the collaboration is dissolved.

In economic terms, a conventional contract is basically an arm's length agreement. Conventional contracts have been applied to the construction industry since a while and includes the following types:

- Fixed Price Contracts (FBC)
- Cost Plus Contracts (CPC)
- Time and Materials (T&M)

Fixed Price Contracts (FBC)

This contracting type has been very popular, where the owner provides a detailed specification of the requirements, and then the winning contractor is obligated to meet the specified requirement at an agreed-on price (Yao, Jiang, Scott, Young, & Talluri, 2010). In theory, most of the risks under this kind of arrangement is shifted to the contractor. According to (FAR, 2020), this contract type places upon the contractor maximum risk and full responsibility for all costs and resulting profit or loss. It provides maximum incentive for the contractor to control costs and perform effectively and imposes a minimum administrative burden upon the contracting parties.

Contracting officers do have flexibility to include award-fee incentives based on factors "other than cost," which include the achievement of specific performance characteristics or schedule reductions, but the fixed-price is generally applied to a firm requirements specification set at the beginning of the program. Change management processes are very rigorous and require contract modifications. According to (Sund & Hausken, 2012) costs associated with moral hazard, adverse selection, monitoring and coordination decrease with the use of an incentive-based contract rather than fixed cost contracts.

- **Firm Fixed Price (FFP):** This is a standard lump sum contract. A statement of work is produced, and a contractor submits a quote for the work. There are no grounds for a change to that price. The contractor assumes all of the risk and insulates the buyer from all unexpected additional work within the scope (Ahsan & Matsukawa, 2012). The bid price in FFP lump sum is the highest of all of the methods, because the risk to the contractor is the highest. All other methods are an attempt to share the vendor's risk to reduce the price. FFP contracts should be used when the scope of the work is well known and not likely to change much.
- **Fixed Price Plus Incentive Fee (FPIF):** This is a lump sum contract just like the FFP; however, it allows for some up-front flexibility based on predefined metrics (Roseke, 2019). There are two components to the price, the firm fixed fee and a bonus/penalty based on some predefined metric. This metric can be anything that is well defined and measurable, such as schedule milestones, technical performance, or actual cost of a certain portion of the work like materials acquisition
- **Firm-Fixed-Price, Level-Of-Effort Term Contracts (FBLE):** This requires the contractor to provide a specified level of effort, over a stated period of time and the owner to pay the contractor a fixed amount. This type is suitable for investigation or study in a specific research and development area. The payment is based on the effort expended rather than on the results achieved.
- **Fixed Price with Economic Price Adjustment (FPEPA):** This is a lump sum contract, but the value is adjusted based on predetermined economic indicators. Adjustment provides for upward and downward revision of the stated contract price upon the occurrence of specified contingencies (FAR, 2020). Economic price adjustments are considering major economic indicators such as inflation and currency fluctuations. Usually this happens on large infrastructure projects that are expected to span several years, or projects that are part of a program in which projects start and stop frequently as per (Roseke, 2019).

Fixed-cost approaches are not inherently incompatible with agile, were cost and schedule are generally fixed parameters, and these drive the scope of development within the product vision. (Opelt, Gloger, Pfarl, & Mittermayr, 2013) suggests an "Agile fixed-price" approach with the main characteristic of a shift to the agile paradigm as more projects are no longer fixed in detail from the start.

Cost Plus Contracts (CPC)

Also termed a cost-reimbursable contract (Roseke, 2019). It is a contract where a contractor is paid for all its allowed expenses, plus additional payment to allow for a profit. It allows for refinement of the requirements based on the evolution of the working system and the priority for functionality defined by the product owner.

(Chen & Gunny, 2014) find that profitability significantly increases during the years that cost-plus contracts are awarded. This type of contract requires adequate organization capability to manage in an effective manner. Active interaction and collaboration will be required to increases the success rate with a flexibility to adjust to changing operational system. These contracts were driven more by the uncertainty of the requirements and the prioritizing of the requirements based on changeable operational need. CPC comprise few items including:

- **Cost Plus Fixed Fee (CPFF):** The CPFF is the standard cost-plus contract where the contractor is reimbursed for costs incurred, and a fixed fee paid in addition to that (Xiang, Zhu, Coit, & Feng,

2017). Hence, there are two components to the contract which is the unit rate (cost reimbursable) and the fixed fee (profit). This type of contract is effective when the scope of work is expected to change significantly. In here the contractor will be shielded from escalating project costs and has a small incentive to introduce efficiencies and reduce the variable part.

- **Cost Plus Incentive Fee (CPIF):** The contractor is rewarded for achieving certain performance targets via changes to the fixed fee. That is, the fixed fee is no longer fixed. These are usually cost based targets, because this contract seeks to incentivize the contractor to reduce the variable (cost reimbursable) part of the budget. (Zhang & Lin, 2018) introduced an optimization model that gives the specific function of target profit and incentive coefficient on target cost and limits the range of profits by setting the upper limit and the specific value at the most likely cost of profit rate.
- **Cost Plus Award Fee (CPAF):** This is like the CPIF contract, except that the bonus/penalty that the bonus/penalty clause is relatively sophisticated and built around subjective and/or various technical criteria. (Braxton, Hetrick, Webb, Whitehead-Scanlon, & Ross, 2017) stated that CPAF contracts employs subjective scoring against established criteria by an Award Fee (AF) panel is more challenging. CPAF contracts tend to be used by governments or large corporations where contract management functions are readily available.

Time and Materials (T&M)

Time and materials contract contain no fixed fee; hence the contractor must price in profit into the unit rates of the individual items. According to (El-adaway, Vance, & Abotaleb, 2020), contractual provisions related to delay and extension of time are often written in difficult language or presented in a scattered manner in construction contracts. This could lead to confusion and misunderstanding by the different parties as to rights and responsibilities. Thus, it is not surprising that poor contract administration is always listed among the top reasons for conflicts, claims, and disputes in the construction industry.

T&M is common on consulting services contracts like engineering, architectural, legal, and professional services. It is also common on small projects where a lot of trust is present because a simple unit rate can be quoted (Roseke, 2019).

NEW CONTRACTING MODELS

According to (Fagundes, 2016), "a lot of contracts, if not most, formalize arm's length transactions, essentially implying there is a distant or strictly professional relationship between the parties". The traditional contracts are run of the mill that might not be suitable for the digital transformation era where the business dynamics are changing frequently. (Forbes & Brady, 2019) stated that written contracts do not always provide satisfactory remedies for unexpected contingencies. Ex-post mechanisms need to be used to manage the contract including incentives, information systems and signals.

Traditional contracts have been complicated but straightforward agreements based on both parties agreeing to perform well defined obligations in exchange for the other party's fulfillment of a duty, which may merely entail the payment of financial compensation.

In her interview (Vitasek K., How to Negotiate a Collaborative Outsourcing Deal, 2014), Kate Vitasek stated that collaboration is certainly an often-heard buzzword these days, and the collaborative outsourcing relationships are gaining traction. The digital transformation era catheterized by the rapid pace in the business world and increasing global competition. This require different contracting types that tend more toward partnership and innovation. Ideally, a strategic collaboration will require contracting that arises from such a relationship to foster a long-lasting, mutually beneficial partnership.

New contracting styles is characterized by the aim of generating a sustainable relation using both proactive and reactive provisions that protect knowledge exchange and work against opportunistic behavior. According to (Petersen & Østergaard, 2017), the contract required today is a partnership arrangement through which the contracting parties achieve sustainable competitive advantage or one could argue a strategic alliance

The Vested Business Model

The Vested business model is accredited to Kate Vitasek and her research team in University of Tennessee. (Vitasek, Ledyard, & Manrodt, 2010). Five rules that, in conjunction with ten steps (or elements), take companies beyond transactional micro-management to a new level of collaboration and value creation, as outlined here, based on (Vitasek K., 2011):

1. **Rule #1: Focus on Outcomes, Not Transactions:** This is a first step it is vital to map potential outcomes to see how well the parties are aligned. The vision and alignment form the basis to draft a "statement of intent (SOI)". Two elements are considered:
    a. Element 1: Business Model Map where the parties will pinpoint the transactions of value, establishing a culture in which the company and the supplier maximize profits by working together more efficiently, no matter who is doing the activity.
    b. Element 2: Shared Vision and Statement of Intent based on the business model mapping, the parties work together on a joint vision that will guide them for the duration of the vested relationship. A cooperative and collaborative mindset is required to handle the conversation between the parties. Parties are required to share what is needed, admit to gaps in capability, and aim to focus on the benefits that the other party can bring to enhance any gaps in capability.
2. **Rule #2: Focus on The What, Not the How:** This lays the foundation for the parties in the Vested partnership to do what they do best while describing intended results.
    a. Element 3: Statement of Objectives/Workload Allocation where every party need to do what this party do best. Depending on the scope of the partnership, the company transfers some or all the activities needed to accomplish relationship goals to the service provider. Together they develop a "statement of objectives (SOO)" that describes intended results, not tasks.
3. **Rule #3: Clearly Defined and Measurable Outcomes:** In an effective, successful relationship, the parties work together to define and quantify desired outcomes then measure performance to determine if the outcomes are achieved
    a. Element 4: Top-Level Desired Outcomes, which is a centerpiece of the entire enterprise because without such mutually defined desired outcomes in place, a vested agreement cannot proceed. Outcomes are expressed in terms of a limited set of high-level metrics. The parties must also define exactly how relationship success is measured.
    b. Element 5: Performance Management, to determine if the outcomes are achieved based on SOI and SOOs and other implemented agreements. The metrics will help align performance to strategy.

4. **Rule #4: Optimize Pricing Model Incentives:** Incentives are a key component, because service providers are taking on risk to generate larger returns on investment. An incentives package delivers the most commercially efficient method of maintaining equitable margins for all parties for the duration of the relationship through a method known as margin matching.
    a. Element 6: Pricing Model and Incentives, to achieve the desired outcomes, the partners must have a properly structured pricing model that incorporates incentives for the best cost and service trade-off. The supplier's profitability is directly tied to achieving mutually agreed outcomes. Suppliers have the authority and autonomy to make strategic investments in innovations, processes, and service reliability that can generate more value.
5. **Rule #5: Insight Versus Oversight Governance Structure:** The four elements associated with Rule 5 provide the tools for parties to manage and operate the vested agreement.
    a. Element 7: Relationship Management which is a structure that creates joint policies to emphasize the importance of building collaborative working relationships, attitudes, and behaviors. The parties monitor the agreement under a flexible governance structure that provides top-to-bottom insights into what is happening.
    b. Element 8: Transformation Management, which is a new relationship model where people and company ecosystems are changing, they are doing things differently, and probably not operating in familiar comfort zones. It is imperative to preserve as much continuity as possible among personnel and teams as the transition progresses into day-to-day implementation and operation.
    c. Element 9: Exit Management when the best plan simply does not work out or is trumped by unexpected events. Business happens, and companies should have a plan when assumptions change. An exit management strategy can provide a template to handle future unknowns.
    d. Element 10: Special Concerns and External Requirements should be there because the governance frameworks are not one-size-fits-all, especially in more technical or complex relationships. Many companies and suppliers must understand and adhere to special requirements and regulatory protocols. A governance framework may need to include additional provisions that address specific market, local, regional, and national requirements.

Some examples of vested relationships that work out according to (Schifferdecker, 2014) are McDonald's award-winning supply chain relationships and Dell- FedEx partnership program. Figure 1 below is presenting the 5 rules

Value Based Contracting

A value-based contract was originated in the healthcare industry and is defined according to (Cantrell, 2017) as "a written contractual agreement in which the payment terms for medication(s) or other health care technologies are tied to agreed-upon clinical circumstances, patient outcomes, or measures" .

The pace of transition from fee-for-service to value-based models varies from one service to another but the shift has begun, and it tends to accelerate rapidly (Eggbeer, Sears, & Homer, 2015). Health systems that are slow to respond with a risk-based value proposition for employers, payers, and other purchasers risk losing market share to competitors that are more actively seeking alternative payment models. According to (Mandal, Tagomori, Felix, & Howell, 2017), value-based contracting can drive utilization patterns and improve clinical outcomes among chronically ill, elderly Medicare Advantage program members.

Figure 1. The Five Rules of Vested Contracts
Source: (Vitasek & Tillman, How to Develop a Successful Outsourcing Contract, 2013)

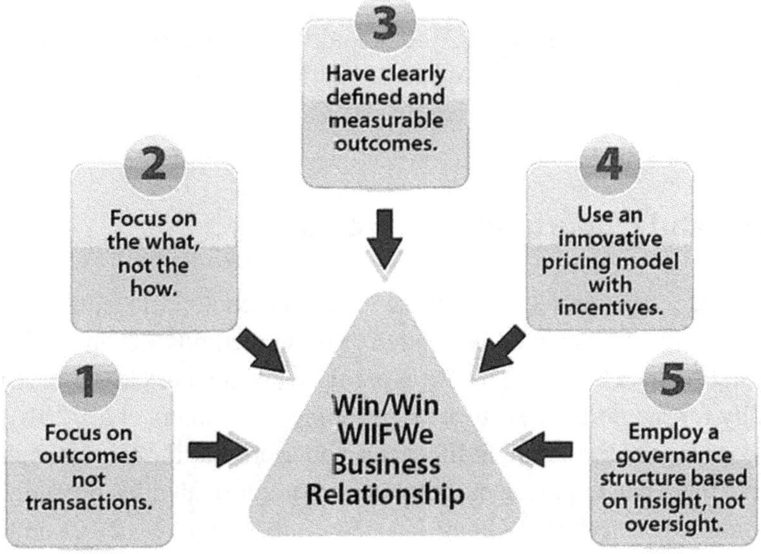

The Definition of Value

Value-based contracting starts with understanding the customer's view of value. In the emerging retail healthcare market for many healthcare services and insurance products, value equates with price, which is becoming a primary factor in consumer decisions (i.e., purchase decisions made directly by consumers, rather than on their behalf by employers, payers, or providers). The value based price, calculated as the discounted present value of expected medical savings plus quality-adjusted life-year gains (Danzon, 2018)

Contract Structure and Design

VBC have common structural characteristics which allow recognizing their alignment to societal health goals and health care affordability (Duhig, Saha, Smith, Kaufman, & Hughes, 2018). Many VBCs are structured around models that are likely to incur high transaction costs relating to the negotiation and specification of outcomes and rely heavily on the relational aspects of contracting (Sanderson, Allen, Gill, & Garnett, 2017). This structure will foster accountability that is measured to calculate the incentive payments. Shared savings can be expressed contractually in an assortment of ways.

According to (Eggbeer, Sears, & Homer, 2015), most value-based contracting is based on three premises:

- Reducing cost by eliminating inappropriate utilization and lowering prices
- Sharing savings or capturing a portion of the value created through lower costs
- Increasing volume through market share gains resulting from enhanced value to the customer

It is worth mentioning that value-based contracts involve far more complexity than fee-for-service contracts. According to (White, 2017), the main risks are that generating the contracts and collecting the data needed are so complex that miscalculations can have large financial implications. It is unclear if the administrative burden required to understand and manage this method will outpace the cost-savings it will generate.

One examples of VBC include the Boeing direct, multiyear, value-based accountable care organization (ACO) contracts with the Providence-Swedish Health Alliance and the University of Washington Medicine Accountable Care Network. Those contracts cover around 27,000 employees and 3,000 retirees in 2015 as per (Stempniak, 2015).

Agile Contracting and Opportunity Contracts

As iterative, incremental, or agile project development methods continue to gain traction in various industries, more and more organizations are taking notice of these methods, because of contractor proposals and program office staff research, outreach, and experience (Wrubel & Gross, 2016). Agile contracting was discussed initially for the iterative software development (Lapham, et al., 2016).

Differences between Agile development lifecycles and more traditional waterfall-based approaches surface throughout the lifecycle, requiring modifications to traditional milestones, documentation, delivery, and progress monitoring activities. (Khong, Yu Beng, Yip, & Fun, 2012). Contracting professionals, however, generally do not receive professional career field training to guide them in developing contracts that support these adaptations (Wrubel & Gross, 2016). So, there is a frequent refrain as program office teams do not feel that they "speak the same language" as contracting officers with whom they must collaborate to create contracts. Speaking the same language will help to satisfy the contracting officer's objectives in protecting the organization interests at an acceptable level of risk.

This agile-system approach focus upon smaller design teams, fewer development phases, and shorter development timetables (Clutterbuck, Rowlands, & Seamons, 2009). This demands a fresh agile contracting approach as the traditional contracting approaches cannot be easily adapted to properly reflect and support the requirements and philosophy of the Agile model. It is thus important to set the stage for understanding how contracting deliverables and structures may need to adapt in various areas such as defining the purpose of the project, the implementation roadmap and how to handle changes and challenges.

Opportunity contracts were suggested by (Shalan & Anaim, 2017) to address many variables that affect the types of contracts that can legally be employed on any given program. It offers an agile approach with a broad view of associated risks and business expectations. It also encourages all stakeholders including the legal practitioners to be involved earlier to widen their scope and evaluate the emerging challenges, risks, values and practices. The main characteristics of opportunity contracts include:

- Starting at the provider terms
- Flexible scope and multi-layered structure
- Incremental deliverables and responsive change management
- Creative contract termination and flexible acceptance criteria

Outcome Based Contracting (OBC) or Performance-Based Contracting (PBC)

This is a type of agreements between providers and customers where providers are paid based on the outcomes they deliver to customers. It have become common for manufacturing firms that are servicing, especially those firms providing advanced services focusing on availability and capability (Hou & Neely, 2018). However, Outcome-based contracting is not a tool by which customers can shift responsibility to their service providers and seek to avoid the effort and time associated with good governance and performance delivery (Paul, 2020).

(Grubic & Jennions, 2018) debate the existence of two types of OBCs: outcomes based on availability (aOBCs) and outcomes based on economic results (eOBCs). The first involve the sale of the availability of a product whereas in the second the customer purchases the functional result of the product. Any way the OBC can be considered as an operational model that requires a strong customer and service provider relationship, trust and a genuine sharing of risk and reward.

According to (Paul, 2020), a true outcome-based model requires a considerable amount of strategic planning from the customer before engaging with service providers. A customer needs to be capable of introspective analysis to understand, develop and communicate its business values and strategic agenda. Strong governance is key in more important when working on an outcome-based model. Governance structures should be developed early in the relationship and be robust with the ability to flex over time in line with the relationship needs and both customer's and service provider's businesses.

Performance-based contracting (PBC) is a business model for the adaptive and innovative delivery of product-service systems. In PBC, the provider is paid according to the service performance with the aim of providing monetary incentives to safeguard possible outcomes as much as possible for the PBC customer (Glas, Henne, & Essig, 2018). Performance-based contracting is a form of contracting that explicitly includes three characteristics (McFall, 2015):

- Clear definition of a series of objectives and indicators by which to measure contractor performance
- Collection of data on the performance indicators to assess the extent to which the contractors are successfully implementing the defined services
- Performance leading to consequences for the contractor, such as provision of rewards or imposition of sanctions.

Rewards can include continuation of the contract in situations in which there is a credible threat of termination, provision of performance bonuses, or public recognition. Sanctions can include termination of the contract, financial penalties, public criticism, and debarment from receiving future contracts.

Selecting and Negotiating Contract Types

It is an exercise of sound judgment to selecting the right contract type. It goes hand by hand to negotiate a contract that will result in reasonable price, moderate contractor risk while managing the overall quality, efficiency, and economical performance. The fixed-price contract, which best utilizes the basic profit motive of business enterprise, shall be used when the risk involved is minimal or can be predicted with an acceptable degree of certainty (FAR, 2020). When a contract is more complex, and the deliverables are not well known the selected contract type need to tie profit to contractor performance. Several factors can be considered including:

- **The Degree of Contractor Flexibility:** will be an important factor in specifying the contract type. The firm-fixed-price make the contractor fully responsible for the performance costs and resulting profit or loss while the cost-plus-fixed-fee make the contractor less responsible for the performance costs.

- **The Ability to Switch Contracts:** In a long-term project, it may be wise to utilize a series of contracts, that can have different forms based on changing circumstances to switch the risk and flexibility margins. If this option is available, it will give the contracting authority an opportunity to mix and match various contracts for every task.
- **Required Resources and Administration Work:** The associated risks and the burden: to manage the selected contract type the organization will need to plan carefully. The fixed cost contracts require an initial planning but once deliverables are moving it will require minimum efforts to generate payments and ensure quality.
- **Planning and Analysis:** Every step should resonate; thus, detailed planning will be required to take appropriate selection and continuous analysis of results should be implemented to measure and evaluate the decisions. Such assessment needs to consider the adequacy of resources that will work every phase.
- **Motivations and Rationale:** It is important to detail the particular facts and circumstances such as complexity of the requirements, uncertain duration of the work, contractor's technical capability and financial responsibility and associated reasoning essential to support the contract type selection.
- **The Price Considerations:** including competition that results in realistic pricing, price analysis that can provide well defined pricing standard and structure. Cost analysis can compensate for the absence of effective price competition. Pricing arrangements is particularly important when uncertainties involved in performance or when the contract type requires price revision while performance is in progress.
- **Requirements' Type and Complexity:** certain types of projects such as research and development include performance uncertainties and changes likelihood which makes it difficult to estimate performance costs in advance. Based on the nature of the project the cost risk may be shifted to the contractor. As product or service descriptions can be defined more clearly the risk levels will be reduced.
- **Urgency and Uncertainty:** When urgency is a primary factor, the contracting authority may choose a contract type that offer incentives tailored to enhance performance. Similar behaviors can be conducted in times of economic uncertainty, where the period of performance or length of production run can extend over a relatively long period resulting in price adjustment or redetermination clauses.
- **Contractor's Technical Capability:** Before agreeing on a contract type, technical and financial capabilities should be evaluated to ensure that contractor is responsible and can handle the contracting obligation in an effective manner. This is important to ensure the quality of technical and administrative deliverables.
- **Trust and Experience:** When awarding a contract, it is important to evaluate the trust level associated with the contractor including the current or past experience with the contractor. The acquisition history is also crucial because the contractor risk usually decreases as the requirement is repetitively acquired.
- **Concurrent contracts:** If performance under the proposed contract involves concurrent operations under other contracts, the impact of those contracts, including their pricing arrangements, should be considered. Similarly, are the extent and nature of proposed subcontracting. If the con-

tractor proposes extensive subcontracting, a contract type reflecting the actual risks to the prime contractor should be selected.

FUTURE RESEARCH DIRECTIONS

Contracting has been very old mechanism to govern the relationship between different business partners. However, as technology is changing everything around us it is doing so to the contracting behaviors. This chapter discussed and challenged the old contracting styles that have been working since long. These styles caused misalignment in multiple technology projects all over the world. This can be further investigated while searching the business failure stories specially when related to technology and innovation.

On the other side new contracting styles are being introduced to accommodate the changes and challenges that are called out by new contracting dynamics. This include agile contracting to handle continuously changing projects, value based contracting which was introduced in health care industry, opportunity contracts which accommodate a wide room for innovations, the vested contracts that encourage multiphase partnership and enforce the win-win scenarios.

However, all these new contracting styles are evolving and still applied to limited use cases. Further investigations will be required to adjust the contracting parameters and the associated negotiation strategies and techniques. This is even more crucial as all new contracting styles are built around trust to promote collaboration and risk sharing. These contracts accept deferring the full detailed planning to consecutive future phases and allow a wide room for transformation, innovation, and change management

CONCLUSION

Human societies depend on value exchange through contracting, outsourcing, and other behaviors. The evolving demands on innovation and transformation are bound to create better ways for contracting based on trust and innovation. The new emerging technologies add plenty of challenge but also create solutions. Debates surrounding the possible use cases are endless. Plenty of parameters have reflections on the deployment scope of the new contracting styles, the associated ecosystem, and the related administration tasks. The journey of innovative contracting will continue, new contracting styles will be introduced, and parameters will be added similarly to what happens in the precious centuries.

REFERENCES

Ahsan, K., & Matsukawa, H. (2012). Project Price Modeling by Optimal Fixed Price Incentive Contract. In *Proceedings of the 2012 International Conference on Industrial Engineering and Operations Management* (pp. 1971-1980). Istanbul, Turkey: International Conference on Industrial Engineering and Operations Management.

Baird, D. (2019). Unlikely Resurrection: Richard Posner, Promissory Estoppel, and the Death of Contract. *The University of Chicago Law Review. University of Chicago. Law School*, 1037–1050.

Bidkar, T. P. (2020, September 1). *What is a Quasi Contract.* Retrieved from http://lawtimesjournal.in: http://lawtimesjournal.in/what-is-a-quasi-contract/

Braxton, P., Hetrick, K., Webb, K., Whitehead-Scanlon, I., & Ross, D. (2017). *Contract Incentives Under Uncertainty:Data-Driven Contract Geometry Best Practices. In 2017 ICEAA Professional Development & Training Workshop.* ICEAA, International Cost Estimating and Analysis Association.

Cantrell, S. A. (2017). AMCP Partnership Forum: Advancing Value-Based Contracting. *Journal of Managed Care & Specialty Pharmacy*, 1096-1102.

Chalkidis, I., & Androutsopoulos, i. (2017). A deep learning approach to contract element extraction. In A. Wyner, & G. Casini (Ed.), *30th International Conference on Legal Knowledge and Information Systems (JURIX 2017)* (pp. 155-165). Luxembourg: IOS Press.

Chalkidis, I., Androutsopoulos, I., & Michos, A. (2018). Extracting contract elements. In *Proceedings of the 16th edition of the International Conference on Articial Intelligence and Law* (pp. 19-28). London: Association for Computing Machinery. 10.1145/3086512.3086515

Chatterjee, C. (2000). *Negotiating Techniques in International Commercial Contracts.* Routledge.

ChenH.GunnyK. (2014). Profitability and Cost Shifting in Government Procurement Contracts. *Management Accounting Section (MAS) Meeting*, 1-33. doi:10.2139srn.2482605

Clutterbuck, P., Rowlands, T., & Seamons, O. (2009). A Case Study of SME Web Application Development Effectiveness via Agile Methods. *The Electronic Journal Information Systems Evaluation, 12*(1), 13–26.

Danzon, P. M. (2018). Affordability Challenges to Value-Based Pricing: Mass Diseases, Orphan Diseases, and Cures. *Value in Health, 21*(3), 252–257. doi:10.1016/j.jval.2017.12.018 PMID:29566830

Darrington, J. W., & Howell, G. A. (2011). Motivation and incentives in relational contracts. *Journal of Financial Management of Property and Construction, 16*(1), 42–51. doi:10.1108/13664381111116070

Du, J., Gelenbe, E., Jiang, C., Zhang, H., & Ren, Y. (2017). Contract Design for Traffic Offloading and Resource Allocation in Heterogeneous Ultra-Dense Networks. *IEEE Journal on Selected Areas in Communications, 35*(11), 2457–2467. doi:10.1109/JSAC.2017.2760459

Duhig, A. M., Saha, S., Smith, S., Kaufman, S., & Hughes, J. (2018). The Current Status of Outcomes-Based Contracting for Manufacturers and Payers: An AMCP Membership Survey. *Journal of Managed Care Speciality Pharma*, 410-415.

Eggbeer, B., Sears, K., & Homer, K. (2015). Finding the 'sweet spot' in value-based contracts. *Healthcare Financial Management Association Journal*, 48-57.

El-adaway, I. H., Vance, R. A., & Abotaleb, I. S. (2020, January 12). Understanding Extension of Time under Different Standard Design-Build Forms of Contract. *Journal of Legal Affairs and Dispute Resolution in Engineering and Construction, 12*(1). Advance online publication. doi:10.1061/(ASCE)LA.1943-4170.0000331

Fagundes, L. (2016, March 3). *Standard Vs. Strategic Contracts*. Retrieved from https://www.contract-works.com/blog/standard-vs.-strategic-contracts#:~:text=A%20lot%20of%20contracts%2C%20if,the%20mill%2C%20standard%20form%20agreements

FAR. (2020, December 1). *Federal Acquisition Regulation*. Retrieved from https://www.acquisition.gov: https://www.acquisition.gov/sites/default/files/current/far/compiled_html/subpart_16.2.html

Forbes, B., & Brady, M. (2019, April 1). Ex-post service contract performance management. *International Journal of Business Performance Management*. doi:10.1504/IJBPM.2019.098634

Fried, C. (2015). *Contract as Promise: A Theory of Contractual Obligation*. Oxford University Press. doi:10.1093/acprof:oso/9780190240158.001.0001

Glas, A., Henne, F., & Essig, M. (2018). Missing performance management and measurement aspects in performance-based contracting: A systematic process-based literature analysis of an astonishing research gap. *International Journal of Operations & Production Management*, *38*(11), 2062–2095. doi:10.1108/IJOPM-09-2016-0571

Gluck, G. (1979). Standard Form Contracts: The Contract Theory Reconsidered. *The International and Comparative Law Quarterly*, *28*(1), 72–90. www.jstor.org/stable/758554. doi:10.1093/iclqaj/28.1.72

Grandori, A., & Furlotti, M. (2009). Facio ut Facias: Associational Contracts for Innovation. *International Studies of Management & Organization*, *39*(4), 81–100. doi:10.2753/IMO0020-8825390405

Grubic, T., & Jennions, I. (2018). Do outcome-based contracts exist? The investigation of power-by-the-hour and similar result-oriented cases. *International Journal of Production Economics*, *206*, 209–219. doi:10.1016/j.ijpe.2018.10.004

Heide, J. B. (1994). Interorganizational Governance in Marketing Channels. *Journal of Marketing*, *85*(1), 71–85. doi:10.1177/002224299405800106

Hietanen, S. (2014). Mobility as a Service"—The new transport model? *Eurotransport*, *12*(2), 2–4.

Hou, J., & Neely, A. (2018). Investigating risks of outcome-based service contracts from a provider's perspective. *International Journal of Production Research*, *6*(6), 2103–2115. doi:10.1080/00207543.2017.1319089

Jittrapirom, V., Caiati, V., Feneri, A.-M., Ebrahimigharehbaghi, S., González, M. J., & Narayan, J. (2017). Mobility as a Service: A Critical Review of Definitions, Assessments of Schemes, and Key Challenges. *Urban Planning*, *2*(2), 13–25. doi:10.17645/up.v2i2.931

Kapsali, M., Roehrich, J., & Akhtar, P. A. (2018). Effective contracting for high operational performance in projects. *International Journal of Operations & Production Management*, 294–325. doi:0.1108/IJOPM-10-2017-0604

Khong, L., Beng, Y. L., Yip, T., & Fun, T. (2012). Software Development Life Cycle AGILE vs Traditional Approaches. In *International Conference on Information and Network Technology* (pp. 162-166). Chennai, India: IACSIT Press.

Kronman, A. (1985). Contract Law and the State of Nature. *Journal of Law Economics and Organization, 1*(1), 5–32. http://www.jstor.org/stable/764905

Kuppa, R. (2018). Negotiating a Contract. *PM World Journal*, 1-11.

Lapham, M. A., Korzec, K., Rosser, L. A., Howard, G., Martin, S., Ryan, M., . . . Capell, P. (2016). RFP Patterns and Techniques for Successful Agile Contracting. Hanscom, MA: Carnegie Mellon University.

Leacock, S. (2011). Fingerprints of Equitable Estoppel and Promissory Estoppel on the Statute of Frauds in Contact Law. Barry University School of Law, 73-133.

Legal Dictionary. (2017, March 25). *Express Contract*. Retrieved from https://legaldictionary.net: https://legaldictionary.net/express-contract/

Lumineau, F. (2015). How Contracts Influence Trust and Distrust. *Journal of Management, 43*(5), 1–25. doi:10.1177/0149206314556656

Lumineau, F. (2017). How Contracts Influence Trust and Distrust. *Journal of Management, 43*(5), 1553–1577. doi:10.1177/0149206314556656

Lumineau, F., & Quelin, B. (2012). An Empirical Investigation of Inter-Organizational Opportunism and Contracting Mechanisms. *Strategic Organization, 10*(1), 55–84. doi:10.1177/1476127011434798

Mandal, A. K., Tagomori, G. K., Felix, R. V., & Howell, S. C. (2017). Value-Based Contracting Innovated Medicare Advantage Healthcare Delivery and Improved Survival. *The American Journal of Managed Care, 23*(2).

McCullough, J. (2020, March 23). *Unilateral vs bilateral contracts*. Retrieved from https://www.jotform.com: https://www.jotform.com/blog/unilateral-vs-bilateral-contract/

McFall, C. (2015, August 25). *Outcome-based contracts – Adding value to the contract life-cycle*. Retrieved from https://pwc.blogs.com/deals/2015/08/outcome-based-contracts.html

Morstyn, T., Teytelboym, A., & Mcculloch, D. M. (2019). Bilateral Contract Networks for Peer-to-Peer Energy Trading. *IEEE Transactions on Smart Grid, 10*(2), 2026–2035. doi:10.1109/TSG.2017.2786668

O'Byrne, S. (2007). The Implied Term of Good Faith and Fair Dealing: Recent Developments. *The Canadian Bar Review*, 53–86.

Opelt, A., Gloger, B., Pfarl, W., & Mittermayr, R. (2013). Agile Contracts: Creating and Managing Successful Projects with Scrum. John Wiley & Sons. doi:10.1002/9781118640067

Paul, M. (2020, August 7). *Understanding Outcome Based Contracting*. Retrieved from https://futureofsourcing.com: https://futureofsourcing.com/understanding-outcome-based-contracts

Petersen, B., & Østergaard, K. (2017). Reconciling contracts and relational governance through strategic contracting. *Journal of Business and Industrial Marketing*, 1–12. doi:10.1108/JBIM-09-2016-0223

Reuer, J. J., & Ariño, A. (2007). Strategic alliance contracts: dimensions and determinants of contractual complexity. *Strategic Management*, 313-330. doi:10.1002mj.581

Roseke, B. (2019, April 23). *Types of Contracts*. Retrieved from https://www.projectengineer.net: https://www.projectengineer.net/types-of-contracts/

Sanderson, M., Allen, P., Gill, R., & Garnett, E. (2017, May 18). New Models of Contracting in the Public Sector: A Review of Alliance Contracting, Prime Contracting and Outcome-based Contracting Literature. *Social Policy and Administration, 52*(5), 1060–1083. doi:10.1111pol.12322

Schaefer, J. A. (2001). Beyond a Definition: Understanding the Nature of Void and Voidable Contracts. *Campbell Law Review*, 193–209.

Schifferdecker, B. (2014, December 1). *Five rules & ten steps to collaborative contracting*. Retrieved from https://www.dhl.com/global-en/home/about-us/delivered-magazine/articles/2014-2015/five-rules-and-ten-steps-to-collaborative-contracting.html

Sefton-Green, R. (2005). *Mistake, Fraud and Duties to Inform in European Contract Law*. Cambridge University Press. doi:10.1017/CBO9780511495052

Shalan, M. A., & Anaim, N. A. (2017). The SMAC Opportunity Contracts: Generating Value From Responsive Agile Risk-Oriented Techniques. In *Mobile Platforms, Design,and Apps for Social Commerce* (pp. 115–134). IGI Global. doi:10.4018/978-1-5225-2469-4.ch008

Stempniak, M. (2015, February 15). *Will Boeing Change Health Care?* Retrieved from https://trustees.aha.org/articles/1020-will-boeing-change-health-care: https://trustees.aha.org/articles/1020-will-boeing-change-health-care

Sund, K. A., & Hausken, K. (2012). Fixed price contract versus incentive-based contract in the oil and gas industry. *International Journal of Global Energy Issues, 35*(5), 371. Advance online publication. doi:10.1504/IJGEI.2012.046727

ToffelM. W. (2008). Contracting for Servicizing. *Harvard Business School Technology & Operations Mgt.*, 1-31. doi:10.2139srn.1090237

Vitasek, K. (2011, August 31). *Vested Outsourcing: A New Business Model*. Retrieved from https://www.bonezonepub.com/196-vested-outsourcing-a-new-business-model?start=2

Vitasek, K. (2014, April 25). *How to Negotiate a Collaborative Outsourcing Deal*. Retrieved from https://www.cio.com/article/2376775/how-to-negotiate-a-collaborative-outsourcing-deal.html

Vitasek, K., Ledyard, M., & Manrodt, K. (2010). *Vested Outsourcing: Five Rules That Will Transform Outsourcing*. Palgrave Macmillan. doi:10.1057/9780230105232

Vitasek, K., & Tillman, J. (2013, December 1). *How to Develop a Successful Outsourcing Contract*. Retrieved from https://www.areadevelopment.com/logisticsInfrastructure/December-2013/collaborative-outsourcing-agreements-vested-model-28272611.shtml

White, C. M. (2017). Potential Benefits and Risks of Value-Based Pricing of Prescription Drugs. *Connecticut Medicine, 28*(10), 587–595.

Wong, J. (2006). Umbrella Clauses in Bilateral Investment Treaties: Of Breaches of Contract, Treat Violations, and the Divide between Developing and Developed Countries in Foreign Investment Disputes. *Geo Mason Legal Review*, 135-150.

Wrubel, E., & Gross, J. (2016). *Contracting for Agile Software Development in the Department of Defense: An Introduction*. Hanscom, MA: Carnegie Mellon University.

Xiang, Y., Zhu, Z., Coit, D. W., & Feng, Q. (2017). Condition-based maintenance under performance-based contracting. *Computers & Industrial Engineering, 111*, 391–402. doi:10.1016/j.cie.2017.07.035

Yao, T., Jiang, B., Scott, Young, T., & Talluri, S. (2010). utsourcing timing, contract selection, and negotiation. *International Journal of Production Research, 48*(2), 305-326. doi:10.1080/00207540903174858

Yu, D. (2020, October 24). Background Concepts and Definitions. *Aircraft Valuation*, 7-31. doi:10.1007/978-981-15-6743-8_2

Zhang, C., & Lin, M. (2018). Optimization of Cost Plus Incentive Fee Contract in Equipment Acquisition Considering Cost Revelation. In *International Conference on Management Science and Engineering (ICMSE)* (pp. 60-66). Frankfurt, Germany: IEEE. doi:10.1109/ICMSE.2018.8744917

Zhang, J., Cao, Q., & He, X. (2019). Contract and product quality in platform selling. *European Journal of Operational Research, 272*(3), 928–944. doi:10.1016/j.ejor.2018.07.023

ADDITIONAL READING

Al-Subhi Al-Harabi, K. M. (1998). Sharing fractions in cost-plus-incentive-fee contracts. *International Journal of Project Management, 16*(2), 73–80. doi:10.1016/S0263-7863(97)00013-6

Heide, J. B., & John, G. (1992). Do norms matter in marketing relationships? *Journal of Marketing, 56*(2), 32–44. doi:10.1177/002224299205600203

Lumineau, F., & Quélin, B. V. (2012). An empirical investigation of interorganizational opportunism and contracting mechanisms. *Strategic Organization, 10*(1), 55–84. doi:10.1177/1476127011434798

Macneil, I. R. (1980). Power, contract, and the economic model. *Journal of Economic Issues, 11*(4), 909–923. doi:10.1080/00213624.1980.11503791

Meinhart, W. A., & Delionback, L. M. (1986). Project management: An incentive contracting decision model. *Academy of Management Journal, 11*, 427–434.

Mesquita, L. F., & Brush, T. H. (2008). Untangling safeguard and production coordination effects in long-term buyersupplier relationships. *Academy of Management Journal, 51*, 785–807.

Müller, R., & Turner, R. (2005). The impact of principle-agent relationship and contract type on communication between project owner and manager. *International Journal of Project Management, 23*(5), 398–403. doi:10.1016/j.ijproman.2005.03.001

Turner, J. R., & Simister, S. J. (2001). Project contract management and a theory of organization. *International Journal of Project Management, 19*(8), 457–464. doi:10.1016/S0263-7863(01)00051-5

Zaghloul, R., & Hartman, F. (2003). Construction contracts: The cost of mistrust. *International Journal of Project Management, 21*(6), 419–424. doi:10.1016/S0263-7863(02)00082-0

KEY TERMS AND DEFINITIONS

Agile Contracts: A new contracting style in which the supplier continually align with customers and other stakeholders on what's being built. This is driven by continuous changes, development discoveries, evolving customer needs, changing technologies, and competitor innovations.

Bilateral Contract: An agreement happened because both parties must make a promise.

Contract Rights: An understanding of how contracts influence trust thus it fosters the interaction between the two contract parties. Those rights may be expressly written such as the exclusive right to use copyrighted material or implicit.

Explicit: Terms that which both parties have explicitly stated the terms of their bargain, either orally or in writing, at the time that the contract was created

Fixed Price Contracts: A very popular contracting where the owner provides a detailed specification of the requirements, and then the winning contractor is obligated to meet the specified requirement at an agreed-on price.

Implicit: Terms that exist based on current contract laws and policies. While they can be written into the agreement, they're usually simply implied by governmental laws or common practices.

Opportunity Contracts: A type of contracts that address many variables that can legally be employed on any given program. It offers an agile approach with a broad view of associated risks and business expectations.

Quasi Contracts: A unique circumstances in which obligations imposed by law to avoid injustice. When no enforceable contract exists, the court may imply one to avoid unjust enrichment on a benefiting party.

Unilateral Contract: An agreement where only one party promises something. The concept of unilateral contracts is important because it has been used by courts to hold a party liable for a promise even when consideration was not given by the other party.

Value-Based Contracts (VBC): A written contractual agreement in which the payment terms for medication(s) or other health care technologies are tied to agreed-upon clinical circumstances, patient outcomes, or measures. This was originated in the healthcare industry and spread to other industries.

Chapter 3
Contract Design and Related Agreements

Hasan Tayyeb
Umm Al-Qura University, Saudi Arabia

ABSTRACT

As we delve into value deconstruction, the number of contractors will increase a great deal, and every specialty will have its own parameters. The contract by its own will not be able to accommodate all clauses and conditions that may be due for changes. Now imagine, what would happen if important information like trade secrets of any corporation or business were to be leaked to competitors? And wouldn't it be so much better to legally oblige to privacy and urge those who consent to keep the information in question completely under wraps? For this reason, it is important to have an ecosystem of agreements such as NDAs, SLAs, and others to complete the chain and allow for efficient governance and risk management considerations. NDAs and confidentiality provisions have groundbreaking propensity. The design of such agreements is fundamental and various parameters must be considered. This chapter directs attention to these subjects and concerns by discussing the various types of complementary agreements and how they can be attached to the original contract to add value and reduce risk.

INTRODUCTION

The deconstruction of value chains has come to define modern business. Business architecture has been transforming in the past couple of years, the players in an industry are organized for value creation when it comes to the ultimate consumer. Technological evolution has changed the long-established pattern of business architecture. Organizations can use deconstruction to gain strategic benefit, but it is necessary to understand the purpose for deconstruction and which parts of the chain are most likely to be affected and how it can be used by the organization to gain a competitive advantage (Dommisse & Oosthuizen, 2004). This will give an insight into the number of contractors and players which includes competitors, suppliers and players from adjacent industries that can compete on different key success factors. In the new model, new players can disrupt the organization by attacking only a specific portion of the whole

DOI: 10.4018/978-1-7998-4501-0.ch003

value chain. This happens when employees intentionally or unintentionally leak confidential information or other players reveal it to unauthorized persons or parties. Sometimes problems emerge when 'external influences' get involved, something that can't be factored into the equation and that's where things go sideways. Value chains are rapidly evolving into value networks, with multiple entry and exit points (Lia & Whalley, 2002). Thus, creating immense complexness and vulnerability for an organization while also posing a huge risk to the information security. The focus is on the interaction between two or more parties.

Contracts form the foundation of all business relationships. Contracts enable both parties to a contract to meet their obligations to deliver the objectives required from the contract. A way for humans to work together and communicate efficiently and effectively. But with value deconstruction, arise a growing number of contracts, increasing convolutions and the constant need for amendments, make it challenging to manage the valuable information in the contracts as well as integrate additional clauses and conditions which may be subject to change. Apart from making the agreement between concerned parties legally binding, contracts can also serve as future references, part of the business' policies, as well as serve as evidence in the event of misunderstandings, complaints or disputes needing litigation proceedings. Organizations are increasingly moving to an "agreement ecosystem" model, where employees across an organization agree to confidentiality and non-disclosure provisions protecting sensitive information.

Embracing formal contracts enables the mitigation of legal risk by ensuring that parties to an agreement know what their obligations and responsibilities are. Confidentiality can be implied, but the other parties may not always be aware of it.

The main aim of this chapter is to shed some light on an issue rising up the chart for causing issues between parties - contractual agreements and the design of these agreements which is of critical importance. Since many contractual parties spend a good deal of time, energy and resources creating contracts that are befitting and to their liking. Furthermore, the main objective of this chapter is to discuss and describe in detail the various types of complementary agreements and how they can be attached to the original contract to add value, reduce risk and ensure data protection.

BACKGROUND

The introduction of new technology and regulatory amendments brought about a phenomenon where parts of the traditional industry value chain started breaking away and either forming new industries or combining with parts of different industries and this break up was titled 'deconstruction'. (Bresser, Heuskel & Nixon, 2000). New concepts of strategy and organization are required to cope with this new business architecture. Confidential information such as customer lists, proprietary technology, pricing information, and marketing plans are critical business assets that can be jeopardized if not managed properly. Contracts are a vital part of building relationships and completing business transactions. A study conducted on what people considered were the most relevant reasons to create contracts found that contracts had many purposes and thus many different reasons for why they are important. Most importantly, contracts are the main source of relationship building for an organization (Concord Editorial, 2018).

A contract as a promise (or a set of promises) that is legally binding; by 'legally binding' we mean that the law will compel the person making the promise ('the promisor') to perform that promise, or to pay damages to compensate the person to whom it was made ('the promisee') for non-performance (Smith S., 2004). In a well-written contract, the written terms evidently define the parties' agreement, their expectations, and their respective risks and obligations. Even if the parties "trust" each other, a written contract provides a guide book of how the parties will make headway, thus ensuring smooth operations and diminished risk of problems (Strickland, 2017).

There has been a boost in the concept of getting employees to enter into agreements consisting of non-disclosure and non-compete clauses, as an indispensable condition to employment. Today a company's most valuable assets are its trade secrets. Agreements consisting of non-disclosure clauses can help prevent employees from disclosing trade secrets or confidential information. And non-compete agreements can protect an organization by restricting potential competition. Confidentiality agreements are contracts entered into by two or more parties in which some or all of the parties agree that certain types of information that is conveyed from one party to the other or that are created by one of the parties will remain confidential (Radack, 1994). Confidentiality agreements protect delicate technical or commercial information from exposure. Parties in the agreement pledge not to disclose information received from the other party. In a case where information has been compromised to another individual or company, the wronged party has motive to claim, 'breach of contract' and solicit injunctive or pecuniary damages. A well-drafted confidentiality agreement can avoid the unwanted and often accidental punitive actions in patent infringement. Lastly, confidentiality agreements specify what information is classified or proprietary and what is not. The type of information that can be included under the umbrella of confidential information is essentially unlimited. Any information that is exchanged between the parties can be regarded as classified, data, techniques, prototypes, software, experimental results, equipment or machinery, algorithms, and blueprints and formulas. Although the law imposes certain obligations of confidentiality on employees, confidentiality provisions in an employment contract make it clear that the organization is committed to confidentiality, and therefore help prevent problems from a legal and practical stance (Kroman, 2013).

An ecosystem of agreements can enable systematic and efficient management of contract creation and implementation with the intention of strengthening financial and operational performance and curtailing risk. Agreements have considerable contribution to a company's financial health and are best described as a strategic weapon in optimizing contract performance and enhancing return on investments. Organizations might be unaware of the fact that contracts help to drive and shape almost every business. Gartner estimates that between 60-80% of all business transactions are governed by contracts or agreements in one form or another, especially across finance, IT, legal dept, purchasing, sales, operations and HR. Therefore, contractual agreements play a vital part in an organization's foundation. If used properly, contracts have the ability to aid organizations reduce costs and improve profitability while mitigating risk.

To turn groups of employees into great teams, an important preliminary move is to form a social contract, an explicit agreement that lays out the ground rules for team members' behaviors. (Riordan & O'Brien, 2012). A contract can cover topics such as how employees will work together, make decisions, communicate, share information, and support each other. Social contracts clearly outline norms for how members will and should "interact" with each other. In business, the key to sharing information safely is making sure that the other party is bound to respect the confidential information provided to them and not use it to the party's detriment. One widespread method to protect the secrecy of confidential information given to another party is through the use of a Non-Disclosure Agreement, which is sometimes also referred to as a "Confidentiality Agreement" or "NDA" (Harroch, 2016).

VALUE DECONSTRUCTION

Over the previous years, integrated value chains have served businesses well and (Stern & Deimler, 2006) believes that they have enabled the sophisticated coordination that growing technical complexity sought for. Furthermore, they organized the dedicated assets, both human and physical, necessary for achieving economies of scale and scope. Although expensive to create, they were a colossal obstacle to competition once they were firmly established. The vertically integrated value chain has been a powerful competitive machine.

Changes in consumer behavior powered by the adoption of emerging Digital Technologies set in motion a rise in latent needs and expose disruption opportunities the Digital Ecosystem. Customers are evolving faster than ever, connected at all times and willing to participate (not as mere reactive consumers), setting up expectations based on what they experience from Digital champions (e.g., Amazon, Netflix, etc.), demanding ubiquitous and hyper-personalized experiences, moving from products to on-demand services and even reformulating the concept of ownership and participation in the business ecosystem – transforming into 'prosumers', thus accelerating the industry disruption loop and revolutionizing the competitive landscape and market dynamics.

Imagine a company building a smart city will require few years for designing and a bunch of years for construction. The technologies are emerging all over this period, furthermore few companies are entering or leaving the market. Thus, you must have flexibility to switch between technologies and companies and to deconstruct the value chain thus you can replace any technology or contractor at any time. Such a scenario is a great motivation for value deconstruction, and it is a trend that is spreading all over the industry and requiring different contracting and ecosystem.

Defining Value Deconstruction

As analysts, mainly in the management consulting arena, observed changes in industries resulting from, amongst other, the introduction of new technology and regulatory amendments, they noticed a phenomenon where parts of the traditional industry value chain started breaking away and either forming new industries or combining with parts of different industries (Bresser, Heuskel, & Nixon, 2000). This disassembling or unbundling was formalized as 'deconstruction'. The end of the last century saw the establishment of vertically integrated value chains that came to define the contemporary business environment. On the flip side, the end of this century is encountering its deconstruction. Markets are meddling with the web of proprietary arrangements that have held these chains together. As they do so, the boundaries defining businesses, companies, and industries are under siege—radically transforming the nature of competition. And thus, new concepts of strategy, contracting and organization are required to address the situation.

The concept of deregulation and deconstruction of integrated value chains in the business landscape rudimentarily means that entire industries may be reshaping and reconstructing and that companies need to embrace strategies grounded in this, in an effort to survive and flourish.

(Vaquero, 2020) writes that, digital disruption is challenging the status quo of traditional industries, generating a continuous stream of innovation and blurring boundaries into digital ecosystems. Customers are demanding experiences that go above and beyond their expectations while budding digital attackers are deconstructing traditional value chains to tackle mature industries, requiring existing companies to drastically transform in order to ensure 'digital adaptability'.

These trends have two simultaneous effects. On one hand, proprietary links give way to markets. Witness the outsourcing trend: companies can now make use of key activities in the value chain without owning them. On the other hand, opportunities for rich communication and collaboration between customers and suppliers are greater than ever. Both these developments undermine vertical integration, replacing it with a highly flexible mix of new coordination mechanisms, ranging from the ruthlessness of the spot market at one extreme to the most strategic of partnerships at the other (Stern & Deimler, 2006). That being the case, to utilize the old model of having a single contractor who handles everything, electromechanical, as for instance is ineffective, alternatively having multiple specialized and dedicated contractors, and engaging in continuous innovation for these systems is more beneficial. Successful orchestrators possess powerful brands and use them to retain control of the lion's share of an industry's value added while minimizing their own assets.

Digital native players like Amazon, Google, Apple or Facebook have become some of the most highly valued companies in the world, leveraging highly modular and asset-light business models to disintermediate traditional value chains and build multi-billion-dollar businesses at a global scale. Digital disruption is significantly affecting revenue pools of established industries, shifting the sources of value from traditional products and services to digitally-enabled, on-demand and even crowdsourced ones (e.g., from mobile phone calls to social media messaging, from owning cars to using on-demand cars, etc.). This fundamental shift in how successful digital value propositions are built reflects the need to reformulate the paradigm under companies to create sustainable value in the new digital business ecosystem.

But maintaining control of the value chain is not an easy task. The orchestrated—those who focus on a specific value-added step, or layer—have every incentive to drive for scale and scope themselves. If they succeed, they seize control of the value chain from the orchestrator, as Intel and Microsoft did with IBM. The business then deconstructs entirely. Each layer becomes a distinct business with its own economics. Some of these layered businesses are highly scale sensitive; subsequently dominating them can be enormously profitable. Others are naturally fragmented; and after deconstruction, profits are hard to come by. The onset of fragmentation can, however, create opportunities for a new kind of player—navigators that help participants cope with the complexity of doing business in a deconstructed world.

The first is deconstruction of value chains: the breakup of vertically integrated businesses, as standards and interoperability replace managed interfaces. And the second is polarization of the economies of mass, meaning that in some activities, economies of scale and experience are evaporating, while in others they are intensifying (Evans, 2014).

The Implications of Deconstruction

According to (Philip Evans, 1999), the competitive implications of deconstruction are profound and wide ranging to include;

1. The traditional definition of businesses and industries—and, therefore, the reference set of competitors, suppliers, and customers—becomes obsolete.
2. Competitive advantage is de-averaged. Businesses in which the economics of one activity are compromised for the sake of the whole will be especially vulnerable.
3. Advantage across the entire value chain no longer matters; it's advantage in each layer that counts. As a result, the new unit of strategic analysis is the layer.

4. Horizontal strategies—those that leverage layer capabilities across previously distinct businesses—become serious alternatives to traditional strategies of vertical integration and customer franchise in a single industry.
5. Managing resource allocation at the layer level requires new ways to evaluate investments and gives birth to a whole new concept of the portfolio. The finer parsing of risk permits imaginative new financial strategies.
6. The boundaries of the corporation become fluid and permeable. Ownership is no longer a condition for effective co-ordination or control.
7. Customers are empowered; brands become vulnerable. Traditional asymmetries of information are challenged by the rise of navigators that search and switch on the customer's behalf.
8. Intermediaries that extract value from controlling a chokepoint in the flow of information are vulnerable to disintermediation.
9. This value deconstruction has a huge impact on contracting styles and the governance and risk setups that require great maturity levels to achieve the required values and avoid getting lost in hassles.

This shows clearly that the implications of the value deconstruction and industry architecture are all about tapping the higher aptitudes of other players. It may require outsourcing innovation to small players, data partnerships or outsourcing processing and facilities management to large providers. This means that the business dynamics are being changed to accommodate innovative ideas and competitive advantages.

Illustrating Value Deconstruction: Asset-Sharing Between Shipping Lines

(Schlingmeyer, 2019) notes that, previously, companies have tried to optimize and extract efficiency gains through value chain integration. Reason being, it is easier to communicate and optimize within a company than with external partners. A typical case from container logistics includes Maersk Line acquiring Damco steering to consolidate the entire value chain up to the last-mile delivery. This is reasoned by the lower transaction costs when communicating within an organization compared to the outside. The risk of "hold-ups" is better manageable when the entire value chain can be observed compared to just a small fraction.

Today, technology and digital platforms reduce transaction costs and eliminate risks. This makes the traditional "company borders" obscure. In the "gig" economy there exist specialists from highly paid professionals such as lawyers and consultants to low-wage uneducated "hands" who choose not to get a job in a company but instead offer their services on platforms such as Uber, Fiverr or Deliveroo. Comically enough, this does not quite fit into the known models of Business to Business (B2B), Business to Consumer (B2C), or even Platform-to-Business (P2B).

Thinking about the future of the shipping industry, value deconstruction is clear in all its aspects. Multiple "neutral" platforms will link together specialized actors along the value chain. Actors on the value chain will be much more specialized than they previously were and instead of seeing mega-carriers covering the transport chain end-to-end, actors such as equipment owner, vessel owner, vessel operator, slot marketer, agents, equipment tracking technology, ports, terminal, truckers, depots and so on, will play a big role.

From an economic viewpoint, in the absence of transaction costs, communication barriers and "holdup risks", it makes hardly any sense to have "vessel operation" and "equipment ownership" implemented by the same party. In the case of equipment management, a pool allows the balancing out of company-specific imbalances and reduction in empty container moves. Container Leasing companies are a prime example where this happens commonly.

What is happening today in the shipping industry is that fully integrated liners act like a "one-stop-shop" and try to offer a platter of services even though their core business is ocean freight. For the most part, forwarders or shippers bring their own containers and only book vessel slots, these containers termed as shipper-owned containers increase flexibility and are a win-win situation for shippers as well as carriers. Forwarders save demurrage charges, while carriers avoid time-consuming planning and can focus on what they're good at which is - moving goods between continents and the sale of vessel slots!

This can stop the race for integration or being the largest and most integrated actor. In the future of shipping, it is more desirable to be highly specialized instead of playing in multiple platforms. From a corporate finance viewpoint, there will be no more "conglomerate cover-up", every activity needs to be performed at par with or better than the best. Because markets will be so efficient, that customers won't be willing to pay for substandard or mediocre pieces of products any longer.

The implications of this are obvious, firms should ensure they are preparing for an eco-system future—or brace themselves for what "eco-systematization" will mean for them. Specifically, they need to dedicate resources to understanding which services are available, as the landscape is evolving quickly. More and more platforms are springing that might evolve into an eco-system of services. Every platform need to decide what differentiates it from the others and exit or source marginal activities. While this has always been a good idea and strategic exercise, it is becoming more important than ever.

However, every player needs to create plug and play architectures, not just in a technical sense, but also in how they contract for short and long durations and to be effective in managing the interrelation with other players. In some cases, they may need to organize themselves into a set of discrete internal services to allow inter-operability with the external market. Zapier is a typical example for pushing plug and play architectures, it is basically an online service that "connects" distinct services to provide additional user value. Easyjet is another example for an "unbundling" of services into micro-services where one can book everything, but don't have to. This will allow better alignment with the market and is profitable areas.

CONTRACT ATTACHMENTS

As (D'Amelio, 2019) rightly said, "contracts are like photographs that capture the details of an agreement at a specific point in time." Nevertheless, conditions change, and even a contract written with a forward-looking perspective, may need to be changed, altered, and revised. To allow a contract to better cope with the prospective changes in the original contract language, there are a set of additional agreements that must be attached to the contract or which could be added later.

The purpose of making another section for additional information is that the information provided in the appendix is not central to the text and usually does not fit into the main text. If this additional information is added into the main document, it makes the document complicated and undecipherable. Thus, such attachments with detailed information can be added in a separate section called 'attachments' that not everyone will want to read.

Attaching or amending a contract must be done carefully, to have a working structure and to only change the parts of the deal that are no longer pertinent while preserving the parts of the deal that do work.

Attachments may exist to list items that will crowd the contract if written in the main body, along with items that are subject to periodic changes. Some other contract amendments are written upon changes to contract price, terms, or scope of services, such as adding or removing work, or changing the terms or duration of a contract. Changes to contracts can occur under a variety of conditions (Minneapolis Government, 2019). Usually there are various documents that can be attached to the contract, which might carry different meanings while being used interchangeably in different occasions or contexts.

Attachment is the umbrella term for a set of documents with common characteristic such as the appendix, annexure, or schedule. This section is detailing few points related to each document.

Schedule

Is the most used label for materials which are attached to a contract. The purpose of a schedule is usually to avoid breaking the continuity of the contract with lots of detailed information. It is a term used for attachments in most practical law standard documents.

A schedule may comprise of the most important legally operative contract terms, for example, a share purchase agreement will usually be a separate schedule containing detailed warranties. Alternatively, a schedule may contain a load of data which will not make sense unless read together with the main body of the agreement.

An Annexure or Annex

This may be considered a report, or a document, separate from the contract. It is often used in international contracts, perhaps where there is a continental law connection. It should be attached to the contract when being signed as part of the contract, to avoid any problems of proof if both parties do not agree on the contents of the annex.

Appendix

This is a group of documents attached at the end of a document, a book, a report, a legal contract, etc. Every appendix contains additional information about the facts and terms mentioned in the main document. It provides supplementary but useful material to the main document.

In contracts, it is used to refer to a document which is attached to but does not form a part of the agreement in any operative sense. The document is attached for reference and often initialed for identification purposes by the parties, but its provisions are not in themselves incorporated into the agreement. Common information in the appendix includes tables; charts; graphs; questionnaires; lengthy derivations of equations; transcripts of interviews; maps; pictures and definitions.

In summary and according to Black's Law Dictionary (Michalsons, 2016):

- **An Appendix** is "a supplementary document attached to the end of a writing",
- **An Annexure** is "something that is attached, such as a document to a report", and
- **A Schedule is** "a written list or inventory; or a statement that is attached to a document and that gives a detailed showing of the matters referred to in the document".

Exhibit

Some legal practitioners would think of the term "exhibit" in the context of legal proceedings, that is, material which is attached to a witness statement or confirmation. However, the term is used for a contract similar to the "appendix", to refer to an attachment of a static nature, for example, a photocopy of an existing document which has been attached for a frame of reference, or as background.

A Supplement

A supplement is an additional document to the contract that does not change the original terms but does add new terms. A supplemental agreement is a legal document that memorializes the settling of a dispute as to the original terms of the contract. A supplemental agreement will describe the dispute and the settlement in an objective manner.

Attachment

(Carlson, 2019) defines the term attachment as referring to the items or documents that are appended to the main document. It is a single document that is combined as a separate document with completely new information to the main document. They are particularly not considered as part of the main document and often recognized to be stand-alone documents by themselves.

The attachment serves a multitude of purposes for a document. It is usually not something that contributes to the understanding of the main work. It follows the introduction of some sort and has information that may be related to the main document but is independent of the document to which it is attached.

Addendum

A contract addendum is an attachment to the initial contract that details any additions to be included as part of the contract. An addendum usually contains items that were not included when the contract was being drafted. Addenda are modifications added to an existing agreement to add or change a few of its terms and conditions. It does not replace the original contract.

(Thompson, 2019) explains that the term "addendum" is often used to add an additional layer of alternative obligations for different kinds of legal relationships. For example, a computer company might have a basic reseller contract, with core terms that apply to all resellers, but then add, say, a "Country Distributor Addendum", or a "Value Added Reseller Addendum", or other addenda which set out obligations describing certain kinds of commercial behavior required of different kinds of resellers.

When parties make a contract, they can add to it or change it by writing a legal addendum. An addendum doesn't replace the original contract; but rather changes minor details that have been incorrectly stated, such as a delivery date or a salary, although it can be used to change more important terms.

An addendum can be used to add stipulated information after the parties have agreed upon the terms of the contract. For example, in real estate contracts, an addendum might be used to add a spouse as a co-owner to a purchase agreement.

Key Differences Between Appendix vs. Attachment

The appendix is also a subcategory of the addendum. The addendum are some documents added at the end of a contract that may be helpful to explain unclear information that a potential reader might encounter and questions that may arise while reading the main work. The appendix is a generally wide term that refers to a series of documents added at the end of a legal contract for further reference and to supplement the main work. However, the main text can be understood without reading the appendix, but for anyone with deep interest for further reference, can always look up the appendix. The appendix is typically arranged in an alphabetical order. It is also important to refer to these appendices in the main document.

Distinct contrasts between an appendix and attachments include:

- The appendix is helpful for further reference of the main work but is not necessarily essential for its understanding while an attachment is not helpful for further reference or the understanding of main work, it is usually uploaded to supplement another document.
- The term appendix refers to a section of subsidiary matter at the end of a book or document, on the flip side, the term attachment refers to items or documents that are appended to the main document.
- The appendix cannot be a stand-alone document conversely, an attachment is a stand-alone document by itself.

HANDLING CHANGE ELEMENTS IN THE CONTRACTS

Contracts should be maintained in the original status and any modification will require certain understanding of accepted techniques. According to (ALDEN, 2019), several methods are commonly used to amend an agreement including:

- **Formatting:** Any changes to the original contract are to be shown using redlines and strikethroughs of the text. Additions are to be indicated with underlined text, and deleted text is crossed out. Most word processing programs have a strikethrough option. The amended information must be preceded by a clarifying statement about the amendment process and an indication of the section to be modified. For example: "The parties agree to amend the Agreement by the following additions (indicated by underlining) and deletions (indicated by strikethroughs): Section 10 is amended to read as follows:"
- **Replacement:** Entire paragraphs and clauses can be replaced by stating the clause that is being replaced, and then adding the new clause that is to replace it.
- **Description:** The portion of the agreement being replaced can be described to clarify the change or replacement. For example: "The rate in the second sentence of the third paragraph is being modified from '$150' to '$175' per hour."

Quick and Handy Amendment Methods

The law gives the parties some freedom and twist room to amend a contract. This includes the quick and convenient method of crossing out terms while the new terms are handwritten on the face of the signed agreement. If both sides initial and date these markings, they are considered to be valid amendments.

However, fleet-footed method should be avoided because it makes the contract incomprehensible which can lead to misunderstandings, disputes, and accusations of fraud.

Correspondingly, a better practice for contract amendments is to write out the changes and make reference to the specific provisions that are changed by the amendment. This is simple and trim and leaves a paper trail should litigation be needed in the future.

Clearly State Reason for Amendment

The reason for the amendment needs to be clearly stated. In the heat of the moment, it may be obvious why certain changes are being made. But, in the future, those very reasons may be forgotten. Thus, clearly stating the reasons for any changes will help keep both parties on the same page.

Stating the reason for amendment has another applicable advantage, it can help settle future disputes. Every contract and amendment should be written bearing in mind that a stranger may need to read and understand the terms of the agreement.

Use Detailed References

When writing a contract amendment, one needs to be detailed. It should be stated that clauses are being changed, where those clauses are located in the contract, and what changes are being made. It is always better to provide every critical detail than not providing enough of it.

Execute the Amendment

For an amendment to be enforceable, it must be executed. Authorized representatives, preferably the same ones who signed the original contract, need to sign and date the amendment. If the amendment is not signed by both sides, it isn't legally valid.

Depending on the contract and the circumstances, it may be technically possible to orally amend a contract. But this almost always leads to disputes and litigation. It is imperative to take the time to execute a written amendment to the contract.

Store Amendment with Original Contract

Once the amendment has been executed, it is not a separate legal document. It becomes a part of the contract. It needs to be placed and stored with the original contract in your Contract Management System (CMS). Most contract management software makes this process easy.

Prepare a Contract Amendment for a Purpose

Legally, an amendment is a change to a contract after it has already been signed. Any changes to a document before it has been signed are known as modifications. A contract amendment may be needed when a handful of sections or clauses need to be changed. For an amendment to be enforceable, both sides must agree to the changes.

If the entire agreement needs to be altered, it is more sensible to formally terminate the contract and execute a new deal. Every time an amendment is made in a contract, the chances of accidentally altering the agreement in unintended ways increase. Common reasons parties amend contracts include changing market conditions, unexpected complications, or a change in the business relationship between the two sides.

Steps to Write an Amendment

For the contract amendments to be clear and usable, few points need to be considered while performing such modifications, this includes, but not limited to, the following steps:

Read the Original Contract

Read the contract that needs to be amended. Make a note of the clauses that need to be deleted, added or changed. Then, create a new blank document, which must be named and styled as "AMENDMENT TO CONTRACT." The addendum can be set out any preferred way – for example, as a letter or matching the font, style, and layout of the original contract. There are a whole lot of templates available for use online.

Describe the Contract

Define the contract the addendum will be changing. For example, if the original contract is an employment contract made between Business X and John Doe dated June 30, 2014, the first paragraph of the addendum may be written as: "This amendment is made between Business X and John Doe, parties to the employment contract dated June 30 2014 ("the Original Agreement")."

List the Deletions and Modifications

List down the clauses in the original contract that have to be deleted. Plain language must be used to do so, for example: "Item 12 of the Original Agreement shall be deleted."

The items in the original contract that need to be modified must be descried in detail. The change must be described in clear and concise words, for instance: "In Item 4 of the Original Contract the word $60,000 shall be deleted and replaced with the word $65,000." Alternatively, when writing an amendment, the clause from the original contract must be copied and any changes using should be depicted by bold text and strikethroughs. Example: "Item 23 of the Original Contract shall be modified by the following additions indicated in bold and deletions indicated by strikethroughs." Then adding the bold and strikethrough text.

Replace Clauses or Write in New Items

Long and complex changes can be made by replacing the old clause with a new one. For example, "Item 8 is replaced in its entirety by the following:" followed by the redrafted clause.

Any new items must be written in. For example, writing, "The following Items shall be added to the Original Contract" which will be followed by the new clauses.

Confirm the Original Contract

It is essential to add words that make it clear that the original contract is still valid. For example, a good option is using the following words: "Except as set forth in this Amendment, the [Original] Agreement is unaffected and shall continue in full force and effect in accordance with its terms. If there is conflict between this amendment and the [Original] Agreement or any earlier amendment, the terms of this amendment will prevail."

Add Signature Blocks

A blank space must be provided for each party to sign their name and extra space below that where each party must print their name and business title, by way of example "Head of Human Resources." Next, the addendum must be proofread and printed, after which the original parties are required to sign and date it.

Restated Agreements

When there is a replacement of an entire contract with an amendment. So, a restated agreement amends and restates, in its entirety, and replaces, the prior contract. In most cases, restated agreements should be refrained from and preference must be given to termination and enactment of a new agreement.

ADDITIONAL AGREEMENT TYPES

According to (Burnett, Norman, & Sycara, 2011), trust is consequential in dynamic multi-agent systems, where agents may periodically come aboard or quit, routinely changing the structure of the society. (Wong, Cheung, Yiu, & Pang, 2007) stated that "although trust has been recognized as a relationship lubricant, its implementation has not attracted the corresponding level of attention".

Several agreements can be added to add multiple layers of trust to the contracting process. Trust deeds are formal agreements through which a trustor vests the ownership rights (title) of one or more assets to one or more trustees for conservation and protection on behalf of one or more beneficiaries of the trust. It normally states the:

- Purpose for which the trust was established and fulfillment of which will terminate the trust,
- Details of the assets placed in the trust,
- Powers and limitations of the trustees, their reporting requirements, and other associated provisions, and
- The trustees' compensations, if any.

A trust agreement expresses the intention behind establishing the trust, the terms that must be satisfied to terminate the trust and the full details of the assets situated in the trust. It also outlines what powers and restrictions the trustees possess and the type of stipulations that may affect them, in addition to any compensation the trustees may receive. The general overview of a trust agreement is that it entitles trustors to exercise authority over their wealth.

Non-Disclosure Agreement (NDA)

Signature of such agreement is done by employees and other relevant parties' who are intended to interact with a company, come in contact with proprietary elements and keep designated company-specific information confidential. The signatories to an NDA are not permitted to disclose, as stipulated in the agreement's language, any information about company research, inventions, or other information designated as proprietary or trade secrets for a specified period of time.

(Conrad, Misenar, & Feldman, 2015) comment on non-disclosure agreements (NDA) as work-related contractual agreements which ensure that, prior to being given access to sensitive information or data, an individual or organization recognizes and comprehends their legal responsibility to maintain the confidentiality of said sensitive information. It is a standard for job candidates, consultants, or contractors to sign NDAs before they are hired. Non-disclosure agreements are largely a directive control.

An NDA builds a confidential relationship between the parties, ordinarily to safeguard any type of confidential and proprietary information or trade secrets. In layman terms, it is a written contract between two parties that prohibits the dissemination or circulation of confidential information shared between the two extremes. It also goes by the names - Confidentiality Agreement (CA), Confidential Disclosure Agreement (CDA), Secrecy Agreement (SA), and Proprietary Information Agreement (PIA).

NDAs have become a recognized aspect of the employee orientation process; it is of utmost importance that all the departments within an organization are aware of and understand the need for non-disclosure agreements. This is particularly high priority for organizations where it is customary for individual departments to engage with external or third-party consultants and contractors.

(Iannarelli & O'Shaughnessy, 2015) believe that, having a non-disclosure agreement is an "easily incorporated" yet integral part of an information governance plan. By simply making such a document a standard practice when hiring new employees—as well as having existent employees sign such an agreement—companies can ensure that their information is legally secured from unauthorized and unsanctioned release. An NDA further protects an organization and its data by spelling out the applicable legal consequences should an employee deliberately spilling protected information, thereby giving the company a clear-cut means of restitution.

Despite the existence of a non-disclosure agreement, should a current or past contractor opt to leak sensitive information regardless, it is highly improbable that they would confess to doing so. Therefore, the victim company should still prepare for having some sort of investigation conducted, either internally or through implementation of the law, to establish the source of the leak before criminal actions or civil restitution can be pursued.

(Moberly, 2014) found that with most NDAs, there are specific provisions describing how confidential information and materials received or exchanged must be handled. When an NDAs are in force, it's prudent that any exchanged documents be clearly marked with the word "confidential." Whenever there is verbal communication between parties, it is a good practice to create a written summary of the exchange and mark those documents.

Usage of Non-Disclosure Agreements

There are countless situations for business that require them to share private and confidential information with other individuals or companies. Companies are likely to need a non-disclosure agreement whenever they are working on a product in development. An NDA is used to ensure that the opposite party has due regard the confidentiality of their information.

NDAs often are lengthy, densely worded documents prepared by lawyers to cover every conceivable situation. For instance, they may deal with the handling of proprietary documents, which are not typically given to usability test participants. In usability testing, the main concern is to have people not talk about what they saw in the session. It is recommended that the legal team be asked to prepare a suitably stripped-down NDA for usability testing.

Although participants should be given the opportunity to read the NDA before signing it, experience indicates that most participants sign it without taking the trouble to read it. If, however, someone wants to take the time to read the NDA before starting the study, it must be sent out in advance.

An "outsider," as is the case of a usability consultant, will also be required to sign an NDA, generally before they can discuss or see the product. Non-disclosure agreements are generally not used if the product is already on the market.

(Marsh, 2009) summarizes some situations where NDAs are applicable, including:

- For protection of a non-patented invention or design that requires to be showcased to potential investors, business partners, or manufacturers for development of a prototype,
- For submission of sensitive financial, and other, business records and information to a prospective purchaser or investor in the business,
- For the presentation of a new product not yet available on the market to a prospective customer, buyer, or licensee,
- For presentation of classified business information to an independent contractor, or outside business, for the purpose of having them provide a service, or
- For disclosure, on an as needed basis, of discreet business information required for an employee to successfully perform his or her duties.

Stakeholders Involvement in NDAs

(Marsh, 2009) highlights that, as there are various situations that may require an NDA, there are also different kinds of such agreements. There are unilateral, mutual, and multilateral agreements.

An NDA can be framed by either of the two methods: a one-way or a two-way agreement. A one-way agreement is the favored method, particularly during the initial discussions with colleagues, superiors' prospective buyers, licensees, or investors. On the other hand, a two-way agreement puts the responsibility of confidentiality on both parties.

A unilateral confidentiality agreement is one-sided agreement that should be used when only one party is revealing classified information for review to another party. Conversely, a mutual confidentiality agreement should be used when both parties are revealing classified information to each other. While, a multilateral confidentiality agreement should be used where three or more parties are entering into a business relationship and each of them is revealing and acquiring classified information.

Important Elements of Non-disclosure Agreement

The type of information to be revealed, to whom it will be revealed, how will it be revealed, the intended use of the revealed information, for how long will it be available, and the measures the receiving party must take all are specific elements that need to be properly addressed in a well drafted NDA.

According to the (International Trade Centre, 2018), every non-disclosure agreement ought to:

- Meticulously and precisely define the nature of the confidential information to be disclosed, not to include the non-essentials and whether or not such information must be labeled as "confidential".
- Lay down the ownership rights to the information being revealed.
- Explain the purpose instigating the disclosure of the classified information.
- Specify information which is not to be categorized as "confidential", such as information already in the public domain.
- Detail the contingencies of the receiving party, say, how they must protect the confidential information, limit its use or release, and hand back or destroy the information provided.
- Declare the interval of time during which the confidential information can be examined, must be handed over, and the duration of the agreement.
- Present countermeasures in circumstances of breach, or threatened breach/ anticipatory breach of the confidential agreement; and
- State a host of miscellaneous standard contract provisions and the nature of the confidential information to be disclosed

Arbitrating an NDA

An NDA can keep a lid on any trade secret, or any information that is not generally known or should remain unrevealed and that provides a business with a competitive edge. However, the use of generic NDA is futile because the court of law is prone to find it to be either overly generalized or vague. When a broad-based, all-purpose NDA is used, besides adversely impacting the value of a company's intellectual property rights, it may also stop the court from enforcing the NDA. All that such an NDA will do is provide the owner of the classified information with cold comfort.

While preparing an NDA, it is vital to specifically describe the nature of the confidential information to be disclosed. When defending an individual accused of misappropriating confidential information, the defense will surely raise one or more of the following arguments:

- The information claimed to be confidential had no value to the competitor.
- The information claimed to be confidential was already in the public domain and in use by others.
- The company made no real effort to keep the alleged confidential information classified.
- The company's definition of what was confidential included everything under the sun and thereby nullified or void for vagueness.

Such points should be kept in mind to avoid pitfalls or skimming the NDA from its value.

Employees' Noncompete Agreements

In most organizations, employees are exposed to information that is sensitive to the organization. All relevant people should be required to sign an NDA in such a case. Although this may not stop all disclosures, it does provide for some recourse and is likely to somewhat discourage people who might consider violating the intent of the agreement.

Some organizations may want to consider implementing noncompete agreements as well. These agreements legally prevent employees from leaving their employer and working for a competitor. Thus, it prevents employees from entering markets reckoned to be in direct opposition with their employer. The concern satisfied by such an agreement is that the person has knowledge that would benefit a competing organization. These agreements can be hard to enforce and should therefore be reserved for key personnel or for those who are reasonably well paid. Since there needs to be a legitimate cause and compensation for affecting a person's potential professional mobility.

Employee Holdover Provision

Some large businesses often ask their employees to sign an employee confidentiality agreement, or proprietary right agreement, that requires the employees to disclose all inventions authored, conceived or reduced to practice for up to one year after the termination of the employee's appointment.

Some of these agreements also state that such inventions will be presumed to be owned by the former employer, and that this presumption may be overcome only if the employee can demonstrate that the invention qualifies for protection under labor code. To satisfy this burden of proof, the employee must testify that the invention, (1) was developed entirely on his/her own without using the employer's equipment, supplies, facilities, or trade secret information; and (2) did not relate at the time of conception or reduction to practice to the creation of the employer's business or actual or evidently foreseeable research or development, or result from any work performed by the employee for the employer.

According to (Marsh, 2009), courts typically rule that these provisions when they extend beyond the date employment terminated are void as an "unreasonable restraint on trade, except to the extent that they relate to ideas and concepts which were based upon trade secrets or confidential information" of the former employer. Therefore, despite the fact that many employee confidential information agreements purport to require disclosure and assignment of inventions developed after the termination of employment, such agreements can only be enforced to the extent that it can be established that the employee's invention is based upon or relates to the trade secrets or confidential information of his or her former employer.

Consultation Work Agreements

In most cases, consultants sign a separate NDA to certify they will not reveal any information gathered during the assignment; at other times, such a provision is included in the project agreement.

Confidentiality is a torch word in business intelligence and information consultancy. The client must rest assured that their request is handled with the strictest confidentiality throughout the project. This means that the name of the client or any details cannot be disclosed to any other party on requests. Inevitably situations where the requested information cannot be obtained without explaining who needs it and for what reason, will emerge. Perhaps this may appear quite harmless, but no information on the client can be supplied in this situation – no matter how urgently needed the information requested for is. In such a situation simply stating the position of an 'information consultant' working for a client on a research project is the best move.

It is often a good idea to offer the client a specific written confidentiality agreement to be signed by the information consultant or researcher that is handling the client's requests. The very act of offering such a written agreement will substantiate the fact that confidentiality issues are not being overlooked.

In Summation

Most businesses are of the mindset that they have to develop their product in a shielded mysterious manner and be sure to conceal all their proprietary information. But in all reality, exhausting excessive time and money creating legal protection for a business, is of no avail, and can drive off potential investors and talent. Nonetheless, using an NDA is a straightforward and reliable way of protecting intellectual property.

Non-disclosure agreements are an invaluable legal framework used to preserve sensitive and classified information from being distributed by the receiver of the information. Companies use these documents to prevent their brainchild from being illegally obtained and leaked by people they are dealing with.

FUTURE RESEARCH DIRECTIONS

Research findings show that over one-third of the U.S. workforce is bound by an NDA. NDAs are now customarily incorporated in the standard employment contracts upon hiring. NDAs can coerce employees to keep quiet about anything from trade secrets to harassment and assault. They have been growing in number as companies become increasingly concerned about competition and prestige. Presently, a large number of organizations employ NDAs and other confidentiality agreements to protect the organization in question from confidential information being revealed to third parties. NDAs restrict competition through their expansive definitions of what must remain confidential and proprietary, consequently, diluting the flexibility of a dissatisfied employee or an employee working in a hostile work environment to change jobs. (Lobel, 2018). It has been noticed that the use of NDAs and confidentiality agreements can be exploited by employers to impose authority and control over employees quitting their positions after they become victims of unwanted conduct during the course of their employment.

Policy makers and law professionals should approve reforms that confine the scope of NDAs in general so as to help employees and promote competition, productivity growth and economic dynamism. As it stands, countless workers keep their lips sealed and end up renouncing alternative employment opportunities due to the threat of litigation. The proposed change is a shot at limiting the magnitude of NDAs and confidentiality agreements in circumstances where they are used immorally and unethically, to conceal acts such as harassment, assault, physical threats, intimidation tactics and racist conduct.

CONCLUSION

Digital technologies, capabilities, and infrastructure provide for richer connections among value chain participants (Hagel, Brown, Wooll, & de Maar, 2016). These connections breed the need to gain protection against the possibility that one party will abuse its power to extract information at the expense of the other. Contractual agreements have the power to protect the business by restricting the other party from performing similar work for a specific period of time within a certain geographical area and also prevent trade secrets from being disclosed, therefore maintaining confidentiality.

Over the last few years, there have been many attempts to make contracts more effective. Experts in the field of law have found the approach of adding attachments to contracts in the form of either exhibits, schedules, or addendums to be highly successful. The primary contract is referred to as a definitive agreement, and the attachments are referred to as ancillary documents. A thorough agreement ecosystem can increase control, increase effectiveness and reduce costs and also provide strategic and competitive advantages. Formal agreements foster trust and collaboration, and legally enforceable agreements are especially useful for highly complex relationships where it is critical to safeguard confidential information and trade secrets and intellectual property.

REFERENCES

Alden, J. (2019, August 15). *Addendum-vs.-amendment-whats-the-difference*. Retrieved from https://www.corridorcompany.com/blog/addendum-vs.-amendment-whats-the-difference

Bresser, R., Heuskel, D., & Nixon, R. (2000). The deconstruction of integrated value chains: practical and conceptual challenges. In R. Bresser, M. Hitt, R. Nixon, & D. Heuskel (Eds.), *Winning strategies in a deconstructing world* (pp. 1–21). John Wiley and Sons.

Burnett, C., Norman, T. J., & Sycara, K. (2011). Trust Decision-Making in Multi-Agent Systems. In T. Walsh (Ed.), *Proceedings of the Twenty-Second International Joint Conference on Artificial Intelligence* (pp. 115-120). Barcelona: Association for the Advancement of Artificial Intelligence.

Carlson, A. (2019, July 26). *Appendix-vs-attachment*. Retrieved from https://www.difference.wiki/appendix-vs-attachment

Conrad, E., Misenar, S., & Feldman, J. (2015). *CISSP Study Guide*. Elsevier Inc.; doi:10.1016/B978-0-12-802437-9.00008-4

D'Amelio, S. (2019, June 21). *how-to-handle-contract-amendments-contraxaware/*. Retrieved April 21, 2020, from https://www.contraxaware.com/blog/how-to-handle-contract-amendments-contraxaware/:https://www.contraxaware.com/blog/how-to-handle-contract-amendments-contraxaware/

Dommisse, W. R., & Oosthuizen, H. (2004). Value chain deconstruction in the United Kingdom retail life insurance industry and resulting strategic options for new entrants to the market. *South African Journal of Business Management*, *35*(4), 11–20.

EvansP. (2014). https://www.bbvaopenmind.com/en/articles/from-deconstruction-to-big-data-how-technology-is-reshaping-the-corporation/

Hagel, J., Brown, J. S., Wooll, M., & de Maar, A. (2016, January 11). *Shorten the value chain*. Retrieved from Deloitte: https://www2.deloitte.com/us/en/insights/focus/disruptive-strategy-patterns-case-studies/disruptive-strategy-value-chain-models.html

Harroch, R. (2016, March 10). *The Key Elements Of Non-Disclosure Agreements.* Retrieved from Forbes: https://www.forbes.com/sites/allbusiness/2016/03/10/the-key-elements-of-non-disclosure-agreements/?sh=267a94e6627d

Iannarelli, J., & O'Shaughnessy, M. (2015). *Information Governance and Security*. Edinburgh: Elsevier Inc.; doi:10.1016/B978-0-12-800247-6.00006-6

International Trade Centre. (2018, November 1). *Cross-border contracting.* Retrieved from https://www.intracen.org/uploadedFiles/intracenorg/Content/Publications/Cross-border%20contracting_final_v2_with%20cover_Low-res.pdf

Kroman. (2013, December 27). *Ten ways to protect your confidential information.* Retrieved from The Globe and Mail: https://www.theglobeandmail.com/report-on-business/small-business/sb-managing/how-to-protect-your-confidential-information/article16072896/

Lia, F., & Whalley, J. (2002). Deconstruction of the telecommunications industry: From value chains to value networks. *Telecommunications Policy*, *26*, 451–472.

Lobel, O. (2018, January 30). *NDAs Are Out of Control. Here's What Needs to Change.* Retrieved from Harvard Business Review: https://hbr.org/2018/01/ndas-are-out-of-control-heres-what-needs-to-change

Marsh, M. (2009, March 1). *California Confidentiality and Non-Disclosure Agreements.* Retrieved from https://www.yourlegalcorner.com/articles.asp?id=66

Michalsons. (2016, February 28). *appendices-annexures-and-schedules.* Retrieved from https://www.michalsons.com/blog/of-appendices-annexures-and-schedules/11774

Minneapolis Government. (2019, December 9). *Contract Amendments Audit – Phase I.* Retrieved April 27, 2020, from https://www.minneapolismn.gov/www/groups/public/@citycoordinator/documents/webcontent/wcmsp-222526.pdf

Moberly, M. D. (2014). *Safeguarding Intangible Assets.* Edinburgh: Elsevier Inc.; doi:10.1016/B978-0-12-800516-3.00007-0

Philip Evans, T. S. (1999). *Blown to Bits: How the New Economics of Information Transforms Strategy* (B. C. Group, Ed.). Harvard Business School Press.

Radack, D. V. (1994). Understanding Confidentiality Agreements. *Journal of the Minerals Metals & Materials Society*, *46*(5), 68.

Riordan, C. M., & O'Brien, K. (2012, April 17). *For Great Teamwork, Start with a Social Contract.* Retrieved from Harvard Business Review Home: https://hbr.org/2012/04/to-ensure-great-teamwork-start

Schlingmeyer, J. (2019, September 13). *Deconstruction-of-the-value-chain.* Retrieved from https://www.globaltrademag.com/deconstruction-of-the-value-chain/

Smith, S. (2004). *Contract Theory: 'Introduction to General Theories' and 'the Justification of Contractual Obligations'.* Oxford University Press. Retrieved from Oxford University Press: http://lib.oup.com.au/he/samples/clarke_cl3e_sample.pdf

Smith, S. (2004). *Contract Theory*. Oxford University Press.

Stern, C. W., & Deimler, M. S. (2006). The Boston Consulting Group on Strategy: Classic Concepts and New Perspectives. John Wiley & Sons.

Strickland, J. (2017, January 31). *The Importance of Construction Contracts and Items to Consider When Preparing Construction Contracts*. Retrieved from Ward and Smith: https://www.jdsupra.com/legalnews/the-importance-of-construction-35239/

The Case for Contracts in 7 Reasons. (2018, April 10). Retrieved from Concord: https://www.concord-now.com/blog/case-for-contracts-7-reasons/

Thompson, J. (2019, May 8). *how-to-write-amendment-contract.html*. Retrieved from https://bizfluent.com/how-4922578-write-amendment-contract.html

Vaquero, P. (2020). *Deconstructing the fundamentals of Strategic Digital plays*. Retrieved from https://www.pablovaquero.com/deconstruct-your-strategic-digital-play/

Wong, W. K., Cheung, S. O., Yiu, T. W., & Pang, H. Y. (2007, August 15). A framework fortrust in construction contracting. *International Journal of Project Management, 26*, 821–829.

Wurster, T. S., & Evans, P. (1999). *Blown to Bits: How the New Economics of Information Transforms Strategy* (B. C. Group, Ed.). Harvard Business School Press.

ADDITIONAL READING

Foss, N. J., & Saebi, T. (2016). Fifteen Years of Research on Business Model Innovation: How Far Have We Come, and Where Should We Go? *Journal of Management*, 1–15.

Frydlinger, D., Hart, O., & Vitasek, K. (2019, September 1). A New Approach to Contracts. *Harvard Business Review*.

Kunreuther, H. (2006). Risk and reaction: Dealing with interdependencies. *Harvard International Review: Global Catastrophe, 28*(3), 17–23.

Manzano, E., & Agugliaro, F. (2019). The Role of Smart Contracts in Sustainability: Worldwide Research Trends. *Sustainability: Environmental Energy Sustainability at Universities*, 1-16. doi:10.3390u11113049

Marshall, A., Mueck, S., & Shockley, R. (2015). *Innovative Analytics (GBE03664-USEN-02)*. IBM.

Moran, A. (2015). *Managing Agile: Strategy, Implementation, Organization and People*. Springer. doi:10.1007/978-3-319-16262-1

Opelt, A., Gloger, B., Pfarl, W., & Mittermayr, R. (2013). *Agile Contracts: Creating and Managing Successful Projects with Scrum*. John Wiley & Sons, Inc. doi:10.1002/9781118640067

KEY TERMS AND DEFINITIONS

Attachment: Contract attachments are added to a contract after it has been drafted. In most cases, attachments do not change the original contract.

Contract: A binding agreement between two or more persons or parties, one that is legally enforceable.

Non-Compete Agreement: A noncompete agreement is a contract between an employee and an employer in which the employee agrees not to enter into competition with the employer during or after employment. These legal contracts prevent employees from entering into markets or professions considered to be in direct competition with the employer.

Non-Disclosure Agreement (NDA): A work-related contractual agreements which ensure that, prior to being given access to sensitive information or data, an individual or organization recognizes and comprehends their legal responsibility to maintain the confidentiality of said sensitive information.

Service-Level Agreement: A service-level agreement (SLA) is a contract between a service provider and its customers that documents what services the provider will furnish and defines the service standards the provider is obligated to meet.

Trade Secrets: Trade secrets are intellectual property (IP) rights on confidential information which may be sold or licensed. They are commercially valuable and known only to a limited group of persons.

Value Deconstruction: When vertically integrated value chains became looser and start to break up. This way, it ends up with different layers fulfilling the same functions as before in the industry. But, this time, each layer contains several independent parties interacting with each other independently and interacting with the rest of the layers.

Chapter 4
Contract Lifecycle Management:
Processes and Benefits

Mohammed Ayedh Algarni
Institute of Public Administration, Saudi Arabia

ABSTRACT

Contract management depends on document-driven processes that, in a paper-based environment, can be laborious and inefficient. The time it takes to approve a contract can be as significant as the content preparation of the contract. Slow, manual contract processing reflects negatively on an organization's ability to provide excellent service. The contract lifecycle is defined differently from an organization to organization or even form department to another. The number of contracts and the associated documents are ramping up in this era of digital transformation. An automated, digital contract lifecycle management (CLM) can reduce the administrative burden on employees and allows legal, financial, sales, and other professionals to make better use of their expertise. This chapter shows how automation can change the organizations' behaviors to view contracts as opportunities for operational improvement and competitive advantage. It shows also how CLM can be integrated with business intelligence (BI) and data analytics systems to provide contract insights and dashboards.

INTRODUCTION

Regardless of the emergence of several startups, medium-sized and large companies, as well as diversifying the size of government organizations; There is a wide and complex set of documents commonly referred to as "contracts" that require effective management according to codified regulations and standards. The definition of contract is "a set of documents, governed and restricted by law, that clearly establish the boundaries, extent, and intent of the executing parties' relationship, along with the rights and responsibilities of the entities involved." (Saxena 2008, 5). According to (Ganes & Nævdal, 2008), "Contracts are used in order to reduce perceived risk between the buyer and the supplier". Verbal agreements and written engagements are contracts that have been agreed by spoken communication or recorded in writing by the parties to evidence their agreement.

DOI: 10.4018/978-1-7998-4501-0.ch004

The technology behind automation can transform passive documents into active drivers of the contracting process to increase productivity without requiring extra staff. Business Process Automation (BPA) and Robotic Process Automation (RPA) facilitates document-based processes and can be an integral part of any Contract Lifecycle Management (CLM) to handle various tasks such as documents filing, creating new folders, and transferring documents between employees. CLM software can eliminate the need for paper-specific tasks like making photocopies and gathering handwritten signatures.

Key elements of the CLM process include identification and management of important contract terms, contract renewals and terminations, tracking and management of spending, compliance, and obligation management. The process is essential for every organization, those who sell goods and services as well as those who buy. It is imperative to have a CLM system in place to manage the entire cycle of contracts to maximize their contractual benefits. Additionally, it can be connected with other intelligence and analytics systems to show the contract data in more presentable formats.

BACKGROUND

Contracts have become a key component in the organization assets to build sustainable competitive advantages, embedded in the organization's vision and strategy, and multilateral business culture (Saxena 2008; Zant & Schlosberg 2002). Contracting is thus "one of the core competencies required by any successful 21st century business" (Cummins 2009). According to (Willcocks,2008,5), more comprehensive and detailed definition of contract is defined as "A contract is a set of documents, governed and restricted by law, that clearly establish the boundaries, extent, and intent of the executing parties' relationship, along with the rights and responsibilities of the entities involved." (Sorsa, 2011) defined contract management, as "an advanced method in which an organization applies quality principles to its business terms, policies, practices and processes in order to improve and optimize the negotiation, execution and governance standards of its contracts" (p. 255-259).

According to (Milosevic. et al, 1995) and (Milosevic, Arnold & O'Connor, 1996) there has been renewed interest in modeling of business contracts in the academic computer science community as well as in the industry. (Anticona, 2020, p.9) defined e-contracting as "a process within an electronic environment where the parties negotiate and use automated communication methods to form their contract; once created, the parties administer and manage the contract through online collaboration systems to elaborate, share, deliver, and approve contractual documents".

According to (Schuhmann & Eichhorn, 2015), the concept of contract management focuses on the contract and its optimal implementation. Thus, it tends to encounter limits when attempting to achieve objectives lying beyond the contract. Specific contracting also exists. (United States Patent No. US20040083119A1, 2004) defined a vendor contract management (VCM) system as a web application used to track obligations, payments and fees under each vendor contract. (Muhammad, Saoula, Issa, & Ahmed, 2019) studied the intends to cover the relationship between contract management and performance characteristics. (Bochicchio & Longo, 2011) discussed the contracts for the cloud that must combine international legal, financial, technical and operational aspects in a concise and expressive form, able to drive the business, but also to minimize any controversy in case of problems.

While Contract Lifecycle Management (CLM) is the most acceptable term that refers to automated contract management, there was phases which defined Contract Management Systems (CMS) as group of software that used to handle or automate the creation, tracking, and monitoring of contracts (Mabey,

2019). Enterprise Contract Management (ECM) terminology was used by (Saxena, 2008) and (Bulacan, 2019) to define the means of streamlining and improving how contracts are stored and reviewed throughout an organization.

Additionally, there is the smart contracts technology that can handle specific set of contracting scenarios. Smart contracts are one of the technological possibilities that came into existence because of blockchain technology. The cryptographer Nick Szabo coined the term smart contract in 1994 in his article (Szabo, 1994), which was defined as "a set of promises, specified in digital form, including protocols within which the parties perform on these promises.". For Szabo, the smart contract was made possible due to the Internet and increasing sophistication of computer processing abilities, which he believed, in time, would lead to a transition of contracts to a purely digitized environment.

At the time of Szabo's prediction, some elements of contracts had already been moving into the digital environment. However, according to (Lauslahti, Mattila, Hukkinen, & Seppälä, 2018) the legal status of these smart-contract-enabled funding mechanisms and smart contracts in general is not well defined. (USA Patent No. US 2018 / 0365686 A1, 2018) showed a registered patent to describe some implementations that are directed to techniques and arrangements for managing the lifecycle of a smart contract. While, a smart contract lifecycle may be adopted by smart contract features, the Contract Lifecycle Management (CLM) will continue to advance for the major bulk of contracts.

FROM CONTRACT AUTOMATION TO SMART CONTRACTS

As organizations move closer towards the transition of the connected enterprise, the role of contracts is clearly evolving, and becoming more integrated into the business processes. There is a growing interest in understanding how contract design and automation can impact efficiencies along the stages and continuous lifecycles of contracts for request, creation, and editing, reviewing and redlining, approval and signature, activation, and amendments, and assessments and review.

As contracts become more performance and outcome based, it is necessary to have an enterprise-class system that can automate the entire process and manage data extraction and validation from contracts and terms throughout their lifecycles. Sell-side contracts often contain integrated agreements and are tightly linked to the sales, channel, and financial transactional processes. They need to integrate with Customer Relationship Management (CRM), Configure Price Quoting (CPQ) systems and the agile performance monitoring tools to enable stakeholders to streamline agreement execution processes and accelerate the quote to cash sales cycles.

Contract automation can be defined as the process of collecting, organizing, classifying, analyzing, preserving, and facilitating the means of return and use of data, information, and documents. It can verify and enforce the negotiation or performance of a transaction or an agreement.

The whole life cycle of a contract consists of several elements that must be considered. The contracting process begins with the creation of the contract and progresses through to negotiation up to the signature.

A smart contract is an interdisciplinary topic that combine aspects of law, economics, management, data, information, and technology. Computer Scientist Nick Szabo's described a smart contract as "a computerized transaction protocol that executes the terms of a contract. The general objectives are to satisfy common contractual conditions, minimize exceptions both malicious and accidental, and minimize the need for trusted intermediaries" (Szabo,1994).

Organizations can implement smart contracts autonomously without the parties being able to interfere and without running in the risk of being tampered, and that what makes smart contracts "smart". It is quite possible that, within a relatively short timeframe, smart contracts increase organizations' profitability and generating transactions based upon economic value rather than party trust alone.

Benefits of Smart Contracts

When reaching a full smart contract that can be executed automatically as a piece of computer code, we can achieve plenty of benefits. According to Mittal, (2020); Molina-Jiménez, et al., (2019); ChainTrade, (2019); and Nzuva, (2019), smart contract offers several benefits and a higher level functional that has recently promoted an increased adoption. These benefits are getting more obvious due to the variety of new systems and the expectation of added values that corresponds with organization's needs. Smart contracts have the following characteristics and benefits:

- **Transparency:** Smart contracts permit the terms and conditions to be fully accessible and visible to all the relevant parties. Once the agreement has been established, there is no way to dispute it.
- **Efficiency:** The automation of settlement and clearance cycle enables more transactions to be processed given the same amount of time.
- **Accuracy:** The terms and conditions of a contract are codified on to a smart contract. This removes any discrepancies in contract interpretation and higher level of accuracy when the contract is being executed.
- **Speed:** Smart contracts promotes two-way messaging communication which allows real-time settlement clearance as compared to the traditional one-way communication used by SWIFT.
- **Guaranteed Outcomes:** They have the potential to significantly reduce or even eliminate the need for litigation and going to courts. By employing self-executing contracts, these parties commit themselves to operate by the rules of the underlying code. This is another attractive feature of automated contracts.
- **Lower cost:** Traditional processing of settlement transactions require high labor and compliance cost. With smart contracts, such costs can be reduced or eliminated.
- **Trust:** The good thing about smart contacts is that they inspire absolute confidence in their execution. The secure, autonomous, and transparent nature of these agreements takes away the possibility of bias, manipulation, or error.
- **Savings:** One of the primary benefits of a smart contract is that they eliminate the need for having a vast chain of middlemen. This means there is no need for lawyers, banks, witnesses, and any other intermediaries.
- **Clear Communication:** When setting up smart contracts, there is a need to detail everything accurately. This means there is no room for miscommunication or misinterpretation. Therefore, they can cut down on efficiency that is lost to gaps in communication.
- **Security:** Smart contracts employ the highest level of data encryption that is currently available, the same as what is used by cryptocurrencies. By doing this, their level of protection is among the best and the most secure on the world wide web.
- **Storage:** Smart contracts are used to record vital details of each transaction. Therefore, wherever an individual's details are used in a contract, they are permanently stored for future reference. These attributes can be easily retrieved in case of nay data loss.

CONTRACT LIFECYCLE MANAGEMENT (CLM)

In this subheading, contract lifecycle management (CLM) and the issues it encompasses are be elaborated. CLM refers to the management of an organization's contracts from inception through achievement, performance, renewal/expiry, and archive. In other words, CLM means managing contracts, documents, agreements, and relationship between entities by perfectly planning all the contract management phases.

The added value of understanding (CLM) is to limit an organization's exposure to risk by reducing missed obligations, increasing compliance with legal requirements, and automating contracts and associated documents. Effective and proactive CLM is achieved using an appropriate software for managing the entire lifecycle. This will lead to considerable improvements in efficiency and cost reduction.

Many organizations have adopted automated systems to manage their documents and contracts to facilitate the contract life cycle process in organized way. Saxena defined the term of an "Enterprise contract management (ECM) as "the process of managing all stages in the lifecycle of enterprise-wide contracts with the goal of minimizing costs and risks, maximizing revenues, streamlining operations, and improving compliance with policies, procedures, regulations, and negotiated terms and conditions" (2008, 12). That Enterprise contract management (ECM) have been developed today as CLM to be more unique from other similar terminologies. The main point in this chapter is indubitably the CLM which depends on several different factors impacting the nature and characteristics of the contract lifecycle. The Steps of contract lifecycle management on the other issues-side is presented in the following sections.

Contract Lifecycle Management Phases

With the progress of the world economy, many companies and organizations find it difficult to manage the rapid development of contract management effectively, including organization's ability to adapt quickly to digital transformation. Obviously, the new technologies can provide huge potential for organizations and companies, to the point where they can enable companies to bypass or leapfrog some traditional businesses work and increasing productivity without increasing their employee numbers.

By understanding of the contract management process and the appropriate systems that enable the integration with other systems, the companies can reduce time spent working on administrative tasks and maximize their strategies to accelerate and automate the deal. Improved contract management systems enable not just more interaction, but also much efficient transmission of crucial data and information that can benefit contract professionals and organizations, and, of course, decision makers more generally.

The fact that contract management systems (CMS) keep getting more efficient, quality and result in newer and information and more effectively and directly. The term CLM is being used more frequently nowadays. Contracts have a lifecycle of their own that resembles the lifecycle of living creations. In general, a contract begins with its creation, maturing, effective and then, eventually comes to an end by either termination or renewal beside storing or repository the contract in the database. CLM goes through several stages which can help guide organization's process at a high level. The key phases in the Contract Lifecycle Management (CLM) process are:

1. **Contract Creation:** In this early stage, contracts will be doing significantly more than just automating aspects of the performance of a contract. It can be speeded up using electronic templates and create better quality final documents. Further, the CLM can identify expected needs, establish

goals, set expectations, and define risks based on previous knowledge. Once the contract elements are established, it will be the time to begin drafting the contract and moving to contract review.

2. **Contract Review:** It is particularly important to review the contract to ensure all the information is up-to-date and all required clauses, are automatically included. Some systems adopt artificial intelligence (AI) to enhance productivity through machine learning (ML), deep learning (DL) and other techniques to extract contract data from legacy contracts and previous scenarios.
3. **Contract Approval:** Setting up the approval a significant process, once automated all stakeholders will be notified as required during the contract negotiation and other phases. Furthermore, the approval levels of the contract can be designed based on contract values, type, or any predefined parameters.
4. **Contract Execution:** Once the contract signed by all parties, demonstrating that the contract become valid and enforceable. Every stakeholder can be notified to start processing. The laws in some countries allow using the electronic contracts directly in their electronic form without any effect on validity. Thus, when the contract is in an electronic form it will be considered enforceable as per the electronic date and timestamps.
5. **Contract Performance:** CLM helps organizations optimize contract performance in multiple areas such as procurement, sales, cost optimization, forecast revenue and even to improve compliance, control, and reporting. This is done by tracking how consistent the business is performing on the digital contracts platform including smart dashboards, alert system, and follow-up systems.
6. **Contract Renewals or Closeout:** This is a crucial part of the CLM which can be integrated with a business intelligence (BI) system to send notifications for contract auto-renewals as configured. Furthermore, it can ensure that the contract has a well-documented closeout process to ensure that all the requirements are completed.
7. **Contract Expiry:** CLM and integrated BI tools can provide proactive alerts and notifications about contract expiry via the BI dashboard. This will provide insights into contracts' expiration to avoid the fines or the penalties. This can be done based on a contract record or a sales module. Also, the notifications can be submitted via variable channels to facilitate the workflow especially when the organization has a huge of dataset.
8. **Contract Storing/Repository:** CLM is very powerful to automate workflows, store, track, edit, and collaborate on content creation for efficiency and productivity. It provides an integrated contracts, documents, and reports repository to support the storing, tracking, retrieval, and management all the contract documents, securely.
9. **Turning Contracts into Data:** The latest developments in contract lifecycle management incorporate data processing to support advanced features such as shared data streams and smart or self-executing contracts that help more efficiently access and assess information embedded in contract. Using the business intelligence functionalities help to extract relevant information accurately and efficiently from contracts. Once analyzed this data can be visualized on BI smart dashboards, which will support business teams and legal staff to improve risk management capabilities and increase the quality of work.

Figure 1 is illustrating the nine phases of contract life cycle management as discussed above.

Figure 1. The Nine Phases of Contract Life Cycle Management

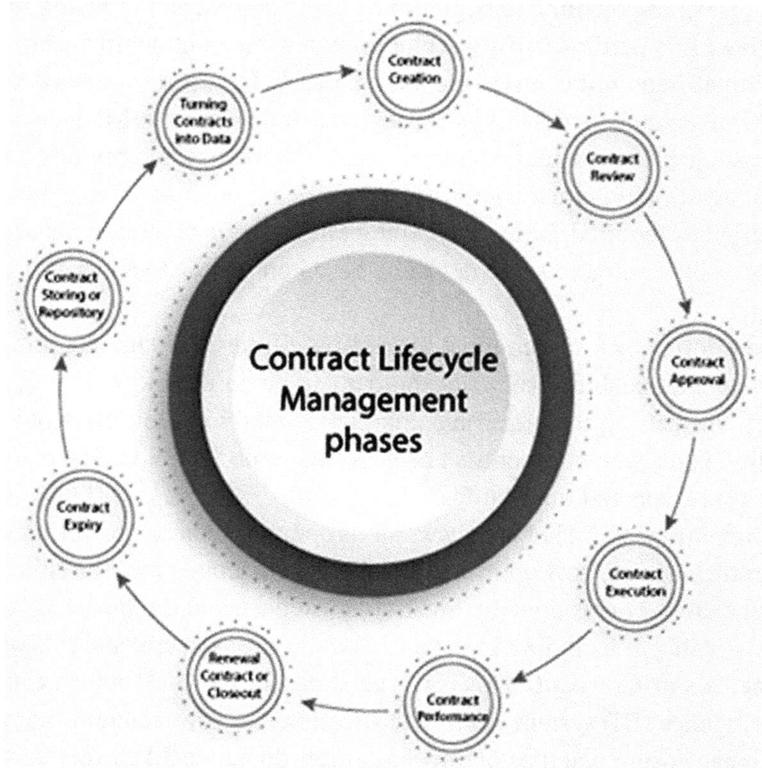

Some Pain Points That Can Be Avoided Through CLM

Technology is coming usually to resolve the pain and the known issues to embark a successful journey. The planning and implementation of CLM need to involve all stakeholders to get their views and avoid disruption. Such involvement will avoid many starts, stops and barriers in the implementation road and will ensure that the right professionals are engaged and that the new technologies are aligned with strategies and policies.

Contracts are one of the elements that affects commercial excellence and financial results. Under-performing contracts may result in losing money, efforts, and times. There are several issues that can be resolved by A CLM compared to the traditional unsatisfactory contract management activities, some of these pain points are articulated below:

Missing or Lost Contracts

The number of contracts that organizations accumulate increases over time and the responsibility to sort and save these documents become a heavy duty. The traditional way of maintaining these contracts and the associated documents prove to be ineffective. In (UN,2020, p.2) United Nations pointed out that "when records are lost or damaged, the office is exposed to several significant risks, such as:

- **Operational Risk:** The inability to meet operational goals and objectives.

- **Financial Risk:** The failure to document financial decisions or expenditures adequately.
- **Reputational or Image Risk:** The loss of status as a reliable, effective, and accountable agency.
- **Physical or Security Risk:** The exposure of personnel and facilities to loss or damage.

Moreover, "records can be lost as a result of disasters such as fires, floods, earthquakes, explosions, military conflicts, or terrorist attacks. Records can also be damaged by emergencies such as power outages, security breaches, or insect infestations" (UN, 2020, p.1). Protecting contracts from loss and damage is essential to ensure that organizations can carry on their work effectively and efficiently. CLM can automate contracts and change them into e-forms that can be easily maintained and protected through digital backups.

The Poor Contracts Repositories

Without a systematic approach to contracts drafting and storage, they become exponentially more difficult to protect. This undoubtedly a harm error that can be damaging to an organization and its mandated responsibilities. It may cause a potential impact on cost, time, or quality. Destroying obsolete records seems like an easy way to mitigate the costs of paper, but without an organized system for retaining records, organizations have no way of knowing when an old contract can be destroyed. According to (UN, 2020, p.1), there are five dangerous potential impacts on traditional ways of dealing with contracts:

- "Not labeling folders, cabinets, or storage boxes clearly, meaning records cannot be found.
- Not securing records when personnel leave their positions, hindering the transition for new personnel.
- Not destroying superseded records systematically, leading to confusion about authoritative versions.
- Not protecting computer systems with up-to-date anti-virus software, risking data damage or loss
- Not imposing strong password controls, leaving gaps in computer security systems".

In contrast, when CLM is used, there will be clear archiving rules and regulations that is built up by the organization, thus it will have no issues when the archive employees retire and leave the organization.

Legal Disputes

Business relationships reach a peak of distrust when legal battles arise. Whether one party fails to uphold a contractual obligation, or the contract language is ambiguous and poorly drafted (Lumineau, 2017; Wagner, 2020). The solution lies in a more transparent and efficiently monitored contract management system. CLM and new technologies might help to reduce claims and disputes in projects because it can automate plenty of activities or processes that mitigate or avoid potential impacts on cost, time, or quality. CLM contributes to monitor legal disputes efficiently and manage the service level agreements, master agreements, and related transactions. Additionally, it leverages automation tools that can support contract authoring and information tracking.

CLM Motivations

Traditionally existing only as paper-based documents with manual or email-based routing for reviews, contracts moved along their lifecycles with a clear delineation of beginning, in-state, and end-state purposes. Once terms were defined, shared, and agreed upon with constituents, they were signed in ink, and either stored away in a file cabinet or scanned into an electronic document repository.

Contract monitoring and control were primarily focused around risk prevention in contract terms. Access to contract documents was likely limited to counsel and separated from scrutiny to actual business performance, obligations, or measurements of returns against the business terms contained within the contracts. The contracting process was typically lengthy, manual, and considered to be solely a legal or administrative function, and a cost of doing business.

Today, companies recognize that contracts remain integral to their legal roots, however, their impact and value to improving overall business performance is directly interrelated, and contracts are increasingly recognized as an imperative asset to the enterprise, and not as simply a cost of doing business.

Implementation of a centralized contract management function saves time and money; high performing companies can close contracts faster; The most efficient contract managers can handle more volumes of contracts, when compared to the least efficient organizations. The effectiveness of Contract Lifecycle Management (CLM), as well as contract design, is growing in importance, and organizations recognize that contracts need to be monitored and measured for various factors including:

- Tactical results pertaining to the contract management process efficiencies
- Standardizing and controlling contract development
- Effectiveness and performance outcomes of contract terms
- Potential costly impacts to risks and compliance
- Managing procurement and sales contracts, IP licenses, and internal agreements
- Automating and accelerating contract lifecycle management from start to finish
- Strengthening operational, contractual, and regulatory compliance
- Creating contracts quickly and easily using pre-approved templates and legal clauses.

Once a contract is signed, its journey within the enterprise is just begins. As terms within the contract are transacted, they should be monitored and measured for performance. The bottom line is that the utilization of enhanced actionable analytics and insights throughout the CLM processes — both pre and post execution — is a vital attribute for CLM and can dramatically improve contract management efficiency and overall impact on business performance

Digital Transformation as a CLM Driver

Changes in business models, such as from a product to a solution as well the knockout of business silos are major driving force for the connected enterprise and renewed perspective towards contract design and effectiveness monitoring. These are all phenomena that are associated with digital transformation.

Contracts are frequently being renegotiated for a more performance and outcomes-based approach. Transformation and innovation trends are expected increase the need and frequency of contract re-negotiations. In addition to being re-negotiated based on performance monitoring results. Currently there is a significant shift in the marketplace towards digital business models with many companies are either during a change, settled on hybrid, or are being born in the new era. Such transformation is also a driving factor new methods of contract construction and design (Nguyen, P. 2013).

As more and more companies shift to the industry 4.0 platforms and change their selling methods, growth in sell-side types of contracts is increasing and driving a strong growth rate for CLM. Such transition is also driving complexities in business models and methods in which companies are contracting with their partners and end customers. This simultaneously causes a rise in complexities with managing contracts, increases in cycle times, and demands for internal governance and a system in place for monitoring the obligations and performance of terms within contracts on a more time-specific and continuous basis.

Usually, the contract cycle times increase significantly based on the level of complexity contained within contracts and can take as longer days to execute. As businesses grow and models evolve and transition to the Industry 4.0 models, complexity within contracts also increases, and contracts may take longer to execute. The type of contract also plays a significant role in complexity as well.

CLM is required also to handle the contracting ecosystem such as non-disclosure agreement (NDA) which may be standard and low in complexity and a service-level agreement (SLA) which may contain many customized clauses, cross multiple business units, or geos. With such complexities, it is vital to remain aware of the impact on overall business performance and to operational efficiencies. Complexity within contracts varies greatly by type of industry and business and is not based mainly on the number of contract pages or volumes. It is greatly related to the amount of authoritative and hierarchal infrastructures that are in place as well as governance and regulation pertaining to the industry or business at hand. The complexity and agility are two digital transformation contracting characteristics that call for CLMs to handle.

Direct CLM Benefits

Automating CLM goes beyond eliminating paper and making contract origination and renewals easier. Managing one contract may be simple enough, but as contract portfolios grow, managing every stage of every contract becomes extremely difficult and ultimately, truly impossible to do well. That is where contract lifecycle management comes in. Automating contract lifecycle management (CLM) is valuable for improving an organization's sourcing process, enhancing control over data,

CLM is becoming a powerful tool for business optimization as pressure grows on modern organizations to develop contract competence. The complex contract landscape and the rising burden of regulatory compliance have further driven the demand for effective management of contractual agreements

The pursuit for an effective CLM system is concluded with the implications drawn from the analysis. Below CLM benefits can assist to improve the current practices and alleviate the CLM understanding.

Reducing Administrative Work

Contract management is a process that is often carried out almost entirely by specialist resource. For example, it's often managed centrally, on behalf of a business, by the legal team. The result of this can often be that highly trained legal professionals spend a disproportionate amount of their time conducting non-specialist work, like basic admin or data entry.

If a business's contract management process is only fundamental, or doesn't have the right technology in place, then it can result in a large amount of manual work for internal teams. CLM can make the difference is helping to better manage the administration side of the work, freeing up the specialists to spend more time applying their training and expertise.

In the case of in-house legal, this could involve below cases which can be automated and then presented for expert assessment

- The automatic extraction of key contract information to create detailed contract records
- The highligh of contract clauses which are either in breach of company policy, or which contain wording that has consistently been red lined in previous contract negotiations
- Gap Analysis to identify missing clauses that should be included
- Interpreting a variety of factors about the contents of a contract and the counterparty to automatically assess contract risk

Improving Document Management

CLM will reduce the outsourced document storage or messy filing cabinets, as the CLM will enable employees to scan paper documents directly into the system using automatic image or optical character recognition (OCR) so that all documentation relevant to the agreement is available from a single location. Additionally, CLM can import electronic contracts from any type and display document status and relevant details. CLM features such as version control allow organizations to keep better track of all contracts from a single platform.

Progressing Commitment to Completion

Using better authoring, review and approval phases with the systematic approach will increase the contract lifecycle completion rate. Some CLM solutions may offer the ability to capture signatures on the go using electronic signatures. Thus, there is no time wasted on getting that final sign-off. In those scenarios the full contract from hire to retire including electronic sign of the agreement can be done with no paperwork.

Streamlining and Simplify the Negotiation Process

Negotiating contracts requires multiple drafts of the same contract, because no matter who drafts the document, the contract always starts off with priorities favoring one party. Negotiations follow, which lead to subsequent drafts with necessary alterations.

Without software to track multiple stages of the contract draft, a company would need to generate a new draft; manually keep track of all the changes; and be certain about the most current draft they should be working with. Keeping track of all these moving parts can be a nightmare for an organization. CLM eliminates this problem. When a draft is stored in the cloud, not only can a single version of the draft be edited online with input from all parties, but the software will track changes as they're made, creating a new version reflecting the edits, and storing previous versions. Both parties can be privy to the alterations, with alerts being sent to notify both parties of any changes.

Accelerating Approvals

After negotiating a contract, the challenge of contract management is to streamline the approval process. CLM can aids this swiftly toward the final approval for acceptable and agreed-upon contracts. Documents can be added to an approval workflow to speed the process along, make sure that everyone is clear on their duty relative to the contract in question, and receive automatic notifications when their task needs to be completed.

A CLM dashboard will shows all needed tasks in a single location, allowing the higher management to make multiple approvals at once for a much quicker and less tedious review process. When a contract has been reviewed, e-signatures make it easier to acquire the proper signature and approval from the proper entity, because they can sign at anytime from anywhere. The team then receives a notification that the proper approver has signed the contract, so they can proceed swiftly with next phases.

Completing Management Control

When an organization automates the contract lifecycle management process, it reduces the likelihood of missed deadlines and terms that go unfulfilled. Alerts generated by the CLM platform accurately inform the team of deadlines, payment due dates, payment amounts, upcoming renewal dates and so forth.

Additionally, terms can be easily searched by team members to monitor compliance. The entire content of the contract, the descriptive elements and the summary sheet can be searched with a comprehensive search algorithm. This drastically reduces the amount of time spent reading through and checking the document. There will be no need to sift through an entire contract to find the terms anymore because the automated process is making it easy to accurately monitor compliance, record past payments to avoid duplication and search for any term within the contract.

Creating Easily Searchable Content

A CLM platform converts legal language within the document into easily searchable text. Everything is accessible, searchable, and accurate to the last saved edit. This makes content easier to search for and identify the terms and conditions of the contract, making it quicker and easier to produce reports as they are requested. This is coming with added security, central storage, collaborative features, and follow-through features. These useful tools bring increased revenue, visibility, collaboration, and efficiency.

Managing Compliance Easily

Compliance is a common challenge for organizations. If a company can't easily track contract terms, then it can't assure those terms are being met. Keeping a close eye on thousands of active contracts is nearly impossible with a manual or paper process. CLM platforms make easy work of this process. Administrators can set reminders for deadlines and configure summaries for each individual contract that points out the more salient terms and conditions to be addressed, with associated dates and reminders.

Also, the entire contract database, including all the content of each contract, can be searched through at any moment, making it fast and easy to find any piece of information or even correlate it with certain specifications. This make it much simpler to monitor compliance.

Handling Contract Reviews

CLM make it easy to perform periodic contract reviews. This will give organizations the opportunity to ascertain what is going well with a particular business relationship, and what is not. This allows an organization to analyze the efficiency of the contract, determine how to improve the contract, and make plans to terminate, renew or revise the contract for the upcoming term.

Recognizing Deviations

Using the guidance from legal team, contract managers spend a considerable amount of time crafting the most appropriate clauses to minimize risk. However, all that hard work is thrown out of the window when an employee intentionally or unintentionally fails to include the appropriate clause or modifies a clause beyond acceptable ranges.

When managing thousands of contracts that might span multiple business divisions and geographies, it's vital to ensure that all parties comply with the terms and clauses contained within contracts. An effective CLM system can monitor and alert administrators if contract deviations occur or if changes to standard clauses are made. CLM can also project the impact of changing standard clauses on overall business performance.

To keep the organization's exposure to contract risk within acceptable ranges, it is important to keep track of instances of deviation from pre-approved clauses and ranges. CLM can customize automated email alerts that notify the appropriate team member when a deviation takes place. This allows swift and timely action to rectify the situation or allow a one-time exception. Additionally, the person causing the deviation can be notified the next time they log in to the software, allowing for awareness of a potential and unintentional omission.

CLM Implementation

Implementing a CLM in an organization will require good discovery, planning and project management. Automating contract lifecycle management requires a solid plan of execution, stakeholder support and willingness from end users to adapt to change. The implementation plan will vary based on multiple factors. For instance, large organizations may need a specialist of contracts system administrator to design affordable templates or wireframes for the contracts, update user data, answer questions and monitor the system database, and security. This will help the organization to avoid the unsuitable software that releases within the prevailing technology stack. Smaller organizations may just need project managers to oversee the implementation of the system.

When organizations are aware early of the issues inherent, they will avoid obstacles and find new solutions to arising problems. moreover, most of organizations try to avoid higher costs for the new system as part of its processes and in accordance with their budget. Contracts are one of the elements commercial excellence and quite a significant element when it comes to financial results. Under-performing contracts may result in losing money, efforts, and times. every day.

There are others several signs point to an unsatisfactory contract management system within several organizations. It is considerable to articulate and assess these pain points to generating improvement to their bottom line. Below elements will help to build and maintain momentum for a successful CLM implementation journey.

Stakeholders Management

Identifying a project owner and project champion is the first critical step toward successful CLM implementation. While the project owner handles daily operations, the project champion shares the vision of automation with stakeholders and gathers support. Both project leaders should be able to effectively communicate with all involved departments to:

- Understand the needs of end users who will be using the new system daily.
- Express the value of automation to stakeholders across the organization, and
- Identify early advocates of automation and enlist their help in gaining support.

The biggest challenge to automating any process is user resistance. This is emphasizing the importance of approaching automation as a strategic business opportunity with clearly expressed benefits. Addressing user concerns before diving into the technical details of the project, will enhance rapid adoption of CLM across the organization.

Securing Buy-In

The project champion should obtain support from all involved departments, not just legal or technology, to realize the full capabilities and cost savings of the CLM implementation. By selecting the right department and stakeholders the impact of CLM would be immediately clear, the committee generated buzz around the project and demonstrated benefits instead of simply talking about them in theory. Potential users will be frequently asking when automation would become available for their departments.

Gathering Relevant Requirements

When office pioneers are ready, the undertaking owner need to acquire data about agreement driven procedures from end client and different partners. Recognizing nuisance focuses helps to separate the basic strides of the procedure from the unimportant ones. The undertaking administrator need to recognize how workers are prepared on contract-driven procedures; how representatives play out their agreement related assignments and the bottlenecks and redundancies in the agreement procedures.

Mapping the Process

The project owner should work to diagram its first contract-driven process and to collaborate with contract stakeholders to make sure essential components and departmental requirements are not lost. Few questions can help to guide decision-making, map out existing contract-driven processes, highlight manual or inefficient steps, and then automate necessary steps during the process reviewing and reengineering:

- When and how is a new contract initiated?
- How to systematically identify and distinguish new, renewed, and legacy contracts?
- Who is involved in the review and approval process for each type of contract?
- Who oversees tracking and monitoring contract deadlines, obligations and compliance?
- How do contracts move through the entire life cycle, from initiation to finalization to archiving?

Training the Staff

Switching from a manual to an automated contract management process requires a significant change in employee behavior, but thorough and engaging training can help facilitate the transition. An engaging training program will be required to successfully establish the CLM across the organization.

Most of the required training will be for the data analysis activities such as collecting, processing, analyzing data and presenting technical reports to build the ability to communicate effectively and concisely. CLM implementation will require being familiar with organization business and technical skills beside a good attention to details to understand the business goals.

Initial orientation is important to prepare staff to perform their duties efficiently and effectively. Typically, training is provided in specific area such as dealing with contracts stages and according to the needs identified by organization, the requirements of the job title or description, the skill level of the employee, and periodically employee evaluated. Thus, training gives staff the direction and skills they need to carry out their assigned tasks (Dahlgaard-Park, S. 2015). There is no benefit of any tool or system in front of employee if no one knows how to use it. (Hoffman & Burks, 2017).

Furthermore, (Druckman, & Bjork, 1994) defined the training as "instruction aimed at procedural knowledge and proficiency, at knowing how to execute the procedures necessary to do a job. It can be distinguished from declarative knowledge, which is knowledge of facts or static information" (p. 140). It is important to provide feedback to the management including reporting in how to assess and improve the training process within organization. This is a part of the commitment to training according to the value and effectiveness of the training program.

Measuring the CLM Performance

Contracts contain a wealth of data that can provide contract managers with valuable insights into their processes. Dates, numbers, and other data points can be used to create key performance indicators (KPIs) and establish benchmarks for evaluating performance. KPIs are required in every organization to leverage, measure, and optimize contract management processes.

CLM systems are designed to take the headache out of manual reporting and tracking, freeing staff from building tiresome spreadsheets that never quite do what's needed. They're used to build relationships, expedite approval processes, and save organizations time and money.

Many organizations do not take full advantage of the efficiencies which a CLM can offer, however. At the end of the day, evaluating CLM performance should be based on the organization's ability to make it a strategic part of its operation. In this case the CLM can go a long way toward helping organizations make decisions about what they need and how to get the most out of the systems they have.

It is important to be aware of seemingly small deviations from optimum performance in contracting can have a big impact over time, which can be bad news for businesses that do not have proper controls in place. It's also important that the CLM system can generate information to support decision-making.

A robust CLM system will track all related KPIs, and also contain tools to measure other factors such as risk and compliance. As a general principle, LM should be able to generate KPIs to ensure that contract management process is SMART (specific, measurable, attainable, relevant, time-constrained) plus being achievable, results-oriented, and time-based across the enterprise.

Every organization need to understand and measure the metrics that are most important to the contract management process and business. Assessing the current state of the organization's contract management practices and putting meaningful measures can lead the way for increased revenue, improved efficiency, and reduced risk. However, contract management may presents a challenge to identify KPIs based on the extreme variability from one type of contract or agreement to the next.

Commercial CLM Software

According to (Gartner, 2020), in the past years, CLM venders used to target specific groups of stakeholders such as legal, procurement or sales, while these days the venders changed their strategies by developing CLM systems and including organization-level solutions with more features that can be used across all contract types.

To give readers a wider vision about commercial CLM software, the author chooses to include some data from (Gartner, 2020) who set strict criteria for inclusion in their magic quadrant including:

- Storing the big data of content and formats over various file types,
- Data governance based on organizational models and KPIs,
- Searchable database across filtering and tagging,
- Ease of accessing the main frontpage and its icons, and
- login permissions according to the active directory or secure with permissions structures.

(Gartner, 2020) have identified plenty of CLM software that fits their criteria and identified 3 dominant leaders mentioned below out of the CLM market that is ranging from smaller startups to more-mature, larger vendors.

- **DocuSign:** It was founded in 2005 and rebranded in 2019 from the "SpringCM". Most of its customers are primarily enterprise and midmarket organizations and was identified according to its software capabilities, understanding its customers' needs, and customers experience and satisfaction score.
- **Agiloft:** It was founded in 1991 as one of the earliest CLMs. It helps its clients to manage buy-side and sell-side contracts' solutions. It is distinguished with chat interfaces that use natural language processing (NLP) that enables self-service contract creation process, searchable system, monitoring, information retrieval, and data analysis.
- **Icertis:** It was founded in 2009 and uses intelligence platform to structure and connect contract information by running artificial intelligence and advanced analytics capabilities to analyst-validated and ensure how an organization runs its contracts. It has also developed advanced capabilities to link supply-side and buy-side contracts to form a holistic view.

According to Figure 2, the three main vendors remained consistent and there are many vendors still working technology and innovation trying to catch up.

Figure 2. Gartner Magic Quadrant for Contract Lifecycle Management (CLM)
Source: (Gartner, 2020)

DATA ANALYTICS AND CONTRACT MANAGEMENT

Considering the development in all fields, the information explosion, and the tremendous technical development that the world has witnessed enormous amount of data and knowledge. The sources and vessels of data and information have diversified, which make it difficult to reach all data sources in a simple manner to achieve goals and make wise decisions. This necessitated the emergence of methodologies that will help the beneficiaries including decision makers, business owners, and researchers to get relevant data and handle various issues.

Data analytics is a methodology for monitoring, processing, analyzing data, and converting it into useful information to achieve successes in making decisions in the correct manner. Data analytics is becoming a powerful tool for business optimization as pressure grows on modern organizations to develop contract competence. The results of data analytics may assist organizations operating a CLM to improve the current practices and reducing obstacles to contracts implementation. The tremendous growth in data affected the business conduct in every organization and country which is looking into data to find means and methods to deal with challenges and find solutions.

(Davenport & Harris, 2007) defined analytics as "the extensive use of data, statistical, and quantitative analysis, explanatory and predictive models, and fact-based management to drive decisions and actions" (p. 7). It is significant for an organization to hire at least one data analyst who can focus solely on the data analytics and to accomplish the data requirements. A data analyst would need to understand the contract processes or contract stages to aid interpreting the results. The data analyst needs to focus on the data analytics tools embedded within the contracts and determine the significant data for the organization.

BUSINESS INTELLIGENCE AND CONTRACT MANAGEMENT

The information and technical development have been reflected in the activities of local and international organizations. Maturity in digital transformation journey became a basic criterion to measure the success of organizations and its management ability to utilize the data collected through various channels and databases, even that outside their automated systems.

Most of the distinguished organizations among their peers placed "information policies" within their strategic objectives, by employing the correct information management process in accordance with scientific and practical standards. This has become one of the secret reasons of success in these organizations.

Today, there is a big need for smart information systems that can help organizations benefit from their data and contribute to transforming them into useful information. These systems will facilitate the identification of their strategic paths and discover errors and missing gaps in their plans and systems. Such systems are powered by the information and knowledge momentum, the multiplicity of channels and systems that can store and transmit information in addition to the emergence of technical systems at the local and global levels.

Organizations tend today to build or adopt an automated information system specialized in data management, information, and decision support, known internationally as the "Business Intelligence (BI)" system. BI performs the role of reading, automatic analysis, comparison, and linking through databases according to the organization's strategic goals. The resulting indicators will measure the performance of the workflow of the organization and its employees in a form of "Key Performance Indicators KPIs".

The KPIs are qualitative and quantitative measure that are usually developed based on the organization's strategic objectives through (numerical or classification indicators). KPIs are built through statistical equations, which in turn contribute to the evaluation of the organization's success and its ability to achieve its strategic goals. This will allow decision-makers to take appropriate decisions based on real and predictive future information.

One of the main objectives of BI is to improve and support decision-making in the organization, which has become one of the most important steps in its course of action. This reflects the BI role in the process of implementing the organization strategies on the ground and measuring performance and achievement. BI goes through four analytics phases as shown in Figure 3.

- **The meta-analysis phase:** explaining what happened?
- **The diagnostic analysis phase:** explaining why did this happen?
- **The predictive analysis phase:** explaining what would happen? and
- **The visualization analysis phase:** which are the highest degrees of business intelligence.

A successful organization must take the four questions - mentioned in the analysis stages - as a measure of its capabilities to support the organization's decision and overcome problems by finding urgent solutions. The results of performance indicators contribute to overcoming obstacles and supporting decision-makers according to solid thoughtful plans.

Figure 3. Values and Difficulties of Big Data Storage and Analysis for Future Business Models
Source: (Shukla, et. al., 2015)

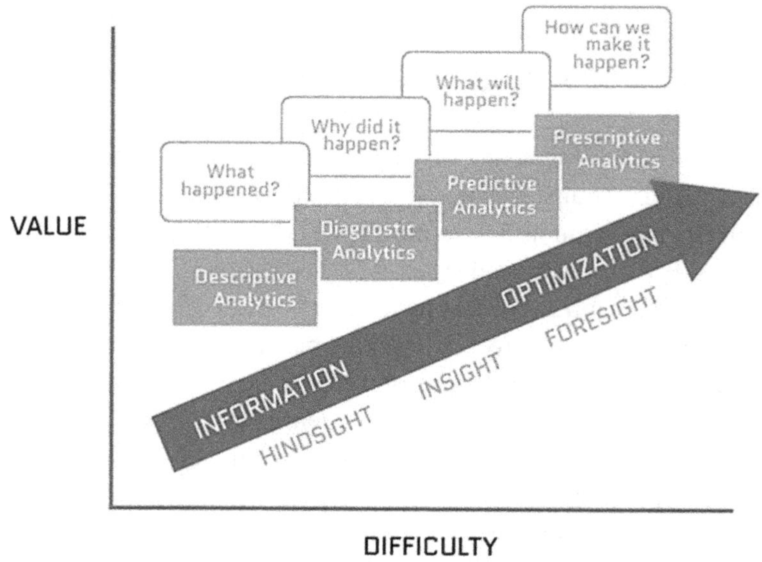

BI system can make significant difference through presenting the contracts' data results after converting them into supportive information for decision-makers in a suitable smart dashboard. Smart organizations are linking their CLM and BI solutions to allow the specialists following broadly the contracts results to show the main contracts' indicators and relevant data for clients, specialists, projects ... etc.

Business Intelligence defined by (Algarni, 2020) as "a comprehensive management system that depends on a set of software, descriptive, predictive and directive analysis through collecting, cleaning and analyzing real data according to the organization's strategies. It also provides useful informational indicators to decision-makers at all levels, through interactive dashboards and flexible reports, that support the organization in making wise decisions aiming to improve business" (p.19). The BI indicators of contracts can play an important role in providing relevant information to support decision-makers and enable them to review the associated indicators on an interactive dashboard and / or flexible easy-to-read reports. The ultimate goal of combining CLM with BI systems is to support the decision makers to reach wise decisions that can improve the business.

FUTURE RESEARCH DIRECTIONS

Contract Lifecycle Management (CLM) can help to adhere and enforce contract archiving and retention rules that will enhance an organization's business operations and its ability to file the necessary reporting. Smart organizations rely on new approaches involving digital contract management and digital storage to keep contracts secure while maintaining version control. However, there is no size that fits all. This will require further exploration to identify processes and tools that can add value to specific industries while considering the size of every organization and its maturity levels.

Usually, the traditional way of building folders and stacking all the physical papers cause losing records and contracts and increase its mandated responsibilities. Some organizations are still lost in papers and they will need to be motivated to utilize new technologies and tools for their sustainability and progression.

CLM systems will require a plan to adopt or implement a new contracts system. The implementation will involve buy-in from top management and other stakeholders. The detailed approach needs to be well structured depending on the size of the organization, its industry, maturity, and other factors that need to be researched case by case.

The relation between Contract Lifecycle Management (CLM) and Business Intelligence (BI) is evolving and require extensive framing, similarly, is the relation with Robotic Process Automation (RPA) and Business Process Automation (BPA). Special research needs to focus on the touch points between CLM and smart contracts which aim to eliminate any human intervention in the contract execution.

CONCLUSION

Contracts play an important role in any organization, but for those without contract automation, contracts are becoming a source of frustration, especially with increased number of contracts and its direct effect on operations. Rather than hire more staff or increase administrative tasks to regain control over contracts, organizations can automate and standardize the contract process.

Contract Lifecycle Management (CLM) streamlines the entire lifecycle of contracts, from internal contract requests to final signatures to archiving. Through electronic document storage, process automation and records management, organizations can transform contract management from a source of inefficiency to a profit powerhouse.

Handling contracts efficiently is crucial in the digital transformation era where the number of contracts are regularly increasing, and where plenty of tasks are being done through limited time contractors, who should be managed and tracked effectively to avoid project overrun. New technologies play a prominent role in facilitating contract procedures, especially when they are transferred digitally, which contributes to the accurate and fast completion of work and enable organization to improve its services electronically while providing excellent services to its customers in a better and tangible way.

As organizations are facing increased challenges in planning and forecasting the future, Contract Lifecycle Management (CLM) and smart contracts contribute to raising the efficiency and effectiveness of the decisions taken. The integration with business intelligence (BI) and other tools boost the organizations' compatibility with the goals and strategies.

REFERENCES

Aksel, K., & Çiftçi, I. (2017). *Smart Contracts (Code Vs. Contract): An Overview of Blockchain Technology and Legal Implications of Smart Contracts from a Turkish Law Perspective, Yegin Ciftci Attorney Partnership*. Retrieved December 12, 2020, from https://www.cliffordchance.com/content/dam/cliffordchance/PDFDocuments/december2017-client-briefing-smart-contracts-(code-vs.-contract).pdf

Algarni, M. (2020). Business Intelligence Informational Support in Saudi Ministries: Exploratory Study. *Journal of Public Administration, Institute of Public Administration, 3*(61), 19.

Anticona, P. (2020). Digital Transformation of Standard Contracts into E-Contracting. *PM World Journal., 5*(1), 40.

Bochicchio, M. A., & Longo, A. (2011). Modelling Contract Management for Cloud Services. In *IEEE 4th International Conference on Cloud Computing* (pp. 332-339). Washington, DC: IEEE. 10.1109/CLOUD.2011.102

Bulacan, B. (2019, April 29). *The 5 W's of Enterprise Contract Management*. Retrieved from https://cloc.org/the-5-ws-of-enterprise-contract-management/

ChainTrade. (2017). *10 Advantages of Using Smart Contracts*. Retrieved December 10, 2020, from https://medium.com/@ChainTrade/10-advantages-of-using-smart-contracts-bc29c508691a

Christian, F. (2020). *Magic Quadrant for Contract Life Cycle Management*. Retrieved December 01, 2020, from http://blog.dayaciptamandiri.com/2020/03/magic-quadrant-for-contract-life-cycle.html

Cummins, T. (2009a). *Commitment Matters. Are complex contracts doomed to fail?* Retrieved September 22, 2020, from https://commitmentmatters.com/2009/11/12/are-complex-contracts-doomed-to-fail/

Cummins, T. (2009b). *Commitment Matters. Poor Contract Management Costs Companies 9% — Bottom Line*. Retrieved September 22, 2020, from https://commitmentmatters.com/2012/10/23/poor-contract-management-costscompanies-9-bottom-line/

Dahlgaard-Park, S. (2015). Training, education, and development of staff. In *The sage encyclopedia of quality and the service economy, 1* (pp. 816–819). SAGE Publications, Inc. doi:10.4135/9781483346366.n225

Davenport, T. H., & Harris, J. G. (2007). *Competing on analytics: The new science of winning*. Harvard Business Review Press.

Druckman, D. E., & Bjork, R. A. (1994). *Learning, remembering, believing: Enhancing human performance*. National Academy Press.

Ganes, A., & Nævdal, S. (2008). *Software Contracting and Agile Development in the Norwegian ICT Industry: A Qualitative Survey* (Unpublished Master dissertation). Norwegian University of Science and Technology (NTNU), Trondheim, Norway.

Gartner, (2020, February 25). Magic Quadrant for Contract Life Cycle Management. Retrieved from https://www.gartner.com/doc/reprints?id=1-1YI5K8JY&ct=200226&st=sb

Hoffman, M., & Burks, S. (2017). *Training Contracts, Employee Turnover, and the Returns from Firm-Sponsored General Training*. Institute of Labor Economics. Retrieved October 08, 2020, from https://www.econstor.eu/bitstream/10419/170819/1/dp10835.pdf

Kondo, Y. (2018). USA Patent No. US 2018 / 0365686 A1.

Lauslahti, K., Mattila, J., Hukkinen, T., & Seppälä, T. (2018). Expanding the Platform: Smart Contracts as Boundary Resources. In A. Smedlund & A. Lindblom (Eds.), *Collaborative Value Co-creation in the Platform Economy* (pp. 65–90). Springer. doi:10.1007/978-981-10-8956-5_4

Lumineau, F. (2017). How contracts influence trust and distrust. *Journal of Management*, *43*(5), 1553–1577. doi:10.1177/0149206314556656

Mabey, R. (2019, July 1). *What is contract management software?* Retrieved from https://blog.juro.com/what-is-contract-management-software/

Milosevic, Z. (1995). An Architecture for Supporting Business Contracts in Open Distributed Systems. *Proceedings of the Second International Workshop on Services in Distributed and Networked Environments (SDNE95)*, 60-67. 10.1109/SDNE.1995.470462

Milosevic, Z., Arnold, D., & O'Connor, L. (1996). *Inter-enterprise Contract Architecture for Open Distributed Systems: Security Requirements*. WET ICE 1996, *Workshop on Enterprise Security*, Stanford, CA.

Mittal, V. (2020). *Smart Contract in Finance Services*. Retrieved December 10, 2020, from https://www.scribd.com/document/488565323/Smart-Contract-in-Financial-Services

Molina-Jiménez, C., Sfyrakis, I., Song, L., Alnakib, N., & Crowcroft, J. (2019). *The Benefits of Deploying Smart Contracts on Trusted Third Parties*. Retrieved December 10, 2020, from https://www.researchgate.net/publication/332165550_The_Benefits_of_Deploying_Smart_Contracts_on_Trusted_Third_Parties

Muhammad, K., Saoula, O., Issa, M., & Ahmed, U. (2019). This study intends to cover the relationship between contract management and performance characteristics. *Management Science Letters*, *9*(8), 1289–1298.

Nguyen, P. (2013). *Contract lifecycle management on the sell-side, a case study in upstream oil and gas industry* (Thesis). Lahit University of Applied Sciences. Retrieved December 01, 2020, from https://core.ac.uk/download/pdf/38085639.pdf

Nzuva, S. (2019). Smart Contracts Implementation, Applications, Benefits, and Limitations. *Journal of Information Engineering and Applications*, *9*(5), 63–75.

Saxena, A. (2008). *Enterprise Contract Management: A Practical Guide to Successfully implementing an ECM solution*. J Ross Publishing.

Schuhmann, R., & Eichhorn, B. (2015). From Contract Management to Contractual Management. *European Review of Contract Law*, *11*(1), 1–21. doi:10.1515/ercl-2015-0001

Schunder, L., & Kitchen, W. (2004). *United States Patent No. US20040083119A1*.

Shukla, G., Radadiya, M., & Akotiya, K. (2015). An emerging trend of big data for high volume and varieties of data to search of agricultural data. *Oriental Journal of Computer Science & Technology*, *8*(2), 121-129.

Sorsa, K. (2011). *Proactive Management and Proactive Business Law. A Handbook*. Retrieved September 25, 2020, from http://julkaisut.turkuamk.fi/isbn9789522162458.pdf

Szabo. (1996). *Smart Contracts: Building Blocks for Digital Markets*. EXTROPY.

Szabo, N. (1994). *Smart Contracts*. Retrieved from https://www.fon.hum.uva.nl/rob/Courses/InformationInSpeech/CDROM/Literature/LOTwinterschool2006/szabo.best.vwh.net/smart.contracts.html

United Nations. (2020). *How do I protect records from loss or damage?* Retrieved from Archives and Records Management Section website: Retrieved December 02, 2020, from https://archives.un.org/sites/archives.un.org/files/RM-Guidelines/guidance_protecting_records_from_loss.pdf

Wagner, R. E. (2020). *Legal Disputes, and Their Resolution*. George Mason University. https://papers.ssrn.com/sol3/papers.cfm?abstract_id=3617045

Zant, C., & Schlosberg, C. (2002). Contract Agreements and Methods of Management. *Pharmaceutical Technology North America, 2002*(1). Retrieved September 22, 2020, from https://cdn.sanity.io/files/0vv8moc6/pharmtech/70fa4ba2f782b7185e9519532534b87b500b81af.pdf

ADDITIONAL READING

Abrahamsson, P., Conboy, K., & Wang, X. (2009). 'Lots done, more to do': The current state of agile systems development research. *European Journal of Information Systems, 281-284*(4), 281–284. Advance online publication. doi:10.1057/ejis.2009.27

Blomqvist, K. (2005). Trust in a Dynamic Environment - Fast Trust as a Threshold Condition for Asymmetric Technology Partnership Formation in the ICT Sector. In K. Blomqvist (Ed.), *Trust in Pressure, Investigations of Trust and Trust Building in Uncertain Circumstances* (pp. 127–147). Edward Elgar Publishing, Inc. doi:10.4337/9781845427962.00011

Foss, N. J., & Saebi, T. (2016). Fifteen Years of Research on Business Model Innovation: How Far Have We Come, and Where Should We Go? *Journal of Management*, 1–15.

Fredette, J., Marom, R., Steiner, K., & Witters, L. (2012). *The Promise and Peril of Hyperconnectivity for Organizations and Societies*. Geneva: World Economic Forum.

Frydlinger, D., Hart, O., & Vitasek, K. (2019, September 1). A New Approach to Contracts. *Harvard Business Review*.

Marttinen, T. (2019, September 4). *Are-you-familiar-with-the-concept-of-contract-value-leakage*. Retrieved July 27, 2020, from https://medium.com/dealsign/are-you-familiar-with-the-concept-of-contract-value-leakage-53bbe1742d73

Shalan, M. (2019). *Risk management for digital transformation contracts. Al-Yamamh University engineering Forum (YUENG2019)*. Al-Yamamh University. Retrieved from https://yueng.yu.edu.sa/wp-content/uploads/2019/02/YUENG2019_paper_6.pdf

Shalan, M., & Anaim, N. (2017). The SMAC Opportunity Contracts: Generating Value From Responsive Agile Risk-Oriented Techniques. In Mobile Platforms, Design, and Apps for Social Commerce (pp. 115-134). Hershey: IGI Global.

Ward, A. M. (2020, July 30). *Dont-let-a-bad-contract-ruin-your-business*. Retrieved from https://www.goingandplank.com/dont-let-a-bad-contract-ruin-your-business/

KEY TERMS AND DEFINITIONS

Block Chain: A technology that is most simply defined as a decentralized, distributed ledger that records the provenance of a digital assets.

Business Intelligence (BI): A comprehensive management system that depends on a set of software, descriptive, predictive, and directive analysis through collecting, cleaning, and analyzing real data according to the organization's strategies. It also provides useful informational indicators to decision-makers at all levels, through interactive dashboards and flexible reports, that support the organization in making wise decisions aiming to improve business.

Business Process Automation (BPA): A technology that enable automation of complex business processes. It automates repeatable, day-to-day tasks and accelerates how work gets done by routing information to the right person at the right time through user-defined rules and actions.

Contract Life Cycle Management (CLM): Contract lifecycle management is the proactive, methodical management of a contract from initiation through award, compliance, and renewal. Implementing CLM can lead to significant improvements in cost savings and efficiency.

Contract Management Systems (CMS): A group of software that used to handle or automate the creation, tracking, and monitoring of contracts. It usually fits into a portfolio of tools used to handle overall vendor or contractor relationships and commonly integrates with customer relation management software, proposal software, accounting software, and e-signature software.

Data Analytics: Data analytics is the science of analyzing raw data to make conclusions about that information. A process can be run to examine data sets in order to find trends.

Enterprise Contract Management (ECM): Enterprise contract management is a means of streamlining and improving how contracts are stored and reviewed throughout an organization. This is usually replacing manual contract archiving systems that is insufficient for your company's needs.

Robotic Process Automation (RPA): A form of business process automation technology based on metaphorical software robots. It can automate mundane rules-based business processes. It is sometimes referred to as software robotics and utilize artificial intelligence.

Smart Contract: A set of promises, specified in digital form, including protocols within which the parties perform on these promises.

Chapter 5
Risk Management for Traditional and Innovative Contracts

Omar A. Shalan
Jerusalem Insurance Company, Jordan

ABSTRACT

Risk management is a very crucial aspect in contracting; it has been an issue since the early days. This is becoming more and more challenging as new dimensions have entered the arena. With a lot of stakeholders working together to produce value, this includes contracts, providers, customers, and end users. The risk management paradigm has shifted and transformed multiple times in the recent years. This chapter is trying to touch on the risks associated with traditional contracts, then move ahead to suggest a design model for risks in innovative contracts. In between, the chapter is touching on points related to outsourcing and governance.

INTRODUCTION

Contracts have its own characteristics and associated behaviors since long time. One important aspect in contracts is related to the engagement with other partners or organizations, which might affect the organization future or operation. This have forced plenty of risk frameworks and discussions in related fields. This chapter have touched several aspects related to the risk management in traditional contracting and the shortcomings out of it. Then it moved to study the outsourcing risks and how to manage a successful outsourcing relation from the risk management point of view.

The chapter also discussed the cost of poor contracting and wrong risk handling in business contracts. It also debates the risk handling practices for digital transformation contracts and other innovative contracting styles. The governance of contracts and contracting is another topic that was conversed, looking at governing contract related activities to achieve greater transparency and participation. In addition to discussing the protection of shareholders' rights and the role of board committees in the risk management of innovative contracts.

DOI: 10.4018/978-1-7998-4501-0.ch005

The main purpose of this chapter is to show various risk management styles starting from traditional contracts, moving into third party partnership contracts, jumping to digital transformation and innovation contracts. It discusses the effects of poor contracting and some behaviors related to risk governance. Some risk management styles and methods were discussed toward the design of transformative blend that can support the movement from traditional to innovative contracts.

BACKGROUND

(P & FD., 2011) have discussed the long-term commercial contracts between governments and private companies to design, build, finance, and/or manage infrastructure projects. The article argued that the success of these contracts from the public's perspective depends upon government's capacity to capture these potential benefits and he concluded that the long-term viability of these complex arrangements is far from guaranteed. (Brown, Potoski, & Van Slyke, 2010) pointed out the "fundamental source of contracting failure is product uncertainty. When the product's cost, quality, and quantity cannot be easily defined, buyers and sellers are unable to clearly and completely define exchange terms". Which is one key aspect of innovative products and digital transformation projects.

(Potoski & Brown, 2005) designed a survey and review to shed light on how public managers should manage contracting and how scholars should further investigate such important subject. Their study was based on dimensions of 64 common municipal services from previous studies of contracting. They investigate how transaction costs factors influence governments' decisions about whether to contract, how to manage contracts, and when contracting is likely to be successful.

(Rahman & Kumaraswamy, 2004) seeks to explore the key legal issues that policy makers may wish to take into account in assessing the merits and risks of digital innovation, with an emphasis on its application to retail payment. (Gruneberg, Hughes, & Ancell, 2007) discuss the extent to which contractors recognize risks and their methods of dealing with them which vary considerably and influenced by the attitudes towards risk. They also touch on risks that are seen as large, uninsurable, and vulnerable to changing client requirements such as that associated with innovative contracting. Among these studies this chapter is trying to connect the dots and summarize few points that can provide value to all stakeholder who are dealing with the contracting risks.

RISK ALLOCATION AND MITIGATION IN THE TRADITIONAL CONSTRUCTION CONTRACTS

The primary process in a traditional contract is based on a buy/sell dipole between contractors, but the decision is based on the best offer and the minimum premium (Kordas, 2015). However, there are other important elements to consider while contracting including triple-constraint parameters such as time, cost and quality.

Successful project management aims at achieving the planned targets for both contractors and project clients. Those activities are often supported by a risk management system based on which contractors identify, assess, monitor, and control any type of risk that may emerge in any stage of the project.

Some risks are commonly managed. Commercial risks associated with safety are covered under both contracts through the employer's liability and public liability which are taken out by the contractor. These may be arranged by the employer where they are not taken out by the contractor. Cover for damage to the works or the existing buildings and their contents can be transferred to the insurance industry. Insolvency protection may be arranged by means of performance bonds. (International Trade Centre, 2018) .

Financial risks and construction go hand by hand. These risks are reduced as the contractor is approaching the project completion. Such risk scope is a huge topic considering underbid projects and embezzlement of project funds (Iqbal, Choudhry, Holschemacher, Ali, & Tamosaitiene, 2015).

Several factors need to be considered while planning a risk management framework for a traditional contract. Some ways can be used to reduce or manage these risks as related to traditional behaviors that are described in this section.

The Zero-Profit Limit

It is extensively reported that the traditional procurement remains inefficient as contractors are obliged to submit tenders approximately on a zero-profit limit and are transferred unrealistic cost risk amounts from their clients. In addition, poor project cost performance is also a common drawback in traditionally procured projects (Ford, 2002). This contractual context suffering from legal disputes and compensation claims leads contractors to embody into their estimate's contingency reserves. These reserves are supposed to perform three tasks: resolve emergencies, control schedule and improve facility.

Contractor Insolvency

Represents a particularly heavy risk borne clients. This risk is typically covered by bonding arrangements. The collapse of any industry and its recent levels of insolvency has led guarantors to limit the rate of cover provided by bonds. (Cunningham, 2015). This problem was causing several failures throughout the history of contracting and building industries.

Specialist Work and Subcontracts

One of the most notable issues in traditional contracts is how specialist work is procured. The nomination process contained in some traditional contracts enables main contractors to appoint subcontractors to carry out specific work packages for, or to supply materials to the main contractor (Akintan & Morledge, 2013). In certain instances, specialists may be 'named subcontractors' where they are selected from a panel of specialists compiled by the main contractor. Contract may contain few or no limitations on the contractor's freedom to obtain specialist subcontractors. The main contractor may exert considerable pressure on specialists to lower their prices in order to submit a competitive tender.

These subcontractors are typically chosen because of their track records for delivering high quality work, and in many instances, because they carry out areas of the detail design. Where a nominated subcontractor is responsible for the design of part of the work, the main contractor will, in general, bear the risk of consequences arising from defective design. The contractor nevertheless retains responsibility for ensuring that the specified standards relating to materials and workers to complied with.

Prime Cost Work

Prime cost sums are included in traditional contracts for works to be carried out by nominated subcontractors or for items to be supplied by nominated suppliers (Smith, 1995). Prime cost rates relate to materials supplied by a nominated supplier that are then fixed by the contractor. Prime cost work is often paid for on a cost reimbursement basis whereby the contractor is paid the nominated subcontractor's or supplier's agreed final account plus tendered sums for attendances and profit. These accounts can be difficult to control and are prone to cost overruns. The contractor has little incentive to control costs under this arrangement which shifts the pricing risk from the contractor to the employer.

The exclusion of nomination provisions also transfers two significant risks previously borne by main contractor: liability for failure of the specialist to perform, and liability for defective design provided by specialists. These risks can be borne by the contractor or retained by the main contractor.

Provisional Work

Provisional sums are included in traditional contracts to cover work or costs which cannot be entirely foreseen, defined or detailed at the time the tendering documents are issued (RICS, 2016). Provisionally measured work typically covers matters such as groundworks, builder's work in connection with services, remedial works, and contingencies whose extent could not be accurately established in advance of opening the existing structure or carrying out a site inspection. Under this arrangement the main contractors bear the quantities risk, and, where provisional sums are used, the pricing risk as well. As is the case with prime cost sums, there is little incentive for contractors to complete work covered by provisional sums efficiently.

One of the central objectives underpinning the traditional contracts is to remove risk inherent in provisional work by providing complete designs in advance of seeking tenders and, consequently, to avoid the need to include provisional work (Miller, Furneaux, Davis, Love, & O'Donnell, 2009) . Such approach may be inappropriate in today contracts

Variations and Change Orders

Changes are invariably made to the building design during its construction and therefore traditional contracts permit variations and change orders. Variations, however, compromise the cost and time certainty of the project. The extent to which variations are needed depends largely on the degree to which the design has been finalized (Hendrickson, 2008). In general, the provisions covering the valuation of variations are similar, but some contracts have a greater emphasis on agreeing the cost of varied works before an instruction is issued. Variations tend to transfer pricing risk from the contractor towards the employer.

Price Variation Provisions

Some traditional contracts identify that the contract sum can be adjusted for price variations to labor and materials arising after the submission of the contractor's tender (The World Bank, 2018). In practice, however, this provision is usually the subject of post-tender negotiations and is deleted from the contract. In effect even very large projects can be covered by this provision and that it will only apply on exceptionally large building projects or in periods of hyperinflation.

Payment Risk

Interim payments are a core contractual obligation. The main contractor's primary contractual obligation is to pay the sub-contractors and deliver the required value. The contractor should be paid promptly and fully in accordance with the contract unless there are valid contractual reasons for withholding part of the payment.

Cash flow is very important for contracting organizations. Most contractors depend on prompt cash-flow for the smooth operation of their business. Traditional contracts set out defined timetables for making payments and late or inadequate certification can cause severe cash flow difficulties, particularly if this occurs on a number of projects (Skaik & Arafat, 2016). In a worst-case scenario these could be a significant factor in leading to a contractor's insolvency. Subcontractors are likewise also vulnerable in these situations as they currently operate on pay-when-paid or extended credit arrangements.

Possible Mitigations for Construction Risks

Construction contracts are a battlefield of risk shifting between property owner, general contractors, and others at the top of the payment chain who are working to insert provisions and languages to shift the risk of the project onto unsuspecting subcontractors and suppliers. Suppliers who issue credit in the absence of a quality credit agreement are swimming with sharks. Common risks prevalent in construction projects include unexpected job conditions, personnel problems, errors in cost estimating and scheduling, delays, financial difficulties, operational problems, inadequate plans and specifications (Baker, Lavers, & Robottom, 2017).

Luckily as the number of contracts are increasing dramatically with digital transformation projects, technology exists that can enable companies to manage these complex requirements without the need for extensive paper-heavy credit departments. Among mitigation possibilities are:

- **Lean on Lien Rights:** The mechanics lien remedy was invented to protecting contractors and suppliers against all financial risk on a project. Mechanics' liens are a unique statutory remedy that can help contractors, subcontractors and suppliers recover unpaid monies on construction projects. The contemporary utility of the equitable lien becomes evident when compared with the trust. (Burns, 2002) The mechanics lien remedy is an encumbrance on real property or a leasehold that acts as security for unpaid labor, material, or construction services (Kelman, Barth, & Bottenfield, 2016) .
- **Right Contract Planning:** Many times, the construction needs to start instantly after the signing of the contract, obliging the hiring company to select only those contractors that can start immediately. To start a contract off the right way, it's first necessary to reserve enough time to prepare the contracting process. It's necessary to define what exactly will be contracted and in which way (Choma, 2008).
- **Credit Agreement:** The first contracting stage of the relationship can have severe consequences down the road in the event of non-payment, so the credit facility team need to examine related documents carefully. Financial risk in the construction industry routinely comes back around to the contract itself, and/or the credit application (Vasilescu, Dima, & Vasilache, 2009).
- **Credit Cascading:** Anyone furnishing labor or materials to a construction project is furnishing on credit. Contractors and subcontractors furnish their labor and materials to the property developers

and then wait for payment. An intelligent construction contractor should check a customer's credit at the beginning of the relationship, and then monitor it throughout the relationship (Blanc-Brude & Makovsek, 2013) .

- **Joint Check Agreements:** A credit gap exists when the customer is without the formal credit to justify the company's risk in furnishing or continue to furnish to that customer thus, he can use this tool to fill the gap. The company skips over the customer and relies on the credit of some other, more stable company.

RISK ALLOCATION AND MITIGATION IN OUTSOURCING CONTRACTS

Outsourcing is a business practice in which services or job functions are conducted by a third party (Dolgui & Proth, 2013). Enterprises should identify arrangements with third party that falls under the definition of outsourcing or direct operational activities that should not be considered as outsourcing.

The Outsourcing Risks

When developing a commercial strategy for outsourcing, the owner should consider which risks it retains and which to transfer. The solution owner should apply appropriate focus and governance to develop the correct approach for risk allocation. Extensive dialogue with potential bidders and discussion of procurement process will be required to satisfy risk allocation and manage it proactively during the contract's term (Uttam & Roos, 2015).

Service providers and outsourcers are in business to deliver services and not to take unreasonable or unnecessary risks. Risk allocation to the supplier is only effective in medium to long term if the risks are quantifiable and manageable (Matook, Lasch, & Tamaschke, 2009). As a rule, "risk should be managed by the party that is best placed to manage that risk." Placing risk with the party best able to manage it will lead to optimal pricing from the suppliers; fewer performance and commercial issues during the contract term; reduced likelihood that the contract fails completely; and a climate of open and honest business dealings for mutual benefit.

On the other side inappropriate risk allocation will make a disruptive influence between the parties throughout the contract term, which may negatively impact performance and relationships.

Defining Critical or Important Functions

While outsourcing the services and products, it will be important to have the right categorization of these activities to consider proper action and especially for critical ones. Functions necessary to perform core business activities should be considered as critical or important. If the outsourcing arrangement relates to a function that is critical or important, number of factors including (Deloitte, 2019):

- Whether a defect or failure in an activity performance would materially impair continuing compliance with the conditions or the continuity of the main services and activities.
- Whether the outsourcing arrangement is directly connected to the provision of main activities or services for which they are authorized.

- The potential impact of any disruption to the outsourced function or failure of the service provider to provide the service at the agreed service levels on a continuous basis on the employers short- and long-term viability, business continuity, operational resilience, resolution planning, resolvability and operational continuity.
- The potential impact of the outsourcing arrangement on the ability to identify, monitor and manage all risks; comply with all legal and regulatory requirements; and conduct appropriate audits regarding the outsourced function.

Added to tis will be the potential impact on the services provided to its clients, the institution's aggregated exposure to the same service provider; and the size and complexity of any business area affected.

Balancing Risks in The Outsourcing Arrangements

The expected benefits and costs of the outsourcing planning, including risks managed should be weighed against any risks that may arise from the proposed outsourcing arrangement (Quélin & Duhamel, 2003). This will help in deciding whether certain roles should be outsourced or not. Business reputation risks should be well considered including the expertise, the capacity of resources, the organizational structure and the ability to meet obligations and to act in a manner consistent with values and code of conduct.

Such assessment should be done in all outsourcing phases. In due diligence phase the potential impact of failed or inadequate services; the risks caused by processes, systems, people or external events and the aggregated risks resulting from outsourcing several functions need to be calculated. Similarly, are the measures implemented to manage and mitigate the risks and the risks associated with sub-outsourcing especially if related to sensitivity and security measures.

During the contracting phase, the outsourcing agreement should set out a clear description of the outsourced function to be provided including the start date, end dates and mobilization timing, the termination rights and governing laws with any conditions and monitoring rights (Cullen, Seddon, & Willcocks, 2006). The reporting obligations of the service provider and the right to inspect and audit the services, functions, or material parts indicating excluded services.

Oversight of outsourced functions need to be an ongoing process to monitor the performance of outsourcing arrangements on a risk-based approach. The availability, integrity and security of data and information needs to be ensured; the application of due skill, care and diligence need to be assured regularly while monitoring the internal concentration risks in line with standards and policies.

Termination rights and the exit strategy should allow the employer to terminate the outsourcing agreement where the provider of the outsourced functions is in a breach of contractual provisions or where barriers capable of altering the performance of the outsourced function are identified (Gozman & Willcocks, 2015). The outsourcing arrangement should facilitate the transfer of the outsourced function to another service provider. The ability to exit outsourcing arrangements without undue disruption to business need to sufficiently documented and tested.

In addition to risk planning, there need to be special considerations for alternative solutions and a nonstop updated register of information on all outsourcing arrangements describing the assessment of the supervisory conditions and assessing conflicts of interest (Westphal & Sohal, 2016).

RISK ALLOCATION IN DIGITAL TRANSFORMATION CONTRACTS

Digital transformation projects are often complex, highly technical and of high value, and can have implementation periods that may span several years (Issa, Hatiboglu, Bildstein, & Bauernhansl, 2018). Projects will also have additional specific risks dependent on the nature of the project and its surrounding circumstances.

In the industry 4.0 dynamics and varied technologies, with differing approaches and risk appetites among contractors, the question is how to measure and handle fair risk allocation in the constantly changing environment (Brocal, González, Komljenovic, Katina, & ebastián, 2019). Risk is a never-ending story and the types of risk factors change because there is always evolution in technology. This is one reason that translating granular factors into high level, intuitive drivers of risk and performance can be extremely powerful.

Contractual Documentations

The volume and nature of contractual documentation will vary as per the project nature, scale and methodologies. A contract will include a compact of rights and obligations between the parties by which the parties allocate responsibilities between themselves in respect of risks that may transpire during the contract's execution.

Risk, in a project delivery context, can be defined as an event or set of circumstances that, should it occur, will influence the achievement of the project's objectives. Risk exists because of uncertainty, and, in any project, the exposure to risk produced by uncertainty must be managed. (Sanchez, Robert, Bourgault, & Pellerin, 2009). Digital transformation projects have a unique circumstances and uncertainties.

The need for fair risk allocation in technology appealing contracts has become a hot topicshalan Huge focus on contracting practices is emerging to understand who is being asked to bear what risk under the contract. Usually owners have tended to shift as much risk as possible to contractors who are willing to accept this and profiting from it but such a trend can't continue in the era of digital transformation.

The Contractual Matrix

Defining this matrix is very crucial for successful digital transformation projects which usually have many features in common such as the alignment of objectives and intent, transparency in all dealings and appropriately tailored risk allocation. Trust need to be built by the industry as a collective approach.

The primary objective of the risk allocation approaches is to set out an approach which drives best value for the products or services that are being procured while maintaining service continuity and ensures the availability of contingency options. This is more important nowadays as projects are becoming more innovative and agile.

The sophisticated risk management tools fail to predict the 2008 crisis and safeguard institutions from its effects because managers relied too heavily on short-sighted models and too lightly on their own expertise and insight (Taran, Boer, & Lindgren, 2013). Innovation contract are working to define a mechanism to optimizing returns and a temptation to allow risk management to re-arrange the list of priorities.

A contractual matrix will focus on proper risk allocation between multiple parties considered in the contract such as contractors, vendors and clients. This will build a strong layer of trust and enhance the innovation capabilities. Ultimately the deliverables will be enhanced in different aspects. A degree of flexibility may be invited as "no human being can possibly foresee all the consequences of an innovation, no matter how obvious they may seem in hindsight" (HBR, 2013).

Risk Transfer

The main cause of issues arising in relation to risk allocation in digital transformation outsourcing is that business departments often do not understand the risk sufficiently to mitigate its impacts. Business then will need to transfer an unknown risk and expect the customer to be responsible for the risk (Rueckel, Krumay, & and Schwarzgruber, 2020).

Typically, the agreed risk positions are reflected in the contract which includes the schedules, the pricing mechanism, and the performance regime. Unknown risk transfer can't be part of legal and commercial discussions until it is formalized and identified.

If a risk materializes during the contract term, the remedy or correction has a cost impact on the contractor. In the past, it has been perceived as a sign of a good negotiation or a good deal if this risk of future costs is passed from the main owner to its suppliers as much as possible. However, in digital transformation contracts this is proved to be very risky.

However, issues arise with this approach if risks are transferred to the supplier without fully understanding how they might best be managed and the impact they could have if transferred inappropriately (Shalan M., 2019).

An example of this is inappropriately passing the full risk of unexpected increases or decreases in volumes to suppliers in output-based contracts, where the suppliers cannot influence that volume, and changes can have a material cost consequence (UK Government, 2020). Sometimes the split of fixed and variable cost, and therefore the supplier's ability to effectively manage its cost base when volumes change, can be the cause of issues. Commonly the labor cost is considered a variable cost, but in the provision of many digital transformation contracts, staff need a level of training or qualification that means this cost may only be semi-variable.

Delivering and Sustaining Value

The primary objective of risk allocation in digital transformation strategy is to set out an approach which can drive best value for the products or services that are being procured, maintain service continuity and ensure that the availability of solid contingency options (Schwertner, 2017).

Two of the key factors that help determine the level of risk to be transferred to a supplier are the level of control the customer wishes to have on the service delivery and the ability of the supply market to bear any risks associated with the delivery of the service or the associated transformation programs (Van Strien, Gelderman, & Semeijn, 2019).

Digital transformation contracts should consider plenty of factors to help determine what level of risk should be transferred. Among them are whether the service is being outsourced for the first time; the maturity of the supply market in delivering similar types of services; the complexity of the services required; the scale of transformation and the extent and quality of supporting data; in addition to the past experience of delivering similar types of services (Cichosz, Wallenburg, & Knemeyer, 2020).

The organizations should identify and document all the key risks which may affect the contract and the delivery of the service. They should then identify which party is best able to manage that risk, including whether it would be best managed jointly. This will help determine the commercial strategy and ensure the correct mechanism to support that strategy.

THE COST OF POOR CONTRACT MANAGEMENT

Contract managers face decisions daily which cost millions of dollars. These decisions are often made in good faith and with justification – but sometimes, due to a lack of awareness of the tools at their disposal, value for the client or contractor is lost. Efficient contract management will result in stronger long-term relationships with clients and vendors and more success in the contractor's business overall (Brown & otoski, 2003).

Contract managers managing large contracts will have many levers at their disposal to make sure they're getting the best value from contracts. But sometimes decisions are made that mean these levers are not fully utilized, leading to the cost of those contracts being notably higher than forecast at contract signature. This ignorance can lead to a significant cost implication for companies, with the IACCM putting the average loss through value leakage due to poor contract management at 9% of annual turnover (Cummins, 2012). Losses occur in a variety of ways from poor contract management practices. Managing contracts throughout their full lifecycle will help reduce losses. Few poor practices are described.

Underperforming Projects

Some contractors do not deliver the contracted work as promised. While most contractors follow the rules, some take advantage of long-term contract situations. This frustrates other potential contractors, who find it unfair that contracts are awarded to another supplier based on the value-added promises, which are then never monitored (Menzies, 2016). A key responsibility of contract managers is to monitor the performance of contracts and gauge them against agreed terms and conditions.

If a vendor mentions cost-saving or value-adding measures in their bid, this can become a deciding factor for the organization to sign a contract. Neglecting to manage the contract effectively will diminish those cost-saving significantly. Checking contracts periodically can ensure that benefits promised at signing are fulfilled over the life of the contract.

Missing Renewals

In some extreme cases, no one realizes when a contract is expiring. This can lead to disruption in service or delivery of products that are fundamental to a business and cost them revenue. More frequently, companies do not renew contracts within a time frame that allows for discounts or a lower rate – something many contractors include when they first negotiate a contract in hopes of establishing a long-term relationship. However, those discounts are often available 30 to 60 days before the contract ends. That deadline is often missed without contract management (FIDIC, 2020).

t's easy to treat auto-renewal or other automatic contract updates as a perk. After all, managers have more pressing things to deal with than pouring over contracts after they are signed (Naughter, 2017). The problem is that this approach sets organizations up to miss opportunities to negotiate better deals.

A smarter strategy is automating aspects of the contract management process, not the contract itself. A timely reminder to review and renegotiate makes contract management more efficient, without sacrificing the opportunity for a better deal.

Loosing Flexibility

A key issue when introducing flexibility to project design is the readiness for changes at any given stage of realizing the project as opposed to the reactive approach applied in traditional project design.

A major drawback of the traditional approach to project design is using average values established in a deterministic way as the basis. This can lead to restricting the possibilities of adapting to the changing environment in which the object functions increased costs during modernization and adaptation when compared to the variant involving flexibility (Kośmieja & Paslawski, 2015).

Costs of Lost Opportunities

The money that goes to underperforming contractors is wasted money. But this issue goes beyond the loss of the money spent (Villanova University, 2020). There is also the opportunity cost which is the loss of money and time that could have been spent on a contractor who completed the job satisfactorily the first time on budget and within the scheduled timeframe.

That is why a system is required to organize all issues and build cases in an efficient manner. Legal counsel will be able to utilize this information to resolve issues and take decisions rather than spending potentially billable hours hunting through filing cabinets. A more organized system can save a lot of money by freeing employee time to work on higher-yield projects.

Scope Creep

Contractors can overwhelm a company with additional costs by increasing the scope of projects. Sometimes these additions come from unforeseen circumstances and other times there are simply additional costs a contract allows them to charge (Amoatey & Anson, 2017). Scope creep can negatively impact project delivery deadlines as well as drive up costs.

The contract is an important document to keep track of a project's timeline. Delays, unexpected extra costs, and contract cancellation can add up to a financial burden for the organization. Effective contract management may catch delays earlier. This allows organizations to course-correct with the original partner or set up a new contract sooner if it becomes clear that a current relationship is failing.

Penalty Costs

Companies held to compliance regulations may face potentially costly penalties if non-compliance incidents occur (Sleiderink, 2015). Managing contracts is especially critical for these organizations so they avoid potential criminal charges.

Even if the organizations are not bound by compliance regulations, they should still be concerned about penalties. Contracts have their own clauses in place to protect both parties from failure to meet expectations. Falling in settling claims and disputes on any contract can turn into a persistent revenue leak.

Missing or Lost Contracts

A whopping 71% of companies are unable to find 10% or more of their contracts (Plimpton, 2008). Lost contracts can be very costly due to penalties, missed renewals, and other revenue-impacting governance. Poorly managed contracts don't just lead to inefficiency and risk. They are also costly in terms of time, revenue, and missed opportunities.

Breach of Contract

Contracts can be breached for a variety of reasons, but sometimes it can happen because contracts are mis-managed. Breach of contract can destroy business relationships and add costs to a project, including damages and attorney's fees. Breaches are commonly the result of poor communication with contractors on benchmarks and goals which can lead to issues down the road (Villanova University, 2020).

SUGGESTING A NEW RISK MODELING METHODOLOGY

Traditional risk models exaggerate historical data and may fail to detect problems with advanced warning. This mindset place extreme confidence in the models and underestimated the importance of individual judgment and personal responsibility. Such combination of short-sightedness and complacency may go disastrous especially, when using standard assumptions and flawed risk calculations.

Such risk models and tools designed to assist managers in tactical medium-term positioning and short-term risk mitigation, however, managers must fully acknowledge that these models provide only a limited view of reality and should not in any circumstance substitute for sound managerial judgment.

An increasing number of Chief Executive Officers (CEOs) see innovation as a key lever for growth and critical to achieving sustained competitive advantage across their business sectors (Analoui & Karami, 2002). To be more innovative, firms increasingly complement their internal innovation capabilities with solutions, ideas, and technologies from external partners such as suppliers and service providers.

It is critical to appraise the contract's potential in order to foster innovation and understand the conditions under which this potential can be fully exploited, given the increased use of outsourcing and external partners in related sectors and their importance in driving innovation in outsourced service delivery.

Some risks are driven by external factors and therefore may be more difficult to be managed by the owner or the supplier. For example, volume change risk is driven by the smart city residences' uptake of a particular service. In such circumstances, the owner may consider that the risk of usage of the service (i.e. volume risk) should not be wholly transferred to the supplier.

Other commercial risks are driven by insufficient data or a lack of transparency or full awareness on the internal and external factors that contribute to the performance of the service (UK Government, 2020). Risk modeling methodology is an important dimension of strategic risk management for the innovative contracting.

Suggested Elements

Digital transformation and innovation projects are demanding a new generation of risk modeling that goes beyond transparency and enhances the ability to see competitive opportunities as well as to recognize the forerunners of economic change. New tools are available, but in order to make the organization truly resilient, managers must radically change their approach to risk decision making. They should pursue a proactive and strategic approach, using insight and foresight to identify and mitigate emerging risks.

A new risk paradigm is crucial practice to support both medium-term positioning as well as strategic decision making in extraordinary circumstances. According to (Angius, et al., 2011) a strategic and holistic risk approach needs to be built around several elements:

- Improved transparency, understanding and modeling of risk
- A clear decision on which risks to "own" and which risks transferring or mitigating
- The creation of a more resilient organization and processes that help the firm to be proactive in risk mitigation
- The development of a true risk culture with superior understanding (insight and foresight) on structural risk.

Insights Rather Than Rigid Rules

According to (Angius, et al., 2011) in the first step, top managers should identify the structural risk drivers of their business and then calculate the quantitative impact of each risk driver on the project performance.

An organization can develop insights that can portray the clearest possible view of its risks by plotting proprietary market and customer data residing in all business areas including sales, customer service, finance, and risk management. Knowledge tools will support gathering and analysis of data while training the organization personal to acquire related skills. Emerging technologies can help in identifying risk factors that are inherently instable and require constant review. The goal will be to reach a point at which the risk unit systematically develops and continuously accesses the full insight available within the organization.

Selective Risk Ownership

While innovation is accelerating, every risk should be properly positioned in terms of its priority and ownership, some risks may be off-loaded. Based on various scenarios and levels of uncertainty, risk managers can decode the insights into an understanding of how underlying risk drivers might evolve.

The risk people should evaluate a reasonable set of consistent scenarios that can evolve and mature based on circumstances and drivers based on the mechanism of "known unknowns". Trained managers can express the appropriate range of uncertainty in designing valid scenarios and producing accurate models. According to (Bin Shawaih, 2016) the actual risk-takers should have a hand in identifying key risk factors and estimating the possible course of their evolution. This will not always be a comfortable setup especially in stressful conditions.

Anticipating Risks With Techniques

Fundamentally, we must recognize that some risks are not foreseeable thus called "unknown unknowns" (Bannerman, 2008). In big projects much can be gained by systematically tapping the organization's knowledge of what could happen in the future which is usually declared as "known unknowns". The aim is not to predict the future, but to focus on detecting early-warning signals to respond sooner.

According to (Angius, et al., 2011) four actions can best safeguard against adverse foreseeable risks: (i) continuously measure the level of each structural risk driver; (ii) derive early-warning indicators to improve assessment of the likelihood of adverse developments; (iii) revise the probability of each scenario and define the reference scenario for action; and (iv) transform the contingency plan into a more detailed action plan if adverse scenarios are increasingly likely.

Knowing How and When to Act

Developing detailed plans for disciplined responses to early-warning triggers is a major hurdle that organizations must overcome. According to (Angius, et al., 2011) such reposes need to be quick and decisive involves two steps: (i) executing the action plan defined for the contingency in question or adapting it as the situation demands especially if an "unknown unknown" occurs, and (ii) monitoring the results and impact of this response.

Contingency plans should fulfill a set of minimum requirements and have a tracker that can help firms monitor the success rate of the action plans once they are launched.

Such planning to act being very crucial for to innovative contracts was not a like in traditional frameworks used by companies for procuring material supply and field services on a primarily transactional basis. That was due to the fact that services performed, or material procured at predetermined prices, rather than performance bases under which the service provider takes a greater share of both risk and reward.

Separating Expectations From Implementation

Innovative contracts need to underline the output, outcome, and quality of the product/service rather than prescribing how it is delivered or which resources to use. To have a common understanding there may be a tie between the external partner's payment and its accomplishments.

According to (Sumo, Kalkman, & Van Weele, 2018), an important element in performance based contracts is the clear separation between the buyer's expectations or the performance goals from the external partner's implementation or how it is achieved. Such contracts need to be characterized by a relatively low degree of contractual detail, as the focus is on the external partner's outcome and a high degree of partner rewards are linked to its performance. Hence, the organization is dependent on the provider and has interest in choosing the "right" external partner.

The overall compensation to the external partner, consisting of the base price and an incentive which may be higher because the risk has shifted to the partner and premium is explicit rather than absorbed into the owner's operating expenditures. The main benefit of such contracts is that it allows freedom for the external partner to deliver the product/service as it sees best. This results in more freedom for the external partner to engage in innovative activities as the partner is stimulated to lower its costs.

In addition, this contract requires little information and knowledge on the inputs and processes required to deliver the product/service. To mitigate risks, it is extremely important to detail and measure the outcome and the performance of the external partner. To successfully implement such collaborative contractual frameworks, (Sumo, Kalkman, & Van Weele, 2018) suggest that companies should emphasize three important stages of engaging with external partners when they want to stimulate innovation: the partner selection phase, the contract design phase, and the contract execution phase.

Outsourcing Considerations

Successful outsourcing arrangements rely on allocating risks between the client and the supplier so that the party best placed to manage the risk is responsible for them (Smit, 2017). The supplier will be responsible for mitigating the chance of the risk arising, managing risk and its impact, and dealing with the consequences both financial and non-financial. It may be appropriate for some risks to be managed by one party rather than another or for some risks to be managed jointly by both parties.

In innovative contracts, multiple levels of contracting might be included especially for services that have a public impact such as smart cities which can have multiple contractors and outsourcing vendors. Although risks may be transferred commercially from the smart city owner to the contractors, the end users do not see it this way. Where there is a long-life public impacting services, the main owner is responsible for the delivery of those services and will always be rightly held to account, whatever the contractual risk position is.

Reputational risk is not a risk that can be transferred (Van, 2013); if services fail or performance falls below acceptable levels, the owner will be held to account in the resident's eyes. Where these services are outsourced, the supplier is also likely to suffer a reputational impact, but this does not lessen the impact on owner as being ultimately responsible for the delivery of that service. Where a contract ends suddenly, for example because the supplier becomes insolvent or cannot fulfil their service obligations, the owner is responsible for maintaining services. To ensure this happens, contingency plans must be put in place by the supplier and maintained and reviewed throughout the life of the contract by the supplier and the owner. In some circumstances, these may also need to be reviewed on a regular basis at a strategic level.

Innovation Considerations

"Innovate or die" (Angel, 2006) has become a well-known impulse for large and small corporations. Utilizing innovation in products and services become the norm in all organizations regardless of the industry, size or geography. Sustained competitive advantage and long-term survival cannot be sustained without innovation. As the overall business structure changes, it is crucial to stay ahead of the curve through innovations.

Innovation in every sector plays a key role in reducing production costs, increasing production efficiency, and ensuring that decommissioning activities are carried out effectively (Daglio, Gerson, & Kitchen, 2014). Firms can engage in innovation through internal innovation practices such as internal development and the research and development teams. However, external partners can enhance and drive innovation in products and services, as well as service outsourcing contexts in which providers innovate to improve and optimize the daily operations.

External relationships may, however, need a solid contracting to avoid opportunistic behavior or coordination failures that may inhibit good performance and innovation activities. Such contracting can't be dependent on bonuses or penalties to enhance performance or mitigate delays. The organization need to put scenarios to avoid the entire project risks including those which are proportional to and limited by the scope of the outsourced work. Contractual frameworks will be required to manage intercompany relationships, improve efficiencies, and mitigate project delays.

RISK GOVERNANCE IN INNOVATIVE CONTRACTS

According to (van Asselt & Renn, 2011), the term 'risk governance' involves the translation of the substance and core principles of governance to the context of risk-related decision-making. Commercial contract is one of the important type of contracts as it can be harmful for the contract parties, therefore contract must be built based on multiple dimensions that include clarity, well documentation and contract certainty.

As the contracts may have huge financial implications, both parties must ensure all terms are clear and unambiguous, also all terms must be clearly expressed and acceptable before signing the contract. The contract documentation must be provided promptly, and the contracts must be cost saving tool and not prejudice to any party. This should be within agreed time scale and without any delay. The governance is the mechanism that will ensure the availability of a business conduct that can be followed expressly, fairly and that is never misleading (Renn, 2008).

(Boholm, Corvellec, & Karlsson, 2012) underscore that risk governance takes place in contexts that are historically, spatially, and institutionally situated. Therefore, one needs to pay attention to the characteristics of this contextuality to understand the social dynamics of governance.

Risk Mitigation Guidelines in Contracting

It is crucial to build an effective and efficient internal control framework to ensure effective day-to-day management and oversight by the management body. This will include also to

- Validate that competent authorities remain able to effectively supervise institutions.
- Create a sound policy and processes that reflect the institution's strategy and risk profile.
- Prepare a proper identification of critical or important functions and suitability of providers
- Confirm that all important risks or important functions are identified, assessed, monitored, managed, reported and, as appropriate, mitigated
- Certify the protection of customer data across the whole institution, including the outsourced functions.
- Arrange appropriate plans for the exit from the contract arrangements of critical or important functions.

The Governance Arrangements Required to Reduce Risks

According to (van Bueren & ten Heuvelhof, 2005), the chances of successful governance increase when governance arrangements are better tuned to the environment that it tries to change. However, a better fit will leave less room for change. Governance arrangements supporting sustainable development are more prone to failure, as they aim at changing that environment. This is a hurdle in innovative contracting that are planning to change the current environments, Solid arrangements will be needed to ensure the success including:

- Identifying the nature and business model of the institution and the scale of the performed activities.
- Having a solid Identify that main contractor should retains full responsibility of compliance.

- Ensuring operational tasks are effectively performed, monitored, and audited
- Certifying that management will be duly informed of relevant planned changes regarding service providers, including a summary of the risk analysis and the impact on service levels.
- Planning a summary of the exit plan for critical or important functions.
- Creating an individual risk profile for every service and the complexity of associated functions.
- Classifying the risks arising from any arrangement and categorizing their criticality and importance.
- Studying the potential impact of the outsourcing on the continuity of activities.

FUTURE RESEARCH DIRECTIONS

Digital transformation is changing the world bringing plenty of opportunities and risks. This chapter discuss plenty of risk dimensions and how it can be handled in terms of innovative contracting. Outsourcing is one major trend in this arena, and it comes with new set of risks considering that most innovative topics are not well defined and even it can't be well defined during the contracting phase. This type of risks will require special frameworks to handle. The old risk mechanisms and methodologies may provide a real basis of study in this area as discussed in this chapter.

Risk and governance are an elaborative structure that affect and influence the business environment very closely. It can make or break business relations and the associated contracting. Every industry may have unique characteristics that need to be considered when customizing the risk and governance structures. This chapter touch on construction and digital transformation, however the floor is open.

Gig workers who are temporary workers will need special risk mitigation scenarios, considering how these workers are increasingly been utilized to run projects and assignments, wherever limited tasks are available or high skilled assignments are there. However, such workers are not permanent employees that adhere to the organization and this situation is creating its own risks. Governance refers to the structures and processes that are designed to ensure accountability, transparency, responsiveness and stability is directly related to the risk and performance structures and will need special attention to control innovative initiatives without jeopardizing the performance.

CONCLUSION

Risk and governance are very vital in the digital transformation era in general and more critical when considering innovation. Contracting is becoming more detailed, phased, and complex as we delve into this era which is characterized by value deconstruction, outsourcing and gig workers. All these parameters lead to larger number of contracts, wider scope and versatile setup which increases the overall risk exposure. Better risk frameworks are required to handle these challenges and cope with these changes.

REFERENCES

Akintan, O. A., & Morledge, R. (2013). Improving the Collaboration between Main Contractors and Subcontractors within Traditional Construction Procurement. *Journal of Construction Engineering*, *11*, 1–11. Advance online publication. doi:10.1155/2013/281236

Amoatey, T., & Anson, B. (2017, January 1). Investigating the major causes of scope creep in real estate construction projects in Ghana. *Journal of Facilities Management, 15*(4), 393–408. doi:10.1108/JFM-11-2016-0052

Analoui, F., & Karami, A. (2002). EOs and development of the meaningful mission statement. *Corporate Governance, 2*(3), 13–20. doi:10.1108/14720700210440044

Angel, R. (2006, January). Putting an Innovation Culture into Practice. *Ivey Business Journal*, 1-5.

Angius, S., Frati, C., Gerken, A., Härle, P., Piccitto, M., & Stegemann, U. (2011, May 1). *Risk modeling in a newparadigm: developing newinsight and foresight onstructural risk.* Retrieved from https://www.mckinsey.com/client_service/risk: https://www.mckinsey.com/client_service/risk/people/~/media/FBFAE9C41A144FCDB9A585126CDD86A4.ashx

Baker, E., Lavers, A., & Robottom, L. (2017). Allocation of Risk in Construction Contracts. *Construction Contracts*, 9. Retrieved from https://www.jdsupra.com/legalnews/allocation-of-risk-in-construction-32247/

Bannerman, P. (2008, December 1). Risk and risk management in software projects: A reassessment. *Journal of Systems and Software, 81*(12), 2118–2133. doi:10.1016/j.jss.2008.03.059

Bin Shawaih, F. (2016, October 1). Risk Management Strategies for dealing with Unpredictable Risk in Saudi Arabian Organisations. In *Requirements of Degree of Doctorate of the Built*. Manchester, UK: College of Science & Technology, School of the Built Environment.

Blanc-Brude, F., & Makovsek, D. (2013). Construction risk in infrastructure project finance. *Procurement and Public-Private Arrangements Conference*, 1-20.

Boholm, Å., Corvellec, H., & Karlsson, M. (2012). The practice of risk governance: Lessons from the field. *Journal of Risk Research, 15*(1), 1–20. doi:10.1080/13669877.2011.587886

Brocal, F., González, C., Komljenovic, D., Katina, P. F., & Sebastián, M. A. (2019). Emerging Risk Management in Industry 4.0: An Approach to Improve Organizational and Human Performance in the Complex Systems. *Complexity in Manufacturing Processes and Systems 2019*. doi:10.1155/2019/2089763

Brown, T., & Potoski, M. (2003, March 1). Contract Management Capacity in Municipal and County Government. *Public Administration Review, 63*(2), 153–164. doi:10.1111/1540-6210.00276

Brown, T. L., Potoski, M., & Van Slyke, D. M. (2010). Contracting for Complex Products. *Journal of Public Administration: Research and Theory, 20*(1), 41–58. doi:10.1093/jopart/mup034

Burns, F. (2002). The Equitable Lien Rediscovered: A Remedy for the 21st Century. *University of New South Wales Law Journal, 25*(2), 1-32.

Choma, A. A. (2008). How to reduce risks in contractors' management. In *PMI® Global Congress 2008—North America*. Denver, CO. Newtown Square, PA: Project Management Institute.

Cichosz, M., Wallenburg, C. M., & Knemeyer, A. M. (2020). Digital transformation at logistics service providers: Barriers, success factors and leading practices. *International Journal of Logistics Management, 3*(2), 209–238. doi:10.1108/IJLM-08-2019-0229

Cullen, S., Seddon, P., & Willcocks, L. (2006, February 1). *Managing outsourcing: The lifecycle imperative*. London, UK, UK: London School of Economics and Political Science.

Cummins, T. (2012, Oct 23). *poor-contract-management-costs-companies-9-bottom-lin*. Retrieved from https://blog.iaccm.com/commitment-matters-tim-cummins-blog/2012/10/23/poor-contract-management-costs-companies-9-bottom-lin

Cunningham, T. (2015). Risk Allocation under the Principal 'Traditional' Irish Forms of Building Contract. Architectural Engineering Commons, 1-16. doi:10.21427/vbqd-mm31

Daglio, M., Gerson, D., & Kitchen, H. (2014). Building Organisational Capacity for Public Sector Innovation. In *OECD Conference "Innovating the Public Sector: from Ideas to Impact"*. Paris: OECD.

Deloitte. (2019). *Risk_outsourcing Guidelines*. Retrieved from https://www2.deloitte.com: https://www2.deloitte.com/content/dam/Deloitte/cy/Documents/risk/CY_Risk_EBA%20outsourcing%20guidelines.pdf

Dolgui, A., & Proth, J.-M. (2013). Outsourcing: Definitions and analysis. *International Journal of Production Research*, *51*(23-24), 23–24. doi:10.1080/00207543.2013.855338

FIDIC. (2020, December 5). *Contracts: basic questions Question/Answer*. https://fidic.org/node/911

Ford, D. N. (2002). Achieving multiple project objectives through contingency management. *Journal of Construction Engineering and Management*, *128*(1), 30–39. doi:10.1061/(ASCE)0733-9364(2002)128:1(30)

Gozman, D., & Willcocks, L. (2015). Crocodiles in the Regulatory Swamp: Navigating The Dangers of Outsourcing, SaaS and Shadow IT. In *Thirty Sixth International Conference on Information Systems*, (p. 20). Fort Worth, TX: Association for Information Systems.

Gruneberg, S., Hughes, W., & Ancell, D. (2007). Risk under performance-based contracting in the UK construction sector. *Construction Management and Economics*, *25*(7), 691–699. doi:10.1080/01446190601164097

HBR. (2013, April 1). *Innovation-risk-how-to-make-smarter-decisions*. Retrieved from https://hbr.org: https://hbr.org/2013/04/innovation-risk-how-to-make-smarter-decisions

Hendrickson, C. (2008). *Project Management for Construction*. Mellon University, Pittsburgh. Retrieved from https://www.cmu.edu/cee/projects/PMbook/

International Trade Centre. (2018). *Cross-border contracting: How to draft and negotiate international commercial contracts*. International Trade Centre, World Trade Organization and the United Nations.

Iqbal, S., Choudhry, R. M., Holschemacher, K., Ali, A., & Tamosaitiene, J. (2015, January). Risk management in construction projects. *Technological and Economic Development of Economy*, *21*(1), 65–78. doi:10.3846/20294913.2014.994582

Issa, A., Hatiboglu, B., Bildstein, A., & Bauernhansl, T. (2018). Industrie 4.0 roadmap: Framework for digital transformation based on the concepts of capability maturity and alignment. In L. Wang (Ed.), *51st CIRP Conference on Manufacturing Systems*. Stockholm: Elsevier. 10.1016/j.procir.2018.03.151

Kelman, L. F., Barth, A. F., & Bottenfield, A. (2016, July 1). *Mechanics-lien-remedies-require-a-sharp-eye*. Retrieved from https://www.cohenseglias.com: https://www.cohenseglias.com/news-article/mechanics-lien-remedies-require-a-sharp-eye/

Kordas, D. (2015). Risk sharing in traditional construction contracts for building projects. A contractor's perspective in the Greek construction industry. Enschede, The Netherlands: University of Twente.

Kośmieja, M., & Paslawski, J. (2015). Flexible Approach in Designing Infrastructure. *Procedia Engineering*, *122*, 104–111. doi:10.1016/j.proeng.2015.10.013

Larsen, M., Pedersen, M., & Andersen, K. V. (2006). IT Governance: Reviewing 17 IT Governance Tools and Analysing the Case of Novozymes A/S. In *Proceedings of the 39th Annual Hawaii International Conference on System Sciences (HICSS'06)* (pp. 1530-1605). Kauia, HI: IEEE. 10.1109/HICSS.2006.234

Matook, S., Lasch, R., & Tamaschke, R. (2009, February 20). Supplier development with benchmarking as part of a comprehensive supplier risk management framework. *International Journal of Operations & Production Management*, *29*(3), 241–267. doi:10.1108/01443570910938989

Menzies, L. (2016, April 29). *Cost-poor-contract-management*. Retrieved from https://www.publicfinance.co.uk/opinion/2016/04/cost-poor-contract-management

Miller, G., Furneaux, C., Davis, P., Love, P., & O'Donnell, A. (2009). *Built Environment Procurement Practice: Impediments to Innovation and Opportunities for Changes*. Australian Government Department of Innovation, Industry, Science and Research. Retrieved from https://eprints.qut.edu.au/27114/1/Furneaux_-_BEIIC_Procurement_Report.pdf

Naughter, T. (2017, May 4). *The True Cost of Poor Contract Management*. Retrieved from https://www.contractworks.com/blog/the-true-cost-of-poor-contract-management#:~:text=Opportunity%20Costs&text=A%20smarter%20strategy%20is%20automating,also%20arise%20within%20the%20organization

P, L., & FD., A. (2011). Long-Term Infrastructure Partnerships: Contracting Risks and Risk-Reduction Strategies. *State and Local Government Review*, *43*(1), 49-59. doi:10.1177/0160323X11400435

Plimpton, L. (2008, June 19). *Do You Know Where Your Contracts Are?* Retrieved from https://www.entrepreneur.com/article/195046

Potoski, M., & Brown, T. L. (2005). Transaction costs and contracting: The practitioner perspective. *Public Performance & Management Review*, *28*(3), 326–351. doi:10.1080/15309576.2005.11051842

Quélin, B., & Duhamel, F. (2003). Bringing Together Strategic Outsourcing and Corporate Strategy: Outsourcing Motives and Risks. *European Management Journal*, *21*(5), 647–661. doi:10.1016/S0263-2373(03)00113-0

Rahman, M. M., & Kumaraswamy, M. M. (2004). Contracting Relationship Trends and Transitions. *Journal of Management in Engineering*, *20*(4), online. Retrieved from https://ascelibrary.org/doi/abs/10.1061/(ASCE)0742-597X(2004)20:4(147)

Renn, O. (2008). *Risk Governance: Coping with Uncertainty in a Complex World*. Earthscan. doi:10.1007/978-1-4020-6799-0

RICS. R. I. (2016, March 14). *Final account procedures.* Retrieved from https://www.rics.org/global-assets/rics-website/media/upholding-professional-standards/sector-standards/construction/black-book/final-account-procedures-1st-edition-rics.pdf

Rueckel, D., Krumay, B., & Schwarzgruber, S. (2020). Outsourcing in the Age of Digital Transformation. In *AMCIS 2020 Proceedings* (p. 24). Atlanta, GA: *Americas Conference on Information Systems (AMCIS)*.

Sanchez, H., Robert, B., Bourgault, M., & Pellerin, R. (2009). Risk management applied to projects, programs, and portfolios. *International Journal of Managing Projects in Business, 2*(1), 14–35. Advance online publication. doi:10.1108/17538370910930491

Schwertner, K. (2017). Digital transformation of business. *Trakia Journal of Sciences, 15*(Suppl.1), 388–393. doi:10.15547/tjs.2017.s.01.065

Shalan, M. (2019). *Risk management for digital transformation contracts. In Al-Yamamh University engineering Forum (YUENG2019).* Al-Yamamh University. Retrieved from https://yueng.yu.edu.sa/wp-content/uploads/2019/02/YUENG2019_paper_6.pdf

Shalan, M., & Anaim, N. (2017). The SMAC Opportunity Contracts: Generating Value From Responsive Agile Risk-Oriented Techniques. In Mobile Platforms, Design, and Apps for Social Commerce (pp. 115-134). Hershey: IGI Global.

Skaik, S., & Arafat, H. (2016). How can contractors warrant timely payments in the UAE construction industry? In RICS Cobra 2016 (p. 11). Royal Institution of Chartered Surveyors.

Sleiderink, W. S. (2015, March 17). *Reducing penalty costs in performance-based contracts. A case study at Thales Nederland B.V.* Drienerlolaan. Enschede, Netherlands: University of Twente. Retrieved from https://essay.utwente.nl/66884/16/W.S.%20Sleiderink(2015),%20Reducing%20penalty%20costs%20in%20Performance-Based%20Contracts,%20MSc.%20Thesis.pdf

Smit, J. (2017). *A Practical Guide on Managing Outsourcing Risk.* Retrieved from https://www.leadmark.nl/wp-content/uploads/2017/04/Guidance-on-Managing-Outsourcing-Risk.pdf

Smith, A. (1995). Subcontractors. In Estimating, Tendering and Bidding for Construction. Macmillan Building and Surveying Series (pp. 81-97). Springer. doi:10.1007/978-1-349-13630-8_7

Sumo, R., Kalkman, J., & Van Weele, A. (2018, April 1). *Innovation through contracting in the oil and gas sector.* Retrieved from https://www.adlittle.jp/sites/default/files/viewpoints/adl_effects_of_contractual_governance_on_innovation_in_the_oil.compressed.pdf

Taran, Y., Boer, H., & Lindgren, P. (2013). Incorporating Enterprise Risk Management in the Business. *Journal of Business Models, 1*(1), 38–60. http://journalofbusinessmodels.com/media/1014/vol-1-no-1-pp-38-60.pdf

The World Bank. (2018). *Contract Management practice.* Washington, DC: The World Bank. Retrieved from http://pubdocs.worldbank.org/en/277011537214902995/contract-management-guidance-september-19-2018-final.pdf

UK Government. (2020, June 1). *Risk Allocation and Pricing Approaches Guidance.* Retrieved from https://assets.publishing.service.gov.uk/government/uploads/system/uploads/attachment_data/file/891148/Risk_Allocation_and_Pricing_Approaches_-_Guidance_Note_-_June_2020.pdf

Uttam, K., & Roos, C. L. (2015). Competitive dialogue procedure for sustainable public procurement. *Journal of Cleaner Production, 86*, 403–416. doi:10.1016/j.jclepro.2014.08.031

Van, D. (2013, May). Reputational risk management in the corporate world. *Keeping Good Companies, 65*(4), 215-220. Retrieved from https://search.informit.com.au/documentSummary;dn=324234888878814;res=IELAPA

van Asselt, M. B., & Renn, O. (2011). Risk governance. *Journal of Risk Research, 14*(4), 431–449. doi:10.1080/13669877.2011.553730

van Bueren, E., & ten Heuvelhof, E. (2005). Improving Governance Arrangements in Support of Sustainable Cities. *Environment and Planning. B, Planning & Design, 32*(1), 47–66. doi:10.1068/b31103

Van Strien, J., Gelderman, C., & Semeijn, J. (2019). Performance-based contracting in military supply chains and the willingness to bear risks. *Journal of Defense Analytics and Logistics, 3*(1), 83–107. doi:10.1108/JDAL-10-2017-0021

Vasilescu, A.-M., Dima, A. M., & Vasilache, S. (2009). Credit analysis policies in construction project finance. *Management & Marketing, 4*(2), 79–94.

Villanova University. (2020, January 16). *What is the Cost of Poor Contract Management?* Retrieved from https://www.villanovau.com/resources/contract-management/what-is-the-cost-of-poor-contract-management/

Westphal, P., & Sohal, A. (2016). 8 17). Outsourcing decision-making: Does the process matter? *Production Planning and Control, 27*(11), 894–908. doi:10.1080/09537287.2016.1159350

ADDITIONAL READING

Abbott, K. W. (2012). Engaging the public and the private in global sustainability governance. *International Affairs, 88*(3), 543–564. doi:10.1111/j.1468-2346.2012.01088.x

Alexander, S. M., Andrachuk, M., & Armitage, D. (2016). Navigating governance networks for community-based conservation. *Frontiers in Ecology and the Environment, 14*(3), 155–164. doi:10.1002/fee.1251

Alles, M., Kogan, A., & Vasarhelyi, M. (2004). *The Law of Unintended Consequences?* (Vol. 1). Assessing the Costs, Benefits and Outcomes of the Sarbanes-Oxley Act. Information Systems Control Journal.

Beasley, M. S., Clune, R., & Hermanson, D. R. (2004). Enterprise Risk Management and the Internal Audit Function. North Carolina State University and Kennesaw State University. Working Paper. December.

Brown, A. E., & Grant, G. G. (2005). Framing the Frameworks: A Review of IT Governance Research. Communications of the AIS. Vol. 15, Article 38.

Cullen-Knox, C., Eccleston, R., Haward, M., Lester, L., & Vince, J. (2016). *Contemporary challenges in environmental governance: the rise of social licence*. Envionmental Policy and Governance.

Kunreuther, H. (2006). Risk and reaction: Dealing with interdependencies. *Harvard International Review: Global Catastrophe*, *28*(3), 17–23.

Moran, A. (2015). *Managing Agile: Strategy, Implementation, Organization and People*. Springer., doi:10.1007/978-3-319-16262-1

Morrison, J. (2014). *The Social License: How to keep your organization legitimate*. Springer.

Tarkoma, S. (2012). *Publish / Subscribe Systems: Design and Principles*. John Wiley & Sons., doi:10.1002/9781118354261

KEY TERMS AND DEFINITIONS

Agile Methodology: A development method and a leadership philosophy that encourages teamwork, self-organization, and accountability to develop a dynamic service that can respond to change and continuously deliver business value.

Governance: Refers to the structures and processes that are designed to ensure accountability, transparency, responsiveness, rule of law, stability, equity and inclusiveness, empowerment, and broad-based participation.

Outsourcing: A common method whereby a third party performs a function on behalf of the Enterprise, often when additional resources (either time, expertise, human resources, service, etc.) are needed.

Risk Frameworks: A skeleton that gives the total enterprise risk management strategy a proper guideline with steps to follow.

Risk Management: The act of handling the risk exposure through mitigation, acceptance, sharing and avoidance. It includes the ability to handle information and technology risks based on stakeholders' risk parameters.

Risk Mitigation: A process that involves taking action to reduce an organization's exposure to potential threats and reduce the likelihood that those threats will happen again or will affect the project deliverables.

Risk Modeling: Usually referrers to quantitative modeling of extreme events and systemic risks through the use of advanced mathematical techniques and multi-agent-based modeling.

Chapter 6
Employee Selection and Recruitment Contracts in the Digital Transformation Era

Akif Lutfi Al-Khasawneh
Balqa Applied University, Jordan

ABSTRACT

The selection and employment processes are considered among the complicated jobs that the human resources department performs. It is related to making specific decisions that are often difficult to withdraw or undo, such decision determine the fate of the organization in terms of human competencies that is selected to conduct the business functions. The employee selection and contracting are changing heavily in the digital transformation era, HR department needs to transform and find new ways to hire and retire based on technology tools. More professionals are looking at limited time jobs rather than permanent jobs as shown in the gig economy. The main objective of this chapter is to highlight hiring, training, and contracting of professionals in this era along with development stages, types, and strategies. In addition, it shows how such activities contributes to increase the effectiveness of employment process as well the organization effectiveness. In the last part will be presented the conclusions, recommendations, and future research suggestions.

INTRODUCTION

The selection and employment process require careful study of all aspects related to the job description and specifications to achieve the organization's goals in general and the job position efficiently and effectively. The main goal of this process is to determine the preferred candidate or setup among individuals applying for the job. This will enhance the ability to make the best decision in choosing individuals who are most distinguished and tuned with the job requirements (French, 2003).

Technology has added new dimensions to the recruitment processes considering the competencies that is required. Legal practitioners are not an exception. Furthermore, the employment contracts also have been changed significantly in this era of digital transformation. Moreover, organizations have different

DOI: 10.4018/978-1-7998-4501-0.ch006

methodologies in terms of choosing the type of work contracts based on their nature of work, policies, organizational strategies and the different workload.

Employment contracts are defined as an official document written between two parties to ensure the rights and duties of each of them. Employment contracts take different types, namely:

- Permanent work contracts: which are not governed by a specific period of time for the work to end, as the employee continues to work with his position in the organization throughout their life span.
- Specific work contracts: in which the start and end period of the work is determined in advance, this can be extended in consent of the parties
- Temporary work contracts: those are labor contracts that finish with the end of the preset task or goal achievement.

This chapter will be discussing the effects of digital transformation on the employment process and associated contracts. It will also describe how align the hiring process to get wider disciplined legal practitioners that can lead to a better contracting style.

BACKGROUND

Digital transformation of human resources is a constant process of using new digital technologies and practices, which recognizes agility (Warner and Wager, 2019). Several studies and literature have reviewed the concept of digital transformation (Mazzone, 2014), (Schwertner, 2017), considering its dimensions; (Seres, Pavlicevic and Tumbas, 2018), its application; and also analyze related items (Schallmo, Williams,and Boardman, 2017), (Ismail, Khater and Zaki, 2017). Although different classification exists for digital transformation (Turchi, 2018), (Matt, Hess and Benliam,2015), they all converge into four main dimensions: technologies - data - processes – individuals (Verina and Titko, 2019).

The human resources field is transforming as well for multiple reasons. The employee gets the flexibility to frequently switch jobs and broaden their portfolio with a wide range of experience (Mandloi, 2020) and traditionally, almost a third of company hires don't work out, despite extensive testing, assessment, and job fit analysis (Launches, 2019). The selection process is an essential sub-stage in the recruitment process and that it is used to select qualified persons from among the group of persons (Dura and Al-Sabbagh, 2008).

This chapter is handling the issue from multiple dimensions, it discusses how the human resources department need to transform as well how to respond to the challenges of the changing workforce. This include creation of agile processes, new hiring practices and the utilization of technology to hire and retain employees

JOB SELECTION

Dura (2008) indicated that the selection process is an essential sub-stage in the recruitment process and that it is used to select qualified persons from among the group of persons who are nominated for the job to be employed in the organization to carry out the workloads. Based on that, we can know the selection of employees as a process whereby a comparison is made between a group of individuals and applicants for the job in order to select the best from them and decide to accept their employment in a specific location in the organization.

It is clear from the above that the recruitment process for workers is based on the selection process, which is a complementary process that plays an executive role through which the decisions of the selection process that play the advisory role and assisting in the recruitment of who is the best are met. In the digital transformation era, the job selection is more driven from the top, designing a strategy requires both tech-savvy leaders from the business and business-savvy leaders from technology. More than ever, companies need to invest in cross-functional knowledge at the executive level on down. The C-suite should need extensive business-related knowledge on the technology side to succeed in executing a digital transformation strategy.

Companies are looking today to hire qualified people with new skills who can think innovatively while acquiring new talents. They hire data scientists' who can think beyond normal resume banks' perimeter and app developers who are able to iterate the selection process through gamification and social collaboration techniques. Such hiring process is directly affecting the organization's ability to setup better contracts to enhance the business potential through using innovative technologies to manage and orchestrate such conversion.

The Importance of Selection and Recruitment Process

The selection process is of great importance in the real administrative work, because it achieves many benefits, especially if the selection process is characterized by integrity, fairness, transparency, and reliance on regulations, laws, standards and scientific foundations. Among these administrative tasks are the following:

- Achieve the conscience's comfort in choosing the most appropriate and best of individuals and applicants for the job and bring them to the organization. That is a legal, ethical and social responsibility.
- Provide an additional number of workers to the organization, which reduces the job burdens for current workers and achieve job stability.
- Provide an opportunity for the organizations to expand their activities and work to increase their market share or improve the level of performance.
- Add specific value from new individuals or workers to the organization to create knowledge diversity qualitative competencies (Patton, et al., 2002).
- Contribute to opening the competition between existing and new hired workers
- Support employee replacement policy (Noe, et al., 2000) by providing an opportunity for the current full-time workers to obtain regular leaves and to achieve certain interests such as finding other job opportunities and going a full-time study.
- Measure the ideal approach to digital age learning consists of which consists of formalized, collaboration and on-the-job training.
- Facilitate the learning about digital transformation and gaining the skills they need. The hiring process should be the good place to start in the business world through triggering flexible and connected learning.

- Show the organization's integrity and social responsibility to the external community and prove that the selection of its employees was made according to the competence and skills of the individuals and not according to sect, racism, mediation or other considerations (Anthony, et al. 1999).

Who Is the Responsible of Selection and Recruitment of the Employees?

The organization concerned with selection or employment differs according to many factors, including the nature of the work in the organization, the size of the organization, the pattern of management, the nature of organizational relationships, the maturity of the organizational structure and the specialization level. Today the innovation and digital transformation behaviors are increasingly becoming defining factors while looking for competencies in human resources, legal staff, and all others.

Factors Affecting the Process of Job Selection

The ability of organizations to attract human competencies varies. Many organizations are distinguished from others in terms of turnover and heavy flow by individuals and job seekers. Some suffer from difficulty in recruiting or attracting talents. Such variation is related to the various circumstances surrounding the organization itself, which are certainly considered as a supportive or obstructive engine through which an individual's behavior is formed. According to (Gomez & Cardy, 1998) the most prominent factors which affects the selection and recruitment process includes the following:

First: The organizational situation: that is, everything relates to the organization's status, privileges, location and status compared to other organizations, in terms of size, nature of work, geographical location, job stability, salaries and wages, rewards and incentives, the system of promotions, social security, health insurance, recreational services for workers and their children, such as education, clubs, unions, bank facilities, loans, consumer markets and housing. These privileges determine the organization's reputation, distinguish it from other organizations and position it among the most attractive position for individuals with distinct and highly distinguished skills.

Second: The economic effect that is divided into two parts:

1. The economic position of the organization in terms of its profit's levels, its returns, market share and competitive position. This reflects directly on its economic strength and prosperity and enhances the volume of cash flows and efficient budgets that allows it to provide the means of luxury and privileges for its workers. This also enhances the individuals desire to be employed and attracted to such organization.
2. The economic situation related to the individual himself (the applicant for employment) and the surrounding economic conditions, problems, and family conditions in terms of levels of poverty, wealth, social status, and so on. Where a person graduates from university, he initiates an application for a job and accept any job without hesitation in usual. Limited people may wait for selected positions only.

Third: Social effect, that is, the culture, values, customs, traditions and trends prevailing in society and the culture of shame which play an influential role in heading towards accepting certain jobs and rejecting other jobs. A certain pattern of positive or negative thinking and behavior towards many special decisions form his positive or negative view of a job, through which the fate of the job is determined for acceptance or rejection.

The business landscape is shifting rapidly with each technology innovations. The human resource professionals are not an exception. They are changing up their tactics in terms of finding—and retaining—the best available talent. From our point of view, other factors can be added in the digital transformation era such as:

- The employee mentoring and learning approaches. Technology acumen is already an important part of the candidate curricula. Corporate learning is rapidly evolving as well and employees would like to engage with organizations which has developed its comprehensive online learning platforms and collaborations hubs. Employees need a flexibility to acquire and access training when they need it, including real-time sessions, sometimes before new solutions are released. The service is required by employees to give them a jump-start in understanding how the latest innovations can benefit their organizations and their own future.
- The work flexibility, some companies allow staff to take as much holiday as they like; no checking with managers, no tracking days off. Such organizations are making such a simple rationale. Since the boundary between work and play has blurred, people can, and do, work anywhere. For highly innovative organizations it's no longer required to meter when staff at work, thus, it's no longer reasonable to meter when we're not. The most striking thing about this is the inherent recognition that digital transformation working practices is not tracking annual leave which is no longer relevant as employees today need different working practices to be effective and innovative.
- The growth mindset, that is a pervasive success factor, and is more important than the need for the latest technology and gadgets. It helps build a culture that accelerates transformation, propelling the business through disruption. This is an exciting opportunity to HR to partner with organization leaders to build an environment that embraces growth hacking and empowers all employees to own innovation in their day-to-day roles. Legal professionals who are drafting contracts are not an exception.

Employment Reasons

There is no doubt that the recruitment process incurs a lot of burdens and efforts on the organization. Organization certainly does not exercise such acts to show off or boast about them or the numbers of workers. Employment process is a result of various motives and reasons that impose the necessity to acquire new employees and additional human capacities to enable the business cycle and achieve excellence on the other hand. According to (Denisi, et al., 2001) the most prominent of these reasons or motives as follows:

- Increasing the size of the organization's business and expanding its activities.
- Designing new sites on the organizational structure.
- Replacing some of the existing employees with new ones for various reasons such as low level of performance or violating employees.
- The termination of some work contracts with some employees.
- The emergence of new job vacancies for various reasons, such as contracting, resignation, job migrations, deaths, etc.

Further to these reasons the digital transformation age is proposing multiple other factors such as:

- The strategic business change, where organizations need to ensure that their human capital remain relevant and are evolving to complement the digital transformation agenda.
- The customer experience and expectations which put a stress on organization to be more customer centric. Organization need to hire new talents that are capable of using data to win, grow and retain their customer base and better serve them.
- Highly specialized tasks that may necessitate new hires if required as full-time jobs or limited time contracts that can be hired to generate certain value and quit.
- Transformation leaders are also required today to see the value in focusing on small 'shapeshifts' towards wider ambition rather than unnecessary complete business overhaul implemented at once. Such leaders can create stories that draws a compelling line between digital initiatives, the organization's vision, and how that ambition translates for individuals.

WORKING PRACTICES IN THE DIGITAL TRANSFORMATION ERA

Generation Z (or Gen Z for short) workers and Millennials are expecting flexible working environments like that they experience in innovation labs or hear about in spin-off ventures and digital giants. Such practices produce enormous value; however, some workers might struggle if such approaches are activated within their organization that's still using old siloed approach. Under these conditions there can be a struggle to make a material impact in the organization.

The working environments and contracting style that is required by Gen Z and Millennials include following behaviors:

Holistic and Customer Centric

Standalone or siloed departments and products are being from past. New startups and power houses are expected to generate a statement to the market with broader business and long-term solution that is a result from collaboration and innovation. A holistic approach that considers how such initiatives will connect and extend across the company is essential. For example, Google has generated multiple products through customer-centric vision that is spreading across the entire company.

Shifts Toward Contemporary Business Cultures

Digital talent is looking for fast-paced, rewarding work, and the flexibility to do it. The concept of a full-time job, with long-term security and big benefits packages are waning in popularity and availability. The independent contractors of today are looking for fun, agile work that gives them a sense of purpose.

Learn and Mix

Today some young may know more than the old. The usual average age of board members is used to be over 60 but this is changing. A new contracted employee may be hired and soon to be accepted in the board who are keen for more technology knowledge. Such cases already exist in new recruits, and reverse mentoring programs can bring this critical learning to the Board. This age mix is affecting all the management and decision-making layers in every leading organizations

Expanding the Scope of Accepted Business Practices

Flexible schedules, work-from-home options—the traditional departmental approach to managing a company is falling by the wayside. Provide the tools for collaboration across all departments, and all types of talent will flourish.

Immediate Response

In the digital transformation era, the demands of customers are changing continuously and same are their expectations. Employees need autonomy and space for self-leadership so they can respond quickly and effectively. Trusting employees enables them to manage their time, without a tight control that characterize the old practices and give them a freedom zone that enables them acting fast to customer expectations.

Reinforcing Skills With Intelligent Behaviors

Embracing new trends of the digital age will only reach their full effectiveness when a collaborative culture is established. Cross-functional learning and creating spaces for motivated talent to make empowered decisions are vital to embracing new business concepts in the digital age.

Softening Line Management Structures

Digital Transformation era have necessitated better connection with customers, opened flows of information and softening line management structures to broaden networks and break silos. Employees are expecting wide connections which facilitate the enterprise social. This will generate new internal ideas as well the strong elaboration with customers which results in direct collaborates with customers to facilitate new products.

Leading Through Inspiration

Talent retention is easier for HR when they can inspire change. Collect feedback in engaging, personal ways, and encourage avenues for digital work to attract the best talent to your organization and keep them there—because they want to be there.

RECRUITMENT CONSIDERATIONS IN THE DIGITAL TRANSFORMATION ERA

The process of recruitment or employment is considered an important and accurate stage in the organization's course of work, because it determines the organization's level in terms of skills that enhance its position, competitive strength and provide it with the opportunity to be distinguished from other organizations.

The Recruitment Process

The administrative procedure that is conducted by human resources in the organization towards the individuals it employs can be very rewarding or conflicting. The employment contract constitutes a legal and moral obligation by the organization towards those individuals concerned with employment, especially after the organization issues an appointment decision. This may be extremely difficult and complicated because there are legal and ethical obligations on the one hand, and the efforts of material and moral organization may incur on the other hand. The organization management and recruitment decision-makers must take into consideration a set of considerations before making the employment decision or selecting employees such as:

- Paying responsibility for recruitment and selecting employees to the human resources as they are specialized with direct channel to the higher management. Hiring decisions need to be away from interference or bias.
- Adhering to job analysis and job description policies to ensure that individuals with consistent job specifications and job description are chosen.
- Studying and analyzing the labor market to choose the most distinguished employment based on various related aspects such as cognitive, epistemological, and ethical behaviors.
- Working according to a clear and accurate methodology and procedures that is defining job needs, descriptions, specifications while advertising and identifying those responsible for employment and providing the appropriate environment for the interview.
- Announcing the job posting through the various channels to ensure that the largest possible number of diverse competencies are obtained to develop alternatives and choose the best.
- Defining the selection and employment process within a clear organizational strategy that is determined through plans, policies, programs, procedures, budgets, laws, and legislations to guarantee correct and fair job rights and duties.

Human resource professionals today need to fully appreciate the value of generalists who can shift gears as fast as technology. They must engage and adapt to the demands of an ever-changing business. More elements are added to the employee selection process in the digital transformation era which includes:

- Hiring an employee who is an advocate to the organization to stimulate engagement and grow the organization reputation among wide audience through digital, social media or offline channels.
- Searching the digital channels which are becoming a major source for high quality talents and thus every organization need to have a related strategy to build relationships with specific influencers who have the ear of targeted talents to come and apply.
- Looking for employees who can increase reach, engagement and innovation through the utilization of emerged technologies and associated bases. A first step is to conduct an audit based on employees' audience size and social activity to identify which persona category they are currently in.

Expected Problems During the Recruitment Process

Organizations in general, and human resources, face many challenges and problems when deciding to employ new workers, especially those with distinct expertise and competencies. Among the most prominent are the following:

- Government intervention in labor and worker policies, is often considered positive for state organizations, population, and human resources, because it aims to organize the activities and protect from any side exploitation. However, some government policies and regulations might lead to challenges in the process of attracting human resources to organizations such as the levels of wages and salaries, laws of residence and borders.
- Competition between organizations in the acquisition of people with creative talents and skills in human resources, which imposes on organizations to bear additional financial burdens to pay them as salaries, incentives and privileges for those with unique specialties and creators of human competencies (Ivancevich, 2001).
- The organization's economic position and status, and its level of prosperity by which it is distinguished in the competition market.
- The societal culture that directs the behavior of workers towards accepting others, interacting with others and harmony with the job, as there are many individuals who are governed by a culture of defect.
- The organization's presence in a natural environment that does not suit people with competencies, such as climatic conditions, various natural disasters, and others (Dessler, 2017).
- Mediation and favoritism in appointments and employee selection.
- High levels of living and low economic conditions, which may lead to the migration of job competencies abroad to improve their standard of living and the level of income.

Digital transformation has added plenty of reasons as people have different attitudes towards innovation, self-learning and technology.

- Digital maturity driving is a key in recruiting, people with tech skills will always be a priority for recruiters, but candidates' business and soft skills are going to be the differentiator between applicants.
- Organizations will need also to decide if they should hire established candidates from the outside or invest in training to nurture from within the companies, especially when it comes to new roles that weren't there a few years ago.
- Microlearning is crucial in current fast paced work environments, thus organizations ae looking for professionals who are self-pushed for self-flexible and on-demand trainings to create the desired value for their selves and their organizations.
- Staying on top of emerging industry trends through maintaining the pace of rapid change and upskilling on a regular basis to stay ahead of the new technologies, strategies, and developments. Organizations need people who can use digital technology to capitalize on emerging opportunities and investments. Digital skills are in demand across sectors and within roles that traditionally did not require them.

- Coach prospects' career decisions in which top talent are increasingly reposition themselves as career coaches who do not focus on just selling the job role, but rather prompt candidates to think about their career goals and where their strengths lie, and then helps them consider their options.
- Adopt a flexible planning strategy against the usual annual, top-down hiring plan, which cannot predict the kind of talent that will be required as needs change. An effective alternative is a bottom-up approach, as managers are far better positioned to provide hiring insights such as how jobs are changing, and the skills required for it.

Requitement Tests

The business landscape is shifting rapidly with each technology innovations, and human resource professionals are changing up their tactics in terms of finding—and retaining—the best available talent. Some of the sweeping new concepts taking root in human resources include reliable testing characteristics to determine the best candidates.

The tests are necessary and very important because they constitute an essential tool in providing the administration with objective information related to individuals applying for jobs and because it reveals the extent of harmony and harmony between job seekers and the candidates themselves, and also enables the human resources department to choose the right among all applicants to occupy jobs, as it reveals the other capabilities and skills for individuals that can be used in the future career strategies, senior positions, and others. To achieve objectivity in the testing process, it must meet few basic conditions:

- **Measurement Reliability:** Which means obtaining fixed results and degrees in time and place, so that they produce the same results if they are re-measured in different time or spatial periods.
- **Validity:** That is, the test measures the elements that were established for measurement. Honesty here measures the validity of the applicant for the job in terms of harmony between the job, its descriptions, and the specifications of its occupant.
- **Prioritization:** Tests need to be able to prioritize candidates based on impact and effort. Such tests need to really measure the business impact of hiring certain staff who can get the ideas to go digital. And start with the ideas that are high impact and low effort.

To be able to know and measure the compatibility of each individual with among other candidate for the job, which tests must be drawn from the job description and job specifications because each job has a test in areas that are different from the other. According to (French, 2003) employment tests that can be carried out by the human resources department may include:

Cognitive Abilities

It includes the additional knowledge that an individual may distinguish from another, such as an individual's knowledge of various languages, or an addition knowledge of an individual in mastery and application of various computer programs and others.

Mental Capacity

This includes intelligence and the intuitive speed with which a person is distinguished from the other / like speed in learning and mastery of work with less time than the other.

Intuitive Capabilities

which includes the extent of the individual's ability to feel, predict and interact with work or others and respond quickly, and the closest we can describe this likewise is that the core of the signal is understood.

Psychological Capacity

It is that which measures the extent of the individual's ability to deal with others in a balanced and logical manner and to control feelings and feelings and that his behaviors are not excessive or impulsive in reactions to others.

Digital Transformation have added few capacities that should be available to succeed in this era, this includes:

Transformational Mindset

When it comes to digital, the stage of mindset in the transformation process is about leadership, strategy and culture with the end goal of the business adopting a culture with digital threaded into its DNA.

Communication and empowerment are crucial to help all employees understand their involvement and help to progress. This will not only engage them in the process, but also enables them to see how it impacts on the success of the business.

Digital Skillset

The fact is there aren't enough people in the workforce with the right digital skills. Despite digital natives and millennials entering the workforce there is still a substantial gap to be filled in the skillsets of organizations.

As digital technologies continue to evolve, the skills that are needed to harness these evolutions needed to be boosted on a continuous basis to filter the platforms or initiatives that may not work with those that will.

Scale and standardization is often an issue where digital skills are no longer confined to particular departments such as marketing. Digital's pervasiveness it is embedded across a business and therefore capabilities need to be instilled across the entire spectrum.

Toolset Learning

People learn in different ways. Some still hold value in classroom settings or workshops while others learn better at their own pace in their own environment through online learning. For some, a combination of the two works well as a classroom or workshop setting incorporates online learning in a blended model.

In recent years and with the development of digital technologies, professionals keen to upskill have turned to online learning. As lives get busier and time is precious, individuals want to be able to learn at their own pace and have access to content as and when they need it.

For many organizations, the added benefit of using digital tools is that they can track what and how people are learning. The popularity of resources can be gauged to see what is most effective while an individual's progress is being tracked.

TRANSFORMING THE HUMAN RESOURCES ROLE FOR THE NEW WORK ERA

Jobs today are in a state of upheaval. Flexible working models and job sharing are on the rise, international and cross-company networking is dramatically increasing the complexity of work, and proven management and organizational models are being put to the test. Companies are increasingly acting as networks and are placing the management of complex teams at the center of organizational structuring. The "organization of the future" has become HR topic number one.

Transforming the HR Department

In todays' environment, HR work must be understood more than ever as a strategic competitive factor. But the reality in many companies still looks very different. The relevance of HR to strategic development has so far hardly been noticed – to say nothing of the efficiency potential of digital technologies.

French, et al. (2019) stated that people can make or break the digital transformation journey. The organization will need people with specific skills, guided by strong leadership, who can collaborate effectively for the project to be successful. During every phase of the HR digital transformation, people will need to be involved actively, this section is showing how people need to be handled during every phase:

Business as Usual

Change doesn't happen in a vacuum - so it's important to get the buy-in of key people within the organization. HR team need to start discussing digital HR as a topic with a small group of potential change agents to create enthusiasm about the matter. At the same time, focus on attracting people with digital capabilities for innovative experimentation.

Presentation and Mobilization

While planning to move toward the digital transformation in HR department, the organization need to train and/or attract people with digital capabilities such as HRIT specialists, HR analysts, technical consultants and software developers in order to execute the desired improvements properly. HR team need also to build alliances with other departments to stimulate integral approaches where possible such as a data warehouse, a KPI dashboard or collaboration tools.

Digital transformation by nature tends to break silos, so the HR need not to be afraid to act form multidisciplinary teams and learn by doing. However, it is crucial to create an impact-effort matrix and focus on making a big impact with small changes.

Formalization and Capacity Building

Once HR have a clear understanding of the digital skill gap in the organization, it's time for action. Integrate new learning and development (L&D) offerings to stimulate digital literacy, and make sure your colleagues understand the necessity of cultivating these new skills. If there are certain skills that can't be trained inside the organization then it must be hired for the future either through employment or agencies.

Strategic Integration

When digital literacy is mandated across all groups working within HR including executives. It will be the time to integrate digital skills within all roles in HR and plan for the future by attracting key digital talent. The new digital HR initiatives need to flourish with regular follow-ups and inspiration. Successes need to be celebrated, and lessons to be learned. It is also important to provide access to on-demand online learning.

Converging and Adaptation

Digital transformation needs to avoid blinkered views. As data analytics becomes increasingly important and complex, more data-savvy people should be trained or hired such as data scientists with HR affinity to work on advanced analyses, or developers to build in-house software solutions.

It is necessary to create a team to be responsible for the continuous delivery and boost of innovation within HR. Adaptation can occur through suggesting innovative ideas for people challenges and challenging current solutions. Regularly the organization will need inputs on skills that will be needed within HR in the future and review the talent gap for digital skills within HR continuously.

Changing Types of Employment Contracts

Organizations differ from others in terms of choosing the type of work contracts according to the organization, the nature of its work, its policy and organizational strategies, as well as the different workload, the extent to which the job specifications are consistent with the job characteristics, the extent of the conviction of the top management and its directions in choosing the work contracts that bring more benefit to the organization.

Employment contracts are defined as a formal document written between the two parties (employers and employees) to ensure the rights and duties of each of them towards the other, and the employment contracts take different types, namely:

Permanent Work Contracts

Which are not governed by a specific period for the end of the work, the employee continues to work in his position in the organization throughout their life span.

Specific Work Contracts

In which the start and end period of the work is determined, that is, there is a specific period and time agreed upon between the employer and the worker, and such type of work contracts can be determined with the consent of the parties for another period of time determined by agreement.

Temporary Work Contracts

These are labor contracts that end with the end of the task or goal that is determined in advance. Where organizations work for this type of contract, in which the nature of the jobs is related to construction projects, contracting and studies.

This digital transformation era is moving away from the permanent work contracts as more people are involved in the Gig economy where employers are looking for flexible skilled workers who can run a required activity and quit. Similarly, professionals need to be hired in certain tasks that falls under their expertise and interest at their schedule rather than working permanently in an organization that might ask them to perform various jobs to fill their work schedule.

New Human Resource Management Dimensions in the New World

Human Resource Management has its focus on the performance of the organization emphasizing the role of business problems resolver. Human resource management is a strategic asset to firms contributing to the competitive advantage of the company. Payne (2010) claims that unless human resource management changes to manage the HR function strategically top management may continue to regard human resources as a drain to the finances of the company. Plenty of challenges are expected today while hiring new talents to get the organization ready for the digital transformation, which includes:

Building an Emerging Digital Corporate Culture

When defining a digital strategy, it is essential to remember that implementation can be undermined by the corporate culture. Various solutions exist for making the company more "digital friendly," promoting buy-in and ensuring the fast adoption of new value-generating behaviors.

This involves raising awareness among teams and new talents, clarifying the changes driven by digital transformation and putting them into perspective. It is important to explain new practices to employees and managers to facilitate adoption and enable greater collaboration, delegation and agility.

Digital transformation is also an opportunity to develop an innovation culture, while avoiding paradoxical demands (e.g. "be creative" vs. "follow the rules").

Helping Managers With Their Own Digital Transformation

This means helping managers update their management styles by challenging and changing their roles and responsibilities. Support must be provided to employees at every level of the hierarchy, especially middle managers who are most often focused on top-down approaches, which are undermined by digitization. In particular, providing constructive criticism and taking a more entrepreneurial, less hierarchical approach are strong indicators of digital management practices.

Reinventing the Workforce Planning

Workforce planning refers to all the programs and tools used to anticipate evolving business needs and their impact on human resources.

Over the next 20 years plenty of jobs will disappear due to the expected wave of automation, workforce planning seems to be making a revival. Competency management systems are re-emerging after a radical methodological overhaul which includes an updated skills assessment in terms of frequency, participants, simplified skills definitions, and other adaptable new approaches.

Developing More Agile HR Processes

The HR function must be prepared to rethink its key processes to better align with business strategy and respond faster through workforce planning. This is required to manage and promote group performance and innovation while simplifying HR processes for jobs, skills and training.

Better exploitation of new technologies is required to manage communities to develop skills and facilitate mobility, develop the employer brand, use big data to identify new trends, digitize processes and documents to free up time and boost productivity.

Rethinking the Employee Experience

While HR teams must remain specialists in their field, they also need to develop marketing skills to position themselves as talent boosters. Improving the employee experience means considering employee satisfaction as key to business performance. It must therefore meet the following needs:

- New digital HR processes
- Improved communications by introducing a corporate social network
- More collaborative work
- A stated principle of goodwill which is the right to make mistakes

FUTURE RESEARCH DIRECTIONS

This chapter have touched the relation between technology and human resources. Both topics have been there for a long time and a lot of researches are there individually for each. However, correlating these two topics altogether has stated to gain potential but still there is a huge room for improvement.

One research topic will be on how to write up a contract for a gig worker who are contracted for a limited period and specific task. Additionally, how to manage his performance and how to go in a dispute if he failed to perform. Another research should focus on how to select and hire a temporary worker. Usually organizations set a probation period of three months to test the newcomer's performance, however this can't be the case for temporary workers.

The open data platforms can provide wealth knowledge about an employee and his performance, every organization should decide if it will be beneficial to subscribe in similar databases. This is an opportunity to study various related behaviors. Another research topic can be directed about how to set up such a database, what fields should be there and how to authenticate and trust such data.

On the other side several research topics are related to building an agile human resources procedures and processes that can handle the new challenges in a flexible and timely manner. Also, to remove unwanted interactions that are coming from different directions.

Research topics in this area are endless and every day a new topic is popping up considering the importance and impact of the human capital and the digital transformation.

CONCLUSION

Digital transformation in human resources must be aligned with the goals of the organization. This calls for long-term measures that require intensive discourse with all participants and should be implemented iteratively. The resources owned by a company such as human capital and technological resources are the main determinants of its value, performance, and sustained competitive advantage. Resources are controlled by an organization and enable the organization to comprehend its strategies that improve its efficiency and effectiveness.

This chapter sense the impact of technology resources on company performance and competitiveness. It showed how these resources can add new capabilities and competitive advantage resulting from the synergy between different sets of resources such as technology and human capital. This will be a step toward a final state in which HR becomes merely a service that is powered by technology and even it can be handled on a smartphone. However, constant adaptation to our way of life, the talent behaviors and progressive technologies will enable a more productive, efficient and healthy working environment.

REFERENCES

Anthony, P. W., Perrewe, L., & Kacmark, M. (1999). Human Resource Management. The Dryden Press.

Denisi, S. A., & Griffin, W. R. (2001). Human Resource Management. Houghton Mifflin Company.

Dessler, G. (2017). *Human Resource Management* (15th ed.). Prentice-Hall.

Dura, A. B., & Al-Sabbagh, Z. N. (2008). *Human Resource Management in the 21st Century: System Approach.* Dar Wael Publishing and Distribution.

Fenech, R., Baguant, P., & Ivanov, D. (2019). Higher Colleges of Technology The changing role of human resource management in an era of digital transformation. *International Journal of Entrepreneurship, 22*(2), 139–149.

French, L. W. (2003). Human Resource Management (5th ed.). Houghton Mifflin Company.

Gomez-Mejia, B., David, B., & Cardy, L. R. (1998). Managing Human Resources. Prentice Hall.

Ismail, M. H., Khater, M., & Zaki, M. (2017). *Digital business transformation and strategy: What do we know so far?* Retrieved on January 11, 2020 from https://pdfs.semanticscholar.org/35b2/bd95aeb8e-6ca0ea0652d0d7fc697eda3362a.pdf

Ivancevich, M. J. (2001). Human resource Management. McGraw-Hill.

Launches, B. (2019, Jan 27). R[REMOVED HYPERLINK FIELD]etrieved April 2020, from https://oliver-dev.s3.amazonaws.com/2019/01/27/12/54/25/916/Tech_Disruptions.pdf

Mandloi, R. (2020, January 13). *Making the Most of Talent in the Gig Economy*. (Retrieved April 24, 2020, from https://www.harvardbusiness.org/making-the-most-of-talent-in-the-gig-economy/

Matt, C., Hess, H., & Benliam, A. (2015). Digital Transformation Strategies. *Business & Information Systems Engineering*, *57*(5), 339–343. doi:10.100712599-015-0401-5

Mazzone, D. M. (2014). *Digital or Death: Digital Transformation – The Only Choice for Business to Survive Smash and Conquar* (1st ed.). Smashbox Consulting Inc.

Moran, A. (2015). *Managing Agile: Strategy, Implementation, Organization and People*. Springer. doi:10.1007/978-3-319-16262-1

Noe, A. R., Hallenbeck, R. J., Gerhart, B., & Wright, M. P. (2000). Human resource Management. Irwin, McGraw-Hill.

Patton, W. D., Wit, L. S., Lovrich, P. N., & Fredericksen, T. P. (2002). Human resource Management. Houghton Mifflin Company.

Payne, J. E. (2010). Survey of the international evidence on the causal relationship between energy consumption and growth. *Journal of Economic Studies (Glasgow, Scotland)*, *37*(1), 53–95. doi:10.1108/01443581011012261

Schallmo, D., Williams, C., & Boardman, L. (2017). Digital Transformation of Business Model-Best Practice, Enablers and Roadmap. International Journal of Innovation Management, 21(8).

Schwertner, K. (2017). Digital transformation of business. *Trakia Journal of Sciences*, *15*(1), 388–393. doi:10.15547/tjs.2017.s.01.065

Seres, L., Pavlicevic, V., & Tumbas, P. (2018).Digital Transformation of Higher Education Competing on Analytics. *Proceeding of INTED conference*. 10.21125/inted.2018.2348

Thierrt, I. (2017). *Companies of the Future: The Issues of Digital Transformation*. Retrieved on December 25,2019 from https://www.researchgate.net/profile/Isckia_Thierry/publication/313105824_White_paper_Companies_of_the_future_The_Issues_of_Digital_Transformation/links/5890566ea6fdcc2351c08eeb/White-paper-Companies-of-the-future-The-Issues-of-Digital-Transformation.pdf?origin=publication_detail

Turchi, P. (2018). *The Digital Transformation Pyramid: A business-driven Approach for Corporate Initiatives*. Retrieved on February 1,2018 from https://www.thedigitaltransformationpeople.com/channels/the-case-for-digital-transformation/digital-transformation-pyramid-business-driven-approach-corporate-initiatives/

Verina, N., & Titko, D. (2019). Digital Transformation: Conceptual Framework. *International scientific conference "Contemporary Issues in Business, Management, and Economics engineering· 2019.*

Warner, K., & Wäger, M. (2018). Building dynamic capabilities for digital transformation: An ongoing process of strategic renewal. *Long Range Planning*, *52*(3), 326–349. Advance online publication. doi:10.1016/j.lrp.2018.12.001

ADDITIONAL READING

Dallas, G. (Ed.). (2004). Governance and risk. New York: McGraw-Hill Companies Inc.

Government, H. (2018, Feb 1). *The_experiences_of_those_in_the_gig_economy*. Retrieved April 24, 2020, from https://assets.publishing.service.gov.uk/government/uploads/system/uploads/attachment_data/file/679987/171107_The_experiences_of_those_in_the_gig_economy.pdf

Grembergen, W. (Ed.). (2003). *Strategies for information technology governance*. Idea Group Publishing.

Kunreuther, H. (2006). Risk and reaction: Dealing with interdependencies. *Harvard International Review: Global Catastrophe*, *28*(3), 17–23.

KEY TERMS AND DEFINITIONS

Contemporary Business Cultures: Such environment is designed for digital talent who are looking for fast-paced, rewarding work, with flexibility to do. This includes fun, agile work that gives the workers a sense of purpose.

Digital Transformation: System of technologies, data, processes, and individuals that aims to improve the performance of organizations and make all of their members and customers more satisfied.

Gig Worker: A temporary worker who are not intersected in permeant hiring who are providing service on temporary basis.

Human Resources Management: Refer to the team and processes which is generally used to hire, measure, and retire staff in various organization. Those employees can be temporary or permeant.

Innovative Contracts: Contracting structure that enables the maximization of opportunities and reduction of risk based on agile and smart features.

New Work Era: An era in which humans and machines can work together to perform the tasks: they can collaborate or chain the jobs till fully completed. Both can be temporary hired and fired.

Chapter 7
Agile IT Department Contracted for New Roles in a New Era

Fawaz Alharbi
Shaqra University, Saudi Arabia

ABSTRACT

The complexity of business and competitive environment enforces organizations to adopt innovative ways for doing business. This drives a new trend of agile organizations that are adaptable to market and technology changes. As a result, 75% of organizations recognized agility as one of the key drivers for their IT strategies. As organizations start adopting digital transformation initiatives, they recognize the necessity to adapt agility in their IT departments as well. However, moving to an agile organization and an agile IT department is more complex than adapting an agile software. This chapter aims to provide an in-depth explanation of agile IT department specifying its features, roles, and differentiation elements from the traditional IT department. Emerging technologies that are crucial in the movement towards an agile IT department are also discussed with possible change management process to facilitate the transition of the agile IT department into profit center that is contracted to add value for the whole organization while working in a feasible partnership mode with the business.

INTRODUCTION

The world is evolving, many rapid changes are affecting the way organizations conduct their business. Organizations are required to adopt agile approaches instead of rigid historical management approaches. One example of the game-changing organizations is Netflix which changes the media and entertainment industry through innovation and agility. Currently, there are 167 million active Netflix customers (Watson, 2020) who consume 140 million hours every day (McPeak, 2018).

Being an agile organization refers to the practices and attributes which allows the organization to be adaptable with market changes (Dahmardeh and Banihashemi, 2010) and to create a solid customer-centric culture (Roberts and Grover, 2012). The agile organization has specific characteristics that are related to the Agile Manifesto values and principles (Beck et al. 2001). A study showed that 75% of

DOI: 10.4018/978-1-7998-4501-0.ch007

organizations stated agility as one of their main drivers for a strategic technology initiative stressing the importance of agility for business (Nuodb, 2017).

One key characteristic of an agile organization is the ability to integrate technology solutions effectively to deliver best values in terms of customers, processes, products development and organization's structure (Seymour, and Coyle, 2016). Digital transformation is changing many aspects of all organizations and affecting all business areas. The implementation of digital transformation requires the utilization of many emerging technologies such as Cloud Computing and Internet of Things (IoT). Organizations willing to adopt digital transformation will need to adopt agile methods to gain the main benefits of digital transformation (Kettunen and Laanti, 2017). The effective implementation of digital transformation implies new requirements and roles of IT department to support innovations (Châlons and Dufft, 2017).

Although agile software methodologies were discussed in many studies, the movement from agile software to an agile organization still requires further actions and investigation (Narayan, 2015) (Fuchs and Hess, 2018). Agile IT department is a vital element in the movement towards the agile organization, thus the understanding of the new roles, structures, technologies of an agile IT department will be very important.

As the adoption of emerging technologies is vital for organizations to be competitive in a changing world, the IT departments should evolve to make quick and right decisions that will increase the collaboration between different stakeholders of organizations.

The chapter will introduce agile IT concept and specify the associated characteristics. The differences between traditional IT and agile IT will be discussed, furthermore new roles and responsibilities of an agile IT department will be explained. The chapter will start by discussing how the IT department can create value by using emerging technologies and the associated benefits. The chapter will discuss also the movement of IT department from cost-center to be profit-center. The required culture and change management of the new movement will be also explained in details in addition to the change management processes.

One main objective of this chapter is to explain how the agile IT department will be contracted to achieve the organization goals while moving away from the practices of the traditional IT department. This can bring many benefits to the organization toward the establishment of a digitally transformed organization that is ready for nowadays rapid business changes.

AGILE IT DEPARTMENT: CONCEPT AND CHARACTERISTICS

This section is intended to discuss the concept of agile IT department and its main characteristics and to explain the differences between agile IT department and the traditional IT department.

Definition

Traditional IT departments are running their projects based on traditional waterfall models such as Software Development Life Cycle (SDLC). Traditional models have their disadvantages such as rigidity during the development process and longtime to produce working prototypes (Stoica, Mircea & Ghilicmicu, 2013). Agile IT department should be developed based on agile methodologies that will act to define the IT as a flexible learning unit which implement agile principles across the entire department to deliver services and respond effectively to the organization's needs (Ambler & Lines, 2016). Agile IT department goes beyond software development to set most of the activities into customer-friendly tasks that will create the required business values. Table 1 presents a comparison between the traditional and agile IT departments.

Table 1. Comparison between traditional IT department and agile IT department

Feature	Traditional IT Department	Agile IT Department
Management style	Command and control	Leadership and collaboration
Communication	Formal	Formal and Informal
Development model	Traditional Software Development Life Cycle	The Evolutionary delivery lifecycle model
Organizational structure	High formalization	Flexible
Team building	Mainly IT staff	Cross-functional teams
Customer involvement	Low	High
Cost	Mainly Capital Expenses (CapEx)	Moving toward Operating Expenses (OpEx)
Architecture	Rigid, new resources require long time to be added	Agile, new resources can be added faster

Source: (Adapted by the author from (Stoica, Mircea & Ghilic-micu, 2013))

MAIN CHARACTERISTICS OF AGILE IT DEPARTMENT

Agile IT department can be characterized as follows:

- **Business Oriented:** Agile IT department goes beyond operation and support to create business values for the entire organization. Acquiring new technologies will be based on the business values they can generate instead of focusing on their technical benefits. One example of business orientation is the Zoom – company for video calling services- that has adopted cloud computing infrastructure which is a technical solution to provide a service that can scale up at any time based on the business needs (Zoom, 2020). With the situation created by COVID-19 panic that generate more online video conference's needs, the company continues to provide and deliver reliable, high-quality services to its customers. The company find it easy to add servers and other equipment to its data centers to align with the increased demand on its services. The results increase the company's shares by 74% this year (CNBC, 2020).
- **Customer Oriented:** One important feature of agile IT department is the ability to collaborate with the customers internally and externally (Châlons and Dufft, 2017). Agile IT department should enforce interaction between the organization and its customers through digital services and underlying digital infrastructure (Tronvoll et al, 2020). Customer co-creation activities are examples of customer orientated approach that can be achieved through agile IT department. More than 58% of businesses are adopting or willing to adopt such activities (Hitachi, 2018). One example of using IT solutions to co-create business activities is 'Co-Create IKEA' which is a digital platform developed by IKEA to encourage customers and fans to design new products (Harvard Business School, 2018).

- **Data Driven:** Advanced technologies allow the IT department to collect a large amount of data about customers and operational activities. Agile IT department should be data-centric to collect the data from various sources, store it efficiently, perform necessary analytics and use it intelligently (Kettunen and Laanti, 2017). An important element of being data-driven department is to make decisions based on real time data (Stoica, Mircea & Ghilic-micu, 2013). This will require an agile IT department to hire staff with new data analytic abilities in addition to the normal technical skills (Tronvoll et al, 2020). Furthermore, some organizations build their entire business models on data or different forms of monetization to generate business value. A German startup company built its entire business model on the correlation analysis between weather conditions and events such as sports games to estimate the demand for fast food orders (Châlons and Dufft, 2017).
- **Strategic alignment:** Agile shift requires new forms of collaboration since it has cross-functional nature. Agile IT department should be involved with other functional and operational strategies in the organization (Châlons and Dufft, 2017). IT department should have a strategic role of in the implementation of digital transformation as well the alignment between IT strategies and digital transformation plans (Matt, Hess, & Benlian, 2015). It is also important to develop applications based on e-business initiatives and business values (O'Brien, & Marakas, 2013). (Setia, Sambamurthy, & Closs, 2008) showed the importance to aligning IT activities with organizational strategy by describing an example of a company producing discretionary home decorating products which failed to align supply chain systems with its operations until it developed an advanced planning and scheduling (APS) systems to integrate number of tasks and activities. This alignment led to improving service level by 5% as the company became more agile.

Figure 1 is Summarizing the main characteristics of an agile IT department.

ROLES AND RESPONSIBILITIES OF AGILE IT DEPARTMENT

Adopting agile philosophy has an impact on the traditional IT department practices and cultures that will lead to a transition of the IT department (Gupta, George, & Xia, 2019). This transition will require shifts from the basic functions of the IT department to new roles and responsibilities. While some of the roles are new, some of them have existed in the traditional IT department but they require enhancement. Agile IT department roles go beyond traditional functions of IT department which was mainly related to technical support and network administration, today it include additional roles such as:

Strategic Planning

The enhancement of IT capabilities is essential towards the movement to the agile organization in which IT department should take part in every strategic planning activities. The strategic role of agile IT department may vary based on the business nature. In tech-savvy mindset businesses, the involvement could be higher than other business (Kettunen and Laanti, 2017). However, agile IT department should involve in all strategic planning activities in all business types. For example, manufacturing firms which focus more on operational technologies have started to think about the strategic use of information technology in their businesses. They started to recognize the importance of service-oriented approaches as well the

Figure 1. Main characteristics of agile IT department

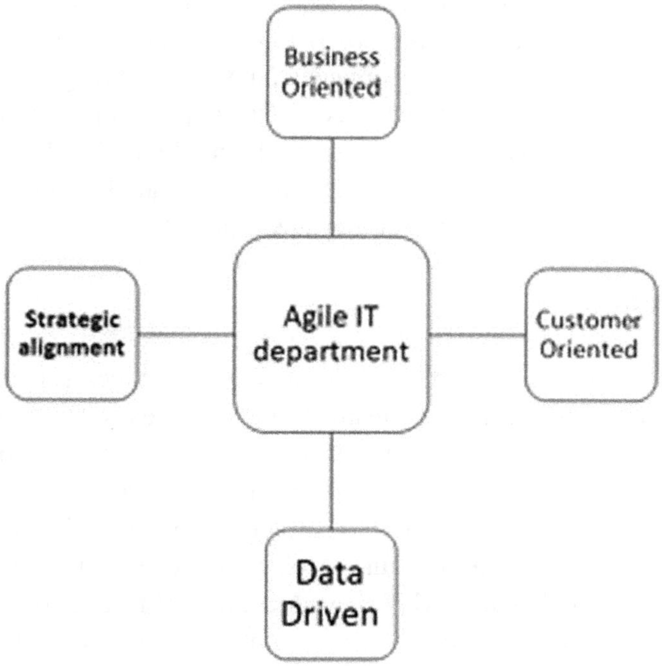

digital service environments (Tronvoll et al, 2020). No doubt that agile IT department should be part of any transition towards industry 4.0 solutions which is a real strategic investment.

Business Enablement

One major issue in traditional organization is that they consider business projects as IT projects, Enterprise Resource Planning is an example, thus the organization is relying solely on the IT department to do related tasks of such project including the planning, design, development, and implementation. Following the implementation, business will start blaming the IT department for any miss functionality. On the contrary, organization that understand the digital transformation reality accept the agile functionality of IT department to act as business enabler conducting specific tasks in coordination with other departments instead of doing the whole job. Emerging technologies and customer centricity allows the IT department to act as business enabling unit and leave a wide room for collaboration, piloting and testing (Werfs, 2013). In some occasions the IT department may procure certain functionalities from a service provider, enhance these services and deliver them to other departments within the organization (Choudhary & Vithayathil, 2013). The agility of the IT department allows to allocate, or transfer resources quickly and easily based on the business needs without waiting a long time for replacements.

Communication's Facilitation

One important feature of agile methodologies is the facilitation of open and effective communication with all stakeholders. Informal communication is playing central roles in agile methods which will have an impact on IT department performance (Stoica, Mircea & Ghilic-micu, 2013). Agile IT department should provide applications to ease the communication between its teams, other departments and among various levels (Hummel, Rosenkranz, & Holten, 2013). It is also important to consider the challenges that may affect the communication flow inside the organization such as having employees in different time zones or various infrastructures such as internet speeds. One important role is to provide greater agility in responding to customers and changing business conditions (Setia, Sambamurthy, & Closs, 2008). IT department should develop or acquire whatever tools to facilitate the communication and integrate required solutions into the organization's technology environments.

Activities Coordination

Collaboration is a basic concept in agile software methodology practices as many solutions were originated from effective collaboration within the teams (Stoica, Mircea & Ghilic-micu, 2013). Based on that, agile IT department should act to coordinate various activities related to innovative initiatives inside agile organizations. Digital transformation activities require a shift from hierarchy mindset toward true partnership which involve different interconnected systems and actors (Kettunen and Laanti, 2017). Agile IT department may provide a supply chain coordination processes to connect business units with technology services providers (Choudhary & Vithayathil, 2013). Effective coordination role of an agile IT department is crucial to ensure that any developed application is fit with the organization needs of all departments (Châlons and Dufft, 2017).

Quality Control

Agile development methods focus on continues improvement when developing software solutions through rapid testing after each iteration (Stoica, Mircea & Ghilic-micu, 2013). Improving IT service quality will have a positive impact on organization agility which will help the organization to reach its goals (Lowry, & Wilson, 2016). The role of agile IT department is to keep streaming the organization value chain with lower cost at better quality or at least without reducing the quality (Kettunen and Laanti, 2017). Service level agreement (SLA) should be designed properly to measure the quality of services within the IT department while exceeding the different performance objectives (Drake, Myung Lee, & Hussain, 2013) and customer expectations (Lowry, & Wilson, 2016).

Value Adding

The use of some technologies such as cloud computing may add another role to the IT department which is creating value out of the incoming services. It is the responsibility of IT staff to incorporate further vale to those services and make them fit to current and future needs of the consuming units inside the organization (Choudhary & Vithayathil, 2013). The delivered values by IT department should be aligned to the organizations' value chain (Kettunen and Laanti, 2017). Customer satisfaction is yet another important value that need to be achieved by the agile IT department.

Agile Governance

The agile practice has direct impact on the governance of IT services inside the IT department and that are delivered to various stakeholders. The new approach of agile governance is a combination of traditional aspects of IT governance combined with values from the agile manifest (Luna et al, 2010). The governance of agile IT department is built around transparency, accountability and responsibility to foster business values, enhance outcomes while maintaining customer satisfaction and effective performance. Ultimately this will enhance or at least maintain a solid business behaviors and core setup (Luna et al, 2014).

Data Management

Although this is a basic role of the IT department, the emerging technologies such as the Internet of Things(IoT) require the agile IT department to manage data more effectively. Data visualization products for example will enhance data management by allowing the database administrators to enquire and build reports without the need for coding (Hughes, 2012). Agile IT department should deal with emerging concepts such as Bigdata or stream data and provide appropriate tools to conduct the required analysis and make the right decisions (Mishra, Lin & Chang, 2015).

ENABLING TECHNLOGIES OF THE AGILE IT DEPARTMENT

The evolving IT industry supports the development of agile IT department. The following section will discuss some enabling technologies and explain how to gain full benefits of each technology:

Cloud Computing

Cloud Computing is an emerging information technology model which impacts many sectors. In this paradigm, IT services (both hardware and software) are delivered on-demand of customers based on specific measurements and self-service style (Marston et al., 2011). Cloud computing model allows customers to provision IT resources automatically and with a minimum human interaction (Simmon, 2018). The payment method related to consuming cloud computing services is usually the pay-per-use model (Vaquero et al., 2008). National Institute of Standards and Technology (NIST) identified five main characteristics of Cloud Computing which are: on-demand self-service, broad network access, resource pooling, rapid elasticity and measured services (Simmon, 2018). NIST also proposed fundamental service models which are: Software as a Service (SaaS), Platform as a Service (PaaS) and Infrastructure as a Service (IaaS). However, Cloud Computing support the delivery of other IT services which develops X as a Service (XaaS) ecosystem; examples include Data as a Service, Security as a Service, Business Processes as a Service, etc. (Duan, 2015). NIST also classified cloud computing based on deployment models into four categories which are: public cloud, private cloud, hybrid cloud and community cloud (Simmon, 2018).

Cloud computing provides many technical and organization advantages that supports agile IT department. Scalability feature of cloud computing provides IT department with the ability to react to an increasing load by increasing the capacity of the system (Ahmad, & Andras, 2018). Elasticity is another feature of cloud computing which refers to the ability to elastically provision IT services and release them up or down based on organization needs (Ahmad, & Andras, 2018). Both features are beneficial to the IT department and offer flexibility to react to customers' needs quickly without the need of investing in extra computing resources (Pauly, 2011).

Additionally, cloud computing improves IT agility by reducing the time between identifying the need for new resources and delivering them. IT competencies of the IT department can be also improved by using cloud services due to the gaining access to the specialized knowledge of cloud providers (Sultan, 2014). A "pay per use" model can also assist agile IT department in optimizing their cost structure to be built around Operating Expenses (OpEx) instead of Capital Expenses (CapEx) while improving the total cost of ownership TCO of IT resources (Chuang et al., 2015). An important advantage of cloud computing is the ability to provide IT staff with access to state-of-the-art technologies that were not previously available because of price and availability issues (Marston et al., 2011). Cloud computing can be a platform for many agile activities since it acts as a facilitator for other technologies such as Bigdata and the Internet of Things (IoT).

SOA (Service Oriented Architecture)

Service-Oriented Architecture (SOA) is an architectural pattern that allows the organization to use software resources more effectively (Tsai et al., 2010). SOA is a software architecture that supports service orientation by designing applications to be composed of services (Goyal, 2012). In SOA, the concept of encapsulation allows for services to be independent of the underlying implementation (Li, WANG, & HAN, 2017). SOA provides many benefits for the business such as reusability of software components (Goyal, 2012, heterogeneity in supporting the enterprise infrastructure since it works across different operating systems (Abdelouhab, Idoughi, & Kolski, 2014), reduction of the development cost (Hamzah et al, 2018). Microservices could be considered as an evolvement of SOA that is utilized in cloud computing and IoT environments to support digital transformation effort in certain sectors such as smart manufacturing (Butzin, Golatowski, & Timmermann, 2016).

SOA can improve the agility of the IT department because it allows the department to act quickly to achieve the rapidly changing business needs. Being loosely coupled, this allows the department to create new services or change the existing ones based on the business's requirements (Tsai et al., 2010). Interoperability and independence of services bring more flexibility, and allow the IT department to adopt new technologies to support the business (Abdelouhab, Idoughi, & Kolski, 2014). SOA can also support the alignment between agile IT department and organization's business processes in a strategic manner as it allows efficient usage of resources (Nichols et al, 2009).

Internet of Things (IoT)

The Internet of Things (IoT) is a system of interrelated digital devices that have the capability to generate, consume and process data with minimal human interaction (Internet Society, 2015). The use of IoT has extended the business side to include daily activities where users can now use IoT devices at their homes (Atzori, Iera, & Morabito, 2017). By the end of 2018, the estimated number of IoT connected devices was about 22 Billion devices around the world and this number is expected to reach more than 50 Billion devices in 2030 (Statista, 2019). The utilization of IoT devices is associated usually with the concept of smart solutions (e.g. smart home, smart city, smart enterprise) (Perera, Liu, & Jayawardena,

2015). IoT can offer many benefits for business such as providing real time information (Perera, Liu, & Jayawardena, 2015), cost-saving (Haller, Karnouskos, & Schroth, 2008) and better resource utilization (Atzori, Iera, & Morabito, 2017). IoT solutions rely on other technologies such as cloud computing since they require specific tools for data storage and analysis.

IoT can be aspiring for agile IT department in many ways. The use of smart sensors will provide the IT department with the ability to proact and detect any issues in their devices. This can improve business performance and increase the asset uptime especially for costly and complicated machines (Haller, Karnouskos, & Schroth, 2008). IoT will also enable the department to collect real time information about different events and devices which will allow the department to provide real time support for its customers (Usländer, & Batz, 2018). Additionally, the IT department can use IoT solutions to create a collaborative environment that make the testing activities more sharable between various devices (Uckelmann, Harrison, & Michahelles, 2011).

Bigdata

Bigdata refers to the large volume of data which is beyond the capability of traditional database software tools to capture, store, manage, and analyze (Manyika, 2011). Bigdata can be categorized based on specific characteristics such as volume (i.e. magnitude of data), variety (i.e. various types of data), Velocity (i.e. speed of data change and generation) (Gandomi, & Haider, 2015). Thus, bigdata requires specific tools for computational and storage processes which all together make a bigdata ecosystem. Example of such an ecosystem is Hadoop which consists of many components such as HDFS (Hadoop Distributed File System) and MapReduce (De Mauro, Greco, & Grimaldi, 2016). Data can be classified based on their sources into internal and external sources or based on their types into structured, unstructured and semi-structured data (Hartmann, 2016). Those categories provide useful information and could create values for the business.

Bigdata can impact agile IT department positively in various ways. Bigdata tools can enrich department knowledge since they allow the department to utilize useful data which was never utilized before (Hartmann, 2016). Bigdata analytic tools offer streaming and real-time processing which can be beneficial for the IT department in some tasks such as network traffic detection (Lopez, Lobato, & Duarte, 2016). Furthermore, bigdata concept can be utilized to create business values of the organization by implementing service models that are related to data analysis such as data-as-a-service and analytics-as-a-service (Hartmann, 2016). Bigdata is also essential to other business initiatives which are related to other technologies such as IoT and AI (Mendonça, & Andrade, 2018).

Artificial Intelligence (AI)

Artificial Intelligence (AI) is the ability of a machine or a program to perform tasks that require intelligence such as speech recognition, images classification, problem-solving (Dinh, & Thai, 2018). AI solutions play an important role in generating strong business impacts and in the accomplishment of digital transformation initiatives (Mendonça, & Andrade, 2018). A report shows that about 77% of global IT leaders indicated that their organizations implemented some AI-related technologies, it also showed that 31% of these organization were able to demonstrate the business value by applying AI solutions (Mindtree, 2019. Some AI applications that have been utilized recently are self-driving vehicles, delivery robots (Dinh, & Thai, 2018) and chatbots (Shirai et al, 2018).

AI and its sub-categories such as machine learning, deep learning, natural language processing (NLP) are applicable to the agile IT departments. AI techniques can also be used to automate some tasks such as the testing function during software development cycles, this will increase the problem-solving speed (Bosch, Olsson, & Crnkovic, 2018). AI may help the agile IT department to increase the customer support hours by using some applications such as chatbots (Shirai et al, 2018). A report showed that 34% of the organizations are developing chatbot applications (Mindtree, 2019). AI applications can also support the predictive maintenance thus reducing the downtime and the overall maintenance cost (Ahmet, 2018). However, the development of AI solutions requires accurate data, and it will be the responsibility of the agile IT department to feed such data (Shirai et al, 2018).

As appeared from the context, the enabling technologies of an agile IT department are interrelated with mutual benefits result from their interaction. Figure 2 summarizes the enabling technologies of agile IT department and their roles.

Figure 2. Summary of enabling technologies for an agile IT department

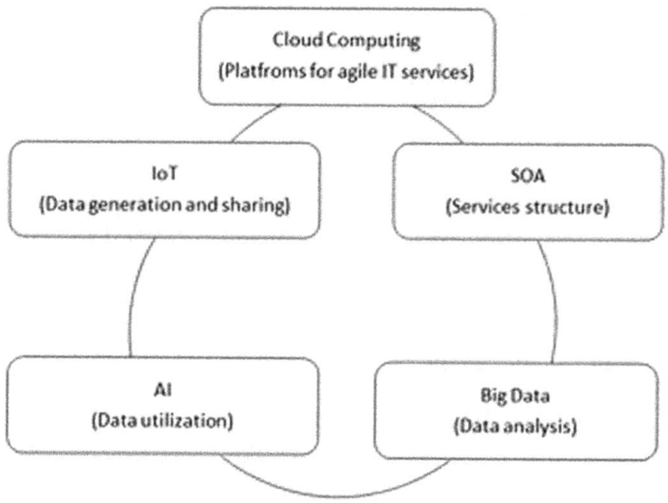

AGILE IT DEPARTMENT: FROM COST-CENTER TO PROFIT-CENTER

As discussed, the agile principles, values and practices will benefit the IT department in many ways. One important transition of the IT department is the change its organizational structure toward the movement from the cost-center to profit-center. A cost center is a unit that generates costs only and is required to save or ultimately not-to exceed the planned costs (Makedon, 2019), A profit center is a unit that has both cost and revenue responsibilities, and is required to generate revenue that exceeds its expenses (Bhattacharyya, 2011).

Historically, dealing with the IT department as a cost center drives its focus on traditional functions such as improving operational capabilities, maintenance activities, new systems' deployment and managing basic services like email (Luftman, Lyytinen & Zvi, 2017). Considering IT as a cost center established a cost structure that aim to meet the allocated budget or save from it (Makedon, 2019). Figure 3 illustrates a conceptual model of the IT department as a cost center, and it shows how the IT department is offering its services to other internal units at no cost. IT department just control the quality of IT services and provide services based on the demand of internal units (Choudhary & Vithayathil, 2013).

Figure 3. 3 Conceptual model of IT department as cost center structure
Source: (Choudhary & Vithayathil, 2013)

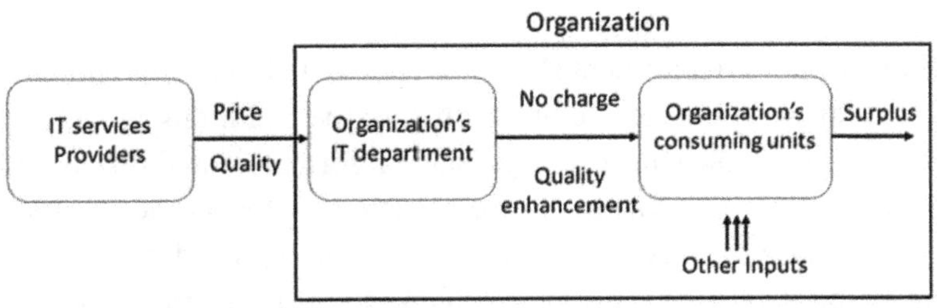

On the other hand, the IT department as a profit center need to be linked to strategic values of the organization and related activities, such as, driving business innovation, enabling digital transformation strategies and improving IT-business collaboration and partnership (Tronvoll et al, 2020). To structure IT department as a profit center, there should be a focus on profit maximization and a control measures for internal price and quality services (Choudhary & Vithayathil, 2013). Figure 4 presents a conceptual model of the profit center structure.

Figure 4. Conceptual model of the IT department as a profit center structure
Adapted by the author from (Choudhary & Vithayathil, 2013)

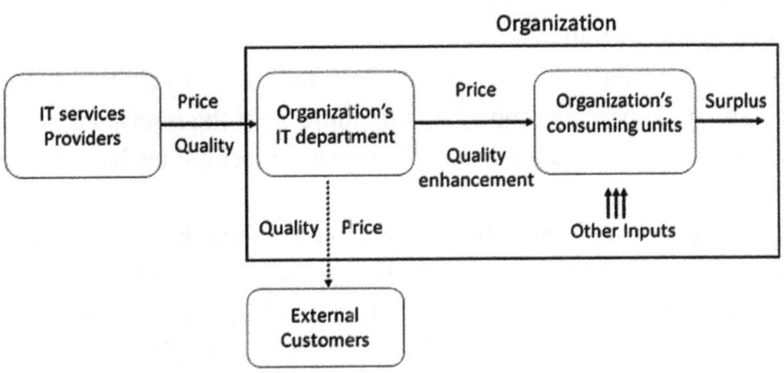

As illustrated in Figure 4, there are two ways to switch IT department into a profit center. First, the IT department to sell its services to internal units based on specific prices while adapting a quality enhancement processes (Choudhary & Vithayathil, 2013). In this structure, the consuming units are internal customers and they pay for the IT department. The profit of the IT department can be calculated as the difference between the costs incurred by IT either through acquiring external services or building them internally and the revenues from selling these services to internal customers (Choudhary & Vithayathil, 2013). Second, the IT department may profit by providing its IT services to external customers (Luftman, Lyytinen & Zvi, 2017). This structure requires the IT department to be competitive with other vendors in the market.

Transition efforts is crucial to move the IT department into a profit-center structure considering its traditional status as a cost center (Langer, 2017). Such transition may be constructed based on agile concepts while utilizing strategic alignment tool such as Strategic Alignment Maturity (SAM) model (Luftman, Lyytinen & Zvi, 2017) with necessary modifications. Transition elements should include:

- **Communication:** Agile IT department should provide collaborative communications to exchange ideas and information with business units. Collaborative solutions include applications such as Slack and Trello where people can access the same information and discuss it immediately.
- **Value analytics:** Agile IT department should be able to offer metrics that are understood by IT and business units. These metrics should be accessed and updated using real time data. Agile IT department should be data-driven decision-making unit and is required to have multiple dashboards through the establishment of business intelligence (BI) tools and even bigdata technologies where applicable.
- **Partnership:** Strategic partnership is important for agile IT department while moving into a profit center since it will be engaged in relations with different parties. This includes IT service providers who can provide high quality, low cost services with sound expertise in their domains. The IT department need also to understand the strategies and value streams of its internal customers in order to provide a better quality services. the department need to receive and send relevant data to achieve proactive responses and actions.
- **Dynamic scoping:** As a profit center IT department should achieve a dynamic and flexible infrastructure to deliver customized solutions to internal and external customers based on emerging technologies where possible to support its dynamic scope. Services from the cloud can help in providing dynamic IT scope as it provides more agility to IT operations and offers on-demand features that enables innovation.
- **Competencies development:** Structuring IT department as a profit center requires human resources that are able to generate competitive advantages for the internal units. IT staff will need to acquire new skills such as data analytics and negotiation techniques besides their computer skills.

It should be noticed that although the agile IT department should be transformed into a profit center, some tasks related cost center concept may continue to exist (Choudhary & Vithayathil, 2013). Agile IT department is required to adopt mixed strategy that combine cost, leadership and differentiation strategies to achieve the best performance (Hitt, Ireland & Hoskisson, 2007). Agile IT department have the advantage to be an internal consultant for the entire organization while acquiring or consuming technology services.

CHANGE MANAGEMENT OF AGILE IT DEPARTMENT

Introducing new IT projects and practices into the organization drive changes in processes and workflows across the organization. Such changes may affect some people in the organization either in their job roles or their position in the organization structure (Voehl & Harrington, 2016). Change management is defined as "*the process, tools, and techniques to manage the people side of change to achieve the required business outcome*" (Voehl & Harrington, 2016, p.6). Many factors can lead to an effective change management such as executive sponsorship, right vendor selection and active user involvement (Altamony, 2016).

Agile IT department is built to be flexible and prone to frequent changes, this require an effective change management during new activities development for the department (Beck et al. 2001). Change management in an agile IT department should consider many actors in the organization not only the IT staff (Luna et al, 2010). Effective change management can mitigate the concerns related to this change and allow for a successful transition toward an agile department (Alharbi, Atkins, & Stanier, 2016). A practical guide to manage the change at the departmental level include the following steps as mentioned in (Cameron, & Quinn, 2011) and (Gupta, George & Xia,2019):

- The various stakeholders of the department should involve effective communications regarding the transition.
- A shared understanding of the desired outcomes should be developed in the department to enable different stakeholders creating a culture to support this transition.
- Common agreement about the implications of such a transition should be circulated.
- The desired values underlying this movement should be identified by various actors.
- Supportive behaviors and practices need to be developed to encourage this movement.
- Clear governance and implementation plan should be settled for effective implementation.

HANDLING THE INTERNAL CUSTOMERS

IT department was seen in the past as department which may hinder innovation more often than they enable it which rise some complaints of business leaders and users about the slow pace of application development, technology that is not aligned with business strategy. However, IT units are transforming into something completely different. It is to establish the basis for coordinating and integrating knowledge that is distributed across the organization and required to build capabilities and products underpinned by IT. Agile IT department is set to work with other units of the organization to create a new concepts with the organization to frame the relation between IT and business units. Few things need to be redefined and one of them are the concept pf internal customer.

Defining the Internal Customers

The very thought of considering employee as customer suggests that internal customers may be have similar characteristics as the external ones. Internal customer relationship is divided into three parts as discussed in Sharma, S. (2016):

- Employees are considered a customer of an organization
- Employees are customer and supplier of each other
- Functional departments are customer and supplier of each other

Employee may be aware of the organization overall objective and mission but may not be fully aware of specific directions of each department. Hence it becomes very important to treat the other departments as customer to the agile IT department.

However, the concept of applying external customers handling tools upon internal customers may not always work as the condition or state may be different. The agile IT department is not trying differentiation techniques here but rather communicating its philosophy and strategies to prepare employee and other stakeholders to successfully face the new structure (Hummel, Rosenkranz, & Holten, 2013).

Organizations encourage employees to adapt an understanding that they need to help each other. The focus is to ensure that employee across departments collaborate in smooth and efficient manner. This will help the organization deliver better practices of total quality management. Therefore, organizations' employees perform their duties without any issues that affect the quality. As for the relationship between IT department and other functional departments, the concept of internal profit and cost centers will be applied. Here IT department will have its own internal targets to achieve and to drive overall business profits.

The Difference Between Cost and Value

In order to increase profitability when considering IT services pricing, it is important to know the difference between cost and value:

- Cost of a product or service is the amount you spend to produce it (Conti, 1998).
- Price is the monetary value of providing the product or service (Economicsonline, 2020).
- Perceived Value which is what customer believes the product or service is worth (Tai, 2011).

Wherever possible, then, IT department as a service provider should set prices that reflect the value they provide – not just the cost.

Selecting the Right Pricing Model for Internal IT Services

It is important to pay attention when choosing a pricing model and it should also be possible to modify it over time and/or/if and when the business model changes. When developing a product, it is often necessary to include various pricing models to develop an optimal total supply at the right viable prices.

The pricing model also differs from pricing strategy, however to some extent, they overlap, and the pricing model is usually a key part of business strategy. The pricing model can often be customized to be fit with perceptions of price. The right pricing model is a challenging schema when handling internal customers, as there can be a need for well-defined thresholds and the internal customers should feel that the price is appropriate and understands how it is generated. Pricing models might include the following:

- **Cost-based pricing:** The price of the product is based on its costs. This pricing model is used to identify the best price for a product or service (Schindler, 2011).
- **Value-based pricing:** Value-based pricing is applicable when the value produced by the product is clearly foreseeable. The value can be in the form of increasing savings, diminishing risks or additional sales. It is not suitable for products where their values are based on emotional value, which are not a "must-have" level (Schindler, 2011).

- **Portfolio-based pricing:** This pricing model is based on the fact that a vast array of products is sold to customers (Dey et al, 2018). The sale of individual products is based on case-by-case at overpriced, undercut prices or given as deal sweeteners. The entirety is the deciding factor. Different product-specific pricing models can be utilized for different portfolio products.
- **Staggered or Volume-based pricing:** Usage-based pricing is often also mentioned. There can be one or more variables (Dey et al, 2018). A basic error is to price the product strongly according to the number of users when the product is targeted for business use and a wide range of users is advised. Cost-base, user-base or value base can be drivers for this pricing.
- **Competitive pricing:** The price of the product is established on the price of competitors (lower) or the price of other products comparable to the product that has the same type of return or buyer profile/purpose (Schindler, 2011).

There are other price models which can be used such as feature-based pricing. razor and blade model, Free product, but services cost. The use of price models is based on the agile IT department needs and the relation between the department and its customer.

Internal Service-Level Agreements (SLAs)

An SLA is traditionally a contract between an organization and an external service provider that mandates specific performance levels. SLAs can be used inside an organization to define levels of performance for many activities such as help desk services, network performance, availability, application performance and availability, internal processes (Silk, 2014).

Internal SLAs between the IT department and other departments offer some benefits to the entire organization. Direct advantages of applying SLA include managing expectations, improving productivity, and increasing employee morale, establishing good relations between IT and other departments.

Defining an Internal SLAs

Creating an internal SLA is a can be achieved through five-step process as discussed in (Kübert, 2011), including;

- Identify requirements and expectations since well-defined the expectations are key elements of effective SLA.
- Define baseline requirements and means of measuring performance.
- Establish a system of rewards and penalties for compliance and noncompliance. rewards and penalties are the incentives to follow the SLA.
- Implement tools to monitor SLA compliance.
- Review SLA contents frequently for timeliness and accuracy. Technology changes quickly, and SLA should reflect these changes in a timely manner.

FUTURE RESEARCH DIRECTIONS

Future research may extend the current research by studying topics related to agile IT department. Digital transformation strategies and their relationship with agile practices are topics which may require further investigation. This is important because many organizations either starting their digital transformation initiatives or planning to make this transition. Agile IT department will take important roles in this transition, thus studying this relation and generated values is a rich research topic. It is also beneficial to investigate the point of view of the IT staff who are working on similar initiatives to have empirical information about this transition.

This chapter is investigating the possibilities of an agile IT department to move forward as a profit center while acting as a business partner, more studies need to be conducted on this topic. For example, the possibility to transit the IT department into an investment unit that can provide services to external organization may enhance the role of agile IT department is an interesting topic for the research. Although some researchers studied the impact of cloud-based services on IT governance structure (Choudhary & Vithayathil, 2013), there is a need to study the impact of combined technologies such as Bigdata and IoT on the governance structure of IT department. Some researchers studied the impact of IT department culture on agile software development practices (Gupta, George & Xia,2019), however, this is still a research topic considering that IT departments are belonging to organizations that are in different domains which can reveal interesting findings.

Another important area for research could be the identification of new skills for IT staff such as problem-solving, negotiation skills to cope with the upcoming changes. This identification should be linked with other areas such as the design thinking process and their roles in digital transformation and agile IT department. One directly related area of research could be the assessment of the existing technological capabilities on the development of agile IT department, as well developing an assessment tool that can measure the department readiness for transformation into agile behaviors.

CONCLUSION

Organizations that wish to survive must stay agile and respond quickly to changes in its marketplace and environment. Many organizations around the world from various domains have already started their digital transformation attempts to improve their business and to stay competitive. Agility is considered as one of the main elements that support the digital transformation journey. Organizations must have an IT department that is structured to be able to respond to the rapid changes while supporting agility.

This chapters provided insights of agile IT department as a unit that applies agile principles and values in all IT department practices. The chapter highlighted also the main characteristics of agile IT department and its new roles and responsibilities. Then, it discussed the enabling technologies which can help in the transition of traditional IT department into an agile IT department. The steps of moving from cost center to profit center are also discussed along with related SLAs, pricing schemes and change management processes.

Ultimately, the chapter showed the importance of restructuring the IT department into an agile department and how this transition can be achieved. Future work includes the development of readiness tool that can measure the agility of the IT department and effects on the organizations.

REFERENCES

Abdelouhab, K. A., Idoughi, D., & Kolski, C. (2014). Agile & user centric SOA based service design framework applied in disaster management. *2014 1st International Conference on Information and Communication Technologies for Disaster Management (ICT-DM)*, 1–8.

Ahmad, A. A.-S., & Andras, P. (2018). Measuring the scalability of cloud-based software services. *2018 IEEE World Congress on Services (SERVICES)*, 5–6. 10.1109/SERVICES.2018.00016

Ahmet, C. (2018). *Artificial Intelligence: How Advance Machine Learning Will Shape The Future Of Our World.* Shockwave Publishing via PublishDrive.

Alharbi, F., Atkins, A., & Stanier, C. (2016). Understanding the determinants of Cloud Computing adoption in Saudi healthcare organisations. *Complex & Intelligent Systems*, *2*(3), 155–171. doi:10.100740747-016-0021-9

Altamony, H., Al-Salti, Z., Gharaibeh, A., & Elyas, T. (2016). The relationship between change management strategy and successful enterprise resource planning (ERP) implementations: A theoretical perspective. *International Journal of Business Management and Economic Research*, *7*(4), 690–703.

Ambler, S. W., & Lines, M. (2016). The disciplined agile process decision framework. *International Conference on Software Quality*, 3–14.

Atzori, L., Iera, A., & Morabito, G. (2017). Understanding the Internet of Things: Definition, potentials, and societal role of a fast evolving paradigm. *Ad Hoc Networks*, *56*, 122–140. doi:10.1016/j.adhoc.2016.12.004

Beck, K., Beedle, M., Van Bennekum, A., Cockburn, A., Cunningham, W., & Fowler, M. (2001). *Manifesto for agile software development.* Academic Press.

Bhattacharyya, D. (2011). *Management Accounting*. Pearson Education.

Bosch, J., Olsson, H. H., & Crnkovic, I. (2018). It takes three to tango: Requirement, outcome/data, and AI driven development. *SiBW*, 177–192.

Butzin, B., Golatowski, F., & Timmermann, D. (2016). Microservices approach for the internet of things. *2016 IEEE 21st International Conference on Emerging Technologies and Factory Automation (ETFA)*, 1–6.

Cameron, K. S., & Quinn, R. E. (2011). *Diagnosing and Changing Organizational Culture: Based on the Competing Values Framework.* John Wiley & Sons, Inc.

Châlons, C., & Dufft, N. (2017). The Role of IT as an Enabler of Digital Transformation. In F. Abolhassan (Ed.), *The Drivers of Digital Transformation: Why There's No Way Around the Cloud* (pp. 13–22). Springer International Publishing. doi:10.1007/978-3-319-31824-0_2

Choudhary, V., & Vithayathil, J. (2013). The Impact of Cloud Computing: Should the IT Department Be Organized as a Cost Center or a Profit Center? *Journal of Management Information Systems*, *30*(2), 67–100. doi:10.2753/MIS0742-1222300203

Chuang, T.-T., Nakatani, K., & Chen, T. T. (2015). An exploratory study of expected business value of cloud computing. *Issues in Information Systems, 16*(4).

CNBC. (2020). *Zoom CFO explains how the company is grappling with increased demand*. Retrieved March 25, 2020, from https://www.cnbc.com/2020/03/18/zoom-cfo-explains-how-the-company-is-grappling-with-increased-demand.html

Conti, C. R. (1998). Can physicians practice cost-effective medicine? *Clinical Cardiology, 21*(1), 2–3. doi:10.1002/clc.4960210101 PMID:9474458

Dahmardeh, N., & Banihashemi, S. A. (2010). Organizational agility and agile manufacturing. European Journal of Economics. *Finance and Administrative Science, 27*, 178–184.

De Mauro, A., Greco, M., & Grimaldi, M. (2016). A formal definition of Big Data based on its essential features. *Library Review, 65*(3), 122–135. doi:10.1108/LR-06-2015-0061

de Mendonça, C. M. C., & de Andrade, A. M. V. (2018). Dynamic Capabilities and Their Relations with Elements of Digital Transformation in Portugal. *Journal of Information Systems Engineering & Management, 3*(3). Advance online publication. doi:10.20897/jisem/2660

Dey, N., Babo, R., Ashour, A., Bhatnagar, V., & Bouhlel, M. S. (2018). *Social Networks Science: Design, Implementation, Security, and Challenges: From Social Networks Analysis to Social Networks Intelligence*. Springer. doi:10.1007/978-3-319-90059-9

Dinh, T. N., & Thai, M. T. (2018). Ai and blockchain: A disruptive integration. *Computer, 51*(9), 48–53. doi:10.1109/MC.2018.3620971

Drake, P. R., Myung Lee, D., & Hussain, M. (2013). The lean and agile purchasing portfolio model. *Supply Chain Management, 18*(1), 3–20. doi:10.1108/13598541311293140

Duan, Y., Fu, G., Zhou, N., Sun, X., Narendra, N. C., & Hu, B. (2015). Everything as a Service (XaaS) on the Cloud: Origins, Current and Future Trends. *2015 IEEE 8th International Conference on Cloud Computing*, 621–628. 10.1109/CLOUD.2015.88

Economicsonline. (2020). *Price – definition*. Retrieved April 22, 2020, from https://www.economicsonline.co.uk/Definitions/Price.html

Fuchs, C., & Hess, T. (2018). Becoming agile in the digital transformation: the process of a large-scale agile transformation. *Thirty Ninth International Conference on Information Systems*.

Gandomi, A., & Haider, M. (2015). Beyond the hype: Big data concepts, methods, and analytics. *International Journal of Information Management, 35*(2), 137–144. doi:10.1016/j.ijinfomgt.2014.10.007

Goyal, V. (2012). Role of SOA & Cloud Computing in IT Industry. *International Journal of Engineering Research & Technology, 1*(6), 1–5.

Gupta, M., George, J. F., & Xia, W. (2019). Relationships between IT department culture and agile software development practices: An empirical investigation. *International Journal of Information Management, 44*, 13–24. doi:10.1016/j.ijinfomgt.2018.09.006

Haller, S., Karnouskos, S., & Schroth, C. (2008). The internet of things in an enterprise context. *Future Internet Symposium*, 14–28.

Hamzah, M. H. I., Baharom, F., Mohd, H., & Omar, M. H. (2018). Evaluation of service-oriented architecture adoption maturity model for sustainable development. *Journal of Telecommunication Electronic and Computer Engineering*, *10*(2–4), 19–22.

Hartmann, P. M., Zaki, M., Feldmann, N., & Neely, A. (2016). Capturing value from big data—A taxonomy of data-driven business models used by start-up firms. *International Journal of Operations & Production Management*, *36*(10), 1382–1406. doi:10.1108/IJOPM-02-2014-0098

Harvard Business School. (2018). *IKEA: crowdsourcing ideas to co-create a better everyday life*. Retrieved March 20, 2020, from https://digital.hbs.edu/platform-digit/submission/ikea-crowdsourcing-ideas-to-co-create-a-better-everyday-life/

Hitachi. (2018). *Co-creating the Future*. Retrieved from https://www.hitachi.eu/sites/default/files/fields/document/sib/whitepapers/cocreatingthefuture-web-updated_17_oct.pdf

Hitt, M. A., Ireland, R. D., & Hoskisson, R. E. (2007). *Strategic Management: Competitiveness and Golbalization*. Thomson South-Western.

Hughes, R. (2012). *Agile Data Warehousing Project Management: Business Intelligence Systems Using Scrum*. Newnes.

Hummel, M., Rosenkranz, C., & Holten, R. (2013). The Role of Communication in Agile Systems Development. *Business & Information Systems Engineering*, *5*(5), 343–355. doi:10.100712599-013-0282-4

Internet Society. (2015). *The Internet of Things (IoT): An Overview*. Retrieved from https://www.internetsociety.org/resources/doc/2015/iot-overview?gclid=EAIaIQobChMIkv3Kyu3L6AIVQUPTCh3DIwFTEAAYASAAEgJCTPD_BwE

Kettunen, P., & Laanti, M. (2017). Future software organizations—Agile goals and roles. *European Journal of Futures Research*, *5*(1), 16. doi:10.100740309-017-0123-7

Kübert, R., Koller, B., Sirvent, R., Ziegler, W., & Hudzia, B. (2011). *Analysis of existing solutions and requirements for SLAs. In OPTIMIS Project, Seventh Framework Programme*. University of Stuttgart.

Langer, A. M. (2017). *Information Technology and Organizational Learning: Managing Behavioral Change in the Digital Age* (3rd ed.). CRC Press. doi:10.1201/9781315143804

Li, J., Wang, P., & Han, Q. (2017). Research on Reuse of Legacy System Based on SOA. *DEStech Transactions on Computer Science and Engineering*.

Lopez, M. A., Lobato, A. G. P., & Duarte, O. C. M. B. (2016). A performance comparison of open-source stream processing platforms. *2016 IEEE Global Communications Conference (GLOBECOM)*, 1–6. 10.1109/GLOCOM.2016.7841533

Lowry, P. B., & Wilson, D. (2016). Creating agile organizations through IT: The influence of internal IT service perceptions on IT service quality and IT agility. *The Journal of Strategic Information Systems*, *25*(3), 211–226. doi:10.1016/j.jsis.2016.05.002

Luftman, J., Lyytinen, K., & Zvi, T. (2017). Enhancing the measurement of information technology (IT) business alignment and its influence on company performance. *Journal of Information Technology, 32*(1), 26–46. doi:10.1057/jit.2015.23

Luna, A., Costa, C., Moura, H., Novaes, M., & Nascimento, C. (2010). Agile governance in information and communication technologies: shifting paradigms. *JISTEM Journal of Information Systems and Technology Management, 7*(2), 311–334. doi:10.4301/S1807-17752010000200004

Luna, A., Kruchten, P., & Pedrosa, EMarcello,, L.G., doa Neto, H. R. d., & Moura, H. P. d. M. (2014). State of the Art of Agile Governance: A Systematic Review. *International Journal of Computer Science and Information Technologies, 6*(5), 121–141. doi:10.5121/ijcsit.2014.6510

Makedon, V., Drobyazko, S., Shevtsova, H., Maslosh, O., & Kasatkina, M. (2019). Providing security for the development of high-technology organizations. *Journal of Security and Sustainability Issues, 8*(4), 757–772. doi:10.9770/jssi.2019.8.4(18)

Manyika, J., Chui, M., Brown, B., Bughin, J., Dobbs, R., Roxburgh, C., & Byers, A. H. (2011). *Big data: The next frontier for innovation, competition*. Academic Press.

Marston, S., Li, Z., Bandyopadhyay, S., Zhang, J., & Ghalsasi, A. (2011). Cloud computing— The business perspective. *Decision Support Systems, 51*(1), 176–189. doi:10.1016/j.dss.2010.12.006

Matt, C., Hess, T., & Benlian, A. (2015). Digital Transformation Strategies. *Business & Information Systems Engineering, 57*(5), 339–343. doi:10.100712599-015-0401-5

McPeak, A. (2018). *5 Lessons Agile Teams Can Learn From Netflix*. Retrieved March 5, 2020, from https://dzone.com/articles/5-lessons-agile-teams-can-learn-from-netflix

Mindtree. (2019). *Make AI Pervasive: A Recent Survey on How to Harness Artificial Intelligence*. Author.

Mishra, N., Lin, C.-C., & Chang, H.-T. (2015). A Cognitive Adopted Framework for IoT Big-Data Management and Knowledge Discovery Prospective. *International Journal of Distributed Sensor Networks, 2015*, 1–12. doi:10.1155/2015/718390

Narayan, S. (2015). *Agile IT organization design: For digital transformation and continuous delivery*. Addison-Wesley Professional.

Nichols, J., Demirkan, H., Goul, M., & Keith, M. (2009). Towards a Theory of Agile Dashboards for Service Oriented Organizations. *AMCIS 2009 Proceedings*, 683.

Nuodb. (2017). *Benchmarking Strategic Technology Initiatives with Software Companies*. Retrieved from http://go.nuodb.com/2016-database-report.html

O'Brien, J., & Marakas, G. (2013). *Introduction to Information Systems*. McGraw-Hill/Irwin.

Pauly, M. (2011). T-Systems' Cloud-Based Solutions for Business Applications. In A. Goscinski, J. Broberg, & R. Buyya (Eds.), *Cloud Computing: Principles and Paradigms*. John Wiley & Sons. doi:10.1002/9780470940105.ch11

Perera, C., Liu, C. H., & Jayawardena, S. (2015). The Emerging Internet of Things Marketplace From an Industrial Perspective: A Survey. *IEEE Transactions on Emerging Topics in Computing*, *3*(4), 585–598. doi:10.1109/TETC.2015.2390034

Roberts, N., & Grover, V. (2012). Investigating firm's customer agility and firm performance: The importance of aligning sense and respond capabilities. *Journal of Business Research*, *65*(5), 579–585. doi:10.1016/j.jbusres.2011.02.009

Schindler, R. (2011). *Pricing Strategies: A Marketing Approach*. SAGE Publications.

Seymour, M., & Coyle, S. (2016). Towards a research agenda for adopting Agile Project Management in Creative Industries. *International Research Workshop on IT Project Management*.

Sharma, S. (2016). Relationship Marketing: Process of Loyal Customer Retention. *Advances in Economics and Business Management (AEBM)*, *3*(4). Retrieved from https://www.krishisanskriti.org/vol_image/08Jun201611064248 Sakshi Sharma 366-368.pdf

Shirai, T., Yamamoto, M., Asano, Y., Fujita, Y., & Tsunami, K. (2018). Dialogue AI for Financial Services. *Hitachi Review*, *67*(5), 550–551.

Silk, D. (2014). *Planning IT*. Butterworth-Heinemann.

Simmon, E. (2018). Evaluation of cloud computing services based on NIST SP 800-145. doi:10.6028/NIST.SP.500-322

Statista. (2019). *Number of internet of things (IoT) connected devices worldwide in 2018, 2025 and 2030*. Retrieved March 27, 2020, from https://www.statista.com/statistics/802690/worldwide-connected-devices-by-access-technology/

Stoica, M., Mircea, M., & Ghilic-micu, B. (2013). Software Development: Agile vs. Traditional. *Informatica Economica*, *17*(4), 64–76. doi:10.12948/issn14531305/17.4.2013.06

Sultan, N. (2014). Making use of cloud computing for healthcare provision: Opportunities and challenges. *International Journal of Information Management*, *34*(2), 177–184. doi:10.1016/j.ijinfomgt.2013.12.011

Tai, Y. (2011). Perceived value for customers in information sharing services. *Industrial Management & Data Systems*, *111*(4), 551–569. doi:10.1108/02635571111133542

Tronvoll, B., Sklyar, A., Sörhammar, D., & Kowalkowski, C. (2020). Transformational shifts through digital servitization. *Industrial Marketing Management*, *89*, 293–305. Advance online publication. doi:10.1016/j.indmarman.2020.02.005

Tsai, W.-T., Sun, X., & Balasooriya, J. (2010). Service-Oriented Cloud Computing Architecture. *2010 Seventh International Conference on Information Technology: New Generations*, 684–689. 10.1109/ITNG.2010.214

Uckelmann, D., Harrison, M., & Michahelles, F. (2011). An Architectural Approach Towards the Future Internet of Things. In D. Uckelmann, M. Harrison, & F. Michahelles (Eds.), *Architecting the Internet of Things*. Springer Berlin Heidelberg. doi:10.1007/978-3-642-19157-2_1

Usländer, T., & Batz, T. (2018). Agile Service Engineering in the Industrial Internet of Things. *Future Internet, 10*(10), 100. doi:10.3390/fi10100100

Vaquero, L. M., Rodero-Merino, L., Caceres, J., & Lindner, M. (2008). A break in the clouds. *Computer Communication Review, 39*(1), 50–55. doi:10.1145/1496091.1496100

Voehl, F., & Harrington, H. J. (2016). *Change Management: Manage the Change or It Will Manage You*. Taylor & Francis Group, LLC.

Watson, A. (2020). *Number of Netflix paying streaming subscribers worldwide from 3rd quarter 2011 to 4th quarter 2019*. Retrieved March 5, 2020, from https://www.statista.com/statistics/250934/quarterly-number-of-netflix-streaming-subscribers-worldwide/

Werfs, M. (2013). *Agile IT Departments – Concepts, Frameworks, Feasibility (Part 1)*. Retrieved March 22, 2020, from https://thinkcreative30.wordpress.com/2013/03/01/agile-it-departments-concepts-frameworks-feasibility-part-1/

Zoom. (2020). *Here's How Zoom Provides Industry-Leading Video Capacity*. Retrieved March 25, 2020, from https://blog.zoom.us/wordpress/2019/06/26/zoom-can-provide-increase-industry-leading-video-capacity/

KEY TERMS AND DEFINITIONS

Agile IT Department: Is a flexible learning unit which implements agile methodology principles across the entire IT department to deliver IT services and response to the organization's needs effectively.

Agile Organization: An organization follows the practices and attributes which allows the organization to be adaptable with any market changes and create customer-driven culture.

AI: Artificial intelligent (AI) is the ability of machine or program to perform tasks requiring intelligence such as speech recognition, images classification, problem-solving.

Bigdata: Bigdata refers to the large volume of data which is beyond the capability of traditional database software tools to capture, store, manage, and analyze.

Cloud Computing: Is an information technology model where IT services (both hardware and software) are delivered on-demand to consumers over a network in a self-service fashion, independent of device and location.

Cost Center: Is a unit that generates costs and is responsible only for non-exceeding (or saving) the planned costs.

IoT: The internet of things (IoT) is a system of interrelated digital devices where these devices have the computing capability to generate, consume and process data with minimal human interaction.

Profit Center: A profit center is a unit that has both cost and revenue responsibilities and generates revenue more than its expenses.

SOA: Service-oriented architecture (SOA): is an architectural pattern that allows an organization to use software resources more effectively.

Chapter 8
Artificial Intelligence Effects on Contracts and Contracting

Fatmah Baothman
King Abdulaziz University, Saudi Arabia

ABSTRACT

Artificial intelligence (AI) will continue to disrupt everything in the future; in the authors' view, AI needs a couple of years for perfect implementation. We need to minimize future AI negative impacts by passing suitable risk avoidance mechanisms for reaching global human satisfaction. Artificial intelligence has a critical role in converting the unstructured documents into structured enterprise data. Through implementing AI in contractual management, enterprises can get assistance in assessing risks and opportunities of businesses. The mission will be to develop and implement an AI strategy for the organization by selecting the best AI techniques and methodology for advancing legal documents' manipulation to assist managers in implementing and generating contracts and contracting analysis.

INTRODUCTION

Contract management is an old field that has been penetrated by various technologies to facilitate its operation and enhance its performance. Plenty of lawyers and assistance work for decades to enforce contracting and investigate related activities. Artificial Intelligence has been evolving and transforming since long time; however, it was not able to penetrate plenty of fields including the contract management.

Nowadays, both fields passed several hurdles and advanced too much. As the level of maturity have increased to comfortable levels, real value is coming out of the joint activities.

According to (Gartner,2020), by 2023, artificial intelligence (AI) will enable 30% faster contract negotiation and document completion processes in organizations that deploy leading contract life cycle management (CLM) solutions. The objective of this chapter is to study few use cases for using AI in contract management, while discussing its pros and cons. Associated processes are also discussed an evaluated to obtain the best behaviors and results.

DOI: 10.4018/978-1-7998-4501-0.ch008

BACKGROUND

Utilizing new technologies can lead to considerable increase in efficiency and thus clear competitive advantage (PWC, 2014). Emerging technologies have reached every aspect and contract management is not an exception. Topics of managing risks in IT contracts or governance and vendor management are prominent take in the extant IT outsourcing literature (Lacity, Khan, & Willcocks, 2009).

Contracts by itself was rigid and hard to manage, especially when companies prepare for changes in business environment and networks in international business contracts (Zhang & Ahtonen, 2016). Assuming complete contracting terms, people are sometimes thinking about an issue the wrong way, while the problem is caused originally because the contract is incomplete. (Hart, 2017). A theory of governance introducing two modes of economic governance (relation-based vs. rule-based) is required to explain strategic management and international business. (Shaomin, Senug Ho & Shuhe, 2004). It is important to understand how flexibility is introduced and adopted in the context of multi-cultural business (Zhang & Ahtonen, 2016).

Under such situations, companies will need to require new skills and tools that will support flexible adaptation to changing circumstances. However, a multi-case study showed that while flexibility is frequently called for in projects, it was rarely prepared for. (Olsson, 2006). In here, artificial intelligence is adding enormous enhancements in such fields. AI can study several factors at the same time and provide real consensus. Several related opportunities are there to utilize AI (Hall & Pesenti, 2017).

ARTIFICIAL INTELLIGENCE PAST CURRENT AND FUTURE

In the 80s, the focus of Artificial Intelligence (AI) was on machine learning enabling business intelligence capabilities to optimize operations and maximize profit. Big data analysis allowed decision support systems for managers; it involved robots that served in the engineering control system to perform repetitive tasks. During the past two decades, AI modified its goal from solving complex problems inside the computer to communications, adaptation, growth, and existence involving human and physical virtual environmental interactions outside the machines. Such modification resulted in the appearance of New AI, which extended its services to cover several disciplines and more advanced methodology. With the AI service and design advancements, many different types of AI evolved, such as cognitive AI, precision AI, explainable AI, and semantic AI. AI has already impacted contracts and contracting analysis, and in the future, we may witness AI innovating even new types of intelligence for systems, humans, and machines.

AI will continue to disrupt everything in the future; in the authors' view, AI needs a couple of years for perfect implementation, we need to minimize future AI negative impacts by passing suitable risk avoidance mechanisms for reaching global human satisfaction. For example, when implementing AI in business, we should demand accountability mechanisms such as Proof-of-accuracy, Proof-of-cooperation, Proof-of-precision, Proof-of-existence, Proof-of-growth, Proof-of-humanity, Proof-of-ethics, Proof-of-empowerment, Proof-of-fairness, Proof-of-wealth. Startups may require different mechanisms such as Proof-of-opportunities, Proof-of-satisfaction, Proof-of-market-security, and Proof-of-activities. Industries would need additional sets of mechanisms such as Proof-of-responsibility, Proof-of-delegation, Proof-of-interaction, Proof-of-assistance, Proof-of-assessment, and Proof-of-equality. Thus, AI regulators, developers, and innovators are responsible not to allow data, machine learning, and decision support systems to manipulate AI systems and decide on the future of humans' without measuring its efficiency. The author believes that the current advancements of AI cognition agents are going to impact even the Turing test concept, method, and technique in the years to come. Nowadays, AI can work in parallel with humans, and assist managers in predictive analysis, empowering them with reliable decisions. Several companies worldwide were already embracing AI during the digital transformation journey and realized that AI offers many advantages to management in contracting, contracting analysis, and implementation; the rest of the chapter discusses this point in detail.

CONTRACT MANAGEMENT AND ANALYSIS

The contract refers to an agreement between two agents in the form of exchange of products or services under specific terms and conditions, including cost, time, specifications, and more. The contract provides an opportunity for both parties to run a business in an exchange of specific compensation (The University of Texas, 2016).

Contract management embraces the entire process form laying the foundation of the business case and realization of prerequisites to maintain a relationship while evaluating the outcome of the performance. (CIPS, 2020). Contract management further encompasses establishing a profound work correlation between client and supplier, which remains to continue and has been spanning over the validity of the contract. The functions of the contract agreement also encompass the task of managing affairs proactively, auguring upcoming stipulation, and responding to the circumstances that rouse in the meantime (Brian, 2018). For example, enabling AI models in contract management systems could add values to management's efficiency and insights. Its supports beyond adjusting terms, enhancing the structure of the contract language, and suggesting the benefits of contract duration and renewal. It involves effective scheduling, improving negotiation workflow process and time, reviewing approvals with each change, determining the number of disagreements, suggesting alignments between contrasts, conducting a fast revision of past contracts. According to Beverly Rich, firms lose between 5% to 40% of values due to inefficiency in contracting. Manual contracts require enormous resources and hundreds of hours to draft, review, approve, process, and negotiate contracts. Thus, AI helps companies to solve challenging issues of business contracts, such as decreasing disputes, improve negotiation, ensuring consistency, and extracting information, assessing risk quicky, tracking records by using predictive analytic and recommender systems, and data mining.

The Process of Initiating a Contract

When two business entities tend to make a joint venture together, a contract embraces the specified course of actions, which are promulgated by both the entities. Contract capacitates them as a blueprint that figures out the obligations and responsibilities of each entity involved in endorsing its particulars. The contract is highly impactful in generating business profits to a greater extent as they make substantial stress on generating revenues and incurring expenses (Business News Daily, 2019). Prominent business companies have realized the viability of refining their abilities to control, dealing, and implementing the conditions of terms, specified in the contract, once the relevant parties endorse a contract. (Cummins, David & Kawamoto, 2011). Business to Business (B2B) services, due to their process orienting nature and their complicated and protracted business operations infer that drafting, procuring, and the procedure of handling the contract has proven to be more intricate in comparison to goods related business operations and transactions. (Zou, et al., 2019). Contract management serves the purpose of guaranteeing that all the groups are acting according to the specified commitments, which have been ratified in the contract after contract award within the mentioned time constraints for executing all the included contract awards (Asian Development Bank, 2018). The contract verification process requires exhaustive working hours and careful due diligence from attorneys. AI contracting tools make the verification process more manageable, and faster-allowing lawyers to focus more on counseling.

For companies to obtain the premeditated objectives of the contracts, most business entities are engaged with ventures by multifold skills and proficiency in the field of management (Muhammad et al. 2019). Some common pitfalls observed when involving varying nature of business units to utilize complicated protocols for contract management. Resultantly, unproductive practices, and a lesser degree of participation by top management are found (Drimalla, 2019). The advent of intelligent automation and cognitive technology has been vigorously taken on by all types of industries and business transactions. For the sake of enhancing the degree of effectiveness in business operations, big companies have earlier brought the technology of Machine Learning (ML), and tools of advanced analytics to have customer life cycle management (CLM) into practice (KMPG, 2019). Contracting technology based on the blockchain model is evolving fast and allowing autonomous re-write and structure rebuilding. Using Intelligent Agents (AI) enable self-negotiations over clauses or terms of contracts, reviewing similar contacts for the past decades, prioritizing tasks, assigning roles, and leading to simpler processes and implementation.

THE INFUSION AND SIGNIFICANCE OF "AI" IN INDUSTRIES

The quest to lead high in the field of smart industrialization has increased among business entities functioning in Europe, the US, and Asia. The industry of manufacturing seems to achieve exemplary milestones in transforming operational units with the digital revolution of technology (Lee, Singh & Azamfar, 2019).

In the present era, AI has brought vigorous innovation in technology that has been replicating human intelligence. AI machines are now more capable of smart thinking and making-decision like humans, as they are equipped with a human level of problem-solving skills (Rahim et al., 2018). Nowadays, machines have cognitive thinking and can take actions more accurately better than humans. AI is fully capitated with the potency to leading the market.

A study of International Data Corporation projected the global spending of acquiring cognitive and AI systems would surpass the worth of USD 57 billion in the year 2021 (Popper et al., 2018). Some small corporations work for providing AI services to already established and functional companies. However, some of the large-scale organizations are also dealing with delivering AI systems. As multifold companies, whether large or small scale, is now engaged with AI in varying nature of business models and contractual arrangements (Hall & Pesenti, 2017).

The industrial revolution can trigger financial and operational impact through enhancing productivity and customer satisfaction. The adoption of Manufacturing 4.0 commenced resulted in the increased productivity with improvement in elasticity and terms of quality and swiftness (Lee, Singh & Azamfar, 2019). The predicted future reflects that the technological spread of AI would be worldwide and prevalent in all societies. Further, it is estimated that AI technology will bring refinement at inaccessibility and production levels. It will be used as a tool for coping with social and structural impediments that have not been countered before, such as: reducing the ratio of birth and population aging (METI, 2018).

Role of AI in Contract Formation

Usually, commercial contracts are based on less degree of knowledge, more critical data, strict legal obligations, specific rights, defined tasks, and regulations. Such agreements redirect the decisions of business, which have been taken erstwhile and may impact the performance in the coming times (Spend matters, 2017). Artificial Intelligence has a critical role in converting the unstructured documents into structured enterprise data. Through implementing AI in contractual management, enterprises can get assistance in assessing risks and opportunities of businesses. AI comprehends the language of the contract and apprehends the meaning of the classes include. AI, through contract management, transform commitment from a simply documented depository to a recognized strategic and tactful machine (Cloudmoyo, 2020).

In the era of 20th century, the involvement of computers, AI, and word processor collaborated and substantiated not only the process of conscripting the contract but also shaped the reality of preparing the drafts through automation by machine (Ying, 2017). Innovations introduced by AI are now contributing much to advancing the contract management processes, operations, and implementation. For instance, when a business entity confers its contract to a contract depositary, the role of AI is to assist on critical levels such as organizing and enhancing its visibility. Microsoft launched the chatting root named as Xiaobing, while, Watson system was established by IBM, to enable detecting the historical records of the cancer patient in various hospitals. In China, Baidu engaged in designing platforms for tiny devices, along with the use of AI for financial sector services (Pan, 2016).

Savelyev's (2017) paper examines the core element between an old-style contract and a technologically driven smart contract. The author terms the smart contract as "agreements existing in the form of software code implemented on the Blockchain platform." However, the existence of a smart contract built on an encoded set of features and functions will massively enhance the process (Savelyev, 2017).

According to (DTA, 2018), by 2025, what people expect will be dramatically different from today. The prevalent usage of AI software can progress the smart approach of firms for developing and managing contracts in three ways: by altering the contracting tools which are used by firms, by inducing the content of contracts and through affecting the procedure of firm for making contracts (Beverly, 2018). There is no doubt that AI will revolutionize the work of legal departments and drastically will change the process of management contracting.

Adopting AI in Contract Management

Financial institutions are more inclined to employ the chatbots to handle daily transactions of banks for ensuring 24/7 customer services. Mostly, chatbots execute the services of personal finance management (PFM) and wealth management. They perform services in wider serviceable zones as described below:

- **Customer Services:** Replying automatically to the simple queries at call centers, recording the events of the loss of card, and re-assigning the PIN's number.
- **Product sales:** Recognition or classification of customers by the system, according to the banking products and purchase behaviors.

- **Transaction:** Serving the transfer of funds autonomously between accounts, payment of bills, and calculating account balance (Rahim, et al. 2018).
- **Prediction:** Assisting management in their responsibilities of future contracting.

Almost all legal AI solutions are now central to dealing with a contract due to emerging technology and vigorous addition in the power of the computer. Conventionally, the legal line of work seems reluctant to change. But the process of adopting change is slow when realizing the fact that technology is a prerequisite, more prevalent, and AI will be dispensing more than generating expenses (Shcherbak, 2018). Concerning AI in the legal profession, a legal AI system, will not only assist experts, and professionals in courts or legal departments in business but may operate in the capacity of intelligent lawyers, smart judges, and automated smart contracts.

Examples of AI in Contracts

AI is prevailing in all forms of businesses and contributing to maximizing the productivity and profitability and quality and accessibility of services goods. It exists in several types while providing varying nature of operations and tasks—prominent examples of AI usages in the contract discussed below.

Intelligent Search

AI helps in searching the contents of the contracts and in acquiring useful results. Moreover, it helps in quickly finding the information and works for investigating and augmenting the communication between robotics and employees (Wisskirchenet al., 2017). Icertis dispenses intellectual search skills through initiating innovative implications for cognitive search. On Azure, an AI-driven feature was created by Microsoft to take out the script from poorly structured data. For instance, if a person related to the health sector and wants to explore data related to the HIPPA privacy rule, Icertis Contract Management (ICM) provides knowledge about the rule which is linked to the protection of patients' information due to the data and cognitive skills (Icertis 2020).

Cloud Computing and Big Data

Edge computing refers to a disseminated open platform over the network edge, which links things and databases. These databases or elements are assimilating the abilities of networks, storage capacities, and applications. This process qualifies the completion of essentials of digitizing the industry such as swift accessibility and simultaneous services, augmenting data, implications for intelligence and guarding the security and privacy. Cloud and edge computing facilitate access to a cost-effective and more comprehensive range of computing resources, including specialized services (Popper, et al., 2018). Big data and cloud computing are the major features of digitized technology. Expansion and growth in developing the sensors, the enhancement and speed in storage capability, and the increase in machine learning, the bulk of data is being prosperous (Li, Hou & Wu, 2017).

Natural Language Processing (NLP)

This is a field of computer science, where AI helps in developing communication between machines, human-to-machines, machines-to-humans in natural languages. Specifically, it is associated with designing a computer program that processes a bulk of natural language data (IATA, 2018). It includes speech recognition; a computer examines the vocalized language and interprets it into writing. The system processes communications in the form of a vocalized query and looks for its answer (Popper, et al., 2018). AI advancements in NLP resulted in the creation of artificial intelligent societies and systems. One prime concern, with these societies, has been the means to establish natural social interaction in dynamic, cross-cultural environments – among human-agents-machines. Such AI technology-enabled speech synthesis, speech recognition, speech verification using voice signatures in generating legal communications for contracting.

Robotics

Productive technologies such as preservative manufacturing, amplified reality, and advancement in robotics are stimuli for augmenting the drive towards machine (M4.0). It is a business archetypal that is more adaptive and ensures reliable headway towards employing new technological designs along with its long- and short-term effects (Lee, Singh, & Azamfar, 2019).

Major field implications of AI are robotics, pattern recognition, medical diagnosis, geological exploration, and machine vision. AI systems that are associated with medical diagnosis and geological exploration work as smart means of mediators, proficient and skilled systems. Big data analysis and intelligent algorithms are swapping the role of humans in service sectors because of their capability of performing multi-dimensional tasks in the same course of time. Moreover, the robots and algorithms cannot fall ill, neither they owe children, nor conferred for annual leaves. Thus, many companies tend to capitalize on the field of robotics and in installing smart software (Wisskirchen, 2018). In my view, it will not be long before legal robots start assisting in the process of emotional contracts and bigdata contracts generations and verifications.

Advantages of AI in Contract Management

The revolution of AI in almost all types of industries have brought augmented profits and highly responsive and improved version of services and goods which have never been experienced and utilized by humankind before. The advantages of AI in contract management are apparent and described as follows:

Reduction of Errors

AI software in contract management can calculate the risk factors in contracts, perform risk analysis more rapidly than a clique of lawyers, and figuring out terms or articles that are sub-optimal. Furthermore, it can eliminate the risk of inaccuracy by humans amid the conscripting and evaluation process (Beverly, 2018). For example, it reduces the vulnerability of errors in the banking sector by augmenting the human role in cyber malfunctioning, compliance, and internal and credit audit (Rahim et al., 2018).

Cost Reduction

Advancement in technology in other arenas is unfolding an environment that is appropriate to the faster adopting of AI. The implication of the contract generator for drafting the CG contracts can assist businesses in spending less time and resources in monetary terms (Ying, 2017). The better quality of AI augments the computers to process data in a fast manner with a less cost-effective method (Mou, 2019).

Reduction in Human Labor

AI is trivial in configuring the set of skills that are necessary by the market. It is estimated to grow more rapidly than human resource skills, which may trigger broadening gaps in the skills of labor and market (IATA, 2018). An AI researcher Tegmark (2017), stated the opportunities of AI and asserted that humans could lead the world towards prosperity by using automation (Buchmeister, Palcic&Ojstersek, 2019). The benefit of AI for employees reduced the burden of work as they do not have to perform tedious manual work. Also, most of the repetitive tasks now performed by automatic systems.

Dematerialization

In diminishing the bar of exploring the bulk amount of data, AI plays an inevitable role. The legal profession, groups like ROSS, Lex Machina, and CaseText, has been utilizing AI to scrutinize the documents of courts and legal records for the information related to particular cases (Hall & Pesenti, 2017).

Manage Complaints

AI can deal automatically with customers' requests, queries, and complaints and for guarantying compliance to regulating (e.g., EU261), enhancing airline assets, diminishing labor-intensive efforts, reimbursement charges, and loss of client devotion (IATA, 2018).

Reduced Training Cost and Risks

The Catapult is an emerging machine learning working out the lab to support companies that are on the initial stage for decreasing the budgets of training machine learning prototypes (Hall & Pesenti, 2017). AI can further forecast what could go wrong during the business process, e.g., payment postponements and right of access to the site. It takes measures to mitigate possible risks. It helps in arranging the closing of the project, assuring that no issue or obligation has not been addressed.

Reduce Accidental Risks

AI reflects that human resources can be saved from executing life-threatening laborer work since robots are taking the place of humans and performing the functions which pose high risks. It has further led towards diminishing the frequency of unpleasant events at the workplace.

FUTURE RESEARCH DIRECTIONS

Artificial Intelligence started very early to add value in the business arena, but there were significant barriers due to immaturity of the surrounding ecosystem. As the surrounding technologies have advances, AI has evolved in multiple dimensions. One important technology is the internet of things (IoT) which is growing exponentially like other technologies. One important dimension is le in using these new innovations is how to manage the stakeholders who are working on was the contract management field in all directions.

This chapter described very few usages of the Ai in the contract management field, to lead to an increased number of research studies in the fields related to using AI for innovative contracting and other dimensions.

This is just a step in this field, but a lot of research is required to explore specific use cases and generate business value. Every scenario will have its own parameters and dimension and every use case can provide a step forward. Every topic discussed in this chapter can generate thorough conclusions, and number of research paths that researchers can follow to advance the utilization of AI in the contracting arena .

CONCLUSION

Artificial Intelligence (AI) will change all business management, processes, and operations. The most significant barriers to advancement may be in obtaining the proper professions within organizations to deploy the correct AI solutions. Without AI, the digital transformation process will remain iterative and never get closer to AI innovation. The mission will be to develop and implement an AI strategy for the organization by selecting the best AI techniques and methodology for advancing legal documents' manipulation to assist managers in implementing and generating contracts and contracting analysis.

REFERENCES

Asian Development Bank. (2018). *Contract Management Guidance Note on Procurement.* Available at: https://www.adb.org/sites/default/files/contract-management.pdf

Beverly, R. (2018, February 18). How AI Is Changing Contracts. *Harvard Business Review, 95*(2), 1–5.

Brian, A. (2018). *The Effectiveness of Contract Management on Contractors' performance (Bachelor's degree).* Kyambogo University.

Buchmeister, B., Palcic, I., & Ojstersek, R. (2019). *Artificial Intelligence in Manufacturing Companies And Broader: An Overview.* Daaam International Scientific Book. doi:10.2507/daaam.scibook.2019.07

Business News Daily. (2019). *The Fundamentals of Contract Management.* Available at: https://www.businessnewsdaily.com/4813-contract-management.html

CIPS (Chartered Institute of Procurement and Supply). (2020). *Contract Management.* Available at:https://www.cips.org/knowledge/procurement-topics-and-skills/developing-and-managing-contracts/contract-management/

Cloudmoyo. (2020). *Applying artificial intelligence to contract management.* Available at https://www.cloudmoyo.com/blog/artificial-intelligence-in-contract-management/

Cummins, T., David, M., & Kawamoto, K. (2011). *Contract and Commercial Management-The Operational Guide.* Van Haren Publishing.

Dabass, J., & Dabass, B. S. (2018). *Scope of Artificial Intelligence in Law.* Academic Press.

Drimalla, R. (2019). *Leverage a Process-Driven Contract Lifecycle Management Method.* Corporate Counsel Business Journal.

DTA (Digital Transformation Agency, Australian Government). (2018). *Digital Transformation Strategy.* Available at: https://dta-www-drupal-20180130215411153400000001.s3.ap-southeast-2.amazonaws.com/s3fs-public/files/digital-transformation-strategy/digital-transformation-strategy.pdf

Gartner. (2020, February 25). *Magic Quadrant for Contract Life Cycle Management.* Gartner. https://www.gartner.com/doc/reprints?id=1-1YI5K8JY&ct=200226&st=sb

Hall, W., & Pesenti, J. (2017). *Growing the artificial intelligence industry in the UK.* Department for Digital, Culture, Media & Sport and Department for Business, Energy & Industrial Strategy. Part of the Industrial Strategy UK and the Commonwealth.

Hart, O. (2017). Incomplete Contracts and Control. *The American Economic Review, 107*(7), 1731–1752. doi:10.1257/aer.107.7.1731

Icertis. (2020). *What Is Contract Intelligence?* Available at: https://www.icertis.com/resource/what-is-contract-intelligence/

International Air Transport Association (IATA). (2018). *Ai in Aviation-Exploring the Fundamentals, Threats, and Opportunities of Artificial Intelligence (Ai) In the Aviation Industry.* White Paper. Available at:https://www.iata.org/contentassets/b90753e0f52e48a58b28c51df023c6fb/ai-white-paper.pdf

KMPG. (2019). *Capture the value of your contracts: Cognitive Contract Management from KPMG and Google Cloud.* Available at: https://assets.kpmg/content/dam/kpmg/uk/pdf/2018/09/capture-the-value-of-your-contracts.pdf

Lacity, M., Khan, S., & Willcocks, L. (2009, September 1). A Review of the IT Outsourcing Literature: Insights for Practice. *The Journal of Strategic Information Systems, 18*(3), 130–146. doi:10.1016/j.jsis.2009.06.002

Lee, J., Singh, J., & Azamfar, M. (2019). Industrial Artificial Intelligence. arXiv preprint arXiv:1908.02150.

Li, G., Hou, Y., & Wu, A. (2017). Fourth Industrial Revolution: Technological drivers, impacts and coping methods. *Chinese Geographical Science, 27*(4), 626–637. doi:10.100711769-017-0890-x

Li, S., Park, S. H., & Li, S. (2004). The Great Leap Forward: The Transition from Relation-Based Governance to Rule-Based Governance. *Organizational Dynamics, 33*(1), 63–78. doi:10.1016/j.orgdyn.2003.11.005

Matters, S. (2017). *Artificial Intelligence in Contract Management: Considerations for Practitioners (Part 1)*. Available at: https://spendmatters.com/2017/01/03/artificial-intelligence-contract-management-considerations-practitioners-part-1-introduction/

METI, Japanese Ministry of Economy, Trade and Industry. (2018). *Contract Guidelines on Utilization of AI and Data: AI Section*. Author.

Mou, X. (2019). *Artificial Intelligence: Investment Trends and Selected Industry Use*. Available at:https://www.ifc.org/wps/wcm/connect/7898d957-69b5-4727-9226-277e8ae28711/EMCompass-Note-71-AI-Investment-Trends.pdf?MOD=AJPERES&CVID=mR5Jvd6

Muhammad, K., Saoula, O., Issa, M., & Ahmed, U. (2019). Contract management and performance characteristics: An empirical and managerial implication for Indonesia. *Management Science Letters*, *9*(8), 1289–1298. doi:10.5267/j.msl.2019.4.012

Olsson, N. O. E. (2006). Management of Flexibility in Projects. *International Journal of Project Management*, *24*(1), 66–74.

Pan, Y. (2016). Heading toward artificial intelligence 2.0. *Engineering (London)*, *2*(4), 409–413.

Popper J., Hermann, J., Cui, K., Bergweiler, S., Weyer, S., Ruskowski, M., Wang, M., Guang, L., Hu, Y.C., Kueh, V., Wang, D., Madigan, M.C., Oppermann, I., Ryu, S.M., Kim, L., Wei, S., Li, R., Du, X., Shang, Y., & Thonet, G. (2018). *Artificial intelligence across industries*. IEC Whitepaper.

PWC. (2014, December 1). *Industry 4.0 - Opportunities and Challanges of the industrial internet.* Retrieved November 10, 2020, from https://www.pwc.nl/en/assets/documents/pwc-industrie-4-0.pdf: https://www.pwc.nl/en/assets/documents/pwc-industrie-4-0.pdf

Rahim, S. R. M., Mohammad, Z. Z., Bakar, J. A., Mohsin, F. H., & Isa, N. M. (2018). Artificial intelligence, smart contract and islamic finance. *Asian Social Science*, *14*(2), 145. doi:10.5539/ass.v14n2p145

Savelyev, A. (2017). Contract law 2.0: 'Smart' contracts as the beginning of the end of classic contract law. *Information & Communications Technology Law*, *26*(2), 116–134. doi:10.1080/13600834.2017.1301036

Shcherbak, S. (2018). *AI in Legal Profession*. Available at: https://synchlaw.se/wp-content/uploads/2018/01/ai_in_legal_profession_latest.pdf

The University of Texas. (2016, November 1). *The University of Texas System Administration*. Available at: https://www.utsystem.edu/sites/default/files/documents/publication/2016/contract-management-handbook/contract-management-handbook.pdf

Wisskirchen, D. G. (2018). *How Artificial Intelligence impacts labour and management.* Available at: https://www.cec-managers.org/wp-content/uploads/2018/06/Script-keynote-speech-Wisskirchen-AI.pdf

Wisskirchen, G., Biacabe, B. T., Bormann, U., Muntz, A., Niehaus, G., Soler, G. J., & von Brauchitsch, B. (2017). Artificial intelligence and robotics and their impact on the workplace. IBA Global Employment Institute.

Ying, H. (2017). *The Art of Contract Drafting in the Age of Artificial Intelligence: A Comparative Study Based on US, UK and Austrian Law*. Transatlantic Technology Law Forum.

Zhang, Y., & Ahtonen, R. (2016). *Flexibility in Contracts and Contractual Practice: Empirical Study in China*. University of Eastern Finland.

Zou, W., Brax, S. A., Vuori, M., & Rajala, R. (2019). The influences of contract structure, contracting process, and service complexity on supplier performance. *International Journal of Operations & Production Management, 39*(4), 525–549. doi:10.1108/IJOPM-12-2016-0756

ADDITIONAL READING

Grembergen, W. (Ed.). (2003). *Strategies for information technology governance*. Idea Group Publishing.

Kark, K., & Vanderslice, P. (2015). CIO as Chief Integration Officer. Deloitte Journal of Tech Trends 2015, 6 (1), 04-19.

Lacity, M., Khan, S., & Willcocks, L. (2009, September 1). A Review of the IT Outsourcing Literature: Insights for Practice. *The Journal of Strategic Information Systems, 18*(3), 130–146. doi:10.1016/j.jsis.2009.06.002

Rigby, D., Sutherland, J., & Takeutchi, H. (2016, May 1). Embracing Agile: How to master the process that's transfroming management. *Harvard Busienss Review*, pp. 1-11.

Shalan, M., & Anaim, N. (2017). The SMAC Opportunity Contracts: Generating Value From Responsive Agile Risk-Oriented Techniques. In J.-É. Pelet, Mobile Platforms, Design, and Apps for Social Commerce (pp. 115-134). Hershey: IGI Global.

Zheng, Z., Xie, S., Dai, H.-N., Chen, W., Chen, X., Weng, J., & Imran, M. (2019). An Overview on Smart Contracts: Challenges, Advances and Platforms. *Future Generation Computer Systems*, 1–19. doi:10.1016/j.future.2019.12.019

KEY TERMS AND DEFINITIONS

Artificial Intelligence: The ability of a computer or a robot controlled by a computer to do tasks that are usually done by humans because they require human intelligence and discernment.

Innovative Contracts: Contracting structure that enables the maximization of opportunities and reduction of risk based on agile and smart features.

Machine Learning: Machine learning is an application of artificial intelligence (AI) that provides systems the ability to automatically learn and improve from experience without being explicitly programmed.

Risk Management: The act of handling the risk exposure through mitigation, acceptance, sharing and avoidance.

Watson System: An IBM supercomputer that combines artificial intelligence (AI) and sophisticated analytical software for optimal performance as a "question answering" machine.

Chapter 9
Regulating Digital Transformation:
Technologies, Scenarios, and Contracts

Belal Hafnawi
Telecommunications Regulatory Commission (TRC), Jordan

ABSTRACT

Digital transformation is the core value of the 4th industrial revolution or Industry 4.0. Although the efforts are focused on utilization and usage of technologies like artificial intelligence, internet of things, cloud computing, and many other technologies. We should focus in parallel on regulating the technologies to provide the proper road map and put the proper regulatory frameworks to remove uncertainties in development, investment, or implementation of technologies. Regulatory effectiveness is very important in saving time and rolling out technologies. In one initiative, regulatory technology (RegTech) will utilize the technology to enhance the regulatory process in financial sector; Regulation 4.0 is another; however, plenty of work is still ahead. Some regulators are keen to facilitate the emerging technologies and to see the consequences immediately, thus they use sandbox thinking in evaluating the impact at a small scale. In summary, this chapter will highlight the different practices and methodologies to regulate the digital transformation in the best way.

INTRODUCTION

As we move forward in the 21st century the importance of digital economy is raising. Digital technologies inspire societies and economies in many ways. Hence it is principally transforming the way we live and work together. It has consequences for the well-being and cohesion of society as a whole, as well as deep impacts for businesses in all sectors, through effects on productivity, employment, skills, income distribution, trade and the environment.

DOI: 10.4018/978-1-7998-4501-0.ch009

Governments and regulators play a major role in encouraging digital innovation and in incentivizing the development of these technologies for the benefit of society. They can foster broad public and consumer interests and limit any potential unintended negative consequences of these developments by providing general rules that reflect societal values and preferences.

However, often, regulatory frameworks lack the agility to accommodate the increasing pace of technological developments. Digital technologies also challenge deeply the way governments regulate by blurring the traditional definition of markets; challenging enforcement; and by transcending administrative boundaries domestically and internationally. As regulators continue to develop their response to disruptive innovation, the regulatory risk –what type of regulatory change will occur in response to innovation –for incumbents is increasing. (OECD, Going Digital in a multilateral world, 2018)

Today throughout the world there is no single generally accepted regulatory framework for digital transformation and industry 4.0, as there are no universal international conventions. However, industry 4.0 has reached such a level of development that can influence the life of all humanity, which suggests inevitable transition in the network from self-regulation to public regulation with the participation of all stakeholders.

This chapter will focus on the importance of regulating digital transformation and best practices designed and used by variant regulators, in addition it shows how to solve problem that could arise, and how to facilitate the deployment and rolling out of emerging technologies.

BACKGROUND

The world is moving forward into huge industrial and technological transformation, hence the movement in addition of being fast should be mature, so have to make the proper Planning and spend enough timing in Regulating the Environments for digital transformation (Brennan & Dobra-Kiel, 2018), which will Influence Regulators to choose the suitable "Fit-For-Purpose" regulatory frameworks (Malyshev & Kauffmann, 2019) to cope with the disruptive nature of digital transformation (Brennan & Dobra-Kiel, 2018) .Also the measurement of the regulatory Effectiveness is highlighted and widely addressed (Bounfour, 2016), (Teague, 2017) and how to cope with The digital transformation imperative. There are many reasons for adopting digital transformation (Bevan, Freiman, Pasricha, Samandari, & White, 2019) which is important in building the proper regulation ecosystem (International Telecommunication Union (ITU), 2019), identification of the Private-Public Partnership is highlighted (EU4Digital, 2020), and drawing the boundaries of Regulatory frameworks (Malyshev & Kauffmann, 2019). The target is to match the current wave of huge transformations in different fields and be ready for regulating the second wave of digital transformation (Malyshev & Kauffmann, 2019).

MOVING TOWARD THE REGULATION 4.0

Driving industry 4.0 or digital transformation ahead will require innovative and "smart" regulatory approaches. Regulation 4.0 is moving ahead to promote better treatment of market participants and to stimulate the spread of services and access to online services and applications without imposing excessive burden on clients and service providers. This needs to call various techniques of co-regulation, self-regulation and, smart motivations.

Nowadays, the promotion of effective and intelligent regulation mechanism of public relations in the field of digital transformation is becoming more urgent. The related business volumes are constantly increasing due to the growth of technology markets, as well as the necessity and possibility to connect an increasing number of devices. Many of the existing business, administrative and social activities are moving towards digital transformation. This tendency is stable and there is no doubt of the need to improve regulatory methods impact.

Planning and Timing Regulatory Environments for Digital Transformation

Digital Transformation and the emerging technologies are evolving fast and so should be the associated regulatory landscape. Today, there is almost no economy that does not have its own, independent regulator whether that is a ministry or regulatory authority. Regulation can help safeguard and protect people, information, and infrastructure. Regulation can foster an environment that encourages and sustains return on investments, and continuous innovation.

Whilst digital transformation typically factors in regulatory compliance based on the current regulatory state of play, it does not tend to factor in regulatory risk. Innovation poses an intrinsic challenge for regulators. Regulate too early and you risk impeding innovation; wait too long and you risk a potentially over-disruptive or harmful, and widespread, innovation reaching consumers and markets (Brennan & Dobra-Kiel, 2018). In the past, due to the incremental nature of innovation, regulators had more time to learn and adapt. Today, as firms are embracing industry 4.0 regulation no one have the time luxury as before.

Influencing Regulators

If regulatory bodies don't have the expertise in newer technologies or processes, they are not expected to regulate digital transformation effectively. At the same time, the companies within the regulators' domain may haven't a grasp on the level of expertise that the regulatory bodies possess. This will necessitate a joint effort to land into sufficient regulations.

Compliance itself is a relatively new industry, so everyone is asking the regulatory bodies when it is expected to have the digital transformation filed fully regulated for client onboarding and remote verification.

According to (Holden, 2020), now, more than ever, we need innovation champions within regulated industries to actively communicate with the regulators. All parties need to promote transparent collaboration to ensure an achievable level of regulation as businesses transform on a continual basis to meet and exceed customer demand for digital experiences.

Regulators need to move in the right direction to encourages the fullest use of responsible digital customer onboarding and delivery of digital services according to the right measures.

Designing Policy Under Uncertainty

Ubiquitous digital devices, connectivity, software, and data are empowering individuals and organizations to change behaviors, relationships, business models, and markets. Better understanding the ways in which digital transformation affects the economy and society is crucial to form a coherent response that is coordinated between tiers of government and across traditional policy domains (OECD, 2018).

At the same time, progress in science and innovation continues to expand the digital frontier and add a new emerging technology every few hours. The extensive use of artificial intelligence, machine learning, big data, sophisticated algorithms, and other emerging technologies is continuing in spite of concerns about bias, accountability and algorithmic transparency. Moreover, plenty of inventions used for medical diagnosis incorporate such embedded components. Similar situation is affecting the production and distribution of goods and services as well as intellectual property systems.

Over the coming years, digital transformation will drive rapid – and potentially accelerating – change on an unprecedented global scale (Perkin & Abraham, 2017). This heightened pace and scale of change means that a broader range of outcomes are possible within a shorter time frame, creating a context of increased complexity and uncertainty for policy making. In this context, individuals, organizations, and governments cannot rely on planning for a future based on a single extrapolation of current trends. Rather, they must explore and prepare for a range of alternative future scenarios to ensure that policy frameworks put in place today will be agile and adaptive in the face of the potential directions that digital transformation could take (Scoblic, 2020).

Designing "Fit-For-Purpose" Regulatory Frameworks

According to (Malyshev & Kauffmann, 2019), digital transformation blurs the usual delineation of markets and sectors, as illustrated by the "new" convergence in telecommunications, media markets and digital platforms. It also confuses the traditional distinction between consumers and producers, as is the case with the rise of individual" prosumers" in the electricity market that both consume and supply energy to the network. This blurring of boundaries affects, inter alia, the scope of the regulators' mandate and activities. The economic properties of digital business also challenge the standard cost-based regulatory models as price formation in the digital economy obeys different rules. New forms of regulatory intervention may be needed to address emerging market failures deriving from information asymmetries in some digital markets. One example is the transactions of personal information exchange in return for "free" digital products or services.

Coping With The Disruptive Nature of Digital Transformation

Three attributes of the current wave of innovation were identified by (Brennan & Dobra-Kiel, 2018) to pose great challenges for regulators, prompting the need for a change of approach: speed, scalability and interconnectedness. Speed and scalability result in fast-moving disruptive innovations that multiply in terms of both market share and time to market. These challenges the traditional cycle of regulation. Interconnectedness, through the rise of business ecosystems – a network of interlinked organizations – results in blurred boundaries between business models, industries, and jurisdictions. This challenges the traditional jurisdictional authority approach of regulators. The current wave of innovation is also altering the profile of risks, posing additional challenges for regulators. This altered profile includes heightened risks concerning data conduct, strategy and profitability, financial stability and financial crime.

Handling the Pacing Problem

Beyond the nature of digital innovation, the sheer pace of technological change itself fundamentally challenges contemporary regulation. The use of digital technologies accelerates interactions, generating economic and social opportunities but also disruptions, and enhances the value of past information, making it more easily accessible and reusable.

According to (Malyshev & Kauffmann, 2019), digital technologies tend to develop faster than the regulation or social structures governing them. While the disconnection between the technological pace and regulation has always been a concern, there is a growing consensus that digital technologies break new "pacing" grounds.

Coping With The Digital Transformation Imperative

Despite this rising regulatory risk, incumbents cannot afford a "wait and see" approach delaying their decisions to invest in digital transformation. Indeed, three interrelated trends in particular underlie the necessity of digital transformation: profitability, customer centricity and competition (Brennan & Dobra-Kiel, 2018).

According to (Teague, 2017), people are working together to apply a modern approach to work with new systems and models, enabled by the right tools. This is crucial to fully exploit massive investment in digital transformation and get the expected return on investment. Digital transformation is enabled by people, processes, and technology. While getting the technology right is important, the people and process issues are often underemphasized. As businesses use digital technologies to intelligently automate more business processes, they also need to contemplate how, where, and why talent should be repurposed. Regulations need to fulfill all three dimensions to get it right.

More Vectors of Digital Transformation That Affect Regulations

To better understand the transformative effects that the use of digital technologies and data can have across the economy and society, this section is listing more vectors that identify key properties of digital transformation. These vectors provide one lens of analysis to ensure that existing or new policies are well-suited to a digital economy and society. Rather than being structurally discrete, the vectors are intertwined and can have differential and reinforcing effects across policy domains. These legal parameters of the digital transformation process go far beyond the familiar General Data Protection Regulations (GPDRs). Business operations will always take place based on legal parameters. These parameters are determined by national and international laws and include directives and regulations. These vectors include, but not limited to:

Data Protection

This includes technical and organizational measures against the improper processing and distribution of data. The measures that need to be enacted depend on the type of data collected such as personal data; pseudonymized data; anonymized data; non-personal data and the publicly available data.

Panoramic Scope and Scaling

Digital transformation and associated functions, both through data flows and through processes enabled by software, lowers the barriers to gaining scope through the ability to combine, process, and integrate digital resources within and across different products and at a global level. The low marginal cost of many digital products allows firms to scale quickly and globally - more easily than with physical products - while making comparably less investment in tangible assets and amassing fewer employees. This has affected the spread of emerging technologies and associated process and innovations.

IT Security

Is a key topic in a digital transformation. Data repositories and networked systems must offer a certain level of security when it comes to the integrity, trustworthiness, and availability of the systems. Directives for ensuring a high common level of security of network and information systems can create a consistent legal framework.

Intangible Capital and the Transformation of Space

Data flows and online platforms are being used to develop the service potential of capital goods, including computers, houses, or cars. This make and new forms of value creation which is decoupled from any specific location. The possibility to move intangible digital value across the global internet undermines conventional constraints of location, distance, and jurisdiction and changes the role that space used to play for production, trade and consumption.

Liability Considerations

Current liability law is applicable if actions can be traced back to people, and product defects can be ascribed to identifiable areas of human misconduct in production and delivery chains. The implementation related directives can lead to harmonization throughout several sectors and countries (The EU Project for Digital Transformation, 2020).

Empowerment at the Edges

The Internet's architecture and digital technologies empower intelligence at the edge of networks, broadening markets and communities and increasingly moving previously centralized responsibility such as privacy and security, to decentralized users. Platforms and ecosystems introduce digital intermediation, for example in e-commerce, social networks, content distribution, or search and storage, leads often to the centralization of flows, access to -and control of data, which in turn can become a strategic asset and competitive advantage.

BOUNDARIES OF REGULATORY FRAMEWORKS

Digital transformation presents great and unprecedented opportunities. However, considerable uncertainty remains on the evolution of such transformative technologies. According to (Malyshev & Kauffmann, 2019), governments should proactively seek a deeper understanding of the potential implications for society as well as of the critical challenges these emerging technologies pose to their rulemaking activity.

Digital transformation presents challenges regulatory enforcement by questioning the traditional notion of liability. In particular, it makes it more difficult to apportion and attribute responsibility for damage or harm caused by the use of technology to end users. A specific example is provided by the difficulty to enforce copyright/property rights with the internet offering new ways to distribute content. Another example is the difficulty of attributing liability to the vendor, the distributor, or the original equipment manufacturer when AI is involved.

Possible Regulatory Responses

The optimum response to digital transformation behaviors is not always to rush into regulation as there is a real risk of getting it wrong. In some cases, a regulatory approach may not even be the best course of action (Malyshev & Kauffmann, 2019). The traditional regulatory policy tools provide important opportunities to pause, consult, question and test the approaches that may help achieve general policy objectives. They can support governments in choosing between regulatory and alternative approaches to promote digital innovation while mitigating the risks. This can range from explicitly preventing the development and use of digital technologies; to adopting a "wait and see" approach in order to discover which perceived risks materialize; or setting fixed-term regulatory exemptions (such as regulatory sandboxes) for innovative entrants.

Given the dynamics of digital transformation, it is likely that the appropriate (mix of) regulatory solutions will require periodic adaptations and constant government monitoring. More than ever, a "whole-of-government" approach to rulemaking is needed to address the institutional challenges raised by digital transformation. In view of their cross-jurisdictional nature, regulating digital technologies calls for increased dialogue and coherence among government bodies. This may potentially require specific institutional responses such as: the establishment of thematic platforms offline and online bringing together key relevant players; and a more prominent role for regulatory oversight in sharing expertise and good practices across policy areas.

Given the level of technical expertise involved, the uncertainty surrounding digital developments and the overwhelming pace of digital transformation, governments need more than ever to actively engage a broad and diverse range of stakeholders, invest in foresight and horizon scanning, initiate regulatory impact assessments early in the policy making process, and carry out regular post implementation reviews. These are important steps to create and sustain regulatory solutions that are evidence-based and to capitalize on the expertise of those who are familiar with the technologies and their implications. Beyond widening the knowledge base for rulemaking, a broader public debate on the fundamental values and preferences of society may help refine the broader goals of regulatory policy

Given the strong cross border effects of the digital economy, solutions limited to the domestic domain will no longer suffice. International regulatory cooperation is needed to avoid arbitrage; protect consumer rights effectively; and promote interoperability across regulatory frameworks and enforcement, whilst creating a favorable environment for the digital economy to thrive. Governments have also recognized the need to address cyber threats and harms together.

Regulatory Design and Architecture

The rise of the digital economy is one of the defining features of the 21st century. Digital technologies affect societies and economies in many ways, including via new means of communication and collaboration; new products that feature a strong service component; the role of data as driver of economic growth; the automation of tasks with artificial intelligence; and the emergence of new business models such as platforms. Digital transformation is therefore fundamentally transforming the way we live and work together. It has consequences for the well-being and cohesion of society as a whole, as well as deep impacts for businesses in all sectors, through effects on productivity, employment, skills, income distribution, trade and the environment.

According to (Brennan & Dobra-Kiel, 2018) the implications towards regulation 4.0 need to consider the risks of innovation. Two scenarios defining the boundaries of the future of regulation could be envisaged based on three factors:

- Risk management which defines the degree to which incumbents demonstrate that they can manage new risks posed by innovation effectively.
- Regulatory design and architecture defining the degree to which the regulatory design is agile and the degree to which the regulatory architecture is an ecosystem, with the latter being far more difficult to achieve.
- Regulatory convergence which is the degree to which the cross-border regulatory framework is harmonized.

The first scenario assumes that above risks are low to medium level. In this case regulation may act as a facilitator, whereby it is anticipatory, enables innovation and enhances competition in markets. This scenario also assumes that targeted transformations can effectively manage the risks related to disruptive innovation. It builds on the future design and architecture features to accommodate for regulatory agility in terms of design and regulatory ecosystem in terms of architecture. In terms of regulatory convergence, this scenario assumes that global integration and international cooperation are progressing

The second scenario assumes that the above risk factors are high to medium level. Regulation acts as a deterrent, whereby it is reactive arises following a challenge for consumers and markets and/or divergent to gaps and inconsistencies. The regulatory framework then aims to de-risk market participants by limiting both the depth and breadth of the applications of disruptive innovation. This scenario assumes that targeted transformations still need to effectively manage the risks related to disruptive innovation. This scenario again builds on the current design and architecture features including the regulatory lifecycle in terms of design and jurisdictional authority in terms of architecture. In terms of regulatory convergence, this scenario assumes that fragmentation, due to national and/or regional protectionism, is on the rise.

Measuring the Regulatory Effectiveness

Governments and regulators play a major role in encouraging digital innovation and in incentivizing plus the development of these technologies for the benefit of society. They can foster broad public and consumer interests and limit any potential unintended negative consequences of these developments by providing general rules that reflect societal values and preferences. Often, however, regulatory frameworks lack the agility to accommodate the increasing pace of technological developments.

Digital technologies also challenge deeply the way governments regulate by blurring the traditional definition of markets; challenging enforcement; and by transcending administrative boundaries domestically and internationally. The pace of digital transformation and its impacts on society and markets have been widely addressed (Bounfour, 2016). Yet much less is understood and said on how the traditional regulatory functions of governments, including the application of good regulatory practices, should evolve with these transformative changes (Teague, 2017). It is therefore timely to engage in such work, especially since the digital transformation is an ongoing process that challenges regulations in place and creates new regulatory needs. Domains such as retail, finance, communication and entertainment have already transformed to some extent. Others, such as healthcare or education, are still expected to change fundamentally with the growing use of data analytics and AI.

Given the level of technical expertise involved, the uncertainty surrounding digital developments and the overwhelming pace of digital transformation, governments need more than ever to actively engage a broad and diverse range of stakeholders, invest in foresight and horizon scanning, initiate regulatory impact assessments early in the policy making process, and carry out regular post implementation reviews. These are important steps to create and sustain regulatory solutions that are evidence-based and to capitalize on the expertise of those who are familiar with the technologies and their implications.

Beyond widening the knowledge base for rulemaking, a broader public debate on the fundamental values and preferences of society may help refine the broader goals of regulatory policy. Regulatory co-operation remains nevertheless challenging because of differing priorities and systems. The regulatory co-operation required to address the challenges of digital transformation will need to consider these political economy factors, as well as make the most of the wide range of possible approaches unilateral, bilateral, and international.

THE CULTURAL CHALLENGES ASSOCIATED WITH REGULATIONS

Digital Transformation is an industry in itself that represents a step-change in the speed at which customer user experience and service innovation is delivered. The customer journey is the process of adapting to new digital methods to increase efficiency and keep up with the rapid changes driven by market demands. Digital onboarding experiences drive competitive differentiation as businesses are redefined from a transactional relationship into a more nuanced relationship between humans and the automated systems and devices they use.

There is much debate around digital transformation and how it has left regulators on the back foot with the various challenges of compliance. There have even been calls for a ‘Regulation 4.0’ to sit alongside Industry 4.0 (Holden, 2020). The velocity at which the commercial world is changing is undeniable, despite the negative impact that regulatory risk can have when onboarding and monitoring customers. This section describes few aspects related to associated cultural aspects.

Adopting Digital Transformation

Organizations which once saw an ever-increasing mountain of compliance regulations and extended human resource ahead of them for any innovation plans, found now a trusted and economic solution to fit their plans for reduced costs against increased expansion into their chosen markets. Adopting digital transformation has allowed businesses to focus on keeping the customer experience at the highest quality, whilst being confident of remaining compliant and reducing resource costs.

Client onboarding alone has accelerated digital transformation are enjoying plenty of benefits including improved customer onboarding, regulatory compliance, competitive advantage, enhanced customer acquisition and operational efficiencies. According to (Bevan, Freiman, Pasricha, Samandari, & White, 2019) a ‘well-executed, end-to-end risk-function transformation can decrease costs by up to 20% while improving transparency, accountability, and employee and customer experience’.

Sandbox Thinking

According to (Rosenworcel, 2013), the technology industry has been extending the idea of the sandbox to all sorts of developments. It means that innovators no longer have to perfect new concepts in obscurity only to bet the farm on launches of large, yet unproven, ideas. Instead, they can set up small experiments to tinker with their projects and expose them to real-world conditions. Think of it like the scientific method: develop an idea, test it, and examine the new result. If what develops is promising, find a way to build it on a larger scale.

Sandbox thinking is popular among startups in Silicon Valley. Testing big ideas on a small scale is a good way to understand the consequences of important policy choices before unleashing them in the world at large. The same idea can be applied by regulators when it comes to digital transformation and emerging technologies.

Delivering Transformation Your Own Way

The hype around digital transformation can be aligned to the typical path of human psychology. Firm promises of what it will deliver can seem endless. However, the reality is based on the organization culture and maturity levels among other factors. Once compliance and regulation are added to the mix it will add another layer of complexity and affect multiple stakeholders.

According to (Holden, 2020), the old saying of 'let's throw another person at the problem' is no longer viable when it comes to Know Your Customer (KYC) and Know Your Business (KYB). Digital transformation requires a fluent change to the culture of the organization, and this might affect the regulations and regulatory bodies which might impede through a focus on risk mitigation. Some industries have a reputation for being averse to change and slow to implement digital solutions. Digital transformation is not a matter of applying new technologies to old problems and that is why regulated industries lag so far behind in the transformation arena.

The Integrated Policy Approaches

As digital transformation cuts across different policy domains and government levels, further seizing its potential benefits may increasingly depend on the capability to strengthen a whole-of-government policy approach. This requires overcoming organizational barriers to integration, sharing and horizontal decision making, a greater emphasis on anticipating potential changes and impacts, and greater use of data and digital technologies in policy making (OECD, 2018).

It is important to change the way policy makers think about digital transformation and in doing so change the way policies are developed in the digital age. Rather than considering narrow policy silos, everyone should support an integrated approach because policy changes in one domain may have implications in another domain. It is essential to be aware of interconnections and relationships across policy domains and to develop digital policy making with them in mind.

Policy Environment and Demand for Innovation

The policy environment plays an important role in encouraging factors that promote the supply and demand for innovation in the economy. Access to finance and markets are among the main challenges experienced by firms aiming to introduce new products or adopt new and improved practices.

Young innovative firms encounter difficulties in obtaining seed and early-stage financing because of uncertain profit expectations and riskier growth perspectives. There are wide differences in the size of venture capital activities across countries (Wilson, 2015). It should be noted that venture and growth capital investments are much less commonly used than other funding sources, such as bank lending, asset-based finance, or trade credit. Governments support innovation by subsidizing the cost of innovation activities in firms.

Institutional and Transboundary Challenges

The traditional institutional framework underpinning regulations – around sector or activity-focused ministries and agencies – is also showing its limits when dealing with the transversal challenges raised by digital transformation (Malyshev & Kauffmann, 2019). Digital technologies can indeed span multiple regulatory regimes, creating the potential for confusion and risks. Moreover, this transformation pays no regard to national or jurisdictional boundaries and drastically increases the intensity of cross-border flows and transactions. It gives businesses global reach while being able to locate various stages of their production processes or service centers across different countries. This feature enables companies to "forum shop" or to avoid compliance when it comes to their physical presence, their internal tax policy, and their policy for data protection or other regulated areas. The mismatch between the transboundary nature of digital transformation and the fragmentation of regulatory frameworks across jurisdictions may undermine the effectiveness of action and therefore people's trust in government. It may also generate barriers to the spread of beneficial digital innovations.

The Private-Public Partnership

It is important to establish Public-Private Partnerships (PPPs) for innovation and emerging technologies. Sound innovation initiatives can include Private-Public Partnership-based projects with multiple stakeholders to support the wide usage of key digital technologies, consolidation of efforts of diverse stakeholders is needed to attain good results. New initiates need to be regulated and established.

According to (EU4Digital, 2020) there is a spectrum of organizational models of innovation support organizations existing today such as:

- Fab-labs – provide start-ups with the first prototyping facilities.
- Accelerators – assist digital companies in growth and scaleup.
- Competence centers – serve as a focal point and a research and development concentration on specific technological areas.
- Digital innovation hubs – provide consulting to small and medium enterprises (SMEs) on digital innovation business models.

Regulating the Second Wave of Digital Transformation

According to (i-scoop, 2020), the first wave of digital transformation focused on the transformation of processes under the guise of Industry 4.0 and opportunities that digital technology provided for automation and data exchange. The second wave will be about the Internet of Things (IoT), machine learning and Artificial Intelligence (AI) as it continues to drive digital transformation to the next level.

Such technologies make it easier to analyze phenomenal amounts of data automatically in a simplified manner, allowing more accurate and useful data results to be delivered, which is of particular interest to the regulated industry. Regulated businesses can take this proactive approach for the benefit of their organization rather than outsourced solutions or a smoke and mirrors approach, digital transformation is no longer a frontage but a real-time solution for businesses that want to continue to grow.

There's no place for "we've always done it that way" in business anymore. That's why digital transformation must be a strategic priority for organizations of all sizes that see demand for self-service and intuitive solutions. There is only one obstacle, inflexibility, but that could soon become a thing of the past if regulators find proper ways to hand or automate these regulations.

THE REGULATION ECOSYSTEM

Regulation can help safeguard and protect people, information, and infrastructure. It can help serve as an equalizer so that all market players benefit from a level playing field. Regulation can foster an environment that encourages and sustains return on investments. However, digital transformation regulations can't stand alone it will require an ecosystem of regulations starting form infrastructure and going beyond the human capital management.

Information and Communication Technologies (ICT) Regulations

According to (International Telecommunication Union (ITU), 2019), there is almost no economy that does not have its own, independent ICT regulator (whether that is the Ministry or regulatory authority), managing vital issues like radio-frequency spectrum allocation, operator licensing and national network and services development in an increasingly complex policy environment. Regulators are dealing with issues such as evolving digital taxation frameworks, infrastructure sharing strategies, consumer trust issues, the blurring of demarcation lines between content development and network operation, network investment issues and getting everyone connected to the benefits of ICTs.

The ICT sector is among the fastest-moving sectors which necessitates fast-moving regulatory responses. On the one hand, ICTs are becoming less visible, but more prevalent, embedded in many sectors and systems beyond ICT. Some markets are consolidating; other markets are proliferating and fragmenting; cyber threats are growing in scope and scale; and growth in mobile subscribers is expanding local access to the Internet. Many countries are expanding the scope of their regulatory frameworks to address the challenges of digital transformation, while monitoring and enforcement are on the rise. On the other hand, collaboration among ICT regulators and regulators from other sectors is also increasing.

New technologies such as artificial intelligence, big data, the app economy, cloud computing, Internet of Things, social media and mobile technology and business models are putting regulatory paradigms to the test. National regulators are faced with new technologies as well as new business and investment models. At the same time, they are conscious that they need to continue to address safeguarding and protecting consumers and infrastructure without hampering innovation or investment.

One regulatory model hardly fits all, and divergent regulatory frameworks in a complex, fast-moving landscape may add complexity, create uncertainty, and discourage investment and innovation.

A national ICT regulatory authority often works with the competition authority, the consumer and data protection authority, the broadcasting authority and any appointed authority dealing with Internet-related issues. ICT regulators also increasingly team up with their peers in other sectors to address regulation for digital transformation. Indeed, digital technologies and services are transforming lives across society, and are now embedded in many sectors and systems beyond ICT. Regulators need to talk across all industries from agriculture, banking, climate change mitigation, education, eGovernment and health, to intelligent transport and smart water management systems.

Building Standards That Fits Industry 4.0

Industrial production is undergoing a radical digital transformation. New advanced manufacturing techniques rely primarily on innovative digital technologies, which cannot work in isolation, but are based on connected ecosystems delivering collective technological breakthroughs. All these new technologies essentially rest on an interconnected 'smart world', where objects, machines, people and the environment are increasingly closely interlinked. The timely and harmonized adoption of technical standards is likely to play a pivotal role in this context.

According to (European Union, 2019), standards can facilitate the ongoing Industry 4.0 journey by promoting compatibility and interoperability between products and processes; they can also transfer information between economic agents or machines, while guaranteeing minimum levels of quality and safety. Crucially, standards can also become accelerators of change, by promoting innovation and the uptake of new digital technologies.

This key role of standards has long recognized in the overall efforts to remove barriers and unlock the growth potential of the economy. Yet, progress in new technologies around the world is accelerating exponentially, and the development of new standards in the field is increasingly taking place. This trend could undermine the future comparative advantage of industries who are not following these standards and weaken its competitiveness in the long term. It therefore calls for a coordinated effort to develop technology standards that are not only more responsive to policy needs but are also agile, open, more strongly linked to research and innovation, and importantly, better joined up.

Handling the Intellectual Property Rights

Progressing digital transformation and networking between companies constantly increases the risk of losing company secrets. Some examples include 3D printing where it is possible to transfer design files and its objects; open innovation if the content of communication between partners can end up in the wrong hands similarly are the cooperation between companies.

Intellectual property rights need to be maintained by regulations to provide innovators with the dominant rights for a certain period in a certain territory. This is not only about the management of how to obtain a patent, but about how to use intellectual property assets in a business strategy for large and small enterprises (EU4Digital, 2020).

Currently, most countries are members of the World Intellectual Property Organization (WIPO). Thus, the legal framework for the procedures of obtaining patents and enforcement as well as the copyright and related rights need to be harmonized. Digital transformation are opening wide doors for cooperation and correlation between these entities.

Regulatory Technology (RegTech)

Failing to meet regulatory obligations can lead not only to punitive action but also to catastrophic results for society at large with the potential to affect a country's economic performance. "RegTech" has sparked a digital transformation of regulatory compliance. According to (Butler & O'Brien, 2020) RegTech is defined as the management of regulatory processes within the financial industry through technology. The main functions of "RegTech" include regulatory monitoring, reporting, and compliance.

Regulations differ depending on product, service, or jurisdiction. Firms walk a tightrope between enterprise-wide compliance management or more siloed approaches. The correct path is not always clear; moreover, regulations and rules are updated continuously – successfully monitoring these changes can mean the difference between compliant activity or damaging costs to both budget and reputation.

According to (Kumar, 2020), monitoring and applying regulations is a process that can be both time-consuming and costly as firms seek to interpret regulations, create new rules, meet current requirements, and answer regulators. It could be argued that RegTech has led to increased regulatory scrutiny, more regulations, and greater expectations. Such solutions are developed, regulators may ramp-up their expectations of firms to implement them.

RegTech solutions have been incorporating cutting-edge technologies in their solutions to ensure that financial firms stay on top of their compliance requirements. Tracking regulations is a huge challenge.

SHOW CASES

According to (Ciligot, 2020), currently, there is no protocol in place to determine the level of regulations a technology or a platform need to meet in terms of safety standards, compliance, protection of rights and interests, and fair competition. This is mainly since todays' business models are drastically different from traditional business models, there is a grey area in terms of what existing regulations apply.

Standards are not policy objectives onto themselves. They are, however, a means to promote economic development, and their role extends to public policy, including fostering increased innovation and productivity. Open standards enhance competition in open markets, support international trade and help reinforce trust among trade actors. Co-operation among standardization actors, encouraged by policy makers, help facilitate market development by promoting diffusion of enabling technologies. This would improve efficiency, foster interoperability, and address needs such as safety, security, and accessibility.

Governments may call for policies that recognize global, open, voluntary standards developed under direct participation models with a view to reinforcing developments among governments in this realm. Specifically, in regard of new emerging technologies and the innovated business models. This section is describing two use cases that can illustrate how regulations need to follow several scenarios to allow for flexibility and maturity.

Show Case: The Platform Governance

In this context of uncertainty and complexity, the (OECD, 2018) has developed four Going Digital Scenarios that represent broad trajectories for the future. None of the scenarios summarized are predictions, and it is assumed that none of them are likely to come about as described. However, these scenarios is can provide a sense of the broader range of future possibilities, and how to use this exploration to develop robust and agile policies, pushing policy thinking beyond what might otherwise be considered and helping policy-makers prepare for the unexpected.

Each scenario serves to highlight potential future policy opportunities and challenges that could emerge or grow. The scenarios also serve as a lens to consider whether current and proposed policies and actions by stakeholders are likely to be successful, under a range of plausible future conditions, in shaping a digital transformation that supports growth and well-being for all.

Scenario 1 "iChoose":

This is a world where individuals have taken their online data and identities into their own hands and are using it increasingly in active ways to further their economic opportunities, civic participation, and personal development.

Governments and firms are at the service of empowered individuals and they have responded with a series of regulations and innovations aimed at giving individuals greater say over their digital lives. This has greatly broadened opportunities, but also created new and larger inequalities. Collective solutions to grand challenges are driven by new grassroots and civil society initiatives working with existing multilateral and corporate structures.

Scenario 2 "Platform Governments"

In this scenario, a number of governments are taking a highly active role in digital transformation and gaining increasing effectiveness and relevance as a result. These governments are developing their own online platforms to manage interactions with citizens, business, and civil society. This provides these governments with a foundation of reliable data on which to build more efficient and responsive public services and to enable a more competitive and productive market economy.

Scenario 3 "Corporate Connectors"

Large global technology firms are becoming one-stop shops for virtually every aspect of our lives. Socializing, shopping, entertainment, health monitoring and diagnosis, many education courses, and even some social security provision are all provided by private sector online platforms. Through their constant interactions with their members, these global corporate ecosystems are better attuned to the popular will and have earned more trust than most governments. On the basis of this legitimacy, they are taking a more active role in global governance and in addressing challenges such as climate change and digital security. Through their new role within society, the corporate connectors have developed means to ensure continued transparency and competition, while citizens hold them accountable to societal goals.

Scenario 4 "Artificial Invisible Hands"

A super-abundance of data, artificial intelligence (AI) and universally accessible tools of digital innovation have created a world where economic activity is highly decentralized and in a constant state of disruption and churn. Automation has advanced rapidly, with AI replacing many of the co-ordination functions previously performed by firms. AI enables humans to understand their motivations and behavior better than they ever could alone and can guide them to make choices that improve their individual and collective well-being. A total loss of privacy is matched with the ability of big data and algorithms to help root out corruption; overcome cognitive biases and selfish interests; and develop solutions to the world's grand challenges. However, questions are intensifying about the future of human autonomy and control in face of the growing capabilities of AI.

The Platform Governance Agenda

Whatever scenario is chosen, there are three dimensions to consider in order to build an effective agenda for the platform governance according to (Owen, 2019) which are the policy coordination, scale of appropriate response and degree of regulatory risk.

The Policy Coordination

There are no single-issue solutions to the challenges of technology and society. In order to address the breadth of policy areas, a combination of content, data and competition policies need to be implemented in coordination across government and between governments. This will demand a coordinated "whole-of-government" effort to bring together a wide range of policies. Most of the confronted challenges are systemic, built into the architecture of digital technologies, therefore public policy response must be holistic and avoid reactions that solve for one aspect of the problem while ignoring the rest.

The Scale of Appropriate Response

Within the platform governance agenda there is a need for multiple scales of responses for different policy issues: national implantation; international coordination; and international collaboration. There is an urgent need for global platform governance, as no single country can shift the structure of the platform economy alone. Platforms are global organizations, which, in the absence of enforced national rules, will default to their own terms of service and business practices.

At the same time, because of the scale of the operation of these companies and the power they have accrued as a result, as well as the complexity of the new governance challenges they present, it is very difficult for any individual country to go it alone on regulation. However, global governance is complicated due to parallel need for subsidiarity in policy responses. Countries can learn from and iterate off each other's policy experimentation. International collaboration will be required to ensure uniform application and enforcement and to overcome collective action problems.

The Degree of Regulatory Risks

The issues that fall under the platform governance agenda are of varying levels of complexity and regulatory risk. Some policies have a high degree of consensus and limited risk in implementation. Data privacy regimes could be updated to provide far greater rights to individuals and greater oversight and regulatory power to punish abuses. Modernized competition policy could be used to restrict and roll back acquisitions and to separate platform ownership from application or product development. Large-scale and long-term civic literacy and critical-thinking efforts could be funded at scale by national governments as well. Other issues, however, such as content moderation, liability, and AI governance, are far more complex and are going to need substantive policy innovation.

The Responsibility Ownership

The largest technology companies globally have grown rapidly over the last 10 years and these "super platforms" are beneficial to society in terms of the expansion in innovation, productivity, consumption, and entrepreneurship.

However, with the fast pace of technology developments, regulators are challenged to protect consumer interests on topics such as trust, security, and fairness in a timely manner. Everyone is seeing these challenges pronounced in public debate around national security, unfair competition, usage of content and consent, and data protection. To tackle these challenges in the future, A report by the World Economic Forum (WEF, 2016) posit four distinct governance models for the platform economy. Each model is characterized by the party that would be responsible for governance

- No one,
- A government or set of governments,
- The platform itself,
- A global, multi-stakeholder community.

The critical questions for leaders to consider going forward include the unintended consequences, both positive and negative, of the platforms and how to protect consumer interests. However, there is still continuous search for an adaptive framework for regulating platforms that can be put in place to continue unlocking societal benefits.

Building an Adaptive Internet of Things (IOT)

The IoT will become as commonplace as electricity in daily life, with many billions of interactive objects connected to devices, equipment, machines, and infrastructure. It is expected to bring many economic and social benefits such as fostering the creation of start-ups, generating new economic value, helping meet the needs of an increasingly elderly population or paving the way for environmentally friendly and inclusive smart cities. At this still early stage, the regulators may have a unique opportunity to help attendant in the IoT in an enabling environment that both promotes its many benefits and addresses the challenges, particularly around safety, security, and privacy.

Encouraging an Interoperable Environment

As a result of the vast diversity of IoT application topic areas and domains, and the vast heterogeneity in their goals and requirements, many IoT devices and techniques will exist, and interoperability will be crucial (Qiu, Chen, Li, Atiquzzaman, & Zhao, 2018). While the current explosion of products and services is the signal of a growing IoT marketplace to some, a fragmented ecosystem with non-interoperable technologies could undermine the efficiencies achieved by large economies of scale and significantly delay the deployment of IoT.

The IoT ecosystem will employ hardware and software from many different vendors, and the ability to employ functionality from many devices and vendors will be key for IoT techniques to reach their full potential. To solve this problem, an effective approach would be to rely on global, voluntary interoperable standards developed by standards development organizations or industry consortia aiming at such interoperability.

Interoperability at the semantic level is an area of particular concern. Standards and vibrant ecosystems fueled by diversity are key to developing semantic interoperability for the IoT. The diversity of potential IoT applications, device technologies, and business and operational models will require flexible approaches, and avoiding tying the IoT ecosystem prematurely to burdensome or conflicting standards, particularly those of a one-size-fits-all nature.

The rapid technology innovation in IoT domain may mean that early approaches will be quickly surpassed. The regulators may wish to agree on the importance of working together to prepare for the IoT and begin to foster a common, interoperable environment in support of it, and the regulatory challenges that the IoT represents. In a second step, governments may consider taking specific collective actions in this regard.

The Open Voluntary Standards

Industry is in the best position to develop the technological standards and solutions to address global IoT ecosystem opportunities and challenges. Governments could encourage national industry to collaborate in globally open standardization efforts to develop technological best practices and standards. Specifically, they could encourage the use of commercially available solutions to accelerate innovation and adoption of IoT deployments. The emphasis on commercially available solutions and market-adopted voluntary standards would allow for faster adoption and increase innovation, bringing the IoT and its benefits to reality sooner.

Public private partnership could leverage existing industry standards and investments and utilize both public and private resources to facilitate the research, leadership, and governance to advance respective nations' IoT vision.

According to (OECD, Key Issues for Digital Transformation in the G20, 2017) report, the IoT will produce a considerable amount of data that can improve productivity across industries through predictive maintenance on equipment and machinery. This data will hold valuable potential to develop important insights into new business risks and opportunities as correlations and associations are made. A challenge will be finding ways to analyze the volume of performance data and information. To keep up with IoT-generated data and gain the promise of its insight, machine learning will be critical. In short, artificial intelligence will emerge as the standard way of managing, interpreting, and acting on IoT.

From a standards perspective, this will bring to the forefront the need for a new type of "hybrid" standard to emerge standards that go beyond technical aspects to encompass trust and ethical dimensions, among others. This will require unprecedented collaboration and co-ordination among multiple disciplines.

Enhancing Core Competencies

Given that ecosystems are critical to the success of the IoT/Industry 4.0, governments may consider policies that support participant actors and companies in enhancing their core competencies while efficiently working together.

Governments could support best practices and policies that enable groups/actors within the variety of forms of standardization to work together more effectively. The various forms of standardization serve a purpose, especially in the ICT sector where there is the need for stability provided by the arena of open standards bodies, a need for coping with fast change and the need for specific intellectual property and marketing environments provided by conglomerates and alliances, and the need for robust community involvement provided by Open-Source Initiative. To tackle the vast emerging standardization needs for largescale systems, such as integrated digital platforms, as well as the IoT, 5G, smart cities, and other smart "Xs" such as homes, vehicles, connected person, government, health, etc. The groups within each arena will need to work together, also more effectively in order to achieve the public good character of standards through open systems. To accomplish this, open standardization is likely to be more appropriate than tightly controlled proprietary solutions (Schoechle, 2009).

As small and medium enterprises (SMEs) could effectively serve as the research engine for technology and application development in Industry 4.0, Governments may consider the merits of policies that support SMEs' integration into the IoT evolutionary process and encourage and promote standards bodies to have open and inclusive processes, with clear rules of engagement that elicit SME participation.

FUTURE RESEARCH DIRECTIONS

Nowadays, massive advances occurred in technology which caused huge digital transformation in many fields and services, the digital development will not stop here but it will continue as technology is getting more mature and complicated. Most of the topics discussed in this chapter will need a continued research and development. The regulators relation with technology producers and providers need to be closer. The influence will be mutual as both will have same target to facilitate the use of technology for the best of nations, however the accelerated interaction will shorten the time needed for deploying the right technology in the suitable time.

In the coming time huge advancement are coming like 6th generation which will provide the state of art massive speed infrastructure which will be an enabler of "unknown services and use cases" that will go clearer by time. The focus will be to adopt new regulations which are dynamic to match the speed of technology.

Regulating digital transformation will open the door for research and development opportunities in technology manufacturing and also in technology consulting firms. The gap will be reduced between all stakeholders while developing new solutions and markets.

Most of topics mentioned in this chapter like Regulation 4.0, data protection and security are moving forward to provide better treatment of market participants and to stimulate the spread of services and access to online services and applications. This is a mutual benefit to clients and service providers. Regulation should be researched and rephrased to enhance involvement and collaboration among all stakeholders. This is increasingly affecting the regulatory practice behaviors and tactics to get more involved and to perform better than before.

Influence and interaction between regulators need to be researched and roles to be developed to have better communications not on the base of best efforts but on the base of mutual policies creation. Uncertainties in regulatory work are there as technology are changing and transforming, hence regulatory frameworks need to be researched to match the right purpose.

Regulatory effectiveness is an important subject to be researched as it will show the impact of regulatory practices on adapting new digital methods to increase efficiency and keep up with the rapid changes driven by market demands. Hence sandbox thinking is introduced to regulators allowing them to test big ideas on a small scale to understand the consequences of important policy choices before unleashing them at large scale, this approach has many research areas that can be of big focus.

Jointly, all the above topics requires plenty of research which is considered part of regulating digital transformation scenarios and innovations as this topic has plenty of dependencies and correlations. The development of effective and acceptable methods for requires the participation of a very wide range of stakeholders.

CONCLUSION

The Fourth Industrial Revolution formed a fundamental change in the way we live and work, it is a new chapter in human development, enabled by advanced technology. Hence the subject of Regulating digital transformation was raised to surface. Governments and regulators are playing a critical rule in motivating digital innovations and adopting new technologies for the benefit of the society.

Moving forward with industry 4.0 require regulators to adopt adaptive regimes and approaches, regulation can help safeguard and protect people, information, and infrastructure. Regulation can foster an environment that encourages and sustains return on investments, and continuous innovation. Regulators require to cope with the disruptive nature of digital transformation in order to overcome the challenges happened with the traditional cycle of regulation.

As digital transformation presents great and unprecedented opportunities, governments should proactively seek a deeper understanding of the potential implications for society to overcome the critical challenges of emerging technologies, it is likely that the appropriate regulatory solutions will require periodic adaptations and constant government monitoring. The pace of digital transformation and its impacts on society and to be reflected in traditional regulatory functions of governments to apply good regulatory practices

It is important to change the way policy makers think about digital transformation and the way policies are developed in the digital era. One consideration is to stop working on narrow policy silos. The policy environment plays an important role to promote the supply and demand for innovation in the economy

Regulating digital transformation is something that is new and dynamic. This impression should be well known to regulators who defines the borders of using technologies, and facilitating interaction between vendors, service providers and end-users. Regulatory framework should be adaptive to match the future change.

REFERENCES

Bevan, O., Freiman, M., Pasricha, K., Samandari, H., & White, O. (2019, April 25). *Transforming-risk-efficiency-and-effectiveness*. Retrieved from https://www.mckinsey.com/business-functions: https://www.mckinsey.com/business-functions/risk/our-insights/transforming-risk-efficiency-and-effectiveness#

Bounfour, A. (2016). *Digital Futures, Digital Transformation*. Springer.

Brennan, S., & Dobra-Kiel, A. (2018, October 22). *Digital-transformation-meets-regulation-4-in-2030-coping-with-disruptive-innovation*. Retrieved from https://blogs.deloitte.co.uk: https://blogs.deloitte.co.uk/financialservices/2018/10/digital-transformation-meets-regulation-4-in-2030-coping-with-disruptive-innovation.html

Butler, T., & O'Brien, L. (2020). Understanding RegTech for Digital Regulatory Complaince. In T. Lynn, J. G. Mooney, P. Rosati, & M. Cummins (Eds.), Disrupting Finance: FinTech and Strategy in the 21st Century (pp. 85-102). Switzerland AG: Springer Nature.

Ciligot, C. (2020, February 24). *platform-governance*. Retrieved from https://learn.g2.com/: https://learn.g2.com/platform-governance

EU4Digital. (2020, January 29). *From start-up ecosystems to innovation funding: EU4Digital begins ICT legislation gap analysis across priority areas*. Retrieved from https://eufordigital.eu/: https://eufordigital.eu/from-start-up-ecosystems-and-innovation-funding-to-intellectual-property-rights-and-the-digitisation-of-industry-eu4digital-begins-ict-legislation-gap-analysis-across-priority-areas/

European Union. (2019, June 1). *Standards and the digitalisation of EU industry*. Retrieved from https://www.europarl.europa.eu/RegData/etudes/BRIE/2019/635608/EPRS_BRI(2019)635608_EN.pdf

Holden, A. (2020, June 25). *the-future-of-compliance-digital-transformation-meets-regulation*. Retrieved from https://www.finextra.com/blogposting/18924/the-future-of-compliance-digital-transformation-meets-regulation

i-scoop. (2020, December 14). *Industry-4-0*. Retrieved from https://www.i-scoop.eu/industry-4-0/

International Telecommunication Union (ITU). (2019, June 1). *Policy and regulatory environments for digital transformation*. Retrieved from https://www.itu.int/: https://www.itu.int/en/mediacentre/backgrounders/Pages/Policy-and-regulatory-environments-for-digital-transformation.aspx

Kumar, S. (2020, May 27). *Digital-transformation-of-regulatory-compliance-for-financial-institutions*. Retrieved from https://gomedici.com/digital-transformation-of-regulatory-compliance-for-financial-institutions

Malyshev, N., & Kauffmann, C. (2019, June 1). *Regulatory-effectiveness-in-the-era-of-digitalisation*. Retrieved from https://www.oecd.org/gov/regulatory-policy/Regulatory-effectiveness-in-the-era-of-digitalisation.pdf

OECD. (2017). Key Issues for Digital Transformation in the G20. In *G20 German Presidency* (pp. 1-165). Berlin, Germany: OECD. Retrieved from https://www.oecd.org/g20/key-issues-for-digital-transformation-in-the-g20.pdf

OECD. (2018, May 30-31). *Going digital in a multilateral world.* Retrieved from http://www.oecd.org/mcm/documents/C-MIN-2018-6-EN.pdf

OECD. (2018). *OECD Reviews of Digital Transformation: Going Digital in Sweden.* Paris: OECD Publishing; doi:10.1787/9789264302259-

Owen, T. (2019, October 28). *introduction-why-platform-governance.* Retrieved from https://www.cigionline.org/articles/introduction-why-platform-governance

Perkin, N., & Abraham, P. (2017). *Building the Agile Business through Digital Transformation.* New York: Kogan Page Publishers.

Qiu, T., Chen, N., Li, K., Atiquzzaman, M., & Zhao, W. (2018, February 8). How Can Heterogeneous Internet of Things Build Our Future: A Survey. *IEEE Communications Surveys and Tutorials*, 2011–2029. doi:10.1109/COMST.2018.2803740

Rosenworcel, J. (2013). Remarks of commissioner - Federal communications commission. In *IEEE GLOBECOM 2013* (pp. 1–3). IEEE.

Schoechle, T. (2009). *Standardization and Digital Enclosure: The Privatization of Standards, Knowledge and Policy in the Age of Global Information Technology.* Hershey, PA: IGI Global; doi:10.4018/978-1-60566-334-0

Scoblic, J. P. (2020, August 1). Learning from the Future: How to make robust strategy in times of deep uncertainty. *Harvard Business Review*, 1–18.

Teague, A. (2017). No Innovation Without Quality. In F. Abolhassan (Ed.), *The Drivers of Digital Transformation* (pp. 73–81). Springer.

The EU Project for Digital Transformation. (2020, Dec. 12). *Legal-parameters-of-digital-transformation/.* Retrieved from https://digital-transformation-tool.eu/legal-parameters-of-digital-transformation/

WEF. W. E. (2016, Jan. 1). *Digital Transformation of Industries.* Retrieved from https://reports.weforum.org/digital-transformation/wp-content/blogs.dir/94/mp/files/pages/files/wef1601-digitaltransformation-1401.pdf

Wilson, K. E. (2015, June 24). *Policy Lessons from Financing Innovative Firms.* doi:10.2139srn.2626741

ADDITIONAL READING

Abrahams, L. (2017). Regulatory imperatives for the future of SADC's "digital complexity ecosystem". The African Journal of Information and Communication, online. doi:10.23962/10539/23578

Jacobs, J. C., Kagermann, H., & Spath, D. (2017). The Future of Work in the Digital Transformation. Munich: acatech – National Academy of Science and Engineering. Retrieved from https://en.acatech.de/publication/the-future-of-work-in-the-digital-transformation-agility-lifelong-learning-and-the-role-of-employers-and-works-councils-in-changing-times/download-pdf?lang=en

OECD. (2019, March 1). Preparing for the Changing Nature of Work. Retrieved from https://www.oecd.org/: https://www.oecd.org/going-digital/changing-nature-of-work-in-the-digital-era.pdf

Stone, M. (2020, December 26). Digital: It is not the future, it is today: Digital transformation in the public sector. Retrieved from https://home.kpmg: https://home.kpmg/xx/en/home/industries/government-public-sector/the-new-reality-for-government/digital-is-not-the-future-it-is-today.html

Von Solms, J. (2020). Integrating Regulatory Technology (RegTech) into the digital transformation of a bank Treasury. Journal of Banking Regulation, online. doi:10.105741261-020-00134-0

WEF. W. E. (2017). Unlocking Digital Value to Society: building a digital future to serve us all. Geneva: World Economic Forum LLC.

World Economic Forum. (2019). Our Shared Digital Future Responsible Digital Transformation – Board Briefing. Geneva: World Economic Forum.

KEY TERMS AND DEFINITIONS

GDPR: General data protection regulations is a legal framework that sets guidelines for the collection and processing of personal information from individuals who live in the European Union (EU).

Industry 4.0: The fourth industrial revolution (or Industry 4.0) is the ongoing automation of traditional manufacturing and industrial practices, using modern smart technology

Pacing Problem: As digital technologies tend to develop in higher speed (pace) faster than the regulation or social structures governing them, causing gap between technology and regulation.

RegTech: Regulatory technology abbreviated "RegTech" is a new technology that Uses information technology to enhance regulatory processes. With its main application in the Financial sector, it is expanding into any regulated business.

Regulation Ecosystem: An ecosystem of regulations starting form infrastructure and going beyond the human capital management.

Sand Box Thinking: A popular methodology for testing big ideas on a small scale to understand the consequences of the ideas before unleashing them in the world at large.

Transformation Imperative: In the current wave of volatility and complexity, organizations must transform, meaning a comprehensive change in strategy, operating model, organization, people, and processes.

Section 2

Technologies at the Heart of Business and Contracting

Chapter 10
Transformation of Human Resources Management Solutions as a Strategic Tool for GIG Workers Contracting

Malek B. Elayan
Institute of Public Administration, Saudi Arabia

ABSTRACT

Recently, organizations are becoming more intelligent, flexible, and efficient by using new digital technologies in human resources management (HRM). The HRM solutions are considered as an important source to support strategic decisions, create value within and across organizations for employees and management. Today, organizations are facing challenges for gig workers to retain the level of progression and development required for business continuity. Gigs are generally self-employed who are very hard to manage without having a solid e-HRMS that can fulfill their needs in addition to the permeate employee needs as well. The main objective of this chapter is to highlight digital transformation in HRM and dive into the e-HRM concept, development stages, types, and strategies. In addition, it shows how e-HRM contributes to increase the effectiveness of human resources. It will also discuss multiple dimensions about the gig work management (GWM) including the contracting methodologies, policies, and behaviors that the e-HRM need to consider for the gig workers.

INTRODUCTION

The accelerating dynamic growth of e-business is causing organizations to face more challenges than they ever had to. Nowadays, the most successful digital leaders realize the power offered by Information Technology (IT) tools for achieving business sought-after ends (Ghazzawi, Al-Khoury & Saman, 2014). Due to the intensive competition between organizations in order to attract and retain the existing professional employees, organizations are becoming more efficient by using "Electronic Human Resource Management" (E-HRM).

DOI: 10.4018/978-1-7998-4501-0.ch010

The e-HRM enables organizations to enhance their HR activities' functionality, thus, bringing benefits of efficiency, cost savings, flexible services, and employee's participation." The importance of e-HRM, is thus being recognized by organizations, specifically with regards to selecting outstanding employees, retaining them, enhancing competition and maintaining good company reputation (Bondarouk, Parry & Furtmueller 2017; Strohmeier, 2007; Ruel, Bondarouk & Looise, 2004).

Organizations strive to cope with new changes and adopt e-HRM in order to survive in the global economy. The main concern of this chapter is where contracting sector stands with respect to the implementation of IT applications, especially in the field of HR, and it is also concerned with determining and evaluating the impact of e-HRM in the context. Hence, the contracting sector is implementing e-HRM in order to ensure a participative HR department administratively and strategically, to achieve its goals precisely and sufficiently in order to tap into the global talent pools as a competitive tool (Alajmi & Alenezi, 2016). Consequently, the main aim of this chapter is to show the digital transformation of HRM solutions as strategic tool for the GIG workers contracting

Through global competition and the desire to increase effective HRM practices in recruiting, selecting, and training talented employees, contracting sector can enhance its performance and create a competitive advantage, specifically, by implementing e-HRM. The chapter's magnitude is acquired from the value of digital transformation of HRM solutions which represents the ultimate investment of IT with HR department at contracting sector, which is considered as a new strategic technological and organizational tool to support the Gig Work Management (GWM). The findings arrived at in this chapter will benefit not only academics, but also HR managers within the context of GWM sector. Furthermore, the chapter could support HR managers; by enabling them to construct HR departments, that is considered to have a strategic significance to any modern business. Additionally, it steers academics in the direction of appreciating the background of e-HRM within the context.

BACKGROUND

According to the literature, there are lots of synonyms for e-HRM. For instance, Ruel, et al. (2004) distinguish; e-HR, virtual HRM, HR Intranet, Web-based HR, Human Resource Information Systems (HRIS) and HR portals. There is a debate going on about the differences between e-HRM and HRIS. Ruel, et al. (2004) excludes HRIS from the synonyms for e-HRM; in their view, HRIS is more focused on the HRM department itself, aiming to improve the processes itself and does not focus on the employees and management. This reason is confirmed by other authors (Bondarouk et al, 2017; Bondarouk, Horst & Engbers, 2009; Bos & Heijden, 2004; Ball, 2001). The author decided to choose "e-HRM" instead of other abbreviations as it is more compatible and relevant with the context of chapter.

The term of e-HRM was first used in the late of 1990's when "e-Commerce" was sweeping the business world"(Lakshmi, 2014). HRM departments using Information and Communication Technology's (ICTs) are becoming an increasingly important phenomenon commonly referred to as e-HRM (Olivas-Lujan & Zapata-Cantu, 2007). E-HRM can be specifically defined as administrative support of the HR function in organizations by using internet technology (Voermans & Veldhoven, 2007). Another definition that used the concept of web-based systems is Panayotopoulou, Vakola, and Galanaki (2007) who defined e-HRM as a web-based solution that takes advantage of the latest web application technology to deliver an online real-time HRM Solution and aims at making information available to managers and employees at anytime and anywhere. E-HRM is defined as a way of implementing HRM strategies in organizations through a conscious and directed support with the full use of web-based technology channels (Parry & Tyson, 2011; Ruel, Bondarouk, & Velde, 2007).

De Alwis (2010) defined e-HRM as the adoption of technology in delivering HRM practices due to the digital revolution in the world to achieve business success, and on another front, Alshibly (2014) argued that achieving more efficient and effective work within HR policies critically relies on e-HRM. Rita and Barbara (2010) indicated that e-HRM refers to the application of ICT for implementing HR strategic policies and practices in organizations or in a broader term; it can be referred to as "the planning, implementation, and application of IT for both networking and supporting actors in their shared performing of HR activities" (Strohmeier, 2007).

E-HRM is an efficient, accessible, reliable and easy to use tool, which - as an implementation support system - leads to quickly maturing the HR function of an organization and work to institutionalize best practices for long-term growth (Srivastava, 2010). As such, it provides an advanced business solution equipped with the capability of managing all process activities, data and information that are needed to successfully manage HR. E-HRM can be used for all HRM functions from traditional activities to transformational activities that add to organizational effectiveness (Parry & Tyson, 2011). It can also be used to manage the whole employee lifecycle from beginning to end.

According to Wyatt (2002) the e-HRM is "an application of any technology enabling managers and employees to have a direct access to HR and other workplace services for communication, performance reporting, team management, knowledge management, learning and other administrative applications". As defined by Ruta (2005: p.35-36) perceived that "e-HRM are vehicles through which HR information and applications can be channeled effectively and efficiently".

In the context of the GWM, gig economy is what others could consider a disruptive industry with new and innovative ways to complete work (Forum, Public Policy, 2019). This is adding a new layer to the e-HRM solutions which is a hot research topic as well. Moreover, it involves the exchange of labor for money between individuals or companies via digital platforms that actively facilitate matching between providers and customers, on a short-term and payment-by-task basis.' (Government, 2018).

DIGITAL TRANSFORMATION OF HUMAN RESOURECS SOLUTION (HRS)

Digital transformation has been described as the use of new digital tools, such as artificial intelligence, mobile, cloud, and blockchain, to create new business models and enhance the customer experience. Digital transformation of HRM is a constant process of using new digital technologies in HRM practices, which recognizes agility as the main tool for the strategic planning of an organization's HRM model and developing e- HRM (Warner and Wager, 2019).

Defining e-HRM

According to Wyatt (2002) the e-HRM is an application of any technology enabling managers and employees to have a direct access to HR and other workplace services for communication, performance reporting, team management, knowledge management, learning and other administrative applications. As defined by Ruta (2005: p.35-36) perceived that "e-HRM are vehicles through which HR information and applications can be channeled effectively and efficiently". Another supportive definition by Lakshmi (2014) identified e-HRM is the complete integration of all HR systems and processes based on common

HR data and information and on interdependent tools and processes, so properly developed e-HRM could provide the data gathering tools, analysis capabilities and decision support resources for HR professionals to hire, pay, promote, terminate, assign, develop, appraise and reward employees. Bondarouk and Ruel (2009: p.507) define e-HRM as "an umbrella term covering all possible integration mechanisms and contents between HRM and IT, aiming at creating value within and across organizations for targeted employees and management"; moreover, based on the extensive literature review of e-HRM, the author examined the different definitions of e-HRM; furthermore, he decided to cover the concept of e-HRM through its main dimensions as shown in Table 1.

Table 1. The Concept of E-HRM and its Main Dimensions

Main Dimensions	Sources
E-HRM is network-technology-based used to improve organizational performance".	AlKerdawy,(2016); Lakshmi, (2014); Voermans & Veldhoven, (2007); Florowski & Olivasalujan- Lujan, (2006); Lepak & Snell (1998) .".
E-HRM is used to decrease administrative efforts and support employees & management".	Alshibly (2014); Parry, (2011); Bondarouk & Ruel (2009); Panayotopoulou, et al.(2007); Ruta (2005)".
E-HRM is used to support HR policies, strategies & practices".	Oswal & Narayanappa (2014); Parry & Tyson (2011);"Ruel, et al. (2007); Ruel, et al. (2004);" Wyatt (2002); Kovach, Hughes, Fagan, & Magitte (2002) ".

Recently, several organizations have moved in the direction of adopting e-HRM and using IT in attracting, retaining, and developing new competencies of HR (AlKerdawy, 2016); several researchers (Bondarouk et al, 2017; AlKerdawy, 2016; Ahmadi, Darayi & Rastgoo, 2014; Babajee, Goolaup & Mamode, 2014; Sharma, 2014; Kulkarni, 2014; Abzari, Radmehr & Shalikar, 2013; & Bondarouk, et al. 2009) have indicated that integrating HR processes with IT can be advantageous towards reaching competitive advantage via e-HRM practices; the author also noticed that e-HRM is designed to increase organizational efficiency and effectiveness, and based on a previous reviews of e-HRM; the author provides the following definition: "Strategic Technical Supportive tool for HRM practices in order to assist the organization in attaining competitive advantage". Therefore, the author develops Figure 1 below to explain the basics of the digital transformation of HRM and its role in supporting for the GIG workers and attaining competitive advantage.

Figure 1. Essentials Elements of digital transformation of HRM and competitive advantage for GWM.

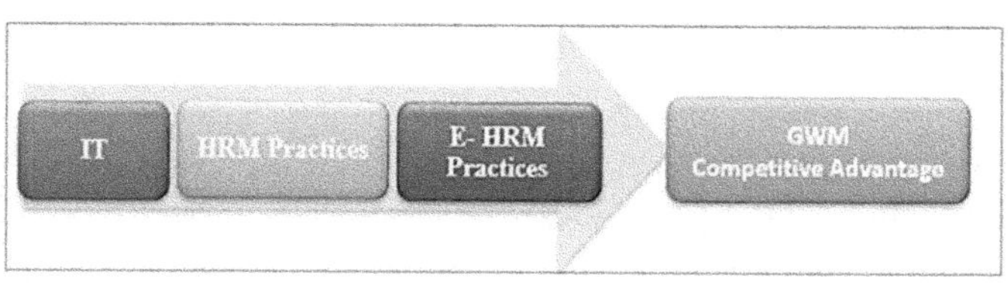

The Stages of e-HRM Development, Its Types and Its Strategies

Table 2 summarizes the main developmental stages of e-HRM as identified by previous readings, and indicates that e-HRM typically starts as a simple transactional or processing tool, developing into an information or decision support tool and finally evolving into a strategic tool that supports transformational efforts"(Ruel, et al., 2004).

Table 2. E-HRM Development Stages

E-HRM Development Stages			Sources
First Stage	Second Stage	Third Stage	
Automation	Information	Transformation	Remenyi Money, & Twite, (1991)
Cost Reduction"	Improve HR Services"	Improve Strategic Orientation"	Ruel et al, (2004)
Transactional	Traditional	Transformational	Wright & Dyer (2000) "
Publishing"	Automation of Transactions"	Transformational of HR	Lengnick-Hall & Moritz (2007) "
Electronic Data Processing"	"Management Information Systems"	Decision Support Systems"	Sanchez & Aguayo (2007)

Source: (Ruel, et al., 2004)

E-HRM Types

Lepak and Snell (1998) suggest that e-HRM types are operational, relational and transformational. On the other hand, others distinguish e-HRM types as transactional, traditional and transformational (Wright & Dyer, 2000), (see Rawash & Saydam, 2012; Reddick, 2009; Ruel, et al., 2004). The connection between the types of e-HRM can be made as follows:

1. **Operational e-HRM:** Concerns impact of IT on automating routine activities in the HR function itself, decreasing the administrative burdens and costs.
2. **Relational e-HRM:** Is about e-HRM tools that support activities in a more advanced HRM area and reduce response times and improve service levels for managers and employees.
3. **Transformational e-HRM:** Focuses on strategic HR activities such as knowledge management and strategic competence management.

It is relevant to distinguish certain e-HRM types, because goals of e-HRM ask for a certain type of e-HRM. For example, an organization that wants to reduce costs has to focus on operational e-HRM, to reduce the administrative burden. A choice for transformational e-HRM will not be the most proper choice in this case. So, out of the e-HRM goals, organizations can make a choice for an e-HRM type. This does not imply that one type is better than another, but organizations have to be aware that the chosen type of e-HRM suits the goals of e-HRM (Lepak & Snell, 1998).

E-HRM Strategies

Voermans and Veldhoven (2007) have categorized the main strategies of e-HRM into three categories as the following:

Replication Strategy (Transactional)

A traditional approach, it is more administrative than strategy-based. Organizations resort to recreating the contents and functions of older systems as a method of updating, via `refreshing' the old system, resulting as such in projects that are not very ambitious and less focus on business value. It is technology centered and focuses more on lower maintenance costs and easier IT support, instead. However, ruling this strategy out as out-dated might not be wise. If implementation is aligned with organizational requirements then the use of this strategy may become justified (Voermans & Veldhoven,2007; Lepak & Snell, 1998).

Enhancement Strategy (Relational)

Instead of refreshing old systems, this strategy attempts to update existing functionality, with a vision in mind (which may include making some features more accessible on the web, like changing biographic or contact details. This method would, thus, help to offer functionality that older systems could not. This approach is considered `low-risk' and results in limited potential negative impact, but may not lead the organization to the status of competitive advantage as projects implementing this strategy usually never go beyond the initial stage and are limited in scope (Voermans & Veldhoven,2007; Lepak & Snell, 1998).

Transformational Strategy (Improve Strategic Orientation)

This strategy is the most involved strategy when it comes to revolutionizing and reconstructing, form the ground up, HR services' delivery model, which may involve using outsourcing, business partnering, and service centers. In other words, technology creates such an environment where managers become more accountable and central personnel are given the chance to take on a more strategic purpose. Generally speaking, the result of implementing this strategy may be the best option for and organization under cost pressure. It will, of course, require sizeable investment in resources and infrastructure, but the payback will be highly compensating in the long run, and will help to establish a new standard in performance (Voermans & Veldhoven, 2007; Lepak & Snell, 1998).

An organization chosen strategy, objectives and environment shall ultimately determine the scope of HR technology (Broderick & Boudreau, 1991). Yeung and Brockbank (1995) define HR objectives by suggesting that one should start at the operational level, move to relational problems, and then move to the transformational level, addressing strategic drivers in the process.

Broderick and Boudreau (1992) suggest the importance of aligning e-HRM strategies with business and HR strategies, since e-HRM strategy and usage is directly related to an organization's overall business and e-HRM strategies, so that is (say) the idea is to be more cost-effective, a transactional e-HRM may be the favored choice, and therefore, an e-HRM replication strategy may be more in the forefront. A focus on innovation in a competitive strategy, on the other hand, focusing attention on good people-management, and thus achieving a more strategic and transformational methodology towards technology.

Organizations that are low-margined will tend to be more cost-focused and will in turn have trouble justifying to themselves the need for a heavy investment in sophisticated people management technologies, whereas the case is the opposite when it comes to organizations focused on technology, IT, or professional services. There is, also, a hint at the importance of an alignment of HR strategies and e-HRM practices, as e-HRM may be influenced by managerial preferences (Voermans & Veldhoven, 2007). Therefore, the idea is that managers will be more supportive of e-HRM if they prefer a more strategic approach to HR Figure 2 illustrates the e-HRM strategies graphically to describe the e-HRM types.

Figure 2. E-HRM Strategies Graphically Describes the e-HRM Types
Source: (Prepared by the Author)

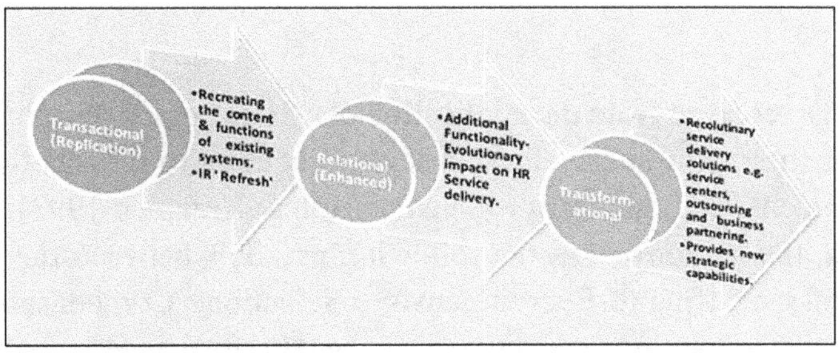

The Outcomes and Benefits of E-HRM

Organizations, nowadays, cannot afford to linger behind in the competitive global marketplace because of its reliance of traditional methods, such as paper and pencil, and the disadvantages that accompany their use (Olivas-Lujan et. al, 2007). Instead, HR processes are minimized if e-HRM is implemented since there will be a great reduction in manual work and paperwork, and there will be an increase in the accuracy of data, which will in turn have positive effects of the efficiency of the HR department, in general, by providing them with extra time to be used for skills development strategic contributions to the organization (Zafar, Shaakat & Mat, 2010). Furthermore, Deshwal (2015) measured e-HRM effectiveness for sustainable development of the organization in this fast, competitive position and indicated that e-HRM aims to transform the HR functions so as to become paperless, more flexible, and help the organization to reduce cost and additional administrative burdens. Lakshmi, (2014) point out that e-HRM plays a critical role in the elimination of unnecessary HR activities.

In addition, e-HRM can create high levels of competence, related to employee learning capacities of new tasks, roles and skills, when the relevant circumstances present themselves (Ruel, et al. 2004). Hence, e-HRM provides the necessary platform for HR departments to upgrade their policies towards web-based technology, in effect supporting both effectiveness and efficiency of HRM (Karampour, Nazari, Alinia & Kameli, 2014). Furthermore, previous studies indicate that e-HRM may be employed to increase the value and effectiveness of HR functions in order to achieve competitive advantage (Strohmeier, 2007; Snell, Stueber, & Lepak, 2002). Accordingly, Table 3 illustrates the outcomes and benefits of e-HRM based on several sources.

Table 3. Overview about E-HRM Outcomes & Benefits

E-HRM Outcomes and Benefits	Sources
Professionalization of the HR Function: should enable e-HRM to gain accurate and detailed information, show early involvement in business strategy and spend more time on activities with a strategic character.	Lepak & Snell, 1998; Snell, et al., 2002; Gardner, Lepak & Bartel, 2003; Buckley, Minette, Joy & Bartl, 2004; Ruel, et al., 2004; Zafar et. al, 2010; Shrivatsava, 2010; Parry & Tyson, 2011; Esakhani, Fani, & Danayifard, 2012; Davoudi & Fartash, 2012; Soltani & Mirzanejad, 2012; Al-dmourl & Al-zu'bi, 2014; Rangarao & Raju, 2014; Karampour, et al., 2014; Lakshmi, 2014; Oswal & Narayanappa, 2014; Deshwal, 2015. Wangpipatwong, Chutimaskul & Papasratorn, 2008.
Cost Effectiveness: refers to the competitiveness of pay levels and employee turnover rate, and to the acceptability of costs resulting from employee resistance such as strikes".	
High Competence: points towards the capacities of employees to learn new tasks and roles if the circumstances require it".	
Higher Congruence refers to the internal organization, the reward system, and the 'input, throughput, and output' of personnel, which need to be structured in the interests of all stakeholders".	
High Commitment: By high commitment workforce is motivated, agreeable, and willing to interact with the management concerning changes in the organization externally and internally".	

The biggest advantage received from the application of e-HRM practice is that it helps to free up HR staff from wasting their time with intermediary roles and helping to refocus their efforts on strategic planning of HR development and organization (Pinsonneault & Kraemer, 1993). Based on the literature about e-HRM practices, the author makes the following parallels between the HRM practices and e-HRM practices, as follows: Staffing (e-Recruitment & e-Selection); Compensation (E-Compensation); Training and Development (e-Training and Developing); and Performance Management (e-Performance Management). In Table 4 below, it will show how e-HRM practices can be support of HRM practices. Then, assumptions are made about the expected benefits of these practices, as illustrated below, which indicate the expected benefits of the e-HRM practices for HRM functions in any organization.

Table 4. Overview About e-HRM Outcomes & Benefits

E-HRM Practices	Expected Benefits
Employment	
e-Recruitment & e-Selection	- "Increasing employee retention levels." - "Increasing the efficiency of the recruitment & selection process, decreasing administrative burdens & minimizing costs." - "Increasing organizational attractiveness & maximizing utilization of the human capital."
Compensation	
"e-Compensation"	- "Effectively designing, administering & communicating compensation programs". - Analyzing market salary data - Process internal information quicker
Training & Development	
e-Training & Development	- More flexible and cost efficient." - Just in time - Control over learning
Performance Management	
"e-Performance Management"	- "Generating KPIs and statistics about performance more easily" - "Enlarging span of control for managers". - "Facilitating the process of writing reviews & generating feedback."

Source: (Bondarouk, et al., 2009)

CONTINGENT AND GIG WORK MANAGEMENT

Worker classification can be tricky, an independent contractor generally performs work for a client without being employed by that client, however, the definition for independent contractors has been broadened by major gig work platforms, making independent contractors a viable resource for most companies.

'The U.S. Bureau of Labor Statistics reports that about 40% of U.S. workers are in non-full-time work situations such as contractor, part-time worker, gig worker, or contingent worker' (Launches, 2019). HR is involved in this workforce only about half the time or less. This "shadow workforce" is simply not being managed well, so there will be an enormous growth in tools to make this easier. That is why companies are putting more money at e-HRMS tools searching for ways to transform their workforce, make people more productive, and improve their quality of hire of those gig workers. A partnership with online platforms can speed up the recruitment process, offer wider access to potential recruits and reduce the cost of hiring workers. However, e-HRM is still required to provide some level of screening, performance management, agile goals follow-up and feedback mechanisms.

New e-HRMS systems combined by artificial intelligence, block chain and other technologies can reads documentation and generates learning assessments automatically, recommend content based on role and experience of others, identify the best coach for an employee in additional to monitoring, assessing candidates on a video interview through facial expressions and even find candidates based on their social profiles and external experiences.

Classifications of Gig Workers

A gig economy offers certain flexibility and freedom for both the employer and the employee. The employer can hire multiple specialists to complete certain tasks and has the option to select freelancers who are hybrid specialists, or even hyperspecialists, in a desired area. Similarly, the employee gets the flexibility to frequently switch jobs and broaden their portfolio with a wide range of experience. (Mandloi, 2020)

The term "gig worker" covers four very different types of the workforce:

- **Highly skilled professionals:** They make their primary living from independent work ; specific work that they are highly skilled in. They include individuals with international experience, consultants, IT professionals, and other such contractors. Often, they make up a minority of the gig economy workforce.
- **Part-time workers:** They are the side hustlers; temporary workers trying to incease their incomes with part-time work or might be unable to find full-time employment. The gigs might not be their primary source of income but fulfill them- could be photography, event planning, administrative work, or personal training.
- **Crowd workers:** Workers who compete to participate in a project and are often only paid if they are among the top participants in a competition. Those workers are sometimes call zero-hour workers.
- **Volunteers:** Academic and nonprofit organizations hire plenty of volunteers who might have great skills, but their ability to deliver is tied to their personal and professional schedules thus it might be hard to get a solid commitment on duration and performance.

The experiences of the gig economy are very much dependent on the circumstances. Gig economy work is highly flexible and this is very much appreciated by those engaged in it; although it is mixed with many feelings that this flexibility is a fair trade-off for any lack of security and employment rights that are resulted. The gig economy is a rapidly developing part of the labour market. The growth of technology has enabled the development of online platforms to facilitate the matching of supply of and demand for work in a range of areas and involving a range of skills.

Contracting Dynamics for Temporary Workers

The gig economy is what others could consider a disruptive industry with new and innovative ways to complete work. This could change how American citizens complete work in the company and redefine contract employment. However, even if various legal concerns arise through a change in the industry, the companies in the country still must abide by certain laws. With a change in these laws to provide for more opportunity and more power over completing work outside the standard day or night shift, legal issues will cause administrations and states to reconsider labor and employment matters.

Gig Worker Contract Issues

Many gig economy workers should consider contractual employment rather than working with a client in a non-legal way. The contract legally binds the two parties together in a working relationship. An employment contract between the two can ensure that the short-term or long-term project has the legal protections that these agreements provide. While not a standard contract for employment as an employee with the company, the independent contractor can use the contract itself to retain continued work until the end date arrives. Additionally, the contract can provide compensation to the freelancer if the other party violates the terms.

Precarious Contracts

As the gig economy progresses into the future, the lean on contractual work rather than standard employment can cause legal issues. The contract agreement can cause a precarious situation when each freelancer uses a contractual relationship for work. These documents can have looser terms and could apply to different scenarios that could increase the possibility of legal problems. One of the primary concerns is the contract breach that can leave a freelancer without payment if the other party decides to cause trouble. Contract terms and provisions may also become unenforceable if a lawyer does not assist in ensuring the document is valid.

Short-Term Engagement

One of several contract issues that gig workers have is that the contracts with a company or client are usually only short-term with few renewals. According to (International Labour Organization (ILO), 2012), gig contractual arrangements are characterized by

- The limited duration of the contract (fixed-term, short-term, temporary, seasonal, day-labor and casual labor)

- The nature of the employment relationship (triangular and disguised employment relationships, bogus self-employment, subcontracting and agency contracts)

This causes a constant search for new work or changes to existing contractual relationships that need to evolve. Some extensions demand lesser pay because the company can find someone else willing to provide the same or similar services for lower payments. Short-term relationships are also a boon with some clients because the freelancer is stuck with the company until the business either breaches the agreement or it ends and the independent contractor is free of the service obligation.

Handling Contract Breaches

Violations to the provisions in a contract are often possible with any gig economy agreement. The client or other party can violate the terms by failing to provide payment, ending the relationship before the contract end date or by altering something that is detrimental to the freelancer. Generally, these are short-term associations that may not require a contract to ensure work, but the breach is often serious enough to seek legal action. If the entity or person violates the terms, this could lead to compensation as stated in the contract for such incidents. If the freelancer hired a lawyer to create the contract, the agreement should contain a provision for compensation in case of a breach.

Employment Litigation

The gig economy does not often provide times when the freelancer can sue the client or any other party. However, if there is a contract between the two parties, this is a possibility. The independent contractor may have a means to enter into a legal process through arbitration, mediation or litigation if there is a contractual relationship between freelancer and an organization and compensation is lost or there are terms violated. The employment contract that provides temporary work with a legal document that has provisions for payment should specify how to proceed through these processes. While part-time work may not be a growing problem at the aggregate level, it may be becoming a bigger issue in sectors that feature more precarious characteristics (CPA Canada, 2018).

The Intermediary

When working through a contract with a client, the gig worker may find the path blocked because of an intermediary involved in the process. This intermediary can take the place of actual contact and full payment with the client. Many will find that they are working with or for a contracting company or with another person that reports or explains the details to the client. This intermediary can cause problems if part of the payment routes to this person or entity which can lower the full amount received. These issues may exist in the contract as an addendum or in language that is confusing for the freelancer. If the gig workers work under multiple contracts, it is possible that many different labels would apply to them at the same time. (ESDC, 2019). These problems can arise because more than one wants services immediately or because there are concerns about some work and deadlines that conflict.

Multiple Clients in One Contract

Sometimes, the freelancer will have multiple clients in a single contract that can create serious issues later. These problems can arise because more than one wants services immediately or because there are concerns about some work and deadlines that conflict. The gig worker may need to reconsider the contract for extensions or if wanting to work with the primary client in the future. Other problems can stem from work that is vastly different which could require more research or not finding a pattern to complete the tasks quicker.

Measuring the Performance

The employer and applicant usually negotiate the terms of a contract for employment. These terms are usually a combination of what both parties want and are a set of each for employment and the business. The classification of an employee is different from a gig worker. The prompt correction of an incorrect classification may help a company avoid or diminish significant financial liability (Kuretzky & Levy, 2019).

Unethical Behaviors

When the individual is unable to perform adequately according to a supervisor or manager, he or she can engage in certain behaviors that may lead to termination. These can include an unwillingness to accomplish goals or tasks, an inability to complete work, making errors or working with a reasonable amount of time and failing to complete duties. An unwillingness or inability to learn how to work or to work with a team. The inability to ensure good judgment prevails, making bad decisions or a lack of judgment. Other behavior can also create the need for termination to include illegal activity.

Handling Violence

A person that engages in illegal activity generally does so from a computer while at work. However, he or she could steal from the business or sell items illegally in the building. Any acts of violence can also require the company to terminate the employment contract. There are terms and provisions for incidents involving violent behavior. Criminal activity with violence is often more than sufficient to fire the person because he or she violated the terms of the employment contract. White-collar crimes and looking up illegal websites on the company computer are both possible termination offenses when performed at work.

Termination Reasoning

When a contract of employment has a term involving performance issues, the individual working at the company must meet these. Generally, they involve accurate statistics that relate to certain tasks such as customer service, tech support or reviews. Others may need to accomplish so much work in a short time. The actual performance can lead to termination if the terms explain that that conclusion is possible. When following the clauses in the contract, the employer can fire the person for any lack of performance with valid reasoning. It is important to have a lawyer look over the contract and ensure the termination is both valid and legal. The fact that an assignment ends does not mean that the employment relationship with the agency ends (Mitchell & Murray, 2017).

Policies and Behaviors to Consider in the Gig Economy

When working in the gig economy, the individual should consider different policies or even to create an entity to ensure better protections in place for taxes or other issues that may arise. The different gigs may even require a contract for each client and various policies to enact and follow based on the situation and the specific client.

Labor Policies

While the person working in the gig economy does not always have the option to work for more than minimum wage, it is important to hold clients and companies accountable for reasonable pay. If there is any possibility that the person paying for the services will either flake out of paying or not provide sufficient monetary income, the gig worker may need to drop the client in the future. Checking the state labor policies and laws is also important to consider even if the person cannot hold the other party accountable or responsible in following these policies.

Insurance in the Gig Economy

Another factor that the freelancer or independent contractor must accomplish alone is acquiring insurance when working in the gig economy. These policies are often more expensive when not obtained through a company or may require more creative thinking. However, having a policy for coverage is often better than going without. When building an entity in the gig economy, it is important to consider how to acquire insurance for both health and dental matters. Sometimes, there are discounted policies available for the independent contractor or through a company policy if the freelancer creates a business.

Legal Matters

Policies that affect the gig worker in a legal context may require the services of a lawyer to remedy or to adjust. Some of these involve contracts, but other problems can arise such as a lawsuit. Certain policies within an agreement can restrict, and others can benefit both the client and the independent contractor. It is vital to have a business lawyer available to help correct mistakes and in avoiding legal violations that can cost the freelancer greatly. By maintaining a relationship with a legal professional, the independent contractor can tackle legal obstacles before they arise. The lawyer can also help prevent violations, mistakes and legal issues that are current or that could happen in the future.

Management of Schedule and Workload

Hiring part-time or shared talent often affects their availability beyond what company leaders have come to expect from a traditional 9-to-5 employee working in an office. You may not have access to them throughout the entire workday, and/or every weekday.

It's important you set expectations upfront with an outsourced hire regarding not just project scope, but how many hours they'll be working and where, as well as how and when you can reach them. Take into account whether you will be their primary client, or if they have a portfolio of clients—and if that portfolio contains any competitors.

Contrary to what many leaders think, you will still need to establish a management structure for this person, as well. While a high-level professional expert should be able to right-size their time, you may need to do so for lower-level contract positions, as well as connect them to the hierarchy of command within your organization.

Ensuring Employment Compliance

Most importantly for a company leader diving into gig labor is to understand how to engage the gig worker within the business while stay compliant with internal and external rules and regulations. It is important to determine how to treat payments for such services including the associated taxes. It is then important to frame the business relationship that exists between the organization and the person performing the services.

The procedures and expertise needed to manage a workforce can become more complicated when a business relies on the speed and flexibility of the gig economy. The role of human resources (HR) therefore becomes extremely important in maintaining visibility of the organization's workforce. Any lack of solid practices can be concerning for HR when they find themselves not being able to report accurately on the use of gig workers because so many are bypassing protocol and being appointed by line managers directly. As soon as management engage a gig worker directly, cutting HR out of the loop and evading their recruitment processes, it can create unchecked risks to security, compliance, and cost control. Some key factors that should be included while measuring compliance should such as:

- **Behavioral:** Does the organization control or have the right to control what the worker does and how the worker does his or her job? Considering that a gig worker is contracted to perform the task. (Dietrich & Anderson, 2012)
- **Financial:** Are the business aspects of the worker's job controlled by the payer? These include things like how a worker is paid, whether expenses are reimbursed, who provides tools/supplies, etc.) (Dietrich & Anderson, 2012)
- **Type of Relationship:** Are there written contracts or employee type benefits such as pension plan, insurance, vacation pay? Will the relationship continue and is the performed work a key aspect of the business where continuous operation is required? ? (Murray, 2019)
- **Visibility:** The gig worker is a significant departure from the traditional employee. Whereas there are defined processes and procedures for employing permanent members of staff, digital platforms allow businesses to appoint freelance workers directly, which sometimes means HR is excluded from the process. The organization need to have necessary policies and procedures to handle such scenarios. (Gross, 2019)
- **Regulations:** The numerous reviews and inquiries into the gig economy will undoubtedly create new regulations and employment laws, which HR teams will need to manage and comply with. They will also need to develop their support strategy to maintain the increasingly diverse and flexible business model that comes with the appointment of gig workers.

- **Management:** As gig workers can pick and choose where and when they work, this can create integration challenges if they are required to collaborate with permanent employees who are confined to set working hours and locations. To overcome this, organizations could include location and working hour requirements in their freelancer agreements or consider remote and flexible working practices for all workers.

Furthermore, as an organisation's percentage of gig workers increases, it can be challenging for HR to retain the level of progression and development required for business continuity. Gig workers cannot be forced to attend training courses or learn new skills as they are generally self-employed. One way HR could uphold succession and progression in a business is to ensure regular reviews of the freelance network to guarantee that there are adequate numbers of gig workers available with the skills required.

WORKPLACE AND HRM TECHNOLOGY CONVERGENCE

The most important and essential part of the eHRM technology landscape used to be its core activities such as payroll, employee management systems and record-keeping systems that was designed as a back-office system used by HR managers, payroll clerks, and HR administrators. Over the last decade, eHRM systems have become useful for employees, with interfaces that let employees use selfservice functionality to manage their information, benefits, and various other tasks. In this era of digital transformation and gig economy, vendors are struggling to transform the eHRM systems into productivity management tools that help employees get their work done.

With such changes, workplace technology vendors such as Microsoft and Google are all getting into HR. (Launches, 2019) The HR tools that used to be a "destination" platforms that employees visited to apply for a job, learn, change their address, or do some other HR-related task, are becoming more of productivity systems including chatbots, messages, and real-time notifications. This can show immediate adoption, tremendously positive re-engineering of the recruitment process.

Introducing Online Platforms

Online platforms, customers and gig workers interact to find the perfect work match; many eHRM systems can integrate or utilize platforms such as Freelancer, Upwork, Bark and Deliveroo. Each platform engages with freelancers and customers in a slightly different way, but generally the customer defines the 'gig' or the nature of the work to be undertaken and places it onto the platform. (Government, 2018) summarizes the main ways in which the customer, online platform, and individual engage with each other; some aspects of the transaction involve all three parties, whereas others involve just two of them in combination.

- **Gig worker and platform:** The gig worker brings their skills and equipment to the work, and liaises with the platform, by building an online profile, induction if required, quality-assurance and sometimes work insurance depending on the nature of the work.
- **Customer and platform:** The customer may use the platform to rate the service provided by the individual and can sometimes access and implement a complaints procedure, should it be necessary.

- **The gig work and customer:** The gig worker and customer interact during the provision of the service or product.
- **The platform, gig worker and customer:** All three parties typically interact in setting pay and making the financial transaction. It was common for the platform to provide an escrow service for payment between the commission and completion of the work.

New Employment Tests

Traditionally, almost a third of company hires don't work out, despite extensive testing, assessment, and job fit analysis (Launches, 2019). That is why technology enabled adding new dimenstions to the gig workers hiring process to reduce the error discovery margins and trajectory, this includes:

- **Innovative Personality Assessments (IPA):** to measure the expected alignment between the workplace behavior and the contraor personality traits, and ultimately to ensure a cultural and team fit criteria.
- **Aptitude Tests:** to measure cognitive ability at work with insights on the candidate's ability to acquire, retain, organize, and apply information in work environments.
- **Technical assessments:** to measure technical skills precisely, candidates immediate fit and producing the results as actionable insights.
- **Dark Personality Tests:** to measure and identify the key negative traits that impact the safety of employees, customers, and work culture.

Introducing the Cross-functional Teams

The traditional hierarchical work model is useful for pay decisions and possibly for traditional careers, but it does not reflect the way people work for innovative tasks. According to (Bersin, 2019) researches show more than 37% of companies are already experimenting with work models based on managing cross-functional teams, setting team goals, and valuing people based on skills and connections rather than job level, title, or tenure. This type of work model is very difficult to implement in traditional HRMS.

New graphical database eHRMS are vastly more powerful for modeling how people interrelate, search for data, communicate, and build different types of relationships with peers, teammates, bosses and subordinates.

The gig economy recruitment needs a speedy and must fit hiring require multiple tools that can help the decision makers. real-time feedback. New eHRMS systems combined by artificial intelleigence, block chain and other technologies can reads documentation and generates learning assessments automatically, recommend content based on role and experience of others, identify the best coach for an employee and monitors, assesses candidates on a video interview through facial expressions and even find candidates based on their social profiles and external experiences.

FUTURE RESEARCH DIRECTIONS

Recently, organizations are becoming more intelligent, flexible, and efficient than other competitors by using new digital technologies, such as artificial intelligence, mobile, cloud, and blockchain in Human

Resource Management (HRM) this will be a very rich field to achieve a sustainable competitive advantages. One more research can target the significance of e-HRM with regards to attracting, developing talented employees and retaining them, as well as enhancing competition and building good company reputation.

Digital transformation is an endless service; thus, it will be great to research more about the related development stages, types and strategies in relation to e-HRMS and Gig workers. Measuring the employee performance using emerging technologies is important as the workplace and e-HRM systems are being merged. This is necessary to protect the organization and ensure that the individual does perform the work necessary for the job and title granted by the business. Additionally, how to contract every category of employees and how to enable the eHRM processes to accommodate such contracting challenges to ensure all workers follow these terms closely or even exceeds the terms to continue working.

CONCLUSION

The HRM solutions have evolved to be an (electronic) as e-HRM throughout multiple development stages, types and strategies. The e-HRM contributes to increase the effectiveness of managing human resources and employee activities. Recently, as an outcome of digital transformation organizations have been facing challenges for gig workers to retain the level of progression and development required for business continuity. Gig workers cannot be forced to attend training courses or learn new skills as they are generally self-employed. E-HRMS is necessary to uphold succession and progression in a business is to ensure regular reviews of the freelance network to guarantee that there are adequate numbers of gig workers available with the skills required. Ultimately it will be very hard to manage gig workers without having a solid e-HRMS that can fulfill the needs of both parties. Policies and behaviors should be injected inside the e-HRM to handle the Gig Work Management (GWM).

REFERENCES

Abzari, M., Radmehr, R., & Shalikar, M. (2013). Analyzing the Effects of E-HRM on the Talent Management Strategies: Medical University of Isfahan as a Case Study. *World of Sciences Journal*, *1*(6), 101–112.

Ahmadi, A., Darayi, M., & Rastgoo, F. (2014). Investigating the Effect of E-HRM on the Successful Implementation of Succession Planning. *Arabian Journal of Business & Management Review*, *4*(1), 65–70.

AL-Dmour, R., & Al-Zu'bi, Z. (2014). Factors Inhabiting & Motivating the Adoption of HRIS in Business Organization. *International Business Research*, *7*(7), 139.

AlKerdawy, M. (2016). The Relationship between HRM Ambidexterity & Talent Management: The Moderating Role of E-HRM. *International Business Research*, *9*(6), 80. doi:10.5539/ibr.v9n6p80

Alshibly, H. (2014). Evaluating E-HRM Success: A Validation of the Information Systems Success Model. *International Journal of HR Studies*, *4*(3), 107. doi:10.5296/ijhrs.v4i3.5929

Alwis, A. (2010). The Impact of E-HRM on the Role of HR Managers. *Ekonomie a Management*, *4*, 47–60.

Babajee, G., Goolaup, R., & Mamode, K. (2014). An Analysis of the Implementation of E-HR Practices at TNT Business Solutions. *Proceedings of 26th International Business Research Conference Imperial College*, 7-8.

Ball, K. (2001). The Use of HRIS: A Survey. *Personnel Review*, *30*(6), 677–693. doi:10.1108/EUM0000000005979

Bersin, J. (2019, January 27). T. & Ruel, H. (2009). E-HRM: Challenges in the Digital Era. *The International Journal of HRM*, *20*(3), 505–514. Retrieved April 2020, from https://www.hrtechnologist.com/

Bondarouk, T., Parry, E., & Furtmueller, E. (2017). Electronic HRM: Four Decades of Research on Adoption & Consequences. *International Journal of Human Resource Management*, *28*(1), 98–131. doi:10.1080/09585192.2016.1245672

Bondarouk, T., ter Horst, V., & Engbers, S. (2009). Exploring Perceptions about the Use of E-HRM Tools in Medium Sized Organizations. In Handbook of Research on E-Transformation & HRM Technologies. Information Science Reference.

Bos, M., & Heijden, H. (2004). E-HRM. In F. Kluytmans (Ed.), *Leerboek Personnel's Management*. Wolters-Nordhoff.

Broderick, R., & Boudreau, J. (1991). The Evolution of Computer Use in Human Resource Management: Interviews with Ten Leaders. *Human Resource Management*, *30*(4), 485–508. doi:10.1002/hrm.3930300405

Broderick, R., & Boudreau, J. (1992). Human Resource Management, Information Technology, & the Competitive Edge. *The Executive*, *6*(2), 7–17. doi:10.5465/ame.1992.4274391

Buckley, P., Minnette, K., Joy, D., & Michaelis, J. (2004). The Use of an Automated Employment Recruiting & Screening System for Temporary Professional Employees: A Case Study. *HRM*, *43*(2), 233–241. doi:10.1002/hrm.20017

Canada, C. P. A. (2018, January 1). Retrieved April 24, 2020, from https://www.cpacanada.ca/-/media/site/operational/sc-strategic-communications/docs/g10475-sc_precarious-employment.pdf?la=en&hash=05185D6F20B709D26C12C966F162EB7F4A3B9992D

Deshwal, P. (2015). Role of E-HRM in Organizational Effectiveness & Sustainability. *IJAR*, *1*(12), 605–609.

Dietrich, M., & Anderson, G. (2012). *The Financial Professional's Guide to Healthcare Reform*. John Wiley & Sons.

Esakhani, A., Fani, A., & Danayifard, H. (2012). Determination of the Relationship between Work Engagement & Employees Organizational Commitment. In General Management Researches (5th ed., pp. 38-23). Academic Press.

ESDC. E. a. (2019, July 29). Retrieved April 24, 2020, from https://www.canada.ca/en/employment-social-development/services/labour-standards/reports/protection-workers-nonstandard.html#h2.3

Florowski, G. & Olivasalujan-Lujan, M. (2006). The Diffusion of HRM-Technology Innovations in US & Non-US Firms. *Personnel Review*, *35*(6), 684–710. doi:10.1108/00483480610702737

Forum, Public Policy. (2019). Retrieved April 24, 2020, from https://ppforum.ca/publications/managing-precarious-work-three-canadian-models-for-rebalancing-bargaining-power-in-the-future-of-work/?utm_source=web&utm_medium=sm&utm_campaign=bnw

Galanaki, E. (2002). The Decision to Recruit on Line: A Descriptive Study. *Career Development International*, *7*(4), 243–251. doi:10.1108/13620430210431325

Gardner, S., Lepak, D., & Bartl, K. (2003). Virtual HR: The Impact of Information Technology on the Human Resource Professional. *Journal of Vocational Behavior*, *63*(2), 159–179. doi:10.1016/S0001-8791(03)00039-3

Ghazzawi, K., Al-Khoury, P., & Saman, J. (2014). The Effect of Implementing Technology in HRM on the Level of Employee Motivation. *HRM Research*, *4*(2), 33–39.

Government, H. (2018, Feb 1). *The_experiences_of_those_in_the_gig_economy*. Retrieved April 24, 2020, from https://assets.publishing.service.gov.uk/government/uploads/system/uploads/attachment_data/file/679987/171107_The_experiences_of_those_in_the_gig_economy.pdf

Gross, E. (2019, August 6). Retrieved April 24, 2020, from https://www.peoplemanagement.co.uk/experts/legal/future-hr-hurdles-gig-economy

International Labour Organization (ILO). (2012). [REMOVED HYPERLINK FIELD]etrieved April 24, 2020, from https://www.ilo.org/actrav/info/WCMS_179787/lang--en/index.htm

Karampour, A., Nazari, Y., Alinia, S., & Kameli, A. (2014). Survey & Comparison of E-HRM Systems in Oil & Gas Companies Lorestan Province. *International Journal of Management & Humanity Sciences*, *3*(1), 1308–1315.

Kovach, A., Hughes, A., Fagan, P., & Maggitti, P. (2002). Administrative & Strategic Advantage of HRIS. Employment Relations Today, 43-48.

Kulkarni, S. (2014). Human Capital Enhancement through E-HRM. *Journal of Management Research*, *3*(1), 59–74.

Kuretzky, B., & Levy, R. B. (2019). Retrieved April 24, 2020, from https://www.business-humanrights.org/en/canada-class-action-lawsuits-over-alleged-misclassification-of-employees-as-independent-contractors-are-increasing-say-lawyers

Lakshmi, C. (2014). Study on E-HRM Practices in Kovai Medical Center & Hospital, Coimbatore. *Journal of Business Management & Social Sciences Research*, *3*(8), 43–47.

Launches, B. (2019, Jan 27). Retrieved April 2020, from https://oliver-dev.s3.amazonaws.com/2019/01/27/12/54/25/916/Tech_Disruptions.pdf

Lengnick-Hall, M., & Moritz, S. (2003). The Impact of e-HR on the Human Resource Management Function. *Journal of Labor Research*, *24*(3), 365–379. doi:10.100712122-003-1001-6

Lepak, D., & Snell, S. (1998). Virtual HR: Strategic HRM in the 21st Century. *HRM Review*, *8*(3), 215–234.

Mandloi, R. (2020). *Making the Most of Talent in the Gig Economy*. Retrieved April 24, 2020, from https://www.harvardbusiness.org/making-the-most-of-talent-in-the-gig-economy/

Mitchell, M., & Murray, J. C. (2017). Retrieved April 24, 2020, from https://files.ontario.ca/books/mol_changing_workplace_report_eng_2_0.pdf

Murray, J. (2019). Retrieved April 24, 2020, from https://www.thebalancesmb.com/what-is-a-common-law-employee-4171936

Olivas-Lujan, M., Ramirez, J., & Zapata-Cantu, L. (2007). E-HRM in Mexico: Adapting Innovations for Global Competitiveness. *International Journal of Manpower*, *28*(5), 418–434. doi:10.1108/01437720710778402

Oswal, N., & Narayanappa, G. (2014). Evolution of HRM to E-HRM towards Organizational Effectiveness & Sustainability. *International Journal of Recent Development in Engineering & Technology*, *2*(4).

Panayotopoulou, L., Vakola, M., & Galanaki, E. (2007). E-HR Adoption & the Role of HRM: Evidence From Greece. *Personnel Review*, *36*(2), 277–294. doi:10.1108/00483480710726145

Parry, E., & Tyson, S. (2011). Desired Goals & Actual Outcomes of EHRM. *HRM Journal*, *21*(3), 335–354.

Pinsonneault, A., & Kraemer, K. (1993). An Assessment of the Use of Survey Research in the Management Information Systems field between (1980 & 1990). *Journal of Management Information Systems*, *10*(2), 75–106. doi:10.1080/07421222.1993.11518001

Rangarao, J., & Raju, S. (2014). E-HRM Add Value to the HRM to Obtain Optimum Potentials from the Available HR. *Indian Journal of Commerce & Management*, *1*(1), 1–9.

Rawash, H., & Saydam, S. (2012). The Impact of E-HRM on Organization's Market Share: An Empirical Study on the Housing Bank for Trade & Finance in Jordan. *International Journal of Business and Social Science*, *3*(24), 113–120.

Reddick, C. (2009). Human Resources Information Systems in Texas City Governments: Scope and Perception of Its Effectiveness. *Public Personnel Management*, *38*(4), 19–34. doi:10.1177/009102600903800402

Remenyi, D., Money, A., & Twite, A. (1991). *A Guide to Measuring & Managing IT Benefits*. NCC, Blackwell Limited.

Rita, B., & Barbara, I. (2010). Generation Y at Work: The Role of E-HRM in Building Positive Work Attitudes. *Proceedings of Third European Academic workshop on e-HRM*, *570*, 378-399.

Ruel, H., Bondarouk, T., & Looise, J. (2004). E-HRM: Innovation or Irritation: An Explorative Empirical Study In Five Large Companies On Web-Based HRM. *Management Review*, *15*(3), 364–380.

Ruel, H., Bondarouk, T., & Van der Velde, M. (2007). The Contribution of E-HRM to HRM Effectiveness: Results from a Quantitative Study in a Dutch Ministry. *Employee Relations*, *29*(3), 280–291. doi:10.1108/01425450710741757

Ruta, C. (2005). The Application of Change Management Theory to HR Portal Implementation in Subsidiaries of Multinational Corporations. *HRM*, *44*(1), 35–53. doi:10.1002/hrm.20039

Sanchez, J., & Aguayo, M. (2007). An Approach to the Satisfaction of Human Resource Information Systems (HRIS): Analysis & Empirical Contrast. *International Journal of Human Resources Development and Management*, *7*(2), 177–214. doi:10.1504/IJHRDM.2007.012862

Sharma, N. (2014). Recruitment Strategies: A Power of E-Recruiting & Social Media. *International Journal of Core Engineering & Management*, *1*(5), 15–35.

Shrivatsava, S. (2010). Shaping Organizations with e-HRM. *International Journal of Innovation, Management and Technology, 1*(1).

Snell, S., Stueber, D., & Lepak, D. (2002). *Virtual HR Departments: Getting Out of the Middle*. CAHRS Working Paper Series, 71.

Soltani, M., & Mirzanejad, R. (2012). E-HRM & Required Infrastructures in its Implementation. *7th Conference on HR Development*, 1-20.

Srivastava, S. (2010). Shaping Organizations with e-HRM. *International Journal of Innovation, Management and Technology, 1*(1), 47–50.

Stone, D., Lukaszewski, K., & Isenhour, L. (2005). E-Recruiting: Online Strategies for Attracting Talent. In *The Brave New World of EHR. HRM in the Digital Age*. Jossey-Bass.

Strohmeier, S. (2007). Research in E-HRM: Review & Implications. *HRM Review, 17*(1), 19–37.

Voermans, M., & Van Veldhoven, M. (2007). Attitude towards E-HRM: An Empirical Study at Philips. *Personnel Review, 36*(6), 887–902. doi:10.1108/00483480710822418

Wangpipatwong, S., Chutimaskul, W., & Papasratorn, B. (2008). Understanding Citizen's Continuance Intention to Use E-government Website: A Composite View of Technology Acceptance Model & Computer Self-Efficacy. The Electronic. *Journal of E-Government, 6*(1), 55–64.

Warner, K. S., & Wäger, M. (2019). Building dynamic capabilities for digital transformation: An ongoing process of strategic renewal. *Long Range Planning, 52*(3), 326–349. doi:10.1016/j.lrp.2018.12.001

Wright, P., & Dyer, L. (2000). *People in the E-business: New Challenges, New Solutions*. Working paper, Vol. 11, Center for Advanced HR Studies, Cornell University.

Wyatt, W. (2002). *E-HR: Getting Results Along the Journey*. Survey Report.

Yeung, A., & Brockbank, W. (1995). Reengineering HR through Information Technology. *People & Strategy, 18*(2), 24.

Zafar, J., Shaakat, M., & Mat, N. (2010). An Analysis of E-HRM Practices: A Case Study of State Bank of Pakistan. *European Journal of Soil Science, 15*, 18–21.

ADDITIONAL READING

Al-Khasawneh, A. L. (2013). The Relation between Human Resource Management (HRM) Strategies and Job Loyalty as Practiced at the Public Relations (PR's) Units in the Government Ministries of Jordan. *Journal of Management Research, 5*(3), 146. doi:10.5296/jmr.v5i3.3689

Alajmi, S., & Alenezi, M. (2016). HRM Practices & Competitive Advantage: The Mediator Role of Person-Organization Fit. *Global Journal of HRM, 4*(1), 65–82.

Aldhmour, F. M., & Eleyan, M. B. (2012). Factors influencing the successful adoption of decision support systems: The context of Aqaba special economic zone authority. *International Journal of Business and Management, 7*(2), 163. doi:10.5539/ijbm.v7n2p163

Amara, N., & Atia, L. (2016). E-Training & Its Role in Human Resources Development. *Global Journal of Human Resource Management*, *4*(1), 1–12.

Antwi, J., Opoku, A., Seth, A., & Margaret, O. (2016). Assessing the HRM Practices of Public Banks From Employees' Perspective: Case Study of Selected Branches of Ghana Commercial Bank, Kumasi. *Global Journal of HRM*, *4*(1), 13–30.

Arkorful, V., & Nelly, A. (2015). The Role of E-learning, Advantages & Disadvantages of its Adoption in Higher Education. *International Journal of Instructional Technology & Distance Learning*, *12*(1), 29–42.

Cappelli, P. (2001). Making the Most of on Line Recruiting. *Harvard Business Review*, *79*(2), 139–146. PMID:11246921

Cardy, R., & Miller, J. (2005). EHR & Performance Management. In H. Gueutal & D. Stone (Eds.), *The Brave New World of EHR. HRM in the Digital Age*. Jossey-Bass.

Cober, R., Brown, D., Levy, P., Keeping, L., & Cober, A. (2003). Organizational Websites: Website Content & Style as Determinants of Organizational Attraction. *International Journal of Selection and Assessment*, *11*(2-3), 158–169. doi:10.1111/1468-2389.00239

Cober, R., Douglas, J., & Levy, P. (2004). Form, Content & Function: An Evaluative Methodology for Corporate Employment Web Sites. *HRM*, *43*(2), 201–218. doi:10.1002/hrm.20015

Davoudi, S., & Fartash, K. (2012). E-HRM: New Avenues which leads to Organizational Success. *Spectrum (Lexington, Ky.)*, *1*(2).

Dessler, G. (2000). *Human Resource Management*. Prentice Hall.

Farid, S., Ahmad, R., Niaz, I., Arif, M., Shamshirband, S., & Khattak, M. (2015). Identification & Prioritization of Critical Issues for the Promotion of e-learning in Pakistan. *Computers in Human Behavior*, *51*, 161–171. doi:10.1016/j.chb.2015.04.037

Hamidianpour, F., Esmaeilpour, M., & Firoozi, H. (2016). Assessing the Impact of Electronic Human Resource Management on Creation of Organizational Agility: A Study in the Bushehr Banks, Iran. *Asian Social Science*, *12*(7), 105. doi:10.5539/ass.v12n7p105

Hogler, R. Henle, C. & Bernus, C. (1998). Internet Recruiting & Employment Discrimination: A Legal Perspective. HRM Review, 8(2).

Kehoe, J., Dickter, D., Russell, D., & Sacco, J. (2005). E-Selection. In H. Gueutal & D. Stone (Eds.), *The Brave New World of EHR. HRM in the Digital Age*. Jossey-Bass.

Kuretzky, B., & Levy, R. B. (2019). https://www.littler.com/publication-press/publication. Retrieved April 24, 2020, from https://www.littler.com/publication-press: https://www.littler.com/publication-press/publication/ontario-canada-companies-beware-class-action-lawsuits-alleging-worker?utm_source=Mondaq&utm_medium=syndication&utm_campaign=View-Original

Marler, J., & Dulebohn, J. (2005). A Model of Employee Self-Service Technology Acceptance. *Research in Personnel & HRM*, *24*, 139–182. doi:10.1016/S0742-7301(05)24004-5

McConnel, B. (2002). Companies Lure Job Seekers. In *New Ways: Corporate Web Sites Snare Applicants on Line* (pp. 1–12). HR News.

Moore, L., Camille, D., & Krista, G. (2011). e-Learning, Online Learning, & Distance Learning Environments: Are they the Same? *The Internet & Higher Education*, *14*(2), 129–135. doi:10.1016/j.iheduc.2010.10.001

Nickel, J., & Schaumberg, H. (2004). *Electronic Privacy*. Trust & Self-Disclosure in E-Recruitment.

Shammot, M. (2014). The Role of HRM Practices Represented by Employee's Recruitment & Training & Motivating in Realization Competitive Advantage. *International Business Research*, *7*(4). Advance online publication. doi:10.5539/ibr.v7n4p55

Tavangarian, D. Leypold, M. Nolting, K. Roser, M. & Voigt, D. (2004). Is E-Learning the Solution for Individual Learning? Electronic Journal of e-Learning, 2(2), 273-280.

KEY TERMS AND DEFINITIONS

Digital Transformation: The use of new digital tools, such as artificial intelligence, mobile, cloud, and blockchain, to create new business models and enhance the customer experience.

Digital Transformation of HRM: The use of new digital technologies in HRM practices, which recognizes agility as the main tool for the strategic planning of an organization's HRM model and developing electronic HRM.

E-Compensation: The extent of linking the performance Appraisal and the compensation system automatically with more transparency by internet technology.

E-HRM: An umbrella term covering all possible integration mechanisms and contents between HRM and IT, aiming at creating value within and across organizations for targeted employees and management.

E-HRM Operational Effectiveness: The extent of reducing administrative costs, saving time, and enhancing the accuracy of data.

E-HRM Relational Effectiveness: The extent of improvement of the services to managers and employees by e-HRM.

E-HRM Strategic Effectiveness: The extent of enhancement of the strategic role of HR in organizations, the assistance in strategic decision making processes and attaining Competitive Advantage by e- HRM.

E-Performance Management: The extent of developing the budget, analyzing the impact of incentive systems and ensuring the fairness of compensation system by internet technology.

E-Recruitment and E-Selection: The extent of recruiting unique talent across world applicants by internet technology and assessment results of selection process could be generated automatically at the same time.

E-Training and Development: The extent of developing online training courses by internet technology.

Gig Economy: It involves the exchange of labor for money between individuals or companies via digital platforms that actively facilitate matching between providers and customers, on a short-term and payment-by-task basis.

Gig Workers: It involves Highly skilled professionals, Part-time workers, and Crowd workers.

Chapter 11
Using Blockchain for Smart Contracts

Sara Jeza Alotaibi
Institute of Public Administration, Saudi Arabia

ABSTRACT

Today's era of globalization and digital transformation has produced many modern technologies that have influenced modern societies, blockchain being one. This chapter will set out definitions and criteria related to what blockchain is, its advantages and limitations, and its relation to the modern techniques used in the conclusion of smart contracts; and the impact of this technology on fighting administrative and financial corruption. Within this chapter, the central focus is on a new form of contracts founded as a result of the challenge of aligning the current system of the contract with the application of blockchain technology (i.e., to replace the idea of credit intermediation in dealing [notary, bank, management] with another thought based on a peer-to-peer system to increase contractual security and to establish the principle of self-implementation of the contract without the need to mediate with others).

INTRODUCTION

Blockchain can be described as an encrypted information program using a unified web transaction log, and it is this that has been designed in a decentralised way to eliminate the need for an intermediary or centralised recording system to track data exchange. This also has eliminated the need for third party or intermediary intervention, and it is according to technology that the largest distributed and open digital record allows for the transfer of the origin of property from one party to another simultaneously, without the need for a broker.

More than a decade has elapsed since the first knowledge of countries and institutions using Blockchain as a guarantor through a reliable and secure database, and, although Blockchain represents the new era of our current and future technical lives, it is still growing and needs more time so as to build user confidence.

DOI: 10.4018/978-1-7998-4501-0.ch011

The progress of countries relies on the provision of different services to their citizens, including those within the health, scientific, and financial sectors—and it is Blockchain that has facilitated the transfer of funds between different countries in an easy and fast way. Blockchain has also massively contributed to the fight against corruption in all its communities—particularly that of financial corruption—through the conclusion of 'smart contracts', which control the movement of digital financial assets between the parties concerned in different countries.

With the above in mind, this chapter will review the use of Blockchain in the conclusion of smart contracts in terms of the novelty of Blockchain technology and the lack of stable technical or legal frameworks at the local and international levels. This, in turn, should create a general theory that governs this modern technology. Notably, smart contracts purpose to maintain transparency in all financial agreements by making all financial transactions more transparent and visible to all, citizens thus being able to monitor the actual allocation of funds and monitor the disbursement of these funds by governments to help reduce corruption—or even future tax evasion.

In order to achieve more logical, realistic, and feasible results, this inductive and descriptive approach will be followed by extrapolating the various facts and events about it on the local and international arenas; indeed, although the attitude of governments, financial regulators, and banks globally range from extreme caution to rigorous acceptance when it comes to cryptocurrencies, the technology behind them (i.e., Blockchain and smart contracts) has been widely accepted as revolutionary, and have been implemented on all levels.

As an example of this, in order to enable cross-border money transfers, a consortium of sixty-one Japanese and South Korean banks successfully tested Blockchain and smart contracts; additionally, Russia's state-controlled Sberbank has assessed Blockchain and the smart contracts that enable it—such an assessment being of high value considering Sberbank has joined a consortium of more than one hundred companies, including leading organizations such as Cisco, Microsoft, etc. In order to make it more accurate and to develop and implement smart contracts for specific companies, the Alliance aims to develop the Blockchain network.

Notably, that there are currently some difficulties and challenges being faced as a result of the traditional methods of concluding contracts (e.g., the absence of laws, legislation, and special regulations), ultimately leaving the banking and commercial arena a safe haven for money laundering. It is because of this that it has become harder to go to smart contracts through the use of Blockchain; indeed, it will contribute significantly to doubling the volume of E-Commerce, as well as to the elimination of piracy and cyberattacks. This will also contribute to the elimination of administrative and financial corruption by combating money laundering.

Despite the support of Blockchain technology as a result of smart contracts, the modernity of technology still brings about a wealth of questions: how will the government decide to regulate such contracts? How will they be taxed? What happens if the contract cannot reach the subject of agreement, or something unexpected happens? If this were to happen when a traditional contract was concluded, it could be cancelled in court, but Blockchain makes the contract applicable regardless of any trying circumstances due to the 'code is law' policy. However, the majority of these issues exist only because of the novelty of smart contracts in the form of technology. With this promise, technology will surely be perfected over time, and will ultimately become an integral part of our society.

This chapter is constructed accordingly: whilst smart contracts and Blockchain will be given a brief summary in Section 2, this will be followed by a corresponding, more detailed elaboration of these in terms of their architecture in Section 3. Finally, whilst Section 4 outlines the advantages, disadvantages, and general traits possessed by smart contracts and Blockchain, Section 5 and Section 6 close the paper by discussing any current use of smart contract and any conclusions drawn from the research, respectively.

BACKGROUND

Having been initially put forward in 1994 by Nick Szabo as 'a set of promises (Hegedus,2018), specified in digital form, including protocols within which the parties perform on these promises' (Mohanta et al., 2018), the first smart contract was actually proposed well in advance of the introduction of Blockchain technology; indeed, in line with this, Bitcoin came into fruition some time after the introduction of 'Bit Gold' (Kuchkovskiy et al., 2019). Bit Gold was put forward in 1998 as a form of digital currency, such a contract operating independently (with the aid of other systems on the same network) via code transferal. It was such a system that became the foundation of Blockchain and smart contract innovation (Mohanta et al., 2018), (Kuchkovskiy et al., 2019).

When considering the public's current perception of what a 'smart contract' is—i.e., one that is inputted into a computer and operates independently—, it is easy to see that there are some far-reaching misconceptions regarding such technology (Singla et al., 2019), (Hegedus,2018),(Pee et al., 2019). Rather, since they operate on the basis of antecedents and consequences (i.e., if this happens, then that will follow), smart contracts would be better thought of as 'conditional transactions'; for instance, if $1,000 is not given by Ahmed on 01/12/20 to Bank A, then transfer this amount from Ahmed's account to Bank A. This is the basis on which such technologies operate (Nagothu et al., 2018).

In turn guaranteeing that it is the only truthful edition available, a transaction must be verified with the aid of the consensus protocol before being placed at the end of the Blockchain (which can thought of as a distributed ledger that records and stores transactions, forming a 'chain' of an entire history) (Ellul et al., 2018). Since these versions of the truth have to be maintained, records can never be altered, earning Blockchain the nickname of 'immutable'. Notably, each file is also encrypted so as to safeguard such documents even more (Leka et al., 2019), (NGUYE et al, 2019).

Acting as the foundation for entities such as Ethereum, Bitcoin, and Hyperledger, Blockchain can be loosely defined as a computer network altering its records on the grounds of pure mathematics, all the computers possessing matching editions of the database (Chen et al.,2019), (Kuchkovskiy et al., 2019). This, in turn, means this system does not require a central agent/server.

To put the use of such a system into context a little more, perhaps the most popular cryptocurrency application utilising Blockchain has been that of Bitcoin—and its wide use is only getting wider and wider (Mohanta et al., 2018), (Chen et al.,2019). Whilst Bitcoin is for decentralised currency, Ethereum—a network that introduced smart contracts and all-round has arguably more potential—focuses on this currency as well as an engine for applications, removing the requirement of a third party (Wang et al., 2018), (Kuchkovskiy et al., 2019).

In the same vein, smart contract—which can be loosely thought of as a code stored within Blockchain's network, stored as Blockchain code lines—categorises the conditions all the contract-using parties agree to, leading to the automatic triggering of the appropriate actions whenever such conditions are abided to (Hu et al., 2019), (Wright et al., 2017). This guarantees any given result by such actions to be the appropriate one, and this major advantage of such a system is felt most prominently by businesses engaged in partnerships (Hu et al., 2019), (Finogeev et al., 2018). In such collaborations, business owners are usually required to instil the use of the previously outlined agreements, in turn ensuring all involved can accurately predict the results without a third party's input—and this is something accessible with this technology (Hu et al., 2019), (Finogeev et al., 2018).

Whilst Blockchain is most commonly known for its ability to employ an additional element of decentralisation not present in other technologies in order to ensure no intermediary parties can tamper with such features—not to mention its proficiency in constructing its own smart contracts—, when it comes to smart contracts within the Blockchain application, they are simply installed programmes that are kept within the technology. Here, the previously outlined conditions are used in order to kickstart token transferrals between users. Intermediary parties are not required in order to allow for such a transaction, leading to smart contracts' nickname of the 'transparent vending machine' (Wright et al., 2017), (Wang et al., 2018).

In order to fully comprehend what smart contracts actually entail, please engage in the following thought exercise to put this into context a little more: imagine you are looking to purchase a vehicle at a car dealership. Here, the transaction process can be a little troublesome: an inability to make the payment outright can lead to the requirement of financing, which then leads to the requirement of a thorough credit check—a time-consuming and inconvenient process, involving correspondences with a wealth of individuals. This will more often than not lead to the vehicle costing a fair chunk more than it would have before due to the effort that is having to be made to facilitate its selling. Smart contracts offer an easier, more convenient alternative to such a process: here, creditors can swiftly assess your credit on the basis of your previously inputted details, and, if the assessment comes back clear and all parties decide they want to continue with the transaction, a smart contract can be drawn up with ease. Within such a contract, the relevant terms will be outlined and agreed upon so as to allow for guaranteed repayment, and all the correct details will be inputted from the relevant people (including the lender and the buyer). The transferral will thus be a simple, automated ordeal, being automatically sent to the Blockchain's records, where it will be available for viewing by the relevant parties whenever wanted (Manimaran et al., 2019), (Wang et al., 2018).

Similarly, draw up the hypothetical of your friend Sara requiring you to send her some goods. Sara is your friend, and so you do trust her—but you do not trust her trucker Ahmed, and it is him who will ultimately be delivering the goods. The distrust between you and Ahmed is mutual, creating complications and issues when it comes to this transaction. This will mean that Ahmed requires you to pay for his delivery service in advance, before you plan to send the goods. An intermediary party may also very well get involved here to ensure the payment and documents are handled appropriately.

As you may already be able to guess, the idea here is that such a situation could be made far easier with the simple use of smart contracts, which would outline the rules necessary (in this case, probably the date of payment and delivery) (Kuchkovskiy et al., 2019). Here, the payment would be carefully stored until delivery was provided by Ahmed, from which point the payment would be automatically transferred to Ahmed's account.

ARCHITECTURE OF BLOCKCHAIN AND SMART CONTRACTS

Blockchain can be generally conceptualised as a linked structure using hash pointers to join documents, imitating a chain structure. Such an idea is not wholly dissimilar to a record book, a limited yet useful resource for storing data—only here, the employed hash points pinpoint other similar past instances of data (Wang et al., 2018), (Kuchkovskiy et al., 2019). All occurring transactions are recorded, publicised, and stored, and are usually connected to one another. Any possessions that have been seen to pass through the system in the past essentially guarantees any future transactions' security (Wang et al., 2018), (Kuchkovskiy et al., 2019).

Figure 1. Blockchain Network and Traditional Network

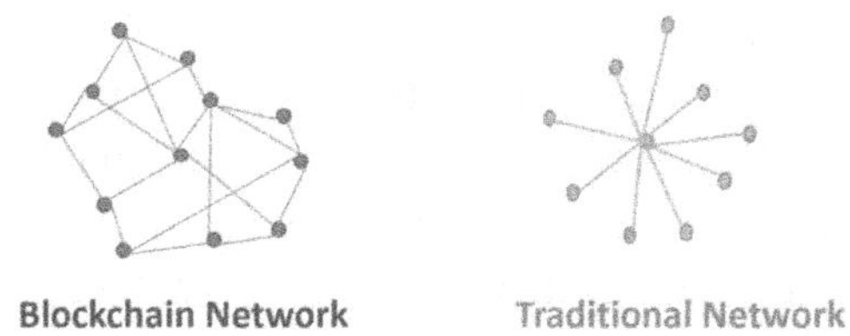

Meanwhile, traditional contracts require a human party's verification to confirm the previously outlined guides have been met, as well as to outline any additional guidelines (Mendi et al., 2019), (Neiheiser et al., 2019). Hence, due to the inconvenience of such a system, the researcher can conclude that this is resource-, time-, and currency-consuming (due to the required human party, the time required to verify the contract, and the financial implications of involving such a human third party, respectively) (Mendi et al., 2019), (Neiheiser et al., 2019).

Figure 2. Traditional Contract

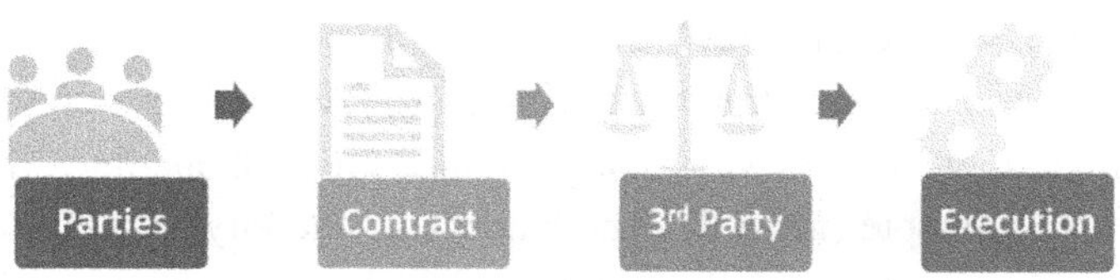

As can be perceived in the for-instance of the implementation of the required stages of verification, the more layers a contract possesses, the more complicated the entire process becomes. This is due to the additional governing required so as to evade any potential disputes. Alternatively, Blockchain stores the smart contract's code, which is then scanned for verification (thus eliminating the need for a human party, instead using cryptographic code). If this comes back clear, the following stages are conducted automatically (Mendi et al., 2019), (Neiheiser et al., 2019).

Figure 3. Smart Contract

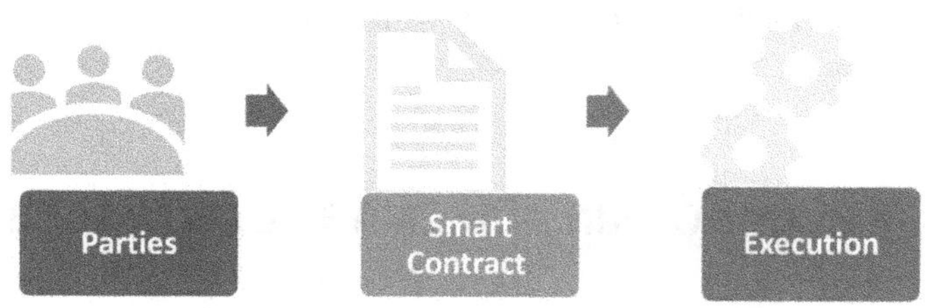

Smart contracts can be defined as agreements possessing previously outlined rules, which are then translated into a computational code (a script). Such a script is then concisely and accurately programmed via Blockchain, this programming script then being used to verify and activate any actions (Aleksieva et al., 2019).

This can be put into context with another for-instance, in which Seller A is selling a product to Buyer B via Shipper C as the deliverer. If the Blockchain system were to be implemented here, the relevant transactions would be made to both Seller A and Shipper C once the system is informed of Buyer B's receipt of the product by the previously agreed Date Z. If, however, this date passes and the product has not been received, this money will simply be returned to Buyer B, and, simultaneously, Manufacturer G will be informed that they need to make another of these productions in order to keep stock supply consistent. All of these processes are automated, and conducted without fuss or confusion from any of the involved parties (Aleksieva et al., 2019).

Indeed, in order to construct such a construct and thus allow for such an above process to take place, there are a variety of aspects that need to be put in place (Aleksieva et al., 2019), (Wang et al., 2019). Initially, guides should be outlined and the ways in which the transactions are automated and the data showcased should all be established within the initial stages (Wang et al., 2019). Furthermore, users additionally need to establish a system for solving any possible future disagreements, finalise a list of rules, and delve into all the possible factors that could refute the implementation of such rules. Such establishments will usually require input from both business stakeholders and developers (Wang et al., 2019).

Every transferral passing through this system hence occurring within the very Blockchain, a smart contract performs within the constraints of a Blockchain (Wang et al., 2018), (Tonelli et al., 2019). Hence, in order to allow for the use of smart contracts, there are a range of stages that need to be undertaken, as follows.

- The smart contract needs to be translated to a programming language in the form of a script by developers, all the while bearing in mind the underpinning logistics of the contract (Wang et al., 2018), (Mendi et al., 2019).
- A distributed network should then be used to send the translated code to the relevant Blockchain—which can, generally speaking, be done by any given system within the network. Notably, the same computer making this transaction should be the same one completing the first stage of translation (Neiheiser et al., 2019), (Tonelli et al., 2019).

Any guidelines agreed upon by the users should then be finalised and detailed in the contract.

Operating in a similar way to decentralisation, the implementation of a contract (as listed above) is conducted in a way that is inherently collaborative; individuals with Internet access can often utilise such a system (the process of the client being downloaded onto the computer called 'mining') (Wang et al., 2018), (Tonelli et al., 2019). The systems used here are frequently referred to as 'nodes', and here, a contract can easily be made and uploaded onto Blockchain (Wang et al., 2018), (Tonelli et al., 2019). A specialised virtual system then looks to perform the code, the contract is financially covered, and transactions are then permitted to be done automatically.

CHARACTERISTICS OF BLOCKCHAIN AND SMART CONTRACTS

It is common knowledge that the insurance industry is one that faces difficulty when it comes to obtaining the public's trust; indeed, a study by YouGov showcased the prominence of this distrust in the US, the results of a poll indicating that whilst 47% of Americans trusted such companies, a comparably high 43% didn't (Mohanta et al., 2018), (Wang et al., 2018). Hence, Blockchain and smart contracts within

Blockchain concerning insurance can be a possible remedy for such distrust in clients, in turn allowing for the more rapid expansion of economies (Tonelli et al., 2019), (Liu et al., 2019). Indeed, when bearing in mind all of the above, the researcher can see that smart contracts boast much of the same benefits of Blockchain in and of itself—namely:

- **Conciseness and Speed:** The coding used by these systems is far more concise than the language used in manually written contracts, thus allowing for these contracts to be less ambiguous and more specific—and, when it comes to allowing for a faster process, the researcher can see that these contracts are automatic and thus compensate for the time that would normally be spent checking for errors and processing essential documents. Further, using a Blockchain-centred ID system, the code implemented here allows for any given insurance company to conduct any wanted risk assessments on a regular basis. Within such a system, any provided IDs are frequently updated with novel data and validated—an automatic, quick process (Wang et al., 2018), (Tonelli et al., 2019).
- **Clear and Smooth:** Within smart contracts, there is very little room for misinterpretation or errors in communication during the process, as all the processes that occur are entirely automatic and have been cross-checked for accuracy multiple times (Aleksieva et al., 2019), (Liu et al., 2019). Smart contracts additionally possess ecological benefits, since they significantly reduce the need for physical paper (since all is done on a virtual system). Hence, with the widespread use of smart contracts, we would be able to perceive not just business benefits, but ecological ones—smart contracts are both profitable and sustainable for the environment.
- **Safety:** The very nature of Blockchain and the way in which it handles transactions and important documents makes it a highly secure system. As discussed previously, all its records—whether from the past, present, or potential future contracts—are all encrypted and organised in a sort of chain where one links to the other (Wang et al., 2019), (Udokwu et al., 2018). Hence, even though their encryption by itself would make them very difficult to hack, this chain structure also means that it would take changing the entire structure in order to access just one document. If this weren't enough, insurers additionally have the option to keep essential documents in multiple sections so that it is very near an impossibility to ever misplace them. All documents and details that ever pass through Blockchain are all stored and tracked diligently, and are always accessible by the corresponding parties. Data is also logged in such a way that it can never be altered or misplaced, and so there is never any room for concern in terms of their security (Wang et al., 2018).
- **Transparency:** Smart contracts are entirely transparent to all of their concerned members. Anyone from the relevant persons will have access to see all the terms and conditions of the agreements. If anyone wants any changes, they have to decide it before the contracts are ready. Once the contract is prepared, there will be no argument on this (Mohanta et al., 2018), (Hu et al., 2019).
- **Trust:** As is often a huge concern for users, it is virtually impossible for any data stored within Blockchain to be changed for personal gain in any way, shape, or form; this is due to the fact that all the stages within the system are conducted automatically and in accordance with a previously established set of guidelines, all related processes being done in a way that is thoroughly secure and with no room for being tampered with. The worry of these details being altered is reduced even further when considering the fact that there actually is no human third party present in a system such as this; all is done automatically within the server. Smart contract structure also means

that it is a very simple matter for any insurance companies to view the stages that have been undertaken thus far, if wanted (Mohanta et al., 2018), (Tikhomirov et al.,2019).
- **Capability:** When combining all the above features of smart contract (conciseness, speed, clarity, smoothness, security, honesty, and trust), it becomes wholly evident that smart contract operation is very efficient and smooth-running. Its very nature (i.e., one that is automatic and conducted within the server itself) means that there is no intermediary third party necessary, and all stages can be easily viewed by the involved parties. All cross-checking and verification processes are undergone within the very system, and claims (in the case of insurance contracts) can also be placed far more easily under this structure. The only possible time-consuming process parties have to engage in is creating a unanimous list of guidelines the system should operate on the premise of in order to ensure smooth operation (Chen et al.,2019), (Wang et al., 2018).

Whilst all of the above advantages to Blockchain are very valid and ultimately create a highly capable system, it seems that all of the excitement surrounding the potential and novelty of such a system has resulted in it still being a wholly misunderstood system by the general public. Hence, the following disadvantages to this system should also be considered and evaluated next to the above listed advantages (Mohanta et al., 2018), (Tonelli et al., 2019):

- **Lack of Clarity in Legal Practice:** Blockchain technology has remained to be a largely unmonitored system, despite its sudden popularity amongst government bodies and the insurance sector—both of which known for being regulated diligently (Mohanta et al., 2018), (Wang et al., 2018). Hence, it is yet to be outlined how Blockchain technology can be used in the insurance industry in a way that corresponds with legal practice (Kuchkovskiy et al., 2019).
- **Restricted Contract Possibilities:** As has been discussed above, every possible mishap needs to be established and solved early on, during the outlining of guidelines, during a smart contract's construction—and this is generally considered to be the main drawback regarding smart contract use (Mendi et al., 2019), (Neiheiser et al., 2019). This is largely due to the fact that such possibilities are frequently much harder to translate into code than they are to simply write in paperwork (Aleksieva et al., 2019), (Cheng et al, 2019). This is even the case in businesses who employ the simplest possible version of smart contract, using the 'if, then' principle within their programming (Wang et al., 2019), (Li et al, 2018).
- **Possible Coding Errors:** Whilst the end product of a smart contract is essentially a smooth-running, effortless system, the actual constructing of that system using the relevant technology is largely complex and technical: their execution is sequential, and so one mistake in its programming will create such a chain reaction that the contract simply will not operate (Tonelli et al., 2019). Hence, even though the end product of smart contracts removes the need for a human intermediary, the development stage does—as established, a potential problem in and of itself (Wang et al., 2018).
- **Complicated Technology:** Considering the above, it is no secret that Blockchain exclusively uses highly advanced, developed technology—and, in line with this, only highly advanced and skilled individuals who are additionally already well-acquainted with the nature of Ethereum will be able to efficiently construct a smart contract (Kuchkovskiy et al., 2019). This is then evidently a job for a rather niche set of people, and the task in and of itself can appear to be a daunting one, necessitating a detailed comprehension of the software being used (Tikhomirov et al.,2019).

BUILDING A SMART CONTRACT AND ITS APPLICATIONS

When bearing in mind the above drawbacks, it is perhaps rather easy to understand why the vast majority of firms feel daunted by the prospect of creating their own smart contracts (Mohanta et al., 2018); however, those in insurance firms should still make the effort to garner as much knowledge as possible concerning what entails smart contract creation—especially if they are ultimately aiming to place their clientele at the forefront of their product creations (Wang et al., 2018). Please see below for a rough sketch of what could be expected from smart contract creation (Tonelli et al., 2019), (Cheng et al, 2019).

1. **Construction:** At this stage, all of the guidelines the smart contract will operate upon are established and translated into the system's code.
    a. **Creating a Token:** During this stage of the construction, all users create their own signature tokens for designated stages with the aid of the Ethereum network. Most notably here, users should evaluate what kind of business logic to employ, as well as the functions that would be most beneficial here.
    b. **Smart Contract Adoption:** Via the Ethereum Virtual Machine, smart contracts are set into motion with the aid of its solidity programming language—formulated specifically for this purpose.
    c. **Assessing:** As much as it is highly advised that smart contracts are first sent to the Blockchain network before full adoption, this may lead to problems in assessment. This problem can be counterbalanced with the use of autotests, which assess the efficacy of a smart contract by replicating a real atmosphere in which a contract would normally be used.
    d. **Validation and Acceptance**: So as to replace the fact that there are no official guidelines for smart contracts in terms of the validation process, developers typically use specific environments in order to cross-check what they have created. Transparency during this stage in terms of what results were reaped so any future financial implications of solving issues could be avoided.

Figure 4. Steps for Building a Smart Contract

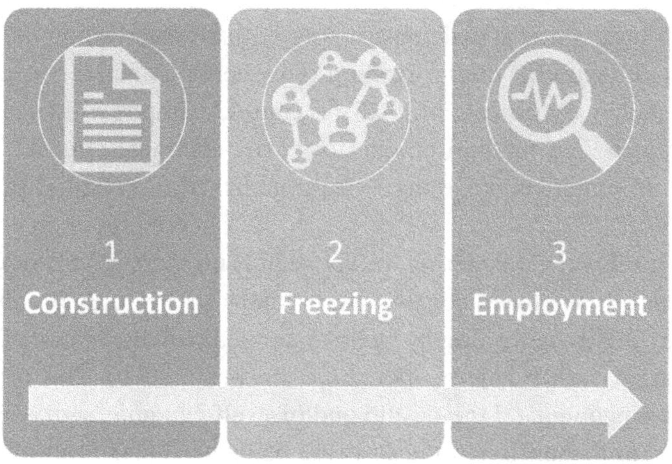

    e. **Deployment:** At this stage (i.e., the contract's deployment to the Ethereum Blockchain), the contract becomes available to all the relevant parties—that is, after the contract code has been transferred to Blockchain and is mined.
    f. **Support:** The inner workings of a given firm's smart contracts should be upkept via the firm's own provided resources
2. **Freezing:** The public ledger makes the smart contract available to the public once it has been sent to the Blockchain, and, at this point, it is a necessity that all relevant parties abide by the previously outlined guidelines—whether that be to undergo a certain monetary transaction, or to send goods to someone else—to keep the ball rolling. It is up until this point—i.e., until these necessary transactions have been made—all other transfers are frozen.
3. **Employment and Finalisation:** The cycle continue of the formulation of transactions and the storing of them in a ledger with the employment of smart contracts—these transactions being, of course, cross-checked according to protocol. Generally speaking, 'employment' is acknowledged to have occurred after all has been unfrozen and any pending transactions given the go-ahead.

Smart contracts are highly versatile in the sense that they can be employed in the vast majority of industries—and this is largely due to the fact that this system actually employs some of the same guidelines as the traditional method (Chen et al.,2019). Some of these are) (Ellul et al., 2018), (Wang et al., 2018):

- **Employment Arrangements:** All firms possess either explicit or implicit demands both for and from their employees in terms of what both parties expect from their business relationship) (Ellul et al., 2018). So as to ensure such expectations are always met within business relationships, smart contracts record and store all discussed terms and conditions within their system—alongside more concrete agreements, such as rate of pay for employees, etc.
- **Safeguarding Copyright:** When group partnerships come about, there is always the possibility that there will be miscommunications surrounding who is doing what and what guidelines should be adhered to—and, since Blockchain obviously stores any agreements made and holds the parties in question responsible for them, these issues will be dramatically reduced, lending the way to better, more effective business partnerships (Mohanta et al., 2018).
- **Internet of Things (IoT):** In turn allowing for smart contracts to fulfil its full potential as a highly effective and strong technology, IoT and Blockchain partnerships creates a better and stronger product, since they both have one primary objective in mind: to implement only the most optimal technologies for industry use (Chen et al.,2019). This combination is thus highly effective through their amalgamation of both hardware and software (Hu et al., 2019).
- **Mortgage System & Real Estate Market:** One of the main industries that have benefitted significantly from the use of smart contracts is the real estate industry—one that usually is known for its time-consuming processes and use of paperwork (Wright et al., 2017). Smart contract implementation here allows for everything to be done within the system, reducing miscommunications and the need for in-person interaction—plus, all mortgage-related transactions will be automated, making for a far smoother long-term process (Manimaran et al., 2019).
- **Government Services:** It is no secret that government services deal with copious amounts of data—specifically in the healthcare sector—, and so smart contracts could be of massive use here, handling, storing, and securing vast amounts of data concerning the public (Finogeev et al., 2018). As would be the case in any other Blockchain system, such files would only be made available to

specific people, and all data concerning test reports, drugs, research, and supplies could be stored safely.

FUTURE RESEARCH DIRECTIONS

Digital Transformation and emerging technologies are creating fast shifts in business paradigms. Emerging technologies are evolving and adding a new dimension every day. One important technology is the blockchain technology which is growing exponentially. Smart contracts are one single case of a wide area of capabilities that can be built around the block chain technology.

This chapter added a single step in this field, but a lot of research is required to deploy the related techniques in specific industries and use cases. Every scenario will have its own parameters and dimension. Every use case can provide specific point for discussion and implementation. Various parameters and dimensions can be applied to create business value.

Every related topic will require plenty of research to reach maturity while studying dependencies and correlations. This will open a wide door for researchers and practitioners to work togother on real life scenarios.

CONCLUSION

As a global market, the smart contracts sector has high expectations in terms of its future performance: 32% CAGR (Combined Annual Growth Rate) being predicted to be generated in the six-year period between 2017 and 2013 (Mohanta et al., 2018), Market Research Future's Smart Contracts Market Research Report indicates toward an estimated $300 being earned by 2024 (Wang et al., 2018). Indeed, whilst the technology of Blockchain and smart contracts are fairly new, they seem to be taking the market industry by storm.

Hence, this chapter barely scratches the surface of Blockchain's potential when it comes to such industries—specifically as a result of their eliminating of the requirement for an intermediary human party, which would normally cast financial and temporal strains. It is due to this potential that a range of businesses have begun making moves towards implementing such a system.

REFERENCES

Aleksieva, V., Valchanov, H., & Huliyan, A. (2019). Application of Smart Contracts based on Ethereum Blockchain for the Purpose of Insurance Services. *2019 International Conference on Biomedical Innovations and Applications (BIA)*, 1-4. 10.1109/BIA48344.2019.8967468

Chen, Y., & Chen, S. S., & Lin, I. (2018). Blockchain based smart contract for bidding system. *2018 IEEE International Conference on Applied System Invention (ICASI)*, 208-211. 10.1109/ICASI.2018.8394569

Cheng, R. (2019). Ekiden: A Platform for Confidentiality-Preserving, Trustworthy, and Performant Smart Contracts. *2019 IEEE European Symposium on Security and Privacy (EuroS&P)*, 185-200. 10.1109/EuroSP.2019.00023

Ellul, J., & Pace, G. (2018). AlkylVM: A Virtual Machine for Smart Contract Blockchain Connected Internet of Things. *2018 9th IFIP International Conference on New Technologies, Mobility and Security (NTMS),* 1-4. 10.1109/NTMS.2018.8328732

Finogeev, A., Vasin, S., Gamidullaeva, L., & Parygin, D. (2018). Blockchain and Smart Contracts for Support the Interaction between the Actors in the Regional Innovation System. *2018 International Conference on System Modeling & Advancement in Research Trends (SMART),* 27-31. 10.1109/SYSMART.2018.8746949

Hegedus, P. (2018). Towards Analyzing the Complexity Landscape of Solidity Based Ethereum Smart Contracts. *2018 IEEE/ACM 1st International Workshop on Emerging Trends in Software Engineering for Blockchain (WETSEB),* 35-39. 10.1145/3194113.3194119

Hu,W., Fan, Z., & Gao, Y. (2019). Research on Smart Contract Optimization Method on Blockchain. *IT Professional, 21*(5), 33-38.

Kuchkovskiy, V., & Shakhovska, N. (2019). Information technology of Blockchain: database, smart contracts, architecture. *2019 IEEE 14th International Conference on Computer Sciences and Information Technologies (CSIT),* 55-59. 10.1109/STC-CSIT.2019.8929885

Leka, E., Selimi, B., & Lamani, L. (2019). Systematic Literature Review of Blockchain Applications: Smart Contracts. *2019 International Conference on Information Technologies (InfoTech),* 1-3. 10.1109/InfoTech.2019.8860872

Li, C., & Palanisamy, B. (2018). Decentralized Privacy-Preserving Timed Execution in Blockchain-Based Smart Contract Platforms. *2018 IEEE 25th International Conference on High Performance Computing (HiPC),* 265-274. 10.1109/HiPC.2018.00037

Liu, Z., & Liu, J. (2019). Formal Verification of Blockchain Smart Contract Based on Colored Petri Net Models. *2019 IEEE 43rd Annual Computer Software and Applications Conference (COMPSAC),* 555-560. 10.1109/COMPSAC.2019.10265

Manimaran, P., & Dhanalakshmi, R. (2019). Blockchain-Based Smart Contract for E-Bidding System. *2019 2nd International Conference on Intelligent Communication and Computational Techniques (ICCT),* 55-59. 10.1109/ICCT46177.2019.8969042

Mendi, A., Erol, T., Safak, E., & Kaym, T. (2019). A Blockchain Smart ContractApplication Framework. *2019 International Symposium on Networks, Computers and Communications (ISNCC)*, 1-4.

Mohanta, B., Panda, S., & Jena, D. (2018). An Overview of Smart Contract and Use Cases in Blockchain Technology. *2018 9th International Conference on Computing, Communication and Networking Technologies (ICCCNT),* 1-4. 10.1109/ICCCNT.2018.8494045

Nagothu, D., Xu, R., Nikouei, S., & Chen, Y. (2018). A Microservice-enabled Architecture for Smart Surveillance using Blockchain Technology. *2018 IEEE International Smart Cities Conference (ISC2),* 1-4. 10.1109/ISC2.2018.8656968

Neiheiser, R., Inácio, G., Rech, L., & Fraga, J. (2019). HRM Smart Contracts on the Blockchain. *2019 IEEE Symposium on Computers and Communications (ISCC)*, 1-6.

Nguyen, V., Pham, H., Tran, T., Huynh, H., & Nakashima, Y. (2019). Digitizing Invoice and Managing VAT Payment Using Blockchain Smart Contract. *2019 IEEE International Conference on Blockchain and Cryptocurrency (ICBC)*, 74-77.

Pee, S., Kang, E., Song, J., & Jang, J. (2019). Blockchain based smart energy trading platform using smart contract. *2019 International Conference on Artificial Intelligence in Information and Communication (ICAIIC)*, 322-325. 10.1109/ICAIIC.2019.8668978

Singla, V., Malav, I., Kaur, J., & Kalra, S. (2019). Develop Leave Application using Blockchain Smart Contract. *2019 11th International Conference on Communication Systems & Networks (COMSNETS)*, 547-549. 10.1109/COMSNETS.2019.8711422

Tikhomirov, S., Voskresenskaya, E., Ivanitskiy, I., Takhaviev, R., Marchenko, E., & Alexandrov, Y. (2018). SmartCheck: Static Analysis of Ethereum Smart Contracts. *2018 IEEE/ACM 1st International Workshop on Emerging Trends in Software Engineering for Blockchain (WETSEB)*, 9-16. 10.1145/3194113.3194115

Tonelli, R., Lunesu, M., Pinna, A., Taibi, D., & Marchesi, M. (2019). Implementing a Microservices System with Blockchain Smart Contracts. *2019 IEEE International Workshop on Blockchain Oriented Software Engineering (IWBOSE)*, 22-31. 10.1109/IWBOSE.2019.8666520

Udokwu, C., Kormiltsyn, A., Thangalimodzi, K., & Norta, A. (2018). The State of the Art for Blockchain-Enabled Smart-Contract Applications in the Organization. *2018 Ivannikov Ispras Open Conference (ISPRAS)*, 137-144. 10.1109/ISPRAS.2018.00029

Wang, P., Liu, X., Chen, J., Zhan, Y., & Jin, Z. (2018). Poster: QoS-Aware Service Composition Using Blockchain-Based Smart Contracts. *2018 IEEE/ACM 40th International Conference on Software Engineering: Companion (ICSE-Companion)*, 296-297.

Wang, S., Ouyang, L., Yuan, Y., Ni, X., Han, X., & Wang, F. (2019, November). Blockchain-Enabled Smart Contracts: Architecture, Applications, and Future Trends. *IEEE Transactions on Systems, Man, and Cybernetics. Systems*, *49*(11), 2266–2277. doi:10.1109/TSMC.2019.2895123

Wright, C., & Serguieva, A. (2017). Sustainable blockchain-enabled services: Smart contracts. *2017 IEEE International Conference on Big Data (Big Data)*, 4255-4264. 10.1109/BigData.2017.8258452

ADDITIONAL READING

Jacobs, T. (2017). *Blockchain: A Step-By-Step Guide For Beginners To Implementing Blockchain Technology And Leveraging Blockchain Programming (Books on Bitcoin, Money,Hidden Economy, FinTech)*. CreateSpace Independent Publishing Platform.

Mukhopadhyay, M. (2018). *Ethereum Smart Contract Development: Build blockchain-based decentralized applications using solidity*. Packt Publishing.

Yuan, M. (2019). *Building Blockchain Apps*. Pearson Education.

KEY TERMS AND DEFINITIONS

Blockchain Platform: A platforms that allow the development of blockchain-based applications. They can either be permissioned or permissionless. They are being used for generalized distributed value exchange, consisting of an expanding list of cryptographically signed, irrevocable transactional records shared by all participants in a network.

Decentralized Autonomous Organization (DAO): Is a digital decentralized autonomous organization or a form of investor-directed venture capital fund. The DAO had an objective to provide a new decentralized business model for organizing both commercial and non-profit enterprises. The code of the DAO is open source.

Innovative Contracts: Contracting structure that enables the maximization of opportunities and reduction of risk based on agile and smart features.

Peer 2 Peer network: A group of computers that are linked together with equal permissions and responsibilities for processing data. Each connected machine has the same rights as its "peers", and can be used for the same purposes.

Risk Management: The act of handling the risk exposure through mitigation, acceptance, sharing and avoidance.

Smart Contracts: A computer code which control the movement of digital financial assets between the parties concerned in different activities based on a predefined rules.

Temper-Proof Transparent Technology: An associated concept with "tamper-proof" enforcement, which means that the smart contract cannot be stopped or modified. Such contract continues to operate irrespective of external events until its pre-set expiration date. It concerns performance and other contractual decisions.

Traditional Contracs: A process that generate trust betwwen two parties to exchange goods and services. The law authorities will need to enforce the contract in case of dispution.

Chapter 12
The Effect of Innovative Contracts on the Business Behaviors in the Context of IoT

Saeed Baselm
Independent Researcher, Saudi Arabia

ABSTRACT

Digital transformation using emerging technologies such as internet of things (IoT) is transforming the way business is conducted within industrial value chains. Consequently, business model innovation and the transition to networked business model are required. Yet, many gaps are being researched to analyze how industrial companies can leverage digital transformation to transform their business models to achieve sustainability benefits. Typically, issues related to value creation and the delivery of business models require more clarification. It is also important to recognize how these components integrate to the sustainability of industrial initiatives. The main objective of this chapter is to pave the way for business behaviors associated with internet of things environment and the related innovative contracts. The discussions and conclusions discussed here will help organizations to establish a long-term, complex relationships with their suppliers, customers, and other value chain actors.

INTRODUCTION

Industry 4.0 reshaping the word and increasingly moving everything to be 'smart' with the use of IoT (Internet of Things), and other emerging technologies. This introduces many advantages such as process automation and optimization. Ultimately this will serve to improve productivity and performance by saving costs, speeding up output, and reducing errors significantly.

The use of digital technologies represents a significant potential for business model innovation in business-to-business (B2B) contexts, while at the same time providing new revenue and value-added opportunities. A major challenge is to find, select and implement customized or preferably configured technology solutions for intended operations. Moreover, exploiting digital transformation goes side by

DOI: 10.4018/978-1-7998-4501-0.ch012

side with business model innovation which requires new products and processes that determine how value is created, delivered, and captured between suppliers, customers, and other value chain players.

This chapter discusses the potential impact of digital transformation on current business models in terms of value creation, delivery, and capture. It also discusses contracting mechanisms in the context of IoT and introduce practical methodologies. Then, it provides insights on the effect of digital transformation and innovative contracts adaption on procurement related business behaviors.

This Chapter is aimed at paving the way for business behaviors in innovative contracts that can work effectively in IoT environments through the combined digital transformation, business model innovation, and sustainability settings. The aim will be to help organizations to establish a long-term, complex relationships with their suppliers, customers and other value chain actors.

BACKGROUND

Digital Transformation using emerging technologies such as Internet of Things (IoT) is transforming the way business is conducted within industrial value chains. Consequently, business model innovation transition is required to maximize digital transformation profits and to achieve sustainability benefits. The term IoT is being used to describe the connectivity of things as "a system of uniquely identifiable and connected constituents" (Ng & Wakenshaw, 2017)

Utilizing new technologies can lead to considerable increase in efficiency and thus clear competitive advantage (PWC, 2014). This shows clearly that the use of digital technologies represents a significant potential for business model innovation in business-to-business (B2B) contexts, while at the same time providing new revenue and value-added opportunities. Those companies that can capitalize on the digital transformation potential driven by big data and analytics will outperform their peers in terms of revenue growth and operating efficiency. Numerous industrial companies are motivated by perceived opportunities and benefits to experiment with innovative business models based on digital technology. (Marshall, Mueck, & Shockley, 2015)

A major challenge for many businesses is to find, select and implement customized or preferably configured technology solutions for their operations. Moreover, there is a new demand from digital technologies and business model innovation to promote continuous improvement in order and keep up with competition and provide consumers with long-term value. Exploiting digital transformation thus goes side by side with business model innovation which requires new products and processes that determine how value is created, delivered, and captured between suppliers, customers, and other value chain players.

Digital Transformation changes necessitate contracting transformation with innovated approaches to get desired benefits, reduce risks and enhance operational controls. More and more companies adopt agile practices to increase speed and flexibility (Gerster & Dremel, 2019); The adoption of agile practices has widespread implications on products, processes, technology, people, and structure that are just beginning to be understood (Highsmith, 2009).

Agile practices can be seen as a response to challenges resulting from the traditional way of development according to "Plan-Build-Run" (Kelker, Gerster, & Dremel, 2018) and the resulting separation between build and run (Rigby, Sutherland, & Takeutchi, 2016). Agile practices can be exemplarily characterized as follows: Formulation of value stories, removing complexity, shortening release cycles to incorporate customer feedback, and the estimation with story points to reduce effort estimation complexity (Abrahamsson, Conboy, & Wang, 2009)

Topics of managing risks in IT contracts or governance and vendor management are prominent take in the extant IT outsourcing literature (Lacity, Khan, & Willcocks, 2009). While IT outsourcing was in the past largely motivated by optimization and cost efficiency, its focus has shifted towards innovation while offshoring activities have declined in importance (Gewald & Schäfer, 2017).

As a result, the digital transformation of business processes, internet of thing (IoT) and cyber-security will have a huge disruptive potential in the upcoming years. Consequently, organizations are motivated to review their strategies to reflect the anticipated implications of digital transformation and to enhance the associated contracting

THE RISE OF INTERNET OF THINGS (IoT)

The term Internet of Things (IoT) is being used to describe the connectivity of things as "a system of uniquely identifiable and connected constituents (termed as Internet-connected constituents) capable of virtual representation and virtual accessibility leading to an internet-like structure for remote locating, sensing, and/or operating the constituents with real-time data/information flows between them" (Ng & Wakenshaw, 2017). Another scientific definition for IOT is attributed to Kevin Ashton "An open and comprehensive network of intelligent objects that have the capacity to auto-organize, share information, data and resources, reacting and acting in face of situations and changes in the environment" (Somayya Madakam, R. Ramaswamy, Siddharth Tripathi, 2015)

IoT can also be considered as a global network which allows the communication between human-to-human, human-to-things and things-to-things, which is anything in the world by providing unique identity to every object. Sensors and actuators embedded in physical objects—from roadways to pacemakers—are linked through wired and wireless networks, often using the same protocols that connects the internet. These networks churn out huge volumes of data that flow to computers for analysis. When objects can both sense the environment and communicate, they become tools for understanding complexity and responding to it swiftly.

IoT can change the world as we know it and will fundamentally alter the business models of many companies and the way consumers interact with these companies and other stakeholders (Fredette, Marom, Steiner, & Witters, 2012). In fact, the progression of its exponential rate impacts all aspects of daily life. It has been estimated that there will be between 25 and 50 billion connected devices by 2020 (Lee & Lee, 2015). New applications in many economic sectors (e.g. finance, insurance, transport...) would surely benefit from the potential of IoT systems to capture process and share a multitude of data instantly and autonomously. This will pave the way for new business opportunities and the emergence of a new kind of 'smart service'.

According to (Langley, et al., 2020), the development of IoT as a network of things interconnected globally opened the way to increased smartness. The ability of smart things to see the environment and act accordingly is one of the key aspects. IoT will transform the world we live in and radically change the model of many businesses and the communication between customers and these companies and other stakeholders. The dynamics of these changes are driven mainly by advances in technology like interconnectivity, big data and artificial intelligence. Moreover, organizations and companies have a significant role to play in deciding how IoT can change communities.

Horizontal vs. Vertical Diffusion

Traditionally, horizontal integration is used when a business grows by acquiring a similar company in their industry at the same point of the supply chain. Vertical integration is when a business expands by acquiring another company that operates before or after them in the supply chain. (York, Dunham, & Ahn, 2012). Rogers' diffusion of innovations theory (DOI), has been regarded as a pivotal framework when it comes to studying and understanding how technological innovations get diffused, and potentially adopted by individuals and/or organizations. (Gomes & Osman, 2019)

Emerging technologies in general and IoT solutions, use the horizontal and vertical diffusions to spread. They can enable the technological infrastructure as needed, from localized sensors to centralized back office systems. IoT is often standardized and can be applied to a wide range of applications with relative ease. It is therefore in the interests of technology-oriented companies to sell their products as widely as possible. This is represented as horizontal diffusion, as an actor attempts to exploit the awareness of a technology to as many customers as possible, regardless of industry or competition. Vertical diffusion aims to improve the company position in the same industry and to expand to other regions or markets. New business models driven mainly by the new information and illustrates the new business benefits to the companies that manufacture, support and service IoT products.

Vertical and horizontal diffusions will happily coexist at one point in time, but as we look forward or study our past, the inconsistency of strategy of industry becomes obvious. As linked products require a wide set of technical know-how, it is similarly difficult to negotiate mutually beneficial partners' agreements. Managers must therefore consider how IoT influence the business model of their own organization, but also note the market logic of their partners. (Saarikko, Westergren, & Blomquist, 2017). This will help organizations to sustain and build its future.

Contributions of IoT in the Development of Legal Disciplines

IoT created a cohesive environment between technology and humans. It is required to enhance the collaboration between stakeholders and combine several factors to produce an effective contract. The new approach of contracting shall consider the massive data flow in the organizations and the inevitable agility and change management practices.

Digital transformation platforms have shifted the working routine from the traditional mode to smart mode which proved to be well-reputed and reliable, in the same time ensuring that these platforms have adequate and strict confidentiality and privacy agreements to protect the rights of all parties. Throughout the contract lifecycle, teams of people must collaborate on various tasks both pre-execution and post-execution. The main contractors may hire specialized their parity for certain activities. Human capital preparations for new contracting styles is also developing to fit between technology based operational activities and adaptive functional strategies utilize advanced technology tools to build the required contracting paradigm.

However, there exist some drawbacks in using mobile and industry 4.0 technologies such as; the lack of trust in contractual relations in terms of the working routine that the various teams follow; the extreme effort it takes to break the power of habit and mindset change requirement and associated culture. Such drawbacks are being eliminated over time.

Finally, there is a need for a proper regulation that, at the same time, provides legal protection to those who opt for a contract and avoids opportunistic or even illegal activities and transactions. This requires specific regulations, considering the existing features of IoT and digital platforms to verify the existence of mechanisms that allow transactions with unscrupulous intentions (Gomes S., 2018). In the popular discourse of IoT technologies and the behaviors associated with digital transformation some expect that the "role of lawyers might shift to producing smart contract templates on a competitive market, [and] contract selling points would be their quality, how customizable they are, and their ease of use". (Cornelius, 2018).

How IoT Will Require a New Business Model

Business model innovation is defined as "Designed, novel, non-trivial changes to the key elements of a company's business model and/or the architecture linking these elements" (Parida, Sjödin, & Reim, 2019). This implies that business model innovation can be focused on introducing novel components into individual elements of the business model as well as across elements, aligning them within an architecture of value creation. (Foss & Saebi, 2016).

Considering the enormous interest in these new concepts which can radically change where we live, how we function and communicate with one another and with organizations. It is not clear how businesses would be impacted by the introduction of IoT. Enterprises who adapt their current business models to the new technologies have significant chances to evolve and are highly competitive. To leverage the advantages, businesses need to build on digital technologies such as artificial intelligence, digital platforms and big data analysis in order to innovate their model.

The IoT poses, however, often significant problems to organizations, including the advancement of system-to-system interoperability, the management of industry partners not collaborated with the new developments, path-dependent, processes and transaction, contractual and liability problems, security risks, loss of control and privacy concerns associated with the data collected and used. Therefore, it is necessary for businesses to consider to what degree smart things are disrupting existing business models and, as part of that, how IoT will impact the value creation of such service ecosystems depending on the configuration and capabilities of smart things. (Langley, et al., 2020)

An important element of this transition is how companies adapt their existing business model to build a new networked business model that fits IoT better. The development of a new business model is therefore concerned with the effects of route dependence as the company progressively tries to extend its existing strategy and value views to the new IoT environment. (Ehret & Jochen, 2017)

IOT AS A CATALYST FOR INNOVATIVE CONTRACTING

A contract is where individuals, groups, firms, institutions and even governments enter into an agreement where each of them is committed to meeting certain conditions. In traditional contracts, the parties shall register and legally agree to comply with the text, in a language appropriate to the jurisdiction or law where the agreement is drafted and if the parties involved consent. The purchase and sale, lease, provision, loan, transportation and working services are some of the most common examples of economic transactions between companies or individuals implemented by means of contracts. However, a question always arises at any time a contract is written, which is a tradeoff that must be addressed—whether or not to make a contract flexible but incomplete or rigid but comprehensive. (Manzano & Agugliaro, 2019).

Traditional projects often include a comprehensive, prescriptive list of what needs to be executed. Conversely, IoT solutions need to avoid these precision and rigidity, but focus on valuable artifacts. They focus on teamwork to manage integration and enhanced respond to innovative development work. Innovative contracts facilitate the gradual deployment of resources and products, either through the implementation or acquisition of predefined delivery intervals and milestones. This approach details how each iteration deployment is carried out, coded, checked, and so on, and how it will be delivered, within a time-boxing of a set reach.

The Need for Innovative IoT Contracts

IoT contracts may be extremely difficult to understand. ICT contracts difficulty is attributed to several reasons. First, they are often distinguished by an abstract language that combines a multitude of technical words. Second, they have often been published with previous technological developments in mind and are therefore not completely appropriate for new technology. Thirdly, the multi-layer market structure will make it difficult to define and analyze all relevant contracts. (La Diega & Walden, 2016)

According to (La Diega & Walden, 2016), IoT contracts should be influenced by two main dependencies. The spectrum of IoT actors, where market power exists within the supply chain, can vary considerably, from a distributor to a software developer, a product producer, or a cloud provider. On the other hand, users are reliant in the sense that they are bound to a contract where flexibility is not feasible and where there is minimal interoperability and portability.

Companies understand that their vendors are important partners in lowering costs, increasing efficiency, and fostering creativity. They regularly speak about the need for cooperative partnerships with mutual goals and risks. However, according to (Frydlinger, Hart, & Vitasek, 2019) they default to a contradictory disposition and a transactional contracting strategy when contract negotiations begin. Contractual clauses–like the "convenience withdrawal," which grants one party full right to terminate the contract after a certain date–are used to attempt to gain an upper hand. These strategies, however, not only provide a false sense of security (because both parties have disproportionate swapping costs to enforce these clauses), they also encourage undesirable actions that compromise the relationship and the contract.

Alternatively, it is suggested to follow a completely different kind of arrangement: a formal contractual framework establishing mutual goals and developing governance structures to keep both parties' expectations balanced over the long term. That covers complicated procurement arrangements, strategic alliances, franchises, public-private partnerships, major construction projects and collective bargaining contracts. This approach is being employed successfully by an increasing number of large companies, such as Dell, Intel, AstraZeneca, and Telia, a Swedish telecoms company (Frydlinger, Hart, & Vitasek, 2019) . This legally enforceable contract was structured from the start to promote cooperation and partnership and is particularly useful for complex relationships in which every situation cannot be expected.

From Traditional to Innovative Contracting Styles

Agile contracts do not determine the exact scope of the project, but the degree of complexity and adjustment varies depending on the price structure from low to high They are progressive contracts, in which no necessary scope is defined beyond one iteration. Unlike target-cost contracts, in which the overall project scope and details are identified at the start as best as possible along with change process. (Vodde & Larman, 2010)

In agile contracting, enterprises and their contractors usually agree to enter into few iterations of implementations, instead of signing a comprehensive contract in advance. This helps the both parties to use a service or product on a trial basis to build trust and to make use of risk coverage. Once the both entities have tested few iterations, they can continue to buy further iterations or improvements as required. In addition, the customer will be given the option to cancel the project within one sprint time. Thus, the client may lose only a limit of one sprint without composing the complete vision. Also, the scope can include sprint changes to add gradual benefits. Some providers incorporate a termination clause into the contract to allow client the option of leaving on predefined iteration notices. (Shalan & Anaim, 2017)

Promoting Sharing Economy

In fact, the integration between Internet of Things (IoT) and innovative contracting can also accelerate sharing market applications. Moreover, the convergence of IoT with blockchains will lead to shared network technologies such as peer-to-peer automatic payment networks and currency exchange platforms. (Zheng, et al., An Overview on Smart Contracts: Challenges, Advances and Platforms, 2019). There are many benefits to the sharing economy: decrease of customer prices by crediting and recycling products, better use of energy, increased quality of service and decreased environmental impacts.

Yet, as a result of this centralization, most modern share markets are plagued by rising consumers transaction costs, anonymity and the unreliability of reputable third parties. Automatic triggers can be an ultimate use case for the integration between IoT systems and smart contracts. IoT can benefit significantly from the smart contracts which is considered as one part of innovative contracts through automation of billing and sizing features. Smart contracts can reshape economy sharing by decentralizing and privacy respecting approach. Practical execution also illustrates the effectiveness of the proposed economic platforms in sharing and exchanging objects without a trusted third party.

Adaptive Rather Than Harsh Change Management

The change management is essentially implicitly tackled within the overall philosophy of the agile approach to allow step reprioritization and incremental adaptation without a rigorous change management process. This area requires considerable care to make change quick and regular and to support the providers displaying more functionalities that are seldom utilized, allowing more value to be achieved from a certain product.

This approach shifts the perspective of the organizations and allows them to look beyond the limits of the contracts towards a larger picture. The change for free contract provision enables customers to adjust the basic priorities free of charge if the overall contract work stays the same. It also helps the clients to add new features if the low priority items of equal work are excluded from the deal. Nonetheless, this does not mean that all forms of change management are given in contractual form. Relevant variations may result from changes in the relationship between the parties, such as the acquisition of a party by another entity. There may also be a fundamental transformation in the corporate direction. (Shalan & Anaim, 2017)

Such approach is very crucial in the IoT industry, because IoT components are cautiously changes and can be used in huge projects that can span over several years. It is expected to have different generation while moving from design to implementation and if operation is included that will be even more diverse.

Avoid Shading

Companies traditionally use contracts to protect them from the abuse of power by one party to take advantages at other's expense— e.g., by increasing or lowering prices unilaterally, changing delivery dates, or requiring more cost-effective terms. The fact that almost every contract contains gaps, omissions, and ambiguities — despite the best efforts of companies to anticipate each scenario — only compounds the hold-up behavior. (Frydlinger, Hart, & Vitasek, 2019)

Shading occurs when a party fails to get the result anticipated from the contract and start blaming the other party for the results or claiming that they neglected to minimize the losses. The aggrieved party sometimes actively, even unintentionally, cuts back on performance to compensate. It highlights the need for frameworks to match expectation or update reference points on unexpected events or changes required over time. According to (Frydlinger, Hart, & Vitasek, 2019), companies are likely to make distorted investments that yield poor results in a reaction to the combined problems of hold-ups and unfinished contracts,. For example, the use of multiple suppliers instead of just one increases costs and so does operating a shadow organization.

PAVING THE WAY TOWARD IOT INNOVATIVE CONTRACTS

Many organizations require long-term, complex relationships for which the vested methodology is well suited. to (Frydlinger, Hart, & Vitasek, 2019). Digital technology isn't just "another technology", it provides opportunities throughout the entire value creation and appropriation process by impacting not only the operational level of business processes, but also the strategic level of business purposes and the ability to produce new value initiatives. (Langley, et al., 2020). Multiple concepts are attached to the journey of building an innovative contract for IoT related industries.

Shared Vision and Objectives

The parties will work together to create a common vision to direct them throughout the partnership. A constructive and mutual strategy opens a dialogue between the participants, which leads to sharing what is required, handling capacity gaps, and focusing on the advantages that the other side can provide to mitigate risks or conflicts. The common teams shall develop a vision and alignment as the basis for a statement of intent. IoT implementation and update is a whole journey that need to be designed as necessary and implemented with results in mind. Updates and upgrades are continuous in this journey.

It is essential to understand the business model and record it. It is important to spend time modeling results and to see how well the parties are in line with the priorities of each other. Together a model should define value exchanges between the partners, which contribute almost inexorably to partnership, commitment and mutual satisfaction share of the market and sustainable benefit. The parties will use it individually to analyze the results once the model is created. Moreover, expectations shall be kept balanced in a dynamic, changing environment by both parties and not just the one with greater power. IoT contract need to clarify the partnership vision and goals along with challenges and roadmap turns.

Business Behaviors

When all parties have trust in the whole process, smart contracts can be enforced under the umbrella of innovative contracting. The integration of supply chains and smart contracts will automate contract rights and obligations throughout the payment, implementation and the delivery. Smart contracts can enable the growth of modern supply chains (Zheng, et al., 2019).

Despite nomenclature, smart contracts use internet protocols to secure, automate and decentralize communication and for the execution and development of agreements. In such contracts, as are currently known, provisions that may grant any person the rights and duties need to be defined and immediately and enforced in agreements. Smart contracts my handle the relation between parties that are not even supposed to recognize one another or have a certain trust in each other. (Gomes S., 2018)

This is crucial for IoT environments. The spread and success of Internet of Things (IoT) is based on the rapidly growing number of applications, and smart contracts may play a pivotal role in IoT. (Schmitt, Mladenow, Strauss, & Schaffhauser-Linzatti, 2019). As smart contracts are being started by a transaction such as data flow, this creates synergies between smart contracts and IoT devices that collect and communicate data. Data from IoT devices could also indicate that a condition for the execution of a further workflow step is fulfilled or serve as verification that a contractual commitment has been performed.

Designing Customers' Experience

Individual organizations are using IoT to improve the efficiency and quality of their decision-making processes. As smart things become adaptable, autonomous and strongly linked to data systems across several domains, changes in industry and institutional arrangements can be noticed. The macro level shifts would lead to global integration, new economic trends and the creation of completely new structures at the highest level of smartness. (Langley, et al., 2020)

According to (Shalan & Anaim, 2017), innovative contracts allow customer experience to be enhanced. This will require that the customer and the development teams to understand the definition of the features clearly. The definition must use a language familiar to the customer rather than a scientific nonsense, also business value should be included in each feature. Business-people should be given sufficient time to discuss, study and develop the design of certain components, otherwise, plans cannot go on, and there will be a bad impression of the value of that part. IoT touch these elements broadly as it is directly affecting business and personal behaviors.

Building the Trust

Trust is often considered the most important factor in the progress of business. Nevertheless, even if trust is common in everyday sense, the conceptual definition of trust is difficult. Everyone sees the importance and role of trust differently and trust is always connected with the situation, making the definition of trust universally impossible (Blomqvist, 2005). Trust and risk sharing are considered key issues in contracting. There is no point in starting the project without any trust between the contracting parties. The level of trust in the often influences the risk-sharing and legal and ethical provisions of contracts. (Laakkonen, 2014). It is important that both parties must make a conscious effort to create an environment of trust — one in which they are transparent about their high-level aspirations, specific objectives and concerns. And if their prior contracting phase led to distrust and a vicious cycle of shading they will focus on how and why this happened. (Frydlinger, Hart, & Vitasek, 2019)

Trust is a complicated concept because situations that are crucial in long-term relationships cannot be addressed perfectly in a written contract and short-term inequalities are unavoidable, which mean that trust in the other party is necessary in any contract. This also suggests that if there is no trust, then trying to contract is unreasonable: it is very unlikely to lead to a (successful) relationship if contracts are not respected. On the other hand, if the negotiating parties have mutual trust, time and efforts will be saved in the negotiations process and contract implementation. Economists also think trust will decrease transaction costs. The idea that trust is important to contracting is thus strengthened by both negative and positive influences.

In IoT environments it is important to consider the trust that customers have in smart things, different parties that use the vast amount of data gathered by smart things. This will help in developing effective business models. (Roman, Najera, & Lopez, 2011) advises that companies disclose in a transparent manner what kind of data is gathered and for which reasons the data is used by different parties.

Creating Value

Digital technology is becoming an integral part of all products and processes, not only driving the internet and social media accounts. Digital transformation and technical advancement are offering products to manufacturers with huge opportunities. Supplementing a product like a car or appliance with IoT sensors and communicative capability will help in obtaining precise location, environmental condition and consumption details.

(Porter & Heppelmann, 2014) shed light on how connected devices impact competitive capabilities. They saw enormous potential for industry leaders to improve their positions by extending their presence in the value chain of integrated product service offerings as holistic solutions. Moreover, they concluded that digital transformation is a way to create higher barriers to market entry for new entrants because incumbents may establish more close service-oriented relationships with customers.

Value creation with IoT will often include many parties in a complicated and interconnected operation. The potential payoff is however important as a linked system can provide valuable information on the location, status and use of new product development. This can be used to enhance logistics performance, operation and maintenance. In addition, a connected device, which allows continuous access for consumer data creates a new layer and allowing users to better understand the actions of their customers thus establishing long-term relationships. (Saarikko, Westergren, & Blomquist, 2017).

Delivering Value

The design of Internet of Things (IoT) solutions are strongly context aware, service-oriented focused, and multidisciplinary. This makes designing IoT solutions complex, often crafted for the specific context in terms of technological choices and business models. (Yaacobi, 2016)

It is thus very crucial to describe how activities and processes are used to deliver the promised value. This includes, for example, the specific delivery resources and capabilities needed (e.g. service support staff, online monitoring systems). Digital business models that have been revised often require the development and application of new capabilities and the revision of operational processes and global delivery activities. Digital capabilities enable continuous improvement of information flow, integration of service activities and centralized monitoring of service processes. As a result, there are fewer delays and more responsive customer service.

In addition, the data collection triggered by IoT systems and the associated storage and sharing will require companies to become more collaborative, facilitating greater transparency of information, inter-company connectivity, and joint data analysis. This allow to track and count, observe and identify, evaluate and act based on previously un-trackable behavior.

Capturing Value

Value capture concerns the revenue model and its financial viability, with due regard to potential revenue streams and the cost structure. Capturing the value of IoT solutions can be increased in various ways— for example, by lower costs, higher revenues, or by capturing new revenue streams. To ensure the profitability of the business model over time, it is very important to set up an appropriate risk management system where financial gains are more than equal to any negative consequences, such as high delivery costs.

Picking the right place to play in an ecosystem is only half the battle. After all, if there is significant competition at the bottleneck stage, then the value created at that stage is likely to be contested at best. (Raynor & Cotteleer, 2015). IoT may have a particularly interesting role in changing the value-capture mechanisms by enabling increased transparency among multiple actors. New revenue models enabled by digital technology will open more flexible and customized pricing that can be changed over time based on operational data. These situations also provide customers the opportunity to choose fixed prices, pay-per-use, or hybrid models, facilitating greater value creation through increased customization and shifts in responsibility.

Focusing on Outcomes Not Transactions

As demand for repeat transactions grew, trade patterns changed, and new transaction-based business models arose. Since then, these transaction-based business structures have been the foundation of traditional business relationships. Traditional outsourcing arrangements usually focus on negotiating deals at a detailed per-transaction level, either on a business basis or on a per-count basis. Unfortunately, many business professionals wrongly assume that a transaction-based business model is the most cost-effective approach. A transaction-based approach cannot achieve a flawless market-based price equilibrium in reliant or multidimensional commercial arrangements.

The evolution of IoT and smart contracts enable companies to pursue various forms of procurement business models, real time activities and direct impact analysis. If you choose to adopt an outcome-based business model, it will be essential to understand that, while the technology is difficult, it's the nontechnical parts that will make business work. This is true for all business-model changes, including the IoT products. (Rossman, 2017)

Setting the Acceptance Criteria

In IoT environment, standardization enables moving between service providers; accordingly, clients are not required to stick to one company. Such an approach reduces the requirements of acceptance criteria that can be accepted incrementally for each operation. This approach relaxes terms of service acceptance and encourages negotiations during the contracting process, preventing major activity. Acceptance process must be contractually transparent. Contract language would help the project advance significantly and facilitate cooperation. Legal professionals participating in a successful project will consider whether the right people engage in the approval and collaborate with the supplier? (Shalan & Anaim, 2017)

Handling Liability and Warranty

The negotiation of liability clauses in every contract is still the most difficult area, and this will not change in innovative contracts. Nonetheless, it reshapes liability by identifying negative findings early and address consequences through the liability model. Smart contracting should proactively reduce exposure to risk of several items, such as cost and reputation, and eliminate consequences. Fixing could be simpler, as the system would have different independent components with less involvements. Similarly, warranty concerns are reduced.

The emergence of the Internet of Things (IoT) is posing significant challenges to the existing product liability framework. Unlike previous liability regimes for "dumb" products, where faults for product failure can clearly percolate up the chain of distribution, it is more difficult to hold retailers, mid-channel distributors, and manufacturers liable for the damages caused by "smart" devices. This difficulty arises because unlike traditional products, IoT devices come with End user License Agreements (EULAs) and other types of software contracts which allow manufacturers to disclaim most, if not all, liability for damages incurred by the usage of IoT products. (Chau & Markel, 2015)

Scheduling Payment

Large-scale Internet of Things (IoT) services such as healthcare, smart cities, and marine monitoring are pervasive in cyber-physical environments strongly supported by Internet technologies and fog computing. (Wen, et al., 2017). Innovative contracts will cover billing and payments including incentives and termination clauses. Although the most common practice is to pay an intermittent charge in addition to set-up fees, where applicable, more sophisticated payment systems can be connected to different IoT portfolios. Pay-per-use frameworks should be structured to suit the needs of the clients and providers.

By collecting and analyzing user data, connected devices make it possible to offer an infinite number of services based on current or upcoming needs. This new technological trend allows companies to move from selling products to selling services linked to device usage.

Creative Contract Termination

The creative contract termination is related to the change control, in that the service provider should be open to change direction. It may be to the point of stopping additional work at the end of any iteration. IoT as part of emerging technologies may trigger special requirements where innovation is continuous, and replacement of sensors may be required every while.

In contrast to traditional contract, legal professionals need to recognize that agreed termination should be seen as a constructive and beneficial occurrence in IoT projects. The main ideas in such methodology are either that the client has a working system for each version, or that both sides will have consistent and up-to-date views on the state of the deliverable. These are crucial points for legal professionals to consider.

Effective Governance Structure

Given the excitement around digital projects, IoT based initiatives rarely go through necessary proper governance checks. Governance is often skipped, and implementation is rushed. While this rule is the most critical rule for successful collaboration among the other rules and elements. A governance structure helps the parties to produce success and sustainable outcomes during agreement execution. A strong governance system provides a company knowledge atmosphere and constructive improvements that will help an organization monitor its operations

Developing a successful IoT strategy requires understanding technology requirements unique to the business (Roe, 2018). Starting with the creation of specific strategies that emphasize the importance of creating collaboration, attitudes and behaviors. In a flexible governance structure, which provides top-to-bottom insights in what happens, the parties are responsible for monitoring this relationship.

Governance addresses the need to manage change, including the transition from existing approaches– and the management of change once the new agreement has been entered. The final element recognizes that all contracts are special and that many companies and service providers must consider and comply with different regulatory requirements and protocols. Additional regulations covering particular sector, state, regional and national criteria may be required in the governance system.

FUTURE RESEARCH DIRECTIONS

Business-technology relationship is transforming the future. Nowadays, deep technology penetrations are creating fast shifts in business paradigms. Emerging technologies are evolving and adding a new dimension every day. One important technology is the internet of things (IoT) which is growing exponentially like other technologies. One big hurdle in using these new innovations is how to manage the stakeholders who are working on such initiatives to create the required values. This chapter attempts to encourage a fruitful discussion that will eventually lead to an increased number of research studies in the field of innovative contracting for IoT and other technologies in general.

This is just a step in this field, but a lot of research is required to deploy the related theories and techniques in specific industries and use cases. Every scenario will have its own parameters and dimension. Every use case can provide a step to portray the full picture. Contracting dimensions need to be applied in every scenario to pave the way for a smooth and fruitful trusted relationship between all stakeholders.

Jointly, all the above topics requires plenty of research which is considered part of the digital transformation and contracting arena that have plenty of dependencies and correlations. The development of effective and acceptable innovative contracting styles requires the participation of a very wide range of stakeholders. To be successful, the research should benefit from various contracting behaviors including the agile, traditional, and innovative. This chapter generates thorough conclusions, and number of research paths that researchers can follow to advance the knowledge in contracting styes related to emerging technologies in general and IoT in particular.

CONCLUSION

Digital transformation appears to be the fastest growing activity for users, and it is expected to play a key role throughout the customer life cycle. IoT among other emerging technologies introduce a new kind of environment which enables people and machines to work with each other and create new circumstances. This chapter clearly demonstrated how IoT related technologies are affecting the contracting style adopted by companies.

Innovative contracting encourages incremental delivery of services which is characterized by iteration development and continuous verification of desired scope. IoT related equipment promoted the usage of complex systems where vertical and horizontal independent contractors are working altogether to operate and manage different aspects independently, to create value from technology and enable business agility. Moreover, the agile contracting approach provides value to cope up with such multi stakeholder environment in an effective manner. Innovative contracting is needed to balance the risks between both parties and give both the incentive to work together towards the success of the joint project.

The innovative contracting affects the business-technology relationship and develop a creative management tools to support the suppliers and the contractor's achievements and compliance. Ultimately this will create an effective setup for planning and implementing IoT related technologies and environments.

REFERENCES

Abrahamsson, P., Conboy, K., & Wang, X. (2009). 'Lots done, more to do': The current state of agile systems development research. *European Journal of Information Systems, 281-284*(4), 281–284. Advance online publication. doi:10.1057/ejis.2009.27

Blomqvist, K. (2005). Trust in a Dynamic Environment - Fast Trust as a Threshold Condition for Asymmetric Technology Partnership Formation in the ICT Sector. In K. Blomqvist (Ed.), *Trust in Pressure, Investigations of Trust and Trust Building in Uncertain Circumstances* (pp. 127–147). Edward Elgar Publishing, Inc. doi:10.4337/9781845427962.00011

Chau, B. K., & Markel, Z. (2015, December 1). *Liability for Home IoT.* Retrieved from[REMOVED HYPERLINK FIELD] https://groups.csail.mit.edu/mac/classes/6.805/student-papers/fall15-papers/Liability%20for%20hone%20IoT.pdf

Cornelius, K. B. (2018). *Standard form contracts and a smart contract future*. Internet Policy Review.

Ehret, M., & Jochen, W. (2017). Unlocking value from machines: Business models and the industrial internet of things. *Journal of Marketing Management, 33*(1-2), 111–130. doi:10.1080/0267257X.2016.1248041

Foss, N. J., & Saebi, T. (2016). Fifteen Years of Research on Business Model Innovation: How Far Have We Come, and Where Should We Go? *Journal of Management*, 1–15.

Fredette, J., Marom, R., Steiner, K., & Witters, L. (2012). *The Promise and Peril of Hyperconnectivity for Organizations and Societies.* Geneva: World Economic Forum.

Frydlinger, D., Hart, O., & Vitasek, K. (2019, September 1). A New Approach to Contracts. *Harvard Business Review.*

Gerster, D., & Dremel, C. (2019). Agile contracts: Learning from an autonomous driving sourcing project. In *Proceedings of the 27th European Conference on Information Systems (ECIS)* (pp. 1-12). AIS Electronic Library (AISeL).

Gewald, H., & Schäfer, L. (2017, February 20). Quo vadis outsourcing? A view from practice. *Journal of Global Operations and Strategic Sourcing, 10*(1), 2–17. doi:10.1108/JGOSS-10-2016-0031

Gomes, R., & Osman, S. (2019). *Managing Organizational Adoption of IoT.* Uppsala, Sweden: Uppsala University. Retrieved November 12, 2020, from http://uu.diva-portal.org/smash/get/diva2:1374639/FULLTEXT01.pdf

Gomes, S. (2018). Smart Contracts: Legal Frontiers and Insertion into the Creative Economy. *Brazilian Journal of Operations & Production Management*, 376-385.

Highsmith, J. A. (2009). *Agile project management: creating innovative products.* Pearson Education.

Kelker, P., Gerster, D., & Dremel, C. (2018). Agile Meets Non-Agile: Implications of Adopting Agile Practices at Enterprises. In *24th American Conference on Infromation Systems* (pp. 1-15). New Orleans, USA: AMCIS 2018 Proceedings.

La Diega, G. N., & Walden, I. (2016, September 25). Contracting for the 'Internet of Things': Looking into the Nest. *European Journal of Law and Technology, 7*(2), 1–29. http://nrl.northumbria.ac.uk/27910/

Laakkonen, K. (2014). *Contracts in Agile Software Development* (Master's Thesis). Aalto University.

Lacity, M., Khan, S., & Willcocks, L. (2009, September 1). A Review of the IT Outsourcing Literature: Insights for Practice. *The Journal of Strategic Information Systems, 18*(3), 130–146. doi:10.1016/j.jsis.2009.06.002

Langley, D. J., Doorn, J., & Ng, C. L. (2020, January). The Internet of Everything: Smart things and their impact on business models. *Journal of Business Research, 122*, 853–863. doi:10.1016/j.jbusres.2019.12.035

Lee, I., & Lee, K. (2015, July 14). The Internet of Things (IoT): Applications, investments, and challenges for enterprises. Business Horizons, 58(4), 431-440. doi:10.1016/j.bushor.2015.03.008

Madakam, Ramaswamy, & Tripathi. (2015). Internet of Things (IoT): A Literature. *Journal of Computer and Communications*, 164-173.

Manzano, E., & Agugliaro, F. (2019). The Role of Smart Contracts in Sustainability: Worldwide Research Trends. *Sustainability: Environmental Energy Sustainability at Universities*, 1-16. doi:10.3390u11113049

Marshall, A., Mueck, S., & Shockley, R. (2015). *Innovative Analytics (GBE03664-USEN-02).* IBM.

Ng, I., & Wakenshaw, S. (2017). The Internet-of-Things: Review and research directions. *International Journal of Research in Marketing*, 2–21.

Parida, V., Sjödin, D., & Reim, W. (2019). Leveraging Digitalization for Advanced Service Business Models: Challenges and Opportunities for Circular Economy. Sustainability Journal, 11(2), 391. doi:10.3390u11020391

Porter, M. E., & Heppelmann, J. E. (2014, November 1). How Smart, Connected Products Are Transforming Competition. *Harvard Business Review, 92*(11), 64–88. https://hbr.org/2015/10/how-smart-connected-products-are-transforming-companies

PWC. (2014, December 1). *Industry 4.0 - Opportunities and Challanges of the industrial internet.* Retrieved November 10, 2020, from https://www.pwc.nl/en/assets/documents/pwc-industrie-4-0.pdf: https://www.pwc.nl/en/assets/documents/pwc-industrie-4-0.pdf

Raynor, M., & Cotteleer, M. (2015, July 27). *The more things change: Value creation, value capture, and the Internet of Things.* Retrieved November 26, 2020, from value-creation-value-capture-internet-of-things.html: https://www2.deloitte.com/us/en/insights/deloitte-review/issue-17/value-creation-value-capture-internet-of-things.html

Rigby, D., Sutherland, J., & Takeutchi, H. (2016, May 1). Embracing Agile: How to master the process that's transfroming management. *Harvard Business Review*, 1-11.

Roe, D. (2018, March 29). *The Governance and Ownership of Internet of Things (IoT).* Retrieved from https://www.cmswire.com/information-management/the-governance-and-ownership-of-internet-of-things-iot/

Roman, R., Najera, P., & Lopez, J. (2011). Securing the Internet of Things. *Computer*, *44*(9), 51–58. doi:10.1109/MC.2011.291

Rossman, J. (2017, January 16). *The Outcome-Based Business Model – Enabled by The Internet of Things.* Retrieved from https://iotbusinessnews.com/2017/01/16/87649-outcome-based-business-model-enabled-internet-things/

Saarikko, T., Westergren, U., & Blomquist, T. (2017). The Internet of Things: Are you ready for what's coming? *Business Horizons*, *60*(5), 667–676. doi:10.1016/j.bushor.2017.05.010

Schmitt, G., Mladenow, A., Strauss, C., & Schaffhauser-Linzatti, M. (2019). Smart Contracts and Internet of Things: A Qualitative Content Analysis using the Technology-Organization-Environment Framework to Identify Key-Determinants. *The 10th International Conference on Emerging Ubiquitous Systems and Pervasive Networks (EUSPN-2019), 160*, 189-196. 10.1016/j.procs.2019.09.460

Shalan, M., & Anaim, N. (2017). The SMAC Opportunity Contracts: Generating Value From Responsive Agile Risk-Oriented Techniques. In Mobile Platforms, Design, and Apps for Social Commerce (pp. 115-134). IGI Global.

Shalan, M. A., & Anaim, N. A. (2017). The SMAC Opportunity Contracts: Generating Value From Responsive Agile Risk-Oriented Techniques. In *Mobile Platforms, Design, and Apps for Social Commerce* (pp. 115–134). IGI Global. doi:10.4018/978-1-5225-2469-4.ch008

Vodde, B., & Larman, C. (2010). *Practices for Scaling Lean & Agile.* Addison-Wesley Professional.

Wen, Z., Renyu, Y., Garraghan, P., Lin, T., Xu, J., & Rovatsos, M. (2017). Fog Orchestration for Internet of Things Services. *IEEE Internet Computing*, 16 - 24. doi:10.1109/MIC.2017.36

Yaacobi, S. (2016, July 21). *Delivering value and monetisation in an Internet of Things environment.* Retrieved July 26, 2020, from https://www.iot-now.com/2016/07/21/50166-delivering-value-and-monetisation-in-an-internet-of-things-environment/

York, A., Dunham, L., & Ahn, M. (2012, January). Vertical Versus Horizontal Integration in the Biopharma Industry. *Advances in Mergers and Acquisitions, 10*, 121–143. doi:10.1108/S1479-361X(2012)0000010010

Zheng, Z., Xie, S., Dai, H.-N., Chen, W., Chen, X., Weng, J., & Imran, M. (2019). An Overview on Smart Contracts: Challenges, Advances and Platforms. *Future Generation Computer Systems*, 1–19. doi:10.1016/j.future.2019.12.019

ADDITIONAL READING

Abram, T. (2009). The hidden values of it risk management. Information Systems Audit and Control Association (ISACA). *Journal, 2009*(2), 40–45. PMID:19480123

Ben Halpert, B. (2011). *Auditing Cloud Computing: A Security and Privacy Guide*. John Wiley & Sons. doi:10.1002/9781118269091

Dallas, G. (Ed.). (2004). Governance and risk. New York: McGraw-Hill Companies Inc.

Dutta, A., Peng, G. C., & Choudhary, A. (2013). Risks in enterprise cloud computing: The perspective of IT experts. *Journal of Computer Information Systems, 53*(4), 39–48. doi:10.1080/08874417.2013.11645649

Grembergen, W. (Ed.). (2003). *Strategies for information technology governance*. Idea Group Publishing.

Kark, K., & Vanderslice, P. (2015). CIO as Chief Integration Officer. Deloitte Journal of Tech Trends 2015, 6 (1), 04-19.

Kunreuther, H. (2006). Risk and reaction: Dealing with interdependencies. *Harvard International Review: Global Catastrophe, 28*(3), 17–23.

Moran, A. (2015). *Managing Agile: Strategy, Implementation, Organization and People*. Springer. doi:10.1007/978-3-319-16262-1

Tarkoma, S. (2012). *Publish / Subscribe Systems: Design and Principles*. John Wiley & Sons. doi:10.1002/9781118354261

Westerman, G., & Hunter, R. (2007). *IT risk: Turning business threats into competitive advantage*. Harvard Business School Publishing.

Zhao, F. (Ed.). (2006). *Maximize business profits through e-partnerships*. IRM Press. doi:10.4018/978-1-59140-788-1

KEY TERMS AND DEFINITIONS

Agile Methodology: A project management approach based on delivering requirements iteratively and incrementally throughout the life cycle.

Horizontal Diffusion: An integration used when a business grows by acquiring a similar company in their industry at the same point of the supply chain.

Innovative Contracts: Contracting structure that enables the maximization of opportunities and reduction of risk based on agile and smart features.

Internet of Things (IoT): The term is being used to describe the connectivity of things as "a system of uniquely identifiable and connected elements capable of virtual representation and virtual accessibility leading to an internet-like structure for remote locating, sensing, and/or operating the constituents with real-time data/information flows between them.

Risk Management: The act of handling the risk exposure through mitigation, acceptance, sharing and avoidance.

Vertical Diffusion: An integration occurred when a business expands by acquiring another company that operates before or after them in the supply chain.

Chapter 13
Contract Guidelines and Scope Building for Digital Transformation and ERP Projects

Mohamed A. Raouf
Gulf Medical Company, Egypt

ABSTRACT

When an organization decides that it is time to invest in a digital transformation journey or even in an enterprise resource planning (ERP) software, it is going to make a big decision. This will significantly impact most elements that contribute to its success and growth. Organized and structured planning and preparation will be required from different aspects. This chapter describes the key success—or failure—factors in implementation focusing on small and medium enterprises (SMEs). SMEs usually have limited time, resources, skills, and budget compared to large firms. Throughout the journey of transformation, they need to focus on scoping and contracting phases distinguishing between digital transformation and regular information technology contracts. This chapter defines the building blocks to have a successful transformation. Contracting and scoping are considered at the heart of managing the complete digital transformation journey.

INTRODUCTION

Removing outdated technologies help organizations to achieve significant business benefits when they seek organizational change management guidelines (Panorama Consulting Group, 2020). The challenge is to have proper scoping that will help in setting the guidelines and scope of digital transformation project and contract. It is imperative to understand what "Industry 4.0" changes in the way we deal with business; and how the role of technology is maximized to boost outcomes. Technology has leveraged to enhance productivity, efficiency, speed of data access and security. Different set of skills and talents are required from employees to handle such transformation and continue to benefit from it afterwards.

DOI: 10.4018/978-1-7998-4501-0.ch013

Acquiring a Business Solution or an Enterprise Resource Planning (ERP), will require real efforts and experience as this can make or break the business. A lot of efforts will be also required to manage stakeholders and run successful implementation journey. Final tuning and performance measurements will require a lot of attention as well.

The Objective of this chapter is to help professionals involved in digital transformation or Enterprise Resource Planning (ERP) projects to define and implement the right scope for such projects. It will also describe the contracting activities related to such initiative.

BACKGROUND

Technology is moving today from "complicated" bulk acting units into "complex" system behaviors comprising multiple independent units. Complex systems are like bird flocks and fish schools that are separate units having a leader to orchestrate their joint behavior (Shalan, 2017)". These separated and integrated units are generally acquired from different providers, generating several risks and complications. According to (Robertson & Langlois, 1995), a central debate in industrial policy today is that between proponents of large vertically integrated firms on the one hand and those of networks of small specialized producers on the other.

A major element of digital transformation is "Change Management". To better picture what change management means just imagine the 1st industrial revolution in the late 18th century in Britain with the mechanization of the textile industry, where labor force were required to learn how to operate machines instead of hand work, managers were required to change their management style to make sure machines uptime is high and production capacity is optimal (Berg, 2005). Bottom line, whomever adapted were very valuable employees for their factories, and whomever failed to adapt, were not suitable to continue in the job (Harris, 2003). Predicting such a change and managing it from the start of transformation, is what is called "change management". (McBeath, 2017) explaining how the structured, strategic, and agile methodologies at the same time are needed to avoid disruption and affecting the organization performance in a negative way. (Loonam & Donagh, 2005) argues for the need for greater inquiry into the field of top management support for the introduction of enterprise information systems.

(Andal-Ancion, Cartwright, & Yip, 2003) discuss the digital transformation for traditional business. According to (Barki, Oktamis, & Pinsonneault, 2005) any ERP implementations fail to achieve their hoped-for benefits and require investments that are often much larger than originally estimated. There is also a need to progress toward more theoretically grounded ERP implementation that rests on the dimensions of breadth, depth, and magnitude. (Ranganathan & Brown, 2006) find that ERP projects with greater functional scope or greater physical scope result in positive, higher shareholder returns. (de Silva & de Oliveira, 2015) argue that eliminating the manual processes is the main tangible benefit wished with the ERP acquisition and that the acquisition plan must preview the discontinuation of the existent systems, replacing all of them for the new management tool to be acquired.

According to (Soffer, Golany, & Dori, 2003), in order to support the ERP implementation process, the model should describe the entire scope of the ERP system's functionality and the alternative business processes it supports, as well as the interdependencies among them. (Soja, 2006) proves the influence of particular factors on the ERP project's success in certain circumstances.

DIGITAL TRANSFORMATION AND INFORMATION TECHNOLOGY CONTRACTS

The main difference between a conventional information technology contract and an innovative contract - done with the objective of digital transformation - is that IT contracts are conducted usually to elevate the organization technical score such as internet bandwidth, datacenter performance, or storage capacity, etc. or to add a missing technical service such as cloud email or security services. Digital transformation is a completely different concept. It aims to integrate digital technology into all areas of business, fundamentally changing how organizations operate and deliver value to customers. It's also a cultural change that requires organizations to continually challenge the status quo, experiment, and get comfortable with failure (The Enterprisers Project, 2020).

Digital transformation puts pressure on organizations' employees to "change" as it challenges their status quo and causes employees to resist the change; either due to perceived risks or due to the habits they are used to make since long times (Adwani, 2001). Nevertheless, it lies on the leaders of change to plan this change and manage it from the early beginning of the transformation. Doing so makes it much easier to imagine these difficulties, plan for them and get prepared to face them. In different words it is crucial to plan for adapting the coming changes before they happen, and this is exactly what "change management" is. Taking a structured, strategic times (Adwani, 2001) and agile way (McBeath, 2017) shall facilitate this journey.

Another key difference between digital transformation and regular IT contracts is that digital transformation is a journey rather than a project, so it takes more time; accordingly, it gets affected by the vast speed of technological advancements. It is important to understand the exponential versus linear speed of technological advancement and to refer to three important laws that are governing technology behaviors today to understand the underlying risk from this fast-technological advancement.

The three laws are Moore's law (1965) for processing power (Powell, 2008); Butter's law (1965) for communication speed (Roser & Ritchie, 2013) and Kryder's law in storage capacity (2005) (Walter, 2005). All these laws stress the exponential advancement in these technology areas. Such trends make digital transformation and contracting quite a difficult task to do, since the contractor needs to be updated with the latest innovations, prices and trends to catch up with technology; plus, this puts pressure on the organization technical and operational employees also to catch up with the big and fast change. This suggests moving more towards an agile implementation versus the big bang theory in implementation; which means building value incrementally "in small steps" with more speed rather than implementing big projects that takes long time to implement, require big change and training from the organization employees and leadership and might be outdated when going live (McBeath, 2017).

Digital transformation contracts are even more challenging; it could potentially involve many new technologies and concepts that are new to business and technical users and difficult to understand. These technologies can also be leveraged to make the best use of it in the digital transformation project that is happening in the organization (Rogers, 2016). In order to have the biggest impact on the organization's performance; these technologies including big data, data analytics, AI "Artificial Intelligence", block chain, IoT "Internet of Things", are added to other technologies as well such as robotics and automation. By the time this book is published, other technologies will be available and could potentially have great impact on our businesses.

KEY SUCCESS AND FAILURE FACTORS IN ERP IMPLEMENTATION

Due to its unique features and accessibility, the focus of implementing digital technology is no longer just to improve internal operations, but to expand internal dimensions, reach customers and external partners, affect services, integrate processes, disrupt markets, and fundamentally change industries (Ivan, Bosilj Vuk, & Spremi, 2019). Since digital transformation is the integration of digital technology into all areas of a business. This fundamentally change how to operate and deliver value to customers. It's a cultural change that requires organizations to continually challenge the status quo, experiment, and get comfortable with failure (McBeath, 2017). It also requires the "involvement" and "understanding" of the different organizational levels and the determination of key failure factors "to avoid them" and the key success factors "to embrace them".

Key Failure Factors

According to (Prasetyo, Lubis, Witjaksono, & Azizah, 2019) the failure rate of ERP implementation in the company is quite high, the results obtained indicate that the failure of ERP implementation ranges from 67% -90%. Thus, it is important to identify the factors that may form obstacles and classify them to help industries to prevent failure in the implementation of ERP projects. Some factors are:

Planning for Value Realization

In many times organizations fail to realize the desired value of implementing a new ERP after going live, on the contrary they realize that they lost many advantages that was available in their old systems and processes. This is mainly due to the lack of vision and planning to target specific success factors from the early stages of the transformation (McBeath, 2017). Realizing value requires the involvement of every single department and role in the organization, each in his area.

Lack of Top Management Support

Achieving the targeted value from transformation require executive decisions that middle management or senior employees might not have the authority to take; this accordingly hinders the opportunity of realizing value of this transformation. (Liu, Wang, & Chua, 2015) Argues that a major reason for IT project failure is the lack of top management support. However, obtaining top management support is often considered outside the IT project team's control.

Culture Resistance

Multinational ERP implementation introduces another dimension of complexity—national differences—into the already complex nature of ERP implementation in the context of global information management (Sheu, Chae, & Yang, 2004). The source of resistance could be due to perceived risks or underlying habits, in both scenarios; this requires; leadership in managing the change to better understand and act slowly to overcome this culture of resistance.

Resource Intensive Nature

ERP implementations require allocating the appropriate workforce, intensive training, top management commitment; moreover, this requirement gets more accentuated when heavy customization of the ERP is required. (Sitalakshmi Venkatraman, 2016)

Long Implementation Time Frame

The extensive utilization of the organization workforce resources may impact the organization's core businesses. (Sitalakshmi Venkatraman, 2016) thus, management should plan resources effectively and sometimes it is important to separate development works from operation teams.

High Cost of Standard ERP Implementation

ERP is well known for its high cost of implementation including, customization, recourses, training and some hidden costs. Thus, financial constraints play a major role in the rejection of ERP by SMEs; ERP vendors strive to offer SMEs a reduced-price solution, but they don't always succeed (Sitalakshmi Venkatraman, 2016) When cost start to rise up the project will suffer in all dimensions.

Key Success Factors

ERP implementation is a way to improve competitive advantage as it is directly affecting the company's performance. (Rahayu & Dillak, 2018). To achieve its success, several key factors to be considered during planning and implementation, including:

Business Plan and Vision

It is important to understand what needs to be achieved at the end of the digital transformation journey. The goal is not to implement an ERP system rather it is to achieve specific objectives to enrich every single department in the organization. (Ifinedo, 2008) argued that ERP systems are different from other information technology implementations; as such, there is a need to provide insights as to how various elements play out in the context of ERP system success.

Business Super Users

One of the most common causes of ERP failure is unrealistic expectations. (Panorama Consulting Group, 2019). This usually comes from the differences in background between technical and business users. To bridge this gap, the company needs a business super user or many super users "one in each department" at least. Superuser is originally a business user but trained technically, his role is to set the business users expectations of what they want to achieve out of the digital transformation journey. As continuous communication is an inevitable factor to achieve the desirable goals; it is highly advisable that this super user to be an elected employee who has exposure on the core processes of the organization or business units.

Previous "Relevant" Experience

It is crucially important that the implementer has previous experience in order to ensure a smooth journey and easy communication between the implementer and the organization. It is important also to understand that there is a big difference between "previous experience" and "relevant previous experience". Digital transformation is a wide terminology that differs in scope significantly between organizations, so "relevant" previous experience is the key question to ask when selecting an implementer. It worth mentioning as well that the importance of previous "relevant" experience varies according to the size and complexity of the organization that is going through the digital transformation journey; the more the organization processes are big and complex the more the digital transformation journey needs an implementer with relevant experience.

Top Management Support

Top management that is committed to listening to business owners and all stakeholders will be effectively involved in the digital transformation journey as it is building a new future for the organization. Top management support will increase the involvement of employees as they feel the management courage to take the right decisions, achieve the planned objectives, and assign the right leaders to manage the change in each department. Such involvement of top management is a must to make the digital transformation happen.

BUDGETING AND SCOPING OF A DIGITAL TRANSFORMATION PROJECT

Technology has proven successful in fostering efficiency and productivity in many application areas and it has also demonstrated great potential to drive innovation in the digital world. However, planning and scoping digital transformation initiatives is a complex task and has been experienced as challenging by many organizations. Plenty of aspects need to be considered, comprising both deep technical knowledge as well as strategic organizational considerations. Digital Transformation plans need to be designed considering business competencies, technology expertise, and social skills, in addition to the full understanding of strategic ambitions and roadmaps. Below are few points that need to be considered.

Vision Planning

A first and foremost milestone in staring a digital transformation project is to "visualize" what value the organization can realize in the future after implementing this transformation (Kurco, Stepanic, & Varga, 2012). The value can be achieving higher conversion rate or higher market share in sales, better response time in customer service, more customers reach in marketing, faster lead time in supply chain, higher profitability and better cash flow for management, higher employees engagement for HR, less stock days for material management, or less receivables days and higher payables days for finance.

Requirements Prioritization

It has been found from literature that SMEs in developing countries consider scope of implementation as one of the highly significant issue when implementing an ERP. (Upadhyay, Basu, Adhikary, & Dan, 2010) . What is mandatory and what can be skipped or postponed out of the collected requirements. A common theme is required when facilitating business process mapping of inter-departmental tasks and responsibilities to increase the understanding among employees. This can result in an improved company culture and generate cross-departmental respect that may have been lacking.

When determining which requirements are most important one need to ensure that team members understand the difference between needs and wants. Requirements can be split into three groups:

- **Mandatory:** These tasks are required to perform a job function or have another outside influence, such as industry regulation. These are non-negotiable.
- **Value-added:** These are requirements that, while important, are not required to perform a task. They typically streamline manual functions (i.e., automatically importing data from an Excel spreadsheet in the correct format).
- **Nice to have:** These are "convenience" requirements, like a button on a screen that enables you to stay on the same screen while completing a task.

Several important business decisions are dependent on above classification. As a result, the prioritization need access to decision makers who can make timely decisions on issues such as terminology and process ownership. Clarifying process ownership is essential as process owners are responsible for validating requirements and ensuring all processes are accounted for within their respective functional areas.

How to Build an Accurate Budgeting Plan?

There are several important elements for the organization executives to set proper expectations of cost versus value realization. Budget forecasting is very important to make sure that the executive management will allocate the "annual" expenditure of transformation base don expected cash flow. Forecasting is directly correlated to the strategy of implementation if it is an agile phased or big bang one-time implementation. The main elements of transformation budgeting could be as follows:

- **Software solutions' cost:** Usually this is the first part of budgeting for transformation project; where the organization identifies the proper software solutions and industry specific solution to buy. This cost can be a one time with service level support purchase or cloud license with monthly or yearly payments.
- **Implementation and customization cost:** This is a bit tricky since it involves resources calculation and time planning. This might involve changes during implementation and hidden costs.
- **Training cost:** Training the internal staff is not the biggest part of budgeting, but it is important to ensure that the organization team is fit, actively involved in the implementation and can foster the achievement of the desired objectives in an efficient manner.
- **Infrastructure cost:** Infrastructure is important to accommodate the software solutions. This includes back up and disaster recovery planning. It can be physical of virtual.

- **Network cost:** It is important to scale the network to fit for implementing the new ERP or digital transformation solutions. This includes the cost of internet connectivity and bandwidth.
- **Security cost:** This is an elaborative cost that is required to assess the required security solutions to ensure protection from internal and external attacks. This is a dynamic matter.

MINDSET SHIFTING AND CHANGE MANAGEMENT

The top management support and understanding of the required change management is very important milestone during transformation. This can only be achieved via active involvement of top management in attending periodic transformation meetings, assigning the proper leaders in each department to manage this change and ensure tackling users' resistance while training them to adopt the change.

Assessing the organization's readiness for change is important for top management to take the right decisions going forward. Knowing how much it is required to increase the organization's change readiness will help to develop a change management strategy and plan. Similarly, it is important to decide on how to communicate with employees and what specific trainings each employee needs. Several activities are required to embark a successful journey (Kurco, Stepanic, & Varga, 2012).

Change Management Components

One of the biggest challenges for business when implementing an ERP solution is not realizing the need for organizational change management. Implementing an ERP solution in any organization implies change and change inevitably will stimulate some resistance.

In a world where everything is connected, organizations can get better results by looking at the whole picture. Taking a holistic approach by connecting people, processes and systems will improve effectiveness and efficiency (Kurco, Stepanic, & Varga, 2012). This ensures people understand the business process change, accept and use the new system. Sticking to change management components will mitigate the challenges that an organization might face when implementing an ERP solution; and here are those components:

Management Buy-In

Buy-in from leadership is fundamental when implementing a new solution. According to (Menon, Muchnick, Butler, & Pizur, 2019), it would necessary to avoid having a general senior leader group and instead add a business leader group, and an IT leader group to get senior leadership perspective from both business and IT. Employees commitment lies where their leadership resides. If the entire leadership team does not buy-in, an ERP implementation will not be successful. An executive who buys into an ERP solution is included in both setting goals and managing issues pre, during, and post an ERP project. When measuring the success of an ERP implementation, executives should use benchmarks to set expectations and establish project achievements.

Communication

Communication within any organization is critical, but often incredibly difficult. According to (Aubert, Hooper, & Schnepel, 2013), communication quality is repeatedly listed among the top success factors to consider when implementing an ERP system. Resistance to a new solution is often caused by lack of communication, as employees struggle to get answers to their questions throughout the ERP project. The more questions that project managers can answer, the more attractive the solution will appear to the employees.

Clearly, it is increasingly important that project and communication teams have a plan as to how they will provide updates and coach managers on how to best deliver the messages to their teams. Language, culture and level of education among end-users have a significant influence on the messaging style.

Training Strategy

Change management plans must be developed to address workforce transition to the new ERP system and decide who will be super-users and trainers. According to (Esteves, 2014) training is one of the most cited critical success factors in the ERP systems implementations A wide-range training strategy should account for local nuances, locations and testing prior to go-live of an ERP solution. A lack of training strategy can have serious implications on the success of an ERP implementation in any organization.

End-user training need to be ongoing and should include classes, workshops, and practical sessions right through the implementation process. Continuous training can be achieved by having readily available access to industry-specific business process modelling. To have high performance of the end users, the organization needs to combine skills, knowledge, and state of readiness.

Employee Engagement

Building employee engagement is one of the key challenges that most ERP implementations fail to address. (Catteeuw, Flynn, & Vonderhorst, 2007) identified employee engagement as an important tool to ensure long-term growth and success. Organizational assessments are critical as they ensure that all issues and opportunities are captured across the company. While this area is often overlooked due to budget constraints, the added expense required for engaging and involving employees leads to quantifiable benefits in the long run. With a proper set of methodologies, the right experienced project sponsors and team members can build the employee engagement and buy-in effectively as required for a successful ERP implementation.

Cultural Considerations

Cultural change should be considered an important factor of any effective ERP organizational change management. Some ERP projects have been deemed unsuccessful due to employee resistance to change, especially in organizations that have employees with very long durations of employment within the company. It is important to recognize these signs early in the process to plan accordingly.

According to (Skok & Döringer, 2002), more recently, there has been an increase in reported ERP failures, suggesting that the implementation issues are not just technical, but encompass wider behavioral factors. Language, education, and demographic differences can have significant impacts on how employees understand and perceive goals, objectives, risks, and benefits of an ERP solution. It is critical that this is taken into consideration when planning for change.

IMPLEMENTATION AND RESOURCING

The author consider top management commitment and change management are the most important things in a digital transformation journey. Project management is the third most important thing. These items will define the implementation strategy and resources allocation.

Implementation Strategy

There are two strategies to implement an ERP system as part of a digital transformation journey, the agile phased approach, or the one-time big bang approach.

- **The agile or phased approach:** Which suggests implementing the project in a step by step approach, it can be one module at a time or one geographical area at a time. The aim of this approach is to get rid of the known risks of failure such as cost, resources allocation and long implementation times, moreover, it makes it easy to manage change and train employees in an adaptable manner. The main drawback of this approach is that it has a continuous nature that it requires continuous planning along the life cycle of the ERP system implementation. (Kurco, Stepanic, & Varga, 2012).
- **The big bang or one-time approach:** Which is preferred for smaller and less complex companies that have an immediate need for solution delivery. Making a big bang implementation at one time might be more efficient in cost but requires higher on a short-term investment, significant allocation of resources, immense change management and might involve disruption of business for a longer period. Going fast might cause the ignorance of important details during implementation specially for SMEs with complex environments or large firms (Kurco, Stepanic, & Varga, 2012)

Planning the Infrastructure and Support

Selecting the right infrastructure is crucial to embark a successful journey, selecting infrastructure should be based on the organization setup, geographical spread, risk factors, operational elements, and other factors. ERP will need a very robust platform to provide reasonable operational effectiveness, security parameters and durability. Such platform is comprising plenty of factors as described here.

Organizations need to choose between the cloud services versus on premise solutions that will require specific hardware infrastructure. Similarly, are network issues, security, and other operational dimensions.

The internal network requirements should be assessed in terms of local network or wireless network; this mandate further security assessment to protect the organization from any security threats. Security assessment should be assessed via a certified security professional. Some other technologies might be also discussed such as IoT solutions which tie back to the location where data is being sent and processed. . (Roemerman, 2019).

Back-up and disaster recovery are increasingly becoming one of the main requirements in any infrastructure considering the increasing threats in telecommunication and cybersecurity. Having a disaster recovery solution for cloud environment system is usually less relevant, while backup is required for both cloud and on-premise infrastructure solutions.

It is highly recommended that the organization infrastructure is always supported by the provider or trusted provider. A crucial point for on-promise support is to consider the End of Support (EOS) date.

Project Management

An experienced individual person or a group should be assigned to manage the project who are called "Project Manager or Solution Manager". Managing the project should be on a cost, time, and quality basis. The project manager needs to coach the technical and business teams and also to handle the top management expectations in terms of time, cost and achievement of the targeted objectives (Kurco, Stepanic, & Varga, 2012)

Technology projects and digital transformation projects are complex projects that require planning thus it is dependent on using the right resources. Two points are noted here:

- Preferably, the project manager needs to have a technical background to understand the IT or transformation project being managed, the project manager may be the "solution manager" as well.
- IT projects implies managing an implicit change. A conventional project of building a residential building is simple because everyone knows what a building is, and everyone knows how to use it. Technology project can't be fully understood by businesspeople. Sometimes "they don't know how to use it". That is why change management is a key success factor.

Building the Team

Building the right team is "THE" most important element of making a successful digital transformation project. It is very crucial to select members with the right set of technical skills or business skills based on the required role, in addition hybrid skills are required at specific tasks or functions. It is also important to have proper communication throughout the project including horizontal communications among the team members and vertical communication with the executive management. A project/ solution manager who has a general understanding of the full picture from the technical and business sides can seamlessly facilitate communication between the key users and the technical team.

The solution manager shall identify the required change management initiatives, propose options to the executive leadership to decide on what options are more suitable for the organization, and propose timelines for implementation. However, it lies on the executive leader's shoulder to enforce these changes in the proper timelines.

It is also mandatory to understand which member of the technical team has the required technical competency for each building block and which member of the business team will be a key user to use this technology in line with the organization vision.

Internal Resources vs. Outsourcing

According to (Olson, 2007), outsourcing has evolved as a viable means to attain cost savings in organizational information technology. An organization may have different models to allocate resources for the ERP project, such as:

Figure 1. The staffing required for an ERP project

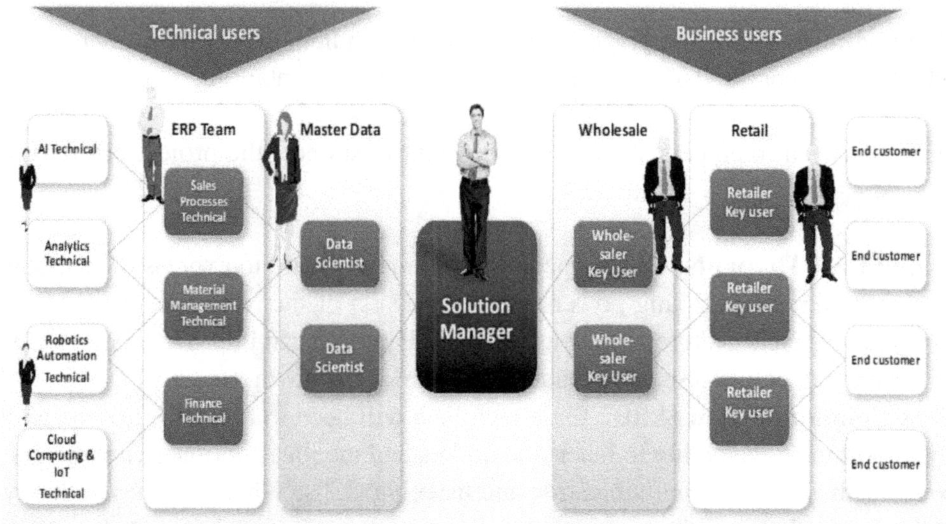

- **Building one's own team:** An organization may decide to have its own "technical" team with high skills if the organization has high turnover or revenues that justifies paying for their salaries or if the organization is part of a bigger holding company where the overheads of the technical team can be distributed over several companies. Continuous training and succession planning are a "must do" in this case. The good thing about having own team is that they are well built up from scratch inside the organization, they understand the organization operations and know its vision. One downside is that retaining the trained staff is not guaranteed.
- **Outsourcing technical and business analysis expertise:** If the organization's revenues can't justify the investment in a company's own team; then it is advised to have immediate access to highly skilled employees who can deliver results immediately and might achieve better results. One bad thing of this option is that the outsourced employees will not be an organization employees thus they have to leave after going live, and the organization "must" depend on a third party either the same outsourced expertise or another one to maintain a good level of support. Good amount of support is usually required post going live and that will cost the organization more investment on the long term.
- **Shared resources model:** This option might be more viable in terms of balancing between the time, cost, and risk of having organizations' own team and the cost and risk of fully outsourcing technical expertise. It will be a moderate approach to have the organizations' own technical expertise and get them trained through the journey of implementation by experts.

Choosing the Level of Competence

When building up the ERP team, it is important to select members based on their level of competence and not necessarily their job title. While it may seem like common sense to choose senior employees in management positions, this can backfire. According to (Sitalakshmi Venkatraman, 2016), there are two primary reasons for this:

- People in these positions tend to be busy, which could make the process take much longer than it should.
- Selecting non-management employees with an understanding of the process can provide motivation, which may be particularly beneficial during the implementation process.

Additionally, the team members should be competent to support the project effectively, thus they need to:

- **Expressing Real Thoughts:** Choose people who are not afraid to express their thoughts so they can have some decision-making power and step outside of their comfort zone. Ideally business teams may have a clear picture of how using an ERP system can improve processes, but they will need to have the courage to stand up and make their ideas known.
- **Excellent Communication Skills:** Team members will need to be more than vocal about ideas. Equally important is the ability to listen and understand the ideas of other team members. Choose employees with excellent communication and listening skills. When it comes to this type of project, everyone should be on the same page for the duration. As a result, every member should have the ability to communicate their thoughts effectively, as well as listen attentively to what others have to say.

CONTRACTING AND NEGOTIATING THE SCOPE OF WORK

The organization needs to sit down and determine exactly why they need to perform digital transformation or ERP implementation. They should write the (As-Is) processes and the (To-Be processes). It is important to avoid scope creep trying to retain the existing processes and doing a major change that requires immense change management that will consume huge resources, trainings, customizations, and cost.

The optimal aim should be to leverage a real implementation of the ERP to achieve the desired outcomes in terms of operational efficiency and better data visualization to facilitate decision making (Okrent & Vokurka, 2004). Some of the key elements to look at during contract and scope of work negotiation are described in this section.

Processes Mapping and Objectives Identification

Successful ERP implementations are not only driven by software but also by business processes. According to (ACC Software Solutions, 2020). Many companies make costly errors during their ERP system implementation. They assume that the new system will fix their broken processes without first determining what's wrong with their processes. Business process re-engineering and improvement is one of the most critical yet often forgotten aspects of implementation projects. Process mapping is more of a flow-charting in a computer program with all stakeholders are identified.

For example in an industrial organization a core six processes can be identified as; quote to cash, procure to pay, plan to perform, manufacturing operations, product life cycle and financial management making (Okrent & Vokurka, 2004). It worth mentioning that for additional processes there are industry specific solutions that exists with ERP providers, industry specific solutions minimize the need for customization and decrease the implementation time and cost (McBeath, 2017). The aim of process mapping is to:

- Understand the (As-Is) processes and draw them in a flowchart manner identifying the participants in the process.
- Identify pain points and bottle necks in current processes.
- Identify processes that need to be eliminated or added to improve operational efficiency and achieve desired outcomes.
- Write the (To-Be) processes and present them to the implementer.

A successful business process mapping exercise will promote transparency and allow organizations to improve their current practices by creating a clear, detailed visual representation of workflows. The organization then need to agree on real achievable objectives and prioritize them for implementation roadmap.

Building Design Document or the "Blueprint"

According to (Remus & Schub, 2003), models and patterns that describe generic processes can build a blueprint for the implementation and support the stepwise integration of business processes into the knowledge life cycle. Blueprints are detailed plans that are required to build something in accordance with the designer's intentions.

Blueprints involves modeling the new process flow and the information required to support it. While the "as-is" process was modeled to indicate information requirements, blueprints will help to create the "to-be" status illustrating how the workflow will be different. The information models, data models, and blueprints will:

- Indicate where the new process will use information that is shared across functional areas of the business.
- Contain models of redesigned organizational structure.
- Show the new process flow along with process team members, the process owners, the case managers, and the process facilitators.
- Specify parts of the organization, which interact with the process personnel.
- Mention detailed technology specifications that are required to support the new process should be defined.
- Point out redesign points that may require an entirely different culture or atmosphere, than what is prevalent in the organization.

It is imperative that this blueprint is signed by the technical users, business owners and executive leadership. This will ensure that all stakeholders are aligned and working towards the same vision and direction to achieve this transformation that is bounded by very specific objectives.

It is important to mention that "Blueprints" are usually a service, which requires an exploration phase by the implementer. It is highly advisable to do the blueprint prior to the contract and scope negotiation with the implementer to minimize any change orders and unexpected financial costs.

Risk Management Planning

There is no risk-free project. A project exists to bring change, with change comes uncertainty, and that means that risks must be considered. Avoiding risk in a project is not an option, the focus must be on risk management.

A research (lumenia consulting, 2020) about risk management in ERP projects looked at some of the most significant risk factors that lead to failed ERP implementations identified the following reasons:

- Ineffective strategic thinking and planning
- Poor project team skills
- Inadequate Business Process Re-engineering (BPR)
- Insufficient change management.
- Low top management involvement

One more reason cited by (Davide Aloini, 2007) for any software project failure is that managers do not properly assess and manage the risks in their projects . Some project managers are dreaming the deliverables without considering the mindset challenges during data gathering and power users creation.

Asking for a Proof of Concept

Seeing is believing; and asking the implementer for a proof of concept using a sample data or limited scope allows the organization to visualize the outcomes before starting to spend time and cost blindly into implementation. (Rijo, Martinho, & Ermida, 2015) stated that proof-of-concept that can be applied in other areas and business processes. The identified gaps need to be covered by proof of concepts.

Most probably, the implementer who insists to do things his way or takes long time to deliver the proof of concept will not be the optimal partner. Working with such implementor will not be that easy because if the proof of concept required a lot of effort from him or many iterations to understand that means a lot of cost and resources was absorbed in this pilot.

Time and Cost Planning

"How long?" is usually the most important and highest-ranking question that end-users ask implementers, the second question is usually "How much it will cost?". The organization need proper planning and various considerations to get the correct answer. According to (Xie, James Allen, & Ali, 2014), ERP implementation cost increases along the time horizon, while performance level increases up to a point and remains unchanged.

Creating and controlling an ERP implementation timeline can be a challenging process if the organization fails to provide the implementer with a full detailed blueprint including well documented processes and specific objectives to achieve. Moreover, the implementation strategy plays a major role in the implementation progress.

System Testing and Acceptance

Determining how the organization technical team and key business users will test and accept the project should be documented in detail. (Amoako-Gyampah & Salam, 2004) presents an extension to the technology acceptance model (TAM) and empirically examines it in an enterprise resource planning (ERP) implementation environment. It is crucial to document what processes are going to be tested and what will be measured such as outcome data, speed, user interface or other parameters.

According to (Youngberg, Olsen, & Hauser, 2009) "To fully exploit the capabilities of complex technologies, businesses must deliberately foster technology acceptance by end users. This deliberate activity must recognize the complexity of factors that influence individuals' perceptions, intentions, and usage of information technology". Testing is a pivotal part of the project commissioning which many organizations miss to include in the scope or sometimes they take it lightly at the time of commissioning or receiving of the project.

Business key users should allocate the necessary time for effective and comprehensive testing including multiple scenarios. Not doing the testing in a proper careful way puts that project at danger after going live, because if business users start discovering many bugs in the system during operation they will need to fix it immediately which may not be possible in a live system. This will put them between two difficult options which is to delay operations to fix these bugs "or" continue with these bugs and live with it bearing the consequences of moving on without proper testing.

Post Go-Live Training and Hyper Support

This is very vital, since it includes training "ALL" users and ensuring they are adapting the new transformation in their daily operations. (Yu, 2005) stated that "a significant insight learned is that end-users across the organization must be educated from the onset of ERP implementation". During this phase, it is required that the project team are highly dedicated to train the organizations' employees and to create training materials including live training manuals, videos, etc....

In order to reduce the burden on the project team, it is highly recommended to train a group of super users in each department who are responsible to train their colleagues within a specific time boundary and answer their questions while conducting operations. The role of superusers is preferred to be voluntary rather than an assignment to spread the culture that helping others is an aptitude rather than a task.

Hyper support is usually the support following the go-live that need to be conducted by technical users. This is either done by the organization technical team or outsourced members. Hyper support is a very busy period because operations are running, users are very stressed and asking for support. As it is difficult to do support while operations are running, managing this tricky period is not easy. That is why putting more emphasis on the testing phase might be more important to reduce the required hyper support post go live.

One reason for unrealistic expectations is that many companies are mainly focused on the technical aspects of implementation. To achieve expected ERP business benefits, the organization must account for the people and process aspects.

THE RIGHT PARTNER AND THE CONTRACT'S NEGOTIATION

The selected vendor can make or break a project in addition to the internal strategies and behaviors. Practically speaking, the primary goal of any ERP vendor or implementer is to sell. Some of them care about delivering quality projects, but this comes as a second priority. In specific words if the organization is not carious about giving the ERP vendor/implementer specific objectives to achieve, the vendor/implementer will not care so much about fixing it. The partners shouldn't be blamed for this. The organization should utilize every effort in the selection, contracting and throughout the implementations.

Setting the Expectations

Setting realistic expectations regarding budget and timeline is primarily a responsibility on the organization itself in the first place not the vendors and not the implementers. The more the organization can be specific of what they want to achieve from the digital transformation, the more the journey will be successful. According to (Helo, Anussornnitisarn, & Phusavat, 2008) ERP project deployment requires careful planning with regard to the change management aspects, but also IT related technical aspects.

The organization should build the requirements around "standard and compliant common practices" not erratic requirements built on previous wrong practices that occurs in the organization. Management, technical and business users need to define their main requirements. Well defined expectations and internal preparations will help the implementer and vendor to provide the organization with a proper and accurate price and timeline as close as possible to reality. The length of the preparation phase depends on many factors, such as:

- Size of the organization, complexity of its processes, the gap analysis (as-is versus to-be),
- The readiness of the technical users and how much training they need for the implementation.
- The enthusiasm of the business users, the selection of super users and their required training
- The top management readiness to do what it takes to change and pay for its cost on top of the transformation contract cost
- Choosing the right time to start based on the organization financial readiness, and employees' readiness.

The organization need to pinpoint the WHY: why do they want to do this transformation, and the HOW: how they are going to do it. Then they can ask the vendor/implementer for a price and timeline. Of course, the organization may utilize external resources when necessary to complete these tasks.

When the requirements are somehow specific; it gives leverage for the implementer to minimize any risk margins for additional requirements that may come from the organization's side and reflects on both the price and timeline as the organization receives.

Building the Request for Proposal, Quotation or Information (RFP/RFQ/RFI)

Once the organization determines the list of vendors and implementers they need to deal with, it is time to send out a Request for Proposal (RFP). It's impossible to put an exact number of how many vendors should be on your list of front-runners; however, keep in mind, that the longer the list, the more time it will take to work through.

A brief, direct RFP should be sent out to the list of front-runners. It should identify the business's most important requirements, short/long-term business goals and provide information about the organization's business process. The vendors can then create a presentation or demonstration for an ERP that meet needs. Request that the RFP be returned in a timely manner, but also be sure to allow them enough time to create a presentation and other deliverables. According to (USA Patent No. US7072857B1, 2006) a well-established process for initiating commercial transactions involves a potential buyer creating what is known as a request for proposal or a request for pricing (RFP) and identifying one or more potential vendors to direct the request to.

Traditionally ERP vendors would create and submit a Request for Information (RFI) to the organization. It often includes dozens, if not hundreds, of detailed questions; this was a tedious process for everyone involved. The organization usually expected to detail all their own information, such as specific requirements, business details, etc. Today, RFIs are shortened with more collaboration are being introduced to answer questions via multiple tools such as workshops and conference calls.

Selecting the Partner

According to (Haddara, 2014) "if an organization selects an inadequate ERP to fit their needs, the project will most likely destine to fail". It is important to create a list of specific criteria the vendor is expected to meet. The list should be elaborative and expandable to accommodate new points that arise while looking into different vendors profiles and proposals. Main component of this matrix might include:

- Total combined price of ERP software, hardware, and customer support
- Scalability, ease of implementation and ease of use
- Functionality and ability to fit scope of business
- Vendor's performance track record in similar industries and platforms
- Potential for growth and quality of documentation
- Ability to work with existing hardware and software if required to
- Total budget expectations including licensing, implementation, and maintenance
- The vendor's financial strength, corporate values, and local presence
- Relevant references or anything else that the team deems pertinent.

The evaluation exercise usually involves assigning a weight or rank to each requirement and score potential vendors accordingly. One of the commonly used methods to compare between vendors is the consulting groups reports.

Asking for Demonstration

ERP vendors who are difficult to work with during the selection/demonstration process will not be any easier to work with during the implementation process. Vendors who come in unprepared manner and give a standard sales demo, may not be able to identify how every organization is unique, and the demo should be as well tailored to each organization goals.

The demonstration will allow the organization team the chance to see the ERP system in action, get an in-depth look at various features and ask any questions they may have. All participants should collaborate with a mentality of "there is no stupid questions". If they need any type of clarification about anything, they should stop the vendor and ask for it. This is also the time to raise any concerns they may have.

Once the demonstration is over, the selection team will need to be ready to give feedback, pay specific attention to whether or not the ERP system will meet each department's needs; also be ready to discuss the look and feel of the ERP system and how easy it is to use. If there are concerns, do not be afraid to contact the vendor.

Negotiating the Contract

To manage conflict a PM must understand the basics of negotiation theory and effective communications (Hudson, Grisham, Srinivasan, & N. Moussa1, 2005). The question that being asked is do we need a "superhero" in technology to be able to negotiate a contract? The simple answer is "No", but it needs special requirements, which includes:

- Gathering the right needs from business owners who are declared as key business users.
- Building the right "Technical Team" and equip all members with the proper set of skills, autonomy" and reliability to continuously be updated in their fields while continue to have the proper understanding of business requirements.
- Having a legal expert who can understand the building blocks of the contract. However, this expert should be aware of the nature of innovative technologies and their role in helping the organization in delivering better results.

FUTURE RESEARCH DIRECTIONS

To build the right scope for a digital transformation or ERP projects the organization need to collect the technical and business information in addition to the unique business process. An encapsulation of "change management" methodologies that are suitable for the specific transformation will form a "glue" that holds the technology blocks together. Connecting technical users and key business users together to work in harmony will maximize the organizational outcomes. This field have been debatable since long time and still need further research to get the maturity level.

Having an "Executive sponsor" is crucial to lead the change management initiatives, enforce them, and promote the "importance and value" of the transformation project. One important topic is how to find the right sponsor who is motivated to understand and mitigate the different risks that can block the project, either financially or operationally. The right sponsor can overcome the political oppositions from different powerful individuals in the organization, which can block implementing a project that has a positive impact on the "whole organization" rather than having a positive impact on one department on the expense of another department. Breaking the silo mentality is very crucial when coming to digital transformation projects but need to be promoted to get people on board.

Digital transformation "Blueprint" comprises all the activities necessary for the reproduction and description of the business operations in an ERP System. These activities commence before the ERP project itself. The blueprint serves as the master plan and becomes a detailed written document. Blueprint shows the business requirements in detail, and serves as the basis for organization, configuration, and development activities. Preparing blueprints that are detailed enough is a huge topic that need research and cooperation from all stakeholders.

An agile or phased approach will help the organization to keep operations running while building new capabilities. Agile practices are more suitable for large and complex organizations, while the big bang approach is appropriate for small organizations who are looking for immediate delivery with less cost upfront. However, every case is unique and the more cases are documented it will be easier for practitioners to utilize these case in similar situations.

The partner selection and contract negotiation are challenging tasks considering the number of variables that need to be considered. This will need a very careful deliberation and very skilled people who are multidisciplined to understand the whole ecosystem and act faithfully for best results. This topic can be further studied and framed.

CONCLUSION

Digital transformation and ERP projects are becoming more crucial to innovate business and create new future for all organizations. The project team need to write down the design document based on dialogues with all stakeholders and proof of concepts in a clear visible manner. Relevant terminologies, written description, descriptive diagrams, and flow charts will be included as necessary.

Defining the project scope is exceptionally important, sometimes, it can be wise to go into a short-term support agreement with remote dedicated resources to build a robust scope of work that is detailed enough. It is also wise to understand any gaps and build proof of concepts for them. This will build trust and confidence and avoid signing an agreement blindly. Ultimately this will serve to avoid having plenty of change requests ahead, which may result in distorted, inconsistent, and costly solution.

It's important to watch out for a technology-focused mindset, plug-and-play prospects and other mindsets that lead to unrealistic expectations. The organization need to make sure that they are not basing timeline and budget on overly optimistic estimates. It is helpful to use benchmarks of what other similar companies have achieved.

Perfect planning and base knowledge will ease selection of the implementation partner and will enhance related negotiation through decreasing the ambiguity and risk levels considerably. A solid scope will make it relatively easy while discussing what resources are needed from the implementer's side and how many work hours should be accounted for and how much the implementer will charge per hour. This will facilitate the contracting experience and outcomes.

REFERENCES

Adwani, A. A. (2001). Change Management Strategies for Successful ERP Implementation. *Business Process Management Journal*, *7*(3), 266–275.

Amoako-Gyampah, K., & Salam, A. (2004). An extension of the technology acceptance model in an ERP implementation environment. *Information & Management*, *41*(6), 731–745. doi:10.1016/j.im.2003.08.010

Andal-Ancion, A., Cartwright, P. A., & Yip, G. S. (2003). The Digital Transformation of Traditional Businesses. *MI Sloan Management Review*, 34-41.

Aubert, B., Hooper, V., & Schnepel, A. (2013). Revisiting the role of communication quality in ERP project success. *American Journal of Business*, *28*(1), 64–85. doi:10.1108/19355181311314770

Barki, H., Oktamis, S., & Pinsonneault, A. (2005). Dimensions of ERP Implementations and Their Impact On ERP Project Outcomes. *Journal of Information Technology Management*, 1–9.

Berg, M. (2005). *The Age of Manufactures, 1700-1820: Industry, Innovation and Work in Britain*. Routledge. doi:10.4324/9780203990971

Calonge, C. (2006). *USA Patent*, (No. US7072857), B1.

Catteeuw, F., Flynn, E., & Vonderhorst, J. (2007). Employee Engagement: Boosting Productivity in Turbulent Times. *Organization Development Journal*, 151–157.

de Silva, S. L., & de Oliveira, S. B. (2015). Planning and Scope Definition to Implement ERP: The Case Study of Federal Rural University of Rio de Janeiro (UFRRJ). *Procedia Computer Science*, *64*, 196–203. doi:10.1016/j.procs.2015.08.481

Esteves, J. M. (2014). An empirical identification and categorisation of training best practices for ERP implementation projects. *Enterprise Information Systems*, *8*(6), 665–683. doi:10.1080/17517575.2013.771411

Haddara, M. (2014). ERP Selection: The SMART Way. *Procedia Technology*, *16*, 394–403. doi:10.1016/j.protcy.2014.10.105

Harris, F. (2003). How many parts to make at once. In M. Lewis & N. Slack (Eds.), *Operations Management: Critical perspective of business management* (pp. 3–9). Routledge.

Helo, P., Anussornnitisarn, P., & Phusavat, K. (2008). Expectation and reality in ERP implementation: Consultant and solution provider perspective. *Industrial Management & Data Systems*, *108*(8), 1045–1059. doi:10.1108/02635570810904604

Hudson, K., Grisham, T., Srinivasan, P., & Moussa, N. (2005). *Conflict Management, Negotiation, and Effective communication Essential Skills for Project Managers*. Retrieved from http://thomasgrisham.com/wp-content/uploads/2020/04/Conflict-Management-Negotiation-and-Effective-Communication-1.pdf

Ifinedo, P. (2008). Impacts of business vision, top management support, and external expertise on ERP success. *Business Process Management Journal*, *14*(4), 551–568. doi:10.1108/14637150810888073

Ivan, L., Bosilj Vuk, V., & Spremi, M. (2019). Mastering the Digital Transformation Process: Business Practices and Lessons Learned. *Technology Innovation Management Review*, *59*(2), 36–50. doi:10.22215/timreview/1217

Kurco, K., Stepanic, D., & Varga, M. (2012). Strategic and Tactical Success Factors in ERP System Implementation. *International Journal of Computers*, *6*(4), 206–214.

Liu, G. H., Wang, E. T., & Chua, C. E. (2015). Leveraging Social Capital to Obtain Top Management Support in Complex, Cross-Functional It Projects. *Journal of the Association for Information Systems*, *16*(8), 707–737. doi:10.17705/1jais.00404

Loonam, J. A., & Donagh, J. M. (2005). Exploring Top Management Support for the Introduction of Enterprise Information Systems: A Literature Review. *Irish Journal of Management*, 163–178.

McBeath, B. (2017, September 6). Retrieved May 9, 2020, from https://www.industryweek.com/sponsored/whitepaper/22024116/agile-erp-concepts-continuous-improvement-through-rapid-incremental-implementation-and-value-realization

Menon, S. A., Muchnick, M., Butler, C., & Pizur, T. (2019). Critical Challenges in Enterprise Resource Planning (ERP) Implementation. *International Journal of Business and Management*, *14*(7), 54–69. doi:10.5539/ijbm.v14n7p54

Olson, D. L. (2007). Evaluation of ERP outsourcing. *Computers & Operations Research*, *34*(12), 3715–3724. doi:10.1016/j.cor.2006.01.010

Panorama Consulting Group. (2019, July 12). Retrieved May 11, 2020, from https://www.panorama-consulting.com/erp-project-plan/

Panorama Consulting Group. (2020). *Panorama Consulting Group 2020 ERP Report*. Panorama Consulting Group. Retrieved May 9, 2020, from https://www.panorama-consulting.com/resource-center/2020-erp-report/?utm_campaign=Popup%20-%202020%20ERP%20Report&utm_source=Popup

Powell, J. R. (2008, August). The Quantum Limit to Moore's Law. *Proceedings of the IEEE*, *96*(8), 1247–1248. doi:10.1109/JPROC.2008.925411

Prasetyo, S., Lubis, M., Witjaksono, R., & Azizah, H. (2019). *Critical Failure Factors in Enterprise Resource Planning (ERP) Implementation: Case Study of PT.Toyota Astra Motor Indonesia*. IEEE. doi:10.1109/ICIC47613.2019.8985720

Rahayu, S., & Dillak, V. (2018). 12 3). Key Success Factor for Successful ERP Implementation in State Owned Enterprises. *IACSIT International Journal of Engineering and Technology*, *7*(4.38), 916–919. doi:10.14419/ijet.v7i4.38.27608

Ranganathan, C., & Brown, C. V. (2006). ERP Investments and the Market Value of Firms: Toward an Understanding of Influential ERP Project Variables. *Information Systems Research, 17*(2). *Online (Bergheim)*, *17*(2), 145–161. Advance online publication. doi:10.1287/isre.1060.0084

Remus, U., & Schub, S. (2003, December 19). A blueprint for the implementation of process-oriented knowledge management. *The Journal of Corporate Transformation*, *10*(4), 237–253. doi:10.1002/kpm.182

Rijo, R., Martinho, R., & Ermida, D. (2015). Developing an Enterprise Architecture Proof of Concept in a Portuguese Hospital. *Procedia Computer Science*, *64*, 1217–1225. doi:10.1016/j.procs.2015.08.511

Robertson, P. L., & Langlois, R. N. (1995). Innovation, networks, and vertical integration. *Research Policy*, *24*(4), 543–562. doi:10.1016/S0048-7333(94)00786-1

Rogers, D. L. (2016). *The Digital Transformation Playbook: Rethink Your Business for the Digital Age*. Columbia University Press. doi:10.7312/roge17544

Roser, M., & Ritchie, H. (2013, January 1). *Technological Progress*. Retrieved from Our World in Data: https://ourworldindata.org/technological-progress

Shalan, M. (2017). *The SMAC Opportunity Contracts: Generating Value From Responsive Agile Risk-Oriented Techniques*. Mobile Platforms, Design, and Apps for Social Commerce. doi:10.4018/978-1-5225-2469-4.ch008

Sheu, C., Chae, B., & Yang, C.-L. (2004). National differences and ERP implementation: Issues and challenges. *Omega*, *32*(5), 61–71. doi:10.1016/j.omega.2004.02.001

Sitalakshmi Venkatraman, K. F. (2016, March 27). Challenges and Success Factors in ERP Implemenatation in Australian SMEs. *MDPI Journal Systems*, 1-18.

Skok, W., & Döringer, H. (2002). Potential Impact of Cultural Differences on Enterprise Resource Planning (ERP) Projects. *The Electronic Journal on Information Systems in Developing Countries*, *7*(1), 1–8. doi:10.1002/j.1681-4835.2002.tb00041.x

Soffer, P., Golany, B., & Dori, D. (2003). ERP modeling: A comprehensive approach. *Information Systems*, *28*(6), 673–690. doi:10.1016/S0306-4379(02)00078-9

Soja, P. (2006). Success factors in ERP systems implementations: Lessons from practice. *Journal of Enterprise Information Management*, *19*(4), 418–433. doi:10.1108/17410390610678331

The Enterprisers Project. (2020, May 26). Retrieved from https://enterprisersproject.com: https://enterprisersproject.com/what-is-digital-transformation#q1

Upadhyay, P., Basu, R., Adhikary, R., & Dan, P. K. (2010, October). A Comparative Study of Issues Affecting ERP Implementation in Large Scale and Small Medium Scale Enterprises in India: A Pareto Approach. *International Journal of Computers and Applications*, *8*(3), 23–28. doi:10.5120/1192-1670

Walter, C. (2005, August 1). Kryder's Law. *Scientific American*, 33-34.

Xie, Y., James Allen, C., & Ali, M. (2014). An integrated decision support system for ERP implementation in small and medium sized enterprises. *Journal of Enterprise Information Management*, *27*(4), 358–384. doi:10.1108/JEIM-10-2012-0077

Youngberg, E., Olsen, D., & Hauser, K. (2009). Determinants of professionally autonomous end user acceptance in an enterprise resource planning system environment. *International Journal of Information Management*, *29*(2), 138–144. doi:10.1016/j.ijinfomgt.2008.06.001

Yu, C. (2005). Causes influencing the effectiveness of the post-implementation ERP system. *Industrial Management & Data Systems*, *105*(1), 115–132. doi:10.1108/02635570510575225

ADDITIONAL READING

Asprion, P. M., Schneider, B., & Grimberg, F. (2018). ERP Systems Towards Digital Transformation. In R. Dornberger (Ed.), *Business Information Systems and Technology 4.0. Studies in Systems, Decision and Control, 141: 15–29*. Springer., doi:10.1007/978-3-319-74322-6_2

Benbasat, I., Goldstein, D. K., & Mead, M. (2012). Digital Transformation: Opportunities to Create New Business Models. *Strategy and Leadership*, *40*(2), 16–24. doi:10.1108/10878571211209314

Brust, L., Antons, D., Breidbach, C. F., & Salge, T. O. 2017. ServiceDominant Logic and Information Systems Research: A Review and Analysis Using Topic Modeling. In *Proceedings of the International Conference on Information Systems*. Association for Information Systems.

Buh, B., Kovačič, A., & Indihar Štemberger, M. (2015). Critical Success Factors for Different Stages of Business Process Management Adoption – A Case Study. *Economic Research-Ekonomska Istraživanja*, *28*(1), 243–258. doi:10.1080/1331677X.2015.1041776

Myers, M. D., & Newman, M. (2007). The Qualitative Interview in IS Research: Examining the Craft. *Information and Organization*, *17*(1), 2–26. doi:10.1016/j.infoandorg.2006.11.001

Niehaves, B., Poeppelbuss, J., Plattfaut, R., & Becker, J. (2014). BPM Capability Development – A Matter of Contingencies. *Business Process Management Journal*, *20*(1), 90–106. doi:10.1108/BPMJ-07-2012-0068

Pellikka, J., & Ali-Vehmas, T. (2016). Managing Innovation Ecosystems to Create and Capture Value in ICT Industries. *Technology Innovation Management Review*, *6*(10), 17–24. doi:10.22215/timreview/1024

Recker, J., Holten, R., Hummel, M., & Rosenkranz, C. (2017). How Agile Practices Impact Customer Responsiveness and Development Success: A Field Study. *Project Management Journal*, *48*(2), 99–121. doi:10.1177/875697281704800208

Sebastian, I. M., Ross, J. W., Beath, C., Mocker, M., Moloney, K. G., & Fonstad, N. O. (2017). How Big Old Companies Navigate Digital Transformation. *MIS Quarterly Executive*, *16*(3), 197–213.

Singh, A., & Hess, T. (2017). How Chief Digital Officers Promote the Digital Transformation of their Companies. *MIS Quarterly Executive*, *16*(1), 1–17.

Spremi, M. (2017). Governing Digital Technology – How Mature IT Governance Can Help in Digital Transformation? *International Journal of Economics and Management Systems*, *2*, 214–223.

Voss, C., Tsikriktsis, N., & Frohlich, M. (2002). Case Research in Operations Management. *International Journal of Operations & Production Management*, *22*(2), 195–219. doi:10.1108/01443570210414329

KEY TERMS AND DEFINITIONS

As-Is Processes: Current state analysis representing a process management strategy that identifies and evaluates a business's current processes. It can focus on an entire business organization or on one or more specific processes within a department or team.

Blueprint: Models and patterns that describe generic processes for the implementation and support the stepwise integration of business processes into the knowledge life cycle. It includes detailed plans that are required to build something in accordance with the designer's intentions.

Business Solution: Technology based solutions designed to integrate multiple facets of a company's business through the interchange of information from various business process areas and related databases. Business solutions are replacing the ERP concept that is usually based on single vendor.

Enterprise Resource Planning (ERP): An integrated suite of modules that are comprehensively devised to digitally sequence and streamline the business functions that include financial management, supply chain management, human resources, customer relations management, cost management and other industry specific modules.

Scooping: An effective ERP scoping process need to build a clear vision and expectation in the mind of the project team and business stakeholders. The strategic objective is to define focus, tactical objectives are to define the statement of work, supporting change control processes and define what should be out of scope.

Scope: Defining what is the project overall, when will the project be complete, how much will it cost, and most importantly, how does it meet the company's strategic goals.

Small and Medium Enterprises (SME): Are businesses whose personnel numbers fall below certain limits, or its revenues or turnover are below a defined threshold.

To-Be Processes: The future state of an organizational or business process. It is the ideal state of how you want your business processes to work and mapping the To-Be processes will structurally clarify how you can get there.

Section 3

Business Cases From the Field

Chapter 14
Enhancing the Contracting Touch Points Through Innovation:
For Architecture Design and Consulting Offices

Solaiman A. Elkhereiji
SAK Engineering Consultants, Saudi Arabia

ABSTRACT

The subject of this chapter revolves around how Industry 4.0 is changing our way of life. The way we communicate, travel, socialize, learn, relax, or do business changed significantly. As a major architecture and design offices, Industry 4.0 technologies are adding new layers to our business every day. This affects the design of offices, houses, communities, and cities. The relation with contractors, customers, and all stakeholders have changed creating new interfaces, channels, and touch points. Terms such as "collective intelligence" or "crowdsourcing" come into the picture with development in the mobile technology, collaboration tools, and Industry 4.0 ecosystem. It is interesting to see how this advanced means are facilitating new mindsets in design architects and construction industry. Customer expectations are being elevated as well. This is adding a lot of touch points with suppliers and consumers, and that is why a new innovative contracts and contracting is required.

INTRODUCTION

The subject of this chapter revolves around how industry 4.0 is changing our way of life. These changes are due to a large extent to contracted designers who invented new interfaces, tools, and devices. When using maps and city guides to gather information on restaurants, museums, or theaters, when communicating with friends and family, in education and health, in shopping and retail store experiences, smartphones enrich our life as well increase and improve our experiences.

DOI: 10.4018/978-1-7998-4501-0.ch014

Industry 4.0 is a trend of automation and data exchange. It created an environment where technology and humans are so closely integrated. Facilitating many different activities and opportunity contracts that enhance the collaboration between stakeholders and combine several factors to produce an effective contract. Major shifts in technology and business dynamics invited the new approach of contracting which evolve around the following pillars:

- The massive data flow in the organizations
- The inevitable agility and change management practices

Mobile technology is currently setting as first option for carrying out most of the businesses, especially, the one related to design and engineering. Most of designers now are aware of that and they have access to the mobile platforms and technology that allow them to proceed and progress their work smoothly and successfully, in collaboration with other teams; local and overseas.

Working routine has been shifted from the traditional mode to smart mode thanks to the digital transformation platforms, which proved to be well-reputed and trust-worthy, with making sure that these mobile platforms have adequate and strict confidentiality and privacy agreements to protect the rights of all parties. Mindset change and cultural differences are gaining more land and can be better controlled over time and in collaboration with other team members actively utilizing mobile platforms and technology.

New styles will enable organizations to accomplish complex tasks in different environments and ecosystems with relative ease. Throughout the contract lifecycle, teams of people must collaborate on various tasks both pre-execution and post-execution. The main contractors may hire specialized second-degree contractors for certain activities. Human capital preparations for new contracting styles is also developing to fit between technology based operational activities and adaptive functional strategies utilize advanced technology tools to build the required contracting paradigm.

However, there exist some drawbacks in using mobile and industry 4.0 technologies such as; the lack of trust in contractual relations in terms of the working routine that the various teams follow; the extreme effort it takes to break the power of habit and mindset change requirement and associated culture. Such drawbacks will be eliminated with time as more people are utilizing the new methodologies.

BACKGROUND

Industry 4.0 related technologies are affecting the design and construction firms (Zaher, 2018). This is expected to challenge the contracting style that is adapted. Building information modeling (BIM) is one of the most promising recent developments in the architecture, engineering, and construction (AEC) industry (Azhar, 2011). One example is the utilization of mobile devices and augmented reality to develop useful applications that client can carry all the time to follow up the progress in his project (Lin, Liu, Tsai, & Kang, 2015).

Industry 4.0 tools and emerging technologies appears to be the fastest growing activity for users (Nowotarski & Paslawski, 2017), and they will play a key role throughout the customer life cycle, especially to enable brands and designers to deepen conversations with their customers. (Oesterreich & Teuteberg, 2016). Stated that despite its potential benefits in terms of improvements in productivity and quality, this concept has not gained much attention in the construction industry. Such tools combine three strong factors which are frequency of use, convenience and emotion. Such tools introduce a new kind of conversations with customers (Larivière, et al., 2013).

Digital Transformation nature has promoted the usage of complex systems where clients enterprise can utilize large numbers of independent components that can be contracted, operated and managed independently, to create value from technology and enable business agility (Shalan & Anaim, 2017). Innovative contracting promotes incremental delivery of services and features through development or acquisition in a pre-defined delivery cycle and milestones which includes iteration delivery with continuous verification within a time-boxing of fixed scope.

According to (Glaiel, 2012), large-scale software engineering organizations have traditionally used plan-driven, heavyweight, waterfall-style approaches for the planning, execution, and monitoring of software development efforts. This approach often results in relatively long development schedules that are susceptible to failure, especially in a rapidly changing environment. Construction projects used to be relatively predictable, while industry 4.0 projects such as smart cities may be highly variable. In traditional projects, legal practitioners spend plenty of time studying problems arising from silo mentality assuming great problems if the project is stopped at any arbitrary point in time (Gardiner, 2005). While the world is changing frequently, agile provides value to cope up with such changes in an effective manner. Agile contracting models are needed to balance the risks between both parties and give both the incentive to work together towards the success of the joint project (Arbogast, Larman, & Vodde, 2012).

For the prescribed situation in contracts, contracting and related human, business and technology factors, plenty of touch points have been described and investigated from construction and design Architects point of view (Kordas, 2015). Among these was the contracting innovation effects on business-technology relationship and how to develop a creative performance management tools to measure the suppliers and the contractor's achievements and compliance. According to (Shalan & Anaim, 2017), few middle circle providers' issues need to be discussed such as responsive change management; creative contract termination; liability and warranty; payment scheduling and faithful and ethical act. This chapter is building on this background to move toward smoothing the touch points in construction projects and contracts.

OUTSOURCING AND TOUCH POINTS

Contracts by itself is a call to organize the relation between multiple stakeholders, usually from different organizations who are acting together to create certain values. Construction contracts is a major area in which touch points need to be managed effectively due to its high cost and the difficulty to return.

Defining Touch Points

Customer touchpoint are always there when a current or potential customer comes into contact with the Design Architects before, during or after they have received the service, or purchased a product.

As a contractor, you don't have a ton of time. Between juggling different subcontractors, lining up your next projects, and putting out fires that come up unexpectedly, you've got a lot on your plate. Industry 4.0 have given a lot of tools that can give a hand.

Smoothing Touch Points

Enhancing the relation between stakeholders will enhance the overall performance of a projects, this can be described as smoothing the touch points between contractors, service providers and clients. In construction projects better collaboration, communication and technology tools utilization will heavily affect the performance of those real projects. The involved parties can effectively share the project data, information, and progress through cloud services, having online meetings, follow up construction activities whether onsite or virtually using webcam streaming to the internet. However, there shall be close monitoring onsite for the consultant to inspect, verify and approve all project activities and materials submittals done by the contractors.

Managing the Outsourcing Activities

With the demand on specialized talents and the pressure to reduce the project costs, organizations are utilizing more offshore or contracted resources. Comparing the benefits of outsourcing against the drawbacks will help to decide if this is something that could work for the business.

Offshore resources can provide very valuable solution for carrying out the design work, especially if subject matter experts (SMEs) are required. However, for the design architects that is responsible for the whole activities, we have to prepare a plan on how to divide the work into elements and components, arrange assignments over the project resources, and how we maintain control over the design work while we are utilizing offshore resources. This plan shall be prepared and shared with project stakeholders prior to utilizing offshore resources.

Some firms prefer to utilize core team for carrying out major tasks, while utilizing limited time employees as per project requirements, budget, and predetermined time frame. This approach may provide some flexibility to expand the workforce as and when needed. However, some control measures shall be proposed to ensure the overall quality of project deliverables are within the acceptance criteria, and to monitor the project progress in terms of time, cost, and quality to achieve all project deliverables successfully.

Although control modes have been studied extensively in traditional contexts, minimal attention has been directed toward understanding how different control modes operate in platform ecosystems (Goldbach, Benlian, & Buxmann, 2018). There are many pros and cons of outsourcing, all of which should be carefully considered before deciding for or against this strategy. As the outsourcing will affect company culture, this isn't something to take lightly. As a business owner we can't focus on the benefits of outsourcing without considering the impact it can have on the ecosystem as a whole.

Benefits of Outsourcing in Construction Projects

Plenty of reasons are available to give a try to outsourced resources, or offshore resources in construction projects which include:

Reducing the Number of Employees

Outsourcing allows to avoid hiring new fulltime resources into the company, which saves money on everything from space allocations, time utilization, employee benefits and training. The company may be interested in a limited high caliper tasks that doesn't require a full-time employee.

Access to A Larger Talent Pool

When hiring an employee, you may only have access to a small, local talent pool. This often means you must compromise. Many companies have found that outsourcing as a tool that gives them access to talent in other parts of the world. If you need specialized help, it often makes sense to expand your search.

Lower Labor Cost

Every company has its own reasons chasing lower labor costs. As a design architects we don't want to trade quality for price but outsourcing often allows us to get the best of both. By searching a global talent pool, it's easier to find the right talent at the right price.

Disadvantages of Outsourcing

Despite the many benefits of outsourcing, the organization should not go down the outsourcing path until they look and measure potential drawbacks:

Lack of Control

Although you can provide direction regarding what you need to accomplish, you give up some control when you outsource. There are many reasons for this, including the fact that you are often hiring a contractor instead of an employee. Since that person is not working on-site, it can be difficult to maintain the level of control you desire.

Communication Issues

This doesn't always come into play, but it's one of the biggest potential drawbacks. Here are several questions to ask:

- What time zone does the person live in and how does this match up with your business hours?
- What is your preferred method of communication? Phone, email, instant messaging?
- Does the person have access to a reliable internet connection?

Problems With Quality

Despite all the benefits of outsourcing, it is only a good thing if you're receiving the quality you expect. Anything less than this will be disappointing. This isn't to say that you can't successfully outsource particular tasks, but you need to discuss the expected quality upfront.

Impact on Company Culture

If you plan on outsourcing, you need to take steps to ensure that it doesn't have a negative effect on company culture. A positive work culture leads to a higher level of productivity, so you don't want to do anything to jeopardize this. Some of the ways outsourcing can negatively affect company culture include:

- Upsetting employees as they may feel they are being replaced
- Confusing employees who don't understand why you are outsourcing particular tasks
- Adding challenges to the daily workflow of the company

Outsourcing doesn't always have a negative impact on company culture, but one need to protect against this before you ever take a step in this direction. This typically means discussing such decisions with employees who could be impacted.

Real Outsourcing Stories in the Design Architects

Plenty of real stories about shifting the business workforce from permanent employees to limited time workers exist, as companies are looking to have different skill sets with flexible approaches and flexibility to expand or change.

Al-Ra'idah Housing Complex Project in Jeddah is an example where SAK Collaborated with Tandem Architects, Pivot International and SPINE to form a joint venture, which not only helped SAK to complete the project with minimum in-house staff but also fostered SAK's innovative design capabilities to deliver an award winning exemplary project.

Choosing Between Partnership, Outsourcing, Offshoring and Gig Workers

In today's economy, it makes sense for the business to explore the idea of offshoring and outsourcing different areas of the business. Before deciding to offshore or outsource, it is vital to understand the advantages and disadvantages of each of the options. Selecting between insourcing where an employee of the company completes a task or business process or outsourcing to have someone external to the company complete the work. Insourcing also has its downfalls, such as the cost, training requirement, scalability, and quick response. Table 1 is showing differences between insourcing and outsourcing options

TECHNOLOGY EFFECTS ON ARCHITECTURE AND CONSTRUCTION FIRMS

In the digital transformation era, it is important to build the right characteristics in the contract to respond to disruption of new technologies while maintaining sustainability. One important aspect will be to handle new technologies that are coming during the implementation but was not considered in the design phase.

While preparing and reviewing the agreement between the consulting firm and client, both entities must ensure that the technological tools and measures are properly defined in the contract agreement, and that all parties are aware of its interpretation. For example, in some design contracts, the client may request the consultant to prepare the design fully using REVIT modules for all disciplines, while in other contracts, the client may ask for design output to be basically using computer aided design in 2D

Table 1. Comparative characteristics of different employment models

	Outsourcing		Insourcing	Freelance	Staff Augmentation
	Offshore	**Nearshore**			
Price	Medium Low	Medium	High	Low	Low
Location	Abroad	Your country	Your country	Abroad or your country	Abroad
Office	Vendor		Yours	Freelancer	Vendor
Management	Vendor		Yours	Yours	Yours
When to use	MVP		Regular dev	MVP/Regular dev	Regular dev
Reliability	Medium		High	Low	High

Source: (Trend Line Global, 2020)

with some 3D shots and perspectives. This is for sure has impact on time and cost and shall be clearly considered in the contract agreement.

However, it is not common to have a case of new technologies that are coming during the implementation but was not considered in the design phase. This may happen in future projects, but it is not common in the design field up to now. Currently, there are some inherent limitations in the construction industry adopting new disruptive technologies, such as the "lack of budget," "upper management's lack of understanding of these technologies," and "design teams' lack of knowledge".

Some managers think that lowering profit margins on construction projects might be a major limiting factor that prevents the industry from adopting new technologies. However, it might be that the lack of availability of cost/benefit analysis or feasibility studies are the actual limiting factors where such technologies should be cost effective over the time. Owners and companies are not willing to invest their money without knowing the true costs and benefits such as time and cost savings and some of them are looking for immediate effect. Among technologies that have affected architects and Design Architectss include the following terms.

Mobile Technologies

With the spread of touch screens over the last years the mobile surpassed desktops in terms of total digital engagement (Narang & Shankar, 2019). According to (Marketing Charts, 2019), smartphones now account for 70% of US digital media time. The convenience of smartphones and tablet devices have completely shifted the digital media landscape in favor of mobile.

We switched from a large horizontal screen and a mouse to a vertical touch screen. According to (Clement, 2019), mobile's screens have become the number one access to the internet and world's internet population is now "Mobile First". Mobile First does not only mean that we spend more than half of our digital time on our smartphones Apps but also because mobile is the fuel that is driving business growth and utility.

The mobile service ecosystem is in a state of fundamental and rapid transformation (Basole & Karla, 2012). Engineering mobile Apps especially shows an immense influence in the design ecosystem in terms of engagement and reach. With all these vendors, suppliers and consumers dealing with mobile and considering mobile first there is a need to suggest a new contracting methodology that fits such a crowd while sustaining value.

Mobile applications gather user data and that is why privacy and security in mobile applications is a very important research. According to ((Silberer & Schulz, 2012) we are now entering the age of computerized mobile communication with diverse possibilities to enlist the services of mobile people mobile customer relationship management becomes a significant concept for generating long-term relationships and increasing customer satisfaction, retention and loyalty.

Nowadays, mobile devices have become so important in construction and design sectors. Phones, tablets and laptops are considered essential for carrying out the work and exchanging the information, data, and reporting to other project stakeholders. For example: at design, we have to maintain a network of communications both local and overseas, mobile services provide us with a smooth way of communications and coordination, as if all teams are being located at same place. This would help delivering the project successfully in a more efficient way, provided that we keep control over the communication by creating project communication plan and maintain this plan over project phases.

On the other hand, designers, contractors, and workers are using mobile devices and applications including maps and city guides to gather information almost about all aspects of life including work and personal matters. For example: locating project sites are determined in a very accurate way by using modern techniques of mobile Global Positioning Systems (GPS) devices then sending and sharing locations of sites through internet to other project stakeholders. Monitoring project progress on construction site by using web-based cameras connected to the internet and transmitting its feed directly to project stakeholders to enable them to observe and monitor the project phases and progress instantaneously.

Even more, mobile platforms nowadays have managed to cross all boundaries between countries and nations to allow the users performing multiple tasks remotely starting from collaborative design, communications, and learning, and even having certificates and university degrees. We currently can have a design team overseas who can work as virtual team, using same tools, communicating with clients and contractors, and having virtual meetings, presenting their work and design, and obtaining client feedback and approval in a very smart way.

Augmenting the Computing Power Through the Cloud

According to (Siddiqui, Alam, & Bokhari, 2012), due to the improved performance of computer systems, Geographic information systems (GIS) are becoming more usual. One more dimension in design and construction is the relation with major engineering firms such as Autodesk, Esri GIS and Geo Media cloud services when uploading and processing images in their cloud. There are certainly many benefits of using platforms of such engineering firms, for example using cloud services can give more efficient and smooth way of dealing with processed data and some activities such as rendering which used to take days and weeks on the Design Architects workstations are performed in minutes or hours if using the optimized supercomputers of those power designers.

Although, there may be a risk of data breach uploading designs to third party, we believe that any uploaded or processed data are being dealt with extreme confidentiality. We trust the excellent international Non-Disclosure Agreements (NDAs) that is governing the uploading and processing of images and layouts.

Another dimension for designers and contractors is using and benefiting from power houses such as Google, Amazon and Microsoft to use cloud computing for normal processing and file on daily basis. Handling of images, maps, files, on-line meetings, and messaging are used frequently as an office automation tools. These services managed to be the first choice for exchange of data and information safely and efficiently, and it guarantees the utmost privacy and confidentiality to its users and saving the designers, contractors, and clients a lot of hassle.

Collective Intelligence or Crowdsourcing

Crowdsourcing, simply referring to the act of outsourcing a task to the crowd, is one of the most important trends revolutionizing the internet and the mobile market at present (Bücheler, Sieg, Füchslin, & Pfeifer, 2010). Designers and project managers are utilizing the concepts of collective intelligence or crowdsourcing to collect ideas about certain design and draw a full picture for sustainable development. Public involvement is a central concern for urban planners, but the challenge for planners is how best to implement such programs, given many difficulties inherent in the typical public involvement process (Brabham, 2009). However, such concepts are not common in that Saudi engineering field, but it can be done on small scale. Applying these concepts may provide a good supply of innovative ideas within a specific time frame.

Virtual (VR), Augmented (AR) and Mixed Reality (MR)

These technologies are already making a huge impact on many industries around the world, and the construction industry is no exception. Augmented, virtual, and mixed reality applications all aim to enhance a user's current experience or reality (Brigham, 2017). Buildings are becoming ever more complicated, and these technologies are helping architects and construction teams improve designs and detect design errors.

To date, architects and design teams greatly improve building design through interactive design and gesture interfacing. According to (Yang & Kang, 2014), Building Information Model (BIM) technology combines a "virtual building" with extended information, removing the necessity to rely on imagination or experience to foresee the completed building. The interface provides hand-based gesture control that allows BIM models to be navigated with ease. These "reality" solutions could correct a range of errors including air-conditioning system design and finding missing elements that have been overlooked during the design phase. They are also being utilized in the construction industry to: -

- Aid 3D modelling of buildings and structures.
- Help improve and innovate BIM (building information modelling) visualization.
- Provide a permanent record of the building and allows clients to explore designs before construction.
- Help seeing through walls for maintenance workers and service engineers.

3-Dimensional (3-D) Printing

Three-dimensional (3D) printing (also known as additive manufacturing) is an advanced manufacturing process that can produce complex shape geometries automatically from a 3D computer-aided design model without any tooling, dies and fixtures (Tay, et al., 2017). Its benefits have already been explored and exploited by various construction companies around the world. The ability to either prefabricate offsite or directly on-site has obvious labor and material cost benefits over more traditional building methods. It also reduces waste and go much beyond the restriction of construction worker shift patterns. Today it's possible for 3D to print an entire house in less than 24 hours.

For good reasons, more and more companies are starting up in the sector to create new, innovative projects with 3D prints. Some are more futuristic while others are very real in the present. As a Design Architects, 3D printing inspires our architects to think of innovative designs that was impossible to implement in normal construction methods.

Robotics

Day by day, robotics is making a bigger impact in the construction industry. Somewhat linked to the impact of 3D printing, robotics is also seeing impressive infiltration into the industry. Research and development in construction robots is intended to extend present capabilities of conventional equipment to an integrated and fully automated system (Kangari, 1991). From robotic bricklayers to laying roads, robots are increasingly finding their place amongst the workforce on construction sites. This is interesting as traditionally the construction industry has seen very little automation, relying largely on manual labor.

By adding robots to the workforce, construction companies are seeing improved construction times and improved quality of builds. According to (Prasath Kumar, Balasubramanian, & Jagadish Raj, 2016) Automated instruments are found to be efficient by reducing average time consumed for major activities by 57.85% of time taken, automated equipment's are found to reduce cost incurred in net working cost by an average of 51.67% Robots are also being used to help demolish buildings too. While currently slower than human demolition crews, they are far safer and cheaper for bringing down concrete structures at the end of its life cycle. Robots are also being developed to help with certain building maintenance like window cleaning.

Modular and Fabricated Construction

Modular and prefabricated solutions are nothing new to the construction industry (Smith, 2010). For example, the end of the Second World War saw something of a 'Cambrian Explosion' in prefab design in war-torn cities across the UK.

While it has fallen out of favor over the last few decades, prefabs have been making something of a comeback in recent years. The promise of faster on-site assembly and higher quality, standardized builds are seen by some as the solution to tackle perceived housing crises around the world.

Advances in high-tech design and construction mean increasing numbers of components that can be manufactured off-site. That means buildings can go up more quickly and quietly, with fewer materials wasted. To accommodate modular housebuilding, developers are building their own factories, and architects are getting ever more ambitious in their designs. Prefabricated construction has been proven effective, environmentally friendly, and labor-friendly (Jiang, Li, Li, & Gao, 2018).

Enhancing Sustainability

For several decades, building regulations have been placing more and more burden on building design to reduce their environmental impact and sustainability (Lechner, 2014). Optimized energy efficiency and a drive for low to zero carbon emissions have driven innovation in building construction and service design for years. In response, new, better thermal performance materials are being developed that promise to make the buildings of the future incredibly well insulated for a fraction of the cost of current solutions.

Industry 4.0 can provide various tools to support this objective. One example from few years ago was the development of a concrete roof that can generate and store energy. Innovations like this should make buildings of the future cheaper to live in and reduce their impact on the environment. Reducing waste or recycling old materials is another area where sustainability is helping drive innovation in the construction industry. One architecture firm announced its plans for a new method of recycling construction waste into ton new reusable building materials.

SAK Head Office Building Jeddah is an example which is currently under construction designed according to the Leadership in Energy and Environmental Design (LEED) standards with target to achieve LEED Certification. The building design will minimize the negative impacts on the environment, reduce energy consumption, minimize potable water consumption, and improve indoor environment quality. Negative impacts on the environment will be minimized by reducing heat island effect, light pollution, storm water management, non-CFC/HCFC refrigerant leakage control, using FSC certified wood, locally available & recycled materials and recycling construction waste materials.

Energy consumption will be reduced by using highly insulated walls, roofs and windows. Similarly, the use of high efficiency VRF AC system, calligraphic screens at windows, LED lights, occupancy sensors, PV panels at the roof and BMS system will further reduce the electricity consumption for the building. Potable water consumption will be minimized by using high efficiency water fixtures/fittings, native low water consumption plants, recycle grey water for flushing toilets, and condensate water from AC system for irrigation.

Indoor environment quality (IEQ) will be improved by using fresh air for the AC system, monitory CO2 levels in interior spaces, and low VOC paints-carpets-composite wood-sealants. IEQ will be further improved by providing individual lighting and AC controls for regularly occupied spaces, views to outside and daylight in the interior spaces. Similarly, air flush before building occupancy, provision of roll on mats to capture dirt and particulates entering the building at entrances, and provision of separate return air system for the housekeeping, photocopying, and printing rooms. Lastly, smoking is prohibited in the building to further improve IEQ.

Enabling the Creative Performance Management for the New Era

Industry 4.0 come with new challenges and opportunities. Outsourcing and gig workers will need profiling, selection and evaluation so that can or can't be hired for future projects. It is crucial to develop a creative performance management tools to measure the suppliers and the contractor's achievements and to reduce friction with them. Performance management is not easy as it varies due to new variation orders and measurement techniques (Kagioglou, Cooper, & Aouad, 2001).

Performance management method for construction companies can be summarized as mentioned below, benefiting from data analysis and storage capabilities:

Measure

Measuring phase defines the necessary perspectives for its performance management based on a concept of BSC (Balanced Score Cards) that sets the objectives of performance. After that step, it deducts success factors, sets the target of performance and measures data with assessment of measurable index. It can add or remove new perspective in need from a criterion of standard perspectives. It is necessary to consider their weight because there would be a difference of importance among perspectives.

Store

In storing phase, it is a step for loading performance data into data warehouse (DW) and it defines fact table which contains measured data and dimension table including descriptive information about fact, and it sets the link for every table. From that, performance data schema is embodied. Data accumulated in DW has two kinds that which are measured data and converted data through extracting, refining stored data in operating system.

Analyze

The analysis phase is a step to make multidimensional analysis applying OLAP (On-Line Analytical Processing) with performance and related data stored in DW. Most of the dimensions have the hierarchical structure. It enables to analyze the data of each level which is required by users. Next, the cube is made, after classifying hierarchical structure of dimension and setting level. The method of cube is decided according to purpose, and situation of their analysis and it analyses with slicing and dicing by preference of users.

Report

It is a phase of creating appropriate pages from results of previous step using tables and pictures without extra programming. In this step, user analyzes information through interaction with system and it displays its report to screen. When analyzing, Extensible Markup Language (xml) formatted data which has been extracted simple information are stored in database of searching system going to be used in next step.

Use

This phase is used to solve problem and support decision-making as a result from analyzed data. In case of application, by using xml, it offers similar contents of searching result as an advertisement from searching system, and tools which offer comparable display that they can get more data and enables their role for helping reasonable decision making.

ADOPTING AND ADAPTING INNOVATIVE CONTRACTS

Each consulting firm has its own business model which suits its objectives and serves its strategic plan. However, consulting firms have to look for ways to improve and develop creative business models to be able to compete with other powerful competitors for innovative projects, and try to adapt to the variable nature of business and rapid pace of transformation in order to have a specific class in the market. Some drawbacks can be related to having some time to adapt to the recently developed business model, and time exerted to improve the learning curve.

This adoption and adaptation come with benefits and drawbacks that will be reflected with or on the creative business models. Here are some of them.

Managing Liabilities and Responsibilities

Project stakeholders are being expanded to include additional layers of contractors, power houses, engineering firms and gig workers. This requires different style to manage liabilities, responsibilities, and quality assurance. According to (Mone, London, & Mone, 2018), creative performance management tools are continuously being developed and enhanced to measure the suppliers and the contractor's achievements against real performance.

This is true and shall be considered in all projects. One of the most critical project phases is the "monitor and control" phase in which the performance and progress of the contractor and suppliers is measured. This is subject to having the project scope well-defined, procurement logs and the approved time schedule while preparing the construction and the procurement management plan by the general contractor and suppliers.

Some tools that usually used include Primavera Project Management and Microsoft Project that can handle procurement logs linked with the project time schedule and periodical reports linked with progress percentages. However, more tools are enquired today to enhance the management of additional stakeholders and various levels of responsibilities and liabilities.

This is crucial to decrease the direct friction and maintain suitable and effective approach for monitoring and measuring the work progress and deliverables, in addition to reporting their performance to project stakeholders, especially the client.

Technology Risk Concerns in Design Architects

Designers shall be aware that there are liabilities and risks for using mobile and other apps to view their design (Juan, Lai, & Shih, 2017). They shall make sure to use trust-worthy apps with strict confidentiality agreements that protect its users from stealing data, designs or altering them. Moreover, designers need to make sure to have their logos on the produced designs, and the files are protected in such way prevents others from changing or manipulating the designs, without permission from the designing firm. Some risks that is directly related to Design Architects include:

Handling Privacy, Security and User Rights

With the spread of technology, privacy and user rights related to mobile applications is crucial especially with applications that is designed to gather user data or show related designs for projects and locations. Designers must ensure that the applications they are using within the firm are trust-worthy, and well-tested by well-reputed firms. Designers shall ensure that these applications have strict confidentiality agreements and non-disclosure agreement (NDAs) to protect the privacy and data confidentiality of the users. Moreover, all the uploaded designs into those applications need to be copyright protected and secured in such way to prevent others from copying or altering the design data.

Responsibility for Real-Time Data Collection and Transmission

The first phase of any design project is data collection including client requirements, site location, site information package, utilities around the site, and carrying out the necessary surveys to collect all the required data. After that, all these data are being transmitted from job site to project managers so that they can start interpreting and analyzing the collected data and surveys, and plan to start the design stages accordingly. However, the project managers are also involved at the stage of data collection as they must coordinate with the client for collecting its requirements and expectations from the project onset.

Technology have added the options of real-time data collection and transmission between the jobsite and project managers back at the office, in addition to collecting data from online resources. All related responsibilities need to be carefully measured and evaluated.

Handling Large Numbers of Independent Components

In design projects, there is a need to subdivide the project into small elements and components, prepare action plans on how and who will execute each component, start the design process, monitor and control it and its outcomes. When the closing phase is reached all the project deliverables need to be validated and approved by client after which we reach the contract closure. All the previous steps and outcomes can be supplied, operated, and managed effectively using smart techniques and mobile platforms.

These techniques may need some scaling to handle the large numbers of independent components that can be supplied, operated, and managed separately in smart designs.

Dealing With Responsive Change Management

According to (Shalan & Anaim, 2017), digital transformation and Industry 4.0 is requiring responsive change management and creative contract termination if the signed contract is not producing the expected value. As many parameters are subject to variation over time or based on client requirements.

Traditionally, if the scope listed in the contract agreement has been subject to, for example scope creep, the Design Architects have to indicate and report that officially to the client, and to ensure that this scope creep will stop and not progress any further. However, when a client violate some of the contract terms relevant to the entitled payment duration, the Design Architects response should be to approach the client to understand the reason for that issue, and try to use all the possible ways to solve it. Such situation needs to be handled on smarter basis today, as clients are changing behaviors and expectation regularly in our fast-moving world.

Extending the Legal Contracts With Commercial Agreements

Some factors can cause project elongation, which may include the duration exerted by client, for review and approval of the design deliverables to be extended beyond the approved design program. Another example from construction projects, that the contractor working onsite has suffered some schedule delays due to procurement delays or the lack of manpower, such cases will eventually cause extending the program, and accordingly the related confidentiality agreements.

Such scenarios need to be extended by commercial agreements such as Service Level Agreements (SLA) especially for innovative or special purpose projects.

Customer Engagements

One major aspect related to digital transformation is the change in contracting style with clients to keep them highly engaged and loyal clients to avoid them from going away to other suppliers.

Industry 4.0 tools can provide improved ways of direct communications and coordination with clients through cloud services and tools which can have the clients on close distance from his project and the engineering firm. For example, in some construction sites, we can provide webcam linked to the internet which provides online streaming of the construction activities and phases all over the project cycle. That way, the client will feel highly engaged and that consultancy firm provides him unique services, in addition to providing periodical progress reports for the project and sharing it with client using mobiles apps and cloud collaboration tools including for example inviting client to attend the progress meetings via online meeting apps. All of that will contribute to the success of project, having the client engaged and fully posted about his project activities and progress.

Hiring New Tools and Techniques

Today there exist a challenge on how to adapt with new generation designs and contracting nature which promoted the usage of complex systems with plenty of tools and stakeholders. Engineering firms are always seeking to develop its design tools using latest software's for drafting drawings, design and engineering. In the design field, it is essential to have a strategy to enhance and improve the existing tools and techniques so that we can offer high-quality services with competitive price while meeting the client predetermined time frame. Training courses are also arranged to provide chance for the designers to develop their abilities and skills.

Avoiding Conflicts From Traditional Contracts

While there are some challenges in adapting to industry 4.0 styles and innovative contracts, there was a lot of conflicts that have arisen in previous projects and there was plenty of consequences and effects that was hard to resolve.

First example for design projects where some conflicts arise due to that the client has not provided all his requirements from the project onset and planning phase, and after progressing with design development, the client demands additional requirements which have negatively affected the design program, and accordingly project budget. At that case, we had indicated that issue and highlighted it to the client illustrating its impact on the design program and project budget, and we had to submit variation order for additional time and charges since these additional requirements have not been incorporated at the concept design stage. After resolving such a conflict, we then progressed to the design development, and submitted it again for client approval.

Second example from construction project, it happened that the construction work has started and we, as the supervision consultant, have noticed the construction work is not progressing as per the approved construction program, and it is suffering from some delays, which may lead to extending the handover date of the project. We instructed the contractor to provide a corrective action immediately that has included to provide a dedicated contractor staff onsite to carry out the planning and procurement tasks, and not to rely only on the contractor head office to accomplish these vital tasks.

FUTURE RESEARCH DIRECTIONS

In this chapter, author showed how emerging technologies are affecting the design and construction firms and how this is dependent on the contracting style that is adapted. The utilization of such technologies including the mobile devices and augmented reality to develop useful applications that client can carry all the time to follow up the progress in his project will be great research.

The customer life cycle management has been a trouble in construction projects because the client may not be able to visualize the final product, or he may not be able to match the dimensions on his own setup. The digital tools introduce a new kind of conversations with customers. This are will need a lot of research as well.

Digital Transformation nature has promoted the usage of complex systems where clients can utilize large numbers of independent components that can be contracted, operated and managed independently, to create value from technology and enable business agility, managing such a huge number of contractors are still in its early start and plenty of dimensions need to be adjusted. Innovative contracting promotes incremental delivery of services and features through development or acquisition in a pre-defined delivery cycle and milestones which includes iteration delivery with continuous verification within a time-boxing of fixed scope, related methodologies need to be framed and their efficiency need to be measured.

Construction projects used to be relatively predictable, while new technology intensive projects may be highly progressive and variable. This will call for agile contracting models to balance the risks between both parties and give both the incentive to work together towards the success of the joint project. The prescribed situations in contracts, contracting and related human, business and technology factors create a lot of touch points that need to be smoothed for a better business-technology relationship. Moreover, few middle circle providers' issues need to be more researched including the shifts in the business workforce including the flexible approaches, elasticity to expand and the ability to build different skill sets.

CONCLUSION

Plenty of touch points, consequences and scenarios resulted due to contract transformation under the pressure of emerging technologies and business dynamics. This chapter have summarized the concepts, mechanisms, trends, forecasts, and consequences related to construction and design architects.

Empirically focused debate on the new era of technology driven innovation and its transformative impact on the design and construction activities and the associated paradigms shifts. Author has demonstrated how the contracting map have been influenced by the digital transformation behaviors and how experiences drawn from this process may be employed in building a business model for innovative contracting to provide a basis for curriculum design for those offices.

Business-technology relationship is transforming the future. This chapter attempts to present an effort and aspires to ignite fruitful discussions that will eventually lead to an increased number of research studies in the field of innovative contracting for design architects. Eventually this is expected to pave the way for a smooth and fruitful trusted relationship between all stakeholders.

REFERENCES

Arbogast, T., Larman, C., & Vodde, B. (2012). *Agile Contracts Primer.* https://agilecontracts.org/

Azhar, S. (2011, July). Building Information Modeling (BIM): Trends, Benefits, Risks, and Challenges for the AEC Industry. *Leadership and Management in Engineering, 11*(3). doi:10.1061/(ASCE)LM.1943-5630.0000127

Basole, R. C., & Karla, J. (2012, March 1). Value Transformation in the Mobile Service Ecosystem: A Study of App Store Emergence and Growth. *Service Science*, *4*(1), 1–88. doi:10.1287erv.1120.0004

Brabham, D. C. (2009). Crowdsourcing the Public Participation Process for Planning Projects. *Planning Theory*, *8*(3), 242–262. doi:10.1177/1473095209104824

Brigham, T. J. (2017). Reality Check: Basics of Augmented, Virtual, and Mixed Reality. *Medical Reference Services Quarterly*, *36*(2), 171–178. doi:10.1080/02763869.2017.1293987 PMID:28453428

Bücheler, T., Sieg, J. H., Füchslin, R. M., & Pfeifer, R. (2010). Crowdsourcing, open innovation and collective intelligence in the scientific method: a research agenda and operational framework. In *Artificial live XII: proceedings of the twelfth international conference on the synthesis and simulation of living systels* (pp. 679 - 686). MIT Press. 10.21256/zhaw-4094

Clement, J. (2019, September 11). *Mobile internet usage worldwide - Statistics & Facts.* Retrieved from https://www.statista.com/topics/779/mobile-internet/

Gardiner, P. D. (2005). *Project Management: A Strategic Planning Approach.* Macmillan International Higher Education. doi:10.1007/978-1-137-07973-2

Glaiel, F. (2012, May 7). *Agile project dynamics: a strategic project management approach to the study of large-scale software development using system dynamics* (Thesis). Massachusetts Institute of Technology, Engineering Systems Division. Retrieved from http://hdl.handle.net/1721.1/79513

Goldbach, T., Benlian, A., & Buxmann, P. (2018). Differential effects of formal and self-control in mobile platform ecosystems: Multi-method findings on third-party developers' continuance intentions and application quality. *Information & Management*, *55*(3), 271–284. doi:10.1016/j.im.2017.07.003

Jiang, L., Li, Z., Li, L., & Gao, Y. (2018). Constraints on the Promotion of Prefabricated Construction in China. *Sustainability.* Retrieved from https://www.mdpi.com/2071-1050/10/7/2516

Juan, Y.-K., Lai, W.-Y., & Shih, S.-G. (2017). Building information modeling acceptance and readiness assessment in Taiwanese architectural firms. *Journal of Civil Engineering and Management*, *23*(2), 356–367. doi:10.3846/13923730.2015.1128480

Kagioglou, M., Cooper, R., & Aouad, G. (2001). Performance management in construction: A conceptual framework. *Construction Management and Economics*, *19*(1), 85–95. doi:10.1080/01446190010003425

Kangari, R. (1991). Advanced robotics in civil engineering and construction. In *Fifth International Conference on Advanced Robotics 'Robots in Unstructured Environments* (pp. 375-378). Pisa, Italy: IEEE. 10.1109/ICAR.1991.240624

Kordas, D.-I. D. (2015, April 20). *Risk sharing in traditional construction contracts for building projects. a contractor's perspective in the Greek construction industry.* Thesis. Arnhem, The Netherlands: University of Twente.

Larivière, B., Joosten, H., Malthouse, E. C., Birgelen, M., Aksoy, P., Kunz, W. H., & Huang, M.-H. (2013). Value fusion: The blending of consumer and firm value in the distinct context of mobile technologies and social media. *Journal of Service Management, 24*(3), 268–293. doi:10.1108/09564231311326996

Lechner, N. (2014). Sustainable environmental control through building design Heating, Cooling, and Lighting. John Wiley & Sons.

Lin, T.-H., Liu, C.-H., Tsai, M.-H., & Kang, S.-C. (2015, November 29). Using Augmented Reality in a Multiscreen Environment for Construction Discussion. *Journal of Computing in Civil Engineering, 29*(6). doi:10.1061/(ASCE)CP.1943-5487.0000420

Marketing Charts. (2019, November 20). *Smartphones Now Account for 70% of US Digital Media Time.* Retrieved from https://www.marketingcharts.com: https://www.marketingcharts.com/digital/mobile-phone-111093

Mone, E. M., London, M., & Mone, E. M. (2018). *Employee Engagement Through Effective Performance Management: A Practical Guide for Managers.* Routledge. doi:10.4324/9781315626529

Narang, U., & Shankar, V. (2019). Mobile Marketing 2.0: State of the Art and Research Agenda. *Marketing in a Digital World, 16*, 97–119. doi:10.1108/S1548-643520190000016008

Nowotarski, P., & Paslawski, J. (2017). Industry 4.0 Concept Introduction into Construction SMEs. *IOP Conference Series. Materials Science and Engineering, 245*, 8981–8999. doi:10.1088/1757-899X/245/5/052043

Oesterreich, T. D., & Teuteberg, F. (2016). Understanding the implications of digitisation and automation in the context of Industry 4.0: A triangulation approach and elements of a research agenda for the construction industry. *Computers in Industry, 83*, 121–139. doi:10.1016/j.compind.2016.09.006

Prasath Kumar, V. R., Balasubramanian, M., & Jagadish Raj, S. (2016). Robotics in Construction Industry. *Indian Journal of Science and Technology, 9*(23), 1–12. doi:10.17485/ijst/2016/v9i23/95974

Shalan, M. A., & Anaim, N. A. (2017). The SMAC Opportunity Contracts: Generating Value From Responsive Agile Risk-Oriented Techniques. In *Mobile Platforms, Design, and Apps for Social Commerce* (pp. 115–134). IGI Global. doi:10.4018/978-1-5225-2469-4.ch008

Siddiqui, S. T., Alam, M. S., & Bokhari, M. (2012). Software Tools Required to Develop GIS Applications: An Overview. In *2012 Second International Conference on Advanced Computing & Communication Technologies* (pp. 51-56). Rohtak, Haryana: IEEE. 10.1109/ACCT.2012.106

Silberer, G., & Schulz, S. (2012). Mobile Customer Relationship Management (mCRM): Constraints and Challenges. In I. R. Association (Ed.), *E-Marketing: Concepts, Methodologies, Tools, and Applications* (pp. 324–340). IGI Global. doi:10.4018/978-1-4666-1598-4.ch020

Smith, R. E. (2010). Prefab Architecture: A Guide to Modular Design and Construction. John Wiley & Sons.

Tay, Y. W., Panda, B., Paul, S. C., Noor Mohamed, N. A., Tan, M. J., & Leong, K. F. (2017). 7 3). 3D printing trends in building and construction industry: A review. *Virtual and Physical Prototyping*, *12*(3), 261–276. doi:10.1080/17452759.2017.1326724

Trend Line Global. (2020, May 7). Retrieved from outsourcing-vs-offshoring-vs-insourcing-what-to-choose-when-hiring-developers/: https://trendlineglobal.net/blog/outsourcing-vs-offshoring-vs-insourcing-what-to-choose-when-hiring-developers/

Yang, C.-C., & Kang, S.-C. (2014). BIM Navigation with Hand-Based Gesture Control on Sites. *Computing in Civil and Building Engineering*, 758-792.

Zaher, M. G., Greenwood, D., & Marzouk, M. (2018). Mobile augmented reality applications for construction projects. *Construction Innovation*, *18*(2), 152–166. doi:10.1108/CI-02-2017-0013

ADDITIONAL READING

Abdul-Rahman, A. 2000. The design and implementation of two and three-dimensional triangular irregular network (TIN) based GIS. PhD thesis, University of Glasgow, UK. 250pp.

Billen, R., Zlatanova, S., Mathonet, P., & Boniver, F. (2002). The Dimensional model: a framework to distinguish spatial relationships. In D. Richardson & P. van Oosterom (Eds.), *Advances in Spatial Data Handling* (pp. 285–298). Springer-Verlag. doi:10.1007/978-3-642-56094-1_21

Cambray, de B., 1993. Three-dimensional (3D) modelling in a geographical database. Proceedings of Auto Carto 11, Bethesda, Maryland, pp.338-347.

Coors, V., & Jung, V. 1998. Using VRML as an Interface to the 3D Data Warehouse. *Proceedings of VRML'98*, New York, pp.121-127. 10.1145/271897.279553

de la Losa, A., & Cervelle, B. (1999). 3D topological modelling and visualisation for 3D GIS. *Computers & Graphics*, *23*(4), 469–478. doi:10.1016/S0097-8493(99)00066-7

Molenaar, M., 1992. A topology for 3D Vector Maps, ITC Journal, 1992-1, pp.25-33.

Pfund, M. 2001. Topologic data structure for a 3D GIS. Proceedings of 3rd International Workshopon Dynamic and Multi-dimensional GIS (Inter. Archives for Photogrammetry and Remote Sensing, Vol.34, Part 2W2), 23-25 May, Bangkok, Thailand, pp.233-237.

Sonnen, D., & Morris, H. 2000. Location in CRM: Linking virtual information to the real world, IDC White Paper, 12pp., http://www.idc.com

Vermeij, M., & Zlatanova, S. 2001. Semi-automatic 3D building reconstruction using Soft Plotter, Proceedings of the International Symposium on "Geodetic, Photogrammetric and Satellite technologies: development and integrated applications", 8-9 November, Sofia, Bulgaria, pp.305-314

Zlatanova, S., Rahman, A.A. and Pilouk, M., 2002. 3D GIS: current status and perspectives.

KEY TERMS AND DEFINITIONS

3D Printing: 3D printing, also known as additive manufacturing, is a method of creating a three-dimensional object layer-by-layer using a computer created design. 3D printing is an additive process whereby layers of material are built up to create a 3D part.

Augmented Reality (AR): An interactive experience of a real-world environment where the objects that reside in the real world are enhanced by computer-generated perceptual information, sometimes across multiple sensory modalities, including visual, auditory, haptic, somatosensory, and olfactory

Building Information Modeling (BIM): A process supported by various tools, technologies and contracts involving the generation and management of digital representations of physical and functional characteristics of places.

Collective Intelligence (CI): A shared or group intelligence that emerges from the collaboration, collective efforts, and competition of many individuals and appears in consensus decision making. The term appears in sociobiology, political science and in context of mass peer review and crowdsourcing applications and is used today in construction and architecture.

Computer-Aided Design (CAD): The use of computers to aid in the creation, modification, analysis, or optimization of a design. CAD software is used to increase the productivity of the designer, improve the quality of design, improve communications through documentation, and to create a database for execution.

Crowdsourcing: Involves obtaining work, information, or opinions from a large group of people who submit their data via the Internet, social media, and smartphone apps. People involved in crowdsourcing sometimes work as paid freelancers, while others perform small tasks on a voluntary basis.

Design Architects: Offices involved in the design and specifications of projects. They use their expertise to evaluate their client's expectations and needs and then develop ideas for the structure. They may be required to do research into local and international laws and building codes.

Geographic Information System (GIS): A conceptualized framework that provides the ability to capture and analyze spatial and geographic data. It analyzes spatial location and organizes layers of information into visualizations using maps and 3D scenes. GIS reveals deeper insights into data, such as patterns, relationships, and situations—helping users make smarter decisions

Revit Architecture: A tool used to coordinate all data inputs (including CAD) and produce federated project deliverables. Both programs are often used within the same firm, with BIM and CAD specialists working on different elements of a project.

Touch Points: A business jargon for any encounter where customers and business engage to exchange information, provide service, or handle transactions.

Virtual Reality (VR): Refers to a computer-generated simulation in which a person can interact within an artificial three-dimensional environment using electronic devices, such as special goggles with a screen or gloves fitted with sensors.

Chapter 15
Contracting Dynamics in Acquiring or Awarding Decisions for Projects and Tenders

Mohamad Raafat Elbardiny
Aqarat Real Estate Development Company, Saudi Arabia

ABSTRACT

The construction sector is large; it engages a variety of professions thus it is a main provider of employment and has a diverse market. The construction sector has a reputation for being conservative, problematic, and inefficient. This should change as we are moving toward industry 4.0 and smart cities that is injecting new tools and business dynamics. This chapter is trying to find methodologies to make an equilibrium between value produced by the contract, the flexibility of contract terms and contracting conditions thus contractors can be controlled in a reasonable matter. We are in here applying concepts and techniques from statics science and structural engineering to calculate PORD or PRCD (the Percentage Profit On Realistic Cashflow Duration) as a new financial modeling parameter that can help financial planners and decision makers to take more realistic decision. This parameter can be used jointly with other financial parameters such as ROI, IRR and NPV.

INTRODUCTION

The construction sector is large; it engages a variety of professions thus it is a main provider of employment and has a diverse market. Examining the role of the construction industry in economic development demonstrated the significant relationship between the construction industry and economic growth (Giang & Pheng, 2011). The objective of the construction sector is to draft the right contracts so that appropriate techniques and organizational structures are used efficiently and thereby positively influence the productivity growth.

DOI: 10.4018/978-1-7998-4501-0.ch015

While moving toward smart cities, there has been a rapidly increasing interest in implementing performance-based contracts and long-term contracts with bundling of design, construction, and maintenance. Implementing these types of contracts can create incentives to build with better quality, increase innovation and decrease cost overruns. (Schjaer-Jacobsen, 2002) set out to examine the possibility of attaining a reasonably useful and realistic picture of the economic consequences of strategic decisions when little is known about the future. The quality of available information to decision-makers renders traditional decision theory and investment calculations obsolete, while demonstrating the representation of economic uncertainties.

Value-based contracting can be applied as an umbrella term for a variety of contracting strategies outside of traditional models. Value-based contracts can take many forms including correlating payment to achievement of goals, objectives, or performance benchmarks, allowing a payment structure that may complement or even replace more traditional milestone-based payments. Contracting agreements should focus on particular services that are being at the core of the contract based on the best evidence. This will help to prove that performance benchmarks are achieved and the agreement between the contracting parties to handle financial risks and rewards are assigned or shared.

Another contracting technique is defined as the equilibrium contracts which characterized by differential efforts between contractors or firms to attain a positive relation between competition and high-powered incentives considering outcomes, risk, or both. These arrangements link the cost of an activity to certain measures of output efficiency. They can take the form of discounts tied to end points or competence guarantees.

This chapter is trying to find methodologies that can lead to an equilibrium between the contract value production and the flexibility of contract terms and conditions. These methodologies are meant so that contractors can be controlled in a reasonable manner while the equilibrium points in the contracts can be managed successfully.

BACKGROUND

The cost benefit analysis (CBA) can be performed primarily with Monte Carlo risk analysis, which is a sophisticated technique. Based on an underlying assumption is that as the number of trials increases the frequencies will converge towards the true underlying probabilities (Boardman, Greenberg, Vining, & Weimer, 2011). Two algorithms to conduct CBA was suggested in (Wang & Liang, 2007) for which it was difficult to obtain exact assessment data such as investment benefit, expenses, project lifetime, gross income, expenses, and depreciation. (Mohamed & McCowan, 2001) proposed a method for modelling the effects of both monetary (construction cost and annual revenue) and nonmonetary (political, environmental, organizational, competition, and market share) aspects of investment options with possibility theory. (Dompere, 2004) studied the discounting process under uncertainty and examined the theory of the fuzzy present value. (Panneerselvam, 2004) developed a cash flow analysis for engineering decisions. (Marnell, 2016) recognized the effects of IRR and the extent it generates open problems or solve investment concerns.

MEASURING PROJECT OR INVESTMENT FEASIBILITY

For a contractor within the construction industry, a feasibility study is undertaken to assess whether it is realistic to carry on certain project. This means that plenty of internal and external parameters will need to be considered. The financial situation and reputation of the company is evaluated, the strengths and weaknesses of the business are taken into consideration.

Construction in developing countries is often encountered with multifarious challenges including contractor's performance due to lack of qualification and resources. (Ahsen Maqsoom, 2019). The unforeseen societal issues may be overlooked if they can have an impact on the project such as economic instability or reasonable competition within the company's field. The likelihood of profit and loss need to be completed. Additional items are also considered such as materials, labor and time required to fulfil the project.

All of this are studied before a decision is made on whether the project will be financially viable and if it is worth undertaking or not. Expert views from architects, engineers and other professionals are required to identify potential pitfalls from an engineering perspective.

The Importance of Conducting a Project Feasibility

Many contracting companies will conduct a feasibility homework to assess the viability of a project before being engaged. Similarly, owners will need to perform such a study before hiring a contractor to perform a task. A feasibility research will give grounds to a project and evaluate it in terms of the strengths, weaknesses, resources, finances and how realistic a project is. Simply, a feasibility exercise assesses the potential, as well as the limitations of an idea. The abuse of the feasibility study may lead to cost and time over runs (Sawsan R. Mohammed, 2019)

Areas of Feasibility Assessment

Feasibility homework is necessary for a successful completion of a project; thus, each construction company should supply a reasonably assessed decision taking everything into consideration for the viability of the project. This can be broken down into layman's terms (Merriam-Webster, 2020) to include below aspects of a feasibility study which make up the whole which include:

- **Technical:** This area assesses how the company will deliver the project based on the hard materials, labor, resources, and any other practical requirements such as transport.
- **Economic:** Loss and profit considerations are an integral area of a feasibility study as, ultimately, the overall goal is that the profit outweighs the cost.
- **Legal:** The legality of a project needs to be looked at to assess whether the construction company will be able to meet the legal requirements of the project.
- **Operational:** To effectively complete a project, there needs to be a plan of action in place. This area of the feasibility study assesses whether the construction company has the ability to manage and execute a complex project.
- **Scheduling**: This area outlines whether the company can execute and deliver a satisfactory product to the client without the quality of the work suffering due to the time constraints laid out.

Financial Ratios to Consider

Big real estate investment projects in general and smart city projects are high yield, long term projects. They require plenty of financial ratios to calculate their feasibility while considering a project for investment or contracting, below is a summary of currently used rations:

Net Present Value (NPV)

Money in the present is worth more than the same amount in the future due to inflation and to earnings from alternative investments that could be made during the intervening time. Present value (PV) and future value (FV) measure how much the value of money has changed over time (Hofstrand, 2013). In other words, a dollar earned in the future won't be worth as much as one earned in the present. The discount rate element of the NPV formula is a way to account for this.

Net present value (NPV) is the difference between the present value of cash inflows and the present value of cash outflows over a period of time. NPV is used in capital budgeting and investment planning to analyze the profitability of a projected investment or project.

Net present value (NPV) is the calculation used to find today's value of a future stream of payments. It accounts for the time value of money and can be used to compare investment alternatives that are similar. The NPV relies on a discount rate of return that may be derived from the cost of the capital required to make the investment, and any project or investment with a negative NPV should be avoided. An important drawback of using an NPV analysis is that it makes assumptions about future events that may not be reliable.

The Internal Rate of Return (IRR) Calculations

The internal rate of return (IRR) is a metric used in capital budgeting to estimate the profitability of potential investments. The internal rate of return is a discount rate that makes the net present value (NPV) of all cash flows from a particular project equal to zero (Maravas & Pantouvakis, 2018). IRR calculations rely on the same formula as NPV does to calculate the equivalent IRR.

Generally speaking, the higher a project's internal rate of return, the more desirable it is to undertake. IRR is uniform for investments of varying types and, as such, IRR can be used to rank multiple prospective projects on a relatively even basis. Assuming the costs of investment are equal among the various projects, the project with the highest IRR would probably be considered the best and be undertaken first.

IRR is sometimes referred to as "economic rate of return" or "discounted cash flow rate of return." The use of "internal" refers to the omission of external factors, such as the cost of capital or inflation, from the calculation (Ranvir, 2020). While IRR is a very popular metric in estimating a project's profitability, it can be misleading if used alone. Depending on the initial investment costs, a project may have a low IRR but a high NPV, meaning that while the pace at which the company sees returns on that project may be slow, the project may also be adding a great deal of overall value to the company. Several variations of IRR exist and among them are the MIRR and FMRR described below.

Modified IRR (MIRR) Calculations

The MIRR more accurately reflects the cost and profitability of a project as the traditional internal rate of return (IRR) assumes the cash flows from a project are reinvested at the IRR itself which usually gives an optimistic estimate (Rangel, Santos, & Savoia, 2015). The modified internal rate of return (MIRR) assumes that positive cash flows are reinvested at the firm's cost of capital and that the initial outlays are financed at the firm's financing cost.

The MIRR is used to rank investments or projects of unequal size. The calculation is a solution to two major problems that exist with the popular IRR calculation.

- The first main problem with IRR is that multiple solutions can be found for the same project.
- The second problem is that the assumption that positive cash flows are reinvested at the IRR is considered impractical in practice.

With the MIRR, only a single solution exists for a given project, and the reinvestment rate of positive cash flows is much more valid in practice. The MIRR allows project managers to change the assumed rate of reinvested growth from stage to stage in a project. The most common method is to input the average estimated cost of capital, but there is flexibility to add any specific anticipated reinvestment rate gives managers more control over the assumed reinvestment rate from future cash flow.

Financial Management Rate of Return (FMRR)

The financial management rate of return (FMRR) is a metric used to evaluate the performance of a real estate investment and pertains to a real estate investment trust (REIT). REITs are shares offered to the public by a real estate company or trust that holds a portfolio of income-producing properties and/or mortgages.

The FMRR is like the internal rate of return and takes into account the length and risk of the investment. The FMRR specifies cash flows (inflows and outflows) at two distinct rates known as the safe rate and the reinvestment rate. (Kobzeff, 2018)

The modified internal rate of return improves on the standard internal rate of return value by adjusting for differences in the assumed reinvestment rates of initial cash outlays and subsequent cash inflows. FMRR takes things a step further by specifying cash outflows and cash inflows at two different rates known as the "safe rate" and the "reinvestment rate."

Safe rates assume that funds required to cover negative cash flows are earning interest at a rate easily attainable and can be withdrawn when needed at a moment's notice (i.e., like from a day of deposit account). In this instance, a rate is "safe" because the funds are highly liquid and safely available with minimal risk when needed. Reinvestment rates include a rate to be received when positive cash flows are reinvested in a similar intermediate or long-term investment with comparable risk. The reinvestment rate is higher than the safe rate because it is not liquid (i.e., it pertains to another investment) and thus requires a higher-risk discount rate.

FMRR also makes an additional assumption not included with IRR and MIRR that positive cash flows occurring immediately prior to negative cash flows will be used to cover that negative cash flow.

Return on Investment (ROI)

To measure the performance and evaluate the efficiency of an investment, Return on Investment (ROI) is usually used to compare the efficiency of several different investments. ROI directly measure the amount of return on a particular investment, relative to the investment's cost. The equation to calculate ROI, the benefit (or return) of an investment is divided by the cost of the investment. The result is expressed as a percentage or a ratio.

ROI is a popular metric because of its versatility and simplicity (Almeida & Santos, 2018). Essentially, ROI can be used as a fundamental measure of an investment's profitability. The ROI calculation that is generated for real estate transaction and associated projects is not too complicated, and it is relatively easy to interpret for its wide range of applications. It is probably worthwhile to go into an investment when the calculated ROI is net positive, the higher ROIs is the better for investors willing to eliminate or select the best options. Negative ROIs imply a net loss.

ROI can be used in conjunction with Rate of Return, which considers the project's time frame and the Net Present Value (NPV) which accounts for differences in the value of money over time, due to inflation to produce a more realistic results.

Some variations in ROI are called the Annualized ROI that is especially useful when comparing returns between various investments or evaluating different investments. The AROI calculation counters one of the limitations of the basic ROI calculation, which is that it does not consider the "holding period" or the length of time that an investment is held.

Another variation is the Social Return on Investment (SROI) which was initially developed in the early 2000s and takes into account broader impacts of projects using extra-financial value (Yates & Marra, 2017). SROI considers social and environmental metrics not currently reflected in conventional financial accounts to help in understanding the value proposition of certain criteria used in socially responsible investing (SRI) practices.

Return on Capital Employed (ROCE)

ROCE examines how efficiently a company uses available capital (CFI, 2020). Capital employed is, in the simplest terms, the total amount of the firm's assets minus current liabilities. It's synonymous with available capital from net profits. The return on capital employed metric is considered one of the best profitability ratios and is commonly used by investors to determine whether a company is suitable to invest in or not. The higher the value of the ROCE, the more efficiently the company is utilizing its capital. ROCE can be very useful for comparing the use of capital by different companies engaged in the same business.

FINANCIAL PERFORMANCE INDICATORS

Every investor or contractor measures himself in a slightly different manner, but certain performance metrics are relevant for most contractors (Goodland & Lam, 2018). Tracking the right key performance indicators (KPIs) can provide insights to help the contractor making the right business decisions and measure his performance and ability to continue the business. According to (Deltek, 2018) some metrics that matter for government contractors are:

- **Revenue:** The revenue recognized by contractors may be influenced by the contract type in effect for each project, as well as by governing guidelines. Contractors often calculate revenue differently for different contracts with countless variations for each primary type. Contractors will want to do revenue analysis by organization, project manager, customer, and specific project.
- **Profit:** Profit is arguably the most important metric for any company and is the ultimate measure of success. As with revenue, the contractor profit is impacted largely by contract type and it is important to assess profitability trends across contract types to ensure pursuing the right type of business.
- **Backlog:** Backlog analytics helps tracking how much work remains and allows measuring whether the contractor is operating above or below budget. It's important that this analytic include not just existing contracts but also those under processing and hope to win.
- **Labor Utilization:** Labor utilization evaluates how efficiently employees are being applied to direct, or billable, projects. The labor utilization analytic can offer insight into which employees are over or underperforming and how staffing levels are appropriate. It's imperative that management can review both direct and indirect components of the metric.
- **Indirect Rates:** Contractors track, at a minimum, two different versions of rates for indirect pools such as fringe, overhead, and general and administrative. The target rate is a contractor's estimated rate based on its budget, while the actual rate is calculated based on incurred costs. Comparing both as the fiscal year progresses is a critical function for contractors and a valuable component of an analytics system.
- **Proposal Win Rate***:* Analytics don't have to be limited to financial data. The ability to win new business, for instance, is paramount to the success of any contractor. Setting targets for proposal win rates across different parts of the company will allow evaluating the performance of business development function.
- **Projects at risk:** Perhaps the greatest potential of an analytics application is to draw attention to areas that need corrective action. Contractors will immediately want to know whether they're operating projects that have the potential to generate losses or put the company out of compliance with contract terms. Examples of risk categories are:
  - Billing in excess of funded contract value
  - Costs incurred after project end date
  - Revenue recognized in excess of contract value
  - Revenue recognized below budgeted amount
- **Cash Flow:** Lack of cash is one of the biggest reasons small businesses fail. A monthly cash flow report and 12-month cash flow projection can help to plan ahead to smooth out the swings in cash flow by accelerating collections, requesting an initial payment prior to starting projects, and carefully planning resource needs and investments. Lines of credit can be helpful, and often necessary, but should be used carefully as the cost of interest to finance operations can cut into profits.
- **Days Sales Outstanding (DSO):** The process of quickly and efficiently recording costs, billing the main client, and receiving payment has a dramatic impact on the success of contractors. Errors in coding vouchers or timesheets, or delays in generating invoices can be devastating to cash flow. Days Sales Outstanding, or DSO, is a measure of the time it takes to collect on an invoice, converting a receivable into cash.
- **Accounts Receivable Aging:** The Accounts Receivable (AR) Aging report helps direct management attention to accounts that are slow to pay. A much slower AR collections than normal can be

a warning sign of taking a greater credit risk in the sales practices or that business may be slowing down. Striving to streamline billing and collection processes may have a huge impact on improving a company's cash flow and is particularly important for small contractors with limited access to cash.

TRACKING THE BIG PICTURE IN CONTRACT FINANCING

According to (Killough, 2020), there are some basic reports that make up the core financial statements of a construction company. Each one of them can be utilized to help contractors improve access to credit, bonding capacity, and cash flow overall.

It can take a long time for payments to flow in the construction industry. As a result, contractors often rely on vendor credit or credit facilities to get through periods of slow or non-payment. The goal should be to run contracting business without using credit which may be difficult especially when working for new customers with their own payment habits. That is why the contractor need to investigate the big picture.

Benefits of Financial Statements

To get the biggest benefit from the financial statements, the contractor must review them regularly. Go over them at least once a month and make sure to compare numbers from one month to another. This will help spotting possible errors and see trends. Looking at past year's reports also can give greater insight into the company's growth (Inghram, 2019).

Financial statements tell contractors and other stakeholders, how well a construction company is doing. A contractor's character, capacity and capital are determined by the numbers reported on the company's financial statements. Commonly referred to as the "three Cs," these indicators provide a foundation to form an opinion on a contractor's past, current and future performance (Boland & McCarthy, 2019). They include:

- Working capital, or access to it, to finance a job and absorb losses (capital).
- Experience, knowledge and equipment to perform the job (capacity); and
- A competent management team to fulfill obligations and contracts (character).

Some general guidelines are useful to explain the contractor's situation in relation to realistic, achievable, and time-sensitive goals. Such indicators are essential to having a positive working relationship. Some of the financial tools and reports related to contracting are mentioned in this section.

Balance Sheet

A balance sheet is used to show the liquidity of a company at a specific moment in time (Spurga, 2004). This is tightened to the company's ability to pay its bills in a timely manner. Balance sheet will show how the companies as managing their risks. Balance sheet is derived at the end of a period such as a quarter or year. The balance sheet has three sections: Assets, liabilities, and equity.

- Assets include bank accounts, accounts receivable, inventory, and any fixed assets owned by the company. The more assets the company have, the better it looks financially.
- Liabilities are money that a company owe including accounts payable which are vendor bills that is not paid yet, loans, and taxes due. The objective is to have as little as possible.
- Equity is defined as the owner's interest in the company assets. Upon liquidation after all the liabilities are paid off, the shareholders own the remaining assets. Equity is often referred to as net assets or assets minus liabilities.

Income Statement (Profit & Loss)

An income statement is a financial statement that shows you the company's income and expenditures. It also shows whether a company is making profit or loss for a given period. The income statement, along with balance sheet and cash flow statement, helps to understand the financial health of the business. (Ittelson, 2009)

The income statement is also known as a profit and loss statement, statement of operation, statement of financial result or income, or earnings statement. To calculate net income or loss for the period, the contractor needs to add or subtract any additional income or expenses that aren't directly related to business activities including tax expense.

The income statement details the income and expense activities during the time period. It starts with revenue for the period, then subtracts the cost of goods sold (COGS), which are expenses that went directly into projects or materials that you sold including direct labor costs. The revenue left over is the gross margin, or gross profit. Subtracting general and administrative expenses will lead to operating income.

The income statement is significant among the major financial statements in that it sheds light on how well the company performed in earning a profit. As such, using the income statement to spot trends that indicate the direction of future profits is a worthwhile exercise.

Cash Flow Statement

The cash flow statement's purpose is to show how much cash a business generates which named as cash inflows and how much cash it's spending which known as cash outflows. (Wong, 2020)

There are two types of cash flow statements: a direct cash flow statement and an indirect cash flow statement. The main difference between the two types of statements lies in how cash flows from operating activities are calculated. Because the direct method is more challenging for businesses that use accrual accounting, most corporations tend to use the indirect method in their cash flow statements. With the indirect method, adjustments are made to convert numbers from accrual basis to cash basis.

There are three types of financial activities on a cash flow report: Operating, Investing, and Financing. Operating activities are the normal day-to-day financial transactions that take place regarding the main business activity. They include sales income, cost of goods sold, administrative expenses, and taxes. Investing activities include fixed asset such as equipment and vehicles purchases and sales. Financing activities include sale of stock and certain long-term debt options.

The cash flow statement shows the net gain or loss in each of the three types of financial activities and arrives at a net gain or loss at the end of the period. This statement can predict how the future will look like based on past periods.

Statement of Retained Earnings

This is defined per (Collins-dictionary, 2020) as the part of a company's profits which is re-invested, rather than being paid out as dividend to shareholders. The statement of retained earnings shows the changes in retained earnings from one point to another.

Retained Earnings are listed on a balance sheet under the shareholder's equity section at the end of each accounting period. To calculate Retained Earnings, the beginning Retained Earnings balance is added to the net income or loss and then dividend payouts are subtracted. It is reported as a separate component of the stockholders' equity section of the balance sheet. The statement of retained earnings can determine if a contractor is over-extended.

Work-In-Progress (WIP) Report

At one time or another, even the best managed contracting firms begin to feel they are slipping off the financial tracks. To the top managers, it seems the company is as busy as ever, maybe busier, but cash flow doesn't reflect it. Many contractors try to front-load their billings so they can get positive cash flow early in a project. This may be good in the beginning of a project. But it can lead to trouble when the end of the project arrives and there isn't much additional income around to pay for costs.

If the contractor's income is being recognized on a percentage-of-completion basis, then it is needed to set up a WIP report in order to reconcile billings and costs every month. WIP report, if properly created, identifies the true value of a project (Ross & Williams, 2012). Without such documentation, contractors can only extrapolate. WIP is valuable for both project managers and financial officers. For project managers, the reports detail what has been billed and what is available to bill. For financial officers, the WIP provide a way to closely monitor a project's schedule of values, total cost estimate, costs to date, and the amount billed to date.

Project managers can utilize this information to proactively manage a project's budget, help guide billing, and help identify any potential overruns. The data combined in a WIP may vary from a contractor to another, but generally it includes the job name, estimated costs, actual costs, percent complete, estimated revenue or contract amount, earned revenue, actual revenue. The difference on each job is then totaled in a groundwork for a period adjustment considering if the project is overbilled or underbilled for the period.

Footnote Disclosures

Financial statement footnotes are explanatory and supplemental notes that accompany a firm's financial statements. The exact nature of these footnotes varies, depending upon the accounting framework used to construct the financial statements (Bragg, 2019). Footnotes are an integral part of the financial statements, so it must be issued along with the financial statements. They are extremely valuable to the financial analyst, who can discern from the footnotes how various accounting policies used by a company are impacting its reported results and financial position.

The footnotes summarize significant accounting policies, business activities, the use of estimates, cash equivalents, methods of accounting used and other key pieces of data. Supplemental schedules give more detailed information that includes but are not limited to the schedule of contract revenue; schedule of general and administrative expenses; schedule of completed contracts; and schedule of Contracts in

Progress. Additional information can be included such as a breakdown of the cost of labor, materials and subcontractors per job, the number and size of jobs in progress, gross profit per job, and job fade.

THE PERCENTAGE PROFIT ON REALISTIC CASHFLOW DURATION: NEW APPROACH

As discussed throughout this chapter, there have been various approaches and ratios that were utilized to support taking the right decision related to acquiring a project or proceeding with and investment considering its feasibility. In this section the author is proposing a new approach called the Cash Inflow (CI) and Cash Outflow (CO) behavior, then we calculate PORD or PRCD (the Percentage Profit On Realistic Cashflow Duration) to determine the feasibility of a project or investment. The author in here is applying concepts and techniques from statics science and structural engineering to calculate PORD or PRCD as a new financial modeling parameter that can help financial planners and decision makers to take more realistic decision. This parameter can be used jointly with other financial parameters such as ROI, IRR and NPV.

Problem Statement

When financial people make the feasibility study to evaluate an investment opportunity, one of the problems they face is determining the right financial ratio that gives the investors the right indicator for the investment decision. However, the problem is how to calculate the duration of the project in selected periods.

The duration of a project is considered as the span between first and last payments regardless to the difference in cash flow behavior for every project. Projects do have same ROI, when they have same total cash inflow and same total cash outflow and have same duration. Also, they will have same Annual ROI, even if there is a big difference in cash flow behavior for every project.

Such indicators will mislead the investment decision if no other realistic indicators are taken into consideration. The most common indicator to solve this problem is IRR that have some disadvantages as specified earlier.

To illustrate the problem let's compare two projects with the different cash flows shown in below figure 1.

In spite the fact that profitability and cash flow for the two projects are totally different the ROI and AROI parameters are giving the same numbers as if they are identical. Both projects will have a duration of 36 periods (months); total cash outflow/inflow of 500M/600M and an ROI/Annual ROI of 20% and 6.7% respectively. Which is totally misleading as the cash flow patterns for the two projects are totally different.

Comparing the cash outflow of two projects, it is obvious that project 1 cash outflow is totally unfavorable as 70% ($350M) of the total cash outflow will be spent in the first 5 months of the cash outflow period which is 24% of the total 21 months. Project 2 on the contrary has a very favorable cash outflow as only 32% ($140M) of the total cash outflow will be spent in the first 14 months which is 67% of the total 21 months cash outflow period.

Looking at the cash inflow of the two projects, it is obvious that project 1 cash inflow is totally unfavorable as 25% ($150M) of the total cash outflow will be received in the first 14 months of the cash outflow period which is 60% of the total 15 months. Project 2 on the contrary has a very favorable cash outflow as 80% ($480M) of the total cash outflow will be spent in the first 14 months which is 47% of the total 15 months cash inflow period.

The cash flow structure is clearly showing that project 2 is totally favorable while the ROI and AROI are both the same. The IRR indicator doesn't give realistic duration regarding to the cash flow as it is considering the duration of cash flow between 1st and last payments without looking on their distribution.

The cash flow paradox is illustrated by figure 2 showing the cash outflow and cash inflow for both projects.

To resolve this paradox, the author is presenting a new concept for the Realistic Cashflow Duration (RCD) which is based on calculating the duration of equivalent cash inflow (DECI) and the duration of equivalent cash outflow (DECO) and finding the difference between both values.

Figure 1. The Cash Flow of Two Projects as an Example To Explain The Problem

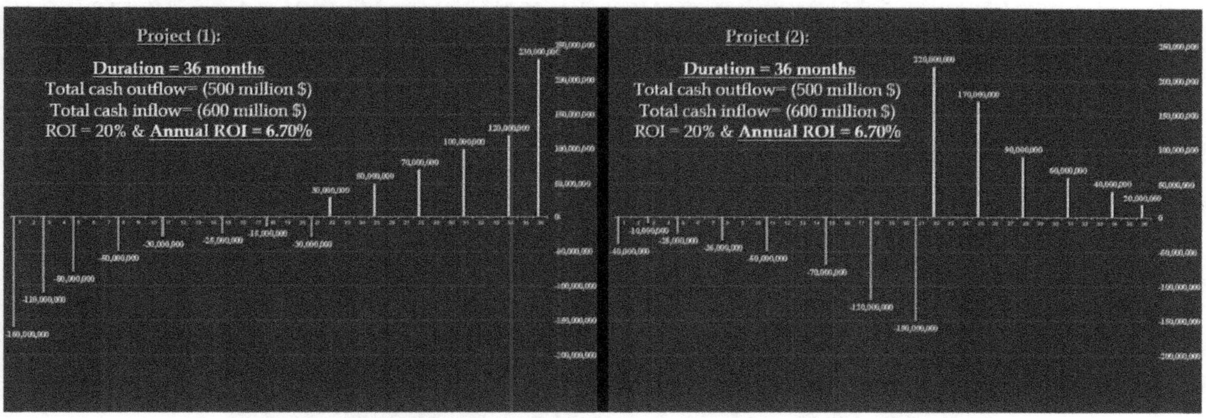

Figure 2. The Cash Inflow and Out Flow Behavior of the Two Projects

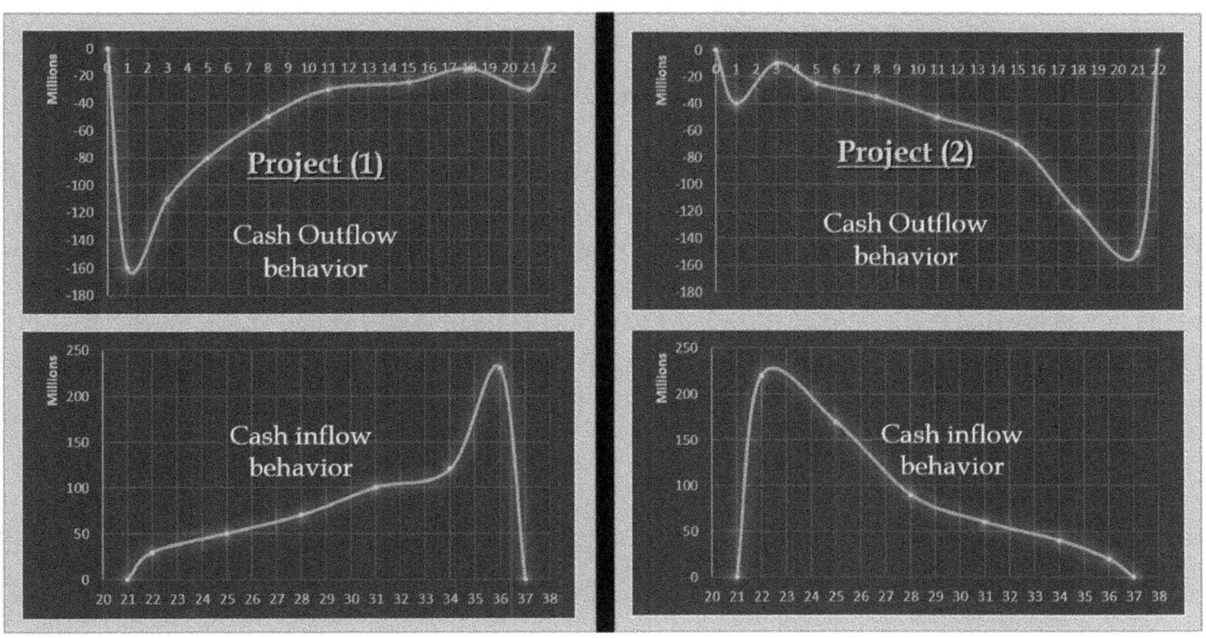

The Origins of the Idea

In Statics science there is a basic idea that two force systems are equivalent if they result in the same resultant force and the same resultant moment. The single force passing through O is equal to the resultant force of the original multi force system.

This idea lead to the concept of reducing the forces to an equivalent force at a defined point, thus instead of dealing with multiple forces you can deal with the equivalent in your calculations and designs.

When a force has the effect of both translating and rotating a body, the extent of the effect depends on how and where the force is applied. It is possible to simplify a system of forces and moments into a single resultant and moment acting at a specified point "O" stands for the origin of forces.

In other words, a system of forces and moments is then equivalent to the single resultant force and moment acting at a specified point "O" which is defined by an equivalent force and point of effect (called arm), below is an example where an equivalent force of 27K Newton acting a distance of 5.926 meters will produce the same result of two forces of 11K and 16K Newton acting at the edges of the 10 meters beam or the 5 distributed forces acting at different points of the beam. Below figure 3 is showing the calculation of the system of forces and moments.

Figure 3. The Example to Calculate The Center Of Equivalent Load To Various Loads

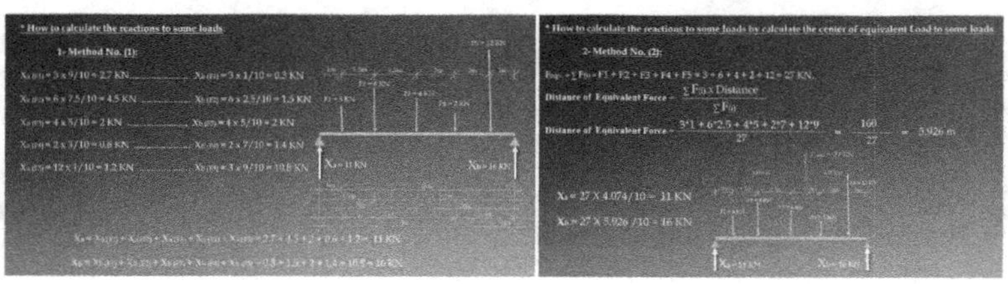

Applying the Equivalent Force System in Cashflow Calculations

We can apply same concepts a technique to calculate realistic duration for investment project.

First, we calculate Duration of Equivalent Cash Outflow (DECO) as the summation of all cash outflows multiplied by the payment slot in defined period unit (months), Second will calculate the Duration of Equivalent Cash Inflow (DECI) as the summation of all cash inflows multiplied by the payment slot in the defined period unit (months), then will calculate the Realistic Cashflow Duration (RCD) as the Duration of Equivalent Cash Outflow (DECO) "minus" the Duration of Equivalent Cash Inflow (DECI), as shown in figure 4.

Figure 4. How to Calculate The Duration Of Equivalent Cash In Flow Or Cash Out Flow

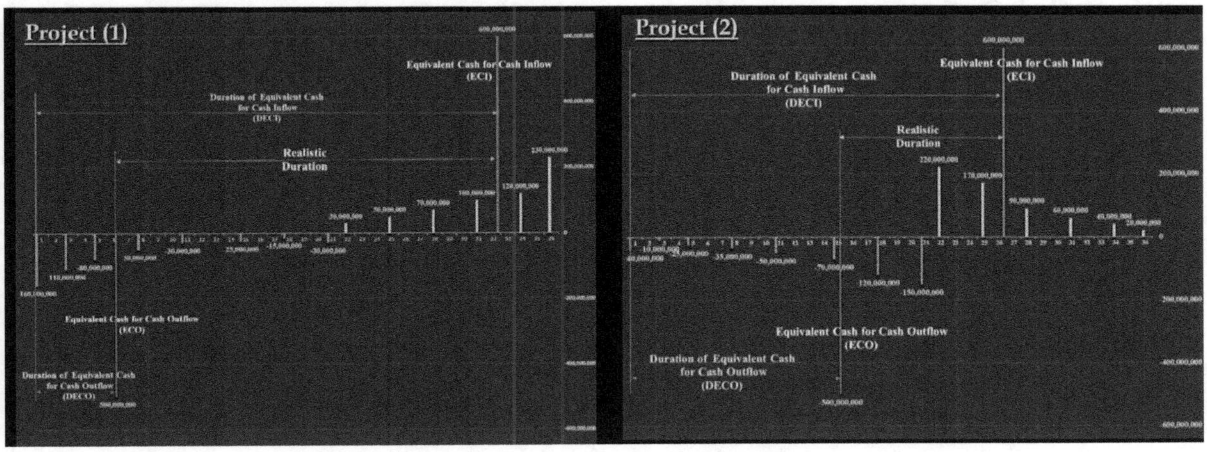

Writing the Equations

Duration of Equivalent Cash Outflow:

$$DECO = \Sigma\left(COF * M\right) / \left(Total\, COF\right) \tag{1}$$

Duration of Equivalent Cash Inflow:

$$DECI = \Sigma\left(CIF * M\right) / \left(Total\, CIF\right) \tag{2}$$

Realistic Cashflow Duration:

$$RCD = DECO \,/\, DECI \tag{3}$$

Where,

DECO is the Duration of Equivalent Cash Outflow
DECI is the Duration of Equivalent Cash Inflow

RCD is the Realistic Cashflow Duration
COF is the Cash Outflow payment
CIF is the Cash Inflow payment
M is The Payment Month Number

For project 1 below table 1 is showing the cash inflow and the cash outflow and the results of their multiplication with the months of duration

Duration of Equivalent Cash Outflow (DECO) = (2,895,000)/ (500,000) = 5.79

Duration of Equivalent Cash Inflow (DECI) = 19,330,000/600,000 = 32.22

Realistic Cashflow Duration (RCD) = 32.22-5.79 = 26.43 months

Table 1. The Cash Inflow and The Cash Outflow and The Results of Their Multiplication

Month	Cash Outflow	Month*Cash Outflow	Month	Cash Inflow	Month*Cash Inflow
1	(160,000)	(160,000)	22	30,000	660,000
3	(110,000)	(330,000)	25	50,000	1,250,000
5	(80,000)	(400,000)	28	70,000	1,960,000
8	(50,000)	(400,000)	31	100,000	3,100,000
11	(30,000)	(330,000)	34	120,000	4,080,000
15	(25,000)	(375,000)	36	230,000	8,280,000
18	(15,000)	(270,000)			
21	(30,000)	(630,000)			
Totals	(500,000)	(2,895,000)	Totals	600,000	19,330,000

For project 2 below table 2 is showing the cash inflow and the cash outflow and the results of their multiplication with the months of duration

Duration of Equivalent Cash Outflow (DECO) = (7,385,000) / (500,000) = 14.77

Duration of Equivalent Cash Inflow (DECI) = 15,550,000 /600,000 = 25.92

Realistic Cashflow Duration (RCD) = 25.92-14.77= 11.15 months

In order to give a very realistic easy to measure indication we have defined the Percentage Profit On Realistic Cashflow Duration (PORD or PRCD) as ROI/RCD in months.

Percentage Profit On Realistic Cashflow Duration:

$$PRCD = ROI \; / \; RCD \quad (4)$$

Where,

PORD or PRCD is the Percentage Profit On Realistic Cashflow Duration
ROI is the return on Investment
RCD is the Realistic Cashflow Duration

As both projects are having the same ROI of 20% , we recalculate the PORD or PRCD (Percentage Profit On Realistic Cashflow Duration) as ROI/RCD = 20/(26.43/12) = 9.08% for project 1 and 20/(11.15/12) = 21.53% for project 2 which is showing a big difference and giving right indications about the project profitability.

Table 2. The Cash Inflow and The Cash Outflow and The Results Of Their Multiplication

Month	Cash Outflow	Month*Cash Outflow	Month	Cash Inflow	Month*Cash Inflow
1	(40,000)	(40,000)	22	220,000	4,840,000
3	(10,000)	(30,000)	25	170,000	4,250,000
5	(25,000)	(125,000)	28	90,000	2,520,000
8	(35,000)	(280,000)	31	60,000	1,860,000
11	(50,000)	(550,000)	34	40,000	1,360,000
15	(70,000)	(1,050,000)	36	20,000	720,000
18	(120,000)	(2,160,000)			
21	(150,000)	(3,150,000)			
Totals	(500,000)	(7,385,000)	Totals	600,000	15,550,000

FUTURE RESEARCH DIRECTIONS

Innovation have reached every aspect of our lives and stretched to business sectors that was considered rigid for a long period of time such as the construction and real estate industries. Business dynamics are also changing frequently considering plenty of emerging technologies that are maturing and evolving continually. Every single effect can be researched and investigated.

Real estate industry is an intensive funding consumer, and it is difficult to return in a started investment. Several financial ratios are considered to evaluate the feasibility of real estate investments; however, some ratios are not accurate in supporting the right decision. Some ratios need to be reevaluated in terms of their viability. This can be reevaluated in several case studies.

The author has suggested a new ratio called Percentage Profit On Realistic Cashflow Duration (PORD or PRCD) which is considering the cashflow behaviors for an investment to evaluate its feasibility. The PORD or PRCD can be used along with other known financial ratios. Although author has tested this approach with several scenarios the method can be further tested in the mathematics modeling and real investment use cases.

CONCLUSION

Real estate investment is changing in the industry 4.0 era, business dynamics are shifting based on new emerging technologies and changing investment models. The real estate investment is taking new shapes such as smart cities which require more operation and longer lives. This calls for new feasibility study approaches and scenarios. The author has suggested a new financial parameter called Percentage Profit On Realistic Cashflow Duration (PORD or PRCD) that can be used along with other financial ratios to enhance the decision-making process.

The PORD or PRCD and RCD parameters was suggested based on a cashflow paradox arising from calculating the real duration of the project in selected periods to measure profitability. The author utilized his engineering sense and his knowledge in the Statics science to invent this technique based on calculating the equivalent force for several forces. The new technique resolved the paradox and can be enhanced further to add more value.

REFERENCES

Ahsen Maqsoom, S. B. (2019). Optimizing contractor's selection and bid evaluation process in construction industry: Client's perspective. *Journal of Construction, 18*(3), 445–458. doi:10.7764/RDLC.18.3.445

Almeida, F., & Santos, J. (2018). *The Business Plan Reference Manual for IT Businesses*. Gistrup, Denmark: River Publishers.

Boardman, A. E., Greenberg, D. H., Vining, A. R., & Weimer, D. L. (2011). Cost-Benefit Analysis: Concepts and Practice (4th ed.). Pearson.

Boland, M., & McCarthy, M. C. (2019, June 18). *Financial Statement Basics: What a Contractor Needs to Know for Surety Bonding*. Retrieved from https://www.constructionexec.com/: https://www.constructionexec.com/article/financial-statement-basics-what-a-contractor-needs-to-know-for-surety-bonding

Bragg, S. (2019, December 22). *Financial statement footnotes*. Retrieved from https://www.accountingtools.com/articles/what-are-financial-statement-footnotes.html

CFI. (2020, November 27). *return-on-capital-employed-roce*. Retrieved from https://corporatefinanceinstitute.com/resources/knowledge/finance/return-on-capital-employed-roce/

Collins-dictionary. (2020, November 29). *Retained-earnings*. Retrieved from https://www.collinsdictionary.com/dictionary/english/retained-earnings

Deltek. (2018, January 29). *10-key-financial-performance-indicators-for-government-contractors*. Retrieved from https://www.deltek.com/en/learn/blogs/government-contracting/2018/01/10-key-financial-performance-indicators-for-government-contractors

Dompere, K. K. (2004). *Cost-Benefit Analysis and the +eory of Fuzzy Decision*. Springer-Verlag.

Giang, D. T., & Pheng, L. (2011, January 1). Role of construction in economic development: Review of key concepts in the past 40 years. *Habitat International, 35*(1), 1–16. doi:10.1016/j.habitatint.2010.06.003

Goodland, H., & Lam, A. (2018, December 1). *Construction-Industry-KPI-report-FINAL*. Retrieved from http://www.constructionfoundation.ca/wp-content/uploads/2019/05/Construction-Industry-KPI-report-FINAL.pdf

Hofstrand, D. (2013, June). *Understanding the Time Value of Money*. Retrieved from Business Development, Starting a Business, Finances: https://www.extension.iastate.edu/agdm/wholefarm/html/c5-96.html

Inghram, Z. (2019, April 24). *3-important-benefits-of-financial-reporting*. Retrieved from https://www.ucpaa.org/3-important-benefits-of-financial-reporting

Ittelson, T. R. (2009). *Financial Statements: A Step-by-step Guide to Understanding and Creating Financial reports*. Career Press.

Killough, D. (2020, January 17). *Construction Accounting 101: How 4 Financial Statements Help You Keep More Money In Your Pocket*. Retrieved from https://www.levelset.com/blog/construction-accounting-how-4-financial-statements-keep-more-money/

Kobzeff, J. (2018, May 22). *The IRR, MIRR, and FMRR Approaches to Investment Analysis*. Retrieved from https://proapod.com/Articles/irr-mirr-fmrr.htm

Maravas, A., & Pantouvakis, J.-P. (2018). *A New Approach to Studying Net Present Value and the Internal Rate of Return of Engineering Projects under Uncertainty with Three-Dimensional Graphs*. Advances in Civil Engineering. doi:10.1155/2018/6108680

Marnell, P. (2016). *Engineering Economics for the 21st Century*. John Wiley & Sons.

Merriam-Webster. (2020, November 27). *"Layman's terms." Merriam-Webster.com*. Retrieved from https://www.merriam-webster.com/dictionary/layman%27s%2

Mohamed, S., & McCowan, A. (2001). Modelling project investment decisions under uncertainty using possibility theory. *International Journal of Project Management*, *19*(4), 231–241. doi:10.1016/S0263-7863(99)00077-0

Panneerselvam, R. (2004). *Engineering Economics*. PHI Learning Pvt. Ltd.

Rangel, A., Santos, J. C., & Savoia, J. R. (2015). Modified Profitability Index and Internal Rate of Return. *Journal of International Business and Economics*, *4*(2), 13–18. doi:10.15640/jibe.v4n2a2

Ranvir, J. (2020). *Project Finance: For the Banker by the Banker*. OrangeBooks Publication.

Ross, A., & Williams, P. (2012). *Financial Management in Construction Contracting*. Wiley-Blckwell.

Sawsan, R., & Mohammed, H. I. (2019). Impact of the Feasibility Study on the Construction Projects. *IOP Conference Series. Materials Science and Engineering*, *518*, 022074. doi:10.1088/1757-899X/518/2/022074

Schjaer-Jacobsen, H. (2002). Representation and calculation of economic uncertainties: Intervals, fuzzy numbers, and probabilities. *International Journal of Production Economics*, *78*(1), 91–98. doi:10.1016/S0925-5273(00)00167-5

Spurga, R. C. (2004). *Balance Sheet Basics: Financial Management for Non-financial Managers*. Penguin Group.

Wang, M. J., & Liang, G. S. (2007). Benefit/cost analysis using fuzzy concept. *The Engineering Economist, 40*(4), 359–376. doi:10.1080/00137919508903160

Wong, B. (2020, July 17). *Income-statement-vs-cash-flow-statement-which-one-should-i-use.* Retrieved from https://www.legalzoom.com/articles/income-statement-vs-cash-flow-statement-which-one-should-i-use

Yates, B. T., & Marra, M. (2017). Social Return On Investment (SROI): Problems, solutions … and is SROI a good investment? *Evaluation and Program Planning, 64*, 136–144. doi:10.1016/j.evalprogplan.2016.11.009 PMID:27979379

ADDITIONAL READING

Akintan, O. A., & Morledge, R. (2013). Improving the Collaboration between Main Contractors and Subcontractors within Traditional Construction Procurement. *Journal of Construction Engineering, 11*, 1–11. Advance online publication. doi:10.1155/2013/281236

Angius, S., Frati, C., Gerken, A., Härle, P., Piccitto, M., & Stegemann, U. (2011, may 1). Risk modeling in a newparadigm: developing newinsight and foresight onstructural risk. Retrieved from https://www.mckinsey.com/client_service/risk: https://www.mckinsey.com/client_service/risk/people/~/media/FBFAE9C41A144FCDB9A585126CDD86A4.ashx

Baker, E., Lavers, A., & Robottom, L. (2017). Allocation of Risk in Construction Contracts. Construction Contracts, 9. Retrieved from https://www.jdsupra.com/legalnews/allocation-of-risk-in-construction-32247/

Bannerman, P. (2008, December 1). Risk and risk management in software projects: A reassessment. *Journal of Systems and Software, 81*(12), 2118–2133. doi:10.1016/j.jss.2008.03.059

Choma, A. A. (2008). How to reduce risks in contractors' management. PMI® Global Congress 2008—North America (p. 7). Denver, CO. Newtown Square, PA: Project Management Institute.

FIDIC. (2020, December 5). https://fidic.org/node/911. (I. F. Engineers, Editor) Retrieved from Contracts: basic questions Question/Answer: https://fidic.org/node/911

Hendrickson, C. (2008). *Project Management for Construction. Pittsburgh, PA.* Mellon University., Retrieved from https://www.cmu.edu/cee/projects/PMbook/

International Trade Centre. (2018). *Cross-border contracting: How to draft and negotiate international commercial contracts.* International Trade Centre, World Trade Organization and the United Nations.

Iqbal, S., Choudhry, R. M., Holschemacher, K., Ali, A., & Tamosaitiene, J. (2015, January). Risk management in construction projects. *Technological and Economic Development of Economy, 21*(1), 65–78. doi:10.3846/20294913.2014.994582

Plimpton, L. (2008, June 19). Do You Know Where Your Contracts Are? Retrieved from https://www.entrepreneur.com: https://www.entrepreneur.com/article/195046

Potoski, M., & Brown, T. L. (2005). Transaction costs and contracting: The practitioner perspective. *Public Performance & Management Review, 28*(3), 326–351. doi:10.1080/15309576.2005.11051842

Rahman, M. M., & Kumaraswamy, M. M. (2004). Contracting Relationship Trends and Transitions. Journal of Management in Engineering, 20(4), online. Retrieved from https://ascelibrary.org/doi/abs/10.1061/(ASCE)0742-597X(2004)20:4(147)

Shalan, M. (2019). *Risk management for digital transformation contracts. Al-Yamamh University engineering Forum (YUENG2019).* Al-Yamamh University., Retrieved from https://yueng.yu.edu.sa/wp-content/uploads/2019/02/YUENG2019_paper_6.pdf

The World Bank. (2018). Contract Management practice. Washington DC: The World Bank. Retrieved from http://pubdocs.worldbank.org/en/277011537214902995/contract-management-guidance-september-19-2018-final.pdf

Westphal, P., & Sohal, A. (2016). 8 17). Outsourcing decision-making: Does the process matter? *Production Planning and Control, 27*(11), 894–908. doi:10.1080/09537287.2016.1159350

KEY TERMS AND DEFINITIONS

Business Dynamics: Strategies for improving the accuracy, timeliness, coverage, and integration of data that are used in constructing aggregate economic statistics. The business activity in this rapidly evolving environment increasingly requires tracking complex interactions among firms, establishments, employers, and employees.

Equilibrium: In statics when all the forces that act upon an object are balanced, then the object is said to be in a state of equilibrium. The forces are balanced if the rightward forces are balanced by the leftward forces.

Feasibility Study: Is undertaken to assess whether it is realistic to carry on certain project. This means that plenty of internal and external parameters will need to be considered including the financial situation, the reputation of the company, strengths, and weaknesses.

Cost Benefit Analysis (CBA): A process used to measure the benefits of a decision or action minus the costs associated with taking that action. A CBA involves measurable financial metrics such as revenue earned, or costs saved because of the decision to pursue a project.

Internal Rate of Return (IRR): A metric used in capital budgeting to estimate the profitability of potential investments. The internal rate of return is a discount rate that makes the net present value (NPV) of all cash flows from a particular project equal to zero.

Profit for the Realistic Cashflow Duration (PRCD): Profit for the realistic cashflow duration is an indication of project profitability based on the realistic cash flow calculations.

Realistic Cashflow Duration (RCD): An effective parameter that will depend on the real Cash Inflow (CI) and Cash Outflow (CO) to determine the feasibility of a project or investment.

Return on Investment (ROI): A metric used to measure the performance and evaluate the efficiency of an investment, Return on Investment (ROI) is usually used to compare the efficiency of several different investments.

Chapter 16
Basic Concepts of Electric Power System Planning:
Contracting for Reliability and Cost Effectiveness

Abdullah Alshaalan
King Saud University, Saudi Arabia

ABSTRACT

Power systems' planning, particularly in developing countries, faces enormous challenges and problems such as defining the future load growth in the face of uncertainties. Renewable energies are coming to the arena and affecting the planning of power and energy systems. The relation between power generation, transmission, and distribution entities, as well as the need for consolidating the dispersed electric utilities in the isolated regions is a prerequisite for future planning. Plenty of technologies, systems, and contractors are coming off the road while an optimal reliability levels need to be achieved. This chapter attempts to display the most tedious and prominent problems and challenges that face innovating the electric power systems which must be based on two major factors, namely reliability and cost. This chapter will help in drafting a new contracting style that mitigate obstacles that face power systems planners and concerned agencies while planning and operating electric power facilities.

INTRODUCTION

Power system planning is an essential and vital topic in the design and operation of power systems. An electric power system consists of a set of components interconnected with each other in some purposeful and meaningful manner. An optimal reliability levels need to be achieved that will guarantee a continuous power flow with a reasonable cost. Usually, the power systems planners and concerned agencies face tremendous difficulties in planning electric power facilities and making sound and appropriate decisions in constructing new power plants or adding new generating units or reinforcing the transmission and distribution networks.

DOI: 10.4018/978-1-7998-4501-0.ch016

Power system planning are changing and the need for consolidating the dispersed electric utilities in the isolated regions is becoming as a prerequisite for future interconnecting regions via local national grids and with other neighboring countries. Renewable energies and new technologies are playing vital role in this regard. An optimal reliability levels can be achieved that will guarantee a continuous power flow with a reasonable cost.

The object of a reliability evaluation is to derive suitable measures, criteria and indices of reliable and dependable performance based on components outage data and configuration. For generation reliability evaluation, the components of interest are the generating units and system configuration which refer(s) to the specific unit(s) operated to serve the present or future load.

This chapter described the indices used to measure generation reliability are probabilistic estimates of the ability of a particular generation configuration to supply the load demand. These indices are better understood as an assessment of system-wide generation adequacy and not as absolute measures of system reliability. With renewable energies and new technologies these indices become more meaningful.

This chapter will also review the types of forecasting of demand for electricity and the importance of accuracy in the preparation of these studies illustrate the foundations that must be taken into consideration when preparing and selecting the methods and models used to prepare these future expectations and explain the basic steps to be followed to conduct such studies.

As the reliability and forecast planning discussed, the main purpose of this chapter is to set the contracting styles that can achieve reliability while accepting new generation technologies and new players who are coming to this market continuously supported by new emerging technologies.

BACKGROUND

Electric Power plays a major role in human life and is considered one of the important means to achieve progress and prosperity in all areas of life (Nicholas, 2009), not surprisingly, that electricity rates are taken to use as one of growth, progress and development of the countries of standards (Wolde-Rufael, 2006).

Planning for power systems is essentially a projection of how the system should grow over a specific period (Masters, 2013), given certain assumptions and judgment about the future loads and the size of investment in generating capacity additions and transmission facilities expansion and reinforcements.

Any plan can become technically and economically obsolete (Schein, 1996). New inventions in electrical utilization equipment or unforeseen industrial, commercial, or residential projects can change load forecast (Schramm, 2006). Breakthroughs in new generation and transmission technologies, unexpected inflation in equipment or labor costs or change of national income can all mean that system plans may take another direction (Stoll, 2007).

In developing countries, power system planning has become more difficult, but more important to provide the necessary information to enable decision to be made today about many years in the future (Wang, Billinton, & Goel, 2002). In almost all cases, planning must be done in the face of many uncertainties, for example: future load patterns, population increase and the economic growth which characterize the developing countries, as well as technical, economic, and environmental constraints (Nakicenovic, Grubler, & McDonald, 1998).

It is also crucial to understand the different ways to prepare the forecast demand for energy and electrical loads due to the daily load curve variations and the methods used to predict in this curve (Jota & Silva, 2011). It is also important to determine appropriate types of power plants and the preparation of the economic drivers of those stations (Lopes, Hatziargyriou, Mutale, & Jenkins, 2007).

Digital transformation and emerging technologies are changing plenty of things around the power generation and distribution (Onyeji-Nwogu, Bazilian, & Moss, 2017). Distributed Renewable Energy Resources (DRESs) are adding new dimensions and challenges (Vezzoli, et al., 2018). One of the most important challenges are the contracting style to cater for flexibility and reliability at the same time.

POWER SYSTEM FORECASTING

The main issue regarding power system planning is to establish basic principles and guidelines to serve as a framework within which the process of planning may proceed. This framework should be flexible, not rigid with broad objectives of finding a plan (or plans) which guarantees a desired degree of a continuous, reliable and least cost service. Good service or, in other words, acceptable reliability level of power system usually requires additions of more generating capacity to meet the expected increase in future electrical demands.

However, in many developing countries with vast, separately populated areas reliability–cost tradeoffs exist between satisfying the fast load growth by investment in additional generating capacity for isolated systems or building transmission networks to interconnect these systems and transfer power between their load centers in case of emergencies and power shortages. Therefore, reliability and cost constraints are major considerations in power system planning process.

The Planning Process

Power system planning is needed especially in developing countries (like Saudi Arabia) to develop and build modern electric power systems. The planning process can be divided into main stages as listed here:

1. **Load forecasting:** which includes population growth, the number of customers and appliances, consumption patterns and the power factor.
2. **Generation planning:** to look at existing power planets, statistical analysis, and reliability indices among other factors to maintain accurate planning. This will help to specify the type and size of generation units and capacity adding stages.
3. **Transmission planning:** through the understanding of existing transmission networks, security, stability and load flow analysis, voltage levels, routing, and interconnections. This will help in scheduling the network reinforcement.
4. **Fixed costs:** including the cost and depreciation of assets, interest rates and other parameters.
5. **Variable costs:** such as fuel cost, maintenance, and spare parts which will derive the operational annual costs
6. **Financial model:** which will help to drive final report about subsidiaries and a long-range verification plan.

The Energy and Electric Loads Forecasting

Because electricity intervention at the present time in many areas affecting human life and the comfort and well-being it is important to predict the future needs of electrical energy and determine the maximum loads to serve as a basis for future planning of power plants, transmission lines and distribution networks for electric power, and this requires the preparation of long, medium and short term plans in order to design programs for future expansions of the systems and electricity facilities to be able to cope with the maximum expected demand for energy and electrical loads during the period of time depends on the quality of the plan (long term- medium term - short term) and the level of appropriate reliability so that the costs of establishing, operating and maintaining these systems are less so can taking into account the economic and technical conditions prevailing.

It is known that the loads and the demand for electrical power are affected by weather conditions, for example, when the air temperature arise, the energy demand and loads will increase due to running the air conditioners, as well as when it goes down the air temperature increased loads due to the operation of heating systems, and from this it is clear that the load is composed of two parts main components: the first part is influenced by weather conditions and the second part of the uninfluenced by weather conditions, so it may be appropriate in some situations and circumstances for future estimates of each part separately then be added to get the total load. Thus, it is clear that the preparation of the Energy and Electric Loads Forecasting studies are the first stages of planning of all kinds (long-term - medium term - short-term).

Electric demand forecast studies based on the concept and objectives of preparing those expectations. There may be a need for future electricity demand at the level of the country or region, or even a small area of those expectations zone setting. There may be a need to prepare a forecast of future demand for electricity to be used in planning for power generating stations or just planning for transmission networks or plan to link a number of electrical systems or for use in the planning of distribution networks to customers.

Preparation of electric demand forecast may be requested in order to prepare an annual budget for part of the project, or one or more projects or planning to arrange for large financial investments for a long period of time may take a number of years may be required. It may be also required to prepare the future demand for electricity as a forecasting of maximum loads (peak) M.W in order to determine the ability of the required power plants or estimate future energy M.W hour or predict the curve of change loads during a certain period of time (a year, for several years, month, day, etc.) in order to choose the right types of power plants.

Accuracy of Demand Forecasting

Preparing of the forecasting of future demand for electric power and loads is the foundation stone on which the planning and design tasks and create electrical projects estimates to determine the capabilities, the right kinds of power plants, transmission and distribution networks capacity, and then connections of customers. Hence the importance of being prepared for future electricity demand largely estimates acceptable accuracy to be as close as possible to reality.

For example, the impact of the results from the study of forecasting of future electricity demand affect the selection and identification of appropriate types of power plants to keep up with those expectations (gas stations, steam, diesel, etc.), and also affects in determining the timetable necessary for the establishment of these stations, as well as in the cost estimates required for the establishment of such stations and financial investments, but that may not later than at the actual impact on a large part of the operation and maintenance costs of these stations.

Take the case of when the forecasting of future electricity demand is less than the actual customers demand, it will cause a shortfall in generation capacity and thus a deficit in feeding some of the electrical loads and then the low level of reliability of the system generation, because in most cases it may be difficult to provide dates of the establishment and installation of power plants and therefore run at specified to meet the rapid growth in loads where the dates they are usually subject to a schedule specified may be difficult to make amendments to it, as well as what it takes it to provide immediate funds ahead of schedule it in advance may be difficult in some cases to ensure those urgent reliability.

On other hand, let's take the case of when the forecasting of future electricity demand is higher than the actual customers demand, this situation will give rise to a provide generation capacity which is no real need for them, which means an increase in costs and financial investment required and thus an increase in the cost of production and sale of units of electric power, also delay the completion dates of creation and preparation of power plants and thus delay the operation until after the planned schedule for operation date in advance, which could also be costly and uneconomic which affects the cost of selling the unit of electrical energy (tariff).

Factors Used in Forecasting

Since the early seventies and forecasting of future electricity demand take attention because it is required to be on the high degree of accuracy and realism to avoid economic and technical risks of its occurrence of reflections and great effects.

Among these factors are price fluctuations and the existence of some kinds of suspicion for the price of future fuel costs, as well as equipment, and rates of economic growth in general. In addition, it has recently been an increased interest from public opinion the issue of the effects of electric power plants and transportation networks to public health and safety of the environment and become a decision determining the stations and their type as well as the future demand for energy, which are built on the basis of these stations is not for companies, institutions and facilities, electricity forecast estimates but it has become a matter of public opinion has sometimes falls within the political issues as well as environmental considerations.

Here it should be noted that in the light of the global financial crisis and low economic growth rates, the effects of lack of precision in the future demand for electricity estimates may have risks and consequences of the worst of cases where high economic growth rates are, for example, the high forecasting of future electricity demand caused in the presence of excess unused generation capacity, and it will take longer time to be placed in service, operation and utilization which may leave a bad economic impacts for a long periods. Also, the low forecasting of future electricity demand impacts may be the worst in such conditions as may be required for long periods of time pass in order to avoid and eliminate the effects of those expectations, and so is the establishment of new stations may take several years to actually can run, this mean we cannot feed some loads and the low level of reliability which may have ill effects on some important, especially the industrial loads.

Thus, it should be taken into account the importance of preparing for future energy demand and electrical loads estimates so that they are as close as much as possible to the actual fact, increasing the importance of the day but is expected to increase the importance and more broadly in the future.

Methods and Models for Future Forecast

There are large number of methods and models that have already been developed and used successfully for the preparation of future electricity demand forecast for the purposes of planning for the electric power systems, however, these methods may vary in terms of:

- The degree of accuracy of the results that can be obtained.
- Conditions appropriate to the implementation conditions.
- The nature of the required data and time periods that can be covered by those models.
- The extent of the flexibility and ease of implementation.

An important factor to consider when choosing the methods and models of forecast is the future demand for electricity length of time that need to be covered in the preparation of these future forecasting, which may require the preparation of forecasts for the period of time in the general limits for the purpose of preparing an annual budget or to prepare a maintenance program (for example, short-term), or the period of time within a few years (medium term), or for more than ten years and up to thirty years (long-term).

Of course, the degree of precision required for the expectations of these cases differ from case to case, so the methods and models required for successful implementation will vary from one state to another, while have to rely on finding a relationship between future demand for loads or energy with appropriate time for periods of time relatively limited and, under certain circumstances electrical systems it is in most cases have to understand and identify the causes that affect the future demand for the loads is an important and necessary energy when prepare plans for long or even medium term.

In addition, the period of time it takes to set up and use those methods and models are often also linked to the period of time covered by those models, which, in cases of planning the short term, it typically takes the accelerate of preparation of such forecasting to be ready during the period of time is relatively shorter than the cases of long planning or medium term, and this is, of course, affects the selection model suitable way.

Regarding to the costs, it is considered one of the fundamental factors that are selected for methods and models of future demand for loads and power forecasts as the cost depends of course on the time required to prepare the forecasts of the loads and the future of energy as well as the expertise needed to fulfill them and devices in addition to the quality of the data required and the degree of precision required.

As for ease of use they relate to various matters such as basic rules on which the model and the extent of its simplicity as well as the steps that follow during the implementation and the required expertise and capabilities available for use, as well as the analysis of the results and the time required methods to get them.

From the above, it is clear that the selection or preparation methods and models appropriate to the forecasting of future demand for electricity depends on a comparison of all the factors and previous rules in terms of advantages and disadvantages for each individual case and that there is no single method can be applied in all cases, and determine the way also depends on experience gained on estimates of future demand for electricity. Therefore, it should be a thorough examination of each individual case, whereby, the selection and more ways and models suited to achieve the desired goal in each case.

LOAD CHARACTERISTICS

Power system planning starts by forecasting the anticipated future loads. It is basically concerned with load forecasting and energy forecasting. Load forecasting is used to define the capacity needed for the system generation, transmission and distribution additions and it is defined as the projection of future load requirements and facilities using a systematic process (methodology) of defining future loads in a sufficient quantitative analysis to permit important system expansion decision to be made. Load forecasting is also needed for budgeting purposes and energy forecast is needed to determine future type of generating units and fuel requirements.

Definitions

Load: A general term referring to the size of electrical power, i.e. W, KW, MW, GW, TW and so on, where W refers to Watt, K is Kilo, M is Mega, G is Giga and T is Tera.

Energy: The amount of energy consumed by the electrical equipment in Wh, the customer (KWh), the city (MWh), the country (GWh), where h refers to hour.

Loads' Classification

Loads can be classified to according to the nature of customers as: Residential, Governmental, Commercial, Industrial, and Municipal and other loads.

- Residential load depends on the domestic activities of the people; Governmental load depends on the daily working hours of the employees.
- Commercial load depends on the commercial activities during the opening hours.
- Industrial load: depends on the time of production and considered to be the most stable load curve.
- Municipal load: Streets lighting loads are typically operated between two periods.

As a result, the total daily load variation curves that comprises of all customers types can be shown below in Figure 1

The energy demanded consumed by the system can be calculated as the area under the load curve, i.e. consumed by the load during the interval of time considered.

Load Duration Curve

Three types of generation units exist usually the Steam (ST), Combined Cycle (CC) and Gas Turbine (GT). Load Duration Curve (LDC) shows the corresponding cost of generation in Saudi Riyal per Kilo Watt (SR/KW) for particular time which is variable with time of operation. The LDC contain three types of loads:

- Base load which is constant all the time of year (normally it is industrial load).
- Intermediate load which is for season period few months in the year.
- Peak load which lasts for short time of day and then disappears.

Figure 1. Typical total daily load variation curve

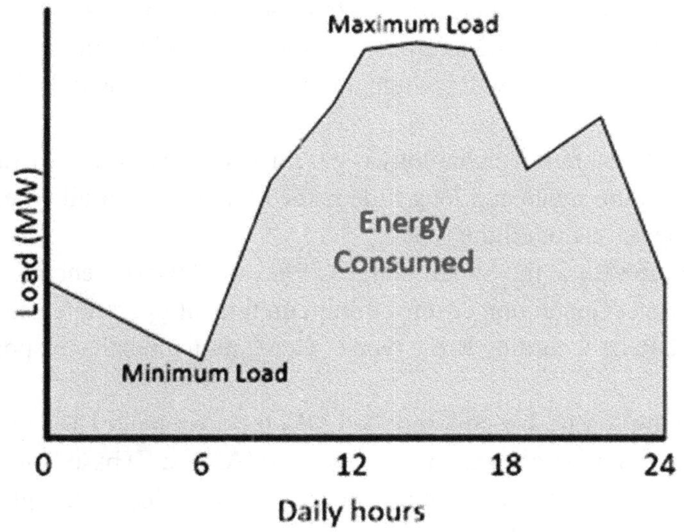

Figure 2. Load duration curve

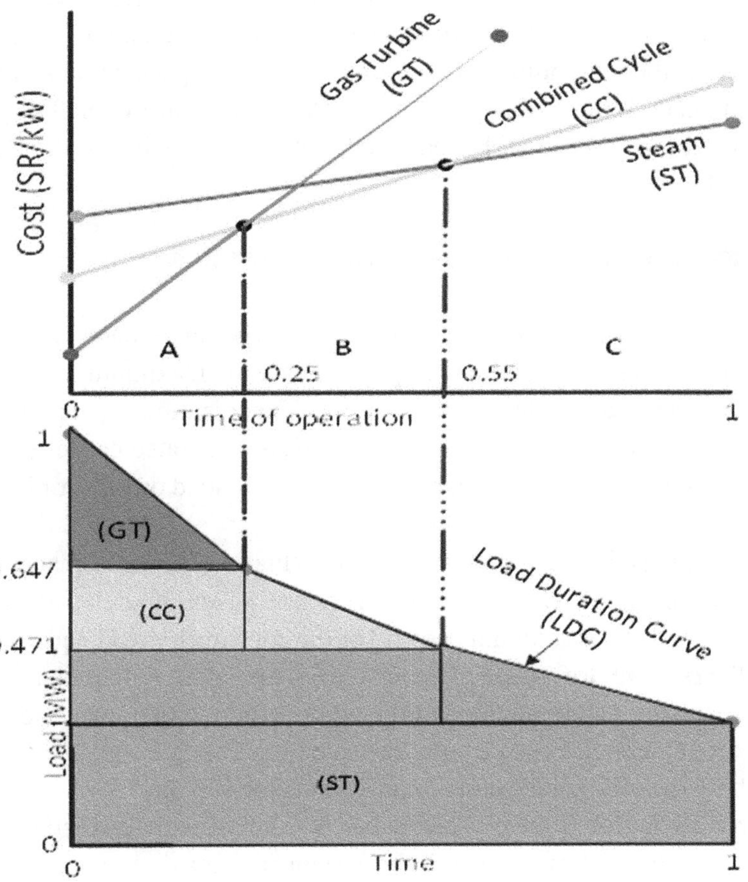

The best generation technology is steam which usually form the base load. Operation cost of steam is low with time, but the main disadvantage of it is that the initial cost is very high. Combined cycle is the best generation technology. The operation cost is lower than steam turbine for Intermediate range, but for longer time the operation cost will be higher than steam turbine and the initial cost of it is lower than steam turbine.

For peak load, the best generation technology is gas turbine, because the operation cost is the lowest for short time but for medium range and long time is the highest cost of all types, the main advantage of it the initial cost is the lowest of all the types.

For maximum operation time, the Steam Unit (ST) has the lowest Generation cost. However, Gas Turbine (GT) has the lowest Generation cost for minimum time of operation. LDC is divided into three zones (Green, Yellow & Red) according to the type of Generation units that respond to load represented in the curve.

To link between the units' variable cost and the LDC, the area under LDC which represents the demanded energy is divided into three segments as illustrated (A, B & C) based on time of operation, 0.25 and 0.55. Time duration and demand are two parameters which define each segment of LDC. Segment A represents the maximum peak load demand (1). Segments B and C represent load at gradually lower level of demand (0.647 and 0.471 respectively).

ST is the most cost effective and efficient unit which assigned as base load unit to meet the load in all Segments A, B and C. ST CC is moderate variable operating cost used in segment B and C if load is more than 47.1% of maximum demand for time lower than base load unit. GT is a peaking load unit as shown in Segment A for the minimum operation time due to its highest variable cost for operation and used if load is more than 64.7% of maximum demand. Base load unit, ST, shall be prevented as possible from cycling, i.e. switching ON and OFF. Peak load unit, GT, is easily and the fastest which could be switched ON and OFF.

Other Factors to Determine the Load Characteristics

- **The load factor (LF):** is measured as the degree of variation of load [L(t)] over a period of time, and can be defined as the ratio of the average load over the maximum load
- **The capacity factor (CF):** is the extent of use of the generating capacity (C) in the Power Plant (PP) and can be defined as average load on power plant over rated capacity of the power plant.
- **The utilization factor (UF):** can be defined as maximum load on power plant over rated capacity of the power plant.
- **The demand factor (DF):** can be defined as the actual maximum demand over connected load. Each device has a maximum capacity for absorption of power. If all devices are run to their fullest extent simultaneously, the maximum demand of the consumer would equal to his connected load.
- **The group diversity factor (GDF):** is defined as the sum of individual consumer maximum loads in the group over maximum load of the whole group. Experience shows that the max loads of individual consumers may not occur at the same time but are spread over time. This holds for consumers whose activities and energy requirements are similar.
- **The peak diversity factor (PDF):** is defined as the sum of individual consumer maximum loads in each group over the maximum load of the system. The maximum load of a system is made up of the individual loads. It is seldom that the peak load of the group occurs at that time.

Reliability Evaluation of Power Generation

Reliability is one of the most important criteria, which must be taken into consideration during all phases of power system planning, design, and operation (Roy Billinton, 1984). A reliability criterion is required to establish target reliability levels and to consistently analyze and compare the future reliability levels with feasible alternative expansion plans (Roy Billinton R. N., 1992). As a measure of power system reliability evaluation in generation planning and energy production, three fundamental indices are widely adopted and used.

- The first reliability index is the Loss of Load Expectation (LOLE) which denotes the expected average number of days per year during which the system is being on outages, i.e. load exceeds the available generating capacity (Endrenyi, 1978).
- The second index is the Expected Demand not Supplied (ϵDNS) which measures the size of load that has been lost due to the severe outages' occurrence. (Al-Shaalan, 2018)
- The third index is the Expected Energy not Supplied (ϵENS), which is defined as the expected size of energy not being supplied by the generating unit(s) residing in the system during the period considered due to capacity deficit or unexpected severe power outages. (Brown, 2009)

The implementations of these indices are now increasing since they are significant in physical and economic terms. The reliability indices are sensitive to basic factors like unit size and unit availability (Wang, 2008). This is particularly useful when comparing the relative reliability of different generation configurations. The system is deemed to operate successfully if there is enough generation capacity (adequate reserve) to satisfy the peak load (maximum demand). Firstly, generation model and load model are convolved (mutually combined) to yield the risk of supply shortages in the system. Secondly, probabilistic estimates of shortage risk are used as indices of bulk power system reliability evaluation for the considered configuration.

ECONOMIC ASPECTS AND CHARACTERISTICS OF POWER GENERATION UNITS

In economic evaluation techniques of electric power system costs, there are several different costs associated with power systems. These include:

- Capital costs which are related to the installation of new generating units. buildings, civil works, cost of materials, interim replacement, and repair, staffing and administration.
- Variable operation costs which are related to the fuel costs.
- Outage costs which are the costs of energy demanded but not served.

There are two main factors to be considered by the system planer when trying to meet these requirements and they are: reliability and costs. There are two main costs to be revaluated and considered in the economic studies of electric power systems. They are the capital costs (SR/kW) of capacity installed and the operating costs (SR/kWh) as shown in Figure 3.

Figure 3. Flowchart for electric power system costs

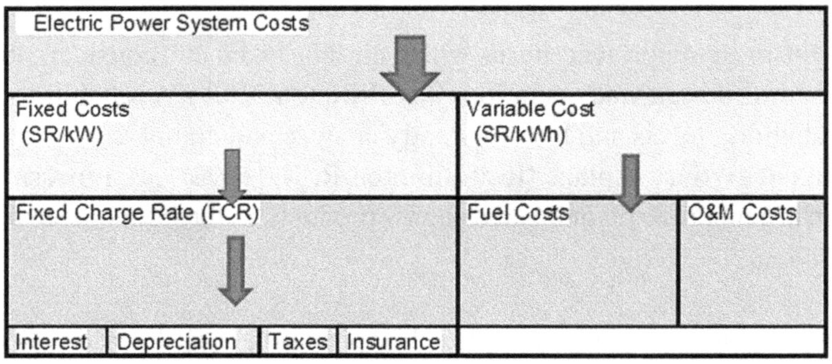

The fixed costs (or total investment) vary directly with the installed plant capacity and overhead and cable transmission lines and do not depend on the hours of operation. These costs include:

- Cost of land.
- Cost of buildings.
- Cost of generating units and their auxiliaries.
- Cost of installation of substations, transformers, control, protection, etc.
- Cost of engineering fees

These costs are paid only once during the life of the project. Therefore, these costs lead to costs that are spent annually over the lifetime of the electric power plant and called "Fixed Charge Rate (FCR)". The annual FCR consists of the interest (or cost of money) on the total investment, taxes, insurance, and depreciation. Depreciation is the most important in the FCR charger as it represents the deterioration (decrease) in the value of the property or asset due to aging, usage, or long operation.

MOVING TOWARDS THE FUTURE POWER AND ENERGY SYSTEMS

Power systems are complex dynamical systems, and scientific research across multiple domains reinforces that such systems have 'critical points' marking a shift to a new regime. As power systems reaching a threshold, various elements will be considered to land on a new stable platform which may require few factors related to markets, policy, regulations, consumer, technology, and business models.

Due to the new circumstances and everywhere in the world, the electric power and utilities sector finds itself pulled to economize and pushed to innovate — two goals that might seem to conflict, but that are actually in harmony. Such pull comes from a prolonged downturn in consumer energy revenue.

Emerging technologies and intensive research and development activities in the recent years are responsible for the development of various new technologies for power generation including fluidized bed combustion systems, gasifier-combined cycle plants, fuel cells and magneto-hydrodynamic power plants, advanced nuclear technologies such as fast-breeder reactor and fusion technology and renewable technologies such as solar, wind, hydro, geothermal, and ocean-thermal conversion plants. Such technologies will change the power generation schemes and plenty of costing and measuring factors.

Some of these technologies are not yet commercialized or demonstrated as much uncertainty lies in the projections of their cost and performance data.

A common theme of desired attributes includes cost-effectiveness, accessibility, reliability, resilience, and increasingly embedding smart, real time control and services. However, it is unlikely that the same transformation will occur everywhere, because in each context the power system of the future emerges from the interacting forces of policy, regulation, global market forces, business model innovation, technological innovation, and consumer behavior.

The Changes of The Electric Power and Utilities Sector

Digital technologies are evolving, and customers are quick to adopt them. Both business and consumer energy users are clear about their expectations. They want to reduce their consumption, and they know that technological controls and data analytics can help them do it. For example, business customers are increasingly interested in managing their energy use patterns.

The technical and economic facts regarding some of the emerging technologies are changing the arena of energy costing. Some technologies are not yet commercialized or demonstrated. Every company in the power and utilities sector, face challenges to close the demand gap and provide value for customers profitably to achieve a future of growth and customer loyalty.

Over the time, a broader array of new technologies including battery storage, microgrids, analytics software, and intelligent substations, will find their way onto the power grid as utility offerings. Utilities have a limited window of opportunity to engage with this trust and establish their new business models, because rivals from other industries are rapidly building their capability and credibility with customers.

To capitalize on this emerging market opportunity, utilities need to move beyond the old commodity-based model (The U.S. Energy Information Administration, 2020). Much of this change will start in the business-to-business domain. As enterprise customers focus on reducing their energy consumption and expanding their mix of options. This will change the contracting for utilities and introduce sophisticated energy management services. This will include merger and acquisition (M&A), partnerships or both. Such changes are leading to a growth path for energy services management to evolve from a basic regulated utility model to one with more flexibility in market participation, offerings of products and services, risk taking, and other factors.

This changing relations between utility providers and customers is reshaping the contracts that is signed between booth entities. This would include more adjustable pricing approaches such as fees-for-service, shared performance gains, and value-based margins. Following an inorganic approach also means shifting from a business model of owning assets and driving return on capital to a model that focuses on product and service volumes that create margins.

Evolutionary Landscape of Power System Transformation

On the spectrum of possibility, the power systems of the future will land on different structure. Considering that Trillions of dollars have been invested in the current structure, legacy systems will transform incrementally utilizing plenty of leapfrog opportunities that employ new technologies, policies, and business models.

According to (Zinaman, et al., 2015), power systems have four modes of innovation:

- **The "Adaptation" mode:** typically, power systems are in the "Adaptation" mode, accommodating incremental changes in demand growth, technology change, and consumer preference. Several forces have the potential to increase the extent and the speed of change, moving power systems into new territory.
- **The Evolution mode:** which implies fundamental changes to power system technologies and actors, during a relatively long period of time and through a sustained incremental change.
- **The Reconstruction mode:** which implies rapid change, but without fundamental changes in power system actors or technologies. For example, introductions of new institutional structures, such as competitive wholesale power markets, with limited change in the generation fleet, tariff structure, or customer interactions.
- **The Revolution mode:** which implies rapid fundamental changes across power systems and might incorporate full competitive markets, services, and real-time rates.

Merger and Acquisition activities may increase as well-capitalized utilities leverage synergies to save costs and expand their geographies, assets, and capabilities. These utilities may also jockey with other energy, infrastructure, and financial groups to establish leading positions in the power market by acquiring smaller players, notably in the renewables sector.

How Digital Transformation Is Affecting the Power and Utility Market

As digital transformation and industry 4.0 is changing the rules, along with the recessionary tailwinds unfold, smaller developers will bring new ideas and attractive assets to the reforming fragmented market and this will help larger utilities to utilize and consolidate later.

Utilities might also develop new services such as behind-the-meter storage solutions to enhance resiliency for critical operations now being performed from a home office. Another idea is to assist businesses in managing their carbon footprint reduction strategies across their networks of employee offices. Virtual agents and home energy management, voice-interactive features, and mobile-friendly options to elevate digital interactions with customers (deloitte, 2020).

The challenges and changes will also strengthen the cybersecure digital solutions to both address short-term challenges and help with long-term resilience. (Thomson, 2020). The related digital capabilities include new technologies such as augmented and virtual reality to help utilities manage a remote workforce and the drones, automation, and asset tracking to boost operational efficiency.

To facilitate and control such technologies, it is required to have an innovative contracting style and a scalable digital contract management tools, that is supported by advanced analytics and cloud based artificial intelligence tools to support corporate and finance functions. All these technologies should be supported by surrounded by cyber defenses to address the increased risk from remote operations.

REALIGNING POWER GENERATION, TRANSMISSION AND DISTRIBUTION

Ancillary services are the services necessary to support the transmission of electric power from generators to consumers given the obligations of control areas and transmitting utilities within those control areas to maintain reliable operations of the interconnected transmission system. (Wikipedia, 2020)

Ancillary services are the specialty services and functions provided by the electric grid that facilitate and support the continuous flow of electricity so that supply will continually meet demand. The term "ancillary services" is used to refer to a variety of operations beyond generation and transmission that are required to maintain grid stability and security. These services generally include, frequency control, spinning reserves and operating reserves. Traditionally ancillary services have been provided by generators; however, the integration of intermittent generation and the development of smart grid technologies have prompted a shift in the equipment that can be used to provide ancillary services.

In the conventional design of the electricity system, the power from the large generators is carried to the transmission systems, while the distribution grid is responsible for the electrification of the loads connected to the medium and low voltage. The frequency and voltage are mainly controlled by the bulk generators by means of providing certain advanced services to the transmission system. (Konstantino, et al., 2020). This centralized approach is becoming outdated, since Distributed Renewable Energy Resources (DRESs) are increasingly connected within the transmission and distribution systems, causing the gradual decommissioning of the conventional synchronous generators (SGs).

This trend results in stability and reliability challenges for grid operators. The problem is becoming more severe considering that most of the DRESs are converter-dominated in some cases, with the absence of any rotational masses, and hence, do not have technical predispositions to provide ancillary services. Furthermore, the DRESs has a highly volatile and intermittent nature due to the dependence on weather conditions. Such situation is flipping over the whole scenario and measures, as the Transmission System Operators (TSOs) who used to be responsible for procuring and using ancillary services in their scheduling and dispatch of generation are no longer the sole players as new players have entered through generators, storage, and flexible loads.

The liberalization of the electricity markets put a focus on the reliability parameters that should be considered with main target of keeping the frequency and voltage within specific safe bands and restoring their values to the normal range after an imbalance occurs. This also identifies possible technical, regulatory and financial barriers that can impede the adoption of these new technologies and behaviors. (NICEIC, 2020)

The Evolving Role of The Distribution System Operators

The current increasing penetration of Distributed Renewable Energy Resources (DRES) in distribution networks impose new challenges in solving the emerging issues at local level including the procurement, development, operation, and maintenance of the distribution grid in order to deliver high quality services to end users. (Zinaman, et al., 2015)

New dimensions are evolving in the distribution systems. The role of the distribution system operators is strengthened in the digital transformation arena. One reason is the smartness of the distribution grid by the wide installation of smart metering infrastructure which develops a new market environment and evolves the future interaction between transmission and distribution service operators.

Following the current market structure, the DRES are mainly connected to inject the available power to the grid, while the market operators remunerate their energy by applying several different pricing schemes such as feed-in-tariff, feed-in-premium, net-metering and net-billing. Such technologies have the potential to provide downward and upward adjustment to the systems, therefore, they should be considered as a powerful tool for balancing the electricity networks.

The DRES can provide a diversity of services having an important economic footprint. In this manner, they can decrease the overall cost of the distribution service providers by enhancing the active distribution management concept, which is opposed to the traditional "fit-and-forget approach". Managing the instantaneous power becomes more important to offer flexibility through active power management leading to incentives stemming and dynamic pricing schemes. This is aligned with the new trends in digital transformation which is affecting every industry and make it possible to take continuous decisions on the spot.

Technical and Financial Evolutions

Technical barriers are one of the most significant barriers related to the current coordination level between the transmission and distribution service providers. Numerous DRESs within the distribution systems are not "visible" and controllable by the transmission service providers thus cannot serve for the efficient provision of ancillary services.

Financial barriers are also crucial as more and more DRES are going to provide ancillary services at the distribution and the transmission system levels. It is thus essential that a proper remuneration scheme is introduced, based on the value estimation of each service. The electricity markets should be developed so that the value of the flexible resources is more visible in market prices and proper investment signals are sent.

Adopting the Distribution and Transmission Services for the New Era

According to (Konstantino, et al., 2020) several activities can be suggested to prepare the stage for the coming transformations while enhancing the system-support functions, these suggestion include;

- Methods for the quantification of each service to be developed, validated, and agreed among the interested stakeholders.
- Techniques need to be developed so that an aggregator can evaluate the aggregated amount of service that can be delivered based on the type, size and location of the DRESs within the distribution system under their responsibility.
- For a number of ancillary services that are meant to be offered within the distribution system, such as contribution to fault-clearing and harmonic mitigation, the quantification methods need to define the starting and ending moments of each service.
- Apart from the development of measurement and quantification methods, the associated costs of investment and operational for each ancillary service need to be evaluated to enable the development of viable business models and associated markets at distribution grid level.
- A rather simple but highly secure information communication technology system is required for the coordinated control of the various DRES within the distribution grid and the accounting of the quantified Ancillary Services. The role of the ICT is mainly the enabling/disabling of an AS in a DRES and the transmission of various set points in relatively large time intervals of the order of minutes.
- A registry containing all the properties of the DRESs within a distribution system should be made and be transparent to the transmission system operators. This will form the basis for further devel-

opment of methods for the estimation of the equivalent models containing both the steady-state and dynamic behavior of the distribution grid considering the technical constraints within it.

Small Sized Power Generation and Metering Contractors

The construction market will show only modest growth in the coming period, with more than half of activity focused on repair, maintenance and improvement. The value of electrical contracting will increase due to demands for more energy efficient buildings because of the increasing energy prices and possible shortages. Customers will be more knowledgeable and, with the rising price of raw materials driving up the cost of construction, they will be encouraging greater competition. There will be opportunities for the electrical contractor who adapts to these changes.

The current worldwide trend is to encourage increased use of small and medium sized contractors to get the benefit of SMART ((Self-Monitoring, Analysis & Reporting Technology) meters will be installed in every home and many buildings to incorporate remote control monitoring with high speed internet allowing specialist centers to take charge of this on behalf of building occupants.

The unifying themes of effective solutions for energy-poor markets are that they are affordable, appropriate, and sufficiently simple. Such solutions can be framed as a continuum of decentralized and customized from the intersection of existing solutions, where novel coordinated strategies are emerging that can potentially accelerate Bottom-of-the-Pyramid solutions

How to Write a Flexible Contract to Manage the Relation Between Entities?

The new power market facilitates the trading of services and improves the competition among different involved stakeholders. Generally, the transmission service operators are the sole purchasers of products in the ancillary services market, while sellers include the prequalified generators and in some cases demand response involving large consumers, aggregators, and storage facilities.

The related procurement methods can be divided in four main categories: compulsory provision, bilateral contracts, tendering and spot markets. In compulsory provision, a class of generators are engaged to provide specific reserves of ancillary services. This engagement rises through the national regulations and network codes, which mandate specific sources to connect to the system. In the case of bilateral contracts, the transmission system operator (TSO) negotiates with each provider the quantity and price of the offered ancillary services. This allows the TSO to buy only a specific amount and to deal with sellers in order to minimize the overall cost.

However, these contracts are usually long-term and possible market conditions changes cannot be considered. The tendering and spot market refer to an ancillary services exchange process characterized from increased competition. The former usually includes long-duration services, while the latter involves shorter and less standardized products.

Further, remuneration includes several components that reflect the different costs of the provision entity. To start with, the fixed allowance and the availability price refer to the cost of the seller to make a specific amount of ancillary services available. Later, the utilization payment and the utilization frequency cost reflect the actual exploitation of the product and the extra cost that may arise each time that the provider is called upon in a specific period of time, respectively.

Finally, the remuneration takes into consideration the opportunity cost that reflects the possible profit loss in the case where the provider could have sold other products instead of the respective ancillary services.

FUTURE RESEARCH DIRECTIONS

This era is built around data. Available data from the most important things on which are appropriate methods and models choose to prepare forecasting the future electricity demand are considered as each method need specific types of data and information, so it is important to use the methods and models that match the quality of information available and the nature of the desired results. Emerging technologies are providing powerful forecasting tools; however such tools need a wide research to be applied to power and energy sectors.

With far greater use of high-tech electrical systems, demand for electrical and communication installations will be high both for installation and when they fail. Installation of local neighborhood power generation and vehicle charging networks will provide new opportunities for electrical contractors, as will the growth of high-speed broadband with networks in every building. Researcher are cautiously investigating the best approach to integrate power generation, electrical vehicles, and communication network for mutual benefit.

Regulatory barriers can have a major effect on the way ancillary services will be provided to the power system in case of increased Distributed Renewable Energy Resources (DRES) penetration, while they can certainly facilitate the establishment of related market at the distribution system level. Technology and size limitations imposed by the present regulations are referred to as one of the main reasons why DRES units and loads are excluded from these markets, even though they could potentially provide the requested services. Making proper regulations in this still field are still evolving and plenty of studies are required in this field from multi discipline professionals who can understand legal and technical dimensions,

The integration between energy storage systems and electrical vehicles may be a key element of the recent progress in smart grids and microgrids to support the stable operation of the distribution grids. These may include voltage regulation and congestion management in addition to the provision of specific active and reactive power profile at the substation level. The contracting styles and dimensions still not mature as of today and will require plenty of research.

CONCLUSION

Planning an efficient power generation and distribution systems ae very crucial for life property. Multiple methodologies and techniques have been applied to reach a reliable power and energy systems. Forecasting played a crucial role as well to provide the right balance between distribution and generation. Digital transformation methodologies and the emerging technologies are adding new dimensions to this industry. Distributed Renewable Energy Resources (DRES) penetration of the market is becoming so huge and innovative in its approaches. Trust and reliability are very defining parameters in this complex environment. This chapter emphasizes the very important role that regulations and contracting can play to reach a robust system that can be utilized efficiently and effectively while balancing costs and risks.

REFERENCES

Al-Shaalan, A. (2018). *Reliability Evaluation and Modeling of Power Systems*. King Saud University.

Brown, R. E. (2009). *Electric Power Distribution Reliability*. Oxfordshire: Taylor & Francis Group, LLC.

Deloitte. (2020, April 1). *Energy-resources/us-2020-power-utilities-midyear*. Retrieved from https://www2.deloitte.com/content/dam/Deloitte/us/Documents/energy-resources/us-2020-power-utilities-midyear.pdf

Endrenyi, J. (1978). *Reliability modelling in electric power systems*. Wiley International Publication.

Jota, P. R., Silva, V. R., & Jota, F. G. (2011). Building load management using cluster and statistical analyses. *International Journal of Electrical Power & Energy Systems*, *33*(8), 1498–1505. doi:10.1016/j.ijepes.2011.06.034

Konstantino, O., Malamaki, K.-N., Gallos, K., Tsitsimelis, A., Dikaiakos, C., Gkavanoudis, S., & Demou, C. (2020, February 18*)*. *Ancillary Services Market Design in Distribution Networks*. Retrieved from https://www.mdpi.com/1996-1073/13/4/917/pdf

Lopes, J. P., Hatziargyriou, N., Mutale, J. D., & Jenkins, N. (2007). Integrating distributed generation into electric power systems: A review of drivers, challenges and opportunities. *Electric Power Systems Research*, *77*(9), 1189–1203. doi:10.1016/j.epsr.2006.08.016

Masters, G. M. (2013). *Renewable and Efficient Electric Power Systems. Hobkens, New Jersy*. John Wiley & Sons.

Nakicenovic, N., Grubler, A., & McDonald, A. (1998). *Global Energy Perspectives*. Cambridge University Press.

NICEIC. (2020, January 1). *NICEIC-and-ECA-2021-Vision-Report*. Retrieved from https://www.niceic.com/Niceic.com/media/Press-Photos/NICEIC-and-ECA-2021-Vision-Report.pdf

Nicholas, S. (2009). *A Blueprint for a Safer Planet: How to Manage Climate Change and Create a New Era of Progress and Prosperity*. Random House.

Onyeji-Nwogu, I., Bazilian, M., & Moss, T. (2017, May 1). *The Digital Transformation and Disruptive Technologies: Challenges and Solutions for the Electricity Sector in African Markets*. Retrieved from Center for Global Development: https://www.cgdev.org/publication/challenges-and-solutions-electricity-sector-african-markets

Roy Billinton, R. N. (1984). *Reliability Evaluation of Power Systems*. Pitman Advanced Publishing Program. doi:10.1007/978-1-4615-7731-7

Roy Billinton, R. N. (1992). *Reliability Evaluation of Engineering Systems*. Springer Science Business Media, LLC. doi:10.1007/978-1-4899-0685-4

Schein, E. H. (1996). Career anchors revisited: Implications for career development in the 21st century. *The Academy of Management Perspectives*, *10*(4), 80–88. doi:10.5465/ame.1996.3145321

Schramm, G. (2006). Electric power in developing countries: status, problems, prospects. *Annual Review of Power*, 307-333.

Stoll, H. (2007). *Least-Cost Electric Utility Planning*. John Wiley & Sons.

The U.S. Energy Information Administration. (2020, January 29). *Annual Energy Outlook 2020 with projections to 2050*. Retrieved from https://www.eia.gov/outlooks/aeo/pdf/AEO2020%20Full%20Report.pdf

Thomson, J. (2020, April 1). *Power-and-utilities-industry-outlook*. Deloitte. Retrieved August 1, 2020, from https://www2.deloitte.com/us/en/pages/energy-and-resources: https://www2.deloitte.com/us/en/pages/energy-and-resources/articles/power-and-utilities-industry-outlook.html

Vezzoli, C., Ceschin, F., Osanjo, L., M'Rithaa, M. K., Moalosi, R., Nakazibwe, V., & Diehl, J. C. (2018). *Designing Sustainable Energy for All: Sustainable Product-Service System Design Applied to Distributed Renewable Energy*. Springer International Publishing AG. doi:10.1007/978-3-319-70223-0

Wang, E. (2008). Outage costs and strategy analysis for hi-tech industries. *International Journal of Quality & Reliability Management, 19*(8-9), 1068–1078.

Wang, P., Billinton, R., & Goel, L. (2002). nreliability cost assessmentof an electric power system using reliability network equivalent approaches. *IEEE Transactions on Power Systems, 17*(3), 49–556.

Wikipedia. (2020, June 13). *Ancillary_services_(electric_power)*. Retrieved from https://en.wikipedia.org: https://en.wikipedia.org/wiki/Ancillary_services_(electric_power)

Wolde-Rufael, Y. (2006). Electricity consumption and economic growth: A time series experience for 17 African countries. *Energy Policy, 34*(10), 1106–1114. doi:10.1016/j.enpol.2004.10.008

Zinaman, O., & Miller, M. (2015, February 1). Retrieved August 15, 2020, from https://www.nrel.gov/docs/fy15osti/62611.pdf

Zinaman, O., Miller, M., & Adil, A. (2015, February 1). *Power Systems of the Future*. Retrieved from https://www.nrel.gov/docs/fy15osti/62611.pdf

ADDITIONAL READING

Billinton, R., & Wacker, L. (2007). *Rural distribution system reliability worth evaluation using individual customer outage cost characteristics. Power Systems Research Group*. University of Saskatche-wan.

Hamachi, K., & Eto, H. (2006). *Cost of power interruptions to electricity consumers in the United States. The International Journal ofEnergy, Department of Energy*. DOE.

Helseth, A., & Holen, A. T. (2008). Impact of energy end use and customer interruption cost on constrained distribution networks. *IEEE Transactions on Power Delivery*, 1. doi:10.1109/TPWRD.2007.909215

Lawton, L. (2006). *A framework and review of customer outage costs: integration and analysis of electric utility outage cost surveys*. Lawrence Berkeley National Laboratory.

KEY TERMS AND DEFINITIONS

Distributed Renewable Energy Resources (DRESs): New power generation systems that are increasingly connected within the transmission and distribution systems, causing the gradual decommissioning of the conventional synchronous generators.

Distribution: The distribution grid is responsible for the electrification of the loads connected to the medium and low voltage.

Forecasting of Demand: An accurate preparation of the power and energy demands that will help in designing the required infrastructure for the future expectations.

Generation: The process of generating power based on statistical analysis, and reliability indices to ensure continuous energy supply.

Outage: The expected average number of days per year during which the system is being on outages, i.e. load exceeds the available generating capacity.

Power System: An electric power system consists of a set of components interconnected with each other in some purposeful and meaningful manner.

Reliability: The object of a reliability evaluation is to derive suitable measures, criteria and indices of reliable and dependable performance based on components outage data and configuration.

Renewable Energy: The energy that can be generated from renewable resources such as Wind and waterfalls. It can affect the procurement, development, operation, and maintenance of the distribution grid.

Transmission: Networks to interconnect these systems and transfer power between their load centers in case of emergencies and power shortages.

Chapter 17
The Transformation of Supplier-Client Relationship:
Real Stories About Tire Business Solutions

Ghassan Wahbe
BridgeStone, UAE

ABSTRACT

Industry 4.0 has affected everything around us. Today we have entered an era where we must move our focus away from traditional business relations and shift instead to solutions that support the virtual enterprise in which independent businesses align to share skills and resources to sharpen their responses to external business opportunities. Manufacturers, suppliers, and clients need to work jointly to create value and share risk instead of settings tight conditions, KPIs that are hard to implement, and start blaming each other. Business solutions are representing a new wave that is built on technology to overcome the inward-looking nature of old systems and promises a great wave of efficiency and reduced costs by streamlining the management processes of external relationships that is based on trust and governed by innovative contracts. This chapter is describing a real virtual enterprise from the business showing how digital transformation is changing the supplier-client contracting relationship.

INTRODUCTION

During the three previous industrial revolutions, plenty of behaviors has emerged to drive efficiency through high levels of standardization, forcing business units and functions to work with common processes. This led to large scale elimination of headcount, especially in administrative tasks, and heralded the era of large-scale outsourcing. When it comes to managing external relationships, systems and processes tends to become a constraint. It was designed to streamline internal operations and since each organization has its own system and it was hard for systems to communicate, even worse they compete. That was a growing problem.

DOI: 10.4018/978-1-7998-4501-0.ch017

Ironically, plenty of the behaviors that cause the success in the past era, need to break down as a result of Industry 4.0 or the digital transformation. Today, business performance relies predominantly on the strength and efficiency of external relationships and the quality of communications and data flows between suppliers and clients. Indeed, there is now increasing focus not only on direct relationships, but rather across entire supply networks or ecosystems. In some cases, this is driven by issues of cost or competitive advantage, in others it is increasingly due to regulatory requirements, reputational risk or market challenges.

The purpose of this chapter is to show how solid partnership and collaboration between the supplier and client will result in a win/win situation that will benefit both entities. Such a partnership is crucial especially with the technology advancement and the need to have more focus on details. The chapter illustrate this situation with a real case from the tire industry in Saudi Arabia.

BACKGROUND

According to (Schwertner, 2017), the ability to digitally reimagine the business is determined in large part by a clear digital strategy supported by leaders who foster a culture able to change and invent the new. New information-technology-based capabilities make it possible to achieve systematic and dramatic gains in business performance (Davidson, 1993). New approaches to business transformation are emerging to address significant need and to serve as successors to reengineering, which has acquired a reputation for being slow and ineffective (Cheyunski F, 1998). These approaches require new, innovative methods that target, integrate, and rapidly implement total business solutions. According to (Groen & Walsh, 2013), many see emerging technologies as a solution vector for the global challenges of the twenty-first century.

As per (Mirani, Moore, & Weber, 2001), suppliers have traditionally managed their relationships in the indirect reseller channel using inefficient, labor-intensive communications processes. Trust and collaboration are key for today business. "Business collaboration" is the great oxymoron of corporate sustainability (Nidumolu, Ellison, Whalen, & Billman, 2014). Organizations focus on trust and collaboration in their pursuit of innovation (Hattori & Lapidus, 2004). (Shaw, 1997) shows how lack of trust is compromising more and more organizations in today's highly competitive environment. The constant development of the automotive industry is inextricably linked to the emergence of larger amounts of tires (Ślusarczyk, Baryń, & Kot, 2016). Looking at this literature, it will be clearly shown that the tire industry like others are moving in the direction of business solutions that are using emerging technologies to create more value. This will require innovative contracting to manage the partnership effectively.

THE BUSINESS SOLUTIONS

This is being applied in different business sectors to handle the network of partners, suppliers, and service centers efficiently. Business solutions are representing a new wave that is built on technology to overcome the inward-looking nature of old systems and promises a great wave of efficiency and reduced costs by streamlining the management processes of external relationships that is based on trust and governed by innovative contracts.

Why Business Solutions Are Important?

In this industry 4.0 era, everyone is talking about business solution. There is different definition that can describe this new terminology of a business solution, but the following can be the most precise: a business solution is a combination of ideas used to help a company achieve its objectives (Kemp, 2009). A business solution comes usually to join the traditional silos comprising marketing, payroll, provided services, auditing, accounting market research and analysis to generate new business value that includes all essential business activities. Businessmen set up companies to solve specific business problems. They specialize in each niche depending on the problems in the market. A business problem is a need that a company strives to provide.

Businesses solutions correct the deficiency of the missing needs in a society. Some relevant solutions include technology evaluation, strategic planning, and the synthesis of complex business information. Businesses develop strategies that are action-oriented to expand the international and domestic markets. Businesses need to identify and manage new property, identify opportunities for growth and leverage technology to serve the customers. Companies restructure their operations and implement changes within their management and operation structures to provide business solutions efficiently. Through these efforts, businesses grow their revenues through marketing, strategic reorganizations, and partnerships.

Do We Really Need Business Solution to Handle the Company-Client Relations?

There is a great importance of intelligent business solutions to empower company-client relations. Companies have embraced new methodologies in adapting to bigger, more dynamic business principles. In a modern world dominated by technology and growing benchmarks for mobilizing financial growth, national to international enterprises continue to find ways making their business accessible for their employees and prized clients.

Truthfully, major corporations install powerful business solutions to increase the communication wavelengths between employee and client – this set-up gives companies flexibility without exhausting resources on expensive modules and prepares employees to the demand imposed by high standards brought by policies dependent on technology and transmission.

Significant breakthroughs within the core of business solutions include the ability of individual employees to efficiently transmit or relay information to key clients. Companies have opened its gates for its employees to remain productive even if they're away from their workstations or conference tables. Effective business solutions motivate employees to focus on important tasks, fueling company growth in the process.

Where to Apply Business Solutions?

The next important thing to know if the business solutions relations with business sectors. It's important to know that a business solution has turned as reel need to majority of sectors, in automotive sector, this business solution has become not just an added value to the whole work process but rather as indispensable need to maintain the business.

The tire industry will not be able to move through without injecting technology in every part, starting from planning and manufacturing, up to the level of distribution and the end customer relation management and this is really happening in every part today.

What Are the Components of a Business Solution in the Tire Industry?

Taking tires as example, where most manufacturers strived to provide the customers with latest advanced solution rather than being a product provider only. It could create a major change in the business model itself, change it from the traditional one known as product provider to a totally new model of service provider including the product.

In the traditional business model, the manufacturer chooses an exclusive supplier or limited number of dealers in each country who sell the tire products to the final client through distribution points. The manufactures continue to support his dealers occasionally and ask for sales increase.

In automotive field, specifically in tires, most of suppliers have turned today as service providers in bid to survive in the market, and in order to maintain their business amid severe competition and huge dumping in the global open markets. The manufacturer has opened communication channels with the major clients to sense their needs and get close feedback.

Introducing A Basket of Solutions

Recently, manufacturers are approaching the clients, mainly the fleets, with basket of solutions that provide safer, more sustainable, and efficient mobility behaviors. Commercial Fleet operators are under constant pressure to maximize their fleet performance whilst minimizing costs. Business solution are offering, combining premium products, extensive services and state of the art digital platforms to provide fleet customers with safer, more sustainable and economically feasible solutions. Such solution is expected to have three components:

Enhancing the Products

Reducing tire costs starts with getting the maximum out of tires' total life. Total tire life is geared around a long first life thanks to superior design features, offering long-lasting robust casing to deliver multiple lives, and multiple retread lives with retread solution. With innovative designs, the manufacturers can help fleet to minimize tire costs over their entire lifecycle.

Adding Services

Increasing preventive maintenance will have a direct impact on the reduction of operational cost. Extensive services include everything fleet need to keep their operations at maximum efficiency: maintenance with tire inspections, monitoring and assistance services provided by the worldwide network of professional technical advice, casing management, and more.

Introducing Digital Platforms

Digital technologies are at the core of value proposition to fleet customers. The combination of digital platforms tailored to individual customer's needs, enable the tire industry to answer the fleets largest pain points around asset tracking, safety, and operational efficiency. Data driven, customized products and service offerings allow for increased vehicle uptime and maximized tire's total life.

UNDERSTANDING A FLEET SOLUTION

Business is becoming more agile and fragile that it requires speed interaction with market changes and challenges. With the current COVID-19 pandemic, now more than ever, it is important to leverage fleet intelligence solutions. (Geotab, 2020). New business models of ride hailing services such as Uber, and ride sharing services are requiring different management similarly are the new approach of subscription model, where a customer subscribes to a class of vehicle, and trades individual vehicles for use according to the day's needs.

Clients and fleet operators are looking to have better data flow in relation to their vehicles, better services without hiring and training a big staff to handle sophisticated technologies and systems. In addition, the business owners are looking for fewer capital expenditures (Capex), more operational expenditures (Opex), reduced costs and enhanced cash flow.

What Are the Dynamics for Fleet Solution?

The goal of systems thinking and system dynamics modeling is to improve the understanding of the ways in which an organization's performance is related to its internal structure and operating policies, including those of customers, competitors, and suppliers and then to use that understanding to design high leverage policies for success. (Sterman, 2000).

There's a rising trend in recent years where companies seek to expand globally and grow more of their service businesses (Erika, 2013). There are many elements companies need to look at such as business practices, regulations, customer preferences, contracts rules, infrastructure and business environments. Tire and fleet industry are not an exception.

In the late 1960s, Firestone Tire & Rubber was one of the best managed companies in its industry. But when French tire maker Michelin introduced the radial tire and shook up the United States market, professor Donald Sull writes that "Firestone's historical success proved its own worst enemy". (Sull, 2000). Today the tire industry needs to continue adapting as autonomous and electric vehicles become more popular (Brown, 2018).

Between those two events, the tire industry has passed through changing business dynamics that affects it dramatically. The global automotive tire market is slated to experience a dynamic growth period owing to the increasing number of innovations in the manufacturing of tires. (Fortune Business Insights, 2019). For example, Goodyear came up with their BH 03 concept tire in 2015, designed to generate electricity through interaction of the materials in the tire. The product is aimed at enhancing the efficiency and capabilities of electric cars. Michelin developed its Vision concept tire that can be 3D printed from biomaterials, is rechargeable, and never blows out. Bridgestone develops technology to reduce tire weight by 10%. (Evans, 2019). Such innovations significantly elevate the market potential and grease the wheels of the global automotive tire market revenues.

Technology, business behaviors, and end user expectations have also changed dramatically. Car manufacturers are looking for enhanced partnerships to cope up with new vehicle types such as autonomous cars which require introduce new challenges for tire manufacturers as they are dealing with additional weights, variable speeds, less rolling resistance and require tires with sensor properties that are able to check pressure and temperature.

What Are the Expected Effects on the Supplier and the Client?

Looking at the major changes, there will be several important changes that affect the client and supplier sides. Business solutions have affected fundamental aspects of both sides and here are some of them.

Total Cost of Ownership

Every solution package has certain cost that need to be added on the total service contract quotation. It is not the cost of the tire only that a hauler need to pay, but it's rather the cost of the full package menu that includes, but not limited to, reporting, headcount's cost, technology related expenses, on site breakdown services in addition to the tire itself.

Cash Flow Status

With this drastic change of business flow, many things have been changed accordingly, and so is the cash flow as well. The hauler has previously to pay to tire's suppliers, rims' supplier, mounting or dismounting expenses to different tires' shops, and of course the high expenses of the staff who was operating and supervising the workshops; it was a big headache to allocate the jobs to the technicians, train them and provide the technical tools as required.

All these costs are now included in one single billed package. With this new business model, owners can easily review and follow-up their expenses, and even save. Time and effort that is given to one single supplier can enable the owners to free themselves to other vital aspect of their daily operation.

The customer can be serviced now through paying monthly amounts compared to unscheduled payments of the traditional solution. Supplier on the other hand will need to hire, build, or rent new service centers and equip them with necessary staff and machines. However, he can enjoy the rotation of some equipment based on his customers base and requirement also he may be able to share these workshops to serve multiple customers.

Return on Investment

Mobile business solutions allow transporters saving time and money providing easy access to relevant data and synchronizing the storage and retrieval of data with complete access control of all the systems. Moreover, employers can gain control of overtime pay and ensure actual work hours are being completed benefiting from timely and accurate data flow. Actually, related applications can be recording all the details such as employee shift start/end time and breaks, truck's start/end trip, service life of each tire on each axle, operation status of each tire, defects report, time spent to change/ air check tires among much other details

Since all the data is captured with time and location stamps. organizations can measure what materials really are consumed on a project and use the time data to develop an accurate history of the length and costs of the project and work rates based on this accurate information. This will help with better quality control and to align with operational cost and strategy planning to eliminate or replace certain routes, functionalities or machines.

User Satisfaction Indices

One of the big benefits is the business processes optimization. A digital and mobile business solution allows client teams to upload reports, forms, documents, and orders with just one click, wherever they are. This technology helps to reduce entry errors and miscommunications which can cost the business time and money. Mobile solutions can also improve the efficiency of an organization and increase productivity.

The flexibility that mobility provides pays off by increasing operational speed of employees. As everything is done through a mobile device with just a few clicks, the process speeds up. Being able to access their work on any device from anywhere increases their efficiency, and eventually delivers better results. This is a valuable improved data accuracy in between hauler's hands.

The digital mobile solutions allow transportations' companies to gather all their data in one place, saving the time spent on data entry and analysis. Consolidating businesses information with a digital mobile solution will also help them to reduce the use of paper forms and to increase the accuracy of the data collected. It can also secure your data storage.

What Are the Expected Benefits Out of Fleet Solutions?

The general aim of fleet solutions is to achieve a punch of benefits which include:

- Reduce fuel costs through the monitoring of fuel usage
- Implement targeted training to improve driver behavior for a safer fleet
- Control access to vehicles for improved security
- Reduce asset theft through live tracking
- Monitor trips to implement better route planning and job assignment
- Meet strict regulations relevant to our both companies
- Track and manage driver hours electronically for better compliance
- Practice preventative maintenance to keep vehicles serviced and safe
- Get visual evidence for crash investigations

REAL BUSINESS CASE SCENARIOS

As we all know, tires was always considered as one of main spending aspect in any fleet, we are going to see a successful case that was implemented in the Kingdom of Saudi Arabia, where operators could witness tremendous benefits upon implementing a solid solution based on technology and collaboration contracting into their business.

One of biggest diary's and juice manufactures in the entire GCC (Gulf Cooperation Council) which owns huge space of farms, warehouses and logistics has entered a period of restructuring and reinvestment that took it from a decentralized structure to a centralized structure.

The aim basically was to establish an efficient, low-cost production so that the consumers can enjoy high-quality products at an affordable price. Benefiting from technology innovations and collaboration contracting. This was never an easy job, in order to reach that goal, there was a long way to go.

As the centralized structure was mature in its architecture and management style to achieve their goals. Delegation of authorities to each department has been widely granted in bid to enable heads of these departments to apply no-cost enhancement programs as an approach to achieve feasible business enhancement while maintaining cost or even attaining cost reduction in their departments.

The customer declared that the best way to enhance service and save money is to find solutions that can bring them more benefits, less expenditure, and to make all parties winners. Every department head has started searching for solid partners who can provide happy trustworthy partnership that can achieve the management goals and strategies while being able to think innovatively and make a profit for himself.

Part of the transformation was to investigate the fleet management that is handling delivery cycle of diary and juice which make more than 100,000 trips a year. This factory is using more than 8,000 vehicles of all sizes, including huge trucks. It is well known that petrol, tires, and oil are the most spending areas for any fleet. The tire supplier proposed a total change in the tire related mechanisms which take the client, the vendor along with manufacturer to a totally new era.

Before, these years, the supplier responsibility was limited to sell tires to the client, dispatch their orders and deliver them to their warehouses. In limited cases, the supplier was offering some free check services for the injured used tires.

The proposed solution has moved the supplier from a product seller to a solution provider in which the products have become part of our service package that are offered to mega big fleets among this region. Such a movement is crucial considering the transformations occurring, the technology advancement and customers willingness to partnership and move to specialized managed services.

More specific, the proposed solution was designed to supply full fledge services along with tires, the solution includes but not limited to:

- Supplying tires as per the measured actual needs considering a set of precise rules and measures instead of manual inspection or periodic changes
- Monitoring the mounting of the tires as per the technical recommendation, and keeping this mount under tight control and enhancement cycle
- Handle all kind of tires' related maintenance utilizing special tools and taking the partners far from the small details that was consuming considerable time, cost and labor in the old setup.
- Consolidating the tire ecosystem supply and payment, thus instead of paying one supplier for the tires, and paying others for rims, filters, mounting services, alignment, and engine set-up, it was gone all in one basket.

As part of the project the customer have moved the ownership of related workshops to the supplier to do everything related to tires' servicing. This includes total handling, monitoring tires performance for each truck, reporting all the details remotely via handheld devices. The accurate data started flowing into the main data center in a timely manner which allowed the customer to log in and check a wealth information such as cost per truck.

The project shows a great value to the customer, and it was an opportunity to seize these fleets with a partner and enjoy great benefits. Headcounts were reduced, the headache of communications with many suppliers was eliminated along with other positive effects that resulted in major savings of time, money, and resources.

This transformation of the company makes the return to previous era an unacceptable thing as they recognize the huge benefits. We know that stepping ahead with such advanced solutions and the evolution of technologies and mindsets have already changed this market, which will not allow returning back to previous methods. This was proved with this client and it was a best occasion to implement a lot of our theories, strategies and actions that is leading ultimately to serve the client in a better way, with lower cost and enhanced efficiencies which make a real great success.

The Road for Success

This success has passed into many stages, phases and action items. Digital innovation is at the core of every business and through solutions suppliers aim to deliver value to their customers by proactively anticipating and addressing their needs and expectations. However, transformation is always a journey that require careful consideration and milestone planning to go through. The business solution journey with the customers passed multiple stages:

Stage 1: Building on Trust and Solid Capabilities

Business partnerships need to be established on trust. When such a big client needs to sign a service deal thy will need to trust their future partner, especially when it comes to a daily operation that can halt the full business. In this case, the supplier was trusted because of the solid name of the manufacturer being represented in addition to the long relationship with this customer full of positive outcomes through the years. The supplier himself have a solid status, full confidence in their products and several implementations around the globe.

Stage 2: Seizing Up the Opportunity and the Customer Pains

It was never easy for a big diary's company to handles all the details pertains to their fleet's workshops allocated in all over the Kingdom of Saudi Arabia and across the Gulf region. Each of these truck trailers needs to have special attention while operating, each peace in the truck has a different service life and so is the tire. Since it's touching the surfaces of the roads the tire can encounter any road hazard or injury that can get it defected and will surely influence the operation, suspend the trip and may be damage the stock inside. This is the worst scenario ever can a milk and diary's hauler face during the operation hour especially in tough circumstances of a country like Saudi-Arabia where temperature can exceed the 50 degrees with a very long span from east to west and north to south.

Under such circumstances an urgent breakdown service is considered as number one pain for such fleet is to detect when and where exactly to expect a sudden defect and how to rescue the situation. This is where the added value of the business solution came from. The client doesn't want to wait for the problem but rather work to prevent it from happening or at least provide a timely fix. With the full menu of services provided by supplier and the associated tools and IoT sensors the failure can be expected, or at least detected at the early beginning. The control center and the driver can be notified to take immediate responses.

Stage 3: Collecting Data and Building Viable Scenarios

In order to have best fleet management, supplier must know all about the mountains of data available with even the most basic tracking and reporting systems. With all this data, it can be tough for the client to determine by his end, where to start and what information is the most important.

As supplier we can't manage the clients' fleet in the dark. Data can shed light on the client operations, exposing weaknesses and illuminating opportunities for improvement. As a supplier we can help in knowing how to effectively leverage data management which is the are many operations are struggling in. As a supplier we manage to utilize the right technologies to capture data and build the intelligence that can be used to boost bottom lines and enjoy myriad other benefits out of these data.

Fleet management technology can gather the important data, help to measure what matters, and enable you to obtain greater value from daily operations through smart changes. Investing in the right technology is the easiest and most effective way to constantly gather and use evolving fleet analytics.

The client's data must be integrated and actionable for the supplier's business to enjoy real returns. Fleet data has never to be ignored, otherwise, we'll be missing an enormous opportunity to boost efficiency, increase the safety of the client fleets, save money, and much more.

The supplier has collected and structured tons of data to get the most out of these fleet management data, and then utilized data science analytics to generate value and plan correctly utilizing proven tips and techniques.

Stage 4: Identifying the Key Performance Indicators (KPIs)

Turning data into an actionable measure is one of the greatest tools to gauge the performance, this happens by seizing the KPI of each entity. The supplier must set list of KPI that can be really SMART (Specific, Measurable, Attainable, Relevant, and Time-Bound) so that the client can track and measure. Utilizing the right business intelligence toolset, the client can get reports every week about the KPI's of the fleet turning their raw data into insight for his advantage. In this case, meaningful KPIs include:

- **Daily Out of Service Trucks:** This number must get always decreased and it's one of best KPI that can tell how good the solution is.
- **Air Pressure Compliance:** Fundamental action, any wrong reading means there are issues in the maintenance.
- **Cost Per Hour:** For individual vehicle, this indicator incorporates both how much it costs to operate an individual truck and how frequently that asset is being utilized. This indicator is of great help in identifying fleets which are expensive as compared to other fleets which are performing the same duty. Cost per hour indicator places all fleets on the same level, thus allowing fleet managers to replace the ones that exceed the set goals. Based on previous data, this cost must show decline after the solution is implemented.
- **Cost Per Unit:** Another great KPI that gives an insight about the operating cost of each asset within the fleet. Cost per unit helps in examining maintenance cost of each vehicle in the fleet.

This can assist fleet managers in removing expensive, unsustainable, problematic, and high maintenance assets.

- **Fuel Economy per Asset:** using this as a performance indicator can help fleet managers identify fleets which indicate high fuel consumption which can be indicators on certain behaviors like speeding and unnecessary idling which the drivers can be trained to avoid.
- **Empty Miles:** A truck driving back empty to the original point after making a delivery is known as deadheading, and the distance travelled when empty is known as empty mileage. Getting a clear picture of empty miles and how fleets are used daily can help fleet managers in optimizing asset utilization and thereby reducing the wasted miles.
- **Preventive Maintenance Compliance:** Completing scheduled maintenance of fleets promptly is an essential thing for fleet managers. Vehicles within the fleet must be repaired regularly to lower long-term maintenance costs and the fleet downtime. This performance indicator helps to track the preventive maintenance practices and gives fleet managers the capability to schedule and undertake maintenance practices on time. In an advanced stage, service provider can rather help client to determine whether buy, retain, rent, or lease and asset.
- **Number of Open Repair Orders:** Too many orders means a weak maintenance behaviors on the road side and data inspection. Such information needs to be very clear to operators and partners to boost efficiency and enhance planning and budgeting.

Additional KPIs include total cost per mile, parts cost per mile, tire cost per mile, fuel cost per mile, miles per gallon, idle time percentage. Even more, the supplier can even develop KPIs around cost per case delivered, cost per delivery, cost per cube, cost per pound of product delivered. In further step the supplier can set KPIs that measure performance that have an indirect effect on cost such as on-time delivery rate, Occupational Safety and Health Administration (OSHA) accident frequency and maintenance facility audit scores.

Stage 5: Negotiating the Deal and Making Consensus

Here is where the supplier and the client need to realize a win-win negotiation, to do so, the supplier make multiple offers simultaneously along with different level of service menus. Also, contingent agreement is badly needed sometimes, especially when clients have different beliefs about the likelihood of future events. The service supplier might be convinced that his firm will deliver a project on time and under budget, for example, but the client may view this proposal as unrealistic. In such situations, a contingent agreement—negotiated "if, then" promises aimed at reducing risk about future uncertainty—offers a way for parties to agree to disagree while still moving forward, to reach Good for You, Great for Me basis (Win-Win Negotiation). Supplier might even propose paying specified penalties for turning the project in late or agree to significantly lower rates if supplier go over budget.

Stage 6: Customer/Vendor Mindset Challenges

Changing mindset of the client after spending years in doing the same routine in his way, is something very challenging, the supplier often work to identify customer expectations. Interview their operational staff and trying to grasp their frustration, and understand, from their perspective, what they are expecting and what's driving it. It was crucial to engage such people in designing the agreement, evaluating processes, and designing measures, to build a common future.

Stage 7: Making Internal Adjustments and New Partnerships

The supplier was supplying tires only. Today, with this complication of total business solution, the supplier need to provide the client with all related tools to reduce their headache and to enrich his basket menu, with this stage, the supplier had to conduct wide consensus and agreement with rims' suppliers, spare-parts suppliers, oil, mounting, dismounting tools and machineries. With these new partnerships, the supplier could only win the contract with this mega diary fleet.

Stage 8: Building Working Prototypes and Identifying Touch Points

Prototypes are one of the most important steps in the design and contracting process. Integrating prototyping deeply into creative process can be transformative. It can make for a more positive, enriching team culture. One basic definition of prototype is a simulation or sample version of a final product, which is used for testing prior to launch. The goal of a prototype is to test products and services before sinking lots of time and money into the final product. Prototyping is essential for resolving usability issues before launch. It can also reveal areas that need improvement.

The supplier did not stop at reporting to client they are doing, nor they stop themselves by conducting seminars. The supplier went to the extra mile ahead and invited the client to visit Osaka city in Japan, where to show him a prototype real case of total fleet management and grant the client's staff a live opportunity on how it works, what are the pros and cons of each detail, having this type of interaction can also facilitate the real penetration to the client.

The Implementation Phase

The implementation of the total tire solution was not an easy task, several steps were designed carefully, tailored for this specific case, and implemented under a wide-open eye of higher management of the manufacturer, the supplier, and the client. Additionally, there were subsequent stages to measure real performance and enhance the quality of this solution, considering that project was the first of its size in the region. Several phases where necessary along the implementation path.

Mobilization Phase

Right after signing the contract, the supplier must reallocate some technical staffs, set new mobile workshops in site, and deliver main necessary machines that can help in deploying the operation phase. It was crucial to decide who will handle what by when and to build the communication route between various entities such as workshops, offices, suppliers, and client.

Paradigm Shift Phase

True collaboration and a paradigm shift are crucial to have business solutions running smoothly. In the traditional model of outsourcing, it was the mindset of "What's in it for ME" but in business solutions the mindset switches to "What's in it for WE." The focus goes from getting the supplier to meet the client needs to both parties finding a way to meet both of their needs.

Instead of saying it's in the contract and it's their problem, the mindset goes to working together to achieve performance and compensation goals. Culture and attitude are everything, and in such situations, it is important to go away from blame and punish environment, or push/pull environment to and open line of communication, where both parties work together to find solutions. Both parties need to be aiming toward positive integrated planning and communications to avoid unpleasant surprises or communicating that are triggered by problems.

To see the benefits of such agreements it can be truly a huge leap of faith for those who have done business with service providers the traditional way. The contract, the business model and the business relationship need to evolve around such new mindset in which collaboration is at the heart. It is vital to shift the paradigm so that everyone truly feel that they have a shared focus on results, continuous improvement, and solutions.

This attitude was built from day one. If there is anything inapplicable, the service provider and the client have to set a meeting and check countermeasures plan to solve it out, especially at first stage, as this is the time to see what indeed is applicable and what not.

Deployment Phase

In this solution the supplier can benefit from the fact that fuel and tires remain _even after implementing a perfect solution_ the key factors and major contributors to fleet's overall operating and maintenance expenses, but with big saving comparing to what was before. Partnership between tire manufacturers, suppliers and clients goes much beyond the supply of new tires.

The supplier has recommended a tailored made program and offer right solution packages by understanding needs of each individual fleet operation. Upon implementing the program, the supplier constantly strive to bring the operation cost down by not only supplying premium products but through offering professional solutions, technology tools and tracking systems. In addition to regular approach through defined tire check services, monitoring programs and close interaction with fleet operators. These continuous activities benefit fleet operators in improving operational efficiency and enhance safety of operation.

The Deployed Components

While every solution should be user friendly and designed with user experience in mind, the complexity is being moved to the heat of the solution where a lot of components, processes and technologies are interacting to make the difference.

The fleet solution that was implemented to the client has many components that are working in harmony to achieve the desired value This basket of solution concept is aimed at providing professional consultancy and customized solution packages to every client, thereby; benefitting him in reducing operation cost and helping him to run business at optimized efficiency. In this particular case the solution was composed of the following components:

The Utilization of Emerging Technologies

A solution was created for yard management as a comprehensive package that includes a full range of premium fleet solution services to address customers' needs. Using the latest IoT (Internet of Things) and cloud technologies facilitates fleet management and enhances operational efficiency. The combination of sensors and a new cloud-based engine enables real-time monitoring of tire pressure and temperature, with a high degree of accuracy and instant alerts when vehicles enter the depot.

Asset management applications utilized a tire audit and performance tracking to deliver end-to-end asset management capabilities to the customers. This allows the client to instantly access tire information to analyze and make informed decisions on optimal tire maintenance and selection.

The system automatically alerts service managers and drivers via email or SMS when abnormal tire air pressure and/or temperature is detected. This positively impact the customers' daily business operations through reduction of tire maintenance costs and occurrences of tire-related breakdowns.

Equipment Selection

In the equipment part, the supplier has introduced a fully loaded package of professional and skilled mobile services for truck tires that can reach every doorstep. The mobile workshop team bring the most specialized and expert assistance to help reduce the client's operating expense. From a single truck to a fleet of heavy vehicles, there should be a team of professionals who are ever ready to serve with the most advanced equipment.

Price Solution

As the service transformation might require high capital expenditure (Capex) at first place to install new equipment and provide necessary services, the supplier have started a marketing initiative that aims to facilitate the understanding of the service offer to the end user while highlighting its uniqueness by stressing its value to the fleet. The price solution was based on three components:

- **Monitor** every fleet with a specific workshop and require only periodical technical support on how to improve on the tire maintenance. In here the supplier acts as a consultant by conducting some tire check service, scrap analysis, prepare report with recommendations and advice fleets on areas to improve on.
- **Maintain** fleets that have already outsourced the tire maintenance services but do not require a high level of reporting thus concentrating on their core business. Here the supplier will provide all tire servicing works such as mounting, balancing, rotation, alignment, repairs at the truck tire center facility or on-site services by assist mobile truck service vans.
- **Manage** the data driven fleets to enable the outsourcing of the entire tire maintenance and require high level of reporting and visibility on every tire. The supplier will provide full range of tire servicing works and comprehensive casing management with individual tire tracking from cradle to grave through necessary tools and submit report to customer

Network Solutions

To collect all necessary information, the supplier used a sophisticated on-board computer, equipped with a fleet management software that collects and transmits driver and vehicle data. An online fleet tracking and information portal will be able to consolidate and analyze all such data then gives access to the authorized member of the client team.

Providing the fleet with emerging technologies related to tire management helped the client to track their tires from cradle to grave, provided various useful reports to understand the performance of each tire and related tire maintenance issue. That was just an amazing utilization of data analytics and data science.

Knowledge Sharing

As continuous training and education is crucial for any transformation program, part of the program was to get people engaged and inspired through continuously enhancing the tire operational knowledge and updating the team with information on the trucking industry and various training programs related to tires.

Upon implementation of the solutions, the supplier needs to keep eying the KPIs and check periodically what was achieved and what not, it was committed for instance that out of service trucks, cost per Kilometer in addition to multiple parameters that are shared with the client.

Product Solutions

With a total solution there will be a need for comprehensive line up of tires for trucks and other vehicles tailored to suit all commercial tire requirement. The manufacturer decides to go with three major categories:

- Main Tire stream
    - Casings that are built to last
    - Maximizing the life of your tires and thus minimizing costs
    - Ingeniously built, using the most advanced technologies
    - Strong structure, Increasing the stability, durability, and multiple retread ability of tires.
- New design tires
    - A long first life, without compromising on performance and safety.
    - Renowned quality.
    - Complete range of steer, drive, and trailer tires, covering all sizes, applications and seasons.
    - Low rolling resistance tires for increased fuel savings and reduced environmental impact.
- Retreaded tires:
    - Similar performance to new, at 30% lower cost. With no compromise on safety.
    - Retreads at a combined know-how, tread design development and dealer's expert use.

The Contracting Focus

This project has a focus on stated and expected results, not tactics. As both the supplier and the client were engaged in a business model that is focused on benefit realization for both parties there was an increased likelihood of meeting goals and objectives because both parties are focused on results and working together in collaboration to achieve a shared result and reduce risks.

According to (Dutt, 2006), the Solow growth model is an exogenous model of economic growth that analyzes changes in the level of output in an economy over time as a result of changes in the population growth rate, the savings rate, and the rate of technological progress. Mutually beneficial, shared incentives drive innovation and cost effectiveness as stated in Solow's Law.

In Solow's Law, business growth is driven by innovation in the business process or technical improvements in products and services. Traditional contracts focus on labor and physical capital in contrary to innovation contracts which is evolving around problem solving, business relationship, results, and solutions. Now both parties are winners as they are interested in other's success, creating an environment of shared risk and reward.

Innovation and Collaboration

This business case was a real illustration of the innovation in contracting and technologies to create a win/win situation that enable the achievement of business objectives for all involved parties. The win/win situation was realized on ground. The maintenance expenses for the first half after signing the agreement was reduced by 12% despite higher mileage.

Proper positioning and maintenance of the tire led to less tire replacement, so despite the increased unit price of tires, total spending on tires decreased by 6% for first half of the year comparing to same operating period of the previous year.

The relationship between various providers were significantly improved, as dispatching/arrival commitment were always on time. While the client was saving money, he also enjoys less hassles and have more time to focus on other part of the business.

Service Level and Confidentiality Agreements

To ensure common ground and same page of understanding both parties agreed to sign a service level agreement (SLA) that details all service items, however this SLA was unique as it was not based on separate transaction but it focused on the whole solution. Similarly to prevent revealing sensitive information that could jeopardize the business in general, the supplier and client agreed to use confidentiality agreements to protect any innovative ideas, effective processes, unique products, or customer information, this is the main future competitive zone that needs to be protected.

Related Vesting and Collaboration Agreements

Before operating the client's workshops and handle the whole fleets' management, the supplier needed to go and evaluate their old used machineries in order to re-sell them and keep the space free to receive the new ones that are planned and budgeted to handle their workshops, not only the machines, but the computers, servers, mobile vans, safety cage and even the soft renovation for the workshop.

This requires a set of agreement that was discussed and agreed jointly between the client and the supplier. The discussion team composed of legal, technical, sales and subject matter experts to reach the right conclusion.

Building and Sustaining B2B Relationship

This case was a jerking knee that could make or break a long-lasting relationship. If the client was looking for a solution that couldn't be supplied by the supplier this will affect the relation heavily. To enhance the motivations of going into a new business model the supplier set an incentive plan for workers in workshops, rewards for best performers and engage another department as well in this contract.

The client and the supplier plan effectively to overcome any hurdles on the way. Upon kicking off the new contract, the client needs to worry about nothing. Just nothing, supplier's staffs were on ground from day one. Keeping stock in the workshop ready. The supplier was monitoring tires performance for each truck on each axle and creating all needed reports and making sure to put all authorized personnel at client side in the loop.

FUTURE RESEARCH DIRECTIONS

The case study shown in this chapter is presenting a special case of building a viable solution based on emerging technologies, digital transformation mindset and sustainable environment. Trust, collaboration, and innovative contracting plays a major role to reach a stable environment. This chapter presented a case in tire industry and discusses all related parameters from plenty of aspects.

Same situation occurs in every industry where digital transformation is making a huge difference in the way people do business and contract with their clients. Every industry has its unique parameters and directions. In addition to its criteria to measure success and failures.

This is a great opportunity for practitioners and researchers who are willing to investigate similar cases and build a viable scenario that will work across those industries.

CONCLUSION

Digital transformation is challenging all industries as organizations are looking to move from Capex (capital expenditure) to Opex (operational expenditure). Organization also need to hire minimum resources to keep their organizations agile and flexible to accommodate more technologies and ideas. Every industry is gaining plenty of insights while internal and external clients are becoming more demanding.

Emerging technologies are accelerating exponentially and plenty of these technologies can be used in a real-life scenario. The increase in contractors and services will call out for more efficient and innovative contracting. Considering these parameters, this chapter demonstrated an applied case in tire industry which utilizes plenty of dimensions and the final results showed clearly how it was beneficial for the suppliers and for the client to move to emerging technologies and innovative contracting.

REFERENCES

Brown, K. (2018, October 5). Retrieved May 1, 2020, from https://www.rubbernews.com/article/20181005/NEWS/181009951/tire-industry-should-prepare-to-adapt-to-automotive-trends

Cheyunski, F. M. J., & Millard, J. (1998). Accelerated Business Transformation and the Role of the Organization Architect. *The Journal of Applied Behavioral Science*, *34*(3), 268–285. doi:10.1177/0021886398343003

Davidson, W. H. (1993). Beyond re-engineering: The three phases of business transformation. *IBM Systems Journal*, *32*(1), 485–499. doi:10.1147j.321.0065

Dutt, A. K. (2006). Aggregate Demand, Aggregate Supply and Economic Growth. *International Review of Applied Economics*, *20*(3), 319–336. doi:10.1080/02692170600736094

Erika, T. (2013, November 13). Retrieved May 1, 2020, from https://www.hitachi.com/rd/sc/story/business_dynamics/index.html

Evans, R. (2019, June 18). Retrieved May 1, 2020, from https://www.tiretechnologyinternational.com/news/research-development/bridgestone-develops-technology-to-reduce-tire-weight-by-10.html

Fortune Business Insights. (2019, November 6). Retrieved May 1, 2020, from https://www.globenewswire.com/news-release/2019/11/06/1941841/0/en/Automotive-Tire-Market-to-Expand-with-Light-Commercial-Vehicles-Production-Set-to-Reach-118-9-Million-Units-by-2025-Fortune-Business-Insights.html

Geotab. (2020, April 14). Retrieved May 1, 2020, from https://www.geotab.com/blog/impact-of-covid-19/

Groen, A., & Walsh, S. (2013). Introduction to the Field of Emerging Technology Management. *Creativity and Innovation Management*, *22*(1), 1–5. doi:10.1111/caim.12019

Hattori, R. A., & Lapidus, T. (2004). Collaboration, trust and innovative change. *Journal of Change Management*, *4*(2), 97–104. doi:10.1080/14697010320001549197

Kemp, S. (2009, March 26). 6 Steps to Better Business Solutions. *Entrepreneur.*

Mirani, R., Moore, D., & Weber, J. A. (2001). Emerging Technologies for Enhancing Supplier–Reseller Partnerships. *Industrial Marketing Management*, *30*(2), 101–114. doi:10.1016/S0019-8501(00)00135-8

Nidumolu, R., Ellison, J., Whalen, J., & Billman, E. (2014, April 1). The Collaboration Imperative. *Harvard Business Review*, 1–10. PMID:24830283

Schwertner, K. (2017). Digital transformation of business. *The Journal of Supercomputing*, *15*, 388–393.

Shaw, R. (1997). Trust in the Balance: Building Successful Organizations on Results, Integrity, and Concern. *Political Science (Wellington, N.Z.)*, 1–10.

Ślusarczyk, B., Baryń, M., & Kot, S. (2016). Tire Industry Products as an Alternative Fuel. *Polish Journal of Environmental Studies*, *25*(3), 1–8. doi:10.15244/pjoes/61543

Sterman, J. (2000). *Business Dynamics: Systems Thinking and Modeling for a Complex World.* Irwin/McGraw-Hill.

Sull, D. N. (2000, November 27). Retrieved May 1, 2020, from https://hbswk.hbs.edu/archive/the-dynamics-of-standing-still-firestone-tire-and-rubber-and-the-radial-revolution

ADDITIONAL READING

Dallas, G. (Ed.). (2004). Governance and risk. New York: McGraw-Hill companies Inc.

Dutta, A., Peng, G. C., & Choudhary, A. (2013). Risks in enterprise cloud computing: The perspective of IT experts. *Journal of Computer Information Systems*, *53*(4), 39–48. doi:10.1080/08874417.2013.11645649

Grembergen, W. (Ed.). (2003). *Strategies for information technology governance*. Idea Group Publishing.

Vodde, B., & Larman, C. (2010). *Practices for Scaling Lean & Agile*. Addison-Wesley Professional.

Wen, Z., Renyu, Y., Garraghan, P., Lin, T., Xu, J., & Rovatsos, M. (2017, Mrch 21). Fog Orchestration for Internet of Things Services. *IEEE Internet Computing*, 16 - 24. doi:10.1109/MIC.2017.36

Yaacobi, S. (2016, July 21). *Delivering value and monetisation in an Internet of Things environment*. Retrieved July 26, 2020, from https://www.iot-now.com/: https://www.iot-now.com/2016/07/21/50166-delivering-value-and-monetisation-in-an-internet-of-things-environment/

KEY TERMS AND DEFINITIONS

Business Solutions: Representing a new wave that is built on technology to overcome the inward-looking nature of old systems and promises a great wave of efficiency and reduced costs by streamlining the management processes of external relationships that is based on trust and governed by innovative contracts.

Fleet Solution: Fleet management is the management of commercial motor vehicles such as cars, vans, trucks, specialist vehicles, forklifts, and trailers private vehicles used for work purposes.

Innovation: Creating new ideas to resolve problems or adding value out of the box

Key Performance Indicators: A quantifiable measure used to evaluate the success of an organization, employee, etc. in meeting objectives for performance.

SMART Goals: A mechanism used to help guide goal setting. SMART is an acronym that stands for Specific, Measurable, Achievable, Realistic, and Timely goals. Once the goals are aligned with the five SMART criteria, this will be an anchor on which to base focus and decision-making.

Tire Industry: The industry of manufacturing and distributing tires for cars and other vehicles, currently it is providing much more complex solutions based on IoT, Data analytics and ither emerging technologies.

Vesting Agreements: In law, vesting is the point in time when the rights and interests arising from legal ownership of a property is acquired by some person. Vesting creates a common responsibility of the contract base on the best owner of every risk.

Viable Scenarios: A scenario capable of becoming actual, useful, practicable solution, that can help business for growth and development reaching a stage of development at which further development can occur independently.

Chapter 18
The Inspiring Contracts:
How to Create Value Through Contracting

Momen Nashar
Oracle, Lebanon

ABSTRACT

Contracts are a powerful and often underutilized way to shape the business while involving all stakeholders. There exist stunning stories where an inspiring contract turns a lose-lose scenario into a successful relationship that fosters significant win-win behaviors. The latter will depend on contracting practices adapted to the level of coordination and the outcomes being sought. Inspiring contractual arrangements can drive a better outcome-based approach that is benefiting everyone. Every business is currently oriented toward value-centered outcomes; contracts can help sustain this approach by incentivizing the desired behavior to reward activities that create value, rather than simply reimbursing costs. Contract discussions should not be adversarial, but they should present an opportunity to align consumers' and providers' values while keeping expenditure under control. This chapter discusses real stories where innovative and inspiring contracting styles generate a vast value and realign the business approaches. This chapter is putting the concept and the story together.

INTRODUCTION

This chapter is unique as it utilizes the story telling method to convey the idea. Contracts and contracting have been going on since quite long time, being verbal or written. Contracting hurdles everywhere, and a lot of people can tell their bad and good stories. Today plenty of ideas are being changed and challenged. The old methodologies are not always the solution for today problems. Emerging technologies are penetrating every corner of the business and live. Innovations are becoming the new norm and new ideas make the difference.

Considering the mentioned points, the author has searched in multidimensions to find real inspiring stories of making a difference by challenging the contracting styles to make a difference. All the stories are based on trust, partnership, and communication. One story is talking about the value-based contract-

DOI: 10.4018/978-1-7998-4501-0.ch018

ing in health care industry which help Boeing and Intel to save a huge amount while keeping every one happy. The other was talking about the unique supply chain of McDonalds and the list goes on.

The main purpose of this chapter is to illustrate how an innovative contracting practice can create a solid win-win situation or even it can turn the losing business relations into a successful relation that will benefit all stakeholders. This chapter is a call for thinking out of the box to create a new innovative and agile contracting style based on trust and partnership rather than transaction-based contracts that based on risk transfer.

BACKGROUND

This chapter utilize a story telling style to pass the ideas. It is collected from different published resources and case studies in different countries. One idea that is illustrated is going around the fact that the main drivers for the successful stories are trust and partnership to share risks and benefits. His is a response to (Lyons, Krachenberg, & Henke, 1990) question "Why then were the parties willing to push this dimension of trust and move from the traditional hierarchical relationships between buyer and supplier to the innovation of relational relationships?". Similar idea is illustrated by (Axelrod, 1984) when he stated "As a result, relationships that encourage or mandate repeated encounters offer a means to develop and test the climate of trust, both internally and externally, that is a prerequisite of cooperation".

Our first story originated in Ukranie and showing how to fight corruption with technology, transparency, and collaboration (Pradhan, 2018). Second story described in detail at (Frey & Schlosser, 1993) and illustrated how ABB and Ford reach the right goal through vested contract that pass multiple phases. Third story illustrated how the business architecture innovation done by TD Bank in cooperation with his partners lead to a win-win situation in which every partner is caring about the others according to (Vitasek, 2016). Fourth story described how the Dell/FedEx relation was transformed from an edge where no company "can squeeze out lemon from the contract" to huge mutual savings and sustained relationship as described by to (Vitasek, Manrodt, Kling, & DeBinedeto, 2018).

One more story discuss how McDonald's supply chain performs shine like a star even throughout troubles, according to (Ovenden, 2020) this is a miracle considering the scale of the task of catering for 69 million customers daily in 36,000 restaurants across 100 countries. The story of Ford $5 minimum wage, which was the news headlines in 1914 according to (Worstall, 2012) showed how Henry Ford launched his innovating employee contracting relationships to enhance his production lines. The idea of moving to partnership while questioning the "the sustainability of the in-house-invent-it-ourselves model" was discussed as Procter & Gamble started looking beyond P&G walls to produce highly profitable innovations that would drive P&G and the parties' value as illustrated in (Vitasek, Manrodt, & Kling, 2012). .

Toward the end of the chapter we discuss how the value based contracting is changing the medical insurance sectors utilizing a partnership model between organizations, employees and service providers as shown in Boeing program (Leader Health Report, 2020) and Intel case (Eggbeer, Morris, & Sukenik, 2016).

REAL STORIES FOR CONTRACTING INSPIRATIONS

This section is describing few real stories, collected around the globe to illustrate the value that can be generated through a unique contracting style, this can turn the subject around and generate huge benefits. In one story from Ukraine a clear and accurate contract evaluation is hugely critical to ensuring that the right business is being awarded the valid contract based on accurate criteria that evaluate the latter technically and commercially. The second story for Ford/ABB created huge value through transparent contracting to share benefits and risks in a win-win mindset.

The third story from TD Bank showed how organizations can evolve their models and allow a juncture with buyers and service providers to build innovative ideas that benefit all stakeholders. And the stories continues to show how an innovative contracting that is coming in different flavors can add value to all stakeholders and change the mindset from "What's in it for Me (WIIFMe)" to "What's in it for We (WIIFWe)".

Open Contracting (ProZorro and DoZorro)

That said, trustworthy firms lose when contracts are awarded based on bribes behind closed doors. Opening procurement contracts and especially government contracts generate powerful dividends for companies, which compels business action to obtain these dividends.

One example coming from Ukraine, where entrepreneurs from the government and private sector came together to combat corruption by improving the public procurement system. The entrenched system of corruption meant that powerful oligarchs had captured the public procurement process through shady deals starting from multi-million-dollar kickbacks on substantial infrastructure projects to inflated prices on day-to-day expenses. According to Pradhan (2018), approximately twenty percent of spending was lost in public procurement due to corruption and limited competition.

A severe action had to be taken to repairing this corrupt system. Entrepreneurs eventually found a systemic approach, which is built on an electronic system (e-system) to monitor the whole cycle. For instance, in Ukrain, they found ProZorro an e-procurement system (Open Contracting, 2016). It's open-source software that enabled both government bodies or anyone else to have proper access to the information. Hence, on one hand, government bodies can conduct procurement deals transparently. On the other hand, information about contracts is easily accessible online in open data fashion for whoever needs the info (bidders, media, etc.). Moreover, a higher level of observation came on when they created a second-generation platform, called DoZorro, which allowed citizens to indicate about any doubtful violations of contract implementation, which enforced the government to take action and respond against such cases.

In South Korea, a solution called KONEPS that it was made for public officials and citizens. The main idea is to prevent people from meeting any procurement or customs services in person anymore. Instead, to do all the work by using online service, it will save time and hinder corruption. Besides, it has improved services for citizens. This Transparent e-procurement generated $6.6 billion inefficiencies for businesses (The Korean Ministry of the Interior, 2016).

The Golden Triangle of Partnership

Innovative contracting is a multi-stakeholder platform for action. Collaboration is essential because there are powerful vested interests and entrenched networks of corruption that benefit from the status quo. These will resist any official opening of contracts. Collaboration across stakeholders, including government, civil society, and the private sector, can play unique roles.

ProZorro and DoZorro systems occur via the cooperation of multiple stakeholders. This what is called "a golden triangle of partnership." Government representatives, businesses, and civil society put together how the systems will work. For instance, Government representatives sat the general rules to govern open contracting and disclosing contract information.

Businesses had multiple tasks, firstly implementing the platform, secondly, support suppliers, and contracting authorities, which supported the coalition. Lastly, civil society's primary role is observing contracts and reporting suspicious transactions or any questionable act.

According to Pradhan (2018), the early results of this partnership were encouraging with promising results over two years period, including:

- 80% of surveyed companies advised that the new system positively impacted their business by increasing the quality of business decisions, lowering administrative costs, and saving time to participate in the procurement.
- Entrepreneurs found that 82% of stakeholders report partial to a significant reduction in corruption of the platform's use.
- There was a 50% growth in companies, including SMEs, bidding for public contracts, attributed to greater trust in the system.
- An estimation of over US $1 billion has been saved by using e-procurement in two years. This has positively impacted the social service; for example, cancer patients received additional, free chemo due to savings from using ProZorro for the procurement of medicines.
- 5,000 cases of suspicious activity reported by civil society. One thousand two hundred of them lead to changing tenders because of feedback, while some included criminal charges.

Creating Value Through Cooperation (ABB-Ford)

Although adversarial practices are very intriguing and ordinarily employed, they do present barriers to create innovative solutions and restrain capturing the embedded process knowledge of suppliers that can reshape industrial organizations. These missed opportunities may dominate any incremental gains from squeezing purchasing costs.

One case study of the Ford-ABB Oak-ville Paint-Finishing Project can reactivate optimism for co-operative and innovative buyer-supplier relationships (Frey & Schlosser, 1993). ABB and Ford have created a genuine, mutually beneficial, win-win relationship and have innovated beyond the current practices of the automotive industry.

The Ford-ABB project was the design and construction of one of the largest automotive paint-finishing plants globally, costing $300 million facilities and supporting 75-cars-per-hour. Paint finishing is a delicate process comprising many steps, each of which compounds the chances of the defect. Also, the pressures of market, technology, and environment have created considerable technical challenges for a paint-finishing facility and call for state-of-the-art responses. The construction of a paint-finishing facility is a complex undertaking, with complicated design and intricate interfaces among the manufacturing processes. A project like the ABB Ford project involves more than thirty different suppliers typically satisfying more than two hundred bid packages with more than one thousand on-site employees. The positive mindset of the client and contractor drive a very interesting journey to create value through innovative contracting.

Setting Up Clear Objectives for Both Parties

The client (Ford) objectives out of this project was clear ahead the line and focused on below items:

- Quality: Ford was planning to use leading-edge paint-finishing technology.
- Timeliness: Benchmarking had also persuaded Ford that it could reduce the time for completion and, as a result, shorten the time for its new products to reach the market.
- Low Price: Ford had committed itself to achieve a 25 percent reduction in the cost of its investment projects capital, and
- No-Risk: Ford did not want to be exposed to the typical risks of cost overruns and time delays. As a result, they decided to offer the project a "turnkey" project to a single, "full-service" contractor.

The contractor (ABB) objectives set also a very clear tone, that was:

- Customer Satisfaction: ABB affirmed its commitment to the business with the proviso that more effective relationships with the automotive companies be developed.
- Profitable Business: ABB worked at developing innovative approaches to doing business in paint finishing and defining solutions for becoming a competent supplier of turnkey projects, and,
- Customary Risk: The financial impact could be significant; therefore, risks had to be minimized. Such a project can make or break the business area's future.

Building an Innovative Structure for Contracting Relationship

Ford and ABB planned ahead to avoid forming their relationship around an initial and often dramatic price negotiation. They structured a series of repeat relationships over an extended period. The cooperative-engineering phase was the foundation for a productive exchange of the sophisticated knowledge and experience they had. This sort of process knowledge is difficult to exchange and transfer because it is embedded in a firm's personnel and infrastructure compared to declarative or factual knowledge. Only sustained relationships allow time for cross-fertilization, the compression of total project time, and the achievement of exceptionally tight schedules. As a result, relationships that encourage or mandate repeated encounters offer a means to develop and test the climate of trust, both internally and externally, which is a prerequisite of cooperation (Axelrod, 1984).

Inventing a Creative Usage of Time

Ford and ABB decided to defer fixing the final specifications and the price until they had made a full investigation of the project and completed a comprehensive and definite design. This approach significantly reduced the self-inflicted risks that are often created by the traditional competitive-bidding process in which the price is the starting point. The risk reduction and the resulting benefits to all parties created the conditions for a genuine win-win situation. In addition, the passage of time before fixing the contract permitted both parties to recognize the benefits of their cooperative relationship.

Creating a Contractual Structure for Sharing Future Savings

Both ABB and Ford would benefit from the savings created by innovative design. The joint venture allowed the sharing of benefits from changes identified during the construction phase. By establishing a well-defined means for dividing mutual gain, all parties focused their attention on creating that gain rather than on the distractions of claiming those gains before they were even created.

Enriching the Purchasing Process

Effective purchasing associated with such contracts should focus more on acquiring a system rather than on acquiring parts, similarly, to focus on minimizing total cost rather than on reducing elemental costs. This will necessitate capturing process knowledge rather than just buying hardware and developing meaningful relationships with a few suppliers rather than enlarging the supplier base. Such purchasing will require engineering managers to become critical players in the purchasing activity. This broadened participation provided the organizational latitude within which mutual value could be created through enriching, internal dialogue.

Building Values Against Challenges

Ford and ABB have established a knowledge link, the value of which will increase with experience. The focus was not to reduce the cost but also to increase profit. From this perspective, innovative solutions suggest further opportunities and overcome specific challenges such as:

- Moving the entire organization to adopt a cooperative mindset and encouraged to shift from competition to cooperation.
- Exchanging of considerable amounts of possibly sensitive information while the control procedures might need to be established.
- Achieving cooperation between equally reliable partners requires the full acceptance and appreciation of differences in expertise among the various parties and preserving those differences that allow for a robust value-adding partnership.

Cultivating Results From Contracting at the Middle Line

The different direction took by ABB and Ford of acting as a joint entity in this project rather than acting as separate entities resulted in a "deferred fixed-price contract" that was conducted as a three-step process that involved:

- Establishing an appropriation price: ABB was convinced that cooperative engineering would enable it to quote an even lower price, maintain its profitability, and not incur any more risk. ABB and Ford agreed to a formula for sharing the cost reductions.
- Executing a three-month cooperative-engineering contract: This allows us to bring both entities distinctive competencies to bear on facility's final design permitting the design to be carried out in the proper sequence. and

- Submitting a final fixed-price bid: The underlying design was substantially different from the original Ford proposal, aggressively seeking solutions beneficial to the project. It resulted in a fixed price that was approximately 25 percent below the initial bid.

The bottom line is that both ABB and Ford were happy and satisfied with the final results, and the final product meets the objectives of both entities and resulted in an iconic example of a vested contract that moves the contracting relation from confrontation to cooperation.

Business Architecture Innovation (TD Bank)

Many organizations are not ready to evolve their models and are finding themselves at a juncture with buyers and service providers asking for innovation. Those organizations are still unwilling to make appropriate investments due to the conventional transaction-based commercial structure of how the companies work together.

Moving Away From Transactional Sourcing

The difficulty is that companies that use the transactional-sourcing business models find that the current way is not impacting their suppliers or service providers' contractual obligations and service levels. However, innovations and efficiencies do not necessarily take place at the pace they need or envision. Suppliers argue that it is risky to invest in an established business because the customer will copy their ideas and bid the work. Therefore, companies ask for solutions that can close the gaps. At the same time, they don't see a real value investing in people, technology, and processes while they do not have a core competency.

That is why vested methodologies can add much value by allowing companies to take a win-win theory. It will transition a highly cooperative relationship purpose-built that contributes to driving innovation against the coveted results. The process enables organizations to move beyond just paying lip service to "collaboration" and "partnership," putting together a win-win agreement and an atmosphere that drives transformative change.

The Vested Facility Management

One great example was the vested contract signed between TD Bank's Enterprise Real Estate (ERE) and an alliance of Brookfield Global Integrated Services (BGIS)/CB Richard Ellis (CBRE) in 2014 (Vitasek, 2016). This contract was a vested facilities management arrangement to cover 25 million square feet of real estate. TD Bank had outsourced its facilities management services to BGIS/CBRE since 2009 with excellent results. Still, the contract was fully restructured to follow the vested rules to align interests through mutually defined desired economics and results.

A formal review started to identify the gaps between the existing outsourcing approach and the vested model as a first step to reviewing the process. The goal was to address how they would incorporate vested rules into their contract and day-to-day operations. For instance, they identified four key desired outcomes to become the focal point of measuring their success. These include providing holistic, world-class real estate services and being an innovative organization.

Innovating the Pricing Model

They also have negotiated a pricing model with incentives to optimize the business, which wasn't an easy task. The pricing model should be fully transparent for both parties and designed to optimize the business. Incentives paying was a new concept for TD Bank that was created to provide BGIS/CBRE teams with an incentive mutually shared if they can carry services that need fewer handoffs or total cost of ownership to deliver particular function. That encourages innovation because while the service provider may increase their expenses to achieve a certain function or renovate a service, they will get an incentive if the total cost of ownership comes in less.

The innovated contract was a real win/win situation for the owner, service provider, and even the end-user. Before the end of the contract's first year, the frugality was huge, and the service catch top score in the facility awards.

Every Dollar, Every Year (Dell/FedEx)

According to (Vitasek, Manrodt, Kling, & DeBinedeto, 2018), as customary in the fast-paced high-tech industry, Dell operated under a procurement strategy of "every dollar, every year," meaning that it used frequent competitive bidding processes to drive down prices. Dell wanted to enhance and expedite their return and change process, therefore, they selected GENCO which is now known as FedEx Supply Chain to assist in this job. Although FedEx Supply Chain gained Dell's respect, still the service levels were high, and Dell could not escape highly competitive cost pressures, so they decided to go outsource. The relation seems fine at the beginning, but by 2011, the honeymoon was over in the relationship.

Driving in the Wrong Direction

First thing toward this step, Dell wanted to consolidate existing sites and create a single refurbishment center. In 2009, FedEx Supply Chain was awarded more than one hundred service level agreements (SLAs) providing the service on behalf of Dell. In addition to three years transaction-based contract of nineteen distinct billable line items. Considering the high pace of change in the high-tech industry, Dell considered a three-year contract a long-term deal. Knowing that Dell operated under a procurement strategy of "every dollar, every year". The arrangements worked fairly-well for a period of time. However, eventually it was hard to sustain due to significant problems. The explanation was complicated. It stemmed from structural challenges like the deal itself. Dell missed every quarter of critical metrics such as cost per box (CPB) for eighteen months in a row and pressed FedEx Supply Chain to proactively invest in innovations to keep up with the fast-paced, high-tech market. FedEx Supply Chain reached a point where it did not believe more savings "could be squeezed out of the lemon."

It was abundantly clear that neither party was happy. The existing contract structure and relationship dynamics put a wedge in the trust level between the two companies toward the end of the contract. A group within Dell wanted to switch the service provider or offshore to a low-cost country as a cure, but others argue that the same contract structure with a new supplier will have the same issues.

Transforming the Relationship

Some people feel strongly a need to consciously challenge years of historical precedent and make changes in contract penalties and incentives. Dell and FedEx Supply Chain appointed a small "Core Team" that would ultimately transform the relationship and transition from a transaction-based contract to a win-win vested business model. The team included leaders who were passionate about the need to think differently about the relationship. Following very tense meetings, both sides ultimately recognize that they can get tremendous value but need to make significant changes operationally under the new vested agreement's transformational nature.

The joint team has created a shared vision, mutually defined desired outcomes, including critical metrics, a pricing model with incentives, and a governance structure, all of which are essential to a successful outsourcing agreement. The team worked to create a relational contract with outcome-based economics. The targeted contract was a flexible framework that allows for the dynamic nature of the business.

Operationally, the two parties collaborated, asking the essential questions: How much money can we save by working together? How can the two companies become more efficient? Dell and FedEx Supply Chain identified 55 initial ideas that would kick-start an entrepreneurial and vested spirit. The views were broad reaching, ranging from business expansion and marketing opportunities to sustainability and creation capacity. The team ultimately agreed they would work on 15 of the highest potential Ponies with the best possible investment return.

From Theory to Economics and Modeling

In conventional outsourcing, companies purchase services for a transactional fee while in vested, buyers and service providers develop a pricing model with incentives that reward the supplier when mutually defined Desired Outcomes are achieved. In short, the supplier is vested in the buyer's success—and vice versa. A win-win pricing model created to move from theory to economics and modeling whiz was hired for this task. The model shifts away from a price per activity to a pricing model that tracked the total profitability of the business based on the mutually defined desired outcomes.

The companies also agreed to create a dynamic baseline that readjusts over time: The rationale was that both parties needed to seek innovations to continue to drive benefits—not just continue to reap rewards in the years after the initial investments and innovations brought value.

As part of the vested methodology, the Core Team set up a vested governance structure that would ultimately help the parties navigate their relationship well post-contract signature—moving from insight governance to versus oversight governance. To have all levels aligned from executive levels to frontline working levels. The responsibility of managers for specific areas is clearly outlined to keep the companies' program and account managers informed. Direct and continuous communication improves information flow and empowers service provider teams.

Cutting the Fruits

The results spoke about itself since the first quarter, and it includes reducing Dell's cost structure by a total of about 44 percent in the first three years and achieved record-high levels for quality targets. The supplier is rewarded for investing in innovation and process improvements because they will get a return.

The key to success is that the vested agreement channeled the parties to look at the bigger picture and align interests.

Results were great, and the win-win behaviors went well beyond economics. One of the best things that happened was the cultural change where the atmosphere inside the operation rooms was 180 degrees different from the past. There becomes a recognition for the importance of relationships, and, most importantly, trust. Another benefit was creating highly collaborative relationship management and transformation management mechanisms that would enable the parties to break down silos both internally and across the companies. Dell and FedEx Supply Chain stopped thinking about "What's in it for Me (WIIFMe)" and embraced the "What's in it for We (WIIFWe)" mindset.

After 6 years the contract was refreshed, while the relationship was more reliable than ever. As the Vested refresh process has enabled both entities to continue seeking alignment and developing mutually defined desired outcomes that will continue to be mutually beneficial to both Dell and FedEx Supply Chain.

Catering For 69 Million Customers Daily (McDonald's Horizontal Supply Chain)

Throughout troubles, McDonald's supply chain performs shine like a star considering the scale of the task. They provide to 69 million customers daily in 36,000 restaurants across 100 countries (Ovenden, 2020). They do so while contesting the company's ultimate goal of always being ready for any item a customer order. Also, restrictions around the time of deliveries as per policy they can't deliver during breakfast and lunch hours.

The Long-Term Supply Chain Strategy

McDonald's supply chain's success rests on the long-term supply chain strategy made by founder Ray Kroc. The foundation of the system is simply a 'win-win' proposition for all parties (Vitasek, Kling, & DeBinedeto, 2012). For instance, the owner, operators, and employees manage the supply chain channel of partners and the restaurants. Those were called the "three legs of the stool," where Kroc believed that if he ensured that restaurant owners/operators and suppliers were all successful, it would translate into success. The obligation has been not only on cost or individual component, but a decision represents long term value that improves things for all parties.

Kroc has always sought about the suppliers who share the same long-term vision he had. That said, many of its supply chain partners have been around since the very beginning. The model has fostered an ambiance of trust, which enabled them to work together and innovate regardless of the costs where they always tried to keep it as low as possible. One of McDonald's most significant distributors is Martin-Brower Company LLC. McDonald's and Martin-Bower have initiated a relationship since 1956 (Ovenden, 2020). They started the business on a low scale delivering paper napkins to Kroc's first restaurant in Des Plaines, Illinois.

Nevertheless, it now provides supplies to almost all its 15,000 locations in North America. Each of its distribution centers includes warehousing, transportation, and logistics services, a range of 250 to 700 restaurants. They often make at least two deliveries to each restaurant a week.

A High Priority on Communication and Collaboration

Necessary to ensuring this happens a high priority on communication and collaboration between all parties. The company continually monitors all things, having transparency to share all data with franchise owners and partners. This includes daily point-of-sale data for each item, inventories, and restaurant stock levels, among other metrics. In general, the McDonald's corporate supply chain team shines at organizing the upstream supply network. It promotes and acts as the channel between outsourced vendors, franchise partners, suppliers, and departmental stores. Mc Donald's uses council meetings to cooperate with suppliers on new product innovation and technology and plant integrity.

A standard supplier performance index is used to manage the expectations with suppliers. The distinction is more behavioral and cultural. Partners favor putting the McDonald's system first when sharing process innovations, product, and staffing support teams with top talent. This close relationship has seen it overcome several crises that could have to halt a lesser organization. For example, the bird flu outbreak affected about 40 million egg-laying hens in 2015. Still, through close collaboration with the egg suppliers, the restaurant could lock inadequate supply at a better-quality rating than the overall industry and ensure regular pricing.

Operating a fully horizontal supply chain is highly effective, but it needs positive relationships with suppliers. McDonald's has shown that by trusting supply chain partners and working closely alongside them, they will reward you.

Innovating Employee Contracting Relationships (Ford $5 Minimum Wage)

In 1903, Ford Motor Company sold the very first car to a doctor in Detroit, Michigan. It was the beginning of Henry Ford's dream. The idea was to make low priced, good cars for the general public. His dream was quoted in his saying: "I want to make a car that anybody can buy."

Before around one century, and precisely on January 5, 1914, the Ford Motor Company introduced an innovative idea in contracting with employees and effectively doubled the pay of his workforce compared to the market benchmark. The minimum five-dollar day plan confused the business, and to this day, historians and business theorists are still arguing the implications of Henry Ford's historic move (Motor City Garage, 2014). The debate continues to this day; however, this provides a different perspective on employee contracting to create value, and it has many innovative ideas as the minimum wage was just 2 Dollars when Ford took his decision. Despite the lengthy debate, the idea was a brilliant contracting style that resolved multiple issues at one shot. May be Ford think of his step from different angles.

Reducing the Staff Turnover

At the time, operators could live for about $2.25 per day, which was considered perfect money to work for nine-hour shifts. The toll was too high for many to bear. Ford's turnover rate was very high (Worstall, 2012). In 1913, Ford hired more than 52,000 employees to keep a workforce of only 14,000. New workers required a high-priced break-in period, making matters more acute for the company and evaded Ford to go with his plan selling his cars at a low price. Severe measures were necessary if he was to keep up this production. Henry Ford wanted loyal workers who would remain.

That level of turnover is hugely expensive, not only the downtime of the production line but also the training costs. Moreover, the search costs to find them. It can indeed be cheaper to pay workers more but to reduce turnover and associated training costs, that is what Ford did.

Building the Right Character

Ford's offer was not only $5 a day, but it was all rather more complicated. The $5-a-day rate was split half pay and a half bonus. The bonus came with character conditions and was enforced by doing things the "American way." They were thought to avoid social ills such as gambling and drinking and to learn English. That cuts the turnover and training time of the labor force and maybe reduced total labor costs.

Efficiency Engineering

The $ 5 a day was not simply nor truly a pay raise scheme, but an employee profit-sharing program. "This is neither charity nor wages, but profit sharing and efficiency engineering," said Ford in announcing the plan (Motor City Garage, 2014). In his view, distributing profits to workers was to lower prices to consumers and increase dividends to shareholders. The result was a greater production at a lower cost.

With the explosive sales of the Model T, Ford's workforce was growing at a phenomenal rate, similarly, Mr. Ford's wealth and even the population of Detroit doubled and then tripled between 1900 and 1920 to meet the demand for factory workers. Ford not only raised wages with his 1914 plan, but he cut the mandatory workday from nine hours to eight. This step-in turn allowed the Highland Park Model T plant to increase from two shifts per day to three. The new system reduced the number of pay grades from over 65 to eight and established payroll authority in a central office. Ford despised piecework and the petty despotism of floor bosses.

Creating a Strong Stakeholder Ecosystem

In 1913 Ford gave back fifty dollars to each person who had bought a Ford car. That made Henry Ford popular with working men. Similarly, he looked at his workers and demonstrated his idea that if workers received good wages, they became better buyers.

While some of the shareholders were concerned as they were tired of seeing profits frittered away on price reductions, rebates for consumers, larger paychecks for workers, investments in an uncertain future, and cleaning up the workers' communities outside the Ford plants. Henry Ford and his team will be remembered as those who maintain a balance within the stakeholders' ecosystem of customers, employees, shareholders, and the economic, political, and social societies they inhabit together. For this elite group, it was business-first supported by a proper communication plan explaining why to maintain a healthy and content stakeholder ecosystem. That was a fantastic unwritten contract to balance risks, opportunities, and benefits for business and among stakeholders.

Contracting for Transformation (P&G and JLL)

Leading the organization into the 21st century, A.G. Lafley has been selected as the CEO of Procter & Gamble (P&G). Innovation became a hallmark under his leadership (Vitasek, Manrodt, & Kling, 2012).

Questioning "The In-House-Invent-It-Ourselves Model"

Lafley questioned the sustainability of the in-house-invent-it-ourselves model. He started looking beyond P&G walls to produce highly profitable innovations that would drive P&G and the parties' value.

P&G extended this thinking by 2003. They worked with suppliers to outsource services providers to reduce costs while ensuring the leading edge of services, especially in areas where P&G lacks a core competency, such as facilities and real estate management. The relationship between P&G and its suppliers had a new twist. It utilized the shared experience to create a genuine win-win mentality sharing the risks and rewards associated with the transformation efforts.

As a result of this strategy, P&G developed a highly strategic facility management outsourcing relationship with Jones Lang LaSalle (JLL), which flipped the conventional outsourcing approach on its head by contracting for transformation instead of contracting day-to-day work.

The model added real business value for both companies that have a long history of delivering results. JLL managed all the offices and technical centers, including security and maintenance. It was a groundbreaking deal that spanned more than 60 countries and included facility management, project management, and strategic occupancy services. P&G desired an outsourcing relationship that challenged the service provider to take care of its buildings and create innovative ideas and take charge of the facilities.

The Tied Client/Provider Profitability

P&G tied the service provider's profitability to its ability to drive success against jointly defined business outcomes. The more successful P&G was the more success for JLL. The deal's size and complexity were a first for both companies, as was the commercial contract approach. Throughout negotiations, both entities have the mentality that a good contract will result from the credit they give to the relationships that drive the right behaviors of transparency and cost pass to align incentives, services, and features.

A long list of potential tasks was unimportant because the whole responsibility was changed. Therefore, JLL's job was to figure out what was needed and how to get it done.

Some formal P&G employees were transferred to JLL and learned how to adapt and accept responsibility as JLL employees and to drive innovations in jobs they had worked for years. Both companies understood that rules and measurements encourage the behavior. Therefore, instead of focusing on tasks and time, they focused on measuring success against P&G's business priorities.

"2 In A Box" Approach

The global team of P&G/JLL developed a pricing model that is fair yet drives accountability and transformation. Key components include cost pass-through if out of control, the base scope of work with management fee at risk and glide path, and shared savings as incentives. This jointly created a "balanced" approach regarding how to measure the business, which was subject to an annual review that allows both organizations to realign the focus based on current business priorities. There was no mention of SLAs (Service Level Agreements) because they do not offer flexibility in such a case, and there were no performance measures related to them.

For far too many companies, it's an afterthought to think about how to manage a deal. Yet, P&G and JLL decided it was essential to design governance inside the agreement itself. In core, they were contractually obligating the firms to manage the business, changes, and relationships proactively. Speaking about one of the most crucial parts of the JLL / P&G governance structure is that the companies live and operate the business following the Vested "Win-Win" philosophy.

Coining the "2 in a Box" Approach

The main idea of the win-win approach is to coin a "2 in a Box" approach. This approach identified both a P&G and a JLL person as owners of the core process. The key idea is that P&G is not successful unless JLL is successful, and vice versa. Shared goals and dreams are harmonious across the relationship. This story showed very interesting points, such as:

- The "2 in a Box" promotes communication at the process level and assures action plans, and business plans are aligned between P&G and JLL.
- While P&G deems all of its outsourcing highly effective, the business relationship with JLL has been, by all factors, wildly successful.
- JLL proved it could balance what some would call a paradox – achieving high service levels AND reducing costs.
- P&G proved it could truly outsource work – manage the WHAT not the HOW, and work for the betterment of both companies.

THE CONNECTED HEALTH CARE

As the Institute of Medicine noted in 2012, healthcare costs in the United States rose 88% during the past 10 years and now consume approximately 18% of the U.S. Gross Domestic Product (GDP) (DeVore, Wilson, & Parsons, 2013)

Medical insurance created clear reasons for frustration, including the increased cost of medical insurance every year and the willingness to influence the wellness and disease management programs for staff. Large employers were unable to bend healthcare cost curves or get their employees satisfied. As a result, the relation deteriorates with third-party administrators, whom they perceive as being unresponsive or unable to rein in medical costs and providers, whom they see as most responsible for high claims expenses.

These frustrations have prompted corporations such as Intel and Boeing to increasingly concentrate on working with providers directly to develop new benefit programs, in an approach that can be pertinently referred to as next-generation health care. This triggers the value-based contracts (VBC) in the health care sector.

Value Based Contracting (VBC)

There are multiple definitions for value-based contracts. However, in a 2017 Academy of Managed Care Pharmacy survey, respondents acknowledged that the term "value-based" contract is "a written contractual agreement in which the payment terms for medication(s) or other health care technologies are tied to agreed-upon clinical circumstances, patient outcomes, or measures." (Services, 2018).

VBCs allow better direct collaboration with provider systems to design new benefit programs. This will apply the style of self-insured employers who are initiating the work directly with providers on profit, plan design, and innovative delivery system reforms. Such movement is inspired by the value deconstruction reforms that are hitting several industries. It is also empowered by emerging technologies, including data analytics and real-time collaboration.

Value-based care growing and the collaborative effort toward these agreements is promising and demonstrates the willingness of healthcare stakeholders to engage in innovative approaches to value-based contracts. (Branning, Lynch, & Hayes, 2019)

A value-focused Strategy should be the culmination of a set of strategic and operational business model alterations required to be successful in the new healthcare environment (Eggbeer, 2015). Successful value-based contracting starts with aligning organizational leadership around a new definition of value and a new business model that touches virtually every aspect of a health system's operations. Next comes a strategic evaluation of risk posture, defining how much risk the value-based contract itself will involve.

Supporting Personal Behavior and Health

Under the VBC model, employers with a strong workforce hope to establish a more effective and efficient model that guarantees employees an excellent healthcare experience, where best personal behavior and health are supported, expected, and eventually rewarded. Compensation for providers is linked to value to diminish the overall costs while enhancing the quality of care and the overall healthcare experience.

Getting started on tracking outcomes is not easy. Addressing this challenge is vital to build an implementation roadmap that captures a shared language for describing, visualizing, and implementing a value-based contract. The problem is to make each concept concrete and relevant, while not oversimplifying complexities. Deep and Direct cooperation between providers and business owners is seen as the most effective means of driving change in health care, according to a white paper published by Intel Corp (DeVore, Wilson, & Parsons, 2013).

Contract Structure and Design

Although value-based contracts are intended to meet specific market and customer needs, they have joint structural characteristics. That said, the structure of many is shadow capitation agreements, which means having no pre-payments. Also, billings hold on as they have under fee for service, depending on what contracts are in place. Accountability is measured, and the incentive payments are reconciled after the contract period.

However, we can express shared savings and global budgets contractually in a variety of ways:

- Health system's total costs of care contrasted with a peer group's total costs of concern over a defined, measured time-period, often inflation-adjusted.
- A cost trend, having the health system agrees to hold the pattern to a specific inflation-measure
- A trend relative to the market, in this case, the health system decides to gain the market medical cost trend by a specific percentage
- Cost guarantees, where attributed beneficiaries' performance is compared with the experiences of a reference group of unassigned beneficiaries.

The Significant Drivers of Healthcare Value

The contract presents a multitude of terms and considerations typically not at play in a conventional fee-for-service payer-provider contract. The following includes attribution models, risk-sharing, quality metrics, network access standards, shared savings methodologies, and reinsurance provisions. Compensation for a mixture of elements is not included in most fee-for-service arrangements. Thus, a well-executed value-based contract has the potential to create a material impact on all significant drivers of healthcare value must consist of:

- **Value-based Benefit Design:** This is crucial for employees to receive cost-sharing or premium reductions if they follow steps to optimize their health or manage or participate in care through a chronic care management program.
- **Integrating Behavioral Health:** This will help to build on the strategic road map, and that's one of the challenges for more organizations today to decide quickly to cope up with the fast market changes.
- **Tailored Networks:** Employees are promoted to use a certain network of lower-cost providers that often provide discounts in return for referrals or are considered high performing based on efficiency and outcome measures.
- **Risk Exposure:** The extent of risk can cover a broad spectrum of small incentive payments. Those are based on provider performance relative to a defined set of competence and quality measures. Health systems can assume full risk for a defined population through a capitated arrangement or ownership of a health plan.
- **Pay-For-Performance:** This can be used with a variety of payment models, from fee-for-service to bundled payments. They can incorporate efficiency metrics that are measured for hospitals and physicians.
- **Shared Savings Arrangements:** Call for distribution of savings that reflect the difference between the actual costs for an attributed population and an agreed-upon target for that population. Many shared savings agreements split savings evenly between the payer and provider, which can translate into a net loss for the provider when the cost of infrastructure investment and the reduction in utilization due to improved care management are considered.

Few Complexities to Handle

VBCs are not an easy task where it is simple for employers to overrate the chance for savings and have irrational expectations for results. In turn, providers may underrate the risk involved in direct contracting. Taking into account the margin discounts employers require, and the complexity involved in setting up an efficient care management system. This includes:

- A shared interest in accelerating adoption of any new payment, disruption, and delivery models.
- Direct relationship with provider systems.
- A focus on elevating the bar on performance.
- Recurring, aligned interventions about payment and benefit redesign.
- Transparency on outcomes and clinical improvement.
- Investment in testing, spreading, and scaling innovations.

Boeing Scenario: Upgrading Care

Boeing Company is one of the biggest multi-national aerospace companies in the world. Boeing has over 500,000 lives covered in 48 states and a $2.5 billion annual healthcare spend. Boeing signed direct, multiyear, value-based accountable care organization (ACO) contracts. In order to improve its employees' healthcare experiences and to control their healthcare costs. This was a prime example of VBC in healthcare.

The contract started in fall 2014. The company began offering about 30,000 of its employees, retirees, and dependents the opportunity of keeping their current health plan or choosing a new narrower network. One year into its efforts, Boeing has found success with the model and worked to apply the VBC model to about 157,000 employees working in all 50 states (Eggbeer, 2015).

The partnership deal covers benefit differentials and incentives such as lower paycheck deductions, more substantial company contributions to health savings accounts, and no copays for primary care visits. This has encouraged members not only to sign up but to stay within partner networks. The employee's choice of plans is voluntary, fitting in with trends in the new retail market where consumers shop among programs on the various health insurance exchanges.

Answering the Questions

Besides, Boeing created a website with cost models for different care options, a provider search function, and FAQs to help employees decide whether the partnership option is proper. Also, Boeing provided a website that offers access to electronic health records, concierge service call centers for scheduling and resolving issues.

Boeing's target is to expand the partnership to other markets as part of an effort to improve member healthcare experiences and to save money. Each contract sets goals for total employee health and medical costs. If costs are higher, suppliers need to foot the bill. On the other side, if prices are lower, they reap the value saved.

VBC has added value that vertically integrated health systems with a strong market presence and the ability to provide a continuum of healthcare services are in the best position to adopt direct relationships with employers. It's an excellent idea to move the insured employee population to the provider and give financial incentives to manage them effectively, which will lower your total costs.

Intel Scenario: The Connected Care

Intel Corp. did significant steps to foster the healthiest employees on the planet. Therefore, they treated health care as if these advances in computing technology were rapidly growing, more vigorous and less cost (Stempniak, 2020). There was a general agreement to do what the performance was, and how it should work together to improve whatever indicators.

A decade ago, Intel's cost trend was running above the national average and was projected to reach $1 Billion by 2012 (Eggbeer, Morris, & Sukenik, 2016). Intel started to create a culture where employees would be engaged in wellness-oriented lifestyles. The new plan involved healthcare delivery and value-based compensation holistically. Moreover, Intel designed the plan to ensure the highest-volume members received the "highest touch care," equal to service in the best private practice.

The Interoperability Standards

Intel considered healthcare as part of its supply chain (Weiler, 2014). The collaborators also developed a value-based compensation structure that included both shared costs and paid for performance that addressed both cost and qualitative factors to align risks and rewards with desired outcomes better.

Intel has included interoperability standards within all healthcare provider contracts. The interoperability helped in ensuring data can flow securely and openly among all members of the provider team. Also, for clinical decision making based on a comprehensive view of different aspects such as current situation, potential drug interactions, and patients' medical history. Interoperability and fluid data exchange are being implemented to ensure providers have efficient yet seamless workflows with thorough, accurate clinical data at the point of care.

In its, VBC Intel showed that standards-based, cross-vendor interoperability is achievable today. It showed that data exchange could be implemented quickly when appropriate rewards and penalties are in place to promote care coordination.

Direct and Deep Methodology

Results for Boeing and Intel VBCs were significant. However, challenges exist to align the financial and patient care goals of employers with providers' financial and business goals. Despite promising results, the VBCs approach remains a learning experience for even the most sophisticated participants and still is best regarded as a work in progress. (Leader Health Report, 2020) suggested a recipe for building successful VBCs which is based on four elements in general:

- **Alignment:** Providers should seek VBCs that address both their pain points and organizations' opportunity areas. Also, it seeks for multi-stakeholder internal alignment and sponsorship around the contract's true value.
- **Data:** organizations always need robust data, analytics, and infrastructure to monitor outcomes and intervention. A value-based contract has to show measurable outcomes aligned to the goals that healthcare systems are focused on.
- **Culture:** Team members must align to drive standardization via product and care delivery. Companies that are successful with standardization work with suppliers and other group purchasing organization to determine how a product measurably contributes to high-quality outcomes.
- **Partnership:** Both suppliers and providers agree it's fundamental to cooperate with a partner capable of connecting suppliers with risk-ready hospitals. However, an industry partner assists the provider to firstly to assess its readiness and data infrastructure to sustain these contracts. Secondly, to connect suppliers with mature organizations that have structure and executive support. Thirdly, to create clear guidelines for outcomes expected and ensure that the supplier will protect the provider if it has not been delivered.

FUTURE RESEARCH DIRECTIONS

The floor is open to apply the lessons learned from each story on similar stories are we are moving into the digital transformation era where new technologies, opportunities and challenge arise every day.

Researches are encouraged o find more inspiring stories to apply for new business structures where applicable. Also, they will need these stories to build new methodologies for innovative contracting and to model these methodologies.

The failure stories also need to be studied to understand the reasons behind every failure and find the path forward. Technology can provide multiple tools and techniques for such analysis. Artificial Intelligence, big data analysis, the open data initiatives and business intelligence tools can be of great help.

CONCLUSION

The learning curve today should go exponential to cope up with technology movement and business innovations. This chapter has shown that failures can be turned into success through wise decisions in which contracting is a key. The stories described in this chapter illustrated inspiring results due to challenged and changed contracting mindset. Of course, the road is full of hurdles, but the destination is full of flowers. Correlation and cooperation, trust and transparency are main elements in any successful and fruitful contracting or partnership. Contract specialists need to think out of the box to create value for all stakeholders. It can be case by case, but always there is a way forward.

REFERENCES

Axelrod, R. (1984). *The Evolution of Cooperation.* Basic Books.

Branning, G., Lynch, M., & Hayes, K. (2019, September). *American Health & Drug Benefits, 12*(5), 232–234. Retrieved July 21, 2020, from https://www.ncbi.nlm.nih.gov/pmc/articles/PMC6979047/ PMID:32015790

DeVore, B. L., Wilson, B. C., & Parsons, J. (2013, January 1). *Healthcare-presbyterian-healthcare-services-whitepaper.pdf.* Retrieved July 22, 2020, from https://www.intel.com/content/dam/www/public/us/en/documents/white-papers/healthcare-presbyterian-healthcare-services-whitepaper.pdf

Eggbeer, W. T. (2015, August 1). *Inding-the-sweet-spot-in-value-based-contracts.* Retrieved July 21, 2020, from https://www.bdcadvisors.com/finding-the-sweet-spot-in-value-based-contracts/

Eggbeer, W. T., Morris, D. E., & Sukenik, C. C. (2016, March 1). Retrieved Jul 21, 2020, from https://www.bdcadvisors.com/next-generation-health-care/

Frey, S. C., & Schlosser, M. M. (1993, October 15). ABB and Ford: Creating Value through Cooperation. *MIT Sloan Management Review*, 65–72.

Health Leaders. (2020, December 2). *Four-keys-building-successful-value-based-supplier-contracts.* Retrieved Jul 21, 2020, from https://www.healthleadersmedia.com/finance/four-keys-building-successful-value-based-supplier-contracts

Lyons, T. F., Krachenberg, A. R., & Henke, J. W. (1990). Mixed Motive Marriages: What's Next for Buyer-Supplier Relations? *Sloan Management Review*, (Spring), 29–36.

Motor City Garage. (2014, January 12). Retrieved June 4, 2020, from https://www.macsmotorcitygarage.com/eight-things-worth-knowing-about-henry-ford-and-the-five-dollar-day/

Open Contracting. (2016, November 28). *Everyone sees everything*. Retrieved from https://medium.com/open-contracting-stories/everyone-sees-everything-fa6df0d00335

Ovenden, J. (2020, January 17). *McDonald's' Supply Chain Success Shows The Benefits Of Collaboration*. Retrieved from https://channels.theinnovationenterprise.com/articles/mcdonalds-supply-chain-success-shows-the-benefits-of-collaboration

Pradhan, S. (2018, May 14). Retrieved July 7, 2020, from https://www.opengovpartnership.org/stories/the-business-imperative-for-open-contracting/

Services, U. D. (2018, May 1). Retrieved July 16, 2019, from https://www.hhs.gov/sites/default/files/AmericanPatientsFirst.pdf

Stempniak, M. (2020, Jul 21). *1020-will-boeing-change-health-care*. Retrieved from https://trustees.aha.org/articles/1020-will-boeing-change-health-care

The Korean Ministry of the Interior. (2016). *Building Better Governance: The Korean Case*. Seoul, Republic of Korea: Korean International Cooperation Division for Good Governance. Retrieved from https://www.mois.go.kr/eng/bbs/type002/commonSelectBoardArticle.do%3Bjsessionid=8YddoT1KCsn7Dl8FrKcOys7l.node10?bbsId=BBSMSTR_000000000022&nttId=56889

Vitasek, K. (2016, June 13). *Procter & Gamble, TD Bank: Vested Outsourcing Success Stories*. Retrieved from https://www.facilitiesnet.com/outsourcing/article/Procter-amp-Gamble-TD-Bank-Vested-Outsourcing-Success-Stories--16660

Vitasek, K., Manrodt, K., Kling, J., & DeBinedeto, W. (2018, June 26). *Dell-FSC-long-teaching-case*. Retrieved from https://www.vestedway.com/wp-content/uploads/2018/07/Dell-FSC-long-teaching-case-June-26-2018-PDF.pdf

Vitasek, K., Kling, J., & DeBinedeto, W. (2012). *McDonalds-Case-Study*. Retrieved from https://www.vestedway.com/wp-content/uploads/2012/09/McDonalds-Case-Study.pdf

Vitasek, K., Manrodt, K., & Kling, J. (2012, September 1). Retrieved July 24, 2020, from https://www.vestedway.com/wp-content/uploads/2012/09/PG-Case-Study.pdf

Weiler, A. (2014, December 3). *Healthcare-is-part-of-our-supply-chain-the-boeing-company*. Retrieved Jul 21, 2020, from https://www.wellpepper.com/healthcare-is-part-of-our-supply-chain-the-boeing-company

Worstall, T. (2012, March 4). Retrieved June 4, 2020, from https://www.forbes.com/sites/timworstall/2012/03/04/the-story-of-henry-fords-5-a-day-wages-its-not-what-you-think/#75ef97ca766d

ADDITIONAL READING

Bloom, N., Eifert, B., Mahajan, A., McKenzie, D., & Robert, J. (2013). Does management matter? evidence from india. *The Quarterly Journal of Economics*, *128*(1), 1–51. doi:10.1093/qje/qjs044

Dallas, G. (Ed.). (2004). Governance and risk. New York: McGraw-Hill companies Inc.

Helper, S. (1991, Summer). How Much Has Really Changed between U.S. Automakers and Their Suppliers? *Sloan Management Review*, 15–28.

Ring, P. S., & Van de Ven, A. H. (1992). Structuring Cooperative Relationships between Organizations. *Strategic Management Journal, 13*(7), 483–498. doi:10.1002mj.4250130702

KEY TERMS AND DEFINITIONS

Open Contracting: It's open-source software that enabled both government bodies and anyone else to have proper access to the information. Hence, on one hand, government bodies can conduct procurement deals transparently. On the other hand, information about contracts is easily accessible online in open data fashion for whoever needs the info (bidders, media, etc.).

Pay-for-Performance: This can be used with a variety of payment models, from fee-for-service to bundled payments. They can incorporate efficiency metrics that are measured for hospitals and physicians.

Transactional: A method of contracting based on measuring cost and quality parameters per transaction. This is an old method that is most common however, it is not suitable for plenty of innovative business scenarios.

Value-Based Contracting (VBC): Allow better direct collaboration with provider systems to design new benefit programs. This will apply the style of self-insured employers who are initiating the work directly with providers on profit, plan design, and innovative delivery system reforms.

Vested Contracts: An innovative contracting style the moves the contracting relation from confrontation to cooperation culture.

Compilation of References

Abdelouhab, K. A., Idoughi, D., & Kolski, C. (2014). Agile & user centric SOA based service design framework applied in disaster management. *2014 1st International Conference on Information and Communication Technologies for Disaster Management (ICT-DM)*, 1–8.

Abrahamsson, P., Conboy, K., & Wang, X. (2009). 'Lots done, more to do': The current state of agile systems development research. *European Journal of Information Systems, 281-284*(4), 281–284. Advance online publication. doi:10.1057/ejis.2009.27

Abzari, M., Radmehr, R., & Shalikar, M. (2013). Analyzing the Effects of E-HRM on the Talent Management Strategies: Medical University of Isfahan as a Case Study. *World of Sciences Journal, 1*(6), 101–112.

Adwani, A. A. (2001). Change Management Strategies for Successful ERP Implementation. *Business Process Management Journal, 7*(3), 266–275.

Ahmad, A. A.-S., & Andras, P. (2018). Measuring the scalability of cloud-based software services. *2018 IEEE World Congress on Services (SERVICES)*, 5–6. 10.1109/SERVICES.2018.00016

Ahmadi, A., Darayi, M., & Rastgoo, F. (2014). Investigating the Effect of E-HRM on the Successful Implementation of Succession Planning. *Arabian Journal of Business & Management Review, 4*(1), 65–70.

Ahmet, C. (2018). *Artificial Intelligence: How Advance Machine Learning Will Shape The Future Of Our World.* Shockwave Publishing via PublishDrive.

Ahsan, K., & Matsukawa, H. (2012). Project Price Modeling by Optimal Fixed Price Incentive Contract. In *Proceedings of the 2012 International Conference on Industrial Engineering and Operations Management* (pp. 1971-1980). Istanbul, Turkey: International Conference on Industrial Engineering and Operations Management.

Ahsen Maqsoom, S. B. (2019). Optimizing contractor's selection and bid evaluation process in construction industry: Client's perspective. *Journal of Construction, 18*(3), 445–458. doi:10.7764/RDLC.18.3.445

Akintan, O. A., & Morledge, R. (2013). Improving the Collaboration between Main Contractors and Subcontractors within Traditional Construction Procurement. *Journal of Construction Engineering, 11*, 1–11. Advance online publication. doi:10.1155/2013/281236

Aksel, K., & Çiftçi, I. (2017). *Smart Contracts (Code Vs. Contract): An Overview of Blockchain Technology and Legal Implications of Smart Contracts from a Turkish Law Perspective, Yegin Ciftci Attorney Partnership.* Retrieved December 12, 2020, from https://www.cliffordchance.com/content/dam/cliffordchance/PDFDocuments/december2017-client-briefing-smart-contracts-(code-vs.-contract).pdf

Alamada-Lobo, F. (2015). The Industry 4.0 revolution and the future of manufacturing execution systems (MES). *Journal of Innovation Management., 3*(4), 16–21. doi:10.24840/2183-0606_003.004_0003

Alden, J. (2019, August 15). *Addendum-vs.-amendment-whats-the-difference*. Retrieved from https://www.corridorcompany.com/blog/addendum-vs.-amendment-whats-the-difference

AL-Dmour, R., & Al-Zu'bi, Z. (2014). Factors Inhabiting & Motivating the Adoption of HRIS in Business Organization. *International Business Research*, *7*(7), 139.

Aleksieva, V., Valchanov, H., & Huliyan, A. (2019). Application of Smart Contracts based on Ethereum Blockchain for the Purpose of Insurance Services. *2019 International Conference on Biomedical Innovations and Applications (BIA)*, 1-4. 10.1109/BIA48344.2019.8967468

Algarni, M. (2020). Business Intelligence Informational Support in Saudi Ministries: Exploratory Study. *Journal of Public Administration, Institute of Public Administration, 3*(61), 19.

Alharbi, F., Atkins, A., & Stanier, C. (2016). Understanding the determinants of Cloud Computing adoption in Saudi healthcare organisations. *Complex & Intelligent Systems*, *2*(3), 155–171. doi:10.100740747-016-0021-9

AlKerdawy, M. (2016). The Relationship between HRM Ambidexterity & Talent Management: The Moderating Role of E-HRM. *International Business Research*, *9*(6), 80. doi:10.5539/ibr.v9n6p80

Almeida, F., & Santos, J. (2018). *The Business Plan Reference Manual for IT Businesses.* Gistrup, Denmark: River Publishers.

Al-Shaalan, A. (2018). *Reliability Evaluation and Modeling of Power Systems*. King Saud University.

Alshibly, H. (2014). Evaluating E-HRM Success: A Validation of the Information Systems Success Model. *International Journal of HR Studies*, *4*(3), 107. doi:10.5296/ijhrs.v4i3.5929

Altamony, H., Al-Salti, Z., Gharaibeh, A., & Elyas, T. (2016). The relationship between change management strategy and successful enterprise resource planning (ERP) implementations: A theoretical perspective. *International Journal of Business Management and Economic Research*, *7*(4), 690–703.

Alwis, A. (2010). The Impact of E-HRM on the Role of HR Managers. *Ekonomie a Management*, *4*, 47–60.

Ambler, S. W., & Lines, M. (2016). The disciplined agile process decision framework. *International Conference on Software Quality*, 3–14.

Amoako-Gyampah, K., & Salam, A. (2004). An extension of the technology acceptance model in an ERP implementation environment. *Information & Management*, *41*(6), 731–745. doi:10.1016/j.im.2003.08.010

Amoatey, T., & Anson, B. (2017, January 1). Investigating the major causes of scope creep in real estate construction projects in Ghana. *Journal of Facilities Management*, *15*(4), 393–408. doi:10.1108/JFM-11-2016-0052

Analoui, F., & Karami, A. (2002). EOs and development of the meaningful mission statement. *Corporate Governance*, *2*(3), 13–20. doi:10.1108/14720700210440044

Andal-Ancion, A., Cartwright, P. A., & Yip, G. S. (2003). The Digital Transformation of Traditional Businesses. *MI Sloan Management Review*, 34-41.

Angel, R. (2006, January). Putting an Innovation Culture into Practice. *Ivey Business Journal*, 1-5.

Angius, S., Frati, C., Gerken, A., Härle, P., Piccitto, M., & Stegemann, U. (2011, May 1). *Risk modeling in a newparadigm: developing newinsight and foresight onstructural risk.* Retrieved from https://www.mckinsey.com/client_service/risk: https://www.mckinsey.com/client_service/risk/people/~/media/FBFAE9C41A144FCDB9A585126CDD86A4.ashx

Anthony, P. W., Perrewe, L., & Kacmark, M. (1999). Human Resource Management. The Dryden Press.

Anticona, P. (2020). Digital Transformation of Standard Contracts into E-Contracting. *PM World Journal.*, *5*(1), 40.

Antonella, P., De Felice, F., Cioffi, R., & Zomparelli, F. (2018). *Fourth Industrial Revolution: Current Practices, Challenges, and Opportunities, Digital Transformation in Smart Manufacturing.* Retrieved on February 16,2020 from https://www.intechopen.com/books/digital-transformation-in-smart-manufacturing/fourth-industrial-revolution-current-practices-challenges-and-opportunities

Arbogast, T., Larman, C., & Vodde, B. (2012). *Agile Contracts Primer.* https://agilecontracts.org/

Asian Development Bank. (2018). *Contract Management Guidance Note on Procurement.* Available at: https://www.adb.org/sites/default/files/contract-management.pdf

Atzori, L., Iera, A., & Morabito, G. (2017). Understanding the Internet of Things: Definition, potentials, and societal role of a fast evolving paradigm. *Ad Hoc Networks*, *56*, 122–140. doi:10.1016/j.adhoc.2016.12.004

Aubert, B., Hooper, V., & Schnepel, A. (2013). Revisiting the role of communication quality in ERP project success. *American Journal of Business*, *28*(1), 64–85. doi:10.1108/19355181311314770

Axelrod, R. (1984). *The Evolution of Cooperation.* Basic Books.

Azhar, S. (2011, July). Building Information Modeling (BIM): Trends, Benefits, Risks, and Challenges for the AEC Industry. *Leadership and Management in Engineering, 11*(3). doi:10.1061/(ASCE)LM.1943-5630.0000127

Babajee, G., Goolaup, R., & Mamode, K. (2014). An Analysis of the Implementation of E-HR Practices at TNT Business Solutions. *Proceedings of 26th International Business Research Conference Imperial College*, 7-8.

Baird, D. (2019). Unlikely Resurrection: Richard Posner, Promissory Estoppel, and the Death of Contract. *The University of Chicago Law Review. University of Chicago. Law School*, 1037–1050.

Baker, E., Lavers, A., & Robottom, L. (2017). Allocation of Risk in Construction Contracts. *Construction Contracts*, 9. Retrieved from https://www.jdsupra.com/legalnews/allocation-of-risk-in-construction-32247/

Ball, K. (2001). The Use of HRIS: A Survey. *Personnel Review*, *30*(6), 677–693. doi:10.1108/EUM0000000005979

Bannerman, P. (2008, December 1). Risk and risk management in software projects: A reassessment. *Journal of Systems and Software*, *81*(12), 2118–2133. doi:10.1016/j.jss.2008.03.059

Barki, H., Oktamis, S., & Pinsonneault, A. (2005). Dimensions of ERP Implementations and Their Impact On ERP Project Outcomes. *Journal of Information Technology Management*, 1–9.

Basole, R. C., & Karla, J. (2012, March 1). Value Transformation in the Mobile Service Ecosystem: A Study of App Store Emergence and Growth. *Service Science*, *4*(1), 1–88. doi:10.1287erv.1120.0004

Bayern, M. (2018). *The 5 biggest challenges to digital transformation and how to overcome them.* Retrieved on January 16,2020 from https://www.techrepublic.com/article/the-5-biggest-challenges-to-digital-transformation-and-how-to-overcome-them

Beck, K., Beedle, M., Van Bennekum, A., Cockburn, A., Cunningham, W., & Fowler, M. (2001). *Manifesto for agile software development.* Academic Press.

Berg, M. (2005). *The Age of Manufactures, 1700-1820: Industry, Innovation and Work in Britain.* Routledge. doi:10.4324/9780203990971

Bersin, J. (2019, January 27). T. & Ruel, H. (2009). E-HRM: Challenges in the Digital Era. *The International Journal of HRM*, *20*(3), 505–514. Retrieved April 2020, from https://www.hrtechnologist.com/

Bevan, O., Freiman, M., Pasricha, K., Samandari, H., & White, O. (2019, April 25). *Transforming-risk-efficiency-and-effectiveness*. Retrieved from https://www.mckinsey.com/business-functions: https://www.mckinsey.com/business-functions/risk/our-insights/transforming-risk-efficiency-and-effectiveness#

Beverly, R. (2018, February 18). How AI Is Changing Contracts. *Harvard Business Review*, *95*(2), 1–5.

Bhattacharyya, D. (2011). *Management Accounting*. Pearson Education.

Bidkar, T. P. (2020, September 1). *What is a Quasi Contract*. Retrieved from http://lawtimesjournal.in: http://lawtimesjournal.in/what-is-a-quasi-contract/

Bin Shawaih, F. (2016, October 1). Risk Management Strategies for dealing with Unpredictable Risk in Saudi Arabian Organisations. In *Requirements of Degree of Doctorate of the Built*. Manchester, UK: College of Science & Technology, School of the Built Environment.

Blanc-Brude, F., & Makovsek, D. (2013). Construction risk in infrastructure project finance. *Procurement and Public-Private Arrangements Conference*, 1-20.

Blomqvist, K. (2005). Trust in a Dynamic Environment - Fast Trust as a Threshold Condition for Asymmetric Technology Partnership Formation in the ICT Sector. In K. Blomqvist (Ed.), *Trust in Pressure, Investigations of Trust and Trust Building in Uncertain Circumstances* (pp. 127–147). Edward Elgar Publishing, Inc. doi:10.4337/9781845427962.00011

Bloomberg, J. (2018). *Digitization and Digital Transformation: Confuse Them at Your Peril*. Retrieved on December 25,2019 from https://www.forbes.com/sites/jasonbloomberg/2018/04/29/digitization-digitalization-and-digital-transformation-confusethem-at-your-peril/#2dd1ce842f2c

Boardman, A. E., Greenberg, D. H., Vining, A. R., & Weimer, D. L. (2011). Cost-Benefit Analysis: Concepts and Practice (4th ed.). Pearson.

Bochicchio, M. A., & Longo, A. (2011). Modelling Contract Management for Cloud Services. In *IEEE 4th International Conference on Cloud Computing* (pp. 332-339). Washington, DC: IEEE. 10.1109/CLOUD.2011.102

Boholm, Å., Corvellec, H., & Karlsson, M. (2012). The practice of risk governance: Lessons from the field. *Journal of Risk Research*, *15*(1), 1–20. doi:10.1080/13669877.2011.587886

Boland, M., & McCarthy, M. C. (2019, June 18). *Financial Statement Basics: What a Contractor Needs to Know for Surety Bonding*. Retrieved from https://www.constructionexec.com/: https://www.constructionexec.com/article/financial-statement-basics-what-a-contractor-needs-to-know-for-surety-bonding

Bondarouk, T., ter Horst, V., & Engbers, S. (2009). Exploring Perceptions about the Use of E-HRM Tools in Medium Sized Organizations. In Handbook of Research on E-Transformation & HRM Technologies. Information Science Reference.

Bondarouk, T., Parry, E., & Furtmueller, E. (2017). Electronic HRM: Four Decades of Research on Adoption & Consequences. *International Journal of Human Resource Management*, *28*(1), 98–131. doi:10.1080/09585192.2016.1245672

Bookbinder, S. (2018). *The Benefits of Digital Transformation (& What They Mean for Sales Professionals)*. Retrieved on March5,2020 from https://www.impactbnd.com/blog/benefits-of-digital-transformation-sales-professionals

Bosch, J., Olsson, H. H., & Crnkovic, I. (2018). It takes three to tango: Requirement, outcome/data, and AI driven development. *SiBW*, 177–192.

Bos, M., & Heijden, H. (2004). E-HRM. In F. Kluytmans (Ed.), *Leerboek Personnel's Management*. Wolters-Nordhoff.

Bounfour, A. (2016). *Digital Futures, Digital Transformation*. Springer.

Brabham, D. C. (2009). Crowdsourcing the Public Participation Process for Planning Projects. *Planning Theory*, *8*(3), 242–262. doi:10.1177/1473095209104824

Bragg, S. (2019, December 22). *Financial statement footnotes*. Retrieved from https://www.accountingtools.com/articles/what-are-financial-statement-footnotes.html

Branning, G., Lynch, M., & Hayes, K. (2019, September). *American Health & Drug Benefits*, *12*(5), 232–234. Retrieved July 21, 2020, from https://www.ncbi.nlm.nih.gov/pmc/articles/PMC6979047/ PMID:32015790

Braxton, P., Hetrick, K., Webb, K., Whitehead-Scanlon, I., & Ross, D. (2017). *Contract Incentives Under Uncertainty:Data-Driven Contract Geometry Best Practices. In 2017 ICEAA Professional Development & Training Workshop*. ICEAA, International Cost Estimating and Analysis Association.

Brennan, S., & Dobra-Kiel, A. (2018, October 22). *Digital-transformation-meets-regulation-4-in-2030-coping-with-disruptive-innovation*. Retrieved from https://blogs.deloitte.co.uk: https://blogs.deloitte.co.uk/financialservices/2018/10/digital-transformation-meets-regulation-4-in-2030-coping-with-disruptive-innovation.html

Bresser, R., Heuskel, D., & Nixon, R. (2000). The deconstruction of integrated value chains: practical and conceptual challenges. In R. Bresser, M. Hitt, R. Nixon, & D. Heuskel (Eds.), *Winning strategies in a deconstructing world* (pp. 1–21). John Wiley and Sons.

Brian, A. (2018). *The Effectiveness of Contract Management on Contractors' performance (Bachelor's degree)*. Kyambogo University.

Brigham, T. J. (2017). Reality Check: Basics of Augmented, Virtual, and Mixed Reality. *Medical Reference Services Quarterly*, *36*(2), 171–178. doi:10.1080/02763869.2017.1293987 PMID:28453428

Brocal, F., González, C., Komljenovic, D., Katina, P. F., & Sebastián, M. A. (2019). Emerging Risk Management in Industry 4.0: An Approach to Improve Organizational and Human Performance in the Complex Systems. *Complexity in Manufacturing Processes and Systems 2019*. doi:10.1155/2019/2089763

Broderick, R., & Boudreau, J. (1991). The Evolution of Computer Use in Human Resource Management: Interviews with Ten Leaders. *Human Resource Management*, *30*(4), 485–508. doi:10.1002/hrm.3930300405

Broderick, R., & Boudreau, J. (1992). Human Resource Management, Information Technology, & the Competitive Edge. *The Executive*, *6*(2), 7–17. doi:10.5465/ame.1992.4274391

Brown, K. (2018, October 5). Retrieved May 1, 2020, from https://www.rubbernews.com/article/20181005/NEWS/181009951/tire-industry-should-prepare-to-adapt-to-automotive-trends

Brown, R. E. (2009). *Electric Power Distribution Reliability*. Oxfordshire: Taylor & Francis Group, LLC.

Brown, T. L., Potoski, M., & Van Slyke, D. M. (2010). Contracting for Complex Products. *Journal of Public Administration: Research and Theory*, *20*(1), 41–58. doi:10.1093/jopart/mup034

Brown, T., & Potoski, M. (2003, March 1). Contract Management Capacity in Municipal and County Government. *Public Administration Review*, *63*(2), 153–164. doi:10.1111/1540-6210.00276

Bücheler, T., Sieg, J. H., Füchslin, R. M., & Pfeifer, R. (2010). Crowdsourcing, open innovation and collective intelligence in the scientific method: a research agenda and operational framework. In *Artificial live XII: proceedings of the twelfth international conference on the synthesis and simulation of living systels* (pp. 679 - 686). MIT Press. 10.21256/zhaw-4094

Buchmeister, B., Palcic, I., & Ojstersek, R. (2019). *Artificial Intelligence in Manufacturing Companies And Broader: An Overview*. Daaam International Scientific Book. doi:10.2507/daaam.scibook.2019.07

Buckley, P., Minnette, K., Joy, D., & Michaelis, J. (2004). The Use of an Automated Employment Recruiting & Screening System for Temporary Professional Employees: A Case Study. *HRM*, *43*(2), 233–241. doi:10.1002/hrm.20017

Bulacan, B. (2019, April 29). *The 5 W's of Enterprise Contract Management*. Retrieved from https://cloc.org/the-5-ws-of-enterprise-contract-management/

Burnett, C., Norman, T. J., & Sycara, K. (2011). Trust Decision-Making in Multi-Agent Systems. In T. Walsh (Ed.), *Proceedings of the Twenty-Second International Joint Conference on Artificial Intelligence* (pp. 115-120). Barcelona: Association for the Advancement of Artificial Intelligence.

Burns, F. (2002). The Equitable Lien Rediscovered: A Remedy for the 21st Century. *University of New South Wales Law Journal, 25*(2), 1-32.

Business News Daily. (2019). *The Fundamentals of Contract Management*. Available at: https://www.businessnewsdaily.com/4813-contract-management.html

Butler, T., & O'Brien, L. (2020). Understanding RegTech for Digital Regulatory Complaince. In T. Lynn, J. G. Mooney, P. Rosati, & M. Cummins (Eds.), Disrupting Finance: FinTech and Strategy in the 21st Century (pp. 85-102). Switzerland AG: Springer Nature.

Butzin, B., Golatowski, F., & Timmermann, D. (2016). Microservices approach for the internet of things. *2016 IEEE 21st International Conference on Emerging Technologies and Factory Automation (ETFA)*, 1–6.

Calonge, C. (2006). *USA Patent*, (No. US7072857), B1.

Cameron, K. S., & Quinn, R. E. (2011). *Diagnosing and Changing Organizational Culture: Based on the Competing Values Framework*. John Wiley & Sons, Inc.

Canada, C. P. A. (2018, January 1). Retrieved April 24, 2020, from https://www.cpacanada.ca/-/media/site/operational/sc-strategic-communications/docs/g10475-sc_precarious-employment.pdf?la=en&hash=05185D6F20B709D26C12C966F162EB7F4A3B9992D

Cantrell, S. A. (2017). AMCP Partnership Forum: Advancing Value-Based Contracting. *Journal of Managed Care & Specialty Pharmacy*, 1096-1102.

Carlson, A. (2019, July 26). *Appendix-vs-attachment*. Retrieved from https://www.difference.wiki/appendix-vs-attachment

Catteeuw, F., Flynn, E., & Vonderhorst, J. (2007). Employee Engagement: Boosting Productivity in Turbulent Times. *Organization Development Journal*, 151–157.

CFI. (2020, November 27). *return-on-capital-employed-roce*. Retrieved from https://corporatefinanceinstitute.com/resources/knowledge/finance/return-on-capital-employed-roce/

ChainTrade. (2017). *10 Advantages of Using Smart Contracts*. Retrieved December 10, 2020, from https://medium.com/@ChainTrade/10-advantages-of-using-smart-contracts-bc29c508691a

Chalkidis, I., & Androutsopoulos, i. (2017). A deep learning approach to contract element extraction. In A. Wyner, & G. Casini (Ed.), *30th International Conference on Legal Knowledge and Information Systems (JURIX 2017)* (pp. 155-165). Luxembourg: IOS Press.

Chalkidis, I., Androutsopoulos, I., & Michos, A. (2018). Extracting contract elements. In *Proceedings of the 16th edition of the International Conference on Articial Intelligence and Law* (pp. 19-28). London: Association for Computing Machinery. 10.1145/3086512.3086515

Châlons, C., & Dufft, N. (2017). The Role of IT as an Enabler of Digital Transformation. In F. Abolhassan (Ed.), *The Drivers of Digital Transformation: Why There's No Way Around the Cloud* (pp. 13–22). Springer International Publishing. doi:10.1007/978-3-319-31824-0_2

Chatterjee, C. (2000). *Negotiating Techniques in International Commercial Contracts*. Routledge.

Chau, B. K., & Markel, Z. (2015, December 1). *Liability for Home IoT.* Retrieved from[REMOVED HYPERLINK FIELD] https://groups.csail.mit.edu/mac/classes/6.805/student-papers/fall15-papers/Liability%20for%20hone%20IoT.pdf

Cheng, R. (2019). Ekiden: A Platform for Confidentiality-Preserving, Trustworthy, and Performant Smart Contracts. *2019 IEEE European Symposium on Security and Privacy (EuroS&P),* 185-200. 10.1109/EuroSP.2019.00023

ChenH.GunnyK. (2014). Profitability and Cost Shifting in Government Procurement Contracts. *Management Accounting Section (MAS) Meeting*, 1-33. doi:10.2139srn.2482605

Chen, Y., & Chen, S. S., & Lin, I. (2018). Blockchain based smart contract for bidding system. *2018 IEEE International Conference on Applied System Invention (ICASI)*, 208-211. 10.1109/ICASI.2018.8394569

Cheyunski, F. M. J., & Millard, J. (1998). Accelerated Business Transformation and the Role of the Organization Architect. *The Journal of Applied Behavioral Science*, *34*(3), 268–285. doi:10.1177/0021886398343003

Choma, A. A. (2008). How to reduce risks in contractors' management. In *PMI® Global Congress 2008—North America*. Denver, CO. Newtown Square, PA: Project Management Institute.

Choudhary, V., & Vithayathil, J. (2013). The Impact of Cloud Computing: Should the IT Department Be Organized as a Cost Center or a Profit Center? *Journal of Management Information Systems*, *30*(2), 67–100. doi:10.2753/MIS0742-1222300203

Christian, F. (2020). *Magic Quadrant for Contract Life Cycle Management*. Retrieved December 01, 2020, from http://blog.dayaciptamandiri.com/2020/03/magic-quadrant-for-contract-life-cycle.html

Chuang, T.-T., Nakatani, K., & Chen, T. T. (2015). An exploratory study of expected business value of cloud computing. *Issues in Information Systems*, *16*(4).

Cichosz, M., Wallenburg, C. M., & Knemeyer, A. M. (2020). Digital transformation at logistics service providers: Barriers, success factors and leading practices. *International Journal of Logistics Management*, *3*(2), 209–238. doi:10.1108/IJLM-08-2019-0229

Ciligot, C. (2020, February 24). *platform-governance*. Retrieved from https://learn.g2.com/: https://learn.g2.com/platform-governance

CIPS (Chartered Institute of Procurement and Supply). (2020). *Contract Management*. Available at:https://www.cips.org/knowledge/procurement-topics-and-skills/developing-and-managing-contracts/contract-management/

Clark, E. (2018).*D igital Transformation:W hat is it?* Retrieved on December 22.2019 from https://er.educause.edu/articles/2018/5/digital-transformation-what-is-it

Clement, J. (2019, September 11). *Mobile internet usage worldwide - Statistics & Facts*. Retrieved from https://www.statista.com/topics/779/mobile-internet/

Cloudmoyo. (2020). *Applying artificial intelligence to contract management*. Available at https://www.cloudmoyo.com/blog/artificial-intelligence-in-contract-management/

Clutterbuck, P., Rowlands, T., & Seamons, O. (2009). A Case Study of SME Web Application Development Effectiveness via Agile Methods. *The Electronic Journal Information Systems Evaluation*, *12*(1), 13–26.

CNBC. (2020). *Zoom CFO explains how the company is grappling with increased demand.* Retrieved March 25, 2020, from https://www.cnbc.com/2020/03/18/zoom-cfo-explains-how-the-company-is-grappling-with-increased-demand.html

Collins-dictionary. (2020, November 29). *Retained-earnings*. Retrieved from https://www.collinsdictionary.com/dictionary/english/retained-earnings

Conrad, E., Misenar, S., & Feldman, J. (2015). *CISSP Study Guide*. Elsevier Inc.; doi:10.1016/B978-0-12-802437-9.00008-4

Conti, C. R. (1998). Can physicians practice cost-effective medicine? *Clinical Cardiology, 21*(1), 2–3. doi:10.1002/clc.4960210101 PMID:9474458

Cornelius, K. B. (2018). *Standard form contracts and a smart contract future.* Internet Policy Review.

Cullen, S., Seddon, P., & Willcocks, L. (2006, February 1). *Managing outsourcing: The lifecycle imperative.* London, UK, UK: London School of Economics and Political Science.

Cummins, T. (2009a). *Commitment Matters. Are complex contracts doomed to fail?* Retrieved September 22, 2020, from https://commitmentmatters.com/2009/11/12/are-complex-contracts-doomed-to-fail/

Cummins, T. (2009b). *Commitment Matters. Poor Contract Management Costs Companies 9% — Bottom Line*. Retrieved September 22, 2020, from https://commitmentmatters.com/2012/10/23/poor-contract-management-costscompanies-9-bottom-line/

Cummins, T. (2012, Oct 23). *poor-contract-management-costs-companies-9-bottom-lin*. Retrieved from https://blog.iaccm.com/commitment-matters-tim-cummins-blog/2012/10/23/poor-contract-management-costs-companies-9-bottom-lin

Cummins, T., David, M., & Kawamoto, K. (2011). *Contract and Commercial Management-The Operational Guide.* Van Haren Publishing.

Cunningham, T. (2015). Risk Allocation under the Principal 'Traditional' Irish Forms of Building Contract. Architectural Engineering Commons, 1-16. doi:10.21427/vbqd-mm31

D'Amelio, S. (2019, June 21). *how-to-handle-contract-amendments-contraxaware/*. Retrieved April 21, 2020, from https://www.contraxaware.com/blog/how-to-handle-contract-amendments-contraxaware/:https://www.contraxaware.com/blog/how-to-handle-contract-amendments-contraxaware/

Dabass, J., & Dabass, B. S. (2018). *Scope of Artificial Intelligence in Law.* Academic Press.

Daglio, M., Gerson, D., & Kitchen, H. (2014). Building Organisational Capacity for Public Sector Innovation. In *OECD Conference "Innovating the Public Sector: from Ideas to Impact"*. Paris: OECD.

Dahlgaard-Park, S. (2015). Training, education, and development of staff. In *The sage encyclopedia of quality and the service economy, 1* (pp. 816–819). SAGE Publications, Inc. doi:10.4135/9781483346366.n225

Dahmardeh, N., & Banihashemi, S. A. (2010). Organizational agility and agile manufacturing. European Journal of Economics. *Finance and Administrative Science, 27*, 178–184.

Danzon, P. M. (2018). Affordability Challenges to Value-Based Pricing: Mass Diseases, Orphan Diseases, and Cures. *Value in Health, 21*(3), 252–257. doi:10.1016/j.jval.2017.12.018 PMID:29566830

Darrington, J. W., & Howell, G. A. (2011). Motivation and incentives in relational contracts. *Journal of Financial Management of Property and Construction, 16*(1), 42–51. doi:10.1108/13664381111116070

Davenport, T. H., & Harris, J. G. (2007). *Competing on analytics: The new science of winning.* Harvard Business Review Press.

Davidson, W. H. (1993). Beyond re-engineering: The three phases of business transformation. *IBM Systems Journal*, *32*(1), 485–499. doi:10.1147j.321.0065

De Mauro, A., Greco, M., & Grimaldi, M. (2016). A formal definition of Big Data based on its essential features. *Library Review*, *65*(3), 122–135. doi:10.1108/LR-06-2015-0061

de Mendonça, C. M. C., & de Andrade, A. M. V. (2018). Dynamic Capabilities and Their Relations with Elements of Digital Transformation in Portugal. *Journal of Information Systems Engineering & Management*, *3*(3). Advance online publication. doi:10.20897/jisem/2660

de Silva, S. L., & de Oliveira, S. B. (2015). Planning and Scope Definition to Implement ERP: The Case Study of Federal Rural University of Rio de Janeiro (UFRRJ). *Procedia Computer Science*, *64*, 196–203. doi:10.1016/j.procs.2015.08.481

Deloitte. (2018). *Digital enablement turning your transformation into a successful journey.* Retrieved on December 23,2019 from https://www2.deloitte.com/content/dam/Deloitte/ie/Documents/Technology/IE_C_HC_campaign.pdf

Deloitte. (2019). *Risk_outsourcing Guidelines.* Retrieved from https://www2.deloitte.com: https://www2.deloitte.com/content/dam/Deloitte/cy/Documents/risk/CY_Risk_EBA%20outsourcing%20guidelines.pdf

Deloitte. (2020, April 1). *Energy-resources/us-2020-power-utilities-midyear.* Retrieved from https://www2.deloitte.com/content/dam/Deloitte/us/Documents/energy-resources/us-2020-power-utilities-midyear.pdf

Deltek. (2018, January 29). *10-key-financial-performance-indicators-for-government-contractors.* Retrieved from https://www.deltek.com/en/learn/blogs/government-contracting/2018/01/10-key-financial-performance-indicators-for-government-contractors

Denisi, S. A., & Griffin, W. R. (2001). Human Resource Management. Houghton Mifflin Company.

Deshwal, P. (2015). Role of E-HRM in Organizational Effectiveness & Sustainability. *IJAR*, *1*(12), 605–609.

Dessler, G. (2017). *Human Resource Management* (15th ed.). Prentice-Hall.

DeVore, B. L., Wilson, B. C., & Parsons, J. (2013, January 1). *Healthcare-presbyterian-healthcare-services-whitepaper.pdf.* Retrieved July 22, 2020, from https://www.intel.com/content/dam/www/public/us/en/documents/white-papers/healthcare-presbyterian-healthcare-services-whitepaper.pdf

Dey, N., Babo, R., Ashour, A., Bhatnagar, V., & Bouhlel, M. S. (2018). *Social Networks Science: Design, Implementation, Security, and Challenges: From Social Networks Analysis to Social Networks Intelligence*. Springer. doi:10.1007/978-3-319-90059-9

Dietrich, M., & Anderson, G. (2012). *The Financial Professional's Guide to Healthcare Reform.* John Wiley & Sons.

Dinh, T. N., & Thai, M. T. (2018). Ai and blockchain: A disruptive integration. *Computer*, *51*(9), 48–53. doi:10.1109/MC.2018.3620971

Dolgui, A., & Proth, J.-M. (2013). Outsourcing: Definitions and analysis. *International Journal of Production Research*, *51*(23-24), 23–24. doi:10.1080/00207543.2013.855338

Dommisse, W. R., & Oosthuizen, H. (2004). Value chain deconstruction in the United Kingdom retail life insurance industry and resulting strategic options for new entrants to the market. *South African Journal of Business Management*, *35*(4), 11–20.

Dompere, K. K. (2004). *Cost-Benefit Analysis and the +eory of Fuzzy Decision.* Springer-Verlag.

Dosi, G. (2017). The blade runner scenario. In La Nueva Revolución de la Producción: La Transformación Digital. Revista de Ciencias y Humanidades (pp. 71–74). Fundación Ramón Areces.

Drake, P. R., Myung Lee, D., & Hussain, M. (2013). The lean and agile purchasing portfolio model. *Supply Chain Management, 18*(1), 3–20. doi:10.1108/13598541311293140

Drimalla, R. (2019). *Leverage a Process-Driven Contract Lifecycle Management Method.* Corporate Counsel Business Journal.

Druckman, D. E., & Bjork, R. A. (1994). *Learning, remembering, believing: Enhancing human performance.* National Academy Press.

DTA (Digital Transformation Agency, Australian Government). (2018). *Digital Transformation Strategy.* Available at: https://dta-www-drupal-20180130215411153400000001.s3.ap-southeast-2.amazonaws.com/s3fs-public/files/digital-transformation-strategy/digital-transformation-strategy.pdf

Duan, Y., Fu, G., Zhou, N., Sun, X., Narendra, N. C., & Hu, B. (2015). Everything as a Service (XaaS) on the Cloud: Origins, Current and Future Trends. *2015 IEEE 8th International Conference on Cloud Computing*, 621–628. 10.1109/CLOUD.2015.88

Duhig, A. M., Saha, S., Smith, S., Kaufman, S., & Hughes, J. (2018). The Current Status of Outcomes-Based Contracting for Manufacturers and Payers: An AMCP Membership Survey. *Journal of Managed Care Speciality Pharma*, 410-415.

Du, J., Gelenbe, E., Jiang, C., Zhang, H., & Ren, Y. (2017). Contract Design for Traffic Offloading and Resource Allocation in Heterogeneous Ultra-Dense Networks. *IEEE Journal on Selected Areas in Communications, 35*(11), 2457–2467. doi:10.1109/JSAC.2017.2760459

Dura, A. B., & Al-Sabbagh, Z. N. (2008). *Human Resource Management in the 21st Century: System Approach.* Dar Wael Publishing and Distribution.

Dutt, A. K. (2006). Aggregate Demand, Aggregate Supply and Economic Growth. *International Review of Applied Economics, 20*(3), 319–336. doi:10.1080/02692170600736094

Economicsonline. (2020). *Price – definition.* Retrieved April 22, 2020, from https://www.economicsonline.co.uk/Definitions/Price.html

Eggbeer, B., Sears, K., & Homer, K. (2015). Finding the 'sweet spot' in value-based contracts. *Healthcare Financial Management Association Journal*, 48-57.

Eggbeer, W. T. (2015, August 1). *Inding-the-sweet-spot-in-value-based-contracts.* Retrieved July 21, 2020, from https://www.bdcadvisors.com/finding-the-sweet-spot-in-value-based-contracts/

Eggbeer, W. T., Morris, D. E., & Sukenik, C. C. (2016, March 1). Retrieved Jul 21, 2020, from https://www.bdcadvisors.com/next-generation-health-care/

Ehret, M., & Jochen, W. (2017). Unlocking value from machines: Business models and the industrial internet of things. *Journal of Marketing Management, 33*(1-2), 111–130. doi:10.1080/0267257X.2016.1248041

El-adaway, I. H., Vance, R. A., & Abotaleb, I. S. (2020, January 12). Understanding Extension of Time under Different Standard Design-Build Forms of Contract. *Journal of Legal Affairs and Dispute Resolution in Engineering and Construction, 12*(1). Advance online publication. doi:10.1061/(ASCE)LA.1943-4170.0000331

Ellul, J., & Pace, G. (2018). AlkylVM: A Virtual Machine for Smart Contract Blockchain Connected Internet of Things. *2018 9th IFIP International Conference on New Technologies, Mobility and Security (NTMS),* 1-4. 10.1109/NTMS.2018.8328732

Endrenyi, J. (1978). *Reliability modelling in electric power systems.* Wiley International Publication.

Erika, T. (2013, November 13). Retrieved May 1, 2020, from https://www.hitachi.com/rd/sc/story/business_dynamics/index.html

Esakhani, A., Fani, A., & Danayifard, H. (2012). Determination of the Relationship between Work Engagement & Employees Organizational Commitment. In General Management Researches (5th ed., pp. 38-23). Academic Press.

ESDC. E. a. (2019, July 29). Retrieved April 24, 2020, from https://www.canada.ca/en/employment-social-development/services/labour-standards/reports/protection-workers-nonstandard.html#h2.3

Esteves, J. M. (2014). An empirical identification and categorisation of training best practices for ERP implementation projects. *Enterprise Information Systems, 8*(6), 665–683. doi:10.1080/17517575.2013.771411

EU4Digital. (2020, January 29). *From start-up ecosystems to innovation funding: EU4Digital begins ICT legislation gap analysis across priority areas.* Retrieved from https://eufordigital.eu/: https://eufordigital.eu/from-start-up-ecosystems-and-innovation-funding-to-intellectual-property-rights-and-the-digitisation-of-industry-eu4digital-begins-ict-legislation-gap-analysis-across-priority-areas/

Eurofound. (2017). *Digitisation of processes. Literature review.* Luxembourg: Publications Office of the European Union.

Eurofound. (2018a). *Game changing technologies: Exploring the impact on production processes and work.* Luxembourg: Publications Office of the European Union.

European Commission. (2019). *Digital transformation.* Retrieved on December 20,2019 from https://ec.europa.eu/growth/industry/policy/digitaltransformation_en

European Union. (2019, June 1). *Standards and the digitalisation of EU industry.* Retrieved from https://www.europarl.europa.eu/RegData/etudes/BRIE/2019/635608/EPRS_BRI(2019)635608_EN.pdf

Evans, R. (2019, June 18). Retrieved May 1, 2020, from https://www.tiretechnologyinternational.com/news/research-development/bridgestone-develops-technology-to-reduce-tire-weight-by-10.html

EvansP. (2014). https://www.bbvaopenmind.com/en/articles/from-deconstruction-to-big-data-how-technology-is-reshaping-the-corporation/

Fagundes, L. (2016, March 3). *Standard Vs. Strategic Contracts.* Retrieved from https://www.contractworks.com/blog/standard-vs.-strategic-contracts#:~:text=A%20lot%20of%20contracts%2C%20if,the%20mill%2C%20standard%20form%20agreements

FAR. (2020, December 1). *Federal Acquisition Regulation.* Retrieved from https://www.acquisition.gov: https://www.acquisition.gov/sites/default/files/current/far/compiled_html/subpart_16.2.html

Fenech, R., Baguant, P., & Ivanov, D. (2019). Higher Colleges of Technology The changing role of human resource management in an era of digital transformation. *International Journal of Entrepreneurship, 22*(2), 139–149.

FIDIC. (2020, December 5). *Contracts: basic questions Question/Answer.* https://fidic.org/node/911

Finance, A. T. C. C. (2015). Industry 4.0 Challenges and Solutions for the Digital Transformation and Use do Exponential Technologies [Audit Tax Consulting Corporate Finance Report]. Zurich, Switzerland: Author.

Finogeev, A., Vasin, S., Gamidullaeva, L., & Parygin, D. (2018). Blockchain and Smart Contracts for Support the Interaction between the Actors in the Regional Innovation System. *2018 International Conference on System Modeling & Advancement in Research Trends (SMART)*, 27-31. 10.1109/SYSMART.2018.8746949

Florowski, G. & Olivasalujan-Lujan, M. (2006). The Diffusion of HRM-Technology Innovations in US & Non-US Firms. *Personnel Review*, *35*(6), 684–710. doi:10.1108/00483480610702737

Forbes, B., & Brady, M. (2019, April 1). Ex-post service contract performance management. *International Journal of Business Performance Management*. doi:10.1504/IJBPM.2019.098634

Ford, D. N. (2002). Achieving multiple project objectives through contingency management. *Journal of Construction Engineering and Management*, *128*(1), 30–39. doi:10.1061/(ASCE)0733-9364(2002)128:1(30)

Foro de Empresas Innovadoras. (2018). Re-industrialización en España: Industria 4.0 y ecosistemas de innovación. Madrid: Author.

Fortune Business Insights. (2019, November 6). Retrieved May 1, 2020, from https://www.globenewswire.com/news-release/2019/11/06/1941841/0/en/Automotive-Tire-Market-to-Expand-with-Light-Commercial-Vehicles-Production-Set-to-Reach-118-9-Million-Units-by-2025-Fortune-Business-Insights.html

Forum, Public Policy. (2019). Retrieved April 24, 2020, from https://ppforum.ca/publications/managing-precarious-work-three-canadian-models-for-rebalancing-bargaining-power-in-the-future-of-work/?utm_source=web&utm_medium=sm&utm_campaign=bnw

Foss, N. J., & Saebi, T. (2016). Fifteen Years of Research on Business Model Innovation: How Far Have We Come, and Where Should We Go? *Journal of Management*, 1–15.

Fredette, J., Marom, R., Steiner, K., & Witters, L. (2012). *The Promise and Peril of Hyperconnectivity for Organizations and Societies*. Geneva: World Economic Forum.

French, L. W. (2003). Human Resource Management (5th ed.). Houghton Mifflin Company.

Frey, S. C., & Schlosser, M. M. (1993, October 15). ABB and Ford: Creating Value through Cooperation. *MIT Sloan Management Review*, 65–72.

Fried, C. (2015). *Contract as Promise: A Theory of Contractual Obligation*. Oxford University Press. doi:10.1093/acprof:oso/9780190240158.001.0001

Frydlinger, D., Hart, O., & Vitasek, K. (2019, September 1). A New Approach to Contracts. *Harvard Business Review*.

Fuchs, C., & Hess, T. (2018). Becoming agile in the digital transformation: the process of a large-scale agile transformation. *Thirty Ninth International Conference on Information Systems*.

Gadi, M. (2016). Left industrial policy and industry 4.0. At progressive industrial policy for the EU? Out-manoeuvring liberalism. Rosa Luxemburgo Stiftung. Brussels Office.

Galanaki, E. (2002). The Decision to Recruit on Line: A Descriptive Study. *Career Development International*, *7*(4), 243–251. doi:10.1108/13620430210431325

Gandomi, A., & Haider, M. (2015). Beyond the hype: Big data concepts, methods, and analytics. *International Journal of Information Management*, *35*(2), 137–144. doi:10.1016/j.ijinfomgt.2014.10.007

Ganes, A., & Nævdal, S. (2008). *Software Contracting and Agile Development in the Norwegian ICT Industry: A Qualitative Survey* (Unpublished Master dissertation). Norwegian University of Science and Technology (NTNU), Trondheim, Norway.

Gardiner, P. D. (2005). *Project Management: A Strategic Planning Approach*. Macmillan International Higher Education. doi:10.1007/978-1-137-07973-2

Gardner, S., Lepak, D., & Bartl, K. (2003). Virtual HR: The Impact of Information Technology on the Human Resource Professional. *Journal of Vocational Behavior*, *63*(2), 159–179. doi:10.1016/S0001-8791(03)00039-3

Gartner, (2020, February 25). Magic Quadrant for Contract Life Cycle Management. Retrieved from https://www.gartner.com/doc/reprints?id=1-1YI5K8JY&ct=200226&st=sb

Gartner. (2020, February 25). *Magic Quadrant for Contract Life Cycle Management*. Gartner. https://www.gartner.com/doc/reprints?id=1-1YI5K8JY&ct=200226&st=sb

Geotab. (2020, April 14). Retrieved May 1, 2020, from https://www.geotab.com/blog/impact-of-covid-19/

Gerster, D., & Dremel, C. (2019). Agile contracts: Learning from an autonomous driving sourcing project. In *Proceedings of the 27th European Conference on Information Systems (ECIS)* (pp. 1-12). AIS Electronic Library (AISeL).

Gewald, H., & Schäfer, L. (2017, February 20). Quo vadis outsourcing? A view from practice. *Journal of Global Operations and Strategic Sourcing*, *10*(1), 2–17. doi:10.1108/JGOSS-10-2016-0031

Ghazzawi, K., Al-Khoury, P., & Saman, J. (2014). The Effect of Implementing Technology in HRM on the Level of Employee Motivation. *HRM Research*, *4*(2), 33–39.

Giang, D. T., & Pheng, L. (2011, January 1). Role of construction in economic development: Review of key concepts in the past 40 years. *Habitat International*, *35*(1), 1–16. doi:10.1016/j.habitatint.2010.06.003

Glaiel, F. (2012, May 7). *Agile project dynamics: a strategic project management approach to the study of large-scale software development using system dynamics* (Thesis). Massachusetts Institute of Technology, Engineering Systems Division. Retrieved from http://hdl.handle.net/1721.1/79513

Glas, A., Henne, F., & Essig, M. (2018). Missing performance management and measurement aspects in performance-based contracting: A systematic process-based literature analysis of an astonishing research gap. *International Journal of Operations & Production Management*, *38*(11), 2062–2095. doi:10.1108/IJOPM-09-2016-0571

Gluck, G. (1979). Standard Form Contracts: The Contract Theory Reconsidered. *The International and Comparative Law Quarterly*, *28*(1), 72–90. www.jstor.org/stable/758554. doi:10.1093/iclqaj/28.1.72

Goldbach, T., Benlian, A., & Buxmann, P. (2018). Differential effects of formal and self-control in mobile platform ecosystems: Multi-method findings on third-party developers' continuance intentions and application quality. *Information & Management*, *55*(3), 271–284. doi:10.1016/j.im.2017.07.003

Gomes, R., & Osman, S. (2019). *Managing Organizational Adoption of IoT*. Uppsala, Sweden: Uppsala University. Retrieved November 12, 2020, from http://uu.diva-portal.org/smash/get/diva2:1374639/FULLTEXT01.pdf

Gomes, S. (2018). Smart Contracts: Legal Frontiers and Insertion into the Creative Economy. *Brazilian Journal of Operations & Production Management*, 376-385.

Gomez-Mejia, B., David, B., & Cardy, L. R. (1998). Managing Human Resources. Prentice Hall.

Goodland, H., & Lam, A. (2018, December 1). *Construction-Industry-KPI-report-FINAL*. Retrieved from http://www.constructionfoundation.ca/wp-content/uploads/2019/05/Construction-Industry-KPI-report-FINAL.pdf

Government, H. (2018, Feb 1). *The_experiences_of_those_in_the_gig_economy*. Retrieved April 24, 2020, from https://assets.publishing.service.gov.uk/government/uploads/system/uploads/attachment_data/file/679987/171107_The_experiences_of_those_in_the_gig_economy.pdf

Goyal, V. (2012). Role of SOA & Cloud Computing in IT Industry. *International Journal of Engineering Research & Technology, 1*(6), 1–5.

Gozman, D., & Willcocks, L. (2015). Crocodiles in the Regulatory Swamp: Navigating The Dangers of Outsourcing, SaaS and Shadow IT. In *Thirty Sixth International Conference on Information Systems*, (p. 20). Fort Worth, TX: Association for Information Systems.

Grandori, A., & Furlotti, M. (2009). Facio ut Facias: Associational Contracts for Innovation. *International Studies of Management & Organization, 39*(4), 81–100. doi:10.2753/IMO0020-8825390405

Groen, A., & Walsh, S. (2013). Introduction to the Field of Emerging Technology Management. *Creativity and Innovation Management, 22*(1), 1–5. doi:10.1111/caim.12019

Gross, E. (2019, August 6). Retrieved April 24, 2020, from https://www.peoplemanagement.co.uk/experts/legal/future-hr-hurdles-gig-economy

Grubic, T., & Jennions, I. (2018). Do outcome-based contracts exist? The investigation of power-by-the-hour and similar result-oriented cases. *International Journal of Production Economics, 206*, 209–219. doi:10.1016/j.ijpe.2018.10.004

Gruneberg, S., Hughes, W., & Ancell, D. (2007). Risk under performance-based contracting in the UK construction sector. *Construction Management and Economics, 25*(7), 691–699. doi:10.1080/01446190601164097

Gupta, M., George, J. F., & Xia, W. (2019). Relationships between IT department culture and agile software development practices: An empirical investigation. *International Journal of Information Management, 44*, 13–24. doi:10.1016/j.ijinfomgt.2018.09.006

Haddara, M. (2014). ERP Selection: The SMART Way. *Procedia Technology, 16*, 394–403. doi:10.1016/j.protcy.2014.10.105

Hagel, J., Brown, J. S., Wooll, M., & de Maar, A. (2016, January 11). *Shorten the value chain.* Retrieved from Deloitte: https://www2.deloitte.com/us/en/insights/focus/disruptive-strategy-patterns-case-studies/disruptive-strategy-value-chain-models.html

Hall, W., & Pesenti, J. (2017). *Growing the artificial intelligence industry in the UK.* Department for Digital, Culture, Media & Sport and Department for Business, Energy & Industrial Strategy. Part of the Industrial Strategy UK and the Commonwealth.

Haller, S., Karnouskos, S., & Schroth, C. (2008). The internet of things in an enterprise context. *Future Internet Symposium*, 14–28.

Hamzah, M. H. I., Baharom, F., Mohd, H., & Omar, M. H. (2018). Evaluation of service-oriented architecture adoption maturity model for sustainable development. *Journal of Telecommunication Electronic and Computer Engineering, 10*(2–4), 19–22.

Harris, F. (2003). How many parts to make at once. In M. Lewis & N. Slack (Eds.), *Operations Management: Critical perspective of business management* (pp. 3–9). Routledge.

Harroch, R. (2016, March 10). *The Key Elements Of Non-Disclosure Agreements.* Retrieved from Forbes: https://www.forbes.com/sites/allbusiness/2016/03/10/the-key-elements-of-non-disclosure-agreements/?sh=267a94e6627d

Hartmann, P. M., Zaki, M., Feldmann, N., & Neely, A. (2016). Capturing value from big data—A taxonomy of data-driven business models used by start-up firms. *International Journal of Operations & Production Management, 36*(10), 1382–1406. doi:10.1108/IJOPM-02-2014-0098

Hart, O. (2017). Incomplete Contracts and Control. *The American Economic Review, 107*(7), 1731–1752. doi:10.1257/aer.107.7.1731

Harvard Business School. (2018). *IKEA: crowdsourcing ideas to co-create a better everyday life.* Retrieved March 20, 2020, from https://digital.hbs.edu/platform-digit/submission/ikea-crowdsourcing-ideas-to-co-create-a-better-everyday-life/

Hattori, R. A., & Lapidus, T. (2004). Collaboration, trust and innovative change. *Journal of Change Management, 4*(2), 97–104. doi:10.1080/14697010320001549197

HBR. (2013, April 1). *Innovation-risk-how-to-make-smarter-decisions.* Retrieved from https://hbr.org: https://hbr.org/2013/04/innovation-risk-how-to-make-smarter-decisions

Health Leaders. (2020, December 2). *Four-keys-building-successful-value-based-supplier-contracts.* Retrieved Jul 21, 2020, from https://www.healthleadersmedia.com/finance/four-keys-building-successful-value-based-supplier-contracts

Hegedus, P. (2018). Towards Analyzing the Complexity Landscape of Solidity Based Ethereum Smart Contracts. *2018 IEEE/ACM 1st International Workshop on Emerging Trends in Software Engineering for Blockchain (WETSEB),* 35-39. 10.1145/3194113.3194119

Heide, J. B. (1994). Interorganizational Governance in Marketing Channels. *Journal of Marketing, 85*(1), 71–85. doi:10.1177/002224299405800106

Helo, P., Anussornnitisarn, P., & Phusavat, K. (2008). Expectation and reality in ERP implementation: Consultant and solution provider perspective. *Industrial Management & Data Systems, 108*(8), 1045–1059. doi:10.1108/02635570810904604

Hendrickson, C. (2008). *Project Management for Construction.* Mellon University, Pittsburgh. Retrieved from https://www.cmu.edu/cee/projects/PMbook/

Hietanen, S. (2014). Mobility as a Service"—The new transport model? *Eurotransport, 12*(2), 2–4.

Highsmith, J. A. (2009). *Agile project management: creating innovative products.* Pearson Education.

Hitachi. (2018). *Co-creating the Future.* Retrieved from https://www.hitachi.eu/sites/default/files/fields/document/sib/whitepapers/cocreatingthefuture-web-updated_17_oct.pdf

Hitt, M. A., Ireland, R. D., & Hoskisson, R. E. (2007). *Strategic Management: Competitiveness and Golbalization.* Thomson South-Western.

Hoffman, M., & Burks, S. (2017). *Training Contracts, Employee Turnover, and the Returns from Firm-Sponsored General Training.* Institute of Labor Economics. Retrieved October 08, 2020, from https://www.econstor.eu/bitstream/10419/170819/1/dp10835.pdf

Hofstrand, D. (2013, June). *Understanding the Time Value of Money.* Retrieved from Business Development, Starting a Business, Finances: https://www.extension.iastate.edu/agdm/wholefarm/html/c5-96.html

Holden, A. (2020, June 25). *the-future-of-compliance-digital-transformation-meets-regulation.* Retrieved from https://www.finextra.com/blogposting/18924/the-future-of-compliance-digital-transformation-meets-regulation

Hou, J., & Neely, A. (2018). Investigating risks of outcome-based service contracts from a provider's perspective. *International Journal of Production Research, 6*(6), 2103–2115. doi:10.1080/00207543.2017.1319089

Hu,W., Fan, Z., & Gao, Y. (2019). Research on Smart Contract Optimization Method on Blockchain. *IT Professional, 21*(5), 33-38.

Hudson, K., Grisham, T., Srinivasan, P., & Moussa, N. (2005). *Conflict Management, Negotiation, and Effective communication Essential Skills for Project Managers.* Retrieved from http://thomasgrisham.com/wp-content/uploads/2020/04/Conflict-Management-Negotiation-and-Effective-Communication-1.pdf

Hughes, R. (2012). *Agile Data Warehousing Project Management: Business Intelligence Systems Using Scrum.* Newnes.

Hummel, M., Rosenkranz, C., & Holten, R. (2013). The Role of Communication in Agile Systems Development. *Business & Information Systems Engineering, 5*(5), 343–355. doi:10.100712599-013-0282-4

Iannarelli, J., & O'Shaughnessy, M. (2015). *Information Governance and Security.* Edinburgh: Elsevier Inc.; doi:10.1016/B978-0-12-800247-6.00006-6

Icertis. (2020). *What Is Contract Intelligence?* Available at: https://www.icertis.com/resource/what-is-contract-intelligence/

IDG. (2018). *State of Digital Business Transformation 2018.* Retrieved on December 15,2019 from https://cdn2.hubspot.net/hubfs/1624046/Digital%20Business%20Executive%20Summary_FINAL.pdf

Ifinedo, P. (2008). Impacts of business vision, top management support, and external expertise on ERP success. *Business Process Management Journal, 14*(4), 551–568. doi:10.1108/14637150810888073

Inghram, Z. (2019, April 24). *3-important-benefits-of-financial-reporting.* Retrieved from https://www.ucpaa.org/3-important-benefits-of-financial-reporting

International Air Transport Association (IATA). (2018). *Ai in Aviation-Exploring the Fundamentals, Threats, and Opportunities of Artificial Intelligence (Ai) In the Aviation Industry.* White Paper. Available at:https://www.iata.org/contentassets/b90753e0f52e48a58b28c51df023c6fb/ai-white-paper.pdf

International Labour Organization (ILO). (2012). [REMOVED HYPERLINK FIELD]etrieved April 24, 2020, from https://www.ilo.org/actrav/info/WCMS_179787/lang--en/index.htm

International Telecommunication Union (ITU). (2019, June 1). *Policy and regulatory environments for digital transformation.* Retrieved from https://www.itu.int/: https://www.itu.int/en/mediacentre/backgrounders/Pages/Policy-and-regulatory-environments-for-digital-transformation.aspx

International Trade Centre. (2018). *Cross-border contracting: How to draft and negotiate international commercial contracts.* International Trade Centre, World Trade Organization and the United Nations.

International Trade Centre. (2018, November 1). *Cross-border contracting.* Retrieved from https://www.intracen.org/uploadedFiles/intracenorg/Content/Publications/Cross-border%20contracting_final_v2_with%20cover_Low-res.pdf

Internet Society. (2015). *The Internet of Things (IoT): An Overview.* Retrieved from https://www.internetsociety.org/resources/doc/2015/iot-overview?gclid=EAIaIQobChMIkv3Kyu3L6AIVQUPTCh3DIwFTEAAYASAAEgJCTPD_BwE

Iqbal, S., Choudhry, R. M., Holschemacher, K., Ali, A., & Tamosaitiene, J. (2015, January). Risk management in construction projects. *Technological and Economic Development of Economy, 21*(1), 65–78. doi:10.3846/20294913.2014.994582

i-scoop. (2020, December 14). *Industry-4-0.* Retrieved from https://www.i-scoop.eu/industry-4-0/

Ismail, M. H., Khater, M., & Zaki, M. (2017). *Digital business transformation and strategy: What do we know so far?* Retrieved on January 11, 2020 from https://pdfs.semanticscholar.org/35b2/bd95aeb8e6ca0ea0652d0d7fc697eda3362a.pdf

Ismail, M. H., Khater, M., & Zaki, M. (2017). *Digital business transformation and strategy: What do we know so far?* Retrieved on January 11,2020 from https://pdfs.semanticscholar.org/35b2/bd95aeb8e6ca0ea0652d0d7fc697eda3362a.pdf

Issa, A., Hatiboglu, B., Bildstein, A., & Bauernhansl, T. (2018). Industrie 4.0 roadmap: Framework for digital transformation based on the concepts of capability maturity and alignment. In L. Wang (Ed.), *51st CIRP Conference on Manufacturing Systems*. Stockholm: Elsevier. 10.1016/j.procir.2018.03.151

Ittelson, T. R. (2009). *Financial Statements: A Step-by-step Guide to Understanding and Creating Financial reports*. Career Press.

Ivancevich, M. J. (2001). Human resource Management. McGraw-Hill.

Ivan, L., Bosilj Vuk, V., & Spremi, M. (2019). Mastering the Digital Transformation Process: Business Practices and Lessons Learned. *Technology Innovation Management Review*, *59*(2), 36–50. doi:10.22215/timreview/1217

Javier-Braña, F. (2019). A fourth industrial revolution? Digital transformation, labor and work organization: A view from Spain. *Economia e Politica Industriale*, *46*(3), 415–430. doi:10.100740812-019-00122-0

Jiang, L., Li, Z., Li, L., & Gao, Y. (2018). Constraints on the Promotion of Prefabricated Construction in China. *Sustainability*. Retrieved from https://www.mdpi.com/2071-1050/10/7/2516

Jittrapirom, V., Caiati, V., Feneri, A.-M., Ebrahimigharehbaghi, S., González, M. J., & Narayan, J. (2017). Mobility as a Service: A Critical Review of Definitions, Assessments of Schemes, and Key Challenges. *Urban Planning*, *2*(2), 13–25. doi:10.17645/up.v2i2.931

Jota, P. R., Silva, V. R., & Jota, F. G. (2011). Building load management using cluster and statistical analyses. *International Journal of Electrical Power & Energy Systems*, *33*(8), 1498–1505. doi:10.1016/j.ijepes.2011.06.034

Juan, Y.-K., Lai, W.-Y., & Shih, S.-G. (2017). Building information modeling acceptance and readiness assessment in Taiwanese architectural firms. *Journal of Civil Engineering and Management*, *23*(2), 356–367. doi:10.3846/13923730.2015.1128480

Kagioglou, M., Cooper, R., & Aouad, G. (2001). Performance management in construction: A conceptual framework. *Construction Management and Economics*, *19*(1), 85–95. doi:10.1080/01446190010003425

Kangari, R. (1991). Advanced robotics in civil engineering and construction. In *Fifth International Conference on Advanced Robotics 'Robots in Unstructured Environments* (pp. 375-378). Pisa, Italy: IEEE. 10.1109/ICAR.1991.240624

Kapsali, M., Roehrich, J., & Akhtar, P. A. (2018). Effective contracting for high operational performance in projects. *International Journal of Operations & Production Management*, 294–325. doi:0.1108/IJOPM-10-2017-0604

Karampour, A., Nazari, Y., Alinia, S., & Kameli, A. (2014). Survey & Comparison of E-HRM Systems in Oil & Gas Companies Lorestan Province. *International Journal of Management & Humanity Sciences*, *3*(1), 1308–1315.

Kelker, P., Gerster, D., & Dremel, C. (2018). Agile Meets Non-Agile: Implications of Adopting Agile Practices at Enterprises. In *24th American Conference on Infromation Systems* (pp. 1-15). New Orleans, USA: AMCIS 2018 Proceedings.

Kelman, L. F., Barth, A. F., & Bottenfield, A. (2016, July 1). *Mechanics-lien-remedies-require-a-sharp-eye*. Retrieved from https://www.cohenseglias.com: https://www.cohenseglias.com/news-article/mechanics-lien-remedies-require-a-sharp-eye/

Kemp, S. (2009, March 26). 6 Steps to Better Business Solutions. *Entrepreneur*.

Kettunen, P., & Laanti, M. (2017). Future software organizations—Agile goals and roles. *European Journal of Futures Research*, *5*(1), 16. doi:10.100740309-017-0123-7

Khong, L., Beng, Y. L., Yip, T., & Fun, T. (2012). Software Development Life Cycle AGILE vs Traditional Approaches. In *International Conference on Information and Network Technology* (pp. 162-166). Chennai, India: IACSIT Press.

Killough, D. (2020, January 17). *Construction Accounting 101: How 4 Financial Statements Help You Keep More Money In Your Pocket.* Retrieved from https://www.levelset.com/blog/construction-accounting-how-4-financial-statements-keep-more-money/

KMPG. (2019). *Capture the value of your contracts: Cognitive Contract Management from KPMG and Google Cloud.* Available at: https://assets.kpmg/content/dam/kpmg/uk/pdf/2018/09/capture-the-value-of-your-contracts.pdf

Kobzeff, J. (2018, May 22). *The IRR, MIRR, and FMRR Approaches to Investment Analysis.* Retrieved from https://proapod.com/Articles/irr-mirr-fmrr.htm

Kondo, Y. (2018). USA Patent No. US 2018 / 0365686 A1.

Konstantino, O., Malamaki, K.-N., Gallos, K., Tsitsimelis, A., Dikaiakos, C., Gkavanoudis, S., & Demou, C. (2020, February 18*). Ancillary Services Market Design in Distribution Networks.* Retrieved from https://www.mdpi.com/1996-1073/13/4/917/pdf

Kordas, D. (2015). Risk sharing in traditional construction contracts for building projects. A contractor's perspective in the Greek construction industry. Enschede, The Netherlands: University of Twente.

Kordas, D.-I. D. (2015, April 20). *Risk sharing in traditional construction contracts for building projects. a contractor's perspective in the Greek construction industry.* Thesis. Arnhem, The Netherlands: University of Twente.

Kośmieja, M., & Paslawski, J. (2015). Flexible Approach in Designing Infrastructure. *Procedia Engineering, 122,* 104–111. doi:10.1016/j.proeng.2015.10.013

Kovach, A., Hughes, A., Fagan, P., & Maggitti, P. (2002). Administrative & Strategic Advantage of HRIS. Employment Relations Today, 43-48.

Kroman. (2013, December 27). *Ten ways to protect your confidential information.* Retrieved from The Globe and Mail: https://www.theglobeandmail.com/report-on-business/small-business/sb-managing/how-to-protect-your-confidential-information/article16072896/

Kronman, A. (1985). Contract Law and the State of Nature. *Journal of Law Economics and Organization, 1*(1), 5–32. http://www.jstor.org/stable/764905

Kübert, R., Koller, B., Sirvent, R., Ziegler, W., & Hudzia, B. (2011). *Analysis of existing solutions and requirements for SLAs. In OPTIMIS Project, Seventh Framework Programme.* University of Stuttgart.

Kuchkovskiy, V., & Shakhovska, N. (2019). Information technology of Blockchain: database, smart contracts, architecture. *2019 IEEE 14th International Conference on Computer Sciences and Information Technologies (CSIT),* 55-59. 10.1109/STC-CSIT.2019.8929885

Kulkarni, S. (2014). Human Capital Enhancement through E-HRM. *Journal of Management Research, 3*(1), 59–74.

Kumar, S. (2020, May 27). *Digital-transformation-of-regulatory-compliance-for-financial-institutions.* Retrieved from https://gomedici.com/digital-transformation-of-regulatory-compliance-for-financial-institutions

Kuppa, R. (2018). Negotiating a Contract. *PM World Journal,* 1-11.

Kurco, K., Stepanic, D., & Varga, M. (2012). Strategic and Tactical Success Factors in ERP System Implementation. *International Journal of Computers, 6*(4), 206–214.

Kuretzky, B., & Levy, R. B. (2019). Retrieved April 24, 2020, from https://www.business-humanrights.org/en/canada-class-action-lawsuits-over-alleged-misclassification-of-employees-as-independent-contractors-are-increasing-say-lawyers

La Diega, G. N., & Walden, I. (2016, September 25). Contracting for the 'Internet of Things': Looking into the Nest. *European Journal of Law and Technology*, *7*(2), 1–29. http://nrl.northumbria.ac.uk/27910/

Laakkonen, K. (2014). *Contracts in Agile Software Development* (Master's Thesis). Aalto University.

Lacity, M., Khan, S., & Willcocks, L. (2009, September 1). A Review of the IT Outsourcing Literature: Insights for Practice. *The Journal of Strategic Information Systems*, *18*(3), 130–146. doi:10.1016/j.jsis.2009.06.002

Lakshmi, C. (2014). Study on E-HRM Practices in Kovai Medical Center & Hospital, Coimbatore. *Journal of Business Management & Social Sciences Research*, *3*(8), 43–47.

Langer, A. M. (2017). *Information Technology and Organizational Learning: Managing Behavioral Change in the Digital Age* (3rd ed.). CRC Press. doi:10.1201/9781315143804

Langley, D. J., Doorn, J., & Ng, C. L. (2020, January). The Internet of Everything: Smart things and their impact on business models. *Journal of Business Research*, *122*, 853–863. doi:10.1016/j.jbusres.2019.12.035

Lapham, M. A., Korzec, K., Rosser, L. A., Howard, G., Martin, S., Ryan, M., . . . Capell, P. (2016). RFP Patterns and Techniques for Successful Agile Contracting. Hanscom, MA: Carnegie Mellon University.

Larivière, B., Joosten, H., Malthouse, E. C., Birgelen, M., Aksoy, P., Kunz, W. H., & Huang, M.-H. (2013). Value fusion: The blending of consumer and firm value in the distinct context of mobile technologies and social media. *Journal of Service Management*, *24*(3), 268–293. doi:10.1108/09564231311326996

Larsen, M., Pedersen, M., & Andersen, K. V. (2006). IT Governance: Reviewing 17 IT Governance Tools and Analysing the Case of Novozymes A/S. In *Proceedings of the 39th Annual Hawaii International Conference on System Sciences (HICSS'06)* (pp. 1530-1605). Kauia, HI: IEEE. 10.1109/HICSS.2006.234

Launches, B. (2019, Jan 27). R[REMOVED HYPERLINK FIELD]etrieved April 2020, from https://oliver-dev.s3.amazonaws.com/2019/01/27/12/54/25/916/Tech_Disruptions.pdf

Launches, B. (2019, Jan 27). Retrieved April 2020, from https://oliver-dev.s3.amazonaws.com/2019/01/27/12/54/25/916/Tech_Disruptions.pdf

Lauslahti, K., Mattila, J., Hukkinen, T., & Seppälä, T. (2018). Expanding the Platform: Smart Contracts as Boundary Resources. In A. Smedlund & A. Lindblom (Eds.), *Collaborative Value Co-creation in the Platform Economy* (pp. 65–90). Springer. doi:10.1007/978-981-10-8956-5_4

Leacock, S. (2011). Fingerprints of Equitable Estoppel and Promissory Estoppel on the Statute of Frauds in Contact Law. Barry University School of Law, 73-133.

Lechner, N. (2014). Sustainable environmental control through building design Heating, Cooling, and Lighting. John Wiley & Sons.

Lee, I., & Lee, K. (2015, July 14). The Internet of Things (IoT): Applications, investments, and challenges for enterprises. Business Horizons, 58(4), 431-440. doi:10.1016/j.bushor.2015.03.008

Lee, J., Singh, J., & Azamfar, M. (2019). Industrial Artificial Intelligence. arXiv preprint arXiv:1908.02150.

Legal Dictionary. (2017, March 25). *Express Contract*. Retrieved from https://legaldictionary.net: https://legaldictionary.net/express-contract/

Leka, E., Selimi, B., & Lamani, L. (2019). Systematic Literature Review of Blockchain Applications: Smart Contracts. *2019 International Conference on Information Technologies (InfoTech),* 1-3. 10.1109/InfoTech.2019.8860872

Lengnick-Hall, M., & Moritz, S. (2003). The Impact of e-HR on the Human Resource Management Function. *Journal of Labor Research*, *24*(3), 365–379. doi:10.100712122-003-1001-6

Lepak, D., & Snell, S. (1998). Virtual HR: Strategic HRM in the 21st Century. *HRM Review*, *8*(3), 215–234.

Li, C., & Palanisamy, B. (2018). Decentralized Privacy-Preserving Timed Execution in Blockchain-Based Smart Contract Platforms. *2018 IEEE 25th International Conference on High Performance Computing (HiPC)*, 265-274. 10.1109/HiPC.2018.00037

Li, J., Wang, P., & Han, Q. (2017). Research on Reuse of Legacy System Based on SOA. *DEStech Transactions on Computer Science and Engineering*.

Lia, F., & Whalley, J. (2002). Deconstruction of the telecommunications industry: From value chains to value networks. *Telecommunications Policy*, *26*, 451–472.

Li, G., Hou, Y., & Wu, A. (2017). Fourth Industrial Revolution: Technological drivers, impacts and coping methods. *Chinese Geographical Science*, *27*(4), 626–637. doi:10.100711769-017-0890-x

Lin, T.-H., Liu, C.-H., Tsai, M.-H., & Kang, S.-C. (2015, November 29). Using Augmented Reality in a Multiscreen Environment for Construction Discussion. *Journal of Computing in Civil Engineering*, *29*(6). doi:10.1061/(ASCE)CP.1943-5487.0000420

Li, S., Park, S. H., & Li, S. (2004). The Great Leap Forward: The Transition from Relation-Based Governance to Rule-Based Governance. *Organizational Dynamics*, *33*(1), 63–78. doi:10.1016/j.orgdyn.2003.11.005

Liu, Z., & Liu, J. (2019). Formal Verification of Blockchain Smart Contract Based on Colored Petri Net Models. *2019 IEEE 43rd Annual Computer Software and Applications Conference (COMPSAC)*, 555-560. 10.1109/COMPSAC.2019.10265

Liu, G. H., Wang, E. T., & Chua, C. E. (2015). Leveraging Social Capital to Obtain Top Management Support in Complex, Cross-Functional It Projects. *Journal of the Association for Information Systems*, *16*(8), 707–737. doi:10.17705/1jais.00404

Lobel, O. (2018, January 30). *NDAs Are Out of Control. Here's What Needs to Change*. Retrieved from Harvard Business Review: https://hbr.org/2018/01/ndas-are-out-of-control-heres-what-needs-to-change

Loonam, J. A., & Donagh, J. M. (2005). Exploring Top Management Support for the Introduction of Enterprise Information Systems: A Literature Review. *Irish Journal of Management*, 163–178.

Lopes, J. P., Hatziargyriou, N., Mutale, J. D., & Jenkins, N. (2007). Integrating distributed generation into electric power systems: A review of drivers, challenges and opportunities. *Electric Power Systems Research*, *77*(9), 1189–1203. doi:10.1016/j.epsr.2006.08.016

Lopez, M. A., Lobato, A. G. P., & Duarte, O. C. M. B. (2016). A performance comparison of open-source stream processing platforms. *2016 IEEE Global Communications Conference (GLOBECOM)*, 1–6. 10.1109/GLOCOM.2016.7841533

Lowry, P. B., & Wilson, D. (2016). Creating agile organizations through IT: The influence of internal IT service perceptions on IT service quality and IT agility. *The Journal of Strategic Information Systems*, *25*(3), 211–226. doi:10.1016/j.jsis.2016.05.002

Luenendonk, M. (2017). *Industry 4.0: Definition, Design Principles, Challenges, and the Future of Employment*. Retrieved on February 28,2020 from https://www.cleverism.com/industry-4-0/

Luftman, J., Lyytinen, K., & Zvi, T. (2017). Enhancing the measurement of information technology (IT) business alignment and its influence on company performance. *Journal of Information Technology*, *32*(1), 26–46. doi:10.1057/jit.2015.23

Lumineau, F. (2015). How Contracts Influence Trust and Distrust. *Journal of Management*, *43*(5), 1–25. doi:10.1177/0149206314556656

Lumineau, F., & Quelin, B. (2012). An Empirical Investigation of Inter-Organizational Opportunism and Contracting Mechanisms. *Strategic Organization*, *10*(1), 55–84. doi:10.1177/1476127011434798

Luna, A., Costa, C., Moura, H., Novaes, M., & Nascimento, C. (2010). Agile governance in information and communication technologies: shifting paradigms. *JISTEM Journal of Information Systems and Technology Management*, *7*(2), 311–334. doi:10.4301/S1807-17752010000200004

Luna, A., Kruchten, P., & Pedrosa, EMarcello,, L.G., doa Neto, H. R. d., & Moura, H. P. d. M. (2014). State of the Art of Agile Governance: A Systematic Review. *International Journal of Computer Science and Information Technologies*, *6*(5), 121–141. doi:10.5121/ijcsit.2014.6510

Lyons, T. F., Krachenberg, A. R., & Henke, J. W. (1990). Mixed Motive Marriages: What's Next for Buyer-Supplier Relations? *Sloan Management Review*, (Spring), 29–36.

Mabey, R. (2019, July 1). *What is contract management software?* Retrieved from https://blog.juro.com/what-is-contract-management-software/

Madakam, Ramaswamy, & Tripathi. (2015). Internet of Things (IoT): A Literature. *Journal of Computer and Communications*, 164-173.

Makedon, V., Drobyazko, S., Shevtsova, H., Maslosh, O., & Kasatkina, M. (2019). Providing security for the development of high-technology organizations. *Journal of Security and Sustainability Issues*, *8*(4), 757–772. doi:10.9770/jssi.2019.8.4(18)

Malyshev, N., & Kauffmann, C. (2019, June 1). *Regulatory-effectiveness-in-the-era-of-digitalisation.* Retrieved from https://www.oecd.org/gov/regulatory-policy/Regulatory-effectiveness-in-the-era-of-digitalisation.pdf

Manda, M., & Dhaou, S. (2019). Responding to challenges and opportunities in the 4th industrial revolution in developing countries. *I EGOV2019.*

Mandal, A. K., Tagomori, G. K., Felix, R. V., & Howell, S. C. (2017). Value-Based Contracting Innovated Medicare Advantage Healthcare Delivery and Improved Survival. *The American Journal of Managed Care, 23*(2).

Mandloi, R. (2020). *Making the Most of Talent in the Gig Economy.* Retrieved April 24, 2020, from https://www.harvardbusiness.org/making-the-most-of-talent-in-the-gig-economy/

Mandloi, R. (2020, January 13). *Making the Most of Talent in the Gig Economy.* (Retrieved April 24, 2020, from https://www.harvardbusiness.org/making-the-most-of-talent-in-the-gig-economy/

Manimaran, P., & Dhanalakshmi, R. (2019). Blockchain-Based Smart Contract for E-Bidding System. *2019 2nd International Conference on Intelligent Communication and Computational Techniques (ICCT),* 55-59. 10.1109/ICCT46177.2019.8969042

Manyika, J., Chui, M., Brown, B., Bughin, J., Dobbs, R., Roxburgh, C., & Byers, A. H. (2011). *Big data: The next frontier for innovation, competition.* Academic Press.

Manzano, E., & Agugliaro, F. (2019). The Role of Smart Contracts in Sustainability: Worldwide Research Trends. *Sustainability: Environmental Energy Sustainability at Universities*, 1-16. doi:10.3390u11113049

Maravas, A., & Pantouvakis, J.-P. (2018). *A New Approach to Studying Net Present Value and the Internal Rate of Return of Engineering Projects under Uncertainty with Three-Dimensional Graphs*. Advances in Civil Engineering. doi:10.1155/2018/6108680

Marketing Charts. (2019, November 20). *Smartphones Now Account for 70% of US Digital Media Time*. Retrieved from https://www.marketingcharts.com: https://www.marketingcharts.com/digital/mobile-phone-111093

Marnell, P. (2016). *Engineering Economics for the 21st Century*. John Wiley & Sons.

Marsh, M. (2009, March 1). *California Confidentiality and Non-Disclosure Agreements*. Retrieved from https://www.yourlegalcorner.com/articles.asp?id=66

Marshall, A., Mueck, S., & Shockley, R. (2015). *Innovative Analytics (GBE03664-USEN-02)*. IBM.

Marston, S., Li, Z., Bandyopadhyay, S., Zhang, J., & Ghalsasi, A. (2011). Cloud computing— The business perspective. *Decision Support Systems*, *51*(1), 176–189. doi:10.1016/j.dss.2010.12.006

Masters, G. M. (2013). *Renewable and Efficient Electric Power Systems. Hobkens, New Jersy*. John Wiley & Sons.

Matook, S., Lasch, R., & Tamaschke, R. (2009, February 20). Supplier development with benchmarking as part of a comprehensive supplier risk management framework. *International Journal of Operations & Production Management*, *29*(3), 241–267. doi:10.1108/01443570910938989

Matt, C., Hess, H., & Benliam, A. (2015). Digital Transformation Strategies. *Business & Information Systems Engineering*, *57*(5), 339–343. doi:10.100712599-015-0401-5

Matters, S. (2017). *Artificial Intelligence in Contract Management: Considerations for Practitioners (Part 1)*. Available at: https://spendmatters.com/2017/01/03/artificial-intelligence-contract-management-considerations-practitioners-part-1-introduction/

Mazzone, D. M. (2014). *Digital or Death: Digital Transformation – The Only Choice for Business to Survive Smash and Conquar* (1st ed.). Smashbox Consulting Inc.

McBeath, B. (2017, September 6). Retrieved May 9, 2020, from https://www.industryweek.com/sponsored/whitepaper/22024116/agile-erp-concepts-continuous-improvement-through-rapid-incremental-implementation-and-value-realization

McCullough, J. (2020, March 23). *Unilateral vs bilateral contracts*. Retrieved from https://www.jotform.com: https://www.jotform.com/blog/unilateral-vs-bilateral-contract/

McFall, C. (2015, August 25). *Outcome-based contracts – Adding value to the contract life-cycle*. Retrieved from https://pwc.blogs.com/deals/2015/08/outcome-based-contracts.html

Mcginnis, D. (2018). *What Is the Fourth Industrial Revolution?* Retrieved on February 20,2020 from https://www.salesforce.com/blog/2018/12/what-is-the-fourth-industrial-revolution-4IR.html

McKeown, N. (2019).*A step- by- step guide to digital Transformation*. Retrieved on December 20,2019 from https://www.ionology.com/wp-content/uploads/2017/03/StepbyStepGuideToDigitalTransformation.pdf

McPeak, A. (2018). *5 Lessons Agile Teams Can Learn From Netflix*. Retrieved March 5, 2020, from https://dzone.com/articles/5-lessons-agile-teams-can-learn-from-netflix

Mendi, A., Erol, T., Safak, E., & Kaym, T. (2019). A Blockchain Smart ContractApplication Framework. *2019 International Symposium on Networks, Computers and Communications (ISNCC)*, 1-4.

Menon, S. A., Muchnick, M., Butler, C., & Pizur, T. (2019). Critical Challenges in Enterprise Resource Planning (ERP) Implementation. *International Journal of Business and Management, 14*(7), 54–69. doi:10.5539/ijbm.v14n7p54

Menzies, L. (2016, April 29). *Cost-poor-contract-management.* Retrieved from https://www.publicfinance.co.uk/opinion/2016/04/cost-poor-contract-management

Merriam-Webster. (2020, November 27). *"Layman's terms." Merriam-Webster.com.* Retrieved from https://www.merriam-webster.com/dictionary/layman%27s%2

METI, Japanese Ministry of Economy, Trade and Industry. (2018). *Contract Guidelines on Utilization of AI and Data: AI Section.* Author.

Michalsons. (2016, February 28). *appendices-annexures-and-schedules.* Retrieved from https://www.michalsons.com/blog/of-appendices-annexures-and-schedules/11774

Miller, G., Furneaux, C., Davis, P., Love, P., & O'Donnell, A. (2009). *Built Environment Procurement Practice: Impediments to Innovation and Opportunities for Changes.* Australian Government Department of Innovation, Industry, Science and Research. Retrieved from https://eprints.qut.edu.au/27114/1/Furneaux_-_BEIIC_Procurement_Report.pdf

Milosevic, Z. (1995). An Architecture for Supporting Business Contracts in Open Distributed Systems. *Proceedings of the Second International Workshop on Services in Distributed and Networked Environments (SDNE95)*, 60-67. 10.1109/SDNE.1995.470462

Milosevic, Z., Arnold, D., & O'Connor, L. (1996). *Inter-enterprise Contract Architecture for Open Distributed Systems: Security Requirements.* WET ICE 1996, *Workshop on Enterprise Security*, Stanford, CA.

Mindtree. (2019). *Make AI Pervasive: A Recent Survey on How to Harness Artificial Intelligence.* Author.

Minneapolis Government. (2019, December 9). *Contract Amendments Audit – Phase I.* Retrieved April 27, 2020, from https://www.minneapolismn.gov/www/groups/public/@citycoordinator/documents/webcontent/wcmsp-222526.pdf

Mirani, R., Moore, D., & Weber, J. A. (2001). Emerging Technologies for Enhancing Supplier–Reseller Partnerships. *Industrial Marketing Management, 30*(2), 101–114. doi:10.1016/S0019-8501(00)00135-8

Miroslava, B. (2018).*Challenges Related to the Digital Transformation of Business Companies.* Paper presented to 6th International Conference: Innovation Management, Entrepreneurship and sustainability(IMES).

Mishra, N., Lin, C.-C., & Chang, H.-T. (2015). A Cognitive Adopted Framework for IoT Big-Data Management and Knowledge Discovery Prospective. *International Journal of Distributed Sensor Networks, 2015*, 1–12. doi:10.1155/2015/718390

Mitchell, M., & Murray, J. C. (2017). Retrieved April 24, 2020, from https://files.ontario.ca/books/mol_changing_workplace_report_eng_2_0.pdf

Mittal, V. (2020). *Smart Contract in Finance Services.* Retrieved December 10, 2020, from https://www.scribd.com/document/488565323/Smart-Contract-in-Financial-Services

Moberly, M. D. (2014). *Safeguarding Intangible Assets.* Edinburgh: Elsevier Inc.; doi:10.1016/B978-0-12-800516-3.00007-0

Mohamed, S., & McCowan, A. (2001). Modelling project investment decisions under uncertainty using possibility theory. *International Journal of Project Management, 19*(4), 231–241. doi:10.1016/S0263-7863(99)00077-0

Mohanta, B., Panda, S., & Jena, D. (2018). An Overview of Smart Contract and Use Cases in Blockchain Technology. *2018 9th International Conference on Computing, Communication and Networking Technologies (ICCCNT)*, 1-4. 10.1109/ICCCNT.2018.8494045

Molina-Jiménez, C., Sfyrakis, I., Song, L., Alnakib, N., & Crowcroft, J. (2019). *The Benefits of Deploying Smart Contracts on Trusted Third Parties*. Retrieved December 10, 2020, from https://www.researchgate.net/publication/332165550_The_Benefits_of_Deploying_Smart_Contracts_on_Trusted_Third_Parties

Mone, E. M., London, M., & Mone, E. M. (2018). *Employee Engagement Through Effective Performance Management: A Practical Guide for Managers*. Routledge. doi:10.4324/9781315626529

Moran, A. (2015). *Managing Agile: Strategy, Implementation, Organization and People*. Springer. doi:10.1007/978-3-319-16262-1

Morstyn, T., Teytelboym, A., & Mcculloch, D. M. (2019). Bilateral Contract Networks for Peer-to-Peer Energy Trading. *IEEE Transactions on Smart Grid, 10*(2), 2026–2035. doi:10.1109/TSG.2017.2786668

Motor City Garage. (2014, January 12). Retrieved June 4, 2020, from https://www.macsmotorcitygarage.com/eight-things-worth-knowing-about-henry-ford-and-the-five-dollar-day/

Mou, X. (2019). *Artificial Intelligence: Investment Trends and Selected Industry Use*. Available at:https://www.ifc.org/wps/wcm/connect/7898d957-69b5-4727-9226-277e8ae28711/EMCompass-Note-71-AI-Investment-Trends.pdf?MOD=AJPERES&CVID=mR5Jvd6

Muhammad, K., Saoula, O., Issa, M., & Ahmed, U. (2019). Contract management and performance characteristics: An empirical and managerial implication for Indonesia. *Management Science Letters*, *9*(8), 1289–1298. doi:10.5267/j.msl.2019.4.012

Muhammad, K., Saoula, O., Issa, M., & Ahmed, U. (2019). This study intends to cover the relationship between contract management and performance characteristics. *Management Science Letters*, *9*(8), 1289–1298.

Murray, J. (2019). Retrieved April 24, 2020, from https://www.thebalancesmb.com/what-is-a-common-law-employee-4171936

Nagothu, D., Xu, R., Nikouei, S., & Chen, Y. (2018). A Microservice-enabled Architecture for Smart Surveillance using Blockchain Technology. *2018 IEEE International Smart Cities Conference (ISC2)*, 1-4. 10.1109/ISC2.2018.8656968

Nakicenovic, N., Grubler, A., & McDonald, A. (1998). *Global Energy Perspectives*. Cambridge University Press.

Narang, U., & Shankar, V. (2019). Mobile Marketing 2.0: State of the Art and Research Agenda. *Marketing in a Digital World*, *16*, 97–119. doi:10.1108/S1548-643520190000016008

Narayan, S. (2015). *Agile IT organization design: For digital transformation and continuous delivery*. Addison-Wesley Professional.

Naughter, T. (2017, May 4). *The True Cost of Poor Contract Management*. Retrieved from https://www.contractworks.com/blog/the-true-cost-of-poor-contract-management#:~:text=Opportunity%20Costs&text=A%20smarter%20strategy%20is%20automating,also%20arise%20within%20the%20organization

Neiheiser, R., Inácio, G., Rech, L., & Fraga, J. (2019). HRM Smart Contracts on the Blockchain. *2019 IEEE Symposium on Computers and Communications (ISCC)*, 1-6.

Newman, D. (2016). *Exploring The Future Of Digital Transformation And Disruption*. Retrieved on January 3,2020 from https://www.forbes.com/sites/danielnewman/2016/03/01/exploring-the-future-of-digital-transformation-and-disruption/#2eeddc375bdc

Ng, I., & Wakenshaw, S. (2017). The Internet-of-Things: Review and research directions. *International Journal of Research in Marketing*, 2–21.

Nguyen, P. (2013). *Contract lifecycle management on the sell-side, a case study in upstream oil and gas industry* (Thesis). Lahit University of Applied Sciences. Retrieved December 01, 2020, from https://core.ac.uk/download/pdf/38085639.pdf

Nguyen, V., Pham, H., Tran, T., Huynh, H., & Nakashima, Y. (2019). Digitizing Invoice and Managing VAT Payment Using Blockchain Smart Contract. *2019 IEEE International Conference on Blockchain and Cryptocurrency (ICBC),* 74-77.

NICEIC. (2020, January 1). *NICEIC-and-ECA-2021-Vision-Report*. Retrieved from https://www.niceic.com/Niceic.com/media/Press-Photos/NICEIC-and-ECA-2021-Vision-Report.pdf

Nicholas, S. (2009). *A Blueprint for a Safer Planet: How to Manage Climate Change and Create a New Era of Progress and Prosperity*. Random House.

Nichols, J., Demirkan, H., Goul, M., & Keith, M. (2009). Towards a Theory of Agile Dashboards for Service Oriented Organizations. *AMCIS 2009 Proceedings*, 683.

Nidumolu, R., Ellison, J., Whalen, J., & Billman, E. (2014, April 1). The Collaboration Imperative. *Harvard Business Review*, 1–10. PMID:24830283

Noe, A. R., Hallenbeck, R. J., Gerhart, B., & Wright, M. P. (2000). Human resource Management. Irwin, McGraw-Hill.

Nowotarski, P., & Paslawski, J. (2017). Industry 4.0 Concept Introduction into Construction SMEs. *IOP Conference Series. Materials Science and Engineering*, *245*, 8981–8999. doi:10.1088/1757-899X/245/5/052043

Nuodb. (2017). *Benchmarking Strategic Technology Initiatives with Software Companies*. Retrieved from http://go.nuodb.com/2016-database-report.html

Nzuva, S. (2019). Smart Contracts Implementation, Applications, Benefits, and Limitations. *Journal of Information Engineering and Applications*, *9*(5), 63–75.

O'Brien, J., & Marakas, G. (2013). *Introduction to Information Systems*. McGraw-Hill/Irwin.

O'Byrne, S. (2007). The Implied Term of Good Faith and Fair Dealing: Recent Developments. *The Canadian Bar Review*, 53–86.

Obeng, E. (2019). *Looking beyond Digital Transformation to the Future of Work*. Retrieved on January 18, 2020 from https://www.eddieobeng.com/wp-content/uploads/2017/02/Future_of_work_in_a-post-Digital_World.pdf

OECD. (2017). Key Issues for Digital Transformation in the G20. In *G20 German Presidency* (pp. 1-165). Berlin, Germany: OECD. Retrieved from https://www.oecd.org/g20/key-issues-for-digital-transformation-in-the-g20.pdf

OECD. (2018). *OECD Reviews of Digital Transformation: Going Digital in Sweden*. Paris: OECD Publishing; doi:10.1787/9789264302259-

OECD. (2018, May 30-31). *Going digital in a multilateral world*. Retrieved from http://www.oecd.org/mcm/documents/C-MIN-2018-6-EN.pdf

OECD. (2019). *Measuring the Digital Transformation: A Roadmap for the future*. Paris: OECD Publishing. Retrieved on January 3,2020 from www.oecd.org/going-digital/measurment-roadmap.pdf

Oesterreich, T. D., & Teuteberg, F. (2016). Understanding the implications of digitisation and automation in the context of Industry 4.0: A triangulation approach and elements of a research agenda for the construction industry. *Computers in Industry*, *83*, 121–139. doi:10.1016/j.compind.2016.09.006

Olivas-Lujan, M., Ramirez, J., & Zapata-Cantu, L. (2007). E-HRM in Mexico: Adapting Innovations for Global Competitiveness. *International Journal of Manpower*, *28*(5), 418–434. doi:10.1108/01437720710778402

Olson, D. L. (2007). Evaluation of ERP outsourcing. *Computers & Operations Research, 34*(12), 3715–3724. doi:10.1016/j.cor.2006.01.010

Olsson, N. O. E. (2006). Management of Flexibility in Projects. *International Journal of Project Management, 24*(1), 66–74.

Onyeji-Nwogu, I., Bazilian, M., & Moss, T. (2017, May 1). *The Digital Transformation and Disruptive Technologies: Challenges and Solutions for the Electricity Sector in African Markets*. Retrieved from Center for Global Development: https://www.cgdev.org/publication/challenges-and-solutions-electricity-sector-african-markets

Opelt, A., Gloger, B., Pfarl, W., & Mittermayr, R. (2013). Agile Contracts: Creating and Managing Successful Projects with Scrum. John Wiley & Sons. doi:10.1002/9781118640067

Open Contracting. (2016, November 28). *Everyone sees everything*. Retrieved from https://medium.com/open-contracting-stories/everyone-sees-everything-fa6df0d00335

Oswal, N., & Narayanappa, G. (2014). Evolution of HRM to E-HRM towards Organizational Effectiveness & Sustainability. *International Journal of Recent Development in Engineering & Technology, 2*(4).

Ovenden, J. (2020, January 17). *McDonald's' Supply Chain Success Shows The Benefits Of Collaboration*. Retrieved from https://channels.theinnovationenterprise.com/articles/mcdonalds-supply-chain-success-shows-the-benefits-of-collaboration

Owen, T. (2019, October 28). *introduction-why-platform-governance*. Retrieved from https://www.cigionline.org/articles/introduction-why-platform-governance

P, L., & FD., A. (2011). Long-Term Infrastructure Partnerships: Contracting Risks and Risk-Reduction Strategies. *State and,Local Government Review, 43*(1), 49-59. doi:10.1177/0160323X11400435

Panayotopoulou, L., Vakola, M., & Galanaki, E. (2007). E-HR Adoption & the Role of HRM: Evidence From Greece. *Personnel Review, 36*(2), 277–294. doi:10.1108/00483480710726145

Panneerselvam, R. (2004). *Engineering Economics*. PHI Learning Pvt. Ltd.

Panorama Consulting Group. (2019, July 12). Retrieved May 11, 2020, from https://www.panorama-consulting.com/erp-project-plan/

Panorama Consulting Group. (2020). *Panorama Consulting Group 2020 ERP Report*. Panorama Consulting Group. Retrieved May 9, 2020, from https://www.panorama-consulting.com/resource-center/2020-erp-report/?utm_campaign=Popup%20-%202020%20ERP%20Report&utm_source=Popup

Pan, Y. (2016). Heading toward artificial intelligence 2.0. *Engineering (London), 2*(4), 409–413.

Parida, V., Sjödin, D., & Reim, W. (2019). Leveraging Digitalization for Advanced Service Business Models: Challenges and Opportunities for Circular Economy. Sustainability Journal, 11(2), 391. doi:10.3390u11020391

Parry, E., & Tyson, S. (2011). Desired Goals & Actual Outcomes of EHRM. *HRM Journal, 21*(3), 335–354.

Patton, W. D., Wit, L. S., Lovrich, P. N., & Fredericksen, T. P. (2002). Human resource Management. Houghton Mifflin Company.

Paul, M. (2020, August 7). *Understanding Outcome Based Contracting*. Retrieved from https://futureofsourcing.com: https://futureofsourcing.com/understanding-outcome-based-contracts

Pauly, M. (2011). T-Systems' Cloud-Based Solutions for Business Applications. In A. Goscinski, J. Broberg, & R. Buyya (Eds.), *Cloud Computing: Principles and Paradigms*. John Wiley & Sons. doi:10.1002/9780470940105.ch11

Payne, J. E. (2010). Survey of the international evidence on the causal relationship between energy consumption and growth. *Journal of Economic Studies (Glasgow, Scotland), 37*(1), 53–95. doi:10.1108/01443581011012261

Pee, S., Kang, E., Song, J., & Jang, J. (2019). Blockchain based smart energy trading platform using smart contract. *2019 International Conference on Artificial Intelligence in Information and Communication (ICAIIC)*, 322-325. 10.1109/ICAIIC.2019.8668978

Perera, C., Liu, C. H., & Jayawardena, S. (2015). The Emerging Internet of Things Marketplace From an Industrial Perspective: A Survey. *IEEE Transactions on Emerging Topics in Computing, 3*(4), 585–598. doi:10.1109/TETC.2015.2390034

Perkin, N., & Abraham, P. (2017). *Building the Agile Business through Digital Transformation*. New York: Kogan Page Publishers.

Petersen, B., & Østergaard, K. (2017). Reconciling contracts and relational governance through strategic contracting. *Journal of Business and Industrial Marketing*, 1–12. doi:10.1108/JBIM-09-2016-0223

Philip Evans, T. S. (1999). *Blown to Bits: How the New Economics of Information Transforms Strategy* (B. C. Group, Ed.). Harvard Business School Press.

Pinsonneault, A., & Kraemer, K. (1993). An Assessment of the Use of Survey Research in the Management Information Systems field between (1980 & 1990). *Journal of Management Information Systems, 10*(2), 75–106. doi:10.1080/07421222.1993.11518001

Plimpton, L. (2008, June 19). *Do You Know Where Your Contracts Are?* Retrieved from https://www.entrepreneur.com/article/195046

Popper J., Hermann, J., Cui, K., Bergweiler, S., Weyer, S., Ruskowski, M., Wang, M., Guang, L., Hu, Y.C., Kueh, V., Wang, D., Madigan, M.C., Oppermann, I., Ryu, S.M., Kim, L., Wei, S., Li, R., Du, X., Shang, Y., & Thonet, G. (2018). *Artificial intelligence across industries*. IEC Whitepaper.

Porter, M. E., & Heppelmann, J. E. (2014, November 1). How Smart, Connected Products Are Transforming Competition. *Harvard Business Review, 92*(11), 64–88. https://hbr.org/2015/10/how-smart-connected-products-are-transforming-companies

Potoski, M., & Brown, T. L. (2005). Transaction costs and contracting: The practitioner perspective. *Public Performance & Management Review, 28*(3), 326–351. doi:10.1080/15309576.2005.11051842

Powell, J. R. (2008, August). The Quantum Limit to Moore's Law. *Proceedings of the IEEE, 96*(8), 1247–1248. doi:10.1109/JPROC.2008.925411

Pradhan, S. (2018, May 14). Retrieved July 7, 2020, from https://www.opengovpartnership.org/stories/the-business-imperative-for-open-contracting/

Prasath Kumar, V. R., Balasubramanian, M., & Jagadish Raj, S. (2016). Robotics in Construction Industry. *Indian Journal of Science and Technology, 9*(23), 1–12. doi:10.17485/ijst/2016/v9i23/95974

Prasetyo, S., Lubis, M., Witjaksono, R., & Azizah, H. (2019). *Critical Failure Factors in Enterprise Resource Planning (ERP) Implementation: Case Study of PT.Toyota Astra Motor Indonesia*. IEEE. doi:10.1109/ICIC47613.2019.8985720

PWC. (2014, December 1). *Industry 4.0 - Opportunities and Challanges of the industrial internet*. Retrieved November 10, 2020, from https://www.pwc.nl/en/assets/documents/pwc-industrie-4-0.pdf: https://www.pwc.nl/en/assets/documents/pwc-industrie-4-0.pdf

Qiu, T., Chen, N., Li, K., Atiquzzaman, M., & Zhao, W. (2018, February 8). How Can Heterogeneous Internet of Things Build Our Future: A Survey. *IEEE Communications Surveys and Tutorials*, 2011–2029. doi:10.1109/COMST.2018.2803740

Quélin, B., & Duhamel, F. (2003). Bringing Together Strategic Outsourcing and Corporate Strategy: Outsourcing Motives and Risks. *European Management Journal*, *21*(5), 647–661. doi:10.1016/S0263-2373(03)00113-0

Radack, D. V. (1994). Understanding Confidentiality Agreements. *Journal of the Minerals Metals & Materials Society*, *46*(5), 68.

Rahayu, S., & Dillak, V. (2018). 12 3). Key Success Factor for Successful ERP Implementation in State Owned Enterprises. *IACSIT International Journal of Engineering and Technology*, *7*(4.38), 916–919. doi:10.14419/ijet.v7i4.38.27608

Rahim, S. R. M., Mohammad, Z. Z., Bakar, J. A., Mohsin, F. H., & Isa, N. M. (2018). Artificial intelligence, smart contract and islamic finance. *Asian Social Science*, *14*(2), 145. doi:10.5539/ass.v14n2p145

Rahman, M. M., & Kumaraswamy, M. M. (2004). Contracting Relationship Trends and Transitions. *Journal of Management in Engineering*, *20*(4), online. Retrieved from https://ascelibrary.org/doi/abs/10.1061/(ASCE)0742-597X(2004)20:4(147)

Ranganathan, C., & Brown, C. V. (2006). ERP Investments and the Market Value of Firms: Toward an Understanding of Influential ERP Project Variables. *Information Systems Research*, *17*(2). *Online (Bergheim)*, *17*(2), 145–161. Advance online publication. doi:10.1287/isre.1060.0084

Rangarao, J., & Raju, S. (2014). E-HRM Add Value to the HRM to Obtain Optimum Potentials from the Available HR. *Indian Journal of Commerce & Management*, *1*(1), 1–9.

Rangel, A., Santos, J. C., & Savoia, J. R. (2015). Modified Profitability Index and Internal Rate of Return. *Journal of International Business and Economics*, *4*(2), 13–18. doi:10.15640/jibe.v4n2a2

Ranvir, J. (2020). *Project Finance: For the Banker by the Banker*. OrangeBooks Publication.

Rawash, H., & Saydam, S. (2012). The Impact of E-HRM on Organization's Market Share: An Empirical Study on the Housing Bank for Trade & Finance in Jordan. *International Journal of Business and Social Science*, *3*(24), 113–120.

Raynor, M., & Cotteleer, M. (2015, July 27). *The more things change: Value creation, value capture, and the Internet of Things*. Retrieved November 26, 2020, from value-creation-value-capture-internet-of-things.html: https://www2.deloitte.com/us/en/insights/deloitte-review/issue-17/value-creation-value-capture-internet-of-things.html

Reddick, C. (2009). Human Resources Information Systems in Texas City Governments: Scope and Perception of Its Effectiveness. *Public Personnel Management*, *38*(4), 19–34. doi:10.1177/009102600903800402

Remenyi, D., Money, A., & Twite, A. (1991). *A Guide to Measuring & Managing IT Benefits*. NCC, Blackwell Limited.

Remus, U., & Schub, S. (2003, December 19). A blueprint for the implementation of process-oriented knowledge management. *The Journal of Corporate Transformation*, *10*(4), 237–253. doi:10.1002/kpm.182

Renn, O. (2008). *Risk Governance: Coping with Uncertainty in a Complex World*. Earthscan. doi:10.1007/978-1-4020-6799-0

Reuer, J. J., & Ariño, A. (2007). Strategic alliance contracts: dimensions and determinants of contractual complexity. *Strategic Management*, 313-330. doi:10.1002mj.581

RICS. R. I. (2016, March 14). *Final account procedures*. Retrieved from https://www.rics.org/globalassets/rics-website/media/upholding-professional-standards/sector-standards/construction/black-book/final-account-procedures-1st-edition-rics.pdf

Rigby, D., Sutherland, J., & Takeutchi, H. (2016, May 1). Embracing Agile: How to master the process that's transfrom-ing management. *Harvard Business Review*, 1-11.

Rijo, R., Martinho, R., & Ermida, D. (2015). Developing an Enterprise Architecture Proof of Concept in a Portuguese Hospital. *Procedia Computer Science*, *64*, 1217–1225. doi:10.1016/j.procs.2015.08.511

Riordan, C. M., & O'Brien, K. (2012, April 17). *For Great Teamwork, Start with a Social Contract*. Retrieved from Harvard Business Review Home: https://hbr.org/2012/04/to-ensure-great-teamwork-start

Rita, B., & Barbara, I. (2010). Generation Y at Work: The Role of E-HRM in Building Positive Work Attitudes. *Proceed-ings of Third European Academic workshop on e-HRM*, *570*, 378-399.

Roberts, N., & Grover, V. (2012). Investigating firm's customer agility and firm performance: The importance of align-ing sense and respond capabilities. *Journal of Business Research*, *65*(5), 579–585. doi:10.1016/j.jbusres.2011.02.009

Robertson, P. L., & Langlois, R. N. (1995). Innovation, networks, and vertical integration. *Research Policy*, *24*(4), 543–562. doi:10.1016/S0048-7333(94)00786-1

Roe, D. (2018, March 29). *The Governance and Ownership of Internet of Things (IoT)*. Retrieved from https://www.cmswire.com/information-management/the-governance-and-ownership-of-internet-of-things-iot/

Rogers, D. L. (2016). *The Digital Transformation Playbook: Rethink Your Business for the Digital Age*. Columbia Uni-versity Press. doi:10.7312/roge17544

Rojko, A. (2014). Industry 4.0 Concepts: Background and Overview. *Journal of Innovation Management*, *11*(5).

Roman, R., Najera, P., & Lopez, J. (2011). Securing the Internet of Things. *Computer*, *44*(9), 51–58. doi:10.1109/MC.2011.291

Roseke, B. (2019, April 23). *Types of Contracts*. Retrieved from https://www.projectengineer.net: https://www.projec-tengineer.net/types-of-contracts/

Rosell, C. D. (2019). *Why Digital Transformation is a Vital Priority for Educational Institutions Today*. Retrieved on January 15,2020 from https://www.cae.net/why-digital-transformation-is-a-vital-priority-for-educational-institutions-today

Rosenworcel, J. (2013). Remarks of commissioner - Federal communications commission. In *IEEE GLOBECOM 2013* (pp. 1–3). IEEE.

Roser, M., & Ritchie, H. (2013, January 1). *Technological Progress*. Retrieved from Our World in Data: https://our-worldindata.org/technological-progress

Ross, A., & Williams, P. (2012). *Financial Management in Construction Contracting*. Wiley-Blckwell.

Rossi, B. (2018). *What will Industry 5.0 mean for manufacturing?* Retrieved on February 25,2020 from https://www.raconteur.net/technology/manufacturing-gets-personal-industry-5-0

Rossman, J. (2017, January 16). *The Outcome-Based Business Model – Enabled by The Internet of Things*. Retrieved from https://iotbusinessnews.com/2017/01/16/87649-outcome-based-business-model-enabled-internet-things/

Roy Billinton, R. N. (1984). *Reliability Evaluation of Power Systems*. Pitman Advanced Publishing Program. doi:10.1007/978-1-4615-7731-7

Roy Billinton, R. N. (1992). *Reliability Evaluation of Engineering Systems*. Springer Science Business Media, LLC. doi:10.1007/978-1-4899-0685-4

Rueckel, D., Krumay, B., & Schwarzgruber, S. (2020). Outsourcing in the Age of Digital Transformation. In *AMCIS 2020 Proceedings* (p. 24). Atlanta, GA: *Americas Conference on Information Systems (AMCIS).*

Ruel, H., Bondarouk, T., & Looise, J. (2004). E-HRM: Innovation or Irritation: An Explorative Empirical Study In Five Large Companies On Web-Based HRM. *Management Review, 15*(3), 364–380.

Ruel, H., Bondarouk, T., & Van der Velde, M. (2007). The Contribution of E-HRM to HRM Effectiveness: Results from a Quantitative Study in a Dutch Ministry. *Employee Relations, 29*(3), 280–291. doi:10.1108/01425450710741757

Ruta, C. (2005). The Application of Change Management Theory to HR Portal Implementation in Subsidiaries of Multinational Corporations. *HRM, 44*(1), 35–53. doi:10.1002/hrm.20039

Saarikko, T., Westergren, U., & Blomquist, T. (2017). The Internet of Things: Are you ready for what's coming? *Business Horizons, 60*(5), 667–676. doi:10.1016/j.bushor.2017.05.010

Sales. (2017). *6 Steps Framework to Implement Digital Transformation in Business.* Retrieved on December 26,2019 from https://www.newgenapps.com/blog/what-is-digital-transformation-steps-to-implement-digital-transformation

Sanchez, H., Robert, B., Bourgault, M., & Pellerin, R. (2009). Risk management applied to projects, programs, and portfolios. *International Journal of Managing Projects in Business, 2*(1), 14–35. Advance online publication. doi:10.1108/17538370910930491

Sanchez, J., & Aguayo, M. (2007). An Approach to the Satisfaction of Human Resource Information Systems (HRIS): Analysis & Empirical Contrast. *International Journal of Human Resources Development and Management, 7*(2), 177–214. doi:10.1504/IJHRDM.2007.012862

Sanderson, M., Allen, P., Gill, R., & Garnett, E. (2017, May 18). New Models of Contracting in the Public Sector: A Review of Alliance Contracting, Prime Contracting and Outcome-based Contracting Literature. *Social Policy and Administration, 52*(5), 1060–1083. doi:10.1111pol.12322

Savelyev, A. (2017). Contract law 2.0: 'Smart'contracts as the beginning of the end of classic contract law. *Information & Communications Technology Law, 26*(2), 116–134. doi:10.1080/13600834.2017.1301036

Sawsan, R., & Mohammed, H. I. (2019). Impact of the Feasibility Study on the Construction Projects. *IOP Conference Series. Materials Science and Engineering, 518*, 022074. doi:10.1088/1757-899X/518/2/022074

Saxena, A. (2008). *Enterprise Contract Management: A Practical Guide to Successfully implementing an ECM solution.* J Ross Publishing.

Schaefer, J. A. (2001). Beyond a Definition: Understanding the Nature of Void and Voidable Contracts. *Campbell Law Review*, 193–209.

Schallmo, D., Williams, C., & Boardman, L. (2017). Digital Transformation of Business Model-Best Practice, Enablers and Roadmap. International Journal of Innovation Management, 21(8).

Schein, E. H. (1996). Career anchors revisited: Implications for career development in the 21st century. *The Academy of Management Perspectives, 10*(4), 80–88. doi:10.5465/ame.1996.3145321

Schifferdecker, B. (2014, December 1). *Five rules & ten steps to collaborative contracting.* Retrieved from https://www.dhl.com/global-en/home/about-us/delivered-magazine/articles/2014-2015/five-rules-and-ten-steps-to-collaborative-contracting.html

Schindler, R. (2011). *Pricing Strategies: A Marketing Approach.* SAGE Publications.

Schjaer-Jacobsen, H. (2002). Representation and calculation of economic uncertainties: Intervals, fuzzy numbers, and probabilities. *International Journal of Production Economics*, *78*(1), 91–98. doi:10.1016/S0925-5273(00)00167-5

Schlingmeyer, J. (2019, September 13). *Deconstruction-of-the-value-chain.* Retrieved from https://www.globaltrademag.com/deconstruction-of-the-value-chain/

Schmitt, G., Mladenow, A., Strauss, C., & Schaffhauser-Linzatti, M. (2019). Smart Contracts and Internet of Things: A Qualitative Content Analysis using the Technology-Organization-Environment Framework to Identify Key-Determinants. *The 10th International Conference on Emerging Ubiquitous Systems and Pervasive Networks (EUSPN-2019), 160*, 189-196. 10.1016/j.procs.2019.09.460

Schoechle, T. (2009). *Standardization and Digital Enclosure: The Privatization of Standards, Knowledge and Policy in the Age of Global Information Technology.* Hershey, PA: IGI Global; doi:10.4018/978-1-60566-334-0

Schramm, G. (2006). Electric power in developing countries: status, problems, prospects. *Annual Review of Power*, 307-333.

Schuhmann, R., & Eichhorn, B. (2015). From Contract Management to Contractual Management. *European Review of Contract Law*, *11*(1), 1–21. doi:10.1515/ercl-2015-0001

Schunder, L., & Kitchen, W. (2004). *United States Patent No. US20040083119A1.*

Schwertner, K. (2017). Digital transformation of business. *The Journal of Supercomputing*, *15*, 388–393.

Schwertner, K. (2017). Digital transformation of business. *Trakia Journal of Sciences*, *15*(1, Suppl.1), 388–393. doi:10.15547/tjs.2017.s.01.065

Scoblic, J. P. (2020, August 1). Learning from the Future: How to make robust strategy in times of deep uncertainty. *Harvard Business Review*, 1–18.

Sefton-Green, R. (2005). *Mistake, Fraud and Duties to Inform in European Contract Law.* Cambridge University Press. doi:10.1017/CBO9780511495052

Seres, L., Pavlicevic, V., & Tumbas, P. (2018).Digital Transformation of Higher Education Competing on Analytics. *Proceeding of INTED conference.* 10.21125/inted.2018.2348

Services, U. D. (2018, May 1). Retrieved July 16, 2019, from https://www.hhs.gov/sites/default/files/AmericanPatients-First.pdf

Seymour, M., & Coyle, S. (2016). Towards a research agenda for adopting Agile Project Management in Creative Industries. *International Research Workshop on IT Project Management.*

Shalan, M., & Anaim, N. (2017). The SMAC Opportunity Contracts: Generating Value From Responsive Agile Risk-Oriented Techniques. In Mobile Platforms, Design, and Apps for Social Commerce (pp. 115-134). Hershey: IGI Global.

Shalan, M., & Anaim, N. (2017). The SMAC Opportunity Contracts: Generating Value From Responsive Agile Risk-Oriented Techniques. In Mobile Platforms, Design, and Apps for Social Commerce (pp. 115-134). IGI Global.

Shalan, M. (2019). *Risk management for digital transformation contracts. In Al-Yamamh University engineering Forum (YUENG2019).* Al-Yamamh University. Retrieved from https://yueng.yu.edu.sa/wp-content/uploads/2019/02/YUENG2019_paper_6.pdf

Shalan, M. A., & Anaim, N. A. (2017). The SMAC Opportunity Contracts: Generating Value From Responsive Agile Risk-Oriented Techniques. In *Mobile Platforms, Design,and Apps for Social Commerce* (pp. 115–134). IGI Global. doi:10.4018/978-1-5225-2469-4.ch008

Sharma, S. (2016). Relationship Marketing: Process of Loyal Customer Retention. *Advances in Economics and Business Management (AEBM), 3*(4). Retrieved from https://www.krishisanskriti.org/vol_image/08Jun201611064248 Sakshi Sharma 366-368.pdf

Sharma, N. (2014). Recruitment Strategies: A Power of E-Recruiting & Social Media. *International Journal of Core Engineering & Management, 1*(5), 15–35.

Shaw, R. (1997). Trust in the Balance: Building Successful Organizations on Results, Integrity, and Concern. *Political Science (Wellington, N.Z.)*, 1–10.

Shcherbak, S. (2018). *AI in Legal Profession*. Available at: https://synchlaw.se/wp-content/uploads/2018/01/ai_in_legal_profession_latest.pdf

Sheu, C., Chae, B., & Yang, C.-L. (2004). National differences and ERP implementation: Issues and challenges. *Omega, 32*(5), 61–71. doi:10.1016/j.omega.2004.02.001

Shirai, T., Yamamoto, M., Asano, Y., Fujita, Y., & Tsunami, K. (2018). Dialogue AI for Financial Services. *Hitachi Review, 67*(5), 550–551.

Shrivatsava, S. (2010). Shaping Organizations with e-HRM. *International Journal of Innovation, Management and Technology, 1*(1).

Shukla, G., Radadiya, M., & Akotiya, K. (2015). An emerging trend of big data for high volume and varieties of data to search of agricultural data. *Oriental Journal of Computer Science & Technology, 8*(2), 121-129.

Siddiqui, S. T., Alam, M. S., & Bokhari, M. (2012). Software Tools Required to Develop GIS Applications: An Overview. In *2012 Second International Conference on Advanced Computing & Communication Technologies* (pp. 51-56). Rohtak, Haryana: IEEE. 10.1109/ACCT.2012.106

Silberer, G., & Schulz, S. (2012). Mobile Customer Relationship Management (mCRM): Constraints and Challenges. In I. R. Association (Ed.), *E-Marketing: Concepts, Methodologies, Tools, and Applications* (pp. 324–340). IGI Global. doi:10.4018/978-1-4666-1598-4.ch020

Silk, D. (2014). *Planning IT*. Butterworth-Heinemann.

Simmon, E. (2018). Evaluation of cloud computing services based on NIST SP 800-145. doi:10.6028/NIST.SP.500-322

Singla, V., Malav, I., Kaur, J., & Kalra, S. (2019). Develop Leave Application using Blockchain Smart Contract. *2019 11th International Conference on Communication Systems & Networks (COMSNETS)*, 547-549. 10.1109/COMSNETS.2019.8711422

Sitalakshmi Venkatraman, K. F. (2016, March 27). Challenges and Success Factors in ERP Implemenatation in Australian SMEs. *MDPI Journal Systems*, 1-18.

Skaik, S., & Arafat, H. (2016). How can contractors warrant timely payments in the UAE construction industry? In RICS Cobra 2016 (p. 11). Royal Institution of Chartered Surveyors.

Skok, W., & Döringer, H. (2002). Potential Impact of Cultural Differences on Enterprise Resource Planning (ERP) Projects. *The Electronic Journal on Information Systems in Developing Countries, 7*(1), 1–8. doi:10.1002/j.1681-4835.2002.tb00041.x

Sleiderink, W. S. (2015, March 17). *Reducing penalty costs in performance-based contracts. A case study at Thales Nederland B.V.* Drienerlolaan. Enschede, Netherlands: University of Twente. Retrieved from https://essay.utwente.nl/66884/16/W.S.%20Sleiderink(2015),%20Reducing%20penalty%20costs%20in%20Performance-Based%20Contracts,%20MSc.%20Thesis.pdf

Ślusarczyk, B., Baryń, M., & Kot, S. (2016). Tire Industry Products as an Alternative Fuel. *Polish Journal of Environmental Studies*, *25*(3), 1–8. doi:10.15244/pjoes/61543

Smit, J. (2017). *A Practical Guide on Managing Outsourcing Risk*. Retrieved from https://www.leadmark.nl/wp-content/uploads/2017/04/Guidance-on-Managing-Outsourcing-Risk.pdf

Smith, A. (1995). Subcontractors. In Estimating, Tendering and Bidding for Construction. Macmillan Building and Surveying Series (pp. 81-97). Springer. doi:10.1007/978-1-349-13630-8_7

Smith, R. E. (2010). Prefab Architecture: A Guide to Modular Design and Construction. John Wiley & Sons.

Smith, S. (2004). *Contract Theory: 'Introduction to General Theories' and 'the Justification of Contractual Obligations'.* Oxford University Press. Retrieved from Oxford University Press: http://lib.oup.com.au/he/samples/clarke_cl3e_sample.pdf

Smith, S. (2004). *Contract Theory*. Oxford University Press.

Snell, S., Stueber, D., & Lepak, D. (2002). *Virtual HR Departments: Getting Out of the Middle*. CAHRS Working Paper Series, 71.

Soffer, P., Golany, B., & Dori, D. (2003). ERP modeling: A comprehensive approach. *Information Systems*, *28*(6), 673–690. doi:10.1016/S0306-4379(02)00078-9

Soja, P. (2006). Success factors in ERP systems implementations: Lessons from practice. *Journal of Enterprise Information Management*, *19*(4), 418–433. doi:10.1108/17410390610678331

Soltani, M., & Mirzanejad, R. (2012). E-HRM & Required Infrastructures in its Implementation. *7th Conference on HR Development*, 1-20.

Sorsa, K. (2011). *Proactive Management and Proactive Business Law. A Handbook*. Retrieved September 25, 2020, from http://julkaisut.turkuamk.fi/isbn9789522162458.pdf

Spurga, R. C. (2004). *Balance Sheet Basics: Financial Management for Non-financial Managers*. Penguin Group.

Statista. (2019). *Number of internet of things (IoT) connected devices worldwide in 2018, 2025 and 2030*. Retrieved March 27, 2020, from https://www.statista.com/statistics/802690/worldwide-connected-devices-by-access-technology/

Stempniak, M. (2015, February 15). *Will Boeing Change Health Care?* Retrieved from https://trustees.aha.org/articles/1020-will-boeing-change-health-care: https://trustees.aha.org/articles/1020-will-boeing-change-health-care

Stempniak, M. (2020, Jul 21). *1020-will-boeing-change-health-care*. Retrieved from https://trustees.aha.org/articles/1020-will-boeing-change-health-care

Sterman, J. (2000). *Business Dynamics: Systems Thinking and Modeling for a Complex World*. Irwin/McGraw-Hill.

Stern, C. W., & Deimler, M. S. (2006). The Boston Consulting Group on Strategy: Classic Concepts and New Perspectives. John Wiley & Sons.

Stoica, M., Mircea, M., & Ghilic-micu, B. (2013). Software Development: Agile vs. Traditional. *Informatica Economica*, *17*(4), 64–76. doi:10.12948/issn14531305/17.4.2013.06

Stoll, H. (2007). *Least-Cost Electric Utility Planning*. John Wiley & Sons.

Stone, D., Lukaszewski, K., & Isenhour, L. (2005). E-Recruiting: Online Strategies for Attracting Talent. In *The Brave New World of EHR. HRM in the Digital Age*. Jossey-Bass.

Strickland, J. (2017, January 31). *The Importance of Construction Contracts and Items to Consider When Preparing Construction Contracts*. Retrieved from Ward and Smith: https://www.jdsupra.com/legalnews/the-importance-of-construction-35239/

Strohmeier, S. (2007). Research in E-HRM: Review & Implications. *HRM Review*, *17*(1), 19–37.

Sull, D. N. (2000, November 27). Retrieved May 1, 2020, from https://hbswk.hbs.edu/archive/the-dynamics-of-standing-still-firestone-tire-and-rubber-and-the-radial-revolution

Sultan, N. (2014). Making use of cloud computing for healthcare provision: Opportunities and challenges. *International Journal of Information Management*, *34*(2), 177–184. doi:10.1016/j.ijinfomgt.2013.12.011

Sumo, R., Kalkman, J., & Van Weele, A. (2018, April 1). *Innovation through contracting in the oil and gas sector.* Retrieved from https://www.adlittle.jp/sites/default/files/viewpoints/adl_effects_of_contractual_governance_on_innovation_in_the_oil.compressed.pdf

Sund, K. A., & Hausken, K. (2012). Fixed price contract versus incentive-based contract in the oil and gas industry. *International Journal of Global Energy Issues*, *35*(5), 371. Advance online publication. doi:10.1504/IJGEI.2012.046727

Szabo, N. (1994). *Smart Contracts*. Retrieved from https://www.fon.hum.uva.nl/rob/Courses/InformationInSpeech/CDROM/Literature/LOTwinterschool2006/szabo.best.vwh.net/smart.contracts.html

Szabo. (1996). *Smart Contracts: Building Blocks for Digital Markets*. EXTROPY.

Tai, Y. (2011). Perceived value for customers in information sharing services. *Industrial Management & Data Systems*, *111*(4), 551–569. doi:10.1108/02635571111133542

Taran, Y., Boer, H., & Lindgren, P. (2013). Incorporating Enterprise Risk Management in the Business. *Journal of Business Models*, *1*(1), 38–60. http://journalofbusinessmodels.com/media/1014/vol-1-no-1-pp-38-60.pdf

Tay, Y. W., Panda, B., Paul, S. C., Noor Mohamed, N. A., Tan, M. J., & Leong, K. F. (2017). 7 3). 3D printing trends in building and construction industry: A review. *Virtual and Physical Prototyping*, *12*(3), 261–276. doi:10.1080/17452759.2017.1326724

Teague, A. (2017). No Innovation Without Quality. In F. Abolhassan (Ed.), *The Drivers of Digital Transformation* (pp. 73–81). Springer.

The Case for Contracts in 7 Reasons. (2018, April 10). Retrieved from Concord: https://www.concordnow.com/blog/case-for-contracts-7-reasons/

The Enterprisers Project. (2020, May 26). Retrieved from https://enterprisersproject.com: https://enterprisersproject.com/what-is-digital-transformation#q1

The EU Project for Digital Transformation. (2020, Dec. 12). *Legal-parameters-of-digital-transformation/*. Retrieved from https://digital-transformation-tool.eu/legal-parameters-of-digital-transformation/

The Korean Ministry of the Interior. (2016). *Building Better Governance: The Korean Case*. Seoul, Republic of Korea: Korean International Cooperation Division for Good Governance. Retrieved from https://www.mois.go.kr/eng/bbs/type002/commonSelectBoardArticle.do%3Bjsessionid=8YddoT1KCsn7Dl8FrKcOys7l.node10?bbsId=BBSMSTR_000000000022&nttId=56889

The U.S. Energy Information Administration. (2020, January 29). *Annual Energy Outlook 2020 with projections to 2050.* Retrieved from https://www.eia.gov/outlooks/aeo/pdf/AEO2020%20Full%20Report.pdf

The University of Texas. (2016, November 1). *The University of Texas System Administration.* Available at: https://www.utsystem.edu/sites/default/files/documents/publication/2016/contract-management-handbook/contract-management-handbook.pdf

The World Bank. (2018). *Contract Management practice.* Washington, DC: The World Bank. Retrieved from http://pubdocs.worldbank.org/en/277011537214902995/contract-management-guidance-september-19-2018-final.pdf

Thierrt, I. (2017). *Companies of the Future: The Issues of Digital Transformation.* Retrieved on December 25, 2019 from https://www.researchgate.net/profile/Isckia_Thierry/publication/313105824_White_paper_Companies_of_the_future_The_Issues_of_Digital_Transformation/links/5890566ea6fdcc2351c08eeb/White-paper-Companies-of-the-future-The-Issues-of-Digital-Transformation.pdf?origin=publication_detail

Thierrt, I. (2017). *Companies of the Future: The Issues of Digital Transformation.* Retrieved on December 25,2019 from https://www.researchgate.net/profile/Isckia_Thierry/publication/313105824_White_paper_Companies_of_the_future_The_Issues_of_Digital_Transformation/links/5890566ea6fdcc2351c08eeb/White-paper-Companies-of-the-future-The-Issues-of-Digital-Transformation.pdf?origin=publication_detail

Thompson, J. (2019, May 8). *how-to-write-amendment-contract.html.* Retrieved from https://bizfluent.com/how-4922578-write-amendment-contract.html

Thomson, J. (2020, April 1). *Power-and-utilities-industry-outlook.* Deloitte. Retrieved August 1, 2020, from https://www2.deloitte.com/us/en/pages/energy-and-resources: https://www2.deloitte.com/us/en/pages/energy-and-resources/articles/power-and-utilities-industry-outlook.html

Tikhomirov, S., Voskresenskaya, E., Ivanitskiy, I., Takhaviev, R., Marchenko, E., & Alexandrov, Y. (2018). SmartCheck: Static Analysis of Ethereum Smart Contracts. *2018 IEEE/ACM 1st International Workshop on Emerging Trends in Software Engineering for Blockchain (WETSEB),* 9-16. 10.1145/3194113.3194115

ToffelM. W. (2008). Contracting for Servicizing. *Harvard Business School Technology & Operations Mgt.,* 1-31. doi:10.2139srn.1090237

Tonelli, R., Lunesu, M., Pinna, A., Taibi, D., & Marchesi, M. (2019). Implementing a Microservices System with Blockchain Smart Contracts. *2019 IEEE International Workshop on Blockchain Oriented Software Engineering (IWBOSE),* 22-31. 10.1109/IWBOSE.2019.8666520

Trend Line Global. (2020, May 7). Retrieved from outsourcing-vs-offshoring-vs-insourcing-what-to-choose-when-hiring-developers/: https://trendlineglobal.net/blog/outsourcing-vs-offshoring-vs-insourcing-what-to-choose-when-hiring-developers/

Tronvoll, B., Sklyar, A., Sörhammar, D., & Kowalkowski, C. (2020). Transformational shifts through digital servitization. *Industrial Marketing Management, 89,* 293–305. Advance online publication. doi:10.1016/j.indmarman.2020.02.005

Tsai, W.-T., Sun, X., & Balasooriya, J. (2010). Service-Oriented Cloud Computing Architecture. *2010 Seventh International Conference on Information Technology: New Generations,* 684–689. 10.1109/ITNG.2010.214

Turchi, P. (2018). *The Digital Transformation Pyramid: A business-driven Approach for Corporate Initiatives.* Retrieved on February 1, 2018 from https://www.thedigitaltransformationpeople.com/channels/the-case-for-digital-transformation/digital-transformation-pyramid-business-driven-approach-corporate-initiatives/

Turchi, P. (2018). *The Digital Transformation Pyramid: A business-driven Approach for Corporate Initiatives.* Retrieved on February 1,2018 from https://www.thedigitaltransformationpeople.com/channels/the-case-for-digital-transformation/digital-transformation-pyramid-business-driven-approach-corporate-initiatives/

Uckelmann, D., Harrison, M., & Michahelles, F. (2011). An Architectural Approach Towards the Future Internet of Things. In D. Uckelmann, M. Harrison, & F. Michahelles (Eds.), *Architecting the Internet of Things.* Springer Berlin Heidelberg. doi:10.1007/978-3-642-19157-2_1

Udokwu, C., Kormiltsyn, A., Thangalimodzi, K., & Norta, A. (2018). The State of the Art for Blockchain-Enabled Smart-Contract Applications in the Organization. *2018 Ivannikov Ispras Open Conference (ISPRAS)*, 137-144. 10.1109/ISPRAS.2018.00029

UK Government. (2020, June 1). *Risk Allocation and Pricing Approaches Guidance.* Retrieved from https://assets.publishing.service.gov.uk/government/uploads/system/uploads/attachment_data/file/891148/Risk_Allocation_and_Pricing_Approaches_-_Guidance_Note_-_June_2020.pdf

United Nations. (2020). *How do I protect records from loss or damage?* Retrieved from Archives and Records Management Section website: Retrieved December 02, 2020, from https://archives.un.org/sites/archives.un.org/files/RM-Guidelines/guidance_protecting_records_from_loss.pdf

Upadhyay, P., Basu, R., Adhikary, R., & Dan, P. K. (2010, October). A Comparative Study of Issues Affecting ERP Implementation in Large Scale and Small Medium Scale Enterprises in India: A Pareto Approach. *International Journal of Computers and Applications, 8*(3), 23–28. doi:10.5120/1192-1670

Usländer, T., & Batz, T. (2018). Agile Service Engineering in the Industrial Internet of Things. *Future Internet, 10*(10), 100. doi:10.3390/fi10100100

Ustundsag, A. & Cevikcan, E. (2018). *Industry 4.0: Managing The Digital Transformation.* . doi:10.1007/978-3-319-57870-5

Uttam, K., & Roos, C. L. (2015). Competitive dialogue procedure for sustainable public procurement. *Journal of Cleaner Production, 86*, 403–416. doi:10.1016/j.jclepro.2014.08.031

van Asselt, M. B., & Renn, O. (2011). Risk governance. *Journal of Risk Research, 14*(4), 431–449. doi:10.1080/13669877.2011.553730

van Bueren, E., & ten Heuvelhof, E. (2005). Improving Governance Arrangements in Support of Sustainable Cities. *Environment and Planning. B, Planning & Design, 32*(1), 47–66. doi:10.1068/b31103

Van Strien, J., Gelderman, C., & Semeijn, J. (2019). Performance-based contracting in military supply chains and the willingness to bear risks. *Journal of Defense Analytics and Logistics, 3*(1), 83–107. doi:10.1108/JDAL-10-2017-0021

Van, D. (2013, May). Reputational risk management in the corporate world. *Keeping Good Companies, 65*(4), 215-220. Retrieved from https://search.informit.com.au/documentSummary;dn=324234888878814;res=IELAPA

Vaquero, P. (2020). *Deconstructing the fundamentals of Strategic Digital plays.* Retrieved from https://www.pablovaquero.com/deconstruct-your-strategic-digital-play/

Vaquero, L. M., Rodero-Merino, L., Caceres, J., & Lindner, M. (2008). A break in the clouds. *Computer Communication Review, 39*(1), 50–55. doi:10.1145/1496091.1496100

Vasilescu, A.-M., Dima, A. M., & Vasilache, S. (2009). Credit analysis policies in construction project finance. *Management & Marketing, 4*(2), 79–94.

Verina, N., & Titko, D. (2019). Digital Transformation: Conceptual Framework. *International scientific conference "Contemporary Issues in Business, Management, and Economics engineering' 2019.*

Verina, N., & Titko, D. (2019). Digital Transformation: Conceptual Framework. *International scientific conference "Contemporary Issues in Business, Management,and Economics engineering' 2019.*

Vezzoli, C., Ceschin, F., Osanjo, L., M'Rithaa, M. K., Moalosi, R., Nakazibwe, V., & Diehl, J. C. (2018). *Designing Sustainable Energy for All: Sustainable Product-Service System Design Applied to Distributed Renewable Energy.* Springer International Publishing AG. doi:10.1007/978-3-319-70223-0

Villanova University. (2020, January 16). *What is the Cost of Poor Contract Management?* Retrieved from https://www.villanovau.com/resources/contract-management/what-is-the-cost-of-poor-contract-management/

Vitasek, K. (2011, August 31). *Vested Outsourcing: A New Business Model.* Retrieved from https://www.bonezonepub.com/196-vested-outsourcing-a-new-business-model?start=2

Vitasek, K. (2014, April 25). *How to Negotiate a Collaborative Outsourcing Deal.* Retrieved from https://www.cio.com/article/2376775/how-to-negotiate-a-collaborative-outsourcing-deal.html

Vitasek, K. (2016, June 13). *Procter & Gamble, TD Bank: Vested Outsourcing Success Stories.* Retrieved from https://www.facilitiesnet.com/outsourcing/article/Procter-amp-Gamble-TD-Bank-Vested-Outsourcing-Success-Stories--16660

Vitasek, K., & Tillman, J. (2013, December 1). *How to Develop a Successful Outsourcing Contract.* Retrieved from https://www.areadevelopment.com/logisticsInfrastructure/December-2013/collaborative-outsourcing-agreements-vested-model-28272611.shtml

Vitasek, K., Kling, J., & DeBinedeto, W. (2012). *McDonalds-Case-Study.* Retrieved from https://www.vestedway.com/wp-content/uploads/2012/09/McDonalds-Case-Study.pdf

Vitasek, K., Manrodt, K., & Kling, J. (2012, September 1). Retrieved July 24, 2020, from https://www.vestedway.com/wp-content/uploads/2012/09/PG-Case-Study.pdf

Vitasek, K., Manrodt, K., Kling, J., & DeBinedeto, W. (2018, June 26). *Dell-FSC-long-teaching-case.* Retrieved from https://www.vestedway.com/wp-content/uploads/2018/07/Dell-FSC-long-teaching-case-June-26-2018-PDF.pdf

Vitasek, K., Ledyard, M., & Manrodt, K. (2010). *Vested Outsourcing: Five Rules That Will Transform Outsourcing.* Palgrave Macmillan. doi:10.1057/9780230105232

Vodde, B., & Larman, C. (2010). *Practices for Scaling Lean & Agile.* Addison-Wesley Professional.

Voehl, F., & Harrington, H. J. (2016). *Change Management: Manage the Change or It Will Manage You.* Taylor & Francis Group, LLC.

Voermans, M., & Van Veldhoven, M. (2007). Attitude towards E-HRM: An Empirical Study at Philips. *Personnel Review, 36*(6), 887–902. doi:10.1108/00483480710822418

Wagner, R. E. (2020). *Legal Disputes, and Their Resolution.* George Mason University. https://papers.ssrn.com/sol3/papers.cfm?abstract_id=3617045

Walter, C. (2005, August 1). Kryder's Law. *Scientific American*, 33-34.

Wang, P., Liu, X., Chen, J., Zhan, Y., & Jin, Z. (2018). Poster: QoS-Aware Service Composition Using Blockchain-Based Smart Contracts. *2018 IEEE/ACM 40th International Conference on Software Engineering: Companion (ICSE-Companion)*, 296-297.

Wang, E. (2008). Outage costs and strategy analysis for hi-tech industries. *International Journal of Quality & Reliability Management, 19*(8-9), 1068–1078.

Wang, M. J., & Liang, G. S. (2007). Benefit/cost analysis using fuzzy concept. *The Engineering Economist, 40*(4), 359–376. doi:10.1080/00137919508903160

Wang, P., Billinton, R., & Goel, L. (2002). nreliability cost assessmentof an electric power system using reliability network equivalent approaches. *IEEE Transactions on Power Systems, 17*(3), 49–556.

Wangpipatwong, S., Chutimaskul, W., & Papasratorn, B. (2008). Understanding Citizen's Continuance Intention to Use E-government Website: A Composite View of Technology Acceptance Model & Computer Self-Efficacy. The Electronic. *Journal of E-Government, 6*(1), 55–64.

Wang, S., Ouyang, L., Yuan, Y., Ni, X., Han, X., & Wang, F. (2019, November). Blockchain-Enabled Smart Contracts: Architecture, Applications, and Future Trends. *IEEE Transactions on Systems, Man, and Cybernetics. Systems, 49*(11), 2266–2277. doi:10.1109/TSMC.2019.2895123

Warner, K., & Wäger, M. (2018). Building dynamic capabilities for digital transformation: An ongoing process of strategic renewal. *Long Range Planning, 52*(3), 326–349. Advance online publication. doi:10.1016/j.lrp.2018.12.001

Watson, A. (2020). *Number of Netflix paying streaming subscribers worldwide from 3rd quarter 2011 to 4th quarter 2019.* Retrieved March 5, 2020, from https://www.statista.com/statistics/250934/quarterly-number-of-netflix-streaming-subscribers-worldwide/

WEF. W. E. (2016, Jan. 1). *Digital Transformation of Industries.* Retrieved from https://reports.weforum.org/digital-transformation/wp-content/blogs.dir/94/mp/files/pages/files/wef1601-digitaltransformation-1401.pdf

Weiler, A. (2014, December 3). *Healthcare-is-part-of-our-supply-chain-the-boeing-company.* Retrieved Jul 21, 2020, from https://www.wellpepper.com/healthcare-is-part-of-our-supply-chain-the-boeing-company

Wen, Z., Renyu, Y., Garraghan, P., Lin, T., Xu, J., & Rovatsos, M. (2017). Fog Orchestration for Internet of Things Services. *IEEE Internet Computing*, 16 - 24. doi:10.1109/MIC.2017.36

Werfs, M. (2013). *Agile IT Departments – Concepts, Frameworks, Feasibility (Part 1).* Retrieved March 22, 2020, from https://thinkcreative30.wordpress.com/2013/03/01/agile-it-departments-concepts-frameworks-feasibility-part-1/

Westphal, P., & Sohal, A. (2016). 8 17). Outsourcing decision-making: Does the process matter? *Production Planning and Control, 27*(11), 894–908. doi:10.1080/09537287.2016.1159350

White, C. M. (2017). Potential Benefits and Risks of Value-Based Pricing of Prescription Drugs. *Connecticut Medicine, 28*(10), 587–595.

Wikipedia. (2020, June 13). *Ancillary_services_(electric_power).* Retrieved from https://en.wikipedia.org: https://en.wikipedia.org/wiki/Ancillary_services_(electric_power)

Wilson, K. E. (2015, June 24). *Policy Lessons from Financing Innovative Firms.* doi:10.2139srn.2626741

Wisskirchen, D. G. (2018). *How Artificial Intelligence impacts labour and management.* Available at: https://www.cec-managers.org/wp-content/uploads/2018/06/Script-keynote-speech-Wisskirchen-AI.pdf

Wisskirchen, G., Biacabe, B. T., Bormann, U., Muntz, A., Niehaus, G., Soler, G. J., & von Brauchitsch, B. (2017). Artificial intelligence and robotics and their impact on the workplace. IBA Global Employment Institute.

Wolde-Rufael, Y. (2006). Electricity consumption and economic growth: A time series experience for 17 African countries. *Energy Policy, 34*(10), 1106–1114. doi:10.1016/j.enpol.2004.10.008

Wong, B. (2020, July 17). *Income-statement-vs-cash-flow-statement-which-one-should-i-use*. Retrieved from https://www.legalzoom.com/articles/income-statement-vs-cash-flow-statement-which-one-should-i-use

Wong, J. (2006). Umbrella Clauses in Bilateral Investment Treaties: Of Breaches of Contract, Treat Violations, and the Divide between Developing and Developed Countries in Foreign Investment Disputes. *Geo Mason Legal Review*, 135-150.

Wong, W. K., Cheung, S. O., Yiu, T. W., & Pang, H. Y. (2007, August 15). A framework fortrust in construction contracting. *International Journal of Project Management*, *26*, 821–829.

World Economic Forum. (2018). *Readiness for the future of production report 2018*. Geneva, Switzerland: Author.

Worstall, T. (2012, March 4). Retrieved June 4, 2020, from https://www.forbes.com/sites/timworstall/2012/03/04/the-story-of-henry-fords-5-a-day-wages-its-not-what-you-think/#75ef97ca766d

Wright, C., & Serguieva, A. (2017). Sustainable blockchain-enabled services: Smart contracts. *2017 IEEE International Conference on Big Data (Big Data)*, 4255-4264. 10.1109/BigData.2017.8258452

Wright, P., & Dyer, L. (2000). *People in the E-business: New Challenges, New Solutions*. Working paper, Vol. 11, Center for Advanced HR Studies, Cornell University.

Wrubel, E., & Gross, J. (2016). *Contracting for Agile Software Development in the Department of Defense: An Introduction*. Hanscom, MA: Carnegie Mellon University.

Wyatt, W. (2002). *E-HR: Getting Results Along the Journey*. Survey Report.

Xiang, Y., Zhu, Z., Coit, D. W., & Feng, Q. (2017). Condition-based maintenance under performance-based contracting. *Computers & Industrial Engineering*, *111*, 391–402. doi:10.1016/j.cie.2017.07.035

Xie, Y., James Allen, C., & Ali, M. (2014). An integrated decision support system for ERP implementation in small and medium sized enterprises. *Journal of Enterprise Information Management*, *27*(4), 358–384. doi:10.1108/JEIM-10-2012-0077

Yaacobi, S. (2016, July 21). *Delivering value and monetisation in an Internet of Things environment*. Retrieved July 26, 2020, from https://www.iot-now.com/2016/07/21/50166-delivering-value-and-monetisation-in-an-internet-of-things-environment/

Yang, C.-C., & Kang, S.-C. (2014). BIM Navigation with Hand-Based Gesture Control on Sites. *Computing in Civil and Building Engineering*, 758-792.

Yao, T., Jiang, B., Scott, Young, T., & Talluri, S. (2010). utsourcing timing, contract selection, and negotiation. *International Journal of Production Research*, *48*(2), 305-326. doi:10.1080/00207540903174858

Yates, B. T., & Marra, M. (2017). Social Return On Investment (SROI): Problems, solutions … and is SROI a good investment? *Evaluation and Program Planning*, *64*, 136–144. doi:10.1016/j.evalprogplan.2016.11.009 PMID:27979379

Yeung, A., & Brockbank, W. (1995). Reengineering HR through Information Technology. *People & Strategy*, *18*(2), 24.

Ying, H. (2017). *The Art of Contract Drafting in the Age of Artificial Intelligence: A Comparative Study Based on US, UK and Austrian Law*. Transatlantic Technology Law Forum.

York, A., Dunham, L., & Ahn, M. (2012, January). Vertical Versus Horizontal Integration in the Biopharma Industry. *Advances in Mergers and Acquisitions*, *10*, 121–143. doi:10.1108/S1479-361X(2012)0000010010

Youngberg, E., Olsen, D., & Hauser, K. (2009). Determinants of professionally autonomous end user acceptance in an enterprise resource planning system environment. *International Journal of Information Management*, *29*(2), 138–144. doi:10.1016/j.ijinfomgt.2008.06.001

Yu, D. (2020, October 24). Background Concepts and Definitions. *Aircraft Valuation*, 7-31. doi:10.1007/978-981-15-6743-8_2

Yu, C. (2005). Causes influencing the effectiveness of the post-implementation ERP system. *Industrial Management & Data Systems*, *105*(1), 115–132. doi:10.1108/02635570510575225

Zafar, J., Shaakat, M., & Mat, N. (2010). An Analysis of E-HRM Practices: A Case Study of State Bank of Pakistan. *European Journal of Soil Science*, *15*, 18–21.

Zaher, M. G., Greenwood, D., & Marzouk, M. (2018). Mobile augmented reality applications for construction projects. *Construction Innovation*, *18*(2), 152–166. doi:10.1108/CI-02-2017-0013

Zant, C., & Schlosberg, C. (2002). Contract Agreements and Methods of Management. *Pharmaceutical Technology North America*, *2002*(1). Retrieved September 22, 2020, from https://cdn.sanity.io/files/0vv8moc6/pharmtech/70fa4ba2f782b7185e9519532534b87b500b81af.pdf

Zhang, C., & Lin, M. (2018). Optimization of Cost Plus Incentive Fee Contract in Equipment Acquisition Considering Cost Revelation. In *International Conference on Management Science and Engineering (ICMSE)* (pp. 60-66). Frankfurt, Germany: IEEE. doi:10.1109/ICMSE.2018.8744917

Zhang, J., Cao, Q., & He, X. (2019). Contract and product quality in platform selling. *European Journal of Operational Research*, *272*(3), 928–944. doi:10.1016/j.ejor.2018.07.023

Zhang, Y., & Ahtonen, R. (2016). *Flexibility in Contracts and Contractual Practice: Empirical Study in China*. University of Eastern Finland.

Zheng, Z., Xie, S., Dai, H.-N., Chen, W., Chen, X., Weng, J., & Imran, M. (2019). An Overview on Smart Contracts: Challenges, Advances and Platforms. *Future Generation Computer Systems*, 1–19. doi:10.1016/j.future.2019.12.019

Zinaman, O., & Miller, M. (2015, February 1). Retrieved August 15, 2020, from https://www.nrel.gov/docs/fy15osti/62611.pdf

Zinaman, O., Miller, M., & Adil, A. (2015, February 1). *Power Systems of the Future*. Retrieved from https://www.nrel.gov/docs/fy15osti/62611.pdf

Zoom. (2020). *Here's How Zoom Provides Industry-Leading Video Capacity*. Retrieved March 25, 2020, from https://blog.zoom.us/wordpress/2019/06/26/zoom-can-provide-increase-industry-leading-video-capacity/

Zou, W., Brax, S. A., Vuori, M., & Rajala, R. (2019). The influences of contract structure, contracting process, and service complexity on supplier performance. *International Journal of Operations & Production Management*, *39*(4), 525–549. doi:10.1108/IJOPM-12-2016-0756

About the Contributors

Mohammad Shalan is a bilingual, multi-discipline business-technology interpreter. Enthusiastic to get more people in the digital transformation train and an optimistic builder in the 4th industrial revolution. A practitioner, author, guest speaker and researcher with published chapters, articles, and presentations. Willing to distilling complex problems into simple solutions, add value and volunteer. Well certified and connected with 9 professional certifications (PMP®, PMI-RMP®, CSX®, CRMA®, ITILF®, CISA®, CGEIT®, CRISC®, CXO®), active membership in 6 well-recognized professional organizations, and distinguished training classes in 16 countries. Adding to his master's degree in telecommunication engineering from University of Jordan. Mohammad is a working professional since 1995 in the Technology industry and Digital Transformation leadership. He is currently working as a head of technology for Aqarat Real Estate Development Company (Omar Kasem Alesayi Group) in Jeddah, Saudi Arabia. Prior to this he has worked in several operational and project management roles at SITA which is a leading multinational technology service provider for airlines and airports. Mohammad Shalan has worked out major operational assignments, portfolios, programs and projects spanning in more than 50 countries and worth more than US$50M. Assignments include distributed activities, numerous dependencies, heavy correspondences, multiple vendors and contractors in multiple disciplines. Mohammad Shalan used to manage multi-nationality, multi-talent, changeable skills, local or geographically distributed staff and project teams. Worked to acquire and transfer knowledge, motivate and inspire teams. Working to be a true digital consultant that brings together the creative and technology capabilities, business acumen, and industry insight needed to help transform the business. Focus areas include IT Service management, digital transformation, enterprise architecture, 4th industrial revolution tools and user experience. In summary, Mohammad Shalan have spent years 'honing skills' in the science and art of soft skills and the required business-technology passions to boost value in a wise manner. He utilizes audit, risk, governance and program/project management to bring a strategic outlook to a business environment.

Mohammed Ayedh Algarni received his Ph.D. in Information Science from the University of North Texas, USA in 2014. He got his master's in Information Management from Emporia State University, Kansas, USA in 2005 and his Bachelor's in Information Science from King Saud University, in Riyadh city in Saudi Arabia in 1999. Currently, he is the chairman of the documents and archives committee and the director general of the information Center in the Institute of Public Administration (IPA), Saudi Arabia. Additionally, he is working as an information technology consultant, committee's member, career adviser and trainer at Institute of Public Administration (IPA). Dr. Mohammad is also an advisor or partner in several projects or companies that is working in information science and emerging technologies fields. Dr. Mohammad is the translator of the book "Business Intelligence, Analytics, and Data Science:

A Managerial Perspective" to Arabic language and the editor of the book "Information management and decision support in organizations" that was published by the Institute of Public Administration Riyadh. Furthermore, he is the author, reviewer, contributor and translator of several articles, journal papers, conference proceeding and other publications. Dr. Mohammad has a wide range of experiences in documentation structuring, information management, business intelligence (BI), data analytics, strategy and governance, and related technology selection. Dr. Mohammad has helped several organizations in public and privet sectors retrieve actionable insights out of their raw data to accelerate decision-making and improve business performance. Dr. Mohammad has got plenty of honors and awards during his journey and is a member of several professional organizations in USA and Saudi Arabia including the Global Information Technology Management Association, the Decision Sciences Institute DSI, the American Library Association and the Saudi Library and Information Association.

* * *

Akif L. Al-Khasawneh, Ph.D. in management from Amman Arab University for higher education, Jordan. Al-khasawneh is associate Professor in Department of Financial and Administrative within the Al-Huson University College at Al-Balqa Applied University in Jordan. His research interests include human resource management, knowledge management, management information system, marketing management, quality management, and other management topics. Professor Al-khasawneh published more than 40 journal articles and 3 books.

Mohamad Raafat Elbardiny is a civil engineer, holding a Bachelor of Civil Engineering from Mansoura University in Egypt since 2000. He is working in AQARAT Real Estate Development Company (a member of Omar Kassem Alesayi Group) since 2002. He has been promoted in several consecutive positions, which provided him a great experience in various fields, such as project management and real estate funds management. Currently he is the director of operations, studies, investment funds, offers and follow-up departments. Due to the diversity of skills he was selected among many important committees at Alesayi Real Estate Group and AQARAT Real Estate Development Company, such as: The Strategic Planning Team of Alesayi Real Estate Group. The Digital Transformation Team of Alesayi Real Estate Group. Offering Projects for Sale Team of AQARAT Real Estate Development Company. Standing Committee for the Preparation and Follow-up of the General Plan and the Budget Forecasting for AQARAT Real Estate Development Company. White Land Fees committee. Mohammad is a PMP certified, and has attended several courses including Agile Certified Practitioner (PMI-ACP) Exam Preparation course.

Fawaz Alharbi is an Assistant Professor of Computer Science and head of the Computer Science Department at the College of Science and Humanities- Harimlae - Shaqra University. He is a Deputy Chairman of the Board at Cloud Computing Association in Saudi Arabia. He was a Consultant of the National Consultancy Task Force for Health Informatics at Saudi Commission For Health Specialties - Saudi Arabia. He received a number of awards for his outstanding performance during his Ph.D. studies and research. He has several publications in cloud computing. His 16 years of experience in scientific research has allowed him to participate as a reviewer in many scientific conferences and scientific committees.

Sara Jeza Alotaibi, Associate Professor in Web Technologies in Institute of Public Administration, and Editor in Chief Journal of Information Technology and Lifelong learning. She was a first female dean of Library Affairs (for male and females) in Saudi Arabia, also she worked as a Dean of University Studied, Vice Dean of University Development, Vice Dean of e-Learning and Distance Learning at Taif University .She has founded the Saudi Lady Geek group, a visiting researcher in Web Lab at University of Southampton, and is the innovative creator Finger ID, a unique system designed to provide users with access to distributed systems through fingerprint, and she creator of three Industrial products from the Saudi Patent Office. She has authored a wealth of published papers and three books in the IT and technical arena, and is a driven, motivated young woman focused on education, self-development, professionalism and, above all, making a difference whilst teaching others how to do the same. She received many local and global awards, and has also been recognised by a variety of institutions and professionals.

Abdullah Alshaalan joined the college of engineering, King University since receiving his doctorate in electrical engineering from the University of Manchester (UK) in 1985. His specialization and research interests fall within the areas of power system planning, reliability evaluation, electrical safety, environmental protection, load management and energy conservation. He participated in many local, regional, and international technical and scientific committees, seminars, conferences and workshops. He offered consultancy services to many governmental and private entities in his areas of specialization. He is an active member in many scientific societies and academic affiliations, including the IEEE as a life SM. He was one of the first founders of Cigrè (Gulf branch). He authored, co-authored and translated several books in various fields of electrical engineering as well as writing articles for public awareness in the safety of electrical installations and energy conservation. Obtained a lot of prizes, trophies and certificates of appreciations for his vast contributions and wide activities aimed at developing and improving the performance of several electricity sectors. Also, supervised many MSc and PhD dissertations and theses. Also, conducted many funded projects for local and foreign agencies. He participated in preparing the Saudi Building Code (Electrical Requirements 401). He is currently working as the supervisor of the “Zamil Industrial Group Chair for Electricity Conservation” at the College of Engineering, King Saud University, Riyadh, Kingdom of Saudi Arabia. Also working as a part-time consultant at the Saudi Arabian Standards Organization (SASO) since 1995.

Saeed Baselm is a Project Management Consultant and Professional (PMP and RMP) with over 20 years of experience in execution of Petrochemical joint venture projects for Saudi Aramco and Rabigh Refining and Petrochemical Company (Petrorabigh). He holds a bachelor’s degree in Engineering from KFUPM and a master’s degree in Computer Engineering from KAU. Saeed is certified Engineering Consultant (Saudi Council of Engineers) and Arbitrator (GCC Commercial Arbitration Centre). Strong background in in defining strategies for professional development/training programs improvement and served in multiple volunteer positions for PMIKSA Chapter.

Fatmah Baothman is Saudi Arabian computer scientist who is the first woman in the Middle East with a Ph.D. in artificial intelligence. She was appointed the board president for the Artificial Intelligence Society. Baothman has worked over 25 years as, and is currently, an assistant professor at King Abdulaziz University Faculty of Computing & Information Technology. Baothman established the women’s Department which is the foundation of the Computer Science College at King Abdulaziz University, and became the first teaching assistant faculty member.

Mohamed Bassyouni is the internal audit manager for Aqarat Real Estate Development Company which is part of Omar Kasem Alesayi Group based in Jeddah, Saudi Arabia. In 1998 he was awarded his bachelor's degree in accounting from Alexandria University in Egypt, and he attended two higher diplomas in computer and advanced financial accounting in 2000 and 2001. Mohammad has a very rich experience in legal accounting and internal audit started with Ibrahim Abdulrazeq office in Egypt in 1998. In 2001 he moved to Jeddah in Saud Arabia as principal auditor in the Office of a Polaris Accounting and he was a chief accountant at Dar Jane International School (pre-kindergarten to high school). In 2004 he started his work as deputy manager of Internal Audit at Al-Naghi Motors Group, before he moved on as the internal audit manager at Aqarat Real Estate Development Company in 2006.

Malek B. Elayan, Assistant Professor and the Specialist of Human Resources Development at Business Administration Department, The Institute of Public Administration (IPA), The Kingdom of Saudi Arabia, Riyadh. His work focuses on Business Management and Human Resources Management courses. has participated in many Conferences locally and international, as Session Chair and Presenter, he has Research interests include HRM Practices, e-HRM and Contemporary Business topics. His work has been published in many high-quality Journals. Elayan with over 10 years of experience in assessing, designing, developing and delivering educational and training courses to improve participants' performance through developing new skills, maximizing understands them, managing the learning function, and measuring the results of educational programs. Elayan, PhD, in HRM at American University-Turkey, CIPD L7 Candidate Advanced Level Certificate in HRM, has Certificate of Professional Trainer (CPT), International Association for People & Performance Development and Training of Trainers (TOT), International Distance Learning Institute (IDLI).

Solaiman A. El Khereiji's background in planning and architectural design is extensive, covering wide range of experience with over Forty years in the Property Development and Construction Industry. In 1978 he founded his own architectural and Engineering Consultancy firm called "Solaiman A. Elkhereiji Consultant" in Saudi Arabia. His involvement in the industry has contributed to the design and supervision of some of the most sophisticated projects in various sectors including healthcare, educational, hospitality, Institutional, Residential, Industrial, leisure, transportation and infrastructure projects. He has been a former Member of the Majlis Al Shoura (the Consultative Committee Member of the Kingdom of Saudi Arabia), Chairman of the Board of Amen Engineering and Former Vice President for PMI in the region. He has been an active member at AIA, New York (USA), Architects Association London (UK), Saudi Council of Engineers and Architects Association of Egypt. He has also given various lectures in Local & International universities including King Fahd University for Petroleum & Minerals in Dahran, King Abdul Aziz University in Jeddah, Taiba University in Madinah, Umm Ul Qura University in Makkah, Dar Al Hikmah University in Jeddah, British Muslim Heritage Centre (UK), Oxford University (UK), Harvard University (USA), Cambridge University (UK), Polytechnic University of Milan (Italy) and Cadi Ayyad University (Morocco), Bogor Agricultural University (Indonesia), Universitas of Indonesia (Indonesia).

Waleed T. Elsigini received PhD degree in the field of Education Technology from Mansoura University, Egypt, in 2012. Since then he works in Education Technology Department, Education Faculty, Mansoura University. W. T. Elsigini is currently an assistance professor of e- learning in E-Learning and Distance Education Deanship at Umm Al-Qura University. He published many studies in the field of instruction technology and e-learning. His current research interests include Commuter assisted instruction, Online courses Design, e-learning environment design, digital transformation in education, distance learning enhancement.

Belal Hafnawi holds MSc of telecommunication from University of Jordan (JU) following his BSc of electrical engineering from University of Jordan (JU). In addition, he has executive certification in management and leadership from Massachusetts institute of technology (MIT) in which he focused on digital transformation strategy and business implications. He has more than 18 years of extensive experience in Management, Leadership, Strategy, Policy Making, Digitization, Technology and Digital Transformation, He is currently a commissioner- board member of telecommunications regulatory commission (TRC) of Jordan and Experienced with Multinational vendors & service Providers (Huawei, Motorola, Nokia, Samsung), Having end to end experience in managing mobile networks. Focused on Management and leadership of emerging technology. He holds also many professional certificates including PMP, Digital Business transformation management, Scrum fundamentals, six sigma, negotiations. He has voluntary membership as board member of EIAC consultation board of King Abdullah II school of engineering, Princess Sumaya University for technology (PSUT), also he has voluntary membership as mentor in MIT Arab SciTech. He is also technology articles writer in local newspapers of Jordan.

Momen Nashar is a scholar-practitioner where he accomplished a doctoral degree program in Management Information Systems from Walden university, USA. Also, he is a certified professional from Harvard Business School (Disruptive Strategies with Professor Clayton Christensen). Momen is well experienced in quantitative and qualitative research methodologies. In his doc study he examined factors that predicts consumers behavior to adopt online shopping in Saudi Arabia. Momen is an information technology expert with more than 10 years of experience. Momen loves to be an education instructor to transfer his professional and educational experience and to help students manage and progress through educational goals, and providing professional, individualized guidance to students.

Mohamed Raouf is the director of service & new technologies at Gulf Medical Co Ltd looking after service, imaging, radiation therapy and information technology. He has a proven track record in medical devices sales and management. He is skilled in emerging technologies, capital equipment, medical devices, consumables, medical projects, healthcare technology, service management and information technology management. Mohamed holds an MBA from IE Business School in Madrid, Spain. IE University is an international institution dedicated to educating business leaders through programs based on core values of global focus, entrepreneurial spirit, and a humanistic approach. Mohamed was awarded his Bachelor of electronics and Communications from University of Alexandria in Egypt in year 2002.

Omar Shalan is a successful professional with strong work ethics and integrity. Executive Underwriting Manager, business and Insurance Trainer with multifaceted skills, competencies, and knowledge. Omar Shalan began his career in 2009, he worked in financial institution underwriting, Marine Underwriting then specialized in Marine liability, cargo, fine art & specie, and Ports & Terminals class of business. He worked with various countries in the UK, America and GCC, he is Chartered Insurance Institute (CII) certified.

Hasan Tayyeb is Civil Engineering Professor, featuring comprehensive experience in the management of construction and engineering projects. Actively conducting research and maintaining a focus on innovation and technical excellence, which is exactly how value is added to construction and engineering.

Ghassan Wahbe is a marketing manager at Bridgestone Middle East and Africa, headquartered in Dubai and based in Kingdom of Saudi-Arabia; oversees market intelligence and develops related plans and strategies, the marketing department was a vital tool for the recent digital transformation program driven by Bridgestone corporation since couple of years back, focusing to create sustainable mobility innovations through advanced technologies and solutions. Prior to this post, Ghassan was handling commercial product sales, in addition to the training, and as a certified trainer, he contributed to improve sales management approaches amid major change of business model in the market, advanced business solution, was one of most important training courses that he was delivering to partner's sales forces, it could help them to penetrate the market with most innovative approaches methods using latest mobility solutions, Ghassan has accomplished economics worked with big top global brands such as Bridgestone, Firestone, goodyear, and other 2nd tier sub-brand, the best moment for him is when he represents the company's public event and starts to talk to public about latest solutions that is changing the concept of new mobility in the world Ghassan is a father of 3 lovely kids enjoy spending the time solving puzzles and travelling with them, he is multidiscipline interested always in exchanging experiences in latest business solution amid this rapid global markets' changes.

Hanaa Abdulraheem Yamani received PhD degree in the field of Computer Science (E-learning) from La Trobe University, Australia, in 2014. Since then she works in E-learning and Distance Education Deanship as a Vice-Dean, Umm Al-Qura University. H.A. Yamani is currently an assistance professor of e- learning in E-Learning at Information Science Department at Umm Al-Qura University. She published many studies in the field of Digital transformation, e-Learning, Digital learning, Distance education instruction technology and Digital competencies. Her current research interests include Commuter assisted instruction, Online courses Design, e-learning environment design, digital transformation in education, distance learning enhancement.

Index

S

T

U

V

W

www.ingramcontent.com/pod-product-compliance
Lightning Source LLC
LaVergne TN
LVHW062111300926
849161LV00010B/2434
* 9 7 8 1 7 9 9 8 4 5 0 1 0 *